X

Philistinism in England and America

MATTHEW ARNOLD

PHILISTINISM IN ENGLAND AND AMERICA

Edited by R. H. Super

ANN ARBOR   THE UNIVERSITY OF MICHIGAN PRESS

Manufactured in the United States of America by
Vail-Ballou Press, Inc., Binghamton, N.Y.

Editor's Preface

The content of the present volume, covering the years 1882–85, is most miscellaneous, but may be said to focus upon Arnold's lecture tour in America in the winter of 1883–84: here are published not only the three lectures he delivered while on that tour, but the essay he wrote about the United States in anticipation of his visit and the one he wrote upon his return. Though only about half the essays in the volume were included in the DeLuxe edition of 1903–4, most of the other items have been republished in the present century, in *Essays in Criticism*, Third Series (Boston, 1910), in *Five Uncollected Essays of Matthew Arnold*, ed. Kenneth Allott (Liverpool, 1953), or in *Essays, Letters, and Reviews by Matthew Arnold*, ed. Fraser Neiman (Cambridge, Mass., 1960). One essay, however, the anonymous "A Septuagenarian Poet," was uncovered by Professor Roger L. Brooks only in 1960 and is here reprinted for the first time. The lectures and public letters included in Appendix I are for the most part trifles, but Arnold's discourse at Toynbee Hall in Whitechapel is a significant statement of his view of the responsibility of the church toward the poor of the East End; it is here for the first time purged of the blunders of the full but garbled report in *The Times*. This and "A Comment on Christmas" are Arnold's last statements on Christian doctrine. A substantial portion of the volume is devoted to Arnold's version of the Book of Isaiah, with its notes—a work of which he was very proud and which deserves the reprinting it has never before received.

When an essay was reprinted in a book under Arnold's supervision, the book version is the one used. Variants from it in earlier versions are recorded in the Textual Notes; these include changes in paragraphing and the change from a semi-colon to a full stop or the reverse, but not other changes in punctuation. In many instances only the single version, from a periodical, appeared in Arnold's lifetime, and for these the only corrections are of obvious misprints or of misquotations by Arnold that significantly misrepresent the original in ways Arnold can hardly have intended. For the first time in this edition, however, with the essay on "Emerson," Arnold's manuscript also has been used as a textual source. (The manuscript of the lectures *On the Study of Celtic Literature*, in the National Library of Wales at Aberystwyth, was not collated when that work was published in the third volume of this edition.) The effect of Arnold's difficult handwriting upon the printed text in this instance does not encourage optimism about the accuracy of minutiae in the vast bulk of Arnold's prose; while he is usually able to correct the printer's errors, he overlooks some, and in several instances where he perceives that the printer has made him say what he did not intend, he has made a fresh accommodation between the printer's misreading and his own meaning.

The Critical and Explanatory Notes follow the pattern of those in previous volumes. When the editor has failed to explain a passage or to identify an allusion, the reason is usually that he has not been able to do so. The notes include rather full cross-references to other essays of Arnold's, and the Index serves also as a means of tracing such cross-references.

It is a pleasure to acknowledge debts to Mr. Norman Colbeck (formerly of Bournemouth), Mrs. Enid Huws Jones, and Professors John Reidy, Wilfred H. Stone, and Carlton F. Wells for kind assistance on matters of detail, and to my former students Theodore L. Colson, Robert C. Lee, Terry Harris Grabar, Michael Ullman, and Jeffrey Welch for doing spade-work with the annotation of various of the essays.

Contents

* *Discourses in America*
† *Letters of an Old Playgoer*

* *Discourses in America*

A Word about America

Mr. Lowell, in an interesting but rather tart essay, "On a certain Condescension in Foreigners," warns off Englishmen who may be disposed to write or speak about the United States of America. "I never blamed England for not wishing well to democracy," he cries; "how should she?" But the criticisms and dealings of Englishmen, in regard to the object of their ill-will, are apt, Mr. Lowell declares, to make him impatient. "Let them give up trying to understand us, still more thinking that they do, and acting in various absurd ways as the necessary consequence; for they will never arrive at that devoutly to be wished consummation, till they learn to look at us as we are, and not as they suppose us to be."

On the other hand, from some quarters in America come reproaches to us for not speaking about America enough, for not making sufficient use of her in illustration of what we bring forward. Mr. Higginson expresses much surprise that when, for instance, I dilate on the benefits of equality, it is to France that I have recourse for the illustration and confirmation of my thesis, not to the United States. A Boston newspaper supposes me to "speak of American manners as vulgar," and finds, what is worse, that the *Atlantic Monthly*, commenting on this supposed utterance of mine, adopts it and carries it further. For the writer in the *Atlantic Monthly* says that, indeed, "the hideousness and vulgarity of American manners are undeniable," and that "redemption is only to be expected by the work of a few enthusiastic individuals, conscious of cultivated tastes and generous desires;" or, as these enthusiasts are presently called by the writer, "rather highly civilised individuals, a few in each of our great cities and their environs." The Boston newspaper ob-

serves, with a good deal of point, that it is from these exceptional enthusiasts that the heroes of the tales of Mr. James and
Mr. Howells seem to be recruited. It shrewdly describes them
as "people who spend more than half their life in Europe, and
5   return only to scold their agents for the smallness of their
remittances;" and protests that such people "will have, and can
have, no perceptible influence for good on the real civilisation
of America." Then our Boston friend turns to me again, says
that "it is vulgar people from the large cities who have given
10   Mr. Arnold his dislike of American manners," and adds, that
"if it should ever happen that hard destiny should force Mr.
Arnold to cross the Atlantic," I should find "in the smaller
cities of the interior, in the northern, middle, and south-
western states, an elegant and simple social order, as entirely
15   unknown in England, Germany, or Italy, as the private life of
the dukes or princes of the blood is unknown in America." Yes,
I "should find a manner of life belonging to the highest civilisation, in towns, in counties, and in states whose names had never
been heard" by me; and, if I could take the writer in the *At-*
20   *lantic Monthly* to see it along with me, it would do him, says
his compatriot, a great deal of good.

I do not remember to have anywhere, in my too numerous
writings, spoken of American manners as vulgar, or to have
expressed my dislike of them. I have long accustomed myself
25   to regard the people of the United States as just the same people with ourselves, as simply "the English on the other side of
the Atlantic." The ethnology of that American diplomatist,
who the other day assured a Berlin audience that the great admixture of Germans had now made the people of the United
30   States as much German as English, has not yet prevailed with
me. I adhere to my old persuasion, the Americans of the United
States are English people on the other side of the Atlantic. I
learnt it from Burke. But from Burke I learnt, too, with what
immense consequences and effects this simple matter—the set-
35   tlement of a branch of the English people on the other side of
the Atlantic—was, from the time of their constitution as an
independent power, certainly and inevitably charged. Let me

quote his own impressive and profound words on the acknowledgment of American independence in 1782:—

> A great revolution has happened—a revolution made, not by
> chopping and changing of power in any of the existing states,
> but by the appearance of a new state, of a new species, in a new
> part of the globe. It has made as great a change in all the rela-
> tions, and balances, and gravitations of power, as the appearance
> of a new planet would in the system of the solar world.

As for my esteeming it a hard destiny which should force
me to visit the United States, I will borrow Goethe's words,
and say, that "not the spirit is bound, but the foot;" with the
best will in the world, I have never yet been able to go to
America, and probably I never shall be able. But many a kind
communication I receive from that quarter; and when one has
much discoursed on equality and on civilisation, and then is
told that in America a lover of these will find just what suits
him, and is invited, and almost challenged, to turn one's eyes
there, and to bear testimony to what one beholds, it seems ungracious or cowardly to take no notice at all of such chal-
lenges, but to go on talking of equality and civilisation just as
if America had never existed. True, there is Mr. Lowell's warning. Englishmen easily may fall into absurdities in criticising
America, most easily of all when they do not, and cannot, see
it with their own eyes, but have to speak of it from what they
read. Then, too, people are sensitive; certainly it would be
safer and pleasanter to say nothing. And as the prophet Jonah,
when he had a message for Nineveh, hurried off in alarm down
to Joppa, and incontinently took ship there for Tarshish in
just the opposite direction, so one might find plenty of reasons
for running away from the task, when one is summoned to
give one's opinion of American civilisation. But Ewald says
that it was a sorry and unworthy calculation, petty human
reason-mongering—*menschliche Vernünftelei*—which made Jonah run away from his task in this fashion; and we will not
run away from ours, difficult though it be.

Besides, there are considerations which diminish its difficulty. When one has confessed the belief that the social system of one's own country is so far from being perfect, that it presents us with the spectacle of an upper class materialised, a mid
5   dle class vulgarised, a lower class brutalised, one has earned the right, perhaps, to speak with candour of the social systems of other countries. Mr. Lowell complains that we English make our narrow Anglicism, as he calls it, the standard of all things; but "we are worth nothing," says Mr. Lowell of himself and
10 his countrymen, "we are worth nothing except so far as we have disinfected ourselves of Anglicism." Mr. Hussey Vivian, the member for Glamorganshire, goes to travel in America, and when he comes back, delighted with the country and the people, he publishes his opinion that just two things are want
15 ing to their happiness—a sovereign of the British type, and a House of Lords:—

If Americans could only get over the first wrench, and elect a king of the old stock, under the same limited constitutional conditions as our sovereigns, and weld their separate states into
20 one compact and solid nation, many of them would be only too thankful. I cannot help suspecting, also, that they would not be sorry to transform their Senate into a House of Lords. There are fortunes amply large enough to support hereditary rank, and men who will not now enter political life upon any consideration
25 would doubtless do their duty as patriotically as our peers, if not compelled to face the dirt of candidature. As to aristocratic ideas being foreign to Americans, I do not believe it for a moment; on the contrary, I believe them to be a highly aristocratic people.

30 I suppose this may serve as a specimen of the Anglicism which is so exasperating to Mr. Lowell. I do not share it. Mr. Hussey Vivian has a keen eye for the geological and mining facts of America, but as to the political facts of that country, the real tendencies of its life, and its future, he does not seem to me to
35 be at all at the centre of the situation. Far from "not wishing well to democracy," far from thinking a king and a House of Lords, of our English pattern, a panacea for social ills, I have

freely said that our system here, in my opinion, has too much
thrown the middle classes in upon themselves, that the lower
classes likewise are thus too much thrown in upon themselves,
and that we suffer from the want of equality. Nothing would
please me better than to find the difficulty solved in America, to   5
find democracy a success there, with a type of equality producing such good results, that, when one preaches equality,
one should illustrate its advantages not from the example of the
French, but, as Mr. Higginson recommends, from the example
of the people of the United States. I go back again to my Bos-   10
ton newspaper:—

> In towns whose names Mr. Arnold never heard, and never will
> hear, there will be found almost invariably a group of people of
> good taste, good manners, good education and of self-respect,
> peers of any people in the world. Such people read the best   15
> books, they interpret the best music, they are interested in themes
> world-wide, and they meet each other with that mutual courtesy
> and that self-respect which belong to men and women who are
> sure of their footing.

This is what we want; and if American democracy gives this,   20
Mr. Lowell may rely upon it that no narrow Anglicism shall
prevent my doing homage to American democracy.

Only we must have a clear understanding about one thing.
This is a case where the question of numbers is of capital importance. Even in our poor old country, with its aristocratic   25
class materialised, its middle class vulgarised, its lower class
brutalised, there are to be found individuals, as I have again and
again said, lovers of the humane life, lovers of perfection, who
emerge in all classes, and who, while they are more or less in
conflict with the present, point to a better future. Individuals   30
of this kind I make no doubt at all that there are in American
society as well as here. The writer in the *Atlantic Monthly*
himself, unfavourable as is his judgment on his country's civilisation in general, admits that he can find a certain number of
"enthusiastic individuals conscious of cultivated tastes and gen-   35
erous desires." Of these "rather highly civilised individuals"
there are, he says, "a few in each of our great cities and their

environs." His rebuker in the Boston newspaper says that these
centres of sweetness and light are rather in the small towns
than in the large ones; but that is not a matter of much importance to us. The important question is: In what numbers are
they to be found? Well, there is *a group* of them, says the
Boston newspaper, in almost any small town of the northern,
middle, and south-western states. This is indeed civilisation. A
group of lovers of the humane life, an "elegant and simple social order," as its describer calls it, existing in almost every small
town of the northern, middle, and south-western states of
America, and this in addition to circles in New York and other
great cities with "a social life as dignified, as elegant and as
noble as any in the world"—all this must needs leaven American society, and must surely, if we can take example from it,
enable us to leaven and transform our own. Leaven American
society it already does, we hear:—

> It is such people who keep the whole sentiment of the land up
> to a high standard. While the few "rather highly civilised indi-
> viduals" are hopping backwards and forwards over the Atlantic
> to learn what is the last keynote which a pinchbeck emperor
> has decided on, or what is the last gore which a man-milliner
> has decreed, these American gentlemen and ladies, in the dignity
> of their own homes, are making America. It is they who main-
> tain the national credit, it is they who steadily improve the stan-
> dard of national education. If Mr. Arnold should ever see them
> in their own homes, it is they who will show him what is the
> normal type of American manners.

Our Boston informant writes so crisply and smartly that one
is unwilling to part with him. I can truly say that I would
rather read him and quote him than join issue with him. He has
seen America, and I have not. Perhaps things in America are as
he says. I am sure I hope they are, for, as I have just said, I
have been long convinced that English society has to transform
itself, and long looking in vain for a model by which we
might be guided and inspired in the bringing forth of our new
civilisation; and here is the model ready to hand. But I own
that hitherto I have thought that, as we in England have to

transform our civilisation, so America has hers still to make; and that, though her example and co-operation might, and probably would, be of the greatest value to us in the future, yet they were not of much use to our civilisation now. I remember, that when I first read the Boston newspaper from which I have been quoting, I was just fresh from the perusal of one of the best of Mr. James's novels, *Roderick Hudson*. That work carries us to one of the "smaller cities of the interior," a city of which, I own, I had never heard—the American Northampton. Those who have read *Roderick Hudson* will recollect, that in that part of the story where the scene is laid at Northampton, there occurs a personage called Striker, an auctioneer. And when I came upon the Boston newspaper's assurances that, in almost every small town of the Union, I should find "an elegant and simple social order," the comment which rose to my lips was this: "I suspect what I should find there, in great force, is Striker." Now Striker was a Philistine.

I have said somewhere or other that, whereas our society in England distributes itself into Barbarians, Philistines, and Populace, America is just ourselves, with the Barbarians quite left out, and the Populace nearly. This would leave the Philistines for the great bulk of the nation; a livelier sort of Philistines than our Philistine midde class which made and peopled the United States—a livelier sort of Philistine than ours, and with the pressure and the false ideal of our Barbarians taken away, but left all the more to himself, and to have his full swing. That this should be the case seemed to me natural, and that it actually was the case everything which I could hear and read about America tended to convince me. And when my Boston friend talks of the "elegant and simple social order established in almost every small town in America, and of the group, in each, of people of good taste, good manners, good education and self-respect, peers of any people in the world," I cannot help thinking that things are not quite so bright as he paints them, and so superior to anything of which we have experience elsewhere; that he is mixing two impressions together, the impression of individuals scattered over the country, real lovers of the humane life, but not yet numerous enough or united enough to

produce much effect, and the impression of groups of worthy
respectable people to be found in almost every small town of
the Union, people with many merits, but not yet arrived at that
true and happy goal of civilisation, "an elegant and simple so-
5   cial order."
   We too have groups of this kind everywhere, and we know
what they can do for us and what they cannot do. It is easy to
praise them, to flatter them, to express unbounded satisfaction
with them, to speak as if they gave us all that we needed. We
10   have done so here in England. These groups, with us, these
serious and effective forces of our middle class, have been extolled as "that section of the community which has astonished
the world by its energy, enterprise, and self-reliance, which is
continually striking out new paths of industry and subduing
15   the forces of nature, which has done all the great things that
have been done in all departments, and which supplies the
mind, the will, and the power for all the great and good things
that have still to be done." So cry the newspapers; our great
orators take up the same strain. The middle-class doers of En-
20   glish race, with their industry and religion, are the salt of the
earth. "The cities you have built," exclaims Mr. Bright, "the
railroads you have made, the manufactures you have produced,
the cargoes which freight the ships of the greatest mercantile
navy the world has even seen!" There we have their industry.
25   Then comes the praise of their religion, their own specially invented and indomitably maintained form of religion. "Let a
man consider," exclaims Mr. Bright again, "how much of what
there is free and good and great, and constantly growing in
what is good, in this country, is owing to Nonconformist ac-
30   tion. Look at the churches and chapels it has reared over the
whole country; look at the schools it has built; look at the ministers it has supported; look at the Christian work which it
has conducted. It would be well for the Nonconformists, especially for the young among them, that they should look back
35   to the history of their fathers, and that they should learn from
them how much is due to truth and how much they have sacrificed to conscience."
   It is the groups of industrious, religious, and unshakeable

Nonconformists in all the towns, small and great, of England, whose praise is here celebrated by Mr. Bright. But he has an even more splended tribute of praise for their brethren of the very same stock, and sort, and virtue, in America also. The great scale of things in America powerfully impresses Mr. 5 Bright's imagination always; he loves to count the prodigious number of acres of land there, the prodigious number of bushels of wheat raised. The voluntary principle, the principle of modern English Nonconformity, is on the same grand and impressive scale. "There is nothing which piety and zeal have 10 ever offered on the face of the earth as a tribute to religion and religious purposes, equal to that which has been done by the voluntary principle among the people of the United States."

I cannot help thinking that my Boston informant mixes up, I say, the few lovers of perfection with the much more numer- 15 ous representatives, serious, industrious, and in many ways admirable, of middle-class virtue; and imagines that in almost every town of the United States there is a group of lovers of perfection, whereas the lovers of perfection are much less thickly sown than he supposes, but what there really is in almost every 20 town is a group of representatives of middle-class virtue. And the fruits by which he knows his men, the effects which they achieve for the national life and civilisation, are just the fruits, be it observed, which the representatives of middle-class virtue are capable of producing and produce for us here in England 25 too, and for the production of which we need not have recourse to an extraordinary supply of lovers of perfection. "It is such people," he says, "who keep the whole sentiment of the land up to a high standard when war comes, or rebellion." But this is just what the middle-class virtue of our race is abun- 30 dantly capable of doing; as Puritan England in the seventeenth century, and the inheritors of the traditions of Puritan England since, have signally shown. "It is they who maintain the national credit, it is they who steadily improve the standard of national education." By national education our informant means popu- 35 lar education; and here, too, we are still entirely within the pale of middle-class achievement. Both in England and in America the middle class is abundantly capable of maintaining the na-

tional credit, and does maintain it. It is abundantly capable of
recognising the duty of sending to school the children of the
people, nay, of sending them also, if possible, to a Sunday
school, and to chapel or church. True; and yet, in England at
5   any rate, the middle class with all its industry and with all its
religiousness, the middle class well typified, as I long ago
pointed out, by a certain Mr. Smith, a secretary to an insurance
company, who "laboured under the apprehension that he would
come to poverty and that he was eternally lost," the English
10   middle class presents us at this day, for our actual needs, and
for the purposes of national civilisation, with a defective type
of religion, a narrow range of intellect and knowledge, a
stunted sense of beauty, a low standard of manners. For the
building up of human life, as men are now beginning to see,
15   there are needed not only the powers of industry and conduct,
but the power, also, of intellect and knowledge, the power of
beauty, the power of social life and manners. And that type of
life of which our middle class in England are in possession is
one by which neither the claims of intellect and knowledge
20   are satisfied, nor the claim of beauty, nor the claims of social
life and manners.

That which in England we call the middle class is in America virtually the nation. It is in America in great measure relieved, as I have said, of what with us is our Populace, and it
25   is relieved of the pressure and false ideal of our Barbarians. It
is generally industrious and religious as our middle class. Its religion is even less invaded, I believe, by the modern spirit than
the religion of our middle class. An American of reputation as
a man of science tells me that he lives in a town of a hundred
30   and fifty thousand people, of whom there are not fifty who do
not imagine the first chapters of Genesis to be exact history.
Mr. Dale, of Birmingham, found, he says, that "orthodox Christian people in America were less troubled by attacks on the orthodox creed than the like people in England. They seemed to
35   feel sure of their ground and they showed no alarm." Public
opinion requires public men to attend regularly some place of
worship. The favourite denominations are those with which
we are here familiar as the denominations of Protestant dissent;

when Mr. Dale tells us of "the Baptists, not including the Free
Will Baptists, Seventh Day Baptists, Six Principle Baptists, and
some other minor sects," one might fancy oneself reading the
list of the sects in *Whitaker's Almanack*. But in America this
type of religion is not, as it is here, a subordinate type, it is the   5
predominant and accepted one. Our Dissenting ministers think
themselves in paradise when they visit America. In that univer-
sally religious country the religious denomination which has
by much the largest number of adherents is that, I believe, of
Methodism originating in John Wesley, and which we know   10
in this country as having for its standard of doctrine Mr. Wesley's fifty-three sermons and notes on the New Testament. I
have a sincere admiration for Wesley, and a sincere esteem for
the Wesleyan Methodist body in this country; I have seen
much of it, and for many of its members my esteem is not only   15
sincere but also affectionate. I know how one's religious connections and religious attachments are determined by the circumstances of one's birth and bringing up; and probably, if I
had been born and brought up among the Wesleyans, I should
never have left their body. But certainly I should have wished   20
my children to leave it; because to live with one's mind, in regard to a matter of absorbing importance as Wesleyans believe
religion to be, to live with one's mind, as to a matter of this
sort, fixed constantly upon a mind of the third order, such as
was Mr. Wesley's, seems to me extremely trying and injurious   25
for the minds of men in general. And people whose minds, in
what is the chief concern of their lives, are thus constantly
fixed upon a mind of the third order, are the staple of the
population of the United States, in the small towns and country
districts above all. Yet our Boston friend asks us to believe, that   30
a population of which this is the staple can furnish what we
cannot furnish, certainly, in England, and what no country
that I know of can at present furnish,—a group, in every small
town throughout the land, of people of good taste, good manners, good education, peers of any people in the world, reading   35
the best books, interpreting the best music, and interested in
themes world-wide! Individuals of this kind America can
doubtless furnish, peers of any people in the world; and in

every town groups of people with excellent qualities, like the representatives of middle-class industry and virtue amongst ourselves. And a country capable of furnishing such groups will be strong and prosperous, and has much to be thankful
5   for; but it must not take these groups for what they are not, or imagine that having produced them it possesses what it does not possess, or has provided for wants which are in fact still unprovided for.

"The arts have no chance in poor countries," says Mr. Low-
10 ell. "From sturdy father to sturdy son, we have been making this continent habitable for the weaker Old World breed that has swarmed to it during the last half-century." This may be quite true, and the achievements wrought in America by the middle-class industry, the middle-class energy and courage, the
15 middle-class religion of our English race, may be full as much as we have any right to expect up to the present time, and only a people of great qualities could have produced them. But this is not the question. The question is as to the establishment in America, on any considerable scale, of a type of civilisation
20 combining all those powers which go to the building up of a truly human life—the power of intellect and knowledge, the power of beauty, the power of social life and manners, as well as the great power of conduct and religion, and the indispens-able power of expansion. "Is it not the highest art of a repub-
25 lic," asks Mr. Lowell, "to make men of flesh and blood, and not the marble ideals of such?" Let us grant it. "Perhaps it is the collective, not the individual humanity," Mr. Lowell goes on, "that is to have a chance of nobler development among us." Most true, the well-being of the many, and not of individuals
30 and classes solely, comes out more and more distinctly to us all as the object which we must pursue. Many are to be made par-takers of well-being, of civilisation and humanisation; we must not forget it, and America, happily, is not likely to let us for-get it. But the ideal of well-being, of civilisation, of humanisa-
35 tion, is not to be, on that account, lowered and coarsened.

Now the New York *Nation*—a newspaper which I read regularly and with profit, a newspaper which is the best, so far as my experience goes, of all American newspapers, and one of the best newspapers anywhere—the New York *Nation* had the other day some remarks on the higher sort of education in America, and the utility of it, which were very curious:—

In America (says the *Nation*) scarcely any man who can af- 5
ford it likes now to refuse his son a college education if the boy
wants it; but probably not one boy in one thousand can say, five
years after graduating, that he has been helped by his college
education in making his start in life. It may have been never so
useful to him as a means of moral and intellectual culture, but 10
it has not helped to adapt him to the environment in which he
has to live and work; or in other words, to a world in which
not one man in a hundred thousand has either the manners or
cultivation of a gentleman, or changes his shirt more than once
a week, or eats with a fork. 15

Now upon this remarkable declaration many comments might
be made, but I am going now to make one comment only. Is it
credible, if there were established in almost every town of the
great majority of the United States a type of "elegant and simple social order," a "group of people of good taste, good man- 20
ners, reading the best books, interpreting the best music, interested in themes world-wide, the peers of any people in the
world," is it credible, with the instinct of self-preservation
which there is in humanity, and choice things being so naturally attractive as they undoubtedly are, is it credible, that all 25
this excellent leaven should produce so little result, that these
groups should remain so impotent and isolated, that their environment, in a country where our poverty is unknown, should
be "a world in which not one man in a hundred thousand has
either the manners or cultivation of a gentleman, or changes his 30
shirt more than once a week, or eats with a fork?" It is not
credible; to me, at any rate, it is not credible. And I feel more
sure than ever that our Boston informant has told us of groups
where he ought to have told us of individuals; and that many
of his individuals, even, have "hopped over," as he wittily says, 35
to Europe.

Mr. Lowell himself describes his own nation as "the most common-schooled and the least cultivated people in the world." They strike foreigners in the same way. M. Renan says that the "United States have created a considerable popu-
5   lar instruction without any serious higher instruction, and will long have to expiate this fault by their intellectual mediocrity, their vulgarity of manners, their superficial spirit, their lack of general intelligence." Another acute French critic speaks of a "hard unintelligence" as characteristic of the people of the
10 United States—*la dure inintelligence des Américains du Nord.* Smart they are, as all the world knows; but then smartness is unhappily quite compatible with a "hard unintelligence." The Quinionian humour of Mr. Mark Twain, so attractive to the Philistine of the more gay and light type both here and in
15 America, another French critic fixes upon as literature exactly expressing a people of this type, and of no higher. "In spite of all its primary education," he says, "America is still, from an intellectual point of view, a very rude and primitive soil, only to be cultivated by violent methods. These childish and
20 half-savage minds are not moved except by very elementary narratives composed without art, in which burlesque and melodrama, vulgarity and eccentricity, are combined in strong doses." It may be said that Frenchmen, the present generation of Frenchmen at any rate, themselves take seriously, as of the
25 family of Shakespeare, Molière, and Goethe, an author half genius half charlatan, like M. Victor Hugo. They do so; but still they may judge, soundly and correctly enough, another nation's false literature which does not appeal to their weak-nesses. I am not blaming America for falling a victim to
30 Quinion, or to Murdstone either. We fall a victim to Murdstone and Quinion ourselves, as I very well know, and the Americans are just the same people that we are. But I want to deliver England from Murdstone and Quinion, and I look round me for help in the good work. And when the Boston newspaper
35 told me of the elegant and simple social order, and the group of people in every town of the Union with good taste and good manners, reading the best books and interpreting the best

music, I thought at first that I had surely found what I wanted, and that I should be able to invade the English realm of Murdstone and Quinion with the support of an overpowering body of allies from America. But now it seems doubtful whether America is not suffering from the predominance of Murdstone and Quinion herself—of Quinion at any rate.

Yes, and of Murdstone too. Miss Bird, the best of travellers, and with the skill to relate her travels delightfully, met the rudimentary American type of Murdstone not far from Denver, and has described him for us. Denver—I hear some one say scornfully—Denver! A new territory, the outskirts of civilisation, the Rocky Mountains! But I prefer to follow a course which would, I know, deliver me over a prey into the Americans' hands, if I were really holding a controversy with them and attacking their civilisation. I am not holding a controversy with them. I am not attacking their civilisation. I am much disquieted about the state of our own. But I am holding a friendly conversation with American lovers of the humane life, who offer me hopes of improving British civilisation by the example of a great force of true civilisation, of elegant and simple social order, developed in the northern, middle, and southwestern states of the Union. I am not going to pick holes in the civilisation of those well-established States. But in a new territory, on the outskirts of the Union, I take an example of a spirit which we know well enough in the old country, and which has done much harm to our civilisation; and I ask my American friends how much way this spirit—since on their borders, at any rate, they seem to have it—has made and is even now making amongst themselves; whether they feel sure of getting it under control, and that the elegant and simple social order in the older States will be too strong for it, or whether, on the other hand, it may be too strong for the elegant and simple social order.

Miss Bird, then, describes the Chalmers family, a family with which, on her journey from Denver to the Rocky Mountains, she lodged for some time. Miss Bird, as those who have read her books well know, is not a lackadaisical person, or in any way a fine lady; she can ride, catch and saddle a horse, "make herself agreeable," wash up plates, improvise lamps, teach knitting. But—

> Oh (she says), what a hard, narrow life it is with which I am
5 > now in contact! A narrow and unattractive religion, which I believe still to be genuine, and an intense but narrow patriotism, are the only higher influences. Chalmers came from Illinois nine years ago. He is slightly intelligent, very opinionated, and wishes to be thought well-informed, which he is not. He belongs to the
10 > straitest sect of Reformed Presbyterians; his great boast is that his ancestors were Scottish Covenanters. He considers himself a profound theologian, and by the pine logs at night discourses to me on the mysteries of the eternal counsels and the divine decrees. Colorado, with its progress and its future, is also a con-
15 > stant theme. He hates England with a bitter personal hatred. He trusts to live to see the downfall of the British monarchy and the disintegration of the empire. He is very fond of talking, and asks me a great deal about my travels, but if I speak favourably of the climate or resources of any other country, he regards it as
20 > a slur on Colorado.
> Mrs. Chalmers looks like one of the English poor women of our childhood—lean, clean, toothless, and speaks, like some of them, in a piping, discontented voice, which seems to convey a personal reproach. She is never idle for one moment, is severe
25 > and hard, and despises everything but work. She always speaks of me as *this* or *that woman*. The family consists of a grown-up son, a shiftless, melancholy-looking youth, who possibly pines for a wider life; a girl of sixteen, a sour repellent-looking creature, with as much manners as a pig; and three hard, unchildlike
30 > younger children. By the whole family all courtesy and gentleness of act or speech seem regarded as *works of the flesh*, if not of *the devil*. They knock over all one's things without apologising or picking them up, and when I thank them for anything they look grimly amazed. I wish I could show them "a more
35 > excellent way." This hard greed, and the exclusive pursuit of gain, with the indifference to all which does not aid in its acquisition, are eating up family love and life throughout the West. I write this reluctantly and after a total experience of nearly two years in the United States. Mrs. Chalmers is cleanly in her
40 > person and dress, and the food, though poor, is clean. Work,

work, work, is their day and their life. They are thoroughly un-
genial. There is a married daughter across the river, just the same
hard, loveless, moral, hard-working being as her mother. Each
morning, soon after seven, when I have swept the cabin, the
family come in for "worship." Chalmers wails a psalm to the   5
most doleful of dismal tunes; they read a chapter round, and he
prays. Sunday was a dreadful day. The family kept the commandment literally, and did no work. Worship was conducted
twice, and was rather longer than usual. The man attempted to
read a well-worn copy of *Boston's Fourfold State*, but shortly   10
fell asleep, and they only woke up for their meals. It was an
awful day, and seemed as if it would never come to an end. You
will now have some idea of my surroundings. It is a moral,
hard, unloving, unlovely, unrelieved, unbeautified, grinding life.
These people live in a discomfort and lack of ease and refine-   15
ment which seem only possible to people of British stock.

What is this but the hideousness, the immense *ennui*, of the
life on which we have touched so often, the life of our serious
British Philistine, our Murdstone; that life with its defective
type of religion, its narrow range of intellect and knowledge,   20
its stunted sense of beauty, its low standard of manners? Only
it is this life at its simplest, rudimentary stage.

I have purposely taken the picture of it from a region outside the settled States of the Union, that it might be evident I
was not meaning to describe American civilisation, and that   25
Americans might at once be able to say with perfect truth that
American civilisation is something totally different. And if, to
match this picture of our Murdstone in other lands and other
circumstances, we are to have—as, for the sake of clearness in
our impressions, we ought to have—a picture of our Quinion   30
too under like conditions, let us take it, not from America at
all, but from our own Australian colonies. The special correspondent of the *Bathurst Sentinel* criticises an Italian singer who,
at the Sydney Theatre, plays the Count in the *Sonnambula;*
and here is the criticism: "Barring his stomach, he is the finest-   35
looking artist I have seen on the stage for years; and if he don't
slide into the affections or break the gizzards of half our Sydney girls, it's a pretty certain sign there's a scarcity of balm in

Gilead." This is not Mark Twain, not an American humourist at all; it is the *Bathurst Sentinel*.

So I have gone to the Rocky Mountains for the New World Murdstone, and to Australia for the New World Quinion. I have not assailed in the least the civilisation of America in those northern, middle, and south-western States, to which Americans have a right to refer us when we seek to know their civilisation, and to which they, in fact, do refer us. What I wish to say is, and I by no means even put it in the form of an assertion —I put it in the form of a question only, a question to my friends in America who are believers in equality and lovers of the humane life as I also am, and who ask me why I do not illustrate my praise of equality by reference to the humane life of America—what I wish to say is: How much does the influence of these two elements, natural products of our race, Murdstone and Quinion, the bitter, serious Philistine and the rowdy Philistine, enter into American life and lower it? I will not pronounce on the matter myself; I have not the requisite knowledge. But all that we hear from America—hear from Americans themselves—points, so far as I can see, to a great presence and power of these middle-class misgrowths there as here. We have not succeeded in counteracting them here, and while our statesmen and leaders proceed as they do now, and Lord Frederick Cavendish congratulates the middle class on its energy and self-reliance in doing without public schools, and Lord Salisbury summons the middle class to a great and final stand on behalf of supernaturalism, we never shall succeed in counteracting them. We are told, however, of groups of children of light in every town of America, and an elegant social order prevailing there, which make one, at first, very envious. But soon one begins to think, I say, that surely there must be some mistake. The complaints one hears of the state of public life in America, of the increasing impossibility and intolerableness of it to self-respecting men, of the "corruption and feebleness," of the blatant violence and exaggeration of language, the profligacy of clap-trap—the complaints we hear from America of all this, and then such an exhibition as we had in the Guiteau trial the other day, lead one to think that Murd-

stone and Quinion, those misgrowths of the English middle-
class spirit, must be even more rampant in the United States
than they are here. Mr. Lowell himself writes, in that very
same essay in which he is somewhat sharp upon foreigners, he
writes of the sad experience in America of "government by   5
declamation." And this very week, as if to illustrate his words,
we have the American newspapers raising "a loud and peremp-
tory voice" against the "gross outrage on America, insulted in
the persons of Americans imprisoned in British dungeons;" we
have them crying: "The people demand their release, and they   10
must be released; woe to the public men or the party that stand
in the way of this act of justice!" We have them turning upon
Mr. Lowell himself in such style as the following: "This Lowell
is a fraud and a disgrace to the American nation; Minister
Lowell has scoffed at his own country, and disowned every-   15
thing in its history and institutions that makes it free and
great."

I should say, for my part, though I have not, I fully own, the
means for judging accurately, that all this points to an American development of our Murdstone and Quinion, the bitter   20
Philistine and the rowdy Philistine, exhibiting themselves in
conjunction, exhibiting themselves with great luxuriance and
with very little check. As I write from Grub Street, I will add
that, to my mind, the condition of the copyright question between us and America appears to point to just the same thing.   25
The American refusal of copyright to us poor English souls
is just the proceeding which would naturally commend itself
to Murdstone and Quinion; and the way in which Mr. Conant
justifies and applauds the proceeding, and continues to justify
and applaud it in disregard of all that one may say, and boldly   30
turns the tables upon England, is just the way in which Murdstone and Quinion, after regulating copyright in the American
fashion, would wish and expect to be backed up. In Mr. Conant they have a treasure: *illi robur et æs triplex* indeed. And
no doubt a few Americans, highly civilised individuals, "hopping 35
backwards and forwards over the Atlantic," much disapprove
of these words and works of Mr. Conant and his constituents.
But can there be constant groups of children of light, joined

in an elegant order, everywhere throughout the Union? for, if there were, would not their sense of equity, and their sense of delicacy, and even their sense of the ridiculous, be too strong, even in this very matter of copyright, for Mr. Conant and his
5   constituents?

But on the creation and propagation of such groups the civilised life of America depends for its future, as the civilised life of our own country, too, depends for its future upon the same thing;—so much is certain. And if America
10   succeeds in creating and installing hers, before we succeed in creating and installing ours, then they will send over help to us from America, and will powerfully influence us for our good. Let us see, then, how we both of us stand at the present moment, and what advantages the one of us has which are
15   wanting to the other. We in England have liberty and industry and the sense for conduct, and a splendid aristocracy which feels the need for beauty and manners, and a unique class, as Mr. Charles Sumner pointed out, of gentlemen, not of the landed class or of the nobility, but cultivated and refined.
20   America has not our splendid aristocracy, but then this splendid aristocracy is materialised, and for helping the sense for beauty, or the sense for social life and manners, in the nation at large, it does nothing or next to nothing. So we must not hastily pronounce, with Mr. Hussey Vivian, that American
25   civilisation suffers by its absence. Indeed they are themselves developing, it is said, a class of very rich people quite sufficiently materialised. America has not our large and unique class of gentlemen; something of it they have, of course, but it is not by any manner of means on the same scale there as here.
30   Acting by itself, and untrammelled, our English class of gentlemen has eminent merits; our rule in India, of which we may well be proud, is in great measure its work. But in presence of a great force of Barbarian power, as in this country, or in presence of a great force of Philistinism, our class of gentlemen,
35   as we know, has not much faith and ardour, is somewhat bounded and ineffective, is not much of a civilised force for the nation at large; not much more, perhaps, than the few "rather civilised individuals" in America, who, according to our

Boston informant, go "hopping backwards and forwards over the Atlantic." Perhaps America, with her needs, has no very great loss in not having our special class of gentlemen. Without this class, and without the pressure and false ideal of our Barbarians, the Americans have, like ourselves, the sense for 5 conduct and religion; they have industry, and they have liberty; they have, too, over and above what we have, they have an excellent thing—equality. But we have seen reason for thinking, that as we in England, with our aristocracy, gentlemen, liberty, industry, religion, and sense for conduct, have 10 the civilisation of the most important part of our people, the immense middle class, impaired by a defective type of religion, a narrow range of intellect and knowledge, a stunted sense of beauty, a low standard of manners; so in America, too, where this class is yet more important and all-pervading than it is 15 here, civilisation suffers in the like way. With a people of our stock it could not, indeed, well be otherwise, so long as this people can be truly described as "the most common-schooled and least cultivated people in the world."

The real cultivation of the people of the United States, as 20 of the English middle class, has been in and by its religion, its "one thing needful." But the insufficiency of this religion is now every day becoming more manifest. It deals, indeed, with personages and words which have an indestructible and inexhaustible truth and salutariness; but it is rooted and grounded 25 in preternaturalism, it can receive those personages and those words only on conditions of preternaturalism, and a religion of preternaturalism is doomed—whether with or without the battle of Armageddon for which Lord Salisbury is preparing—to inevitable dissolution. *Fidelity to conscience!* cries the popular 30 Protestantism of Great Britain and America, and thinks that it has said enough. But the modern analysis relentlessly scrutinises this conscience, and compels it to give an account of itself. What sort of a conscience? a true conscience or a false one? "Conscience is the most changing of rules; conscience is 35 presumptuous in the strong, timid in the weak and unhappy, wavering in the undecided; obedient organ of the sentiment which sways us and of the opinions which govern us; more

misleading than reason and nature." So says one of the noblest
and purest of moralists, Vauvenargues; and terrible as it may be
to the popular Protestantism of England and of America to
hear it, Vauvenargues thus describes with perfect truth that
5   conscience to which popular Protestantism appeals as its supposed unshakeable ground of reliance.

And now, having up to this point neglected all the arts of the
controversialist, having merely made inquiries of my American friends as to the real state of their civilisation, inquiries
10   which they are free to answer in their own favour if they like,
I am going to leave the advantage with them to the end. They
kindly offered me the example of their civilisation as a help to
mend ours; and I, not with any vain Anglicism, for I own our
insular civilisation to be very unsatisfactory, but from a desire
15   to get at the truth and not to deceive myself with hopes of
help from a quarter where at present there is none to be found,
have inquired whether the Americans really think, on looking
into the matter, that their civilisation is much more satisfactory
than ours. And in case they should come to the conclusion,
20   after due thought, that neither the one civilisation nor the
other is in a satisfactory state, let me end by propounding a
remedy which really it is heroic in me to propound, for people
are bored to death, they say, by me with it, and every time I
mention it I make new enemies and diminish the small num-
25   ber of friends that I have now. Still, I cannot help asking
whether the defects of American civilisation, if it is defective,
may not probably be connected with the American people's
being, as Mr. Lowell says, "the most common-schooled and
the least cultivated people in the world." A higher, larger cul-
30   tivation, a finer lucidity, is what is needed. The friends of
civilisation, instead of hopping backwards and forwards over
the Atlantic, should stay at home a while, and do their best to
make the administration, the tribunals, the theatre, the arts,
in each State, to make them become visible ideals to raise, purge
35   and ennoble the public sentiment. Though they may be few
in number, the friends of civilisation will find, probably, that
by a serious apostolate of this kind they can accomplish a good
deal. But the really fruitful reform to be looked for in Amer-

ica, so far as I can judge, is the very same reform which is so urgently required here—a reform of secondary instruction. The primary and common schools of America we all know; their praise is in every one's mouth. About superior or University instruction one need not be uneasy, it excites so much   5
ambition, is so much in view, and is required by comparatively so small a number. An institution like Harvard is probably all that one could desire. But really good secondary schools to form a due proportion of the youth of America from the age of twelve to the age of eighteen, and then every year to   10
throw a supply of them, thus formed, into circulation—this is what America, I believe, wants, as we also want it, and what she possesses no more than we do. I know she has higher schools, I know their programme: Latin, Greek, German, French, Surveying, Chemistry, Astrology, Natural History,   15
Mental Philosophy, Constitution, Book-keeping, Trigonometry, etc. Alas, to quote Vauvenargues again: "*On ne corrigera jamais les hommes d'apprendre des choses inutiles!*" But good secondary schools, not with the programme of our classical and commercial academies, but with a serious programme—a pro-   20
gramme really suited to the wants and capacities of those who are to be trained—this, I repeat, is what American civilisation in my belief most requires, as it is what our civilisation, too, at present most requires. The special present defects of both American civilisation and ours are the kind of defects for   25
which this is a natural remedy. I commend it to the attention of my friendly Boston critic in America; and some months hence, perhaps, when Mr. Barnum begins to require less space for his chronicles of Jumbo, my critic will tell me what he thinks of it.   30

An Eton Boy

"It is becoming a mania with him," people will say; "he has schools on the brain!" Yes, I have certainly made secondary schools my theme very often, and for the public ear the attractions of this theme are not inexhaustible. Perhaps it is time that I quitted it, but I should like the leave-taking to be a kind one. I have said a great deal of harm of English secondary instruction. It deserves all the blame that I have cast upon it, and I could wish everybody to grow more and more impatient of its present condition amongst us. Necessarily, as I wished to make people dissatisfied with the thing, I have insisted upon its faults; I have insisted upon the faults of the civilisation which goes along with it, and which is in a considerable measure the product of it. But our actual secondary schools, like our actual civilisation, have the merit of existing. They are not, like all projects for recasting them, an ideal; they have the merit of existing. They are the *modus vivendi*, as the phrase now is, the schools and the civilisation are the *modus vivendi* found by our nation for its wants, and brought into fact, and shape, and actual working. The good which our nation has in it, it has put into them, as well as the bad. They live by the good in them rather than by the bad. At any rate, it is to the good which dwells in them, and in the nation which made them, that we have to appeal in all our projects for raising them, and for bringing them nearer to the ideal which lovers of perfection frame for them.

Suppose we take that figure we know so well, the earnest and nonconforming Liberal of our middle classes, as his schools and his civilisation have made him. He is for disestablishment; he is for temperance; he has an eye to his wife's sister; he is a member of his local caucus; he is learning to go up to Birmingham every year to the feast of Mr. Chamberlain. His inadequacy is but too visible. Take him, even, raised, cleared, refined, ennobled, as we see him in Dr. Alexander Raleigh, the late well-known Nonconformist minister of Stamford Hill, whose memoir has recently been published. Take Dr. Raleigh, as he himself would have desired to be taken, dilating on a theme infinitely precious to him—*the world to come.* "My hope of that world seems to be my religion. If I were to lose it, this whole life would be overcast in a moment with a gloom which nothing could disperse. Yet a little while, and we shall be sorrowless and sinless, like the angels, like God, and, looking back on the struggles and sorrows of earth, astonished that things so slight and transient could have so much discomposed us." This transference of our ideal from earth to the sky—this recourse, for the fulfilment of our hopes and for the realisation of the kingdom of God, to a supernatural, future, angelic, fantastic world—is, indeed, to our popular religion the most familiar and favourite conception possible. Yet it is contrary to the very central thought and aim of Jesus; it is a conception which, whether in the form of the new Jerusalem of popular Judaism, or in the form of the glorified and unending tea-meeting of popular Protestantism, Jesus passed his life in striving to transform, and in collision with which he met his death. And so long as our main stock and force of serious people have their minds imprisoned in this conception, so long will "things so slight and transient" as their politics, their culture, their civilisation, be in the state in which we see them now: they will be narrowed and perverted. Nevertheless, what a store of virtue there is in our main body of serious people even now, with their minds imprisoned in this Judaic conception; what qualities of character and energy are in such leaders of them as Dr. Raleigh! Nay, what a store of virtue there is even in their civilisation itself, narrowed and stunted though it be! Imperfect as it is, it has founded itself, it has made its way, it exists; the good which is in it, it has succeeded in bringing forth and establishing against a thousand hindrances, a thousand difficulties. We see its faults, we contrast it with our ideal; but our ideal has not yet done as much. And for making itself fact, this civilisation has found in its Judaic conceptions the requisite guidance and stimulus, and probably only in conceptions of this kind could it have done so.

5   Take, again, that other type which we have accustomed ourselves to call, for shortness, the Barbarian. Take it first in its adult and rigid stage, devoid of openness of mind, devoid of flexibility, with little culture and with no ideas, considerably materialised, staunch for "our traditional, existing social arrangements," fiercely ready with the reproach of "revolution"
10   and "atheism" against all its disturbers. Evidently this is the very type of personage for which Jesus declared entrance to the kingdom of God to be well-nigh impossible. Take this type in its far more amiable stage, with the beauty and freshness of youth investing it; take it unspoiled, gay, brave, spirited, generous; take it as the Eton boy. "As Master of the Beagles," so
15   testifies the admiring record of such a boy in the *Eton College Chronicle*, "he showed himself to possess all the qualities of a keen sportsman, with an instinctive knowledge of the craft."
20   The aged Barbarian will, upon this, admiringly mumble to us his story how the battle of Waterloo was won in the playing-fields of Eton. Alas! disasters have been prepared in those playing-fields as well as victories; disasters due to inadequate mental training—to want of application, knowledge, intelligence, lucidity. The Eton playing-fields have their great charms, not-
25   withstanding; but with what felicity of unconscious satire does that stroke of "the Master of the Beagles" hit off our whole system of provision of public secondary schools; a provision for the fortunate and privileged few, but for the many, for the nation, ridiculously impossible! And yet, as we said of the
30   Philistine and his civilisation, so we may say of the Barbarian and his civilisation also: What merits they have, what a store of virtue! First of all, they have the grand merit of existing, of having—unlike our ideal society of the future—advanced out
35   of the state of prospectus into the state of fact. They have in great part created the *modus vivendi* by which our life is actually carried forward, and by which England is what it is. In the second place, they have intrinsic merits of nature and

character; and by these, indeed, have mainly done their work in the world. Even the adult and rigid Barbarian has often invaluable qualities. It is hard for him, no doubt, to enter into the kingdom of God—hard for him to believe in the sentiment of the ideal life transforming the life which now is, to believe in it and come to serve it—hard, but not impossible. And in the young the qualities take a brighter colour, and the rich and magical time of youth adds graces of its own to them; and then, in happy natures, they are irresistible. In a nature of this kind I propose now to show them.

The letters and diary of an Eton boy, a young lieutenant in the army who died of dysentery in South Africa, came the other day into my hands. They have not been published, but they were printed as a record of him for his family and his friends. He had been with his regiment little more than a year; the letters and diary extend over a space of less than two months. I fell in, by chance, with the slight volume which is his memorial, and his name made me look through the pages; for the name awakened reminiscences of distant Oxford days, when I had known it in another generation. The passing attention which his name at first drew was presently fixed and charmed by what I read. I have received permission to give to the public some notice of the slight and unpretending record which thus captivated my interest.

Arthur Clynton Baskerville Mynors was born in 1856, of a Herefordshire family. His bringing-up was that of an English boy in an English country house. In January, 1870, he went to Eton, and left at Election, 1875. "His life here," says the short record of him in the *Eton College Chronicle*, "was always joyous, a fearless keen boyhood, spent *sans peur et sans reproche*. Many will remember him as fleet of foot and of lasting powers, winning the mile and the steeplechase in 1874, and the walking race in 1875. As Master of the Beagles in 1875 he showed himself to possess all the qualities of a keen sportsman, with an instinctive knowledge of the craft." After leaving Eton he joined the Oxford militia, and at the beginning of 1878 obtained a commission in the 60th Rifles. He had been just a year

with his battalion when it was sent to South Africa. He sailed on the 19th of February, and on the 25th of April he died of dysentery at Fort Pearson, Natal. For these two months we have his letters and diary, written to his father and mother at
5   home. I wish to let him tell his own story as far as possible, and we will begin with his first letter.

                                    " 'DUBLIN CASTLE,' *February 20th.*
      "MY DEAR PAPA,
          "We were all safe on board last night, and steamed down the
10   Thames, and anchored for the night. The boat is a beautiful one, it goes very smooth as yet; we have passed Dover and Folkestone, and are now off Dungeness. To-night we reach Dartmouth at twelve, and wait till twelve next day. There is an *oudacious* crowd on board with all the men, and nothing to do.
15   The cabins we sleep in are the most extraordinary, two of us, bed and all, in a place about as big as the dining-room table at home, and when it's rough, as far as I can see, we must tumble out; still, it is rather fun. The skipper is a first-rate fellow, lets us do what we like on board. He expects we shall get to Natal
20   about the 18th or 19th of next month; we are sailing about eleven knots an hour, I wish we were going faster. It is very windy and cold on deck; the band played, which enlivened us a little. We have mess as usual, only at six o'clock. I have fitted all my things on your belt, and they do capitally. Please give my love
25   to mamma and everybody that is staying at Durrant's, especially Aunt Ellen, and thank them all for everything they have given me. We stop at Madeira, when I will write to you again; so good-bye till then.
                            "Ever your most affectionate son,
30   "ARTHUR."

      The next letter is written four days later.

                                    " 'DUBLIN CASTLE,' *February 24th.*
      "MY DEAR MAMMA,
          "Many thanks for your letters, which I found waiting at Dart-
35   mouth, where we arrived after rather a rough voyage. There were no end of people there assembled to see us off, and when we started we were lustily cheered by crowds on the shore; the

band played 'Should old acquaintance,' &c., and we soon lost sight of England. Friday night everybody was ill, as the sea was rough. Saturday, in the Bay of Biscay, it was awful; the waves were mountains high—a grand sight—so much so, that the upper decks were washed over by the sea all day. I was awfully ill; in 5 fact, so was everybody. On Saturday morning at 4 A.M. I was on watch; luckily for me it was much calmer. I found two of the horses had died in the night, and that several hammocks and other things had been washed overboard. I was awfully glad when we got out of the Bay. I'll never go to sea again if I can 10 help it. Sunday was bright and sunny; everybody came up on deck after the bad weather, and we had quite a jolly day, steaming with a strong wind behind at about twelve and a half miles, or knots I should say, an hour. I was on duty that day. We consigned the poor horses to the deep. This morning was lovely, 15 and we had a regular tropical shower, the weather, by-the-bye, getting much warmer. It's most absurd, since we started none of us have shaved; we are (not myself) all growing beards. It is awfully slow, nothing to do but read. The men also have nothing to do. I wish we were at Natal, I do so detest the sea. It 20 keeps very rough all the time, and the ship rolls horribly. The men have an awfully bad time of it; packed so close, they have scarcely room to breathe. All the officers and passengers have dinner, &c., together, down-stairs, in a stuffy place, not so bad to look at, but when it is full of sickly females, and no one in 25 the best of humours, it's perfectly unbearable. Still we live in hopes of getting to Natal soon, where I hope we shall have some better fun. We get to Madeira to-morrow night at ten o'clock, and wait for about three hours for stores and the mails. I sent you a picture of the vessel. I hope you got it safe. I hope 30 you were none the worse for waiting in the cold and seeing me off at Tilbury. I have no more to say, but, with best love to papa and all,

"I am ever, dear Mamma,

"Your affectionate son, 35

"ARTHUR."

Madeira is reached and left; they have a week "awfully hot," during which "I have been learning signalling, which will probably come in useful in the bush." The line has now been crossed, they are approaching Cape Town.

40

"It has been getting much cooler the last few days, and to-
day quite a breeze and rather rough; the ship is getting lighter,
and consequently rolls more. We had some pistol practising yesterday, and a nigger entertainment last night, which was great
fun. I spend the day mostly in reading, but it is awfully slow,
nothing to do. . . . So far, we have had a capital passage, but
the trade winds are dead against us now. I wonder how you are
all getting on; you will soon begin fishing at Aberedw. Have
the hounds had any sport, and how are grandpapa and grandmamma? Please let granny have my letter, and tell her I would
write, only one letter answers the purpose as there is so little
to say; but I want lots of letters, to hear what is going on at
home and at Bosbury. We are all ready to land at Natal; all our
weapons are as sharp as needles. I wish we were there. You will
hear plenty of news (even if I don't write often, as there may
be no way of conveying the letters), as there are three correspondents going up to the front. The *Graphic* correspondent
has taken one or two drawings of our men on board ship, so
you may see them; I advise you to take it in. I have written very
badly, but must make excuse that the sea is rough to-day. Remind Charles about planting the gorse in the cock-shoots, where
the trees are bitten off by the rabbits. I don't fancy the mosqui-
toes in Natal. I believe there are swarms of them there, so I
am going to buy a mosquito net at Cape Town. My next letter
will probably be from Durban, in a week's time or so."

"For something to do," he copies out, to send with this letter,
the verses written by a passenger on the burial of a private
soldier who died on board. Then comes Cape Town, "a horrid
place, very hot and dirty," but with the Table Mountain to
make amends; "the rocks were rather like the Craigy rocks,
only much larger and bolder." Then Cape Town is left, and
they are in the last stage of their voyage.

"On Sunday morning I went to church at the cathedral, rather
a fine building for Cape Town. Had to go on board at one
o'clock, and we sailed at two o'clock. We passed the Cape of
Good Hope about six o'clock in the afternoon. The coast all
along looked rugged and bare, very mountainous in the background, and rocks jutting boldly out. Rounding the point, the

sea became very rough, and has been ever since. At dinner nothing can stand up, knives, forks, tumblers, bottles, everything sent
flying about. There are no end of porpoises and dolphins all
along the coast; they come swimming and jumping by the side
of the vessel. Rounded Cape D'Agulhas about three in the morn-   5
ing; only saw the lighthouse. Monday was still rough, and we
kept in sight of shore all day. We practised revolver-shooting
most of the afternoon. To-day it rained all the morning . . .
the country opposite us looks much flatter, and is quite green on
the slopes of the hills. We amuse ourselves by looking through   10
our field-glasses at the shore—we are now about three miles
from it; enormous great sand-hills along the beach, and woody
at the back. We have seen a few houses and some cattle, otherwise the country looks uninhabited. We passed Algoa Bay this
morning. . . . I shall be very glad when we have landed, as this   15
is the slowest work I ever went through in my life; we sail along
pretty fast, do about two hundred and seventy to three hundred
miles in twenty-four hours. Another of the horses is very ill
from the rough weather; I expect he will die before he gets on
shore. The men and officers are none the worse for the journey,   20
but I expect we shall get very foot-sore at first. We are in awfully bad training, as we can't get any exercise. How is poor
old Martha? Give her my love. I suppose you are just beginning
summer; here the winter is beginning. I believe in the winter-time
there is no rain at all."   25

On Friday, the 21st of March, they are at Durban, and in
tents; "the country looks beautiful; like Wales, only all the
hills are bush." On Saturday they start to relieve Colonel Pearson, surrounded by the Zulus at Fort Ekowe. On Saturday, the
22nd, "went by train twelve miles, encamped, had dinner in   30
dark; slept four hours, up at two o'clock in the dark." Then a
diary gives a record of the march.

"*Sunday morning.*—Started at 4 A.M., to march in utter darkness; unpitched camp, packed up and off; marched six miles on
awful bad road to Verulam; the hilliest and prettiest country I   35
ever saw; forded two rivers; stopped eight hours at Verulam;
bathed, washed my clothes, and started at three o'clock P.M.,
our baggage drawn by oxen, sixteen to twenty oxen in each

waggon. Went to church at Verulam. Niggers awful-looking
beasts, tall, strong, and active; wear no clothes at all, except very
few round the waist. The battalion bathed in the Umdloti River.
No more news about the war. Weather very hot from 9 A.M. till
5   3 P.M. The march to Victoria was fearful, dreadfully hot; the
sun right on our heads; and carrying our ammunition and arms,
almost heart-breaking. We got there just in time to see to pitch
our tents and tumble into bed for a few hours, and on
    "*Monday morning*—Up at 2.20 in the dark, see nothing and
10   find nothing; started, crossed and bathed in the Tongaati, up to
our waists crossing, so wet and wretched. One halt for mid-day
in Compensation Flat in the sun, no shade to be found and no
rest; waited till 2.30 and marched nine miles, the longest and
weariest I ever marched; the men were almost dead with heat.
15   Had only coffee and tea twice a day, and nothing else, unless
we passed a public-house or shed, which were few and far between; and then what we bought was awfully dear. Still we
scrape along; and at last at seven o'clock we got to our camping-
place; put tents up in the dark; had some salt tinned beef and
20   muddy water, and went to bed. Up next morning at 2.30 to a
minute; lowered and packed our tents and off at 4 A.M.; crossed
and bathed in the Umhlali, which, we being pretty dirty from
heat, refreshed us much; and then encamped at eight o'clock
at the Umvoti River, up to our knees. Very, very hot; we
25   washed some of our clothes, and this time a native who owned
a mill was very kind and gave us some beer. We boiled our
tinned meat and made soup; started much refreshed, and in
much better spirits. The country very hilly and hot; Indian corn
up to one's head in the fields. Some plantations of sugar-cane
30   also in the country, which, when picked, was sweet and juicy.
The Zulus or niggers here are scarcely human beings; naked and
their skins like leather; awful beasts to look at and very hideous.
That afternoon we passed Stanger Camp, and halted a mile and a
half from the camp. The men just beginning to get into condition
35   again; since they left the ship they had been in very bad training
for marching, owing to no exercise on board ship. Next morning
we got up at 2.45, and down tents, and crossed a river (shoes
and stockings off), and marched by New Gelderland about
seven or eight miles by seven o'clock, and encamped by the
40   Monoti River, where alligators and hippopotami are numerous;
we bathed notwithstanding. It was hotter than ever; the country

beautiful and hilly; no fences; mostly grass about as high as
your thigh. We heard yesterday that the column going to relieve Pearson had crossed the Tugela, and was waiting for us
before starting. . . . We shall cross the Tugela to-morrow.
"*Thursday*, 27th.—A spy was caught yesterday at Fort Pearson   5
in the camp. No one knows where the Zulu armies are; one day
they are seen at one place, another at another; one meal lasts
them for three days, and the bush they can creep through like
snakes. Being nothing but Zulus (natives) about the country
here, they come and watch us; in fact, they know everything   10
that goes on. They are awfully wily; they are never to be caught
in an open country, and never will be unless at Ulundi; the only
time they will attack their enemy is before daybreak, and at
night when we encamp, and then they won't attack a very
big force.   15
"My dear papa and mamma, I send you my diary."

Finding that they have still to wait a day at Fort Pearson,
he writes a letter to accompany his diary, and gives an account
of the military situation.

"We shall cross the river to-morrow or next day, and then we   20
relieve Pearson. They can signal from here to them. Pearson
says he is pretty well off, but has nine officers and one hundred
and fifty men ill with dysentery. When Pearson is relieved, we
by ourselves stay here; the other regiments return and make a
depôt between Fort Pearson and Ekowe, where Pearson is en-   25
camped, and carry stores and provisions there; then we shall
march to Ulundi, the king's kraal. At first it is a pretty clear
road to Pearson, but afterwards there is a large bush which we
have to get through to get at him. We shall be at Ekowe for
about three weeks. We are about four miles from the sea, and   30
the river is about a quarter of a mile across. Everything looks
like business. Colonel Hopton, when we march up, remains in
command here, and at Fort Tenedos, the other side of the river.
I saw him this morning; he asked after everybody at home. It is
very jolly getting here, and having a day's rest, and some bread   35
and fresh meat. All in very good spirits. Everything I have, and
the rest of us, is washing and drying. My camp equipage is first
rate—everything I want. The Zulus are very fine men, use as-

segaies and rifles of some sort. They treat the wounded fearfully; spear them through and through—at least, their women do. I enclose my diary of the month as I have no time to copy it."

On Friday, the 28th of March, the Tugela is crossed, and the diary recommences.

"We crossed the Tugela, being towed across. The men bivouacked and spent an awful night in pouring rain. Colonel Hopton gave me a bed in his tent. Most of the officers stood up in the rain all night. Next day,

"*Saturday*, March 29th—We started for Ekowe and marched about twelve miles. The column was five to six miles long, and we went awfully slow. There we laagered with shelter-trench outside. It would have taken 100,000 Zulus to take it. I and Keith (Turnour) on outpost duty all night (blue funk), and both tired and wet. Luckily no enemy came. Returned to camp tired, after the column had marched off.

"*Sunday*, March 30th.—Started at ten. Much delay caused by waggons crossing a brook. Warm march. Burnt a lot of kraals on the way. Enemy flying in small detachments. Arrived at Amatakula River, one mile from river on Natal side. Great bother about laager being put up, and much confusion. Early to bed. Bright moonlight till twelve.

"*Monday*, March 31st.—Under arms at four, expecting attack early. Enemy moving. Very hot; no wind; no shade. A buck ran into camp this morning and was assegaied, after much sport amongst the natives. Rumour of Cetewayo having offered peace; not believed, one word of it. Got into camp about 5.30, where we bivouacked.

"*Tuesday*, April 1st.—Under arms at four. Marched about eight o'clock with great care, Zulus having been seen by scouts hovering about. This morning the order of advance was—

"57th.
"The sailors with a Gatling and rocket.
"Ourselves.
"Our train.
"Rear Guard, 99th.
"Marines and 91st.
"Two Regiments of Natives,

protecting our waggons on the flanks. We were drawn up ready
to receive the enemy twice, but they retreated. We reached our
camping-place about four o'clock; laagered as usual, and made
entrenchments round it, only making them nearly double the
height. About one hour after we got in, it began to thunder, 5
and the rain came down in torrents, wetting us through. Our
feet had been wet for the last two days; in fact, we are never
dry. No clothes to change, or anything, as now we have only
got with us what we have got on, a mackintosh sheet, and a
great-coat. We slept as well as we could. Had the sentries 10
doubled, the enemy being expected to attack us next morning.

"*Wednesday*, April 2nd.—Under arms at four; and just as
day was beginning to break, our pickets reported the enemy advancing. Everything was got into readiness; the trenches manned;
the pickets recalled. We saw the enemy coming out of a dingle 15
in files, and, opening out, they surrounded us in most splendid
skirmishing order. The bravest fellows I ever saw. Our face
was attacked first, as they had not had time to get round to the
other side. At about 6.20 the first shot was fired, and soon all
our men were blazing away; shots whizzing over our heads, the 20
Gatling at the corner pounding it into them. They advanced at
the double, creeping in shelter of the grass. We were so strong
they could do nothing. Still they advanced within twenty yards,
where afterwards some were picked up dead. Our men were
awfully frightened and nervous at first, could not even speak, 25
and shivered from funk; so we, the officers, had enough to do
to keep the men cool. We repulsed them in about twenty minutes; whilst on our flanks and rear, where the other regiments
were, the battle was still going on. Two of our companies were
then taken round to relieve the other side, one of which was 30
mine, so we marched under their fire to the rear face, and acted
as a support. It was soon all over. We repulsed them on all sides.
The native cavalry and native contingent were then let loose to
pursue them; which they did, assegaieing most of the wounded
on their way and not doing much damage to the enemy. There 35
ought to have been a great many more killed, but all the men
were nervous and excited, and had not been under fire before.
We counted and buried four hundred and seventy-four, but a
great many were found the same day by our scouts, wounded
and hiding in bushes some miles off. We finished at about 7.10, 40
and the rest of the day we were burying them, and our own five

poor fellows, and one officer, Johnson, of the 99th. I think we
had thirty wounded. In our regiment one man was killed; he
was in my company—shot right through the head; and Colonel
Northey badly wounded, the shot entering at the shoulder and
5   lodging itself in his back. It was got out. He is very weak; I
only hope he may recover. Three other men in the regiment
were wounded. It was a fearful sight—so many of these brave
chaps lying about, dead and covered with blood and gore. They
must have had a great many more wounded, whom they took
10 away with them. I myself did not quite like the first few shots
as they whizzed about over our heads, but found I had such
a lot to do to keep the men in order and telling them when to
shoot, that I did not mind it a bit.''

This was the affair, or "battle," of Ginghilovo; and surely
15 never was such an affair described with a more prepossessing
simplicity, modesty, and humanity. The next day, the 3rd of
April, Ekowe was reached and Pearson relieved. On the 5th of
April young Mynors with his battalion marched back to the
scene of their recent action, Ginghilovo, where a fort was to
20 be established for a base of operations. And now, with the
common mention of bad weather and trying climate, comes
the ominous mention of sickness also.

"*Saturday*, April 5th.—We left Ekowe quite empty, having
burnt the king's brother's kraal the day before. We halted for
25 two hours, as our line of waggons with Pearson's was so long.
It was awfully hot. The country is perfectly lovely; such grass
and woods, hills, most beautiful flowers and trees; if only inhabited, it would be one of the most charming countries in the
world. The climate is bad. So hot in the day-time and cold at
30 night. Dew like rain. I saw, on our route to-day, after halting
in the sun for a couple of hours, six or seven fellows fall out
from sunstroke.
"*Sunday*, April 6th.—Poor Colonel Northey died. We had a
scare, or rather false alarm, at about 3.30 in the morning. Colonel
35 Pemberton has got dysentery. We began half-rations to-day.
Men not in good health.''

That night the second instalment of diary is sent off by the
courier from Ginghilovo, with a letter of a few lines, written

by moonlight. "I hope this will find you all well at home. Here there is nothing but hard work, and very little to eat from morning till night. I am afraid it will be a long affair." The same Sunday night the diary is resumed.

"GINGHILOVO.—We came back here in the morning, after leaving Pearson to our right, who was going straight back to the Tugela to recruit his troops. We encamped about three-quarters of a mile from where we had had our battle. Passing the ground the stench was fearful, owing to natives who had dragged themselves off and died.

"*Monday*, April 7th.—Colonel Pemberton still remains on the sick list; and several of the officers have been suffering more or less from diarrhœa, caused by bad water. In my last letter I said we were on half-rations; but it only lasted for about two days, as we have got some more sent us. In the afternoon we moved up a small hill into a first-rate position, but water bad and a mile off, and even that not likely to last long. We have also on the next hill another laager for the natives and bullocks. It is, of course, a necessity to keep them out of the camp, because they make the place smell so. In the daytime it is awfully hot, the sun having such power; and at night cool, and very heavy dews wet you through if you did not wear a mackintosh. The men begin to improve in spirits, but it will be awfully slow here for a fortnight on the saltest of pork and hard biscuit, pork unfit to eat.

"*Wednesday*, April 9th.—I was on duty from 3 to 4 A.M. Another scorching-hot day. A great deal of long grass has been burnt about the country, of course by the Zulus. Captain Tufnell—who was assuming command of the regiment, as we had no other officers—also very ill. We sit in the shade under the waggons out of the sun. Of course we cannot go much more than a couple of hundred yards from the camp, except in armed parties, so we find it rather dull. I got your letter from Mereworth, and was very glad to get it; always like having as much news as possible, as we seldom see a paper. . . . I walked round our new fort this afternoon. It is very strong, so to say, and would keep any Zulu army in the world off.

"*Thursday*, April 10th.—My company was on outpost duty, so I was out all day long, and did not do much but keep a look-out. Most of the troops suffering from dysentery and want

of sustenance. We expect a convoy soon, as we have only six
days' more provisions. Awfully hot again to-day. The country
all round our fort is more or less plain to the N., S., and E.,
where the King feeds his cattle. To the W. it is very mountainous, very like Scotland, only hills, I should say, higher. We see
the Zulu fires at night in the distance. I wish we could get from
here, but I believe we have to wait until all the forces are ready
to advance. I don't know whether I told you about the native
contingent. They are all black like niggers, and awful-looking
beasts; have scarcely any clothes on at all. They are armed with
rifles, but are very bad shots; the only good they are is after a
victory to pursue the enemy, as they are very active; also they
do not make bad scouts; they are very sharp-sighted, and can
hear very quickly. We must in the end give the Zulus a thrash-
ing, but the hard thing is to find them. We can never attack
them, because we don't know where they are, and they will take
good care only to attack us when we are in the bush or crossing
rivers, and perhaps at night. When they advance at close quarters, they come like cavalry; but of course any English army can
stop them if properly handled.

"Now, my dear papa and mamma, I must finish off. I hope this
will catch the mail on Tuesday. I hope all the farms, &c., are
doing well. With very best love to all, Martha, Jubber, and
Pussy,

"I am, ever your affectionate son,
                                      "ARTHUR."

On the night of Saturday, the 12th of April, poor boy, after
being on duty all the previous day, Good Friday, "in the other
laager where the niggers live," he was himself seized by sickness. On the 13th he writes home:—

"I was taken awfully seedy in the night with diarrhœa, and
to-day, Easter Sunday, I was obliged to go on the sick list, as
my complaint had turned more to dysentery. The bad water
and lowering food and bad climate are enough to kill anybody;
still we struggle on, the same for everybody. Our native runners
who take the post were yesterday chased on their way to the
Tugela, and had to return here. A convoy with provisions has
arrived here all safe; so far so good, as long as it lasts. We
expect to be here a month or six weeks doing nothing, unless we

have to alter the position of our fort owing to the scarcity of
water. The nights get colder, and the sun is hotter than any
English sun in the day-time. . . . When we left England we
were 700 strong, and now we figure about 628, caused mostly
by men gone to hospital. Some two or three of our cattle die   5
every night, also a horse or two; consequently, being only just
covered with earth for burial, there are numerous unhealthy
smells. I tried to get leave with Hutton to go shooting some
buck which had been seen, but was refused as not being safe.
We got our first English papers on Thursday, and very glad we   10
were to get them. By-the-bye, have you been fishing, and what
sport? Please tell me everything. How are grandmamma and
grandpapa? I have not heard of or from them. I hope you send
them my scribbles; I daresay they are very hard to make out,
but having only a blanket and sheet (waterproof) with us, there   15
is very little paper to be got. What I write with now is a pen I
bought, which you dip in water and it writes as you see. How
is Jubber, and how is Edmund Carew? The Zulus around us
amuse themselves by burning grass, I suppose with the idea to
starve our cattle. Lord Chelmsford has gone back to Durban. All   20
the troops have arrived safe, the 17th only losing three horses
on their journey. The niggers brought us in some sweet potatoes
yesterday which are horrible things, still they are of the vegetable description. . . . The Colonel is still suffering from dysentery, also Tufnell; so Cramer, the second captain, is in com-   25
mand of us. I should very much like to have the *Hereford Times*
forwarded to me, as it would give me all the county news. We
had service this morning for the first time since we left the
'Dublin Castle;' every other Sunday we have been marching. We
killed an enormous snake the other day, about five or six feet   30
long. Two rhinoceroses have been seen near here feeding; I
wish I could get a shot at them, but can't get leave to get out.
Has Colonel Price had much sport with the hounds, and how
are all the horses, colts, mares, &c.? How does the Cwm get on;
I wish I was there; also the ravens, everything? Colonel Northey   35
is a great loss; he was married, too, and his wife a very nice
person. Tell grandpapa I find the little book he gave me very
useful; also your Bible, which I always carry with me. To-day
is Easter Sunday, and a convoy has just been sighted; they say
we shall get the mail. I know I am writing great bosh, but have   40
nothing else to do. If you happen to see Mr. Walsh, please

thank him for my revolver; I find it very useful, and it shoots
first rate, also remember me to Aunt Ellen, and tell her she does
not know how much I am indebted to her. . . . Several fellows
have followed my idea of writing a diary and posting it; it
seems very lazy and undutiful of me, but it is perhaps better
than nothing. I do wish you could be here for a day or two to
see the country, and the trees and shrubs that grow wild,
just like a flower garden. I should say the grass here is better
for feeding than any in England, one could easily mow three or
four crops of hay in the year. The only thing, or one of the few
things, the Zulus cultivate is Indian corn, what they call mealies;
also a few fields of sugar-cane here and there. We are not many
miles from the sea, as we can hear it when the wind is the
right way, from six to ten miles I daresay.

"*Monday.*—Convoy arrived all safe last night. By the mail
poor Keith Turnour heard he had lost his father. I was awfully
sorry, as I could not do any work, being still on the sick list.
My dysentery still sticks to me with bad pain in my inside, but
I feel otherwise well in myself. I slept under a cart last night—
quite a luxury, as it keeps the dew off. To-day we are burning
the grass round our laager, so that the Zulus cannot set fire to
it and attack us at the same time. The men have had fresh meat
the last two days, as several bullocks have come up from Tugela.
They are killed at eight in the morning, and eaten at one. We
got some jam up last night, so we are doing pretty well now.
The only thing I wish is that the Zulus would attack us again.
It is getting quite slow doing nothing. Captain Tufnell is off the
sick list to-day, and takes command of the regiment. How are
Uncle Tom and Aunt Conty getting on? Having no end of fun,
I'll be bound. Our laager is about twenty miles from Fort Pearson on the Tugela, and sixteen miles from the now abandoned
Ekowe, which we can see with our telescopes. We are all becoming very learned cooks, as we cook all our meat, salt meat,
&c., make soup and different things of them. The worst of it is
we have very few materials to cook in, mostly provided by the
waggon conductors. We made some mealie cakes of Indian corn,
which were first rate at the time, but awfully indigestible afterwards; I'm afraid the fault of the cooking; I wish I had taken
lessons from Miles before I left.

"*Tuesday*, April 15th.—The convoy of empty waggons left
at six to go to Tugela. Spent a very bad night, suffering from

diarrhœa, and felt much weaker to-day; still I hope I shall get over it soon. Some of the fellows got leave to shoot, and they shot five golden plovers, or grey kind of plovers, which are very acceptable to our larder. I felt awfully dull, nothing to do but sit under a cart out of the sun and try to sleep. The scouts went 5 out some six or seven miles to-day and burnt several kraals. Four Zulu women and a boy were brought in yesterday, the most hideous creatures I ever saw, more like wild animals. I am going to post my letter to-night, so as to be certain to catch the mail. I hope you are all well, and love to everybody. 10
"Ever your most affectionate son,
"ARTHUR."

P.S.—I was very glad to get a letter from you and papa last night, of March 11th. I am exceedingly sorry to hear of grandmamma's attack. It must indeed have been very serious. I only 15 hope she may recover for some time, and be well when I get home again. I had rather a better night last night, but am still very weak. Sorry to hear 'Masquerade' is a roarer. Have not had grandpapa's and Elinor's letters yet: must have missed the mail." 20

He never got home, and he wrote no more; the cold nights, and heavy dews, and suns "hotter than any English sun," had done their work. On the 24th of April he was sent to the hospital at Fort Pearson, where Colonel Hopton, a Herefordshire neighbour, was in command; the poor boy died on the 25 day following, and in a letter to his father Colonel Hopton relates the end.

"Yesterday morning I got a note from an officer of the 60th, Gunning, who appears to have been told by Arthur that he knew me, informing me that he, Arthur, was very ill with dysentery, 30 and that the doctor had sent him to Fort Pearson in hopes that the change of air would do him good, and asking me to meet the convoy on arrival here and get Arthur at once into the hospital. I met the empty convoy of waggons last evening, as they approached our camp, and got the one with Arthur in it over 35 the river (Tugela) as soon as I could, and sent it up to hospital. This morning early I went to see him, having first asked the doctor in charge about him. He at once told me he feared the

worst. When I saw him I did not think he could recover. His servant was with him, who was very attentive to him. We gave him what medical comforts could be got, such as beef-tea and champagne. I stayed with him all the morning, until 2 P.M., and
5 at his request I read and prayed by his stretcher side; he was then quite sensible and followed all I said, and repeated some of the prayers after me. All this time he was very weak, and hardly able to raise himself up, although his servant told me that yesterday he was able to stand and walk. The disease for some days
10 seems to have taken hold of him. He passed nothing but pure blood, and when I first saw him was reduced almost to a skeleton. About 2 P.M., having changed his shirt and made him as comfortable as I could, I left him, telling him I would come back soon. Some time afterwards I got a message from him ask-
15 ing me to go back, which I did, about 5.30 P.M. I found a Captain Cardew, one of the staff officers, with him. He had just read the fourteenth chapter of St. John to him, which he listened to, and asked Cardew to read slowly, so that he might follow. A doctor was also with him. They told me that the end was ap-
20 proaching. We all stayed with him till about 7 P.M., when he gave a little sigh and passed away; he was not sensible for the last hour, but appeared not to suffer any pain. When I was with him in the morning, I said: 'Arthur, I shall write by the post to-night, to tell your mother how ill you are.' He said: 'Yes,
25 please, Colonel, write to mamma.' It was at this time that he asked me to read to him and repeated after me the Lord's Prayer."

A little more is added by a friend and brother officer, Lieutenant Hutton, a corporal from whose company had helped the dying boy's servant in his attendance on his master.

30 "The corporal at the boy's request had on several occasions read to him both from the Bible and Prayer Book, and as the corporal expressed himself to me, he seemed always more peaceful and happy afterwards. His servant Starman was most struck by the heroic and resigned way in which his master bore the
35 pain of his disease shortly before his death. Knowing the end was approaching, and seeing his master inclined to move, Starman got up and was about to smooth his pillow for him, when the boy, with a smile that as he said he will never forget, turned

and whispered: 'Hush, don't touch me, I am going to heaven;' and so fell asleep."

On the 26th of April, the day after his death, Arthur Mynors was buried under a mimosa-tree, on a grassy slope looking down to the sea over the lovely valley of the Tugela. On the 5 2nd of May some men of his regiment, the 60th, put a small rough wooden cross over his grave, with this inscription:—

IN MEMORY OF
LIEUT. MYNORS,
3/60,   10
WHO DIED APRIL 25, 1879,
AGED 22 YEARS.

It was a happy nature that, by the banks of the Tugela, passed thus early away—a happy and beautiful nature. His simple letters and diary, which we have been following, show 15 him to us better than any admiring description. They show a nature fresh, wholesome, gay; an English boy with the tastes of his age and bringing up, with a keen love of sport, with a genuine love for the country, a genuine eye for it—Greek in his simplicity and truth of feeling, Greek in his simplicity and 20 truth of touch. We see him full of natural affection, and not ashamed of manifesting it; bred in habits of religion, and not ashamed of retaining them; without a speck of affectation, without a shadow of pretension, unsullied, brave, true, kind, respectful, grateful, uncensorious, uncomplaining; in the time 25 to act, cheerfully active; in the time to suffer, cheerfully enduring. So to his friends he seemed, and so their testimony shows him—testimony which by its affectionate warmth proves the character which could inspire it to have been no ordinary one. "I am sure you and anybody who knew him," writes a 30 brother officer, "will be grieved beyond measure to hear of the death of our dear Bunny Mynors, of dysentery. I can't tell you what a loss he is to us, as he was such a favourite with us all. He had endeared himself in his short stay of a year with men and officers alike, more than is given to the lot of most of 35

us." "He had all the qualities," says another, "of a good soldier
and a leader of men, combined with a perfect temper, thorough
unselfishness, and a genial cheery manner." "The life and soul
of the mess," writes the adjutant of his battalion, himself an
5 Etonian, "keen at all sports and games, and a universal favourite
wherever we have been quartered—it seems hard to lose him.
But when I add that in all professional matters he was most
earnest, and so keen to be well up in his work, strict and yet
with a perfect manner, a favourite with his men, and, as all ad-
10 mit, the most promising boy Eton has sent to our ranks for
many a day—when I add this, I feel that not only we who
knew him, but all the battalion, must grieve, and will do so for
the loss of one who promised to be such a credit to his regiment. . . . The old school may well grieve for so fine a char-
15 acter as his who has just been taken from us. I know no finer
fellows, or those who do their work so well, as those like
Mynors, who never said an unkind word of any one, and consequently no one ever said any word except of praise or love
for them." "Such as they," to the same effect says his tutor,
20 Mr. Warre, who has gained and kept the loving regard and
trust of so many generations of his Eton pupils, as he gained
and kept those of young Mynors; "such as *they* have from
others the love that they deserve."

Natures so beautiful are not common; and those who have
25 seen and possessed the bright presence of such a boy, while
they mourn their irreparable loss, cannot but think most of his
rareness, his uniqueness. For me, a stranger, and speaking not
to his friends but to the wide public, I confess that when I
have paid my tribute of sympathy to a beautiful character and
30 to a profound sorrow, it is rather to what he has in common
with others that my thoughts are drawn, than to what is
unique in him. The order of things in which he was brought
up, the school system in which he was educated, produce, not
indeed many natures so sweet as his, but in all good natures
35 many of his virtues. That school system is a close and narrow
one; that order of things is changing, and will surely pass away.
Vain are endeavours to keep it fixed for ever, impotent are re-
grets for it; it will pass away. The received ideas which fur-

nished the mind of Arthur Mynors, as they in general furnish
the minds of English boys of his class, and which determine
his and their intellectual vision, will change. But under the old
order of things, and with its received ideas, there were bred
great and precious virtues; it is good for us to rest our eyes   5
upon them, to feel their value, to resolve amid all chances and
changes to save and nourish them, as saved and nourished they
can be. Our slowness of development in England has its excellent uses in enabling indispensable virtues to take root, and
to make themselves felt by us to be indispensable. Our French   10
neighbours have moved faster than we; they have more lucidity, in several important respects, than we have; they have
fewer illusions. But a modern French school-boy, Voltairian
and emancipated, reading *La Fille Elisa* and *Nana*, making it
his pastime to play tricks on his chaplain, to mock and flout   15
him and his teaching—the production of a race of lucid schoolboys of this kind is a dangerous privilege. When I lay down
the memoir of Dr. Raleigh I feel that, crude and faulty as is
the type of religion offered by Puritanism, narrow and false
as is its conception of human life, materialistic and impossible 20
as is its world to come, yet the seriousness, soberness, and
devout energy of Puritanism are a prize, once won, never to be
lost; they are a possession to our race for ever. And in taking
leave of the letters and diary of Arthur Mynors, I feel that this
natural and charming boy, too, has virtues, he and others like   25
him, which are part of the very tradition and life of England;
which have gone to make "the ancient and inbred integrity,
piety, good-nature, and good-humour of the English people," [1]
and which can no more perish than that ideal.

[1] Burke.

A Septuagenarian Poet *

Mr. Tennyson and Mr. Browning, as we all of us note admiringly, are septuagenarian poets—septuagenarian poets carrying on unchanged into their later verse their lifelong manner and qualities. A septuagenarian poet far less celebrated, Mr.
5 William Bell Scott, has just given us a charming little volume, in which he departs entirely from the manner and qualities of a former poetical work (a work which Emerson and Mr. Swinburne have praised highly, and which its author appears himself to have regarded as his principal achievement), the
10 "Year of the World," a philosophical poem on "Redemption from the Fall." The author tells us that "the scheme of the poem—namely, the descent of the soul from a simple and unconscious state into the antagonistic and concrete, and its reascent, or the readjustment of the human with the divine
15 nature, which is the profound idea of all religions and philosophy—is less a subject for the analytic than the imaginative faculty." It may be so; but the proof of the pudding, according to the homely proverb, is in the eating.

> And thus the Hierarch of the Phantasy
20 > This shattered image of the soul reforms
> By sensuous tools—and man adores himself—
> But everlasting fate holds all; and time
> Scatters the chaff as doth the winnowing fan
> After the wearied flail. Not this, not this!

25 *Not this, not this,* indeed! No theory regarding the proper subjects for the imaginative faculty will ever prevent people

* "A Poet's Harvest Home." By William Bell Scott. (London: Elliot Stock, 1882.)

whose taste is sane from crying out *not this!* when a strain of
such kind is offered to them as poetry.

But some forty years ago we happened to fall in with a
poem by Mr. Scott, written in quite another manner—written
with what the old Scotch poet Barbour, in some lines which 5
Mr. Scott has taken as the motto for his present volume, excellently calls

> . . . . the soothfastness
> That shows the thing just as it was.

That poem was "Rosabel." The life of Rosabel, poor girl, had 10
its misadventure, and the poem had its misadventure too. It dis-
appeared; it emerged again with a new name; it suffered one
knows not what of chance and change. But the original Rosabel
lives in our memory, and will live there always.

> On saunters Rosabel, 15
> Avoided, gazed at; once a time
> She was the harvest-queen. . . .

Oh! the indescribable charm of "soothfastness," to borrow
Barbour's word; soothfastness in the poet's personages, soothfastness in his treatment of them. "Rosabel" had soothfastness; 20
"the heroic efforts of Lyremnos, the Energy," in the "Year of
the World," are sadly wanting in them.

And now, after his seventieth birthday, Mr. Scott comes to
us with soothfast work again; with a little volume in which on
a few simple matters he discourses with great plainness of 25
speech. He has no "Revenge," no "Despair"; and we will
frankly own that to "Despair" we ourselves prefer, as septuagenarian work, the following

OLD, OLD STORY
> It seems but yesterday 30
> The sweet light voice, a living lute,
> The sweet slim figure, struck one mute.
> Matilda was the lovely name;
> Within a neat red-pencilled frame

I wrote it in my first verse book
Snugly kept in secret nook!

She came to us beneath the wing
Of her mamma, whose bonnet wide
Was an epitome of Spring—
So long since, I must even confide,
The great scoop'd bonnet was just then
Adored by fashion and by men.
Well I remember wondering
How this frank angel ever came
From such a broad-wing'd pompous dame!

And after forty years depart,
Child and mamma drop on us here.
Can the slim figure and light heart
Beneath the same broad wing appear
Again in this far-distant year?
Ah, no! the ladies seem the same,
But the bonnet is quite different;
Matilda is the pompous dame,
And this her daughter Millicent!

Good heavens! it is indeed just so
Time reproduces all his toys;
Here is the pair of long ago
Touching the hearts of other boys.
And am I then to moralise,
With satire in my rhymes and eyes?
The sonsy matron! suppose we
Ask *her* now what she thinks of *me?*

I would indeed like well to see
What Matilda thinks, or thought of me
In that romantic early year
When her fine name I held so dear,
Or so at least made it appear
In my long-hid first verses' book.
I'll try to wile her out to look
At the sundial or the bees,

And underneath the quivering trees
I shall touch on ancient things,
That so long since lost all their wings,
Or rather, to tell truth, I'd say,
Used them long since to fly away.—   5
I did at once, and I must own
A faintly sentimental tone
Stole o'er my reminiscences,
As we pass'd, repass'd the bees:
I said her child recall'd her so—   10
Revived in me the long ago.
The age was just about the same
When we once played a charming game,
Now quite gone out, upon the grass;
And here again the bees we pass,   15
Though she forgets to turn her head,
But answers in a cheerful mood,
Her daughter is both fair and good.
The gravel crunch'd beneath her tread
While she went on, and thus she said: 20

"Your memory's good for long ago,
I often wish that mine were so;
But when a girl is wed, like me,
And carried quite away to town,
The rest soon fades away, you see;   25
The birds gone, soon the nest blows down.
Your brother James, now dead, and I
Had some flirtations certainly;
He was the red-hair'd one, and tall,
I can't remember *you* at all."   30

I made reply, some sidelong mutter;
We turn'd, we join'd the rest at tea,
She ate three folds of bread and butter.
She had *never* thought at all of me.

Sometimes, with the same plainness, the tone is graver and   35
deeper, as in

AN AUTUMN EVENING

Dinner and day together go,
    As round the table still we dwell.
Watching the sun descending low,
5   Our faces shine with day's farewell.

This is the moment of all time
    When stillness reigneth over all,
When life calms down, the highest lime
    Moves not, nor any leaf dares fall.

10   Shall we sit still in low-voiced talk,
    Anticipating lamp and book,
Or once more take a sauntering walk
    Hillward to catch the sun's last look?

The lambs and sheep have parted long;
15   No anxious bleat nor moor-hen's call
Is heard, nor robin's autumn song;
    Absolute silence reigns o'er all—

Over the orange-tinted brae
    Against that wondrous north-west sky;
20 Over the far sea golden-grey
    Where no horizon we descry. . . .

Now we return with noiseless tread,
    These cottage-doors are shut betimes;
Listen . . . this is old John Grimes—
25   He reads before he goes to bed.

He reads a chapter of the Book
    Of Books, to comfort his old wife;
Happily in this far Scotch nook
    Faith still trims the lamp of life.

30 But there our own high windows shine!
    The evening fire is lit, we see.
Wayfaring shoes let us resign,
    And you will sing that hymn to me.

Or a pathos is added, as in

ADIEU

Farewell! it is not much to say,
When bright night follows pleasant day,
And when the traveller takes his way   5
From friendly hearth to hearth of friend.
But yet with each change we portend
Some grief, some hand-long cloud of care
We ought to shelter from, or share.
Parting eyes are over-kind;   10
The lamb-lost ewe's bleat fills the air,
The plover's plaint is in the wind.

"Rose-Leaves" has the same kind of charm as "Adieu"; and it
brings in a name which we have pleasure in saluting with
honour: the name of Miss Christina Rossetti, the sister of the   15
artist and poet whom we have just lost:—

Once a rose ever a rose, we say.
    One we loved, and who loved us,
Remains beloved though gone from day.
    To human hearts it must be thus.   20
The past is sweetly laid away!

Sere and seal'd for a day and year,
    Smell them, dear Christina, pray.
So nature treats its children dear,
    So memory deals with yesterday.   25
The past is sweetly laid away!

Or even, along with pathos, there is the touch of weirdness, of
otherworldness; but still, still, "great plainness of speech."

TO THE DEAD

Gone art thou? gone, and is the light of day   30
Still shining; is my hair not touch'd with gray?
—But evening draweth nigh, I pass the door
And see thee walking on the dim-lit shore.

Gone art thou? gone, and weary on the brink
Of Lethe waiting there? O do not drink!
Drink not, forget not, wait a little while!
I shall be with thee; we again may smile.

5   It would be pleasant to go on; but the columns of the *St.
James's Gazette* are required, alas! for Egypt, and Ireland, and
the Gladstone Ministry, and other miseries of that sort. If the
reader wants more of our septuagenarian poet, let him send
for his volume.

Literature and Science

Practical people talk with a smile of Plato and of his absolute ideas; and it is impossible to deny that Plato's ideas do often seem unpractical and impracticable, and especially when one views them in connexion with the life of a great work-a-day world like the United States. The necessary staple of the life of   5
such a world Plato regards with disdain; handicraft and trade and the working professions he regards with disdain; but what becomes of the life of an industrial modern community if you take handicraft and trade and the working professions out of it? The base mechanic arts and handicrafts, says Plato, bring   10
about a natural weakness in the principle of excellence in a man, so that he cannot govern the ignoble growths in him, but nurses them, and cannot understand fostering any other. Those who exercise such arts and trades, as they have their bodies, he says, marred by their vulgar businesses, so they have   15
their souls, too, bowed and broken by them. And if one of these uncomely people has a mind to seek self-culture and philosophy, Plato compares him to a bald little tinker, who has scraped together money, and has got his release from service, and has had a bath, and bought a new coat, and is   20
rigged out like a bridegroom about to marry the daughter of his master who has fallen into poor and helpless estate.

Nor do the working professions fare any better than trade at the hands of Plato. He draws for us an inimitable picture of the working lawyer, and of his life of bondage; he shows how   25
this bondage from his youth up has stunted and warped him, and made him small and crooked of soul, encompassing him with difficulties which he is not man enough to rely on justice and truth as means to encounter, but has recourse, for help

out of them, to falsehood and wrong. And so, says Plato, this poor creature is bent and broken, and grows up from boy to man without a particle of soundness in him, although exceedingly smart and clever in his own esteem.

One cannot refuse to admire the artist who draws these pictures. But we say to ourselves that his ideas show the influence of a primitive and obsolete order of things, when the warrior caste and the priestly caste were alone in honour, and the humble work of the world was done by slaves. We have now changed all that; the modern majesty consists in work, as Emerson declares; and in work, we may add, principally of such plain and dusty kind as the work of cultivators of the ground, handicraftsmen, men of trade and business, men of the working professions. Above all is this true in a great industrious community such as that of the United States.

Now education, many people go on to say, is still mainly governed by the ideas of men like Plato, who lived when the warrior caste and the priestly or philosophical class were alone in honour, and the really useful part of the community were slaves. It is an education fitted for persons of leisure in such a community. This education passed from Greece and Rome to the feudal communities of Europe, where also the warrior caste and the priestly caste were alone held in honour, and where the really useful and working part of the community, though not nominally slaves as in the pagan world, were practically not much better off than slaves, and not more seriously regarded. And how absurd it is, people end by saying, to inflict this education upon an industrious modern community, where very few indeed are persons of leisure, and the mass to be considered has not leisure, but is bound, for its own great good, and for the great good of the world at large, to plain labour and to industrial pursuits, and the education in question tends necessarily to make men dissatisfied with these pursuits and unfitted for them!

That is what is said. So far I must defend Plato, as to plead that his view of education and studies is in the general, as it seems to me, sound enough, and fitted for all sorts and conditions of men, whatever their pursuits may be. "An intelligent

man," says Plato, "will prize those studies which result in his
soul getting soberness, righteousness, and wisdom, and will less
value the others." I cannot consider *that* a bad description of
the aim of education, and of the motives which should govern
us in the choice of studies, whether we are preparing ourselves   5
for a hereditary seat in the English House of Lords or for the
pork trade in Chicago.

Still I admit that Plato's world was not ours, that his scorn
of trade and handicraft is fantastic, that he had no conception
of a great industrial community such as that of the United   10
States, and that such a community must and will shape its education to suit its own needs. If the usual education handed
down to it from the past does not suit it, it will certainly before
long drop this and try another. The usual education in the
past has been mainly literary. The question is whether the   15
studies which were long supposed to be the best for all of us
are practically the best now; whether others are not better.
The tyranny of the past, many think, weighs on us injuriously
in the predominance given to letters in education. The question
is raised whether, to meet the needs of our modern life, the   20
predominance ought not now to pass from letters to science;
and naturally the question is nowhere raised with more energy
than here in the United States. The design of abasing what is
called "mere literary instruction and education," and of exalting what is called "sound, extensive, and practical scientific 25
knowledge," is, in this intensely modern world of the United
States, even more perhaps than in Europe, a very popular design, and makes great and rapid progress.

I am going to ask whether the present movement for oust-
ing letters from their old predominance in education, and for   30
transferring the predominance in education to the natural sciences, whether this brisk and flourishing movement ought to
prevail, and whether it is likely that in the end it really will
prevail. An objection may be raised which I will anticipate.
My own studies have been almost wholly in letters, and my   35
visits to the field of the natural sciences have been very slight
and inadequate, although those sciences have always strongly
moved my curiosity. A man of letters, it will perhaps be said,

is not competent to discuss the comparative merits of letters
and natural science as means of education. To this objection
I reply, first of all, that his incompetence, if he attempts the
discussion but is really incompetent for it, will be abundantly
visible; nobody will be taken in; he will have plenty of sharp
observers and critics to save mankind from that danger. But
the line I am going to follow is, as you will soon discover, so
extremely simple, that perhaps it may be followed without
failure even by one who for a more ambitious line of discussion would be quite incompetent.

Some of you may possibly remember a phrase of mine
which has been the object of a good deal of comment; an observation to the effect that in our culture, the aim being *to
know ourselves and the world*, we have, as the means to this
end, *to know the best which has been thought and said in the
world*. A man of science, who is also an excellent writer and
the very prince of debaters, Professor Huxley, in a discourse
at the opening of Sir Josiah Mason's college at Birmingham,
laying hold of this phrase, expanded it by quoting some more
words of mine, which are these: "The civilised world is to be
regarded as now being, for intellectual and spiritual purposes,
one great confederation, bound to a joint action and working
to a common result; and whose members have for their proper
outfit a knowledge of Greek, Roman, and Eastern antiquity,
and of one another. Special local and temporary advantages
being put out of account, that modern nation will in the intellectual and spiritual sphere make most progress, which most
thoroughly carries out this programme."

Now on my phrase, thus enlarged, Professor Huxley remarks that when I speak of the above-mentioned knowledge as
enabling us to know ourselves and the world, I assert *literature*
to contain the materials which suffice for thus making us know
ourselves and the world. But it is not by any means clear, says
he, that after having learnt all which ancient and modern literatures have to tell us, we have laid a sufficiently broad and deep
foundation for that criticism of life, that knowledge of ourselves and the world, which constitutes culture. On the contrary, Professor Huxley declares that he finds himself "wholl

unable to admit that either nations or individuals will really advance, if their outfit draws nothing from the stores of physical science. An army without weapons of precision, and with no particular base of operations, might more hopefully enter upon a campaign on the Rhine, than a man, devoid of a knowledge of what physical science has done in the last century, upon a criticism of life."

This shows how needful it is for those who are to discuss any matter together, to have a common understanding as to the sense of the terms they employ,—how needful, and how difficult. What Professor Huxley says, implies just the reproach which is so often brought against the study of *belles lettres*, as they are called: that the study is an elegant one, but slight and ineffectual; a smattering of Greek and Latin and other ornamental things, of little use for any one whose object is to get at truth, and to be a practical man. So, too, M. Renan talks of the "superficial humanism" of a school-course which treats us as if we were all going to be poets, writers, preachers, orators, and he opposes this humanism to positive science, or the critical search after truth. And there is always a tendency in those who are remonstrating against the predominance of letters in education, to understand by letters *belles lettres*, and by *belles lettres* a superficial humanism, the opposite of science or true knowledge.

But when we talk of knowing Greek and Roman antiquity, for instance, which is the knowledge people have called the humanities, I for my part mean a knowledge which is something more than a superficial humanism, mainly decorative. "I call all teaching *scientific*," says Wolf, the critic of Homer, "which is systematically laid out and followed up to its original source. For example: a knowledge of classical antiquity is scientific when the remains of classical antiquity are connectedly studied in the original languages." There can be no doubt that Wolf is perfectly right; that all learning is scientific which is systematically laid out and followed up to its original sources, and that a genuine humanism is scientific.

When I speak of knowing Greek and Roman antiquity, therefore, as a help to knowing ourselves and the world, I mean more than a knowledge of so much vocabulary, so much grammar, so many portions of authors in the Greek and Latin languages. I mean knowing the Greeks and Romans, and their life and genius, and what they were and did in the world; 5   what we get from them, and what is its value. That, at least, is the ideal; and when we talk of endeavouring to know Greek and Roman antiquity, as a help to knowing ourselves and the world, we mean endeavouring so to know them as to satisfy this ideal, however much we may still fall short of it.

10   The same also as to knowing our own and other modern nations, with the like aim of getting to understand ourselves and the world. To know the best that has been thought and said by the modern nations, is to know, says Professor Huxley, "only what modern *literatures* have to tell us; it is the criticism 15   of life contained in modern literature." And yet "the distinctive character of our times," he urges, "lies in the vast and constantly increasing part which is played by natural knowledge." And how, therefore, can a man, devoid of knowledge of what physical science has done in the last century, enter hopefully 20   upon a criticism of modern life?

Let us, I say, be agreed about the meaning of the terms we are using. I talk of knowing the best which has been thought and uttered in the world; Professor Huxley says this means knowing *literature*. Literature is a large word; it may mean every- 25   thing written with letters or printed in a book. Euclid's *Elements* and Newton's *Principia* are thus literature. All knowledge that reaches us through books is literature. But by literature Professor Huxley means *belles lettres*. He means to make me say, that knowing the best which has been thought and 30   said by the modern nations is knowing their *belles lettres* and no more. And this is no sufficient equipment, he argues, for a criticism of modern life. But as I do not mean, by knowing ancient Rome, knowing merely more or less of Latin *belles lettres*, and taking no account of Rome's military, and political, 35   and legal, and administrative work in the world; and as, by knowing ancient Greece, I understand knowing her as the giver of Greek art, and the guide to a free and right use of reason and to scientific method, and the founder of our mathematics and physics and astronomy and biology,—I understand knowing her as all this, and not merely knowing certain Greek poems, and histories, and treatises, and speeches,— so as to the knowledge of modern nations also. By knowing modern nations, I mean not merely knowing their *belles lettres*, but knowing also what has been done by such men as Copernicus, Galileo, Newton, Darwin. "Our ancestors learned," says Professor Huxley, "that the earth is the centre of the visible universe, and that man is the cynosure of things terrestrial; and more especially was it inculcated that the course of nature had no fixed order, but that it could be, and constantly was, altered." But for us now, continues Professor Huxley, "the notions of the beginning and the end of the world entertained by our forefathers are no longer credible. It is very certain that the earth is not the chief body in the material universe, and that the world is not subordinated to man's use. It is even more certain that nature is the expression of a definite order, with which nothing interferes." "And yet," he cries, "the purely classical education advocated by the representatives of the humanists in our day gives no inkling of all this!"

In due place and time I will just touch upon that vexed question of classical education; but at present the question is as to what is meant by knowing the best which modern nations have thought and said. It is not knowing their *belles lettres* merely which is meant. To know Italian *belles lettres* is not to know Italy, and to know English *belles lettres* is not to know England. Into knowing Italy and England there comes a great deal more, Galileo and Newton amongst it. The reproach of being a superficial humanism, a tincture of *belles lettres*, may attach rightly enough to some other disciplines; but to the particular discipline recommended when I proposed knowing the best that has been thought and said in the world, it does not apply. In that best I certainly include what in modern times has been thought and said by the great observers and knowers of nature.

There is, therefore, really no question between Professor Huxley and me as to whether knowing the great results of the modern scientific study of nature is not required as a part of

our culture, as well as knowing the products of literature and
art. But to follow the processes by which those results are
reached, ought, say the friends of physical science, to be made
the staple of education for the bulk of mankind. And here
5   there does arise a question between those whom Professor
Huxley calls with playful sarcasm "the Levites of culture,"
and those whom the poor humanist is sometimes apt to regard
as its Nebuchadnezzars.

The great results of the scientific investigation of nature we
10 are agreed upon knowing, but how much of our study are
we bound to give to the processes by which those results are
reached? The results have their visible bearing on human life.
But all the processes, too, all the items of fact, by which those
results are reached and established, are interesting. All knowl-
15 edge is interesting to a wise man, and the knowledge of nature is interesting to all men. It is very interesting to know,
that, from the albuminous white of the egg, the chick in the
egg gets the materials for its flesh, bones, blood, and feathers;
while, from the fatty yolk of the egg, it gets the heat and en-
20 ergy which enable it at length to break its shell and begin the
world. It is less interesting, perhaps, but still it is interesting, to
know that when a taper burns, the wax is converted into carbonic acid and water. Moreover, it is quite true that the habit
of dealing with facts, which is given by the study of nature,
25 is, as the friends of physical science praise it for being, an
excellent discipline. The appeal, in the study of nature, is constantly to observation and experiment; not only is it said that
the thing is so, but we can be made to see that it is so. Not
only does a man tell us that when a taper burns the wax is
30 converted into carbonic acid and water, as a man may tell us,
if he likes, that Charon is punting his ferry-boat on the river
Styx, or that Victor Hugo is a sublime poet, or Mr. Gladstone the most admirable of statesmen; but we are made to
see that the conversion into carbonic acid and water does
35 actually happen. This reality of natural knowledge it is, which
makes the friends of physical science contrast it, as a knowledge of things, with the humanist's knowledge, which is, say
they, a knowledge of words. And hence Professor Huxley is

moved to lay it down that, "for the purpose of attaining real culture, an exclusively scientific education is at least as effectual as an exclusively literary education." And a certain President of the Section for Mechanical Science in the British Association is, in Scripture phrase, "very bold," and declares that if a man, in his mental training, "has substituted literature and history for natural science, he has chosen the less useful alternative." But whether we go these lengths or not, we must all admit that in natural science the habit gained of dealing with facts is a most valuable discipline, and that every one should have some experience of it.

More than this, however, is demanded by the reformers. It is proposed to make the training in natural science the main part of education, for the great majority of mankind at any rate. And here, I confess, I part company with the friends of physical science, with whom up to this point I have been agreeing. In differing from them, however, I wish to proceed with the utmost caution and diffidence. The smallness of my own acquaintance with the disciplines of natural science is ever before my mind, and I am fearful of doing these disciplines an injustice. The ability and pugnacity of the partisans of natural science make them formidable persons to contradict. The tone of tentative inquiry, which befits a being of dim faculties and bounded knowledge, is the tone I would wish to take and not to depart from. At present it seems to me, that those who are for giving to natural knowledge, as they call it, the chief place in the education of the majority of mankind, leave one important thing out of their account: the constitution of human nature. But I put this forward on the strength of some facts not at all recondite, very far from it; facts capable of being stated in the simplest possible fashion, and to which, if I so state them, the man of science will, I am sure, be willing to allow their due weight.

Deny the facts altogether, I think, he hardly can. He can hardly deny, that when we set ourselves to enumerate the powers which go to the building up of human life, and say that they are the power of conduct, the power of intellect and knowledge, the power of beauty, and the power of social life

and manners,—he can hardly deny that this scheme, though drawn in rough and plain lines enough, and not pretending to scientific exactness, does yet give a fairly true representation of the matter. Human nature is built up by these powers;
5   we have the need for them all. When we have rightly met and adjusted the claims of them all, we shall then be in a fair way for getting soberness and righteousness, with wisdom. This is evident enough, and the friends of physical science would admit it.
10   But perhaps they may not have sufficiently observed another thing: namely, that the several powers just mentioned are not isolated, but there is, in the generality of mankind, a perpetual tendency to relate them one to another in divers ways. With one such way of relating them I am particularly concerned
15   now. Following our instinct for intellect and knowledge, we acquire pieces of knowledge; and presently, in the generality of men, there arises the desire to relate these pieces of knowledge to our sense for conduct, to our sense for beauty,—and there is weariness and dissatisfaction if the desire is baulked.
20   Now in this desire lies, I think, the strength of that hold which letters have upon us.

All knowledge is, as I said just now, interesting; and even items of knowledge which from the nature of the case cannot well be related, but must stand isolated in our thoughts,
25   have their interest. Even lists of exceptions have their interest. If we are studying Greek accents, it is interesting to know that *pais* and *pas*, and some other monosyllables of the same form of declension, do not take the circumflex upon the last syllable of the genitive plural, but vary, in this respect, from the common rule. If we are studying physiology, it is interest-
30   ing to know that the pulmonary artery carries dark blood and the pulmonary vein carries bright blood, departing in this respect from the common rule for the division of labour between the veins and the arteries. But every one knows how we seek
35   naturally to combine the pieces of our knowledge together, to bring them under general rules, to relate them to principles; and how unsatisfactory and tiresome it would be to go on for

ever learning lists of exceptions, or accumulating items of fact which must stand isolated.

Well, that same need of relating our knowledge, which operates here within the sphere of our knowledge itself, we shall find operating, also, outside that sphere. We experience, as we go on learning and knowing,—the vast majority of us experience,—the need of relating what we have learnt and known to the sense which we have in us for conduct, to the sense which we have in us for beauty.

A certain Greek prophetess of Mantineia in Arcadia, Diotima by name, once explained to the philosopher Socrates that love, and impulse, and bent of all kinds, is, in fact, nothing else but the desire in men that good should for ever be present to them. This desire for good, Diotima assured Socrates, is our fundamental desire, of which fundamental desire every impulse in us is only some one particular form. And therefore this fundamental desire it is, I suppose,—this desire in men that good should be for ever present to them,—which acts in us when we feel the impulse for relating our knowledge to our sense for conduct and to our sense for beauty. At any rate, with men in general the instinct exists. Such is human nature. And the instinct, it will be admitted, is innocent, and human nature is preserved by our following the lead of its innocent instincts. Therefore, in seeking to gratify this instinct in question, we are following the instinct of self-preservation in humanity.

But, no doubt, some kinds of knowledge cannot be made to directly serve the instinct in question, cannot be directly related to the sense for beauty, to the sense for conduct. These are instrument-knowledges; they lead on to other knowledges, which can. A man who passes his life in instrument-knowledges is a specialist. They may be invaluable as instruments to something beyond, for those who have the gift thus to employ them; and they may be disciplines in themselves wherein it is useful for every one to have some schooling. But it is inconceivable that the generality of men should pass all their mental life with Greek accents or with formal logic. My friend Pro-

fessor Sylvester, who is one of the first mathematicians in the world, holds transcendental doctrines as to the virtue of mathematics, but those doctrines are not for common men. In the very Senate House and heart of our English Cambridge I once
5 ventured, though not without an apology for my profaneness, to hazard the opinion that for the majority of mankind a little of mathematics, even, goes a long way. Of course this is quite consistent with their being of immense importance as an instrument to something else; but it is the few who have the
10 aptitude for thus using them, not the bulk of mankind.

The natural sciences do not, however, stand on the same footing with these instrument-knowledges. Experience shows us that the generality of men will find more interest in learning that, when a taper burns, the wax is converted into car-
15 bonic acid and water, or in learning the explanation of the phenomenon of dew, or in learning how the circulation of the blood is carried on, than they find in learning that the genitive plural of *pais* and *pas* does not take the circumflex on the termination. And one piece of natural knowledge is added to
20 another, and others are added to that, and at last we come to propositions so interesting as Mr. Darwin's famous proposition that "our ancestor was a hairy quadruped furnished with a tail and pointed ears, probably arboreal in his habits." Or we come to propositions of such reach and magnitude as those
25 which Professor Huxley delivers, when he says that the notions of our forefathers about the beginning and the end of the world were all wrong, and that nature is the expression of a definite order with which nothing interferes.

Interesting, indeed, these results of science are, important
30 they are, and we should all of us be acquainted with them. But what I now wish you to mark is, that we are still, when they are propounded to us and we receive them, we are still in the sphere of intellect and knowledge. And for the generality of men there will be found, I say, to arise, when they
35 have duly taken in the proposition that their ancestor was "a hairy quadruped furnished with a tail and pointed ears, probably arboreal in his habits," there will be found to arise an invincible desire to relate this proposition to the sense in us

for conduct, and to the sense in us for beauty. But this the
men of science will not do for us, and will hardly even profess
to do. They will give us other pieces of knowledge, other
facts, about other animals and their ancestors, or about plants,
or about stones, or about stars; and they may finally bring us 5
to those great "general conceptions of the universe, which are
forced upon us all," says Professor Huxley, "by the progress
of physical science." But still it will be *knowledge* only which
they give us; knowledge not put for us into relation with our
sense for conduct, our sense for beauty, and touched with 10
emotion by being so put; not thus put for us, and therefore,
to the majority of mankind, after a certain while, unsatisfying,
wearying.

Not to the born naturalist, I admit. But what do we mean
by a born naturalist? We mean a man in whom the zeal for 15
observing nature is so uncommonly strong and eminent, that
it marks him off from the bulk of mankind. Such a man will
pass his life happily in collecting natural knowledge and
reasoning upon it, and will ask for nothing, or hardly anything,
more. I have heard it said that the sagacious and admirable 20
naturalist whom we lost not very long ago, Mr. Darwin, once
owned to a friend that for his part he did not experience the
necessity for two things which most men find so necessary to
them,—religion and poetry; science and the domestic affections,
he thought, were enough. To a born naturalist, I can well 25
understand that this should seem so. So absorbing is his occupation with nature, so strong his love for his occupation, that he
goes on acquiring natural knowledge and reasoning upon it,
and has little time or inclination for thinking about getting it
related to the desire in man for conduct, the desire in man for 30
beauty. He relates it to them for himself as he goes along, so
far as he feels the need; and he draws from the domestic
affections all the additional solace necessary. But then Darwins
are extremely rare. Another great and admirable master of
natural knowledge, Faraday, was a Sandemanian. That is to 35
say, he related his knowledge to his instinct for conduct and
to his instinct for beauty, by the aid of that respectable Scottish
sectary, Robert Sandeman. And so strong, in general, is the

demand of religion and poetry to have their share in a man, to associate themselves with his knowing, and to relieve and rejoice it, that, probably, for one man amongst us with the disposition to do as Darwin did in this respect, there are at least
5 fifty with the disposition to do as Faraday.

Education lays hold upon us, in fact, by satisfying this demand. Professor Huxley holds up to scorn mediæval education, with its neglect of the knowledge of nature, its poverty even of literary studies, its formal logic devoted to "showing how
10 and why that which the Church said was true must be true." But the great mediæval Universities were not brought into being, we may be sure, by the zeal for giving a jejune and contemptible education. Kings have been their nursing fathers, and queens have been their nursing mothers, but not for this.
15 The mediæval Universities came into being, because the supposed knowledge, delivered by Scripture and the Church, so deeply engaged men's hearts, by so simply, easily, and powerfully relating itself to their desire for conduct, their desire for beauty. All other knowledge was dominated by this supposed
20 knowledge and was subordinated to it, because of the surpassing strength of the hold which it gained upon the affections of men, by allying itself profoundly with their sense for conduct, their sense for beauty.

But now, says Professor Huxley, conceptions of the universe
25 fatal to the notions held by our forefathers have been forced upon us by physical science. Grant to him that they are thus fatal, that the new conceptions must and will soon become current everywhere, and that every one will finally perceive them to be fatal to the beliefs of our forefathers. The need of
30 humane letters, as they are truly called, because they serve the paramount desire in men that good should be for ever present to them,—the need of humane letters, to establish a relation between the new conceptions, and our instinct for beauty, our instinct for conduct, is only the more visible. The Middle Age
35 could do without humane letters, as it could do without the study of nature, because its supposed knowledge was made to engage its emotions so powerfully. Grant that the supposed knowledge disappears, its power of being made to engage the

emotions will of course disappear along with it,—but the emotions themselves, and their claim to be engaged and satisfied, will remain. Now if we find by experience that humane letters have an undeniable power of engaging the emotions, the importance of humane letters in a man's training becomes not less, but greater, in proportion to the success of modern science in extirpating what it calls "mediæval thinking."

Have humane letters, then, have poetry and eloquence, the power here attributed to them of engaging the emotions, and do they exercise it? And if they have it and exercise it, *how* do they exercise it, so as to exert an influence upon man's sense for conduct, his sense for beauty? Finally, even if they both can and do exert an influence upon the senses in question, how are they to relate to them the results,—the modern results,— of natural science? All these questions may be asked. First, have poetry and eloquence the power of calling out the emotions? The appeal is to experience. Experience shows that for the vast majority of men, for mankind in general, they have the power. Next, do they exercise it? They do. But then, *how* do they exercise it so as to affect man's sense for conduct, his sense for beauty? And this is perhaps a case for applying the Preacher's words: "Though a man labour to seek it out, yet he shall not find it; yea, farther, though a wise man think to know it, yet shall he not be able to find it." [1] Why should it be one thing, in its effect upon the emotions, to say, "Patience is a virtue," and quite another thing, in its effect upon the emotions, to say with Homer,

τλητὸν γὰρ Μοῖραι θυμὸν θέσαν ἀνθρώποισιν—[2]

"for an enduring heart have the destinies appointed to the children of men"? Why should it be one thing, in its effect upon the emotions, to say with the philosopher Spinoza, *Felicitas in eo consistit quod homo suum esse conservare potest*— "Man's happiness consists in his being able to preserve his own essence," and quite another thing, in its effect upon the emotions, to say with the Gospel, "What is a man advantaged, if he gain the whole world, and lose himself, forfeit himself?"

[1] *Ecclesiastes*, viii. 17.   [2] *Iliad*, xxiv. 49.

How does this difference of effect arise? I cannot tell, and I am not much concerned to know; the important thing is that it does arise, and that we can profit by it. But how, finally, are poetry and eloquence to exercise the power of relating the modern results of natural science to man's instinct for conduct, his instinct for beauty? And here again I answer that I do not know *how* they will exercise it, but that they can and will exercise it I am sure. I do not mean that modern philosophical poets and modern philosophical moralists are to come and relate for us, in express terms, the results of modern scientific research to our instinct for conduct, our instinct for beauty. But I mean that we shall find, as a matter of experience, if we know the best that has been thought and uttered in the world, we shall find that the art and poetry and eloquence of men who lived, perhaps, long ago, who had the most limited natural knowledge, who had the most erroneous conceptions about many important matters, we shall find that this art, and poetry, and eloquence, have in fact not only the power of refreshing and delighting us, they have also the power,—such is the strength and worth, in essentials, of their authors' criticism of life,—they have a fortifying, and elevating, and quickening, and suggestive power, capable of wonderfully helping us to relate the results of modern science to our need for conduct, our need for beauty. Homer's conceptions of the physical universe were, I imagine, grotesque; but really, under the shock of hearing from modern science that "the world is not subordinated to man's use, and that man is not the cynosure of things terrestrial," I could, for my own part, desire no better comfort than Homer's line which I quoted just now,

τλητὸν γὰρ Μοῖραι θυμὸν θέσαν ἀνθρώποισιν—

"for an enduring heart have the destinies appointed to the children of men"!

And the more that men's minds are cleared, the more that the results of science are frankly accepted, the more that poetry and eloquence come to be received and studied as what in truth they really are,—the criticism of life by gifted men, alive and active with extraordinary power at an unusual number of points;—so much the more will the value of humane letters, and of art also, which is an utterance having a like kind of power with theirs, be felt and acknowledged, and their place in education be secured.

Let us therefore, all of us, avoid indeed as much as possible any invidious comparison between the merits of humane let- 5 ters, as means of education, and the merits of the natural sciences. But when some President of a Section for Mechanical Science insists on making the comparison, and tells us that "he who in his training has substituted literature and history for natural science has chosen the less useful alternative," let us 10 make answer to him that the student of humane letters only, will, at least, know also the great general conceptions brought in by modern physical science; for science, as Professor Huxley says, forces them upon us all. But the student of the natural sciences only, will, by our very hypothesis, know nothing of 15 humane letters; not to mention that in setting himself to be perpetually accumulating natural knowledge, he sets himself to do what only specialists have in general the gift for doing genially. And so he will probably be unsatisfied, or at any rate incomplete, and even more incomplete than the student of 20 humane letters only.

I once mentioned in a school-report, how a young man in one of our English training colleges having to paraphrase the passage in *Macbeth* beginning,

"Can'st thou not minister to a mind diseased?" 25

turned this line into, "Can you not wait upon the lunatic?" And I remarked what a curious state of things it would be, if every pupil of our national schools knew, let us say, that the moon is two thousand one hundred and sixty miles in diameter, and thought at the same time that a good paraphrase for 30

"Can'st thou not minister to a mind diseased?"

was, "Can you not wait upon the lunatic?" If one is driven to choose, I think I would rather have a young person ignorant about the moon's diameter, but aware that "Can you not wait

upon the lunatic?" is bad, than a young person whose education had been such as to manage things the other way.
Or to go higher than the pupils of our national schools. I
have in my mind's eye a member of our British Parliament who
comes to travel here in America, who afterwards relates his
travels, and who shows a really masterly knowledge of the
geology of this great country and of its mining capabilities, but
who ends by gravely suggesting that the United States should
borrow a prince from our Royal Family, and should make him
their king, and should create a House of Lords of great landed
proprietors after the pattern of ours; and then America, he
thinks, would have her future happily and perfectly secured.
Surely, in this case, the President of the Section for Mechanical
Science would himself hardly say that our member of Parliament, by concentrating himself upon geology and mineralogy,
and so on, and not attending to literature and history, had
"chosen the more useful alternative."
If then there is to be separation and option between humane
letters on the one hand, and the natural sciences on the other,
the great majority of mankind, all who have not exceptional
and overpowering aptitudes for the study of nature, would
do well, I cannot but think, to choose to be educated in humane letters rather than in the natural sciences. Letters will
call out their being at more points, will make them live more.
I said that before I ended I would just touch on the question
of classical education, and I will keep my word. Even if
literature is to retain a large place in our education, yet Latin
and Greek, say the friends of progress, will certainly have to
go. Greek is the grand offender in the eyes of these gentlemen.
The attackers of the established course of study think that
against Greek, at any rate, they have irresistible arguments.
Literature may perhaps be needed in education, they say; but
why on earth should it be Greek literature? Why not French
or German? Nay, "has not an Englishman models in his own
literature of every kind of excellence?" As before, it is not on
any weak pleadings of my own that I rely for convincing the
gainsayers; it is on the constitution of human nature itself, and
on the instinct of self-preservation in humanity. The instinct

for beauty is set in human nature, as surely as the instinct for knowledge is set there, or the instinct for conduct. If the instinct for beauty is served by Greek literature and art as it is served by no other literature and art, we may trust to the instinct of self-preservation in humanity for keeping Greek as 5 part of our culture. We may trust to it for even making the study of Greek more prevalent than it is now. Greek will come, I hope, some day to be studied more rationally than at present; but it will be increasingly studied as men increasingly feel the need in them for beauty, and how powerfully Greek art 10 and Greek literature can serve this need. Women will again study Greek, as Lady Jane Grey did; I believe that in that chain of forts, with which the fair host of the Amazons are now engirdling our English universities, I find that here in America, in colleges like Smith College in Massachusetts, and 15 Vassar College in the State of New York, and in the happy families of the mixed universities out West, they are studying it already.

Defuit una mihi symmetria prisca,—"The antique symmetry was the one thing wanting to me," said Leonardo da Vinci; 20 and he was an Italian. I will not presume to speak for the Americans, but I am sure that, in the Englishman, the want of this admirable symmetry of the Greeks is a thousand times more great and crying than in any Italian. The results of the want show themselves most glaringly, perhaps, in our architec- 25 ture, but they show themselves, also, in all our art. *Fit details strictly combined, in view of a large general result nobly conceived;* that is just the beautiful *symmetria prisca* of the Greeks, and it is just where we English fail, where all our art fails. Striking ideas we have, and well-executed details we have; 30 but that high symmetry which, with satisfying and delightful effect, combines them, we seldom or never have. The glorious beauty of the Acropolis at Athens did not come from single fine things stuck about on that hill, a statue here, a gateway there;—no, it arose from all things being perfectly combined 35 for a supreme total effect. What must not an Englishman feel about our deficiencies in this respect, as the sense for beauty, whereof this symmetry is an essential element, awakens and

strengthens within him! what will not one day be his respect
and desire for Greece and its *symmetria prisca,* when the scales
drop from his eyes as he walks the London streets, and he sees
such a lesson in meanness as the Strand, for instance, in its
5   true deformity! But here we are coming to our friend Mr.
Ruskin's province, and I will not intrude upon it, for he is its
very sufficient guardian.

And so we at last find, it seems, we find flowing in favour
of the humanities the natural and necessary stream of things,
10 which seemed against them when we started. The "hairy
quadruped furnished with a tail and pointed ears, probably
arboreal in his habits," this good fellow carried hidden in his
nature, apparently, something destined to develop into a
necessity for humane letters. Nay, more; we seem finally to
15 be even led to the further conclusion that our hairy ancestor
carried in his nature, also, a necessity for Greek.

And therefore, to say the truth, I cannot really think that
humane letters are in much actual danger of being thrust out
from their leading place in education, in spite of the array of
20 authorities against them at this moment. So long as human
nature is what it is, their attractions will remain irresistible. As
with Greek, so with letters generally: they will some day
come, we may hope, to be studied more rationally, but they
will not lose their place. What will happen will rather be that
25 there will be crowded into education other matters besides,
far too many; there will be, perhaps, a period of unsettlement
and confusion and false tendency; but letters will not in the
end lose their leading place. If they lose it for a time, they
will get it back again. We shall be brought back to them by
30 our wants and aspirations. And a poor humanist may possess
his soul in patience, neither strive nor cry, admit the energy
and brilliancy of the partisans of physical science, and their
present favour with the public, to be far greater than his own,
and still have a happy faith that the nature of things works
35 silently on behalf of the studies which he loves, and that, while
we shall all have to acquaint ourselves with the great results
reached by modern science, and to give ourselves as much
training in its disciplines as we can conveniently carry, yet the

majority of men will always require humane letters; and so much the more, as they have the more and the greater results of science to relate to the need in man for conduct, and to the need in him for beauty.

A Liverpool Address *

Among the documents with which I was favoured in order that
I might acquaint myself, before coming to speak here, with the
origin and aims of the Liverpool University College, was a
programme of our present proceedings, in which I read, I
5 think, that you were to have Lord Derby in the chair, and an
address from an eminent man of science. Lord Derby—who
has been just now introducing me to you with words prompted
by his kindness, and for which I cordially thank him—Lord
Derby you have. Lord Derby you have, but the eminent man
10 of science you have not. You have, in his stead, many people
would tell you, a nearly worn-out man of letters, with one
nostrum for practical application, his nostrum of public schools
for the middle classes; and with a frippery of phrases about
sweetness and light, seeing things as they really are, knowing
15 the best that has been thought and said in the world, which
never had very much solid meaning, and have now quite lost
the gloss and charm of novelty.
   I am sorry for the disappointment of any one who may have
come here hoping for an eminent man of science, but finds in-
20 stead of him the personage who has just been described. In
several important points the description does not lack truth. To
call a man worn out is always, perhaps, invidious and harsh,
because in human nature there are to the very last such wonderful powers of recovery. And, again, to one person a phrase
25 may convey more meaning than it will to another. But one
does undoubtedly advance in age; phrases such as "sweetness
and light" have undoubtedly been often used by me, and have

* Delivered at the opening of the Session of University College, Liverpool.

now lost the gloss of novelty; and the one practical suggestion
which for years I have been reiterating may be said to be that
of public schools for the middle classes.

I wish I could promise to change my old phrases for new
ones, and to pass from my one practical suggestion to some   5
other. I wish I saw a prospect, that, within the term of life
which can yet remain to me, phrases such as "sweetness and
light," "seeing things as they really are," were likely to cease
to sum up, to my mind, crying needs for our nation. I wish
that the persistent call for public schools for the middle classes   10
might, within the same limits of time, become unnecessary and
impertinent. But I fear there is no chance of this happening.
What has been the burden of my song hitherto, will probably
have, so far as I can at present see, to be the burden of it till
the end.   15

I suppose it was because he knew how much I had talked
about education for the middle classes, that the Principal of
your College asked me to come and speak at the opening of its
session. His name revived memories in me of much kindness
shown to me and mine in former days at Harrow, and I should   20
have been sorry to refuse a request of his. But apart from this
private motive, any one who has been preaching in the wilderness for I know not how many years on the need of educating
the middle classes, may be glad of an opportunity for acknowledging and praising what you have done in Liverpool. Your   25
school board and your elementary schools have a reputation
so high, that you might well be ashamed if your provision for
secondary or intermediate education were no better than the
provision for it in many or most towns of England. But yours
is better than theirs, very much better. In your Collegiate   30
School, and in the schools of the Royal Institution, and of
your Institute, you have schools providing for the education of
the middle classes in your city; schools known beyond the
bounds of Liverpool itself, schools of good and high standing,
schools considerable enough to come within the influence of   35
public opinion, and which offer sound guarantees for their efficiency. I do not know that the provision is entirely sufficient
for your needs. If it is, then your advantage in comparison with

the rest of England is still more conspicuous. I should like to
extend the calculation which, for the purposes of the Education
Act, the Government made; and as we calculated what in
each locality was the population requiring elementary schools,
5   and what was the provision of proper schools of that kind,
so to inquire also what in each locality is the population requiring secondary schools, and how far proper secondary
schools are provided for it. I feel sure that your Collegiate
School and your Royal Institution and Institute schools would
10   come under the denomination of proper secondary schools. But
I am not so sure that they would be found quite enough for
your needs. In any case, however, your provision is far more
adequate to the need than the provision in England generally,
and you may well be proud of it.
15   After secondary schools and their studies come the higher
schools with university studies. Secondary and higher schools
are closely connected with each other. Without good secondary schools you cannot have good universities; without good
universities you cannot have good secondary schools. You
20   have a School of Art, you have a School of Science. But your
direct provision for university studies in Liverpool itself was,
until lately, the Queen's College connected with the Liverpool
Institute. For twenty-seven years that college has been at
work; for a part of that time, as I understand, with day classes,
25   latterly with evening classes only. But it has now, in fact, been
given up;—that is to say, it has relinquished its name, and it
has united its classes with the other evening classes of the Institute. I find that the council of the College, announcing this in
their last report, declare: "In no instance whatever, in Europe
30   or America, has a college of the description of Queen's College
had any material success, except when supported by endowments sufficient to render the teachers practically independent
of the fees received from students." That is water to my mill,
as the Germans say; for I have always contended for some kind
35   of public institution and endowment for each description of
schools. But for the present let me pursue my review of what
you have done for higher schools in Liverpool.
Well, Queen's College has been given up, but you have

founded University College. Four years ago a town's meeting
was convened to consider "the desirability of establishing a
College in Liverpool to provide such instruction in all the
branches of a liberal education as will enable residents in the
town and neighbourhood to qualify for degrees in arts and   5
sciences at some of the existing universities; and at the same
time to give such technical instruction as would be of immediate service in professional and technical life." Your town's
meeting unanimously approved the project, and a committee
was nominated to draw up a scheme for the proposed College.   10
Four splendid donations, each of 10,000*l*., head a subscription
list the most satisfactory, I think, that I have ever seen, and
which now exceeds 100,000*l*. For the site and buildings the
corporation of Liverpool has voted a grant to the College of
30,000*l*. more. A Royal Charter has been obtained, the chairs   15
endowed have been filled, while professors from the distinguished School of Medicine in connection with your Royal
Infirmary are united in the senate with the newly endowed
professors and form the medical faculty of the College. In the
present year a beginning was made of college-work, with more   20
than five hundred students attending the different courses of
lectures. It is a gratifying, an animating history.

I am reproached with always harping on the need of public
schools for the middle classes, and I have owned to you that
upon this theme I have, in truth, harped a good deal. By pub-   25
lic schools I am understood to mean State-founded, State-paid,
and State-regulated schools only. Now to State intervention
many people in England, and I think our Chairman among
them, are much disinclined. For my part I am not disposed to
argue questions of this kind in the abstract. I want to see cer-   30
tain things done, and I look around for effective means of doing them. When I came back from the Continent, after seeing
the provision of schools both secondary and higher for the
middle classes in a country like Germany, I looked attentively
at the sort of provision made in England, and it naturally oc-   35
curred to me that the State might, to the great benefit of the
middle classes, organise secondary and higher instruction here,
as it has organised it abroad. The difficulty of duly proportion-

ing and co-ordering the supply of schools according to the
need, can hardly, perhaps, be got over without legislative organisation. The difficulty arises, of course, in respect to the supply of secondary schools far more than of higher schools or
5 universities. The task of providing for secondary instruction
is a far vaster business than the other. The universities required
for a country are very few in number compared with the secondary schools required. They have to be provided in far
smaller number, and at the same time they are more in the pub-
10 lic eye, than secondary schools; they are more imposing, they
have much more in them to engage and gratify the pride of
founders. The far harder business of providing secondary
schools is also, therefore, humbler and less attractive. All this
should be considered before people deny the need or the ex-
15 pediency of having recourse to legislation and to the State for
organising education for the middle classes.
    But a man must be a fanatic on behalf of State interference—
as some English people, perhaps, are fanatics in opposition to it
—if he refuses to accept what meets his wishes in essentials be-
20 cause it does not bear a particular brand, and if he will not
approve of a school as a public school unless the State makes
and maintains it. For my part, I call a school public if I find
it standing in the public eye, open to the wholesome influences
of public opinion, and affording proper guarantees. Your Col-
25 legiate School in Liverpool is, I believe, what is called a proprietary school. The proprietary system cannot, in my opinion,
be at all relied upon for producing throughout the country the
supply of secondary schools needed. I should not myself have
been disposed beforehand to betake myself to that system for
30 supplying the needs of even this one city. But the Collegiate
school has been established, it exists, it succeeds. It stands in the
public eye; it feels the wholesome stimulus and the wholesome
check of public opinion; it gives sufficient guarantees by the
character of its governors, by the distinction of its teachers, by
35 the work of its scholars. Well, then, it is what I call a public
school. It is a school which the State, if the Legislature were to
impose on Government the duty of seeing that our supply of
secondary schools be sufficient as well as our supply of elemen-

tary schools, might at once recognise as a public school, and, taking note of its guarantees, interfere with it no further so long as those guarantees were maintained. The same with University College. One gets larger and easier, I hope, in one's treatment of questions as one advances in age; that is one of the consolations, perhaps, for wearing out. But I am sure that I should at no time have hesitated to recognise the claims of this College to the title of a public higher school, or have wished for it any other mode of creation than that which it has had. I might have doubted whether the age of endowment were not passed, whether such a splendid subscription list as yours were any longer possible. But to refuse to be satisfied with an institution like this because it draws its main support from the munificence of individuals, and has no grant from the State, would never have entered into my head. Oxford and Cambridge were created by the munificence of individuals. They stand in the public eye, they more and more feel the pressure of public opinion, they afford due guarantees. Therefore they are public higher schools. You will do the same and be the same. If we are to desire public endowment, you have by the grant of your municipality public endowment in that very form in which it is best for schools—in the form of local and municipal endowment. A municipal grant proves more surely than a State grant that a local want is genuine. I should be glad, perhaps, if the State, organising secondary and higher instruction, were to assign to institutions such as this and Owens College some Regius Professorships, just as I should be glad if it were to assign to institutions such as your Collegiate School some bursaries or scholarships. But this is to be desired for the sake of adding to the efficiency of such institutions, and of giving to them a yet more honourable standing; not for the sake of conferring upon them thus, for the first time, a public character. You have that already, and you do not require an act of the State to give it to you.

Nay, partisan of State intervention as I am, I will show my candour by frankly owning that probably, if you had gone to the State for a university, and if you had prevailed, you would have got something less good, less useful, than what you have

given to yourselves. You would have got, probably, an Examining Board, a repetition of the London University. If it were not for the increasing width of view, that easiness of old age of which I have spoken, if I had still the impetuosity and aggres-
5   siveness of youth, I should have been apt to say, perhaps, as to that London model of a higher school, to you and to other people in like case with you: "Save yourselves from this untoward university!" At present I indulge in no sally of the kind, because, with age, one learns to take a larger view of things;
10 and I accustom myself to dwell on the high value of some of the degrees of the London University, and on the utility, for certain purposes, of others, and I regard the London University with great respect. Still, I am glad you are what you are, and not a reproduction of the London University. I will tell
15 you why. In the first place, the most valuable function of a university or higher school is not to examine for degrees or to confer them. Its far more valuable function is to bring young men into personal contact with teachers of high mental gifts and high attainments, and to raise and form the pupil by that
20 contact. You do not confer degrees. It does not much matter. You do what is more important. By the chairs which you have endowed or are endowing you provide for that personal presence and effect of the teacher, that communication between him and the learner, which is so desirable. The degrees will
25 come, but the training is more than the stamp put upon it.
    Then I have a second point. Your leanings here seem to me, so far as I can judge from the reports and documents which I have been reading, to have been hitherto towards the examinations of the London University, and principally towards its
30 matriculation examination. But this type of matriculation examination is not a good one. A matriculation examination may be said to set the standard for the condition of culture in which a young man is to be thought ripe for passing on from the secondary school to the higher school or university. Now, the
35 standard thus set by the matriculation examination of the London University is, in my opinion, inadequate. It should be compared with the standard set by the leaving examination, or examination for the certificate of ripeness, enabling a boy on quitting school to enter a German university. I will not say that

the mathematics, the natural philosophy, and the chemistry of the London matriculation examination are too much; I will say only that the Latin and other literary matters are far too little. That is, they are far too little for a young man who has passed through a proper secondary school, though they may be quite enough for a young man from an elementary school and evening classes, or a young man from a so-called modern or commercial school. The Latin is just the inevitable book or two of Cæsar *De Bello Gallico*—not a work to speak much to the young, though Cæsar as a man is so interesting. And this is all that a boy who has passed through a proper secondary school is supposed to know of Greek or Latin literature! The thing is ridiculous. The Oxford and Cambridge local examinations correspond in character with the examination in question. But the Oxford and Cambridge local examinations are not matriculation examinations. They do not give admission to the university. Therefore they do not tend to set an inadequate standard for the work of secondary schools. I hope that you and Owens College, I hope that the new northern University, may keep up the standard of teaching, both in the secondary schools and in your own colleges, by making the passage examination from school to university an adequate one, and adequate in letters as well as in mathematics and natural science only.

But letters must not absorb me on the present occasion. I must not forget that this is, in strictness, the opening of the annual session of the School of Medicine, now the medical faculty of University College. This is properly their day and their meeting. To some extent they have sunk themselves in the College, and the College owes them a good deal. The zeal of the gentlemen of the medical profession in Liverpool for establishing the new College, their willingness to unite their own prosperous and esteemed School of Medicine with it, have been of signal service, I am told, to your institution. We ought to put the medical faculty forward on the present occasion, though they do not put themselves forward. But in my opinion nothing can be more appropriate and desirable, at the opening of this new College in Liverpool, than to put them and some characters of their studies forward.

Long ago, when I was occupying myself with things which

seem now much out of my line, and when I had even thoughts
of studying medicine, I fell in with two sentences of two eminent men in high honour with all surgeons and physicians,
which made a deep impression upon me, which I carefully
5 wrote down, and have never forgotten. One is an exhortation
by Sir Astley Cooper to a young student: "That, sir, is the way
to learn your business; *look for yourself,* never mind what
other people may say; no opinion or theories can interfere with
information acquired from dissection." The other is a saying,
10 more brief, of the great John Hunter: *"Don't think;* try and
be patient."

I cannot easily say for how much light and help I feel myself indebted to those two sentences. Sir Astley Cooper's words
are words to stand for ever before the mind of a man setting
15 himself to see things as they really are—to stand for ever before his mind to save him from doubt and discouragement. And
the brief and profound saying of John Hunter points to the
simplicity of truth, the simplicity with which things are seen
when they are seen as they really are. We labour at words and
20 systems, and fancy that we are labouring at the things for the
sake of which those exist. But in truth we are often only labouring at the artificial and difficult forms under which we
choose to try to think things, and the things themselves must
be seen simply if we are to see them at all.

25 So through Sir Astley Cooper and John Hunter, and the
help afforded me by them, I connect the medical faculty with
one of my maxims, the maxim of seeing things as they really
are. I must claim the sympathy of the medical faculty with
another phrase of mine also, the too familiar phrase of sweet-
30 ness and light; a phrase in which they, as I shall show them, are
likewise interested, and which has great import for this new
College.

Lord Jeffrey, visiting Liverpool in 1813 and scanning with
those sharp eyes of his the place and its inhabitants, seems to
35 have put himself into communication, as I am doing now, with
the doctors. He asked a most intelligent physician of Liverpool,
he tells us, about a body of citizens here, the most serious, respectable, and prosperous in the town, and this is the extraor-

dinary statement which the physician made to him, after practising amongst them, says Lord Jeffrey, for twenty years. "He
informs me that few of the richer sort live to be fifty, but die
of a sort of atrophy. They eat too much, take little exercise,
and, above all, have no nervous excitement." 5
The criticisms of Lord Jeffrey himself, brilliant as he was,
are not always solid; and perhaps he fascinated his friend the
physician, beguiled him somewhat from his sobriety, and made
him utter here a criticism more startling than solid. Still the
physician and Lord Jeffrey, when they thus insist upon the bad 10
effects of the want of "nervous excitement," as they call it, do
touch, I suppose, on what is really the weak point in the life
of these great business places of the north of England. They
touch on the same thing which I meant, when not long ago I
spoke, in a phrase warmly resented by Mr. Goldwin Smith, 15
of "the hideousness, the immense ennui," of a type of life too
prevalent both here and in America. If it is a fact of physiology, that health cannot in general be maintained without nervous excitement, we must add, I think, that the true and
perfect balance of health cannot be attained without nervous 20
excitement of divers kinds. Money-making is not enough by
itself. Industry is not enough by itself. Seriousness is not enough
by itself. I speak now of the kinds of stimulus most in use with
people of our race, and above all in business communities such
as Liverpool. Respectable these kinds of stimulus may be, use- 25
ful they may be, but they are not by themselves sufficient.
The need in man for intellect and knowledge, his desire for
beauty, his instinct for society, and for pleasurable and grace-
ful forms of society, require to have their stimulus felt also, felt
and satisfied. You know better than I can, how far adequate 30
provision has hitherto been made in Liverpool for all this. But
I imagine you are by no means satisfied with the sort of stimulus which the resources, pleasures, and amusements of this
great city, this port and passage place of the world, at present
afford to your people, and above all to the young. You would 35
own that the standard of life, as the political economists say,
that the standard of life, in respect to these sources of stimula-
tion, is at present pitched far too low. Well, in establishing this

College you are on the way to raise it higher, to introduce a
better balance of activities. You provide by this College a direct
stimulus and satisfaction to the need in human nature for intellect and knowledge. But you at the same time provide in-
5   directly a powerful help to the desire for beauty and to the
social spirit. For intellectual culture quickens the wish for a
proper satisfaction to these; and if by means of this College intellectual culture becomes a power among you, without doubt
it will gradually affect and transform the amusements, plea-
10   sures, society, even the aspect and architecture, of Liverpool.
The sweetness and amenity of life, then, will probably be increased by this College. That will be an indirect product of it;
but its direct natural product is of higher importance still. This
product, if I am to sum it up in one word, is *lucidity*. Doctors
15   are the natural friends of lucidity. At any rate, the most valuable quality which a doctor can have is lucidity. Suffer me,
therefore, to say, at this solemnity in which the medical faculty
have so large a share, that if there is a word which I should like
to plant in your memories, and to leave sticking there after I
20   am gone, it is this word *lucidity*. If I had to fix upon the great
want at this moment of the three principal nations of Europe,
I should say that the great want of the French was morality,
that the great want of the Germans was civil courage, and that
our own great want was lucidity. Our own want is of course
25   what concerns us the most. People are apt to remark the defects which accompany certain qualities, and to think that the
qualities cannot be desirable because of the defects which they
see accompanying them. There is no greater and more salutary
lesson for men to learn, than that a quality may be accom-
30   panied naturally, perhaps, by grave dangers, that it may actually present itself accompanied by terrible defects, and yet
that it may be itself indispensable.
Let me illustrate what I mean by an example of which we
shall all readily feel the force. Seriousness is a quality of our
35   nation. Perhaps seriousness is always accompanied by certain
dangers. But, at any rate, many of our French neighbours
would say that they find our seriousness accompanied by so
many false ideas, so much prejudice, so much that is disagree-

able, that it cannot have the value which we attribute to it. And yet we know that it is invaluable. Follow the same mode of reasoning as to the quality of lucidity. The French have a natural turn for lucidity, as we have a natural turn for serious-ness. Perhaps a natural turn for lucidity carries with it always certain dangers. Be this as it may, it is certain that we see in the French, along with their lucidity, a want of seriousness, a want of reverence, and other faults, which greatly displease us. Many of us are inclined, in consequence, to undervalue their lucidity, or to deny that they have it. We are wrong; it exists, as our seriousness does; it is valuable, as our seriousness is valuable. Both the one and the other are valuable, and, in the end, indispensable.

What is lucidity? It is negatively that the French have it; and we will now concern ourselves, therefore, with its negative characters only. Negatively, lucidity is the perception of the want of truth and validness in notions long current; the per-ception that they are no longer possible, that their time is fin-ished and they can serve us no more. All through the last cen-tury a prodigious travail for lucidity was going forward in France. Its principal agent was a man whose name excites gen-erally repulsion in England, Voltaire. Voltaire did a great deal of harm in France. But it was not by his lucidity that he did harm; he did it by his want of seriousness, his want of rever-ence, his want of sense for much that is deepest in human na-ture. By his lucidity he did good. We all of us admire Luther. Conduct is three-fourths of life, and a man who works for conduct, therefore, works for more than a man who works for intelligence. But, having premised this, we may say that the Luther of the eighteenth century and of the cultivated classes was Voltaire. As Luther had an antipathy to what was im-moral, so Voltaire had an antipathy to what was absurd. Both had faults—great faults. But both of them made war upon the object of their antipathy with such masterly power, with so much conviction, so much energy, so much genius, that they carried their world with them;—Luther his Protestant world, and Voltaire his French world and the cultivated classes throughout the continent of Europe generally.

Voltaire had more than the negative lucidity of which we have been speaking. With all his faults, he had the conception which we have already mentioned, the large and true conception that a number and equilibrium of activities is requisite for man. *Il faut donner à notre âme toutes les formes possibles*, is a maxim with him. And this maxim he really and truly applied in practice, "advancing," as Michelet finely says, "in every direction with a marvellous vigour and with that conquering ambition which Vico called *mens heroica.*" Nevertheless Voltaire's signal characteristic is his lucidity, his negative lucidity.

There was great and free intellectual movement in England at the beginning of the eighteenth century; indeed, it was from England that the movement passed into France. But our nation had not that strong natural bent for lucidity which the French have; its bent was towards other things in preference. Our leading thinkers had not the genius and passion for lucidity which distinguishes Voltaire. In their free enquiry they soon found themselves coming into collision with a number of established facts, beliefs, conventions. Thereupon all sorts of practical considerations began to sway them; the danger signal went up, they often stopped short, turned their eyes another way, or drew down a curtain between themselves and the light. "It seems highly probable," says Voltaire, "that nature has made thinking a function of the brain, as vegetation is a function of trees; that we think by the brain, just as we walk by the feet. So our reason, at least, would lead us to conclude, if the theologians did not assure us of the contrary; *such, too, was the opinion of Locke, but he did not venture to announce it.*"

The French Revolution came, with its horrors; England grew to detest France, and was cut off from the Continent; did great things, gained much, but not in lucidity. The Continent was reopened, the century advanced, time and experience brought their lessons, lovers of free and clear thought such as the late Mr. John Stuart Mill arose amongst us; but one could not say that they have by any means founded among us the reign of lucidity. We are fond of boasting that in no country in the world do men hold their convictions with so much energy as in England. True, but one may also put the proposition in another shape, and say: "In no country in the world is so much nonsense so firmly believed." Consider that movement of which we are hearing so much just now; look at the Salvation Army and its operations. You will see numbers, funds, energy, devotedness, excitement, conversions—and a complete absence of lucidity. A little lucidity would make the whole movement impossible. The movement takes for granted, as its basis, what is no longer possible or receivable; its adherents proceed, in all they do, upon the assumption that this basis is perfectly solid, and neither see that it is not solid, nor ever even think of asking themselves whether it is solid or not.

Or take a very different movement from that of the Salvation Army, a movement of far higher dignity, reach, and import. We have all had before our minds lately the long, laborious, devoted, influential, pure, pathetic life of Dr. Pusey, which has just ended. Many of us have also been reading, in the two lively volumes of that acute but not always good-natured rattle, Mr. Mozley, an account of that great movement which took from Dr. Pusey its earlier name. Of its later stage of Ritualism you have had in this county of Lancashire a now celebrated experience. The movement is full of interest. It has produced men to be respected, men to be admired, men to be loved—produced men of learning, men of genius, men of goodness and charm. But can one resist the truth that lucidity would have been fatal to it? The movers of all those questions about apostolical succession, church, patristic authority, primitive usage, symbolism, postures, vestments—questions so passionately debated, and on which I will by no means seek to cast ridicule—do they not all begin by taking for granted something no longer possible or receivable, build on this basis as if it were indubitably solid, and fail to see, that, their basis not being solid, all they build upon it is fantastic?

I by no means say that negative lucidity is by itself a satisfying possession. It is very far indeed from being this. But I say that it is inevitable and indispensable, and that it is the condition of all serious construction for the future. Without it, at present, a man or a nation is intellectually and spiritually all abroad. If we see it accompanied in France by much that we

shrink from, we should reflect that in England it will have influences joined with it which it has not in France—the natural
seriousness of our people, their sense of reverence and respect,
their love for the past. Come it must; and here, where it has
5 been so late in coming, it will probably be for the first time
seen to come without danger.

Capitals are natural centres of mental movement and sources
of lucidity. And it is natural, too, for the classes with most
leisure, most freedom, most means of cultivation, most con-
10 versance with the wide world, to have lucidity, though often
they have it not. To generate a spirit of lucidity in provincial
towns, and among the middle classes, bound to a life of much
routine and plunged in business, is more difficult. Schools and
universities—universities with serious studies, with disinterested
15 studies, universities connecting these studies the one with the
other, and continuing them into the years of manhood—are in
this case the best agency we can use. It may be slow, but it is
sure. Such an agency you are now going to employ. May this
College fulfil all your expectations! May your students, in
20 the words which I was quoting just now, "advance in every
direction with a marvellous vigour, and with that conquering
ambition which Vico called *mens heroica!*" And among the
many good results of this, may one result be the apparition in
our midst of that indispensable spirit, the spirit of lucidity!

A French Worthy

We will permit ourselves to distinguish three types of French-men. The Frenchman of one type is the Frenchman of our received notions, gay and free and bold of spirit, positive (as the phrase is), social, sensual. This is the common Gaulish, or rather Gallo-Roman type. Then there is the type of French- 5 man grave and austere, self-introspective, meditative, spiritual. We have only to think of Port Royal. Finally, there is again the type with nothing Puritan, but yet with a genuine and serious bent for a well-ordered life, for morality; and of this type we may take personages so various as Mdme. de Sévigné, 10 the Chancellor Daguesseau, Vauvenargues, Joubert, Littré, as representative. It will seem strange that one should speak of Mdme. de Sévigné as having anything very serious about her. But whoever will closely follow the life and nature of this famous woman, both in general contrast with that of the world 15 in which she moved, and in particular contrast with the emi-nently Gaulish life and nature of her cousin Bussy-Rabutin, will convince himself that strongly characterizing Mdme. de Sévigné, with all her gaiety, all her wit, all her lightness, is an antipathy to moral disorder. The other personages named along with her 20 have the same antipathy; Port Royal, of course, has it; and it points to a strain of race more serious than the Gaulish. It points probably to a German strain brought in by the Franks and appearing in the French people. French personages char-acterized by this strain are not of the Gaulish type; of what 25 type shall we call them? To talk of a Frankish type sounds pedantic, to talk of an old-French type suggests something superannuated and obsolete: let us say that the French per-sonages of whom we are speaking are morally, by contrast with the Gaulish type of the majority around them, of a Germanic type.

Of this type was an old functionary of primary instruction who died in France this year, and of whom the *Journal des Instituteurs* has recently published a notice—M. Rapet. A less showy life than M. Rapet's, and a more laborious one, can hardly be imagined. He was born in 1805, in the Department of the Ain; his father was a bookseller. He went to school at the Lycée Louis-le-Grand, in Paris; turned his attention to the natural sciences, the modern languages, and education; travelled in Switzerland and Germany, and became acquainted with the Père Girard, Pestalozzi, and Fellenberg. He attracted the notice at Lyons of the Baron Degerando, at that time prominent as an economist and philanthropist. On his recommendation M. Rapet was appointed, after the passing of M. Guizot's school law in 1833, director of the primary normal school at Périgueux. He remained there thirteen years. In 1847 he was made an inspector of primary schools in Paris, in 1861 an inspector-general. In the latter years of his life he had retired from active service, but was continually employed on commissions dealing with popular education.

All questions connected with popular education interested M. Rapet. Normal schools in France, school management, teachers' conferences, teachers' newspapers, all of them owe him much. He was one of the founders of the *Bulletin de l'Instruction Primaire*, now the *Journal des Instituteurs*. His "Cours d'Études des Écoles Primaires" is or was in the hands of nearly all the primary schoolmasters of France. He was a man of detail, a man of painful labour, often working sixteen and eighteen hours out of the twenty-four. His papers on the condition of the labouring classes and on Pestalozzi were crowned by the Institute. Its prize of 10,000 f. was given to his "Manuel de Morale et d'Économie Politique" for the use of workpeople. M. Cousin told the Commission which had to award the Prix Halphen, a prize founded to reward signal services to popular education, that they had no need to go looking about for the proper prizeman: "Il est tout trouvé, et chacun le nomme: c'est M. Rapet." M. Guizot had previously pointed him out as the man whose practical acquaintance with primary schools was greater and more valuable than that of any one else in France.

But it is above all on account of his type of character that we wish to call attention to him. He is well described as follows by the writer of the notice in the *Journal des Instituteurs*, an old friend and colleague: "Alike as a public and as a private man he had *un même culte du vrai et de l'être, une même horreur du fictif et du paraître*." There was something brusque in his manner, there was at times even something harsh: it came from his horror of phrase, of vanity deluding itself and others, of unsoundness and turpitude cloaked under *tant de qualités charmantes*, and from his impatience at meeting them continually. "How true is what you say," he writes to M. Ambroise Rendu from Périgueux, "that *seriousness* in thought and action is our want almost everywhere! It is so in the highest spheres, and it is so in what surrounds me in this place. People pose and make professions; they are men of outside seeming and of apparent success; but men of reality and of duty, no. Provided they can *seem*, they do not care to *be*. And in education this is just what is fatal." Brusque as he was, and at times harsh, the students who passed through M. Rapet's hands at Périgueux, the teachers who came in contact with him as inspector, were conscious, many of them, of finding in this man a virtue which they found nowhere else, and could never forget what they owed to him.

M. Rapet was uneasy at the secularization of popular instruction which accompanies in France its present rapid extension. "I give them ten years," he said a few months before his death, "to show what they will make of it." That there is ground for anxiety his adversaries themselves admit. We have a striking testimony from another inspector-general, who has been an able promoter of the recent changes, a strong advocate of "education compulsory, secular, and free." He says: "We must admit that we are in presence of a vast gap which I here point out merely; dogmatic religion withdraws from our schools, and there is nothing at present to take its place. . . . If our democracy is not to be, what its detractors call it, a regime of mediocrity of soul and of vulgarity of character—that is to say, of decadence—there is no time to lose; we must find a way of uniting, as at this moment we do not unite, *education* with *instruction*."

5   M. Rapet was for retaining the usual religious instruction in schools, and for continuing to charge the teacher with the duty of giving it. His biographer remarks that his language on this subject, though in agreement with that of Royer-Collard, Guizot, Cousin, Villemain, Salvandy, is now absolutely *démodé*,
10 gone out of fashion. The difficulty of doing as M. Rapet wished has indeed become in France almost insuperable. The state of things there in regard to religion is entirely unlike the state of things in this country. We know what is the general character of the religious instruction now given in schools.
15 M. Renan tells us in his latest volume that "the negation of the supernatural has become an established article of faith with every cultivated mind," and he adds that even among the uncultivated the same negation is daily coming more and more to prevail. As to France, he is probably in great measure right.
20 As to England and America, the truth is very far indeed from being as he says. These countries may have their difficulties in store for them in the future; that is another matter. But meanwhile the actual condition of things in France is such that to retain the usual religious instruction in French schools seems
25 impossible. To attempt it would probably only heighten animosities and thicken confusion. The "immense gap" exists, indeed; but it will hardly now be filled as M. Rapet wished. How it is to be filled is a question involving the whole future of France, but by no means easy of solution. Only one may
30 predict that it will not be solved by the Frenchman of the Gaulish type, as we have called it, affirming himself more and more, and filling the gap with his new religion of "patriotism and civic virtue." The more numerous type tends to crowd out the less numerous and to efface it. The gifts and graces of
35 her Gaulish type of character France may be pretty sure of having always with her; the type of Germanic character once intermingled with it she cannot be so sure of retaining. Yet few things can be more certain than that her best hope for the

future lies in the persistence and multiplication of this type; lies in her producing greater numbers of Frenchmen equipped not only with *qualités charmantes,* but with the seriousness, conscience, and sense of duty which were so admirable in M. Rapet.   5

At the Princess's

An "Old Playgoer" sends us the following:—

I am a sexagenarian who used to go much to the Princess's some five-and-thirty years ago, when Macready had an engagement there. I remember it as if it were yesterday. In spite of his faults and his mannerism, Macready brought to his work so much intellect, study, energy, and power, that one admired him when he was living, and remembers him now he is dead. During the engagement I speak of, Macready acted, I think, all his great Shakspearian parts. But he was ill supported, the house was shabby and dingy, and by no means full; there was something melancholy about the whole thing. You had before you great pieces and a powerful actor; but the theatre needs the glow of public and popular interest to brighten it, and in England the theatre was at that time not in fashion.

After an absence of many years I found myself at the Princess's again. The piece was "The Silver King." Perhaps I ought to have gone to see "The Lights o' London;" but the lyric of Mr. Sims with which the streets were placarded, in order to charm us to "The Lights o' London," had, to my aged mind, an unpleasant touch of *le faux*—that danger, as the critic tells us, of the romantic artist:—"Comme chaque genre de composition a son écueil particulier, celui du genre romanesque, c'est le faux." At any rate, I resisted the charm of Mr. Sims, and stayed away from "The Lights o' London." But "The Silver King" I have just now been to see, and I should like to record some of my impressions from it while they are fresh.

It was another world from the old Princess's of my remembrance. The theatre itself was renewed and transformed; in-

94

stead of shabby and dingy, it had become decorated and brilliant. But the real revival was not in the paint and gilding, it was in the presence of the public. The public was there; not alone the old, peculiar public of the pit and gallery, with a certain number of the rich and refined in the boxes and stalls, and with whole, solid classes of English society conspicuous by their absence. No, it was a representative public, furnished from all classes, and showing that English society at large has now taken to the theatre.

Equally new was the high general level of the acting. Instead of the company with a single powerful and intelligent performer, with two or three middling ones, and with the rest moping and mowing in what was not to be called English but rather stagese, here was a whole company of actors, able to speak English, playing intelligently, supporting one another effectively. Mr. Wilson Barrett, as Wilfred Denver, is so excellent that his primacy cannot be doubted. Next after him, so far as the piece now acting is concerned, I should be inclined to put Mr. Charles Coote, as Henry Corkett. But it is the great merit of the piece that the whole is so effective, and that one is little disposed to make distinctions between the several actors, all of them do their work so well.

And the piece itself? It is not Shakspeare, it is melodrama. I have seen it praised as though it were not melodrama, not sensational drama at all, but drama of a new and superior kind, bordering upon poetic drama, and even passing into it. With this praise I cannot quite agree. The essential difference between melodrama and poetic drama is that one relies for its main effect upon an inner drama of thought and passion, the other upon an outer drama of, as the phrase is, sensational incidents. "The Silver King" relies for its main effect upon an outer drama of sensational incidents, and so far is clearly melodrama, transpontine melodrama. But for this outer drama, no less than for the inner drama which we have opposed to it, there is needed an exposition by means of words and sentiments; and in the exposition of the melodrama of Messrs. Jones and Herman, there is nothing transpontine. The critics are right, therefore, in thinking that in this work they have some-

thing new and highly praiseworthy, though it is not exactly what they suppose. They have a sensational drama in which the diction and sentiments do not overstep the modesty of nature. In general, in drama of this kind, the diction and senti-
5 ments, like the incidents, are extravagant, impossible, transpontine; here they are not. This is a very great merit, a very great advantage. The imagination can lend itself to almost any incidents, however violent; but good taste will always revolt against transpontine diction and sentiments. Instead of giving
10 to their audience transpontine diction and sentiments, Messrs. Jones and Herman give them literature. Faults there are in "The Silver King;" Denver's drunkenness is made too much of, his dream is superfluous, the peasantry are a little tiresome, Denver's triumphant exit from Black Brake Wharf puzzles us.
15 But in general throughout the piece the diction and sentiments are natural, they have sobriety and propriety, they are literature. It is an excellent and hopeful sign to find playwrights capable of writing in this style, actors capable of rendering it, a public capable of enjoying it.
20   Another excellent sign should be noticed too. As everybody was said to know how that the city of the Ephesians was a worshipper of the great goddess Diana, so we may say that everybody knows how that, if not the city of the French, yet their modern drama, like their lighter newspapers, their novels,
25 and their art in general, is a worshipper of the great goddess Lubricity. We imitate and adapt French pieces, and whether the adapter wishes it or not, some traces of the goddess can hardly fail to pass into his work. It is refreshing to find a native piece without the vestige of an appeal to her; and to find this
30 piece, too, admirably given by the actors, passionately enjoyed by the audience. So at least it seems to your obedient servant.

An Old Playgoer at the Play

Twice at the Olympic! At last I have seen "Forget-me-Not." If the renovated and crowded house, at the Princess's, was quite unlike the house of my recollections, I must own that the Olympic is dingy and shabby enough to correspond to them perfectly. Nor was the house full. But then "Forget-me-Not" 5 has been given seven hundred and something times, and one is the very Epimenides of playgoers to be seeing it for the first time now.

The piece of Messrs. Grove and Merivale is full of clever things. The dialogue is always pointed and smart, sometimes 10 quite brilliant. The piece has life from its ability and verve, and it is effectively acted besides. What can one want more? Well, the talent of the authors, the talent of the actors, makes one exacting. The dialogue is so incisive, Miss Geneviève Ward is so powerful, that they make one take them seriously, make 15 one reflect. Now the moment one deliberates, "Forget-me-Not" is, I will not say lost, but considerably compromised.

That Monsieur and Mdme. de Mohrivart should have kept a gambling-house, that their blameless son should have married Rose Verney, that Rose should have become a widow, that her 20 disreputable father-in-law should have been killed by one of his victims, that his wife should desire to be whitewashed, and to this end should seek to extort the aid of Rose's sister, Alice Verney, for getting into society, all this is admissible enough. But the gist of the play lies in the pressure which Mdme. de 25 Mohrivart can put upon Alice, and the force of the pressure which Mdme. de Mohrivart can put upon Alice lies in Article 148 of the French Code. For by this article Mdme. de Mohrivart has the power, if she chooses to exert it, of making

her son's marriage with Rose Verney invalid in France. But
the marriage is good in England. Rose lives with her English
friends and on her English fortune; her worthy French connections have no effects, and their social status is all gone to
5   ruin. Under these circumstances, Mdme. de Mohrivart's threatened invocation of Article 148 has by no means the substantial
force which, for our authors' purpose, it requires. Why all this
terror and dismay, for why should Rose live in France at all?
To live in the Capital of Pleasure without effects and with
10   execrable connections, for the mere satisfaction of belonging
to a nation where, like the lady of whom M. Blowitz told us
the other day, one can name one's child Lucifer Satan Ver-
cingetorix, is surely no such irresistible object of longing to an
English girl. It is the last thing Alice Verney would naturally
15   desire for her sister, or her sister for herself. But then Mdme.
de Mohrivart's power over the sisters has no basis.

I have seen, too, the new piece by Mr. Hamilton Aïdé, "A
Great Catch." If the piece of Messrs. Grove and Merivale
wants motive, that of Mr. Hamilton Aïdé wants development.
20   It has not the terse and sparkling dialogue of "Forget-me-
Not," but it is better grounded and more substantial. It has one
character which strongly attracts sympathy, Mrs. Henry de
Motteville; and another which might easily be made to do so,
Sir Martin Ingoldsby. But Sir Martin does not produce his due
25   effect, and the piece does not produce its due effect, from a
want of development. Why Mr. Hamilton Aïdé should develop the humours of his supernumeraries so copiously, and
the relations of his main characters so sparingly, I do not understand. The truth is, the piece requires another act, if not
30   two. Mrs. Henry de Motteville is a widow who has in her
youth known Sir Martin Ingoldsby as Richard Carlton. Her
father was his benefactor; the young people loved one another.
But Richard Carlton robs his benefactor, causes his ruin and
death, leaves his daughter to her fate, flies to Australia, then re-
35   appears in England some years later, a prosperous and powerful man. At the height of his prosperity, Mrs. Henry de Motteville recognizes him and can unmask him. But his conduct is
not really what it has seemed; and, above all, his heart and that

of Mrs. de Motteville still vibrate to each other. At the last moment he exculpates himself and she relents. Here are elements of strong interest, and Mr. Hamilton Aïdé should have thrown all his power into their development. But they are summarily indicated in the last scene; they are not prepared, established, made to produce their due effect. Mr. Hamilton Aïdé's play is seen with pleasure as it is; but I cannot but think he might treble its effect by a more complete use of the resources which he has created but does not employ.

The Olympic company, on the whole, like that at the Princess's, surprises by the merits of its acting an Epimenides who has been asleep all these years. Mr. Vernon is good as Sir Horace Welby, and good, too, in the more difficult part of Sir Martin Ingoldsby. Miss Lucy Buckstone is pleasing and sympathetic. Mr. Beerbohm Tree is excellent as a young nobleman of the period. Miss Geneviève Ward is a host in herself. External advantages go for much, and in "A Great Catch" Miss Geneviève Ward has three "arrangements," an arrangement in black, an arrangement in grey, and an arrangement in red, of which the arrangement in red is the most irresistible, but every one of them is charming. Her intellectual qualities are as eminent as these external advantages. Her cynicism, coolness, and scorn, her energy, invective, and hate, are unsurpassable. Have her pathos and tenderness quite the sincerity of these qualities, and therefore quite the power? Perhaps not; but one should see her in a more favourable part before deciding. Her elocution is admirable; she has an intonation supremely distinct, intelligent, and effective. A slight nasality, certainly; but perhaps this, like the transplanted French idioms in the novels of Mr. Howells, will be the English of the future. However this is, whatever the future may be or whatever the present, the gifts of Miss Geneviève Ward will always make their possessor a fine actress.

AN OLD PLAYGOER

Isaiah of Jerusalem:
Introduction

The time approaches for the revised version of the Old Testament to make its appearance. Before it comes, let us say to ourselves and say to the revisers that the principal books of the Old Testament are things to be deeply enjoyed, and which
5 have been deeply enjoyed hitherto. It is not enough to translate them accurately; they must be translated so as also to be deeply enjoyed, and to exercise the power of beauty and of sentiment which they have exercised upon us hitherto. Correct information by itself, as Butler profoundly says, is "really the least
10 part" of education; just as religion, he adds, "does not consist in the knowledge and belief even of fundamental truths." No; education and religion, says Butler, consist mainly in our being brought by them "to a certain temper and behaviour." Now, if we are to be brought to a temper and behaviour, our affections
15 must be engaged; and a force of beauty or of sentiment is requisite for engaging them.

Correct rendering is very often conspicuously absent from our authorised version of the Old Testament; far more often and far more conspicuously, indeed, than from our authorised
20 version of the New. Correct information as to the meaning, therefore, far oftener fails us in reading or hearing the Old Testament; and the need for revision is great. But what a power is in the words as they stand, imperfectly as we may often comprehend them, impossible as it may often be to at-
25 tach a clear meaning to them! It can be said for them, at any rate, that they connect themselves with truths which have a surpassing grandeur and worth for us, and that they lend themselves to the connexion with a splendour of march and sound worthy of the great objects with which we connect them.

Take, for instance, the two short lessons from Isaiah which we hear in church on Christmas Day. Hardly any one can feel that he understands them clearly as he hears them read; indeed, as they now are, they cannot be understood clearly. But they connect themselves strikingly and powerfully with the great event which the festival of Christmas commemorates, and they have a magnificent glow and movement. "For every battle of the warrior is with confused noise and garments rolled in blood; but this shall be with burning and fuel of fire." No one of us understands clearly what this means, and indeed a clear meaning is not to be got out of the words, which are a mistranslation. Yet they delight the ear, and they move us. Professor Robertson Smith brings an amended translation: "For the greaves of the warrior that stampeth in the fray, and the garments rolled in blood, shall be cast into the fire as fuel for the flame." Yes, we understand; but the charm of the thing is rudely shaken. Mr. Cheyne brings us a translation more close and correct still: "For every boot of him that trampleth noisily, and the cloak rolled in blood, are for burning, the fuel of fire." The charm has altogether vanished, if we receive these words to supersede the old words; the charm has vanished, never to return.

Mr. Cheyne and Professor Robertson Smith read their Isaiah in the original Hebrew, and in the Hebrew they enjoy him. Their translation of him, like their notes and commentaries on him, are designed to give correct and exact information as to his meaning. But such correct information is in the present case, as Butler has told us, "really the least part" of the matter; the main thing is the effect of a wonderful work of poetry and prophecy upon the soul and spirit. And this they themselves, as I have said, get by reading it in the Hebrew. But the mass of English readers, who know no Hebrew, how are they to get as fully as possible, for their soul and spirit, the effect of this wonderful work? Granted that they get some of it even from the present imperfect translation in our Bibles; but we must allow that they do not and cannot get it at all fully. Such translation as that of which I have quoted specimens above will not give it them more fully. It will give them more correct knowl-

edge of Isaiah's meaning; but his effect upon their soul and
spirit it will even impair, and render less than it is now. What
is to be done? Can nothing be done to give it to them more
fully?

5   Such is the question which, with the revised version of the
New Testament in my hands, and the revised version of the
Old Testament in prospect, I keep asking myself about Isaiah.
Taking him merely as poetry and literature,—which is not, I
will readily add, to take him in his entirety,—I consider the
10   question very important. I rate the value of the operation of
poetry and literature upon men's minds extremely high; and
from no poetry and literature, not even from our own Shakespeare and Milton, great as they are and our own as they are,
have I, for my own part, received so much delight and stimulus
15   as from Homer and Isaiah. To know, in addition to one's native literature, a great poetry and literature not of home
growth, is an influence of the highest value; it very greatly
widens one's range. The Bible has thus been an influence of the
highest value for the nations of Christendom. And the effect of
20   Hebrew poetry can be preserved and transferred in a foreign
language, as the effect of other great poetry cannot. The effect
of Homer, the effect of Dante, is and must be in great measure
lost in a translation, because their poetry is a poetry of metre,
or of rhyme, or both; and the effect of these is not really
25   transferable. A man may make a good English poem with the
matter and thoughts of Homer or Dante, may even try to reproduce their metre, or to reproduce their rhyme; but the
metre and rhyme will be in truth his own, and the effect will
be his, not the effect of Homer or Dante. Isaiah's, on the other
30   hand, is a poetry, as is well known, of parallelism; it depends
not on metre and rhyme, but on a balance of thought, conveyed by a corresponding balance of sentence; and the effect
of this can be transferred to another language. Hebrew poetry
has in addition the effect of assonance and other effects which
35   cannot perhaps be transferred; but its main effect, its effect of
parallelism of thought and sentence, can. I ask myself, therefore, this question: How can the effect of this best of a great

poetry and literature, an effect of the highest worth and power, an effect which can in a great degree be preserved in translation, and which our old version does preserve, but renders imperfectly,—how, to the mass of English people, who do not know Hebrew, may the effect of Isaiah be so rendered and 5 conveyed as that they may feel it most fully?

[1]

First and foremost in importance, for the attainment of such an end, is this rule:—that the old version is not to be departed from without necessity. It comes from a great flowering-time of our literature, and has created deep and powerful senti- 10 ments; it is still the prime agent on which we have to rely for the attainment of our prime object, that Isaiah may be enjoyed fully. Increase of knowledge enables us to see mistakes in the old version and to correct them; but only mistakes, real mistakes, should be corrected, and they should be corrected 15 gently. I once said that I would forbear to alter the old version of Isaiah where it made sense, whether the sense made was that of the original or not. I went too far; where the sense given by the old version is another sense from that of the original, alteration is required. But we should use a large and liberal 20 spirit in judging what constitutes a departure from the sense of the original. If the general sense is preserved, we should be satisfied. We should not regard ourselves as called to a trial of skill in which he succeeds best who renders the original most literally and exactly. At least, if we choose to engage in a 25 trial of skill of such a kind, we should say to ourselves that all we can hope to produce in this way is what may be called aids to the study of Isaiah,—capable of being of great use, perhaps, to students, but the mass of mankind are not students, and the mass of mankind want something quite different. To meet the 30 wants of the mass of mankind, our trial of skill must be, to succeed in altering as little as possible and yet altering enough, and in altering enough and yet leaving the reader with the impression that we have not altered at all, or hardly at all. Only thus can our revised version, under the actual conditions of the case, have charm; and it is essential that it should have charm.

The first chapter of Isaiah really and strictly requires, for our purpose as thus laid down, three changes and three changes only. In verse 17, *relieve the oppressed* should be *correct the oppressor;* in verse 25, *thy tin* should be *thine alloy;* and in verse 31, for *the maker of it* we should read *his work.* Two or three other very slight changes besides may be desirable, in order to bring out the effect better; but these are the only changes which can be called indispensable. To re-write the chapter, if the reader we have in view is the great public, not the sifting and curious student, is fatal. If the authorised version had succeeded in giving the chapters which follow as happily as in giving the first chapter, the task of a reviser would be easy indeed. But this high standard of success is not maintained; and consequently, in the chapters which follow there is much more need of change than in the first chapter. Still our rule should always be to alter as little as possible. What can be gained, or rather what is not lost, by changing, "But Ahaz said, I will not ask, neither will I tempt the Lord," into, "But Ahaz said, I will not ask, neither will I put Jehovah to the test"? Here no change was needed at all. Where change is needed, our ideal should be a case such as one which is presented in the sixteenth verse of the thirtieth chapter, where the change of a letter [1] is all that is required to effect a needful improvement, and to effect it admirably.

Undoubtedly the use of *Jehovah* or *Jahve,* instead of *The Lord,* is inadmissible in a version intended, not to be scanned by students, but to be enjoyed by the mass of readers. *Jehovah* and *Jahve* have a mythological sound, and to substitute them for *The Lord* disturbs powerful sentiments long and deeply established already. *The Eternal* is in itself a better equivalent than *The Lord* for *Jehovah;* it is adopted in one of the French versions. And in many of the familiar texts which a man has present to his mind and habitually dwells upon, he will do well to adopt it; he will find that it gives to the text a fuller and deeper significance. But there are combinations to which

[1] *Fly* for *flee.*

it does not lend itself without some difficulty, and to which *The Lord* lends itself better; and at any rate, to banish this accustomed reading, and to substitute for it everywhere *The Eternal,* would be too radical a change. There would be more loss to the sentiment, from the disturbing shock caused to it by so great a change, than gain from the more adequate rendering.

The old translators of Isaiah, with the notion that a prophet is, above everything, a man who makes supernatural predictions, lean always to the employment of the future tense; they use it excessively. But it is unnecessary and pedantic to change always, in order to mark that a prophet is *not*, above everything, a man who makes supernatural predictions, their future tenses into presents. The balance of the rhythm is often deranged and injured by the correction, without any compensating advantage. For, in truth, the present, the past, and the future, are all of them natural and legitimate tenses of prophecy. Sometimes the prophet may be said to intend them all, to use them all; and often one of them will serve to render him as well as another. "Therefore my people are gone into captivity, because they have no knowledge: and their honourable men are famished, and their multitude dried up with thirst. Therefore hell hath enlarged herself, and opened her mouth without measure: and their glory, and their multitude, and their pomp, and he that rejoiceth, shall descend into it." [1] Here preterites, presents, and futures are mingled together; but the general sense is adequately given, and nothing is gained by endangering the rhythm of these fine verses through turning all the tenses into presents. But sometimes the futures of the old version hinder our adequately seizing the sense, and then they are to be altered. "Behold, their valiant ones shall cry without: the ambassadors of peace shall weep bitterly." [2] The magnates of Judah have been sent to Lachish to make Hezekiah's submission to Sennacherib; the ambassadors are returned and are at the gate of the capital, bringing with shame and consternation the tidings that the Assyrian, after accepting their submission

---

[1] Isaiah, v, 13, 14.   [2] *Ibid.*, xxxiii, 7.

and presents, insists further on the surrender of Jerusalem. "Behold, Judah's valiant ones cry without: the ambassadors of peace weep bitterly." The prophet is not predicting; he sees and hears the envoys weeping at the city gate. In a case of this
5   kind the future tense impairs the effect, and must be altered.

[II]

The first requisite, then, if we are to feel and enjoy the book of Isaiah aright, is to amend the authorised translation without destroying its effect. And the second requisite is to understand the situation with which the book deals, the facts to which it
10   makes reference, the expressions which it employs;—to do this, and to do it without losing oneself in details. All sorts of questions solicit the regard of the student of Isaiah: questions of language, questions of interpretation, questions of criticism, questions of history. The student has the Assyrian inscriptions
15   offering themselves to him on one side, and the great controversy as to the arrangement of the book of Isaiah offering itself to him on the other. Now, all kinds of knowledge are interesting, some kinds of knowledge are fascinating; and the book of Isaiah invites us towards kinds of knowledge which are
20   peculiarly fascinating. But there is the same danger here which there is in the apparatus of philological study which accompanies and guards for us, in our boyhood, the entrance upon Greek. There is the danger of our losing ourselves in preliminaries, and of our being brought, by the pursuit of an impossible perfection, to miss our main design. Perfection is the
25   ideal, thoroughness in preparation is most precious. But there is the danger, also, of forgetting how short man's time is, how easily he is diverted and distracted from his real aim, how easily tired. How many boys learning Greek never get beyond that
30   philological vestibule in which we are kept so assiduously, never arrive at Greek literature at all! The adult student of Isaiah is exposed to the risk of a like misfortune. The apparatus to Isaiah is so immense, that the student who has to handle it is in danger of not living long enough to come ever to enjoy
35   the performance of Isaiah himself.

Four names stand out from among the names of Isaiah's commentators. They are all of them the names of Germans. Mr. Cheyne is the first Englishman who has given us a commentary on Isaiah of like seriousness and sound knowledge with theirs, and he would himself be the foremost to profess his obligations to them. The four Germans are Vitringa, Gesenius, Ewald, Delitzsch; and of these four, again, two stand out most prominently,—Ewald and Delitzsch. Both are invaluable; to both we owe all gratitude. Ewald kindles and inspires us most, Delitzsch instructs us most. But at what a length he instructs us, and with what discursiveness! Life being so short as it is, and the human mind so shallow a vessel, can it be well to make us read a closely-printed page of imperial octavo about the different kinds of wounds and their treatment, in connexion with the "wounds and bruises and putrefying sores" [1] spoken of by Isaiah? Can it be necessary, in connexion with Isaiah's phrase, "though your sins be as scarlet," [2] to give us another like page on the mystical character of red and white to this sort of effect: "Blood is the colour of fire and therefore of life; blood is red, because life is a fire-process?"

No, it is not necessary; and we must be careful not to let ourselves be lost in excursions of this kind. Still, it is very requisite to understand the situation with which the book of Isaiah deals, the facts to which it makes reference, the expressions which it employs. For instance, the mystic names of Isaiah's sons, *Shear-jashub* and *Maher-shalal-hash-baz*, are of the very highest significance. One of them, the name of *Shear-jashub*, governs the whole book. Yet not one in twenty among ordinary readers or hearers of Isaiah knows what they mean. However, the chief drawback to our right enjoyment of Isaiah is our ignorance of that whole situation of things which the book supposes, rather than our ignorance of the meaning of particular expressions. Verses and passages from Isaiah are far more generally known, and far more present to the minds of most of us, than passages from the Greek and Latin classics. But they stand isolated in our minds, without our having any

---

[1] Isaiah, i, 6.   [2] *Ibid.,* i, 18.

firm grasp of the facts to which they refer, or any clear view
of the situation of things which they suppose. Cultivated people have in general a much clearer and more connected notion
of the important moments and situations in Greek and Roman
5   history,—of the Persian war, the rise of Athens, the Peloponnesian war, the Sicilian expedition, the Roman Republic, the
Punic wars, Cæsar and the Empire,—than they have of the
historical moment and situation with which Isaiah had to deal.
But we cannot appreciate Isaiah unless we have before our
10 minds this moment and situation.

Its history is well given in Professor Robertson Smith's recent work on the Prophets; but our purpose requires a narrative which will go into two or three pages, not a narrative
spreading itself through a series of chapters. Let us try here to
15 sketch the situation. There is some uncertainty in the chro-
nology; the old received dates of the Jewish kings have in
some cases to be corrected from data furnished by the Assyrian
inscriptions. But, at any rate, the period with which we have
to deal is the last half of the eighth century before Christ.
20 From 750 to 700 B.C. is the period of Isaiah's activity. The chief
countries concerned are Judah, Israel, Assyria, Syria, Egypt,
Ethiopia. Babylon for most of this period is as yet, though
again and again rising in revolt, a vassal kingdom of Assyria.
The great personages of the history are four successive kings
25 of Assyria,—Tiglath-pileser, Shalmaneser, Sargon, and Sennacherib; two successive kings of Judah,—Ahaz and Hezekiah;
the king of Syria, Rezin; Pekah, king of Israel; the king of
Egypt, whom Isaiah calls by the general dynastic name of
Pharaoh only; and the king of Ethiopia. The main events of
30 our fifty years' period are the conquest of Samaria, the capital
of the kingdom of Israel, by the Assyrians in 721 B.C., and
the failure of Sennacherib to possess himself of Jerusalem
in 701.

Of the final scope of Isaiah's ideas, so far as we can appre-
35 hend it, and of the character and grandeur of his prophetic deliverances, I do not here speak. Here I only deal with his
prophecy so far as our presentment of the historical situation
requires. Isaiah's centre of action was Jerusalem. He was of

noble, by some accounts of even royal birth. To his native country of Judah the long reign of Uzziah, the grandfather of Ahaz, had been a time of great power, wealth, and prosperity. The rival kingdom of Israel under the reign of the second Jeroboam, in part contemporary with the reign of Uzziah, had 5 likewise been conquering, rich, and prosperous. Never since the death of Solomon, and the separation of the ten tribes from Judah, had the two kingdoms enjoyed so much prosperity. But when Isaiah began his career, the tide of the northern kingdom's prosperity had long since turned. The king of Israel 10 was now the subordinate ally of the king of Syria; and the two kings, fearing extinction by their great military neighbour on the north, Assyria, which was pressing hard upon them, desired to unite Syria, Palestine, and Egypt in resistance to Assyria's progress, and for this purpose to force the king of 15 Judah into an alliance with them. At the end of Uzziah's reign the design was already formed. It was maturing during the reign of his son Jotham. And about the year 732 B.C., soon after the accession of Jotham's son, Ahaz, the kings of Syria and Israel appeared with an army in Judah, resolved to bend 20 Ahaz to their will.

The outward and seeming prosperity of Judah had continued until the death of Jotham. On this outward prosperity the eyes of Isaiah in his early manhood rested; but it exercised no illusion upon him, he discerned its unsoundness. He saw his 25 country with "an upper class materialised,"—an upper class full of cupidity, hardness, insolence, dissoluteness. He saw the lower class, the bulk of the people, to be better, indeed, and more free from vice than the upper class; he saw it attached in its way to the old religion, but understanding it ill, turning it 30 into a superstition and a routine, admitting gross accretions and admixtures to it;—a lower class, in short, fatally impaired by bad example and want of leading. Butler's profound words, so true for at any rate the old societies of the world, cannot but here rise to the mind:—"The behaviour of the lower rank 35 of mankind has very little in it original or of home growth; very little which may not be traced up to the influence of others, and less which is not capable of being changed by such

influence. This being their condition, consider now what influence, as well as power, their superiors must, from the nature of the case, have over them. And experience shows that they do direct and change the course of the world as they
5   please. Not only the civil welfare but the morals and religion of their fellow-creatures greatly depend upon them."

In his first deliverances,[1] soon after the year 740, Isaiah denounced as unsound the still existing outward prosperity of Judah, his country. Ahaz came to the throne; and the young
10 king, and the governing class surrounding him, now began freely to introduce from the neighbouring nations worships and rites, many of which had for their vicious adopters the attraction of being also dissolute or cruel orgies. Then fell the blow of invasion. The kings of Syria and Israel overran the
15 country of Judah; and, amid the consternation pervading Jerusalem, the famous meeting of Isaiah with Ahaz took place "at the end of the conduit of the upper pool, in the highway of the fuller's field." [2]

Three names, which are to be found in the chapter relating
20 Isaiah's interview with Ahaz and in the chapter immediately following it, sum up for us the judgment of Isaiah upon this emergency, and indeed upon the whole troublous future discovering itself to his thoughts. These three names are *Immanuel, Shear-jashub, Maher-shalal-hash-baz*. Immanuel means,
25 as everybody knows, "God with us." Shear-jashub and Maher-shalal-hash-baz are the names of Isaiah's two sons. The meaning of Shear-jashub is given in a subsequent chapter: "The remnant shall return." *Return*, not in the physical sense, but in the moral,—be converted, come to God. The third name, Maher-
30 shalal-hash-baz, means, "Spoil speedeth, prey hasteth."

Spoil speedeth, prey hasteth. The kingdoms which the chosen people has made for itself, their world which now is, with its prosperities, idolatries, governing classes, oppression, luxury, pleasures, drunkards, careless women, systems of
35 policy, strong alliances, shall pass away; nothing can save it. Strokes of statesmanship, fluctuations of fortune, cannot change

---

[1] Isaiah, ii–v.   [2] *Ibid.*, vii, 3.

the inevitable final result. The present invasion by Rezin and Pekah is nought. The kings of Syria and Israel will disappear; their plans will be frustrated, their power destroyed. But no real triumph is thus won, no continuance secured, for Judah as it is, for Judah's king and governing classes as they are. Assyria, the great and colossal power, the representative and wielder of "the kingdoms of this world" now, as Babylon and Rome became their representatives afterwards,—Assyria is behind. Swiftly and irresistibly this agent of the Eternal is moving on, to ruin and overwhelm Judah and Judah's allies. "He shall pass through Judah; he shall overflow and go over." [1] *Spoil speedeth, prey hasteth.*

And, nevertheless, *God is with us.* In this Jerusalem, in this city of David, in this sanctuary of the old religion, God has been known, righteousness loved, the root of the matter reached, as they never have been in the world outside. The great world outside has nothing so indispensable to mankind, no germ so precious to mankind, as the "valley of vision" has. Therefore "he that believeth shall not take flight;" there is laid by the Eternal "in Zion for a foundation a stone, a tried stone, a precious corner-stone, a sure foundation." [2] *God is with us.*

But it is the *remnant* shall return; the remnant, and the remnant only. Our old world must pass away, says Isaiah to his countrymen; God is with us for the making of a new world, but how few of us may take part in that making! Only a *remnant!* A remnant sifted and purged by sharp trial, and then sifted and purged afresh! "Even if yet there shall be a tenth, it shall return and shall be burned; but as a terebinth tree, and as an oak, whose substance is in them when they are cut down, so the stock of that burned tenth shall be a holy seed." [3] Against this seed the kingdoms of the world, the hosts of self-seeking and unrighteous power, shall not finally prevail; they shall fail in their attacks upon it, they shall founder. It shall see a king of its own, who shall reign not as Ahaz, but "shall reign in righteousness;" it shall see a governing class, not like

[1] Isaiah, viii, 8.   [2] *Ibid.*, xxviii, 16.   [3] *Ibid.*, vi, 13.

the ministers and nobles of the court of Ahaz, but of whom "a man shall be as an hiding-place from the wind and a covert from the tempest;" where "the vile person shall no more be called noble, nor the worker of mischief said to be worthy."
5   It shall see the lower people with a religion no longer blind and gross; "the tongue of the stammerers shall be ready to speak plainly." [1] Amidst such a society it "shall see the king in his beauty, shall behold the land spreading very far forth." [2] *The remnant shall return.*

10   The final scope of these ideas of Isaiah, and what is really their significance and their greatness, I do not, as I have said, attempt to discuss here. But they give us, just as they stand, the clue to his whole book and to all his prophecy. Let us pursue our summary of the historical situation with their
15   aid. They will enable us to make very brief what remains to be said.

Ahaz heard, but was not convinced. He had a more short and easy way than Isaiah's. He put himself into the hands of the king of Assyria. In 731 B.C. Tiglath-pileser, after chastising
20   the kingdom of Israel, crushed the kingdom of Syria, and received the homage of Ahaz at Damascus. Shalmaneser, Tiglath-pileser's successor, determined to make an end of the subjected but ever restless kingdom of Israel, and formed the siege of Samaria, which was taken by his successor Sargon in 721.
25   Three years before this destruction of the northern kingdom, Hezekiah had succeeded his father Ahaz upon the throne of Jerusalem. Hezekiah was a man of piety; but the governing class remained as they were before, and controlled the policy of their country. Judah was tributary to Assyria, and owed to
30   Assyria its deliverance from a great danger. But the deliverer and his designs were extremely dangerous, and made Judah apprehensive of being swallowed up presently, when its turn came. The neighboring countries,—Phœnicia on the north, Moab, Ammon, and the Arabian nations on the east, Philistia
35   on the west, Egypt and Ethiopia on the south,—shared Judah's apprehensions. There were risings, and they were sternly

[1] Isaiah, xxxii, 1, 2, 5, 4.   [2] *Ibid.*, xxxiii, 17.

quelled; Judah, however, remained tranquil. But the scheme of an anti-Assyrian alliance was gradually becoming popular. Egypt was the great pillar of hope. By its size, wealth, resources, pretensions, and fame, Egypt seemed a possible rival to Assyria. Time went on. Sargon was murdered in 705; Sennacherib succeeded him. Then on all sides there was an explosion of revolts against the Assyrian rule. The first years of Sennacherib's reign were spent by him in quelling a formidable rising of Merodach Baladan, king of Babylon. The court and ministers of Hezekiah seized this opportunity for detaching their master from Assyria, for joining in the movement of the insurgent states of Palestine and its borders, and for allying themselves with Egypt.

All this time Isaiah never changed his view of the situation. The risings were vain, the Egyptian alliance could not profit. Of his three great notes he kept reiterating the sternest one, and insisting upon it: *Spoil speedeth, prey hasteth.* He repeated it to Moab and Arabia, to Tyre and Philistia, to Egypt and Ethiopia. The great stream of Assyrian conquest will assuredly submerge you, he said, and you cannot escape from it.—But of what avail, then, could Egypt and Ethiopia be to help Judah?

Nay, and the stream must overflow Judah also. In the year 701, Sennacherib, victorious in Babylonia, marched upon Palestine. For Judah also was now the note true: *Spoil speedeth, prey hasteth.* But for Judah Isaiah had those two other notes besides, constantly alternating with the darker one: the notes of *God with us* and of *The remnant shall return.* Higher still those notes rose when the invader appeared in Judæa, confident, overbearing, unscrupulous, perfidious, and demanded the surrender of Jerusalem. Jerusalem, so Isaiah prophesied, the invader should never enter; a disaster should befall him, he should return in discomfiture to his own land.

Sennacherib's enterprise against Jerusalem presently failed. His own account of the failure is not the same as the Jewish account: any more than the account of the battle of Albuera in Napier's history is the same as the account of it in the *Victoires et Conquêtes de l'Armée Française.* But from the Assyrian account itself it is sufficiently manifest that the enterprise failed,

and that Sennacherib returned to his own land unsuccessful. It was a great triumph for Isaiah. And undoubtedly it gave him for the moment a commanding influence, and contributed not a little to the final accomplishment of religious reforms
5   which were dear to his heart. Shall we ask whether it enabled him to behold a king reigning in righteousness, and a governing class like the shadow of a great rock in a weary land? Shall we ask whether he even expected it to enable him to do this? No; we will not now pursue further his own conceptions
10 as to the fulfilment of his own prophecies,—prophecies "impatient," as Davison says, "for the larger scope." We will not interrogate him as to his own view, as years rolled on with him, of his splendid promises of Immanuel and of the Remnant. He had put his Immanuel too soon by seven centuries. Too soon
15 by far more than seven centuries had he put his reign of the saints, for it is not come about even yet. Men, as has been truly said, "are impatient, and for anticipating things;" even great prophets are "for anticipating things." But with inspired faith and sure insight Isaiah foresaw Immanuel and the reign of
20 saints; he foresaw and foretold them; he established the ideal of them for ever. The movement and upshot of history has, in part, brought his immortal prophecy true already, and will unfold its accomplishment more and more. We do well to love the exalted belief that in nothing will the prophecy of this
25 sublime seer finally fail, in nothing will it come short.

    At present, however, I do but give a summary of the historical situation which ought to be ever present to our minds in reading Isaiah. I will conclude the summary by saying that he lived on into the reign of Hezekiah's son Manasseh, and that he
30 is said to have been put to death by Manasseh. One tradition attributes his death to offence given to the fanaticism of a narrow religiosity by his large and free language. Whether his death was caused by the hatred of a religious party, or by the hatred of that governing class which in former reigns he had
35 so unsparingly assailed, we shall never know. A Puritan terror, an aristocratical terror, a Jacobin terror,—a great soul may easily become an object of fear and hatred to each and all of them. By any one of them he may easily perish. In one or the other of them, probably, Isaiah sank.

The events and personages of the historical situation of which I have thus given the rapid summary should be as familiar to us, if we are ever rightly to enjoy Isaiah, as the events and personages of those passages of history with which we are most conversant. 5

[III]

The third requisite for a full enjoyment of Isaiah is to have the book so arranged that we can read his prophecies in their right order and in their right connexion. It is demonstrable that the book is not so arranged now; and although in re-arranging it there is danger of being fantastic and rash, and 10 many critics have succumbed to this danger, yet some re-arrangement is absolutely necessary, and, if made with sobriety, fairness, moderation, and caution, must be of signal benefit.

Whoever has once acquainted himself with the history of the times during which Isaiah lived, must be struck with the 15 close connexion in which his first thirty-nine chapters mostly stand with that history. They are called forth by it and turn upon it. The prophet announces judgments and blessings to come, he delineates an ideal future; but the positive history with which he deals is the history passing before his eyes,—the 20 names, actors, and events are those of that history. He does not profess to exhibit the positive history of future centuries.

In the twenty-seven chapters which conclude the Book of Isaiah, and in certain chapters occurring amongst the first thirty-nine, this course of proceeding is changed. The names, 25 actors, and events, are no longer contemporary with the prophet, like Ahaz, Hezekiah, the Assyrian invasion; or else ideal creations like Immanuel. No, they are actual names and events of a time more than one hundred and fifty years after Isaiah's death,—Cyrus, the Medes and Persians, the fall of 30 Babylon. Instead of insight profound indeed and most admirable, but still natural, we have supernatural prediction.

People say: As a fact, supernatural predictions are not made, names of future actors in human affairs, details of future events, are not foreknown. And the conviction of this has led a great 35

and ever-growing majority of serious critics to conclude that in our present Book of Isaiah the deliverances of two distinct prophets have got joined together;—the deliverances of one prophet whose centre was Jerusalem, and who had before his
5 eyes the events of the year 700 B.C. and of the half century preceding it, and of another prophet whose centre was Babylon, and who had before his eyes the events of a time one hundred and sixty years later. These critics have been led in the same way to attribute prophecies in the Book of Daniel, which
10 were supposed to come from a Daniel living at the time of the Babylonian Captivity, to a much later prophet. As a matter of fact, supernatural predictions are not, it is said, made. But the point on which I, for my part, desire to insist, is a different one. I do not now urge that supernatural predictions are
15 not, in fact, made, and that therefore we must separate the latter part of our Book of Isaiah from the earlier. What I urge is rather this: by separating the two prophets now joined together in our Book of Isaiah, and by letting each prophet deal with his own proper time, we enable ourselves to feel the Book not less
20 deeply and fully, but more; we increase our enjoyment of it.

It is characteristic of the prophet whom we call Isaiah of Jerusalem to deal with the history passing before his eyes, and to show his insight by seizing that history's tendency and sure issue. His regards are on Jerusalem in the latter half of the
25 eighth century before Christ; as the regards of the prophet who follows him, in the last twenty-seven chapters of our Book of Isaiah, are on Babylon about a hundred and sixty years later. The younger prophet has several differences distinguishing him from the older. The younger prophet has more copiousness,
30 pathos, and unction than his predecessor; he has less fire, energy, and concentration. He is much more general; and he engages in outpourings, for which the stress of matter and of exposition allows his predecessor hardly any room. These are in themselves reasons for separating the two prophets and for
35 reading each by himself. But a reason far more decisive is supplied by the incomparably greater effectiveness which each will be found to acquire when read in connexion with his own time. So incomparably greater does the effectiveness of the

elder prophet, in especial, become when he is so read, that the reader who imagined himself to know Isaiah previously will be astonished and charmed; he will feel that he now really knows him for the first time, so new will be his sense of this great prophet's beauty and power.

In the last twenty-seven chapters of the Book of Isaiah we are in another world from the world of the first part. The centre, as I have already said, is Babylon, not Jerusalem; the posture of events, the state of the world, is quite different. Above all, the prophet's ideal helper, saviour, and restorer, is different. With the original Isaiah, he is a prince of the house of David, a Rod out of the stem of Jesse, a Branch of the Eternal beautiful and glorious; smiting the earth with the rod of his mouth, and with the breath of his lips slaying the wicked. With the prophet of the last twenty-seven chapters he is the Servant whom man despiseth, whom the people abhorreth, the servant of tyrants; who strives not, nor cries, nor causes his voice to be heard in the street. The ideal has been transformed.

Now, to my mind it seems a more impressive thing, as it is certainly a more natural thing, that the later ideal should have developed itself, with the change of time and circumstances, out of the former, and should have come from a later prophet, than that both ideals should have proceeded from one and the same prophet. However, it may be contended, pursuant to the old fashion of explaining these things, that Isaiah in a preternatural way foresaw the state of the world a hundred and fifty years after his own death, and himself transformed his Messianic ideal accordingly. Religious people, for the most part, are agreed to say that they are edified by a belief of this sort; for my part, I am simply bewildered by it. But still, on this supposition, the later matter is at least kept separate from the earlier, the two are not jumbled up together. At the end of the thirty-ninth chapter there is a pause, and then (though without one of those prefaces which the original Isaiah is accustomed in a transition of this kind to employ) the Babylonian Isaiah begins. The march of the work, as regards order, is at least artistically natural, if we admit this supposition. But who can suppose that a writer of Isaiah's genius, whether he had

supernatural prevision or not, would ever have so perverted
the march of his work, have so spoiled it artistically, as to thrust
in suddenly, without any connexion at all, the thirteenth chapter and the chief part of the chapter following, about Babylon
and the death of Belshazzar, in the midst of chapters relating
entirely to Assyria and to a history nearly two hundred years
before Belshazzar's; and then again abruptly to return, towards
the end of the fourteenth chapter, to Assyria and the history of
the eighth century before Christ? The supernatural itself is less
bewildering than a supposition like this, and to read Isaiah in so
perverse an arrangement greatly impairs one's enjoyment of
him.

But how, then, did the two or more prophets get joined together? To understand this, we must keep in mind that the
Book of Isaiah did not assume its present shape until the time
of Ezra, two hundred and fifty years after the date of the
original Isaiah, and nearly a hundred years after the fall of
Babylon. Ezra edited the sacred books; and even critics like
Delitzsch, who claim unity of authorship for the whole Book of
Isaiah, admit that there were interpolations in the books edited
by Ezra. Now, in our Book of Isaiah itself there is one interpolation so remarkable, that Delitzsch singles it out and en-
larges upon it. At the beginning of the thirty-sixth chapter it is
said that "in the fourteenth year of king Hezekiah Sennacherib
king of Assyria came up against all the defenced cities of
Judah." But we know that Sennacherib's invasion took place in
the year 701 B.C., and that this year was not the fourteenth year
of Hezekiah but the twenty-third or twenty-fourth. In the
thirty-eighth and thirty-ninth chapters comes the account of
Hezekiah's sickness and of Merodach Baladan's embassy to him
to congratulate him on his getting well. Now, the fourteenth
year of Hezekiah is quite right as the year of Hezekiah's sickness, for his reign was twenty-nine years long, and he reigned
fifteen years after his sickness. It is also quite admissible as the
year of the embassy of Merodach Baladan, who at that time
was in revolt against Sargon and in special need of Hezekiah's
friendship. Therefore, while certainly the narrative in the
thirty-sixth chapter, as this narrative stood originally, cannot

have begun with assigning for its events the date of the fourteenth year of Hezekiah, the narrative in the thirty-eighth and
thirty-ninth chapters may perfectly well have begun in that
manner, for this narrative relates events earlier by ten or twelve
years than the events of the other. But Hezekiah's sickness and   5
Merodach Baladan's embassy were required by the arranger in
Ezra's time to stand last, in order to form the transition to the
Babylonian prophecies of the last part of the Book. The
narratives, therefore, were transposed, and the date was transferred to the beginning of that narrative which now stood   10
first, although for that narrative it is clearly inadmissible. Delitzsch himself receives this explanation of the erroneous date as
necessary; and it is evidence of an *arrangement* of contents
actually taking place, at the first authoritative editing of the
Book of Isaiah,—an arrangement more or less plausible, but   15
erroneous.

Plausible it was, at a time when no man doubted but that a
prophet was, above all, one who utters supernatural predictions,
and when the rules of due sequence and ordinance for a work
of genius might indeed move the maker of it himself, but were   20
certainly not likely to trouble his arrangers. Isaiah had left his
sublime deliverances to fructify in the minds of his disciples.
One disciple, separated by three or four generations from the
master, but living constantly with his prophecies and nourished
upon his spirit, produced at the crisis of Babylon's fall a proph-   25
ecy of Israel's restoration as immortal as Isaiah's own. This
disciple named not himself. Whether he intended his work to
become joined with Isaiah's, and to pass among men with the
authority of that great name, we cannot know. But his contemporaries joined the disciple's work with the master's, and by   30
Ezra's time the conjunction was established.

It was a conjunction which that age might readily make. The
younger prophet, as I have before said, is without some of the
qualities of the elder; he is more given to generalities and to
outpouring. Above all, by his time it had become evident that   35
the prince of the house of David, the royal and victorious Immanuel, whose birth Isaiah announced to be imminent, whose
childhood should witness the chastisement of Ephraim, whose

youth the visitation of Judah, but who in his manhood should
reign in righteousness over a restored and far-spreading kingdom of the chosen people,—that this Immanuel's date was put
too soon, and that the characters assigned to him required, I
5   will not say some change, but some addition. Isaiah himself,
however, had given the sign and uttered the word on which,
for this addition, the insight of his successor seized. "The
meek," Isaiah in his picture of the ideal future had said, "shall
increase their joy in the Eternal, and the *poor* among men shall
10   rejoice in the Holy One of Israel."[1] The word was here given.
Possessing himself of it, the disciple of Immanuel's prophet
fixed the new ideal of the *Servant*, despised and rejected of
men, but anointed and sent "to preach good tidings unto the
meek."[2] This stricken Servant's work is the condition of the
15   victorious Immanuel's reign, and must precede it.

The Jewish nation could not receive the transformed ideal.
Jesus, Christianity, the destruction of Judaism, were necessary
to its triumph. Nevertheless the unknown prophet of the Babylonian Captivity had announced it; and there it henceforth
20   stood, set up for ever. *Mansueti possidebunt terram.*

The Jewish nation, I say, could not receive the new ideal.
Yet it could not but be profoundly stirred and transported by
this ideal's unknown promulgator, although without truly com-
prehending him. It could not but feel the spirit and power of
25   Isaiah in his disciple. There was the same irresistible eloquence,
the same elate emotion, the same puissance of faith and joy.
Isaiah was his inspirer among the prophets, his parent source,
his only equal. The conjunction of the disciple with the master
easily followed.

30   Besides this great prophecy of Israel's restoration after the
fall of Babylon, other shorter prophecies of a similar date
were in circulation. Whether they proceed from the same
author as the great prophecy which fills the last twenty-seven
chapters of the Book of Isaiah, cannot be determined with cer-
35   tainty. What is certain is, that even those which do not manifestly give their own date, yet lend themselves to the circum-

---

[1] Isaiah, xxix, 19.   [2] *Ibid.*, lxi, 1.

stances of the younger prophet's time better than to those of his predecessor's time; that they do not suit, but mar, the plan of composition which appears to govern the original Isaiah's Book; and that they have, besides, those characters of generality and of outpouring which mark, as has been already said, the disciple rather than the original Isaiah. We shall find that their effect is felt best if we read them as subsidiary to the great prophecy which ends the Book, and as, like that prophecy, the work of a prophet formed upon Isaiah, but living amid other events, and a century and a half later;—a prophet whose centre was Babylon, and who may most fitly be called *Isaiah of Babylon,* as the original Isaiah, whose centre was Jerusalem, may be called *Isaiah of Jerusalem.*

The shorter and isolated prophecies had, like the great prophecy of Israel's restoration which now ends our Book of Isaiah, the Isaian eloquence, the Isaian spirit and power. They, too, associated themselves in men's minds and affections with the original Isaiah's work, and the arrangers in Ezra's time finally incorporated them with it. But as these arrangers placed the great Babylonian prophecy at the end, where Merodach Baladan's embassy afforded a natural transition to it, so they placed the isolated prophecies in the connexion which they thought most natural for them. One division of the original Isaiah's prophecies consisted of *Burdens,* or oracular sentences of doom, pronounced against different nations. Among these burdens was placed the isolated prophecy having for its title *The Burden of Babylon* and celebrating the death of Belshazzar.[1] Another division of prophecies consisted of *Woes* pronounced upon a number of nations; and here were inserted those other single prophecies of the Babylonian epoch for which insertion was desired, and which seemed to find here their own rubric and their most suitable place.

Some change of arrangement, then, we find forced upon us by regard to possibility, to probability, to the genius and art of the author with whom we have to deal. We have to detach from Isaiah of Jerusalem the great prophecy of restoration

[1] Isaiah, xiii–xiv, 23. Chapter xxi, 1–12 is of like date, and its present place is due to the same cause.

which fills the last twenty-seven chapters. We have to disen-
gage from him, and to read in connexion with the restoration
prophecy, several shorter single prophecies which are intermingled with Isaiah's prophecies in the first thirty-nine chap-
5 ters. To these shorter prophecies we may give names from
their subject-matter. Taken in the order in which they now
stand in our Bibles, these prophecies are as follows:—*The King
of Babylon* (xiii–xiv, 23); *The First Vision of Babylon's Fall*
(xxi, 1–10); *Early Days of Return* (xxiv–xxvii); *Edom and
10 Israel* (xxxiv, xxxv). Read where they at present stand, these
prophecies interrupt the natural and impressive march of
Isaiah's work, throw the attentive reader out, confuse and ob-
struct our understanding and our enjoyment. Removing them
from the place where they now stand, and reading them in an-
15 other connexion, we are enabled to enjoy much more these
prophecies themselves, and to enjoy much more, also, the original Isaiah thus disengaged from them.

Re-arrangement to this extent may be called necessary. One's
first impulse naturally is to receive a book as it comes to us,
20 and from all unsettlement of it one is averse. But we have to
get over this natural conservatism in the present case, because
so much more embarrassment to our understanding is created,
so much more check given to our full enjoyment of Isaiah, by
rejecting all re-arrangement than by accepting it. Mr. Cheyne,
25 who was formerly inclined to follow Ewald in all his tem-
erities, but who in his recent edition of Isaiah shows a moderation which, like his learning, deserves cordial acknowledgment,
—Mr. Cheyne seems now disposed to leave *The King of Babylon* and *The First Vision* in the connexion where in our Bibles
30 they stand. He still sees that prophets do not supernaturally
mention names and incidents posterior to their own time. He
knows that if Isaiah of Jerusalem wrote *The King of Babylon*
and *The First Vision,* then the subject of these prophecies cannot be Belshazzar and the taking of Babylon by Cyrus. He is
35 disposed to think, however, that the prophecies may possibly
relate to the rising, in Sargon's time, of Merodach Baladan
against Assyria, and that they may be left, therefore, to stand
with the contemporary prophecies of Isaiah. But a greater

shock is given to our sense of probability and possibility, our enjoyment is more spoiled, by having to dissociate the exhortation to Elam and Media from the Medo-Persian troops of Cyrus and to think it fortuitous, by having to dissociate the splendid "proverb against the king of Babylon" from the epoch-making death of Belshazzar, and to connect it with some unknown incident of an obscure struggle, than by taking the two prophecies away from Isaiah and attributing them to a younger prophet. So, too, with *Edom and Israel* and with *Early Days of Return.* Some disturbance and shock is given to our feelings by meddling with the traditional arrangement, and by removing these prophecies from the place where they stand now. But nevertheless much more is gained than lost by doing it. They suit the history of the sixth century before Christ so much better than that of the eighth, they are so much less effective where they stand now than in connexion with Babylon's fall and the conquests of Cyrus, their very generality, which makes it not impossible to assign them to the eighth century, is so alien to the method of the original Isaiah,—that the balance of effect, the balance of satisfaction, the balance of enjoyment, is decisively in favour of removing them.

But tradition ought to go for something, and we should respect it where we can. If, in order to enjoy fully a great work, it is necessary, on the one hand, to have our sense of order and possibility satisfied, so also is it necessary for our enjoyment, on the other hand, that we should read our text with some sense of security. We are so constituted by nature that our enjoyment of a text greatly depends upon our having such a sense of security. This law of our nature Ewald totally disregards. No one can read Ewald's Isaiah with a sense of security. Ewald was a man of genius. He deeply felt Isaiah's grandeur himself, and he admirably helps us to feel it deeply too. But he was violent and arbitrary. He freely alters the text, striking things out when they do not suit him, and inserting things of his own where he thinks they will be an improvement. Above all, he re-arranges the Book of Isaiah from one end to the other, and literally turns it, as the saying is, inside out. He is supremely confident in his own perception and judgment. He will tell you

how many different prophets we hear speaking in the *Burden of Moab*, how many they are, and of what date each of them is, and exactly where each of them leaves off and the other begins. Like other critics of his school, like the professors of the so-
5   called higher criticism generally, after producing reasonings which do really prove that a thing *might* have been so and so, he then jumps straight to the conclusion that they prove that so and so it *must* have been. Often and often one feels Ewald to be brilliant, ingenious, impassioned, profound, but not in
10 the least convincing; and one reads his Isaiah with a disturbed and uneasy sense of its being a fantastic Isaiah; one reads it without security. This is, as I have already said, a great draw-back upon one's pleasure. It is a drawback to which the solid English reader is especially sensible; and the solid English reader,
15 I think, is right. But whether he is right or not, the drawback is strongly felt. Lowth's rashness in emendation has prevented his great services in the promotion of a better understanding of Isaiah from being widely useful. Lowth was a bishop of the Church of England, a Hebraist, and a man of fine taste and
20 accomplishments. He had the qualifications and the authority requisite for propagating in England a truer understanding of Isaiah, but one cannot say that he has done it. He failed to do it because of the liberties he allowed himself to take with his author. Lovers of their Bible desire, in reading their Isaiah, to
25 read him with a sense of security.

      All meddling with the letter itself of the text is, in my opinion, undesirable. The case is one where the feeling that liberty is taken with the text does more damage than any amendment of the text can do good. There has been suggested
30 a brilliant emendation for a passage in the twenty-third chapter: to read, at the thirteenth verse, "Behold the land of the *Canaanites*," instead of "Behold the land of the *Chaldeans*." I would resist the temptation of making it. A tolerable sense can be got out of the reading *Chaldeans*, and when once we begin
35 to change the text for the sake of bettering, as we think, the sense, where are we to stop? Again, in an important passage of the seventh chapter, the text, as it stands, has something em-barrassing. "For the head of Syria is Damascus, and the head of

Damascus is Rezin; and within threescore and five years shall Ephraim be broken, that it be not a people; and the head of Ephraim is Samaria, and the head of Samaria is Remaliah's son. If ye will not believe, surely ye shall not be established." [1] Ewald urges that the words "And within threescore and five years shall Ephraim be broken, that it be not a people," are superfluous, and that afterwards one expects the words, "But the head of Judah is Jerusalem, and the head of Jerusalem is Jehovah;" and he boldly omits the former sentence and inserts the latter. Other editors who do not follow the example of his boldness so far as to insert the new words of Ewald's own invention, yet go so far with him as to strike out the words which he condemns as superfluous. But it is better, I think, to get out of the existing text what meaning can be got out of it, than to create the sense of insecurity which comes when the reader perceives the text to be treated with licence.

The same respect for existing facts, the same dread of the fantastic, which should govern us in dealing with the actual text of the prophecies of Isaiah, should govern us, also, in dealing with their re-arrangement. Some re-arrangement there must be;—this, I think, has been proved and must be admitted. The balance of enjoyment in reading these prophecies, even the balance of security in reading them, is in favour of it. But the existing fact goes, after all, for something. The Book of Isaiah comes to us in an arrangement which it has had ever since Ezra's time. Probably the Book must before Ezra's time have already had its present arrangement in great part, since that is the most natural reason which we can suppose for Ezra's adopting it. Portions engaged with the names and events of a history long posterior to that history with which Isaiah was engaged, we are compelled to think an appendage to the original Book, or insertions in it. But that which remains, when these portions are removed, is the original Book of Isaiah. At all events, it is safest for us now to treat it as such. We do well, when we pass to the body of prophecies concerned with the very history with which Isaiah was engaged, to take the text as it stands, the arrangement as it stands, the history as it

[1] Isaiah, vii, 8, 9.

stands. Some critics suppose an invasion of Judæa by Sargon of which history tells us nothing; others transfer the opening chapter to the middle of the Book, because the history with which the second and following chapters deal seems anterior to
5   the history implied in the first chapter. Sargon *may* have invaded Judæa; the first chapter *may* have originally stood in the middle of the Book. But it is not necessary to our adequate understanding of the Book to admit either conjecture, while to adapt the Book to such conjectures is fatal to all secure enjoy-
10 ment of it. We make it something fantastic, and it loses power over us.

Until we come to the thirty-sixth chapter, at any rate, there is no difficulty in receiving the arrangement of the original Isaiah's prophecies mainly as it now stands. It is evident that
15 they were uttered at different times. But we shall read them most naturally and with most satisfaction if we conceive them to have been collected in their present arrangement by Isaiah himself in his old age, and at the moment when his influence was highest, shortly after the discomfiture of Sennacherib.
20 The Book falls into several groups or divisions,—divisions quite independent, of course, of the actual distribution into chapters, which comes to us not from Jewish antiquity at all, but from the Catholic Middle Age. The first chapter, however, is one of the real divisions into which the Book falls. It
25 is a *Prelude*, an introductory piece opening the way and striking the tone for all which follows, and establishing the point of view from which Isaiah, about the year 700 B.C., wished the series of his prophecies to be read and the history of the preceding half century to be regarded. Then comes a division
30 to which we may give for title one of the headings here employed by our Bibles: *Calamities coming upon Judah.* This prophecy (occupying chapters ii–v in our Bibles) belongs to the time of Jotham and of Isaiah's early career, when Jewish society was to outward view still prosperous. What follows
35 next, the *Vision*, is exactly the sixth chapter in our version, as the *Prelude* is exactly the first. The *Vision* dates from a yet earlier time than the prophecy in Jotham's reign, and marks the outset of Isaiah's public career, his call to deal with the state

of things declared in the prophecy preceding. After the *Vision* comes a group of prophecies to which we may most fitly give the great name of *Immanuel*. Occupying chapters vii–xii in our Bibles, they date from the reign of Ahaz and from the invasion of Judah by the kings of Syria and Israel; they set forth Isaiah's view of this crisis, and of the future to follow it. After *Immanuel* comes a division of prophecies best designated by Isaiah's own term, the *Burdens;*—a series of oracular sentences of doom upon the nations engaged in making the history which the prophet had before his eyes. Here, as has been already said, the *Burden of Babylon* was in Ezra's time inserted. The original *Burdens* of our Isaiah begin with the twenty-fourth verse of the fourteenth chapter, and with a sentence of doom upon Assyria. They extend through the nine chapters which in our Bibles follow, but an insertion has to be disengaged from them: the *Burden of the Desert of the Sea*, or first vision of the fall of Babylon, in chapter xxi.[1] Between the *Burdens* and the succeeding division of prophecies, the *Woes*, comes an insertion [2] conceived in the spirit of these divisions, but with far greater generality, and pointing, so far as amidst this generality we can at all make out clearly the times and events indicated, to a later era,—the era of Cyrus. The *Woes* (this title again, like that of the *Burdens*, is supplied by a dominating phrase of Isaiah's own using)—the *Woes*, of which the purport is sufficiently explained by the name, extend from the beginning of our twenty-eighth chapter to the end of our thirty-third. They are followed by another insertion,[3] of like character with the insertion which introduces them, and which should, like that, be separated from them. This insertion occupies two chapters, the thirty-fourth and thirty-fifth.

For the division which follows, the natural title is *Sennacherib*, since that personage is the main subject of it. This division contains one of Isaiah's noblest prophecies, which, together with the history accompanying it, is repeated in the Book of Kings with but slight variation. I have already noticed

---

[1] Verses 1–10. [2] Named by me *Early Days of Return*.
[3] Named by me *Edom and Israel*.

the demonstrable error of date which occurs at the outset. Undoubtedly Isaiah never assigned Sennacherib's invasion of Judah to the fourteenth year of king Hezekiah. We have seen how this error was probably caused, and that it shows later arrangers to have been busy with this part of the book. Shall we, with Ewald and others, retain of this division only Isaiah's famous prophecy in answer to the threatenings of Sennacherib, and put aside the rest altogether? We know, indeed, from the Book of Chronicles that Isaiah wrote history, and the historical style of the division in question is worthy of him. On the other hand, it is difficult to conceive so great a master of effect concluding such a whole as that which he had formed out of the combined series of prophecies hitherto enumerated, with a mixed division such as *Sennacherib*. It is difficult; and moreover, in order to admit it, we must further suppose that Isaiah finally arranged his Book of prophecies, not about 700 B.C., when he was seventy years old, but after the death of Sennacherib in 680 B.C., when Isaiah was ninety. For the murder of Sennacherib by his sons is mentioned in the thirty-seventh chapter. To suppose all this is to suppose things by no means likely; and their improbability, joined to the error in date at the outset, may well make us regard with suspicion Isaiah's authorship of this division as a whole. Still it is not absolutely impossible that this part too should be his; that at ninety years of age he should have arranged his prophecies with this *Sennacherib* to conclude them, and that the error of date at the beginning, together with a transposition of the matters recorded, should afterwards have crept in. There *Sennacherib* now stands in the Book of Isaiah, and it is not absolutely impossible that Isaiah should have himself put it there. At any rate we have no more fitting place to which we may move it. It belongs to his time, it deals with the men and events of his age and not with those of the age of Babylon's fall. It is best to accept it provisionally where it stands, and to let it conclude the Book of the original Isaiah. With the fortieth chapter we pass to another age and world from his, and to prophecies which will not be attributed to him by any one who has been enabled to understand rightly the original Isaiah and his line of prophecy.

Thus, then, I have attempted to answer as clearly and fairly as I could my own question: How may we best enjoy Isaiah? Let me end by summing up the results reached.   5
First, we must respect, not in profession only, but in deed and in truth, the wording and rhythm of the old version. Such change as the change of, "Therefore saith the Lord, the Lord of hosts, the mighty One of Israel," [1] into "Therefore this is the utterance of the Lord, Jehovah of Hosts, the Hero of   10
Israel," is not to be thought of. In passages of this kind, indeed, the old version needs no change at all. Often it needs change, but no great change. "Before the child shall know to refuse the evil and choose the good, the land that thou abhorrest shall be forsaken of both her kings." [2] This is intelligible, but it departs   15
too far from the original. It deserves, however, no such total subversion as that which Mr. Cheyne inflicts: "Before the boy shall know how to reject the evil and choose the good, deserted shall the land become, at the two kings whereof thou art horribly afraid." Sometimes the old version is not even in-   20
telligible. "Go, ye swift messengers, to a nation scattered and peeled, to a people terrible from their beginning hitherto; a nation meted out and trodden down, whose land the rivers have spoiled." [3] Or again, in a more celebrated passage: "Never-theless the dimness shall not be such as was in her vexation,   25
when at the first he lightly afflicted the land of Zebulun and the land of Naphtali, and afterward did more grievously afflict her by the way of the sea, beyond Jordan, in Galilee of the nations." [4] Passages like these miss at present the right sense of the original entirely, and they must be reconstructed so far as   30
to enable them to give it. But even this reconstruction may be effected without loss of the present fine rhythm and fine diction of these passages, and must be so effected, if Isaiah is to be enjoyed.
Secondly, we must know the historical situation which   35

[1] Isaiah, i, 24.   [2] *Ibid.*, vii, 16.   [3] *Ibid.*, xviii, 2.   [4] *Ibid.*, ix, 1.

Isaiah had before him to deal with, and we must keep it
present to our minds. By so doing we shall much increase our
enjoyment of this greatest of the prophets.

    And our sense of that situation, and of Isaiah's own power-
5 ful and characteristic line of prophecy, will be greatly enhanced if, thirdly, we separate from the Book of Isaiah one
large work now appended to it, and several short works now
mixed up with it; and if we then, disregarding the division into
chapters, read what remains as one combined whole, made up
10 of seven successive pieces, as follows: *Prelude, Calamities
for Judah, Vision, Immanuel, The Burdens, The Woes, Sennacherib.*

    To publish their Isaiah with this arrangement is not possible
for the company of revisers, however successful may be their
15 translation of him. And therefore I have thought that the present volume might be useful. It may be objected that to correct
the translation of Isaiah a skilled Hebraist is required, and
that I am not a skilled Hebraist. Certainly I am not. But the
meaning of Isaiah has so long been the object of the most
20 minute and attentive investigation by skilled Hebraists, that
what is required for a work like the present is not so much
that its author should himself be a great Hebraist capable of
making fresh discoveries of his own; it is rather that he should
be Hebraist enough, and at the same time critic enough, to fol-
25 low intelligently the researches of great Hebraists, and to
judge and choose among the results reached by them. This,
to the best of my power, I have done. I have also sought to
exhibit Isaiah in that arrangement which seems desirable, and
with the historical elucidations which I consider indispensable.
30 The reader will find that the interpretation finally adopted for
any passage is, if necessary, explained, but is not compared
with other rival interpretations,—is not discussed or defended.
The reason is, that my paramount object here is to get Isaiah
enjoyed; and the right way to get a great author enjoyed is to
35 raise not as much discussion as possible over his meaning, but
as little as possible.

Address to the Wordsworth Society
May 2nd, 1883

At your last year's meeting you did me the honour, although I was not a member of your Society, to elect me your President for this year. I had declined to join the Wordsworth Society for the same reason that I decline to join other societies—not from any disrespect to their objects or to their promoters, but because, being very busy and growing old, I endeavour to avoid fresh engagements and distractions, and to keep what little leisure I can for reflexion and amendment before the inevitable close. When your election of me came, however, I felt that it would be ungracious to decline it; and, as generally happens, having decided to accept it and to join you, I soon began to find out a number of excellent reasons for doing what I had resolved to do. In former days, you know, people who had in near view that inevitable close of which I just now spoke, people who had had their fill of life's business and were tired of its labour and contention, used to enter a monastery. In my opinion they did a very sensible thing. I said to myself: Times and circumstances have changed, you cannot well enter a monastery; but you can enter the Wordsworth Society. The two things are not so very different. A monastery is under the rules of poverty, chastity, and obedience. Well, and he who comes under the discipline of Wordsworth comes under those same rules. Wordsworth constantly both preached and practised them. He was "frugal and severe;" he ever calls us to "plain living and high thinking." There you have the rule of poverty. His chosen hero and exemplar, the Pedlar of *The Excursion*, was formed and fashioned by the Scottish Church having held upon him in his youth, with a power which endured all his life long, "the strong hand of her purity." There you have the rule of chastity. Finally, in an immortal ode, Wordsworth tells us how he made it his heart's desire and prayer to live the "bondman of duty in the light of truth." There you have the rule of obedience. We live in a world which sometimes, in our morose moments, if we have any, may almost seem to us, perhaps, to have set itself to be as little poor as possible, and as little chaste as possible, and as little obedient as possible. Whoever is oppressed with thoughts of this kind, let him seek refuge in the Wordsworth Society.

As your President, it is my duty not to occupy too much of your time myself, but to announce the papers which are to be read to you, and to introduce their readers. It was hoped that a paper would have been read by Lord Coleridge. There was an additional reason for joining your Society! But the paper has had to be put off, alas, till next year. There is a reason for continuing to belong to you! Mr. Stopford Brooke—whose published remarks on Wordsworth, as on other great English writers, we all know, and excellent they are—Mr. Stopford Brooke, I am glad to say, will read us a paper. Mr. Aubrey de Vere—who has given us more interesting and trustworthy reports of Wordsworth in his old age than any one except Miss Fenwick—Mr. Aubrey de Vere has prepared a paper, which will be read by our Secretary—if he is not more properly to be called the author of our being—Professor Knight. If Professor Knight's work in founding us (I may say in passing) had even had no other result than the production of those photographs of Wordsworth which appear in the Society's Transactions of last year, that result alone would have been a sufficient justification of his work. Other matters, besides the papers which I have mentioned, will come before you, and I must leave way for them. But suffer me, before I sit down, to say seriously and sincerely what pleasure I find in the testimony afforded by the prosperity of your Society, and by the numbers present here to-day, to the influence of Wordsworth. His imperfections, the mixture of prose with his poetry, I am probably more disposed than some members of this Society to admit freely. But I doubt whether any one admires Wordsworth more than I do. I admire him, first of all, for the very simple and solid reason that he is such an exceedingly great poet. One puts him after Shakespeare and Milton. Shakespeare is out of comparison. Milton was, of 5 course, a far greater artist than Wordsworth; probably, also, a greater force. But the spiritual passion of Wordsworth, his spiritual passion when, as in the magnificent sonnet of farewell to the River Duddon, for instance, he is at his highest, and "sees into the life of things," cannot be matched from Milton. I 10 will not say it is beyond Milton, but he has never shown it. To match it, one must go to the ocean of Shakespeare. A second invaluable merit which I find in Wordsworth is this: he has something to say. Perhaps one prizes this merit the more as one grows old, and has less time left for trifling. 15 Goethe got so sick of the fuss about form and technical details, without due care for adequate contents, that he said if he were younger he should take pleasure in setting the so-called art of the new school of poets at nought, and in trusting for his whole effect to his having something important to say.[1] 20 Dealing with no wide, varied, and brilliant world, dealing with the common world close to him, and using few materials, Wordsworth, like his great contemporary the Italian poet Leopardi, who also deals with a bounded world and uses few materials—Wordsworth, like Leopardi, is yet so profoundly 25 impressive, because he has really something to say. And the mention of Leopardi, that saddest of poets, brings me, finally, to what is perhaps Wordsworth's most distinctive virtue of all —his power of happiness and hope, his "deep power of joy." What a sadness is in those brilliant poets of Italy—what a 30

[1] See Eckermann, *Gespräche mit Goethe,* ii. 260-2:—"Es ist immer ein Zeichen einer unproductiven Zeit, wenn sie so ins Kleinliche des Technischen geht, und eben so ist es ein Zeichen eines unproductiven Individuums, wenn es sich mit dergleichen befasst. . . . Wäre ich noch jung und verwegen genug, so würde ich absichtlich gegen alle solche 35 technische Grillen verstossen . . . aber ich würde auf die Hauptsache losgehen, und so gute Dinge zu sagen suchen, dass jeder gereizt werden sollte, es zu lesen und auswendig zu lernen."

sadness in even the sweetest of them all, the one whom Wordsworth specially loved, the pious and tender Virgil!

> Optima quæque dies miseris mortalibus ævi
> Prima fugit—

5   "the best days of life for us poor mortals flee first away;"
subeunt morbi, "then come diseases, and old age, and labour,
and sorrow; and the severity of unrelenting death hurries us
away." *Et duræ rapit inclementia mortis.*[1] From the ineffable,
the dissolving melancholy of those lovely lines, let us turn our
10   thoughts to the great poet in whose name we are met together
to-day; to our Westmoreland singer of "the sublime attractions of the grave," and to the treasure of happiness and of
hope—

> [Of] hope, the paramount *duty* which Heaven lays,
15 > For its own honour, on man's suffering heart—

which is in him. We are drawn to him because we feel these
things; and we believe that the number of those who feel
them will continue to increase more and more, long after we
are gone.

---

20   [1] Optima quæque dies miseris mortalibus ævi
       Prima fugit; subeunt morbi, tristisque senectus
       Et labor; et duræ rapit inclementia mortis.
                        VIRGIL, *Georgics*, iii. 66–8.

An Old Playgoer on "Impulse"

Like "society" in general, I have been to see "Impulse."
Nothing, apparently, could be more to the taste of "society"
than this piece. That alone is a reason for going to see it. And
what impression did it leave, what remained in the mind after
seeing it? Chiefly, to tell the truth, this sentence of the "Imi-   5
tation:" *Multa oportet surdâ aure pertransire, et quæ tuæ
pacis sunt magis cogitare.* A piece more perfectly unprofitable
it is hard to imagine. But it is worth pausing upon, because its
production and its popularity bring well to light the want of
clear vision, the turn for the half-true and for the factitious,   10
characteristic of English "society."

"Impulse" is founded, as its author, Mr. Stephenson, honestly
informs us, upon a French piece. French pieces have their
reason for existing in the state of society which they reflect
and interpret. All people want to know *life*, above all the life   15
which surrounds them and concerns them; and we come to
the novel and to the stage-play to help us to what we want.
French plays and French novels do undoubtedly render for
French people the life which surrounds them. Those productions have this merit, at any rate. George Sand declares that   20
"Madame Bovary" is not at all an immoral work, but, on the
contrary, a useful one. Good and useful, after reading "Madame Bovary" in the family circle, Madame Sand and her
family circle, so she tells us, judged this reading to be. But
why? Because of the numberless Madame Bovarys, "les in-   25
nombrables madame Bovary en herbe," at the present moment springing up everywhere throughout the provincial life
of France, with their immense crop of "maris imbéciles" and
of "amants frivoles" to attend them. That, says George Sand,

is M. Flaubert's defence for writing his book, and that is the
reason for reading it—that it holds the mirror up to French
nature. Of course the same plea may even more confidently be
urged for plays and novels rendering the life of Paris. They
5   may be full of immoralities, but at any rate they hold the
mirror up to nature, they do render the life of Paris.

I am far from saying that I agree with Madame Sand that a
book is good reading, even for grown men and women, because
it faithfully represents actual life. It must have a quality in it
10   besides to make it so. "Manon Lescaut," which has this quality,
is good reading; I would not say that "Madame Bovary" has
the quality, or that it is good reading. All this, however, we
need not discuss now. What is certain is that the French play,
the French novel, render the actual life of the French. One
15   may rate the work of M. Alexandre Dumas the younger, or of
M. Sardou, as low as one pleases. One may even refuse to call
it literature. Of course it is not literature as the comedy of
Shakspeare and of Molière is literature; it is not even literature
as the comedy of Beaumarchais and of Sheridan is literature;
20   perhaps it is not to be called literature at all. But that it renders
French life one cannot deny, and that the French public,
wishing to see its life rendered, should follow with eagerness
and pleasure this rendering, one cannot wonder.

But "Impulse"—what life does it render? What does it say
25   to all these wearers of attractive toilettes, to all these charming
faces and figures, to all this "society" a little wanting in soul
and very much wanting in clear vision, which frequent it?
Something half-true, factitious, and unmeaning. The English
provinces really do not teem with "des innombrables madame
30   Bovary en herbe:" the most salient features of English society
are really not the "mari imbécile" and the "amant frivole."
The "society" newspapers and their emancipated and brilliant
staff may regret that the fact should be so, but so it is.
Madame Bovarys, instead of being countless in our country
35   neighbourhoods, are almost unknown there; the "amant frivole," instead of being a stock element in our married life, is
rare and unimportant. That fraction of our society for which
the French play and novel are a rendering of its own life is so

small as to be quite unimportant. This is proved, indeed, by the transformation which the French play undergoes before the English playwright can present it to the charming faces, figures and toilettes of our boxes and stalls. Virtue has to triumph; the "amant frivole" has to come to grief. Ingenious playwright! ingenuous "society"! Know this, as to your "amant," as to your Victor de Riel: that, as your French guides would tell you, "c'est à prendre ou à laisser." Where he exists, where he is an institution, matters may well enough pass as they pass in the genuine French play; logic and experience are in favour of their so passing. Where he is an exotic, nothing can make him tolerable; defeated or triumphant, he equally makes the piece, of which he is the centre, unpleasant, makes it ridiculous.

"Impulse" is, in truth, in itself a piece intensely disagreeable. It owes its success to the singularly attractive, sympathetic, and popular personalities of Mr. and Mrs. Kendal. While they are on the stage it is hard to be dissatisfied. One must feel, nevertheless, even while liking Mr. Kendal, that the young English gentleman, whom one so well knows, with sterling qualities but no philosopher, does not talk quite so like a fool as Captain Crichton. Mrs. Kendal, as Mrs. Beresford, one could accept with entire pleasure if one could understand so winning and sensible a person having so little influence with her sister, or being so easily baffled by circumstances. Perhaps a sympathetic actress might have made the ungrateful part of Mrs. Macdonald not quite repulsive, not quite impossible. At present Mrs. Macdonald makes the impression, not of an interesting victim of passion, but of a personage morbid and perverse; and every scene between her and Victor de Riel is a misery. Victor de Riel is not ill acted; on the contrary, this exotic "amant" is well acted—too well. The fatal likeness to the "similis turpissima bestia nobis," which so struck Alfieri in the passion-driven Frenchman, forces itself upon the mind; and the more passionate the love-making, the more that likeness forces itself on us. Why should cool-headed people hide their conviction that this sort of drama is detestable, even though the journals of "society" call to one another, deep to deep, "Edmund" to "Henry," that it is very good? One can imagine the grim

5

10

15

20

25

30

35

colleague of "Henry" surveying the "society" which enjoys this half-true, factitious, and debilitating art, and waving "Henry" aside while he himself cries sternly to their common constituents, the Northampton populace, "Arise, ye Goths, and
5   glut your ire!"

AN OLD PLAYGOER

An Old Playgoer at the Lyceum

History tells us that the Sultanas of the famous Sultan Ouloug-beb would not hear the philosophical romance of "Zadig," but preferred to it an interminable succession of idle tales. "How can you prefer," asked the sage Sultan, "a heap of stories utterly irrational, and which have nothing in them?" The Sultanas answered: "It is just on that very account that we prefer them" ("c'est précisément pour cela que nous les aimons").

By what magic does Mr. Irving induce the Sultanas to listen to Shakspeare? From the utterances of Captain Crichton, Mrs. Beresford, and Mrs. Macdonald, how does he manage to wile them away to the talk of Benedick and Beatrice—of Benedick, capable of looking pale "with anger, with sickness, or with hunger, not with love;" of Beatrice, "upon my knees every morning and evening that God may send me no husband"? The truth is, in a community so large as ours you may hope to get a demand for almost anything—not only for "Impulse" at the St. James's, or for the "Biography" of Mr. Archer and the "Early Days" of Mr. Marwood among visitors to Epsom, but even for the fantastic—Mr. Labouchere would add, the tiresome—comedy of Shakspeare at the Lyceum.

Fantastic, at all events, it is. It belongs to a world of fantasy; not to our world, palpitating with actuality, of Captain Crichtons, and Fred. Archers, and Marwoods. It so belongs to a world of fantasy that often we have difficulty in following it. "He set up his bills here in Messina, and challenged Cupid at the flight; and my uncle's fool, reading the challenge, subscribed for Cupid, and challenged him at the bird-bolt." Who understands without a commentary? Even where the wit is more evident and we can follow it, it is still the wit of another

139

world from ours, a world of fantasy. "He that hath a beard is
more than a youth; and he that hath no beard is less than a
man: and he that is more than a youth is not for me; and he
that is less than a man, I am not for him; therefore I will even
5 take sixpence in earnest of the bearward, and lead his apes into
hell."

But Mr. Labouchere deals hardly with himself in refusing to
enter this Shakspearian world because it is a world of fantasy.
Art refreshes us, art liberates us, precisely by carrying us into
10 such a world, and enabling us to find pleasure there. He who
will not be carried there loses a great deal. For his own sake
Mr. Labouchere should "away to St. Peter for the heavens"
with Beatrice; should let it be revealed to him "where the bach-
elors sit, and there live we as merry as the day is long." With
15 his care for seating his colleague and for reconstructing society, can he live as merry as the day is long now?

So salutary is it to be carried into a world of fantasy that I
doubt whether even the comedy of Congreve and Wycherley,
presented to us at the present day by good artists, would do us
20 harm. I would not take the responsibility of recommending its
revival, but I doubt its doing harm, and I feel sure of its doing
less harm than pieces such as "Heartsease" and "Impulse." And
the reason is that Wycherley's comedy places us in what is
for us now a world wholly of fantasy, and that in such a
25 world, with a good critic and with good actors, we are not
likely to come to much harm. Such a world's main appeal is
to our imagination; it calls into play our imagination rather
than our senses. How much more is this true of the ideal comedy of Shakspeare, and of a world so airy, radiant, and spiritual
30 as that of "Much Ado about Nothing"!

One must rejoice, therefore, at seeing the Sultanas and society listening to Shakspeare's comedy; it is good for them to
be there. But how does Mr. Irving bring them? Their natural
inclination is certainly more for a constant "succession of idle
35 tales" like the "Dame aux Camélias" or "Impulse." True; but
there is at the same time something in human nature which
works for Shakspeare's comedy, and against such comedy as
the "Dame aux Camélias" or "Impulse;" something prompting us

to live by our soul and imagination rather than by our senses. Undoubtedly there is; the existence of this something is the ground of all hope, and must never, in our impatience at men's perversions, be forgotten. But to come into play it needs evocation and encouragement; how does Mr. Irving evoke it? 5

It is not enough to say that "Much Ado about Nothing," in itself beautiful, is beautifully put upon the stage, and that of ideal comedy this greatly heightens the charm. It is true, but more than this is requisite to bring the Sultanas. It is not enough to say that the piece is acted with an evenness, a general level 10 of merit, which was not to be found five-and-twenty years ago, when a Claudio so good as Mr. Forbes Robertson, or a Don Pedro so good as Mr. Terriss, would have been almost impossible. This also is true, but it would not suffice to bring the Sultanas. It cannot even be said that they are brought because certain leading or famous characters in the piece are given with a 15 perfection hitherto unknown. The aged eyes of an "Old Playgoer" have seen the elder Farren and Keeley in the parts of Dogberry and Verges. Good as is Mr. Irving's Benedick, those who have seen Charles Kemble as Benedick have seen a yet 20 better Benedick than Mr. Irving. It is, however, almost always by an important personality that great things are effected; and it is assuredly the personality of Mr. Irving and that of Miss Ellen Terry which have the happy effect of bringing the Sultanas and of filling the Lyceum. 25

Both Mr. Irving and Miss Ellen Terry have a personality which peculiarly fits them for ideal comedy. Miss Terry is sometimes restless and over-excited, but she has a spiritual vivacity which is charming. Mr. Irving has faults which have often been pointed out, but he has, as an actor, a merit which 30 redeems them all, and which is the secret of his success: the merit of delicacy and distinction. In some of his parts he shows himself capable, also, of intense and powerful passion. But twenty other actors are to be found who have a passion as intense and powerful as his, for one other actor who has his 35 merit of delicacy and distinction. Mankind are often unjust to this merit, and most of us much resist having to exhibit it in our own life and soul; but it is singular what a charm it exercises

over us. Mr. Irving is too intelligent, and has too many of an actor's qualities, to fail entirely in any part which he assumes; still there are some parts for which he appears not well fitted, and others for which he appears fitted perfectly. His true parts
5 are those which most display his rare gift of delicacy and distinction; and such parts are offered, above all, in ideal comedy. May he long continue to find them there, and to put forth in them charm enough to win the Sultanas to art like "Much Ado about Nothing," as a change from art like "Fédora" and "Im-
10 pulse"!

                                        AN OLD PLAYGOER

Numbers;
or
The Majority and the Remnant

There is a characteristic saying of Dr. Johnson: "Patriotism is the last refuge of a scoundrel." The saying is cynical, many will even call it brutal; yet it has in it something of plain, robust sense and truth. We do often see men passing themselves off as patriots, who are in truth scoundrels; we meet with talk and proceedings laying claim to patriotism, which are these gentlemen's last refuge. We may all of us agree in praying to be delivered from patriots and patriotism of this sort. Short of such, there is undoubtedly, sheltering itself under the fine name of patriotism, a good deal of self-flattery and self-delusion which is mischievous. "Things are what they are, and the consequences of them will be what they will be; why, then, should we desire to be deceived?" In that uncompromising sentence of Bishop Butler's is surely the right and salutary maxim for both individuals and nations.

Yet there is an honourable patriotism which we should satisfy if we can, and should seek to have on our side. At home I have said so much of the characters of our society and the prospects of our civilisation, that I can hardly escape the like topic elsewhere. Speaking in America, I cannot well avoid saying something about the prospects of society in the United States. It is a topic where one is apt to touch people's patriotic feelings. No one will accuse me of having flattered the patriotism of that great country of English people on the other side of the Atlantic, amongst whom I was born. Here, so many miles from home, I begin to reflect with tender contrition, that perhaps I have not,—I will not say flattered the patriotism of my own countrymen enough, but regarded it enough. Perhaps that is one reason why I have produced so very little effect upon them. It was a fault of youth and inexperience. But it would be unpardonable to come in advanced life and repeat the same error here. You will not expect impossibilities of me. You will not expect me to say that things are not what, in my judgment, they are, and that the consequences of them will not be what they will be. I should make nothing of it; I should be a too palpable failure. But I confess that I should be glad if in what I say here I could engage American patriotism on my side, instead of rousing it against me. And it so happens that the paramount thoughts which your great country raises in my mind are really and truly of a kind to please, I think, any true American patriot, rather than to offend him.

The vast scale of things here, the extent of your country, your numbers, the rapidity of your increase, strike the imagination, and are a common topic for admiring remark. Our great orator, Mr. Bright, is never weary of telling us how many acres of land you have at your disposal, how many bushels of grain you produce, how many millions you are, how many more millions you will be presently, and what a capital thing this is for you. Now, though I do not always agree with Mr. Bright, I find myself agreeing with him here. I think your numbers afford a very real and important ground for satisfaction.

Not that your great numbers, or indeed great numbers of men anywhere, are likely to be all good, or even to have the majority good. "The majority are bad," said one of the wise men of Greece; but he was a pagan. Much to the same effect, however, is the famous sentence of the New Testament: "Many are called, few chosen." This appears a hard saying; frequent are the endeavours to elude it, to attenuate its severity. But turn it how you will, manipulate it as you will, the few, as Cardinal Newman well says, can never mean the many. Perhaps you will say that the majority *is*, sometimes, good; that its impulses are good generally, and its action is good occasionally. Yes, but it lacks principle, it lacks persistence; if to-day its good impulses prevail, they succumb to-morrow; sometimes it goes right, but it is very apt to go wrong. Even a popular orator, or a popular journalist, will hardly say that the multitude may be trusted to have its judgment generally just, and its action generally virtuous. It may be better, it is better, that the body of the people, with all its faults, should act for itself, and control its own affairs, than that it should be set aside as ignorant and incapable, and have its affairs managed for it by a so-called superior class, possessing property and intelligence. Property and intelligence cannot be trusted to show a sound majority themselves; the exercise of power by the people tends to educate the people. But still, the world being what it is, we must surely expect the aims and doings of the majority of men to be at present very faulty, and this in a numerous community no less than in a small one. So much we must certainly, I think, concede to the sages and to the saints.

Sages and saints are apt to be severe, it is true; apt to take a gloomy view of the society in which they live, and to prognosticate evil to it. But then it must be added that their prognostications are very apt to turn out right. Plato's account of the most gifted and brilliant community of the ancient world, of that Athens of his to which we all owe so much, is despondent enough. "There is but a very small remnant," he says, "of honest followers of wisdom, and they who are of these few, and who have tasted how sweet and blessed a possession is wisdom, and who can fully see, moreover, the madness of the multitude, and that there is no one, we may say, whose action in public matters is sound, and no ally for whosoever would help the just, what," asks Plato, "are they to do? They may be compared," says Plato, "to a man who has fallen among wild beasts; he will not be one of them, but he is too unaided to make head against them; and before he can do any good to society or his friends, he will be overwhelmed and perish uselessly. When he considers this, he will resolve to keep still, and to mind his own business; as it were standing aside under a wall in a storm of dust and hurricane of driving wind; and he will endure to behold the rest filled with iniquity, if only he himself may live his life clear of injustice and of impiety, and

depart, when his time comes, in mild and gracious mood, with
fair hope."

Plato's picture here of democratic Athens is certainly
gloomy enough. We may be sure the mass of his contempo-
5 raries would have pronounced it to be monstrously over-
charged. We ourselves, if we had been living then, should most
of us have by no means seen things as Plato saw them. No, if
we had seen Athens even nearer its end than when Plato wrote
the strong words which I have been quoting, Athens in the
10 very last days of Plato's life, we should most of us probably
have considered that things were not going badly with Athens.
There is a long sixteen years' administration,—the administration of Eubulus,—which fills the last years of Plato's life, and
the middle years of the fourth century before Christ. A tem-
15 perate German historian thus describes Athens during this
ministry of Eubulus: "The grandeur and loftiness of Attic
democracy had vanished, while all the pernicious germs contained in it were fully developed. A life of comfort and a
craving for amusement were encouraged in every way, and
20 the interest of the citizens was withdrawn from serious things.
Conversation became more and more superficial and frivolous.
Famous courtesans formed the chief topic of talk; the new in-
ventions of Thearion, the leading pastry-cook in Athens, were
hailed with loud applause; and the witty sayings which had
25 been uttered in gay circles were repeated about town as matters of prime importance."

No doubt, if we had been living then to witness this, we
should from time to time have shaken our heads gravely, and
said how sad it all was. But most of us would not, I think,
30 have been very seriously disquieted by it. On the other hand,
we should have found many things in the Athens of Eubulus
to gratify us. "The democrats," says the same historian whom
I have just quoted, "saw in Eubulus one of their own set at
the head of affairs;" and I suppose no good democrat would
35 see that without pleasure. Moreover, Eubulus was of popular
character. In one respect he seems to have resembled your own
"heathen Chinee"; he had "guileless ways," says our historian,
"in which the citizens took pleasure." He was also a good

speaker, a thorough man of business; and, above all, he was very skilful in matters of finance. His administration was both popular and prosperous. We should certainly have said, most of us, if we had encountered somebody announcing his resolve to stand aside under a wall during such an administration, that he was a goose for his pains; and if he had called it "a falling among wild beasts" to have to live with his fellow-citizens who had confidence in Eubulus, their country, and themselves, we should have esteemed him very impertinent.

Yes;—and yet at the close of that administration of Eubulus came the collapse, and the end of Athens as an independent State. And it was to the fault of Athens herself that the collapse was owing. Plato was right after all; the majority were bad, and the remnant were impotent.

So fared it with that famous Athenian State, with the brilliant people of art and intellect. Now let us turn to the people of religion. We have heard Plato speaking of the very small remnant which honestly sought wisdom. *The remnant!*—it is the word of the Hebrew prophets also, and especially is it the word of the greatest of them all, Isaiah. Not used with the despondency of Plato, used with far other power informing it, and with a far other future awaiting it, filled with fire, filled with hope, filled with faith, filled with joy, this term itself, *the remnant*, is yet Isaiah's term as well as Plato's. The texts are familiar to all Christendom. "Though thy people Israel be as the sand of the sea, only a remnant of them shall return." Even this remnant, a tenth of the whole, if so it may be, shall have to come back into the purging fire, and be again cleared and further reduced there. But nevertheless, "as a terebinth tree, and as an oak, whose substance is in them, though they be cut down, so the stock of that burned tenth shall be a holy seed."

Yes, the small remnant should be a holy seed; but the great majority, as in democratic Athens, so in the kingdoms of the Hebrew nation, were unsound, and their State was doomed. This was Isaiah's point. The actual commonwealth of the "drunkards" and the "blind," as he calls them, in Israel and Judah, of the dissolute grandees and gross and foolish common people, of the great majority, must perish; its perishing was the necessary stage towards a happier future. And Isaiah was right, as Plato was right. No doubt to most of us, if we had been there to see it, the kingdom of Ephraim or of Judah, the society of Samaria and Jerusalem, would have seemed to contain a great deal else besides dissolute grandees and foolish common people. No doubt we should have thought parts of their policy serious, and some of their alliances promising. No doubt, when we read the Hebrew prophets now, with the larger and more patient temper of a different race and an augmented experience, we often feel the blame and invective to be too absolute. Nevertheless, as to his grand point, Isaiah, I say, was right. The majority in the Jewish State, whatever they might think or say, whatever their guides and flatterers might think or say, the majority were unsound, and their unsoundness must be their ruin.

Isaiah, however, does not make his remnant confine itself, like Plato's, to standing aside under a wall during this life and then departing in mild temper and good hope when the time for departure comes; Isaiah's remnant saves the State. Undoubtedly he means to represent it as doing so. Undoubtedly he imagines his Prince of the house of David who is to be born within a year's time, his royal and victorious Immanuel, he imagines him witnessing as a child the chastisement of Ephraim and the extirpation of the bad majority there; then witnessing as a youth the chastisement of Judah and the extirpation of the bad majority there also; but finally, in mature life, reigning over a State renewed, preserved, and enlarged, a greater and happier kingdom of the chosen people.

Undoubtedly Isaiah conceives his remnant in this wise; undoubtedly he imagined for it a part which, in strict truth, it did not play, and could not play. So manifest was the non-fulfilment of his prophecy, taken strictly, that ardent souls feeding upon his words had to wrest them from their natural meaning, and to say that Isaiah directly meant something which he did not directly mean. Isaiah, like Plato, with inspired insight foresaw that the world before his eyes, the world of actual life, the State and city of the unsound majority, could not stand. Unlike Plato, Isaiah announced with faith and joy a leader and a remnant certain to supersede them. But he put the leader's coming, and he put the success of the leader's and the remnant's work, far, far too soon; and his conception, in this respect, is fantastic. Plato betook himself for the bringing in of righteousness to a visionary republic in the clouds; Isaiah, —and it is the immortal glory of him and of his race to have done so,—brought it in upon earth. But Immanuel and his reign, for the eighth century before Christ, were fantastic. For the kingdom of Judah they were fantastic. Immanuel and the remnant could not come to reign under the conditions there and then offered to them; the thing was impossible.

The reason of the impossibility is quite simple. The scale of things, in petty States like Judah and Athens, is too small; the numbers are too scanty. Admit that for the world, as we hitherto know it, what the philosophers and prophets say is true: that the majority are unsound. Even in communities with exceptional gifts, even in the Jewish State, the Athenian State, the majority are unsound. But there is "the remnant." Now the important thing, as regards States such as Judah and Athens, is not that the remnant bears but a small proportion to the majority; the remnant always bears a small proportion to the majority. The grave thing for States like Judah and Athens is, that the remnant must in positive bulk be so small, and therefore so powerless for reform. To be a voice outside the State, speaking to mankind or to the future, perhaps shaking the actual State to pieces in doing so, one man will suffice. But to reform the State in order to save it, to preserve it by changing it, a body of workers is needed as well as a leader;—a considerable body of workers, placed at many points, and operating in many directions. This considerable body of workers for good is what is wanting in petty States such as were Athens and Judah. It is said that the Athenian State had in all but 350,000 inhabitants. It is calculated that the population of the kingdom of Judah did not exceed a million and a quarter. The scale of things, I say, is here too small, the numbers are too scanty, to give us a remnant capable of saving and perpetuating the community. The remnant, in these cases, may influence the world and the future, may transcend the State and survive it; but it cannot possibly transform the State and perpetuate the State: for such a work it is numerically too feeble. Plato saw the impossibility. Isaiah refused to accept it, but facts were too strong for him. The Jewish State could not be renewed and saved, and he was wrong in thinking that it could. And therefore I call his grand point this other, where he was altogether right: that the actual world of the unsound majority, though it fancied itself solid, and though most men might call it solid, could not stand. Let us read him again and again, until we fix in our minds this true conviction of his, to edify us whenever we see such a world existing: his indestructible conviction that such a world, with its prosperities, idolatries, oppression, luxury, pleasures, drunkards, careless women, governing classes, systems of policy, strong alliances, shall come to nought and pass away; that nothing can save it. Let us do homage, also, to his indestructible conviction that States are saved by their righteous remnant, however clearly we may at the same time recognise that his own building on this conviction was premature.

That, however, matters to us little. For how different is the scale of things in the modern States to which we belong, how far greater are the numbers! It is impossible to overrate the importance of the new element introduced into our calculations by increasing the size of the remnant. And in our great modern States, where the scale of things is so large, it does seem as if the remnant might be so increased as to become an actual power, even though the majority be unsound. Then the lover of wisdom may come out from under his wall, the lover of goodness will not be alone among the wild beasts. To enable the remnant to succeed, a large strengthening of its numbers is everything.

Here is good hope for us, not only, as for Plato's recluse, in departing this life, but while we live and work in it. Only, before we dwell too much on this hope, it is advisable to make sure that we have earned the right to entertain it. We have earned the right to entertain it, only when we are at one with the philosophers and prophets in their conviction respecting the world which now is, the world of the unsound majority; when we feel what they mean, and when we go thoroughly along with them in it. Most of us, as I have said already, would by no means have been with them when they were here in life, and most of us are not really with them now. What is saving? Our institutions, says an American; the British Constitution, says an Englishman; the civilising mission of France, says a Frenchman. But Plato and the sages, when they are asked what is saving, answer: "To love righteousness, and to be convinced of the unprofitableness of iniquity." And Isaiah and the prophets, when they are asked the same question, answer to just the same effect: that what is saving is to "order one's conversation right"; to "cease to do evil"; to "delight in the law of the Eternal"; and to "make one's study in it all day long."

The worst of it is, that this loving of righteousness and this delighting in the law of the Eternal sound rather vague to us. Not that they are vague really; indeed, they are less vague than American institutions, or the British Constitution, or the civilising mission of France. But the phrases sound vague because of the quantity of matters they cover. The thing is to have a brief but adequate enumeration of these matters. The New Testament tells us how righteousness is composed. In England and America we have been brought up in familiarity with the New Testament. And so, before Mr. Bradlaugh on our side of the water, and the Congress of American Freethinkers on yours, banish it from our education and memory, let us take from the New Testament a text showing what it is that both Plato and the prophets mean when they tell us that we ought to love righteousness and to make our study in the law of the Eternal, but that the unsound majority do nothing of the kind. A score of texts offer themselves in a moment. Here is one which will serve very well: "Whatsoever things are true, whatsoever things are elevated, whatsoever things are just, whatsoever things are pure, whatsoever things are amiable, whatsoever things are of good report; if there be any virtue, and if there be any praise; have these in your mind, let your thoughts run upon these." [1] That is what both Plato and the prophets mean by loving righteousness, and making one's study in the law of the Eternal.

5   Now the matters just enumerated do not come much into the heads of most of us, I suppose, when we are thinking of politics. But the philosophers and prophets maintain that these matters, and not those of which the heads of politicians are full, do really govern politics and save or destroy States. They
10   save or destroy them by a silent, inexorable fatality; while the politicians are making believe, plausibly and noisily, with their American institutions, British Constitution, and civilising mission of France. And because these matters are what do really govern politics and save or destroy States, Socrates maintained
15   that in his time he and a few philosophers, who alone kept insisting on the good of righteousness and the unprofitableness of iniquity, were the only real politicians then living.

I say, if we are to derive comfort from the doctrine of *the remnant* (and there is great comfort to be derived from it),
20   we must also hold fast to the austere but true doctrine as to what really governs politics, overrides with an inexorable fatality the combinations of the so-called politicians, and saves or destroys States. Having in mind things true, things elevated, things just, things pure, things amiable, things of good report;
25   having these in mind, studying and loving these, is what saves States.

There is nothing like positive instances to illustrate general propositions of this kind, and to make them believed. I hesitate to take an instance from America. Possibly there are some peo-
30   ple who think that already, on a former occasion, I have said enough about America without duly seeing and knowing it. So I will take my instances from England, and from England's neighbour and old co-mate in history, France. The instance from England I will take first. I will take it from the grave
35   topic of England's relations with Ireland. I am not going to reproach either England or Ireland. To reproach Ireland here would probably be indiscreet. As to England, anything I may

[1] *Philippians*, iv. 8.

have to say against my own countrymen I prefer to say at home; America is the last place where I should care to say it. However, I have no wish or intention now to reproach either the English or the Irish. But I want to show you from England's relations with Ireland how right the philosophers and 5 prophets are. Every one knows that there has been conquest and confiscation in Ireland. So there has elsewhere. Every one knows that the conquest and the confiscation have been attended with cupidity, oppression, and ill-usage. So they have elsewhere. "Whatsoever things are just" are not exactly the 10 study, so far as I know, of conquerors and confiscators anywhere; certainly they were not the study of the English conquerors of Ireland. A failure in justice is a source of danger to States. But it may be made up for and got over; it has been made up for and got over in many communities. England's 15 confiscations in Ireland are a thing of the past; the penal laws against Catholics are a thing of the past; much has been done to make up for the old failure in justice; Englishmen generally think that it has been pretty well made up for, and that Irishmen ought to think so too. And politicians invent Land Acts 20 for curing the last results of the old failure in justice, for insuring the contentment of the Irish with us, and for consolidating the Union: and are surprised and plaintive if it is not consolidated. But now see how much more serious people are the philosophers and prophets than the politicians. *Whatsoever* 25 *things are amiable!*—the failure in amiability, too, is a source of danger and insecurity to States, as well as the failure in justice. And we English are not amiable, or at any rate, what in this case comes to the same thing, do not appear so. The politicians never thought of that! Quite outside their combina- 30 tions lies this hindrance, tending to make their most elaborate combinations ineffectual. Thus the joint operation of two moral causes together,—the sort of causes which politicians do not seriously regard,—tells against the designs of the politicians with what seems to be an almost inexorable fatality. If there 35 were not the failure in amiability, perhaps the original failure in justice might by this time have been got over; if there had not been the failure in justice, perhaps the failure in amiability

might not have mattered much. The two failures together
create a difficulty almost insurmountable. Public men in England keep saying that it will be got over. I hope that it will
be got over, and that the union between England and Ireland
5   may become as solid as that between England and Scotland.
But it will not become solid by means of the contrivances of
the mere politician, or without the intervention of moral
causes of concord to heal the mischief wrought by moral
causes of division. Everything, in this case, depends upon the
10 "remnant," its numbers and its powers of action.

My second instance is even more important. It is so important, and its reach is so wide, that I must go into it with some
little fulness. The instance is taken from France. To France
I have always felt myself powerfully drawn. People in England
15 often accuse me of liking France and things French far too
well. At all events I have paid special regard to them, and am
always glad to confess how much I owe to them. M. Sainte-
Beuve wrote to me in the last years of his life: "You have
passed through our life and literature by a deep inner line,
20 which confers initiation, and which you will never lose." *Vous
avez traversé notre vie et notre littérature par une ligne inté-
rieure, profonde, qui fait les initiés, et que vous ne perdrez
jamais.* I wish I could think that this friendly testimony of
that accomplished and charming man, one of my chief bene-
25 factors, were fully deserved. But I have pride and pleasure in
quoting it; and I quote it to bear me out in saying, that whatever opinion I may express about France, I have at least been
a not inattentive observer of that great country, and anything
but a hostile one.

30 The question was once asked by the town clerk of Ephesus:
"What man is there that knoweth not how that the city of the
Ephesians is a worshipper of the great goddess Diana?" Now
really, when one looks at the popular literature of the French
at this moment,—their popular novels, popular stage-plays,
35 popular newspapers,—and at the life of which this literature
of theirs is the index, one is tempted to make a goddess out of
a word of their own, and then, like the town clerk of Ephesus,
to ask: "What man is there that knoweth not how that the city

of the French is a worshipper of the great goddess Lubricity?" Or rather, as Greek is the classic and euphonious language for names of gods and goddesses, let us take her name from the Greek Testament, and call her the goddess Aselgeia. That goddess has always been a sufficient power amongst mankind, and her worship was generally supposed to need restraining rather than encouraging. But here is now a whole popular literature, nay, and art too, in France at her service! stimulations and suggestions by her and to her meet one in it at every turn. She is becoming the great recognised power there; never was anything like it. M. Renan himself seems half inclined to apologise for not having paid her more attention. "Nature cares nothing for chastity," says he; *Les frivoles ont peut-être raison;* "The gay people are perhaps in the right." Men even of this force salute her; but the allegiance now paid to her, in France, by the popular novel, the popular newspaper, the popular play, is, one may say, boundless.

I have no wish at all to preach to the French; no intention whatever, in what I now say, to upbraid or wound them. I simply lay my finger on a fact in their present condition; a fact insufficiently noticed, as it seems to me, and yet extremely potent for mischief. It is well worth while to trace the manner of its growth and action.

The French have always had a leaning to the goddess of whom we speak, and have been willing enough to let the world know of their leaning, to pride themselves on their Gaulish salt, their gallantry, and so on. But things have come to their present head gradually. Catholicism was an obstacle; the serious element in the nation was another obstacle. But now just see the course which things have taken, and how they all, one may say, have worked together for this goddess. First, there was the original Gaul, the basis of the French nation; the Gaul, gay, sociable, quick of sentiment, quick of perception; apt, however, very apt, to be presumptuous and puffed up. Then came the Roman conquest, and from this we get a new personage, the Gallo-Latin; with the Gaulish qualities for a basis, but with Latin order, reason, lucidity, added, and also Latin sensuality. Finally, we have the Frankish conquest and the

Frenchman. The Frenchman proper is the Gallo-Latin, with Frankish or Germanic qualities added and infused. No mixture could be better. The Germans have plenty of faults, but in this combination they seem not to have taken hold; the Germans seem to have given of their seriousness and honesty to the conquered Gallo-Latin, and not of their brutality. And mediæval France, which exhibits the combination and balance, under the influence then exercised by Catholicism, of Gaulish quickness and gaiety with Latin rationality and German seriousness, offers to our view the soundest and the most attractive stage, perhaps, in all French history.

But the balance could not be maintained; at any rate, it was not maintained. Mediæval Catholicism lost its virtue. The serious Germanic races made the Reformation, feeling that without it there was no safety and continuance for those moral ideas which they loved and which were the ground of their being. France did not go with the Reformation; the Germanic qualities in her were not strong enough to make her go with it. "France did not want a reformation which was a moral one," is Michelet's account of the matter: *La France ne voulait pas de réforme morale.* Let us put the case more favourably for her, and say that perhaps, with her quick perception, France caught sense, from the very outset, of that intellectual unsoundness and incompleteness in the Reformation, which is now so visible. But, at any rate, the Reformation did not carry France with it; and the Germanic side in the Frenchman, his Germanic qualities, thus received a check. They subsisted, however, in good force still; the new knowledge and new ideas, brought by the revival of letters, gave an animating stimulus; and in the seventeenth century the Gaulish gaiety and quickness of France, the Latin rationality, and the still subsisting German seriousness, all combining under the puissant breath of the Renascence, produced a literature, the strongest, the most substantial and the most serious which the French have ever succeeded in producing, and which has, indeed, consummate and splendid excellences.

Still, the Germanic side in the Frenchman had received a check, and in the next century this side became quite atten-

uated. The Germanic steadiness and seriousness gave way more and more; the Gaulish salt, the Gaulish gaiety, quickness, sentiment, and sociability, the Latin rationality, prevailed more and more, and had the field nearly to themselves. They produced a brilliant and most efficacious literature,—the French literature 5
of the eighteenth century. The goddess Aselgeia had her part in it; it was a literature to be praised with reserves; it was, above all, a revolutionary literature. But European institutions were then in such a superannuated condition, straightforward and just perception, free thought and rationality, were at such 10
a discount, that the brilliant French literature in which these qualities predominated, and which by their predominance was made revolutionary, had in the eighteenth century a great mission to fulfil, and fulfilled it victoriously.

The mission is fulfilled, but meanwhile the Germanic qual- 15
ity in the Frenchman seems pretty nearly to have died out, and the Gallo-Latin in him has quite got the upper hand. Of course there are individuals and groups who are to be excepted; I will allow any number of exceptions you please; and in the mass of the French people, which works and is 20
silent, there may be treasures of resource. But taking the Frenchman who is commonly in view,—the usual type of speaking, doing, vocal, visible Frenchman,—we may say, and he will probably be not at all displeased at our saying, that the German in him has nearly died out, and the Gallo-Latin 25
has quite got the upper hand. For us, however, this means that the chief source of seriousness and of moral ideas is failing and drying up in him, and that what remains are the sources of Gaulish salt, and quickness, and sentiment, and sociability, and sensuality, and rationality. And, of course, the play and 30
working of these qualities is altered by their being no longer in combination with a dose of German seriousness, but left to work by themselves. Left to work by themselves, they give us what we call the *homme sensuel moyen*, the average sensual man. The highest art, the art which by its height, depth, 35
and gravity possesses religiousness,—such as the Greeks had, the art of Pindar and Phidias; such as the Italians had, the art of Dante and Michael Angelo,—this art, with the training

which it gives and the standard which it sets up, the French
have never had. On the other hand, they had a dose of German
seriousness, a Germanic bent for ideas of moral duty, which
neither the Greeks had, nor the Italians. But if this dies out,
5   what is left is the *homme sensuel moyen*. This average sensual
man has his very advantageous qualities. He has his gaiety,
quickness, sentiment, sociability, rationality. He has his horror
of sour strictness, false restraint, hypocrisy, obscurantism, cre-
tinism, and the rest of it. And this is very well; but on the
10   serious, moral side he is almost ludicrously insufficient. Fine
sentiments about his dignity and his honour and his heart,
about the dignity and the honour and the heart of France, and
his adoration of her, do duty for him here; grandiose phrases
about the spectacle offered in France and in the French Re-
15   public of the ideal for our race, of the *épanouissement de l'élite
de l'humanité*, "the coming into blow of the choice flower of
humanity." In M. Victor Hugo we have (his worshippers must
forgive me for saying so) the average sensual man impassioned
and grandiloquent; in M. Zola we have the average sensual man
20   going near the ground. "Happy the son," cries M. Victor
Hugo, "of whom one can say, 'He has consoled his mother!'
Happy the poet of whom one can say, 'He has consoled his
country!'" The French themselves, even when they are sever-
est, call this kind of thing by only the mild name of emphasis,
25   "*emphase*,"—other people call it fustian. And a surly Johnson
will growl out in answer, at one time, that "Patriotism is the
last refuge of a scoundrel"; at another time, that fine sentiments about *ma mère* are the last refuge of a scoundrel. But
what they really are is the creed which in France the average
30   sensual man rehearses, to do duty for serious moral ideas. And,
as the result, we have a popular literature and a popular art
serving, as has been already said, the goddess Aselgeia.

    Such an art and literature easily make their way everywhere.
In England and America the French literature of the seven-
35   teenth century is peculiarly fitted to do great good, and nothing but good; it can hardly be too much studied by us. And
it is studied by us very little. The French literature of the
eighteenth century, also, has qualities to do us much good,

and we are not likely to take harm from its other qualities; we may study it to our great profit and advantage. And it is studied by us very little. The higher French literature of the present day has more knowledge and a wider range than its great predecessors, but less soundness and perfection, and it exerts much less influence than they did. Action and influence are now with the lower literature of France, with the popular literature in the service of the goddess Aselgeia. And this popular modern French literature, and the art which corresponds to it, bid fair to make their way in England and America far better than their predecessors. They appeal to instincts so universal and accessible; they appeal, people are beginning boldly to say, to Nature herself. Few things have lately struck me more than M. Renan's dictum, which I have already quoted, about what used to be called the virtue of chastity. The dictum occurs in his very interesting autobiography, published but the other day. M. Renan, whose genius I unfeignedly admire, is, I need hardly say, a man of the most perfect propriety of life; he has told us so himself. He was brought up for a priest, and he thinks it would not have been in good taste for him to become a free liver. But this abstinence is a mere matter of personal delicacy, a display of good and correct taste on his own part in his own very special circumstances. "Nature," he cries, "cares nothing about chastity." What a slap in the face to the sticklers for "Whatsoever things are pure"!

I have had to take a long sweep to arrive at the point which I wished to reach. If we are to enjoy the benefit, I said, of the comfortable doctrine of the remnant, we must be capable of receiving also, and of holding fast, the hard doctrine of the unsoundness of the majority, and of the certainty that the unsoundness of the majority, if it is not withstood and remedied, must be their ruin. And therefore, even though a gifted man like M. Renan may be so carried away by the tide of opinion in France where he lives, as to say that Nature cares nothing about chastity, and to see with amused indulgence the worship of the great goddess Lubricity, let us stand fast, and say that her worship is against nature, human nature, and that it is ruin. For this is the test of its being against human nature, that for human societies it is ruin. And the test is one from which there is no escape, as from the old tests in such matters there may be. For if you allege that it is the will of God that we

5   should be pure, the sceptical Gallo-Latins will tell you that they do not know any such person. And in like manner, if it is said that those who serve the goddess Aselgeia shall not inherit the kingdom of God, the Gallo-Latin may tell you that he does not believe in any such place. But that the sure

10 tendency and upshot of things establishes that the service of the goddess Aselgeia is ruin, that her followers are marred and stunted by it and disqualified for the ideal society of the future, is an infallible test to employ.

The saints admonish us to let our thoughts run upon what-

15 soever things are pure, if we would inherit the kingdom of God; and the divine Plato tells us that we have within us a many-headed beast and a man, and that by dissoluteness we feed and strengthen the beast in us, and starve the man; and finally, following the divine Plato among the sages at a humble

20 distance, comes the prosaic and unfashionable Paley, and says in his precise way that "this vice has a tendency, which other species of vice have not so directly, to unsettle and weaken the powers of the understanding; as well as, I think, in a greater degree than other vices, to render the heart thoroughly cor-

25 rupt." True; and once admitted and fostered, it eats like a canker, and with difficulty can ever be brought to let go its hold again, but for ever tightens it. Hardness and insolence come in its train; an insolence which grows until it ends by exasperating and alienating everybody; a hardness which

30 grows until the man can at last scarcely take pleasure in any-thing, outside the service of his goddess, except cupidity and greed, and cannot be touched with emotion by any language except fustian. Such are the fruits of the worship of the great goddess Aselgeia.

35   So, instead of saying that Nature cares nothing about chas-tity, let us say that human nature, *our* nature, cares about it a great deal. Let us say that, by her present popular literature, France gives proof that she is suffering from a dangerous and

perhaps fatal disease; and that it is not clericalism which is
the real enemy to the French so much as their goddess; and if
they can none of them see this themselves, it is only a sign of
how far the disease has gone, and the case is so much the
worse. The case is so much the worse; and for men in such   5
case to be so vehemently busy about clerical and dynastic intrigues at home, and about alliances and colonial acquisitions
and purifications of the flag abroad, might well make one borrow of the prophets and exclaim, "Surely ye are perverse"!
perverse to neglect your really pressing matters for those sec-   10
ondary ones. And when the ingenious and inexhaustible M.
Blowitz, of our great London *Times*, who sees everybody and
knows everything, when he expounds the springs of politics
and the causes of the fall and success of ministries, and the
combinations which have not been tried but should be, and   15
takes upon him the mystery of things in the way with which
we are so familiar,—to this wise man himself one is often
tempted, again, to say with the prophets: "Yet the Eternal also
is wise, and will not call back his words." M. Blowitz is not
the only wise one; the Eternal has his wisdom also, and some-   20
how or other it is always the Eternal's wisdom which at last
carries the day. The Eternal has attached to certain moral
causes the safety or the ruin of States, and the present popular
literature of France is a sign that she has a most dangerous
moral disease.   25
Now if the disease goes on and increases, then, whatever sagacious advice M. Blowitz may give, and whatever political
combinations may be tried, and whether France gets colonies
or not, and whether she allies herself with this nation or with
that, things will only go from bad to worse with her; she will   30
more and more lose her powers of soul and spirit, her intellectual productiveness, her skill in counsel, her might for war,
her formidableness as a foe, her value as an ally, and the life
of that famous State will be more and more impaired, until it
perish. And this is that hard but true doctrine of the sages   35
and prophets, of the inexorable fatality of operation, in moral
failure of the unsound majority, to impair and destroy States.
But we will not talk or think of destruction for a State with

such gifts and graces as France, and which has had such a place in history, and to which we, many of us, owe so much delight and so much good. And yet if France had no greater numbers than the Athens of Plato or the Judah of Isaiah, I do not see how she could well escape out of the throttling arms of her goddess and recover. She must recover through a powerful and profound renewal, a great inward change, brought about by "the remnant" amongst her people; and, for this, a remnant small in numbers would not suffice. But in a France of thirty-five millions, who shall set bounds to the numbers of the remnant, or to its effectualness and power of victory?

In these United States (for I come round to the United States at last) you are fifty millions and more. I suppose that, as in England, as in France, as everywhere, so likewise here, the majority of people doubt very much whether the majority is unsound; or, rather, they have no doubt at all about the matter, they are sure that it is not unsound. But let us consent to-night to remain to the end in the ideas of the sages and prophets whom we have been following all along; and let us suppose that in the present actual stage of the world, as in all the stages through which the world has passed hitherto, the majority is and must be in general unsound everywhere,—even in the United States, even here in New York itself. Where is the failure? I have already, in the past, speculated in the abstract about you, perhaps, too much. But I suppose that in a democratic community like this, with its newness, its magnitude, its strength, its life of business, its sheer freedom and equality, the danger is in the absence of the discipline of respect; in hardness and materialism, exaggeration and boastfulness; in a false smartness, a false audacity, a want of soul and delicacy. "Whatsoever things are *elevated*,"—whatsoever things are nobly serious, have true elevation,[1]—that perhaps, in our catalogue of maxims which are to possess the mind, is the maxim which points to where the failure of the unsound majority, in a great democracy like yours, will probably lie. At any rate let us for the moment agree to suppose so. And the philosophers and the prophets, whom I at any rate am dis-

1 ″Οσα σεμνά.

posed to believe, and who say that moral causes govern the standing and the falling of States, will tell us that the failure to mind whatsoever things are elevated must impair with an inexorable fatality the life of a nation, just as the failure to mind whatsoever things are just, or whatsoever things are amiable, or whatsoever things are pure, will impair it; and that if the failure to mind whatsoever things are elevated should be real in your American democracy, and should grow into a disease, and take firm hold on you, then the life of even these great United States must inevitably suffer and be impaired more and more, until it perish.

Then from this hard doctrine we will betake ourselves to the more comfortable doctrine of *the remnant.* "The remnant shall return;" shall "convert and be healed" itself first, and shall then recover the unsound majority. And you are fifty millions and growing apace. What a remnant yours may be, surely! A remnant of how great numbers, how mighty strength, how irresistible efficacy! Yet we must not go too fast, either, nor make too sure of our efficacious remnant. Mere multitude will not give us a saving remnant with certainty. The Assyrian Empire had multitude, the Roman Empire had multitude; yet neither the one nor the other could produce a sufficing remnant any more than Athens or Judah could produce it, and both Assyria and Rome perished like Athens and Judah.

But you are something more than a people of fifty millions. You are fifty millions mainly sprung, as we in England are mainly sprung, from that German stock which has faults indeed,—faults which have diminished the extent of its influence, diminished its power of attraction and the interest of its history, and which seems moreover just now, from all I can see and hear, to be passing through a not very happy moment, morally, in Germany proper. Yet of the German stock it is, I think, true, as my father said more than fifty years ago, that it has been a stock "of the most moral races of men that the world has yet seen, with the soundest laws, the least violent passions, the fairest domestic and civil virtues." You come, therefore, of about the best parentage which a modern nation can have. Then you have had, as we in England have also had,

but more entirely than we and more exclusively, the Puritan
discipline. Certainly I am not blind to the faults of that discipline. Certainly I do not wish it to remain in possession of the
field for ever, or too long. But as a stage and a discipline, and
5   as means for enabling that poor inattentive and immoral creature, man, to love and appropriate and make part of his being
divine ideas, on which he could not otherwise have laid or kept
hold, the discipline of Puritanism has been invaluable; and the
more I read history, the more I see of mankind, the more I
10 recognise its value. Well, then, you are not merely a multitude
of fifty millions; you are fifty millions sprung from this excellent Germanic stock, having passed through this excellent
Puritan discipline, and set in this enviable and unbounded
country. Even supposing, therefore, that by the necessity of
15 things your majority must in the present stage of the world
probably be unsound, what a remnant, I say,—what an incomparable, all-transforming remnant,—you may fairly hope
with your numbers, if things go happily, to have!

Emerson

Forty years ago, when I was an undergraduate at Oxford, voices were in the air there which haunt my memory still. Happy the man who in that susceptible season of youth hears such voices! they are a possession to him for ever. No such voices as those which we heard in our youth at Oxford are 5 sounding there now. Oxford has more criticism now, more knowledge, more light; but such voices as those of our youth it has no longer. The name of Cardinal Newman is a great name to the imagination still; his genius and his style are still things of power. But he is over eighty years old; he is in the Oratory 10 at Birmingham; he has adopted, for the doubts and difficulties which beset men's minds to-day, a solution which, to speak frankly, is impossible. Forty years ago he was in the very prime of life; he was close at hand to us at Oxford; he was preaching in St. Mary's pulpit every Sunday; he seemed about 15 to transform and to renew what was for us the most national and natural institution in the world, the Church of England. Who could resist the charm of that spiritual apparition, gliding in the dim afternoon light through the aisles of St. Mary's, rising into the pulpit, and then, in the most entrancing of 20 voices, breaking the silence with words and thoughts which were a religious music,—subtle, sweet, mournful? I seem to hear him still, saying: "After the fever of life, after wearinesses and sicknesses, fightings and despondings, languor and fretfulness, struggling and failing, struggling and succeeding; after all 25 the changes and chances of this troubled, unhealthy state,—at length comes death, at length the white throne of God, at length the beatific vision." Or, if we followed him back to his seclusion at Littlemore, that dreary village by the London road,

and to the house of retreat and the church which he built
there,—a mean house such as Paul might have lived in when
he was tent-making at Ephesus, a church plain and thinly sown
with worshippers,—who could resist him there either, welcom-
5 ing back to the severe joys of church-fellowship, and of daily
worship and prayer, the firstlings of a generation which had
well-nigh forgotten them? Again I seem to hear him: "The
season is chill and dark, and the breath of the morning is
damp, and worshippers are few; but all this befits those who
10 are by profession penitents and mourners, watchers and pil-
grims. More dear to them that loneliness, more cheerful that
severity, and more bright that gloom, than all those aids and
appliances of luxury by which men nowadays attempt to make
prayer less disagreeable to them. True faith does not covet
15 comforts; they who realise that awful day when they shall see
Him face to face, whose eyes are as a flame of fire, will as little
bargain to pray pleasantly now, as they will think of doing so
then."

Somewhere or other I have spoken of those "last enchant-
20 ments of the Middle Age" which Oxford sheds around us, and
here they were! But there were other voices sounding in our
ear besides Newman's. There was the puissant voice of Carlyle,
so sorely strained, over-used and misused since, but then fresh,
comparatively sound, and reaching our hearts with true, pa-
25 thetic eloquence. Who can forget the emotion of receiving in
its first freshness such a sentence as that sentence of Carlyle
upon Edward Irving, then just dead: "Scotland sent him forth
a herculean man; our mad Babylon wore and wasted him with
all her engines,—and it took her twelve years!" A greater voice
30 still,—the greatest voice of the century,—came to us in those
youthful years through Carlyle: the voice of Goethe. To this
day,—such is the force of youthful associations,—I read the
Wilhelm Meister with more pleasure in Carlyle's translation
than in the original. The large, liberal view of human life in
35 *Wilhelm Meister*, how novel it was to the Englishman in those
days! and it was salutary, too, and educative for him, doubtless,
as well as novel. But what moved us most in *Wilhelm Meister*
was that which, after all, will always move the young most,—

the poetry, the eloquence. Never surely was Carlyle's prose so beautiful and pure as in his rendering of the Youths' dirge over Mignon!—"Well is our treasure now laid up, the fair image of the past. Here sleeps it in the marble, undecaying; in your hearts, also, it lives, it works. Travel, travel, back into life! Take along with you this holy earnestness, for earnestness alone makes life eternity." Here we had the voice of the great Goethe;—not of the stiff, and hindered, and frigid, and factitious Goethe who speaks to us too often from those sixty volumes of his, but of the great Goethe, and the true one.

And besides those voices, there came to us in that old Oxford time a voice, also, from this side of the Atlantic,—a clear and pure voice, which for my ear, at any rate, brought a strain as new, and moving, and unforgettable, as the strain of Newman, or Carlyle, or Goethe. Mr. Lowell has well described the apparition of Emerson to your young generation here, in that distant time of which I am speaking, and of his workings upon them. He was your Newman, your man of soul and genius visible to you in the flesh, speaking to your bodily ears, a present object for your heart and imagination. That is surely the most potent of all influences! nothing can come up to it. To us at Oxford Emerson was but a voice speaking from three thousand miles away. But so well he spoke, that from that time forth Boston Bay and Concord were names invested, to my ear, with a sentiment akin to that which invests for me the names of Oxford and of Weimar; and snatches of Emerson's strain fixed themselves in my mind as imperishably as any of the eloquent words which I have been just now quoting. "Then dies the man in you; then once more perish the buds of art, poetry, and science, as they have died already in a thousand thousand men." "What Plato has thought, he may think; what a saint has felt, he may feel; what at any time has befallen any man, he can understand." "Trust thyself! every heart vibrates to that iron string. Accept the place the divine providence has found for you, the society of your contemporaries, the connexion of events. Great men have always done so, and confided themselves childlike to the genius of their age; betraying their perception that the Eternal was stirring at their heart, working

through their hands, predominating in all their being. And we
are now men, and must accept in the highest spirit the same
transcendent destiny; and not pinched in a corner, not cowards
fleeing before a revolution, but redeemers and benefactors,
5   pious aspirants to be noble clay plastic under the Almighty
effort, let us advance and advance on Chaos and the Dark!"
These lofty sentences of Emerson, and a hundred others of like
strain, I never have lost out of my memory; I never *can* lose
them.
10   At last I find myself in Emerson's own country, and looking upon Boston Bay. Naturally I revert to the friend of my
youth. It is not always pleasant to ask oneself questions about
the friends of one's youth; they cannot always well support it.
Carlyle, for instance, in my judgment, cannot well support such
15   a return upon him. Yet we should make the return; we should
part with our illusions, we should know the truth. When I
come to this country, where Emerson now counts for so
much and where such high claims are made for him, I pull
myself together, and ask myself what the truth about this
20   object of my youthful admiration really is. Improper elements often come into our estimate of men. We have lately
seen a German critic make Goethe the greatest of all poets,
because Germany is now the greatest of military powers, and
wants a poet to match. Then, too, America is a young country;
25   and young countries, like young persons, are apt sometimes to
evince in their literary judgments a want of scale and measure.
I set myself, therefore, resolutely to come at a real estimate of
Emerson, and with a leaning even to strictness rather than to
indulgence. That is the safer course. Time has no indulgence;
30   any veils of illusion which we may have left around an object
because we loved it, Time is sure to strip away.

I was reading the other day a notice of Emerson by a serious
and interesting American critic. Fifty or sixty passages in
Emerson's poems, says this critic,—who had doubtless himself
35   been nourished on Emerson's writings, and held them justly
dear,—fifty or sixty passages from Emerson's poems have already entered into English speech as matter of familiar and uni-

versally current quotation. Here is a specimen of that personal sort of estimate which, for my part, even in speaking of authors dear to me, I would try to avoid. What is the kind of phrase of which we may fairly say that it has entered into English speech as matter of familiar quotation? Such a phrase, surely, as the "Patience on a monument" of Shakespeare; as the "Darkness visible" of Milton; as the "Where ignorance is bliss" of Gray. Of not one single passage in Emerson's poetry can it be truly said that it has become a familiar quotation like phrases of this kind. It is not enough that it should be familiar to his admirers, familiar in New England, familiar even throughout the United States; it must be familiar to all readers and lovers of English poetry. Of not more than one or two passages in Emerson's poetry can it, I think, be truly said, that they stand ever-present in the memory of even many lovers of English poetry. A great number of passages from his poetry are no doubt perfectly familiar to the mind and lips of the critic whom I have mentioned, and perhaps of a wide circle of American readers. But this is a very different thing from being matter of universal quotation, like the phrases of the legitimate poets.

And, in truth, one of the legitimate poets, Emerson, in my opinion, is not. His poetry is interesting, it makes one think; but it is not the poetry of one of the born poets. I say it of him with reluctance, although I am sure that he would have said it of himself; but I say it with reluctance, because I dislike giving pain to his admirers, and because all my own wish, too, is to say of him what is favourable. But I regard myself, not as speaking to please Emerson's admirers, not as speaking to please myself; but rather, I repeat, as communing with Time and Nature concerning the productions of this beautiful and rare spirit, and as resigning what of him is by their unalterable decree touched with caducity, in order the better to mark and secure that in him which is immortal.

Milton says that poetry ought to be simple, sensuous, impassioned. Well, Emerson's poetry is seldom either simple, or sensuous, or impassioned. In general it lacks directness; it lacks concreteness; it lacks energy. His grammar is often embar-

rassed; in particular, the want of clearly-marked distinction
between the subject and the object of his sentence is a frequent cause of obscurity in him. A poem which shall be a
plain, forcible, inevitable whole he hardly ever produces. Such
5 good work as the noble lines graven on the Concord Monument is the exception with him; such ineffective work as the
"Fourth of July Ode" or the "Boston Hymn" is the rule.
Even passages and single lines of thorough plainness and commanding force are rare in his poetry. They exist, of course;
10 but when we meet with them they give us a slight shock of
surprise, so little has Emerson accustomed us to them. Let me
have the pleasure of quoting one or two of these exceptional
passages: —

> So nigh is grandeur to our dust,
15 > So near is God to man,
> When Duty whispers low, *Thou must,*
> The youth replies, *I can.*

Or again this: —

> Though love repine and reason chafe,
20 > There came a voice without reply:
> " 'Tis man's perdition to be safe,
> When for the truth he ought to die."

Excellent! but how seldom do we get from him a strain
blown so clearly and firmly! Take another passage where his
25 strain has not only clearness, it has also grace and beauty: —

> And ever, when the happy child
> In May beholds the blooming wild,
> And hears in heaven the bluebird sing,
> "Onward," he cries, "your baskets bring!
30 > In the next field is air more mild,
> And o'er yon hazy crest is Eden's balmier spring."

In the style and cadence here there is a reminiscence, I
think, of Gray; at any rate, the pureness grace and beauty of
these lines are worthy even of Gray. But Gray holds his high

rank as a poet, not merely by the beauty and grace of passages in his poems; not merely by a diction generally pure in an age of impure diction: he holds it, above all, by the power and skill with which the evolution of his poems is conducted. Here is his grand superiority to Collins, whose diction in his best poem, the "Ode to Evening," is purer than Gray's; but then the "Ode to Evening" is like a river which loses itself in the sand, whereas Gray's best poems have an evolution sure and satisfying. Emerson's "Mayday," from which I just now quoted, has no real evolution at all; it is a series of observations. And, in general, his poems have no evolution. Take for example his "Titmouse." Here he has an excellent subject; and his observation of Nature, moreover, is always marvellously close and fine. But compare what he makes of his meeting with his titmouse with what Cowper or Burns makes of the like kind of incident! One never quite arrives at learning what the titmouse actually did for him at all, though one feels a strong interest and desire to learn it; but one is reduced to guessing, and cannot be quite sure that after all one has guessed right. He is not plain and concrete enough,—in other words, not poet enough,—to be able to tell us. And a failure of this kind goes through almost all his verse, keeps him amid symbolism, and allusion, and the fringes of things, and in spite of his spiritual power deeply impairs his poetic value. Through the inestimable virtue of concreteness, a simple poem like "The Bridge" of Longfellow or the "School Days" of Mr. Whittier is of more poetic worth, perhaps, than all the verse of Emerson.

I do not, then, place Emerson among the great poets. But I go further, and say that I do not place him among the great writers, the great men of letters. Who are the great men of letters? They are men like Cicero, Plato, Bacon, Pascal, Swift, Voltaire,—writers with, in the first place, a genius and instinct for style; writers whose prose is by a kind of native necessity true and sound. Now the style of Emerson, like the style of his transcendentalist friends and of the "Dial" so continually,— the style of Emerson is capable of falling into a strain like this, which I take from the beginning of his "Essay on Love:" "Every soul is a celestial Venus to every other soul. The heart

has its sabbaths and jubilees, in which the world appears as a
hymeneal feast, and all natural sounds and the circle of the
seasons are erotic odes and dances." Emerson altered this sentence in the later editions. Like Wordsworth, he was in later
5 life fond of altering; and in general his later alterations, like
those of Wordsworth, are not improvements. He softened
the passage in question, however, though without really mending it. I quote it in its original and strongly-marked form.
Arthur Stanley used to relate that, about the year 1840, being
10 in conversation with some Americans in quarantine at Malta
and thinking to please them he declared his warm admiration
for Emerson's "Essays," then recently published. However,
the Americans shook their heads, and told him that for home
taste Emerson was decidedly too *greeny*. We will hope, for
15 their sakes, that the sort of thing they had in their heads was
such writing as I have just quoted. Unsound it is indeed, and
in a style almost impossible to a born man of letters.

It is a curious thing, that quality of style which marks the
great writer, the born man of letters. It resides in the whole
20 tissue of his work, and of his work regarded as a composition
for literary purposes. Brilliant and powerful passages in a
man's writings do not prove his possession of it; it lies in their
whole tissue. Emerson has passages of noble and pathetic eloquence, such as those which I quoted at the beginning; he has
25 passages of shrewd and felicitous wit; he has crisp epigrams; he
has passages of exquisitely touched observation of nature. Yet
he is not a great writer; his style has not the requisite wholeness
of good tissue. Even Carlyle is not, in my judgment, a great
writer. He has surpassingly powerful qualities of expression,
30 far more powerful than Emerson's, and reminding one of the
gifts of expression of the great poets,—of even Shakespeare
himself. What Emerson so admirably says of Carlyle's "devouring eyes and portraying hand," "those thirsty eyes, those
portrait-eating, portrait-painting eyes of thine, those fatal per-
35 ceptions," is thoroughly true. What a description is Carlyle's of
the first publisher of *Sartor Resartus*, "to whom the idea of a
new edition of *Sartor* is frightful, or rather ludicrous, unimag-
inable"; of this poor Fraser, in whose "wonderful world of Tory

pamphleteers, Conservative Younger-brothers, Regent Street Loungers, Crockford Gamblers, Irish Jesuits, drunken reporters, and miscellaneous unclean persons (whom nitre and much soap will not wash clean) not a soul has expressed the smallest wish that way!" What a portrait, again, of the well-beloved John Sterling! "One, and the best, of a small class extant here, who, nigh drowning in a black wreck of Infidelity (lighted up by some glare of Radicalism only, now growing *dim* too), and about to perish, saved themselves into a Coleridgian Shovel-Hattedness." What touches in the invitation of Emerson to London! "You shall see blockheads by the million; Pickwick himself shall be visible,—innocent young Dickens, reserved for a questionable fate. The great Wordsworth shall talk till you yourself pronounce him to be a bore. Southey's complexion is still healthy mahogany brown, with a fleece of white hair, and eyes that seem running at full gallop. Leigh Hunt, man of genius in the shape of a cockney, is my near neighbour, with good humour and no common-sense; old Rogers with his pale head, white, bare, and cold as snow, with those large blue eyes, cruel, sorrowful, and that sardonic shelf chin." How inimitable it all is! And finally, for one must not go on for ever, this version of a London Sunday, with the public-houses closed during the hours of divine service! "It is silent Sunday; the populace not yet admitted to their beer-shops, till the respectabilities conclude their rubric mum-meries,—a much more audacious feat than beer." Yet even Carlyle is not, in my judgment, to be called a great writer; one cannot think of ranking him with men like Cicero and Plato and Swift and Voltaire. Emerson freely promises to Carlyle immortality for his histories. They will not have it. Why? Because the materials furnished to him by that devouring eye of his and that portraying hand were not wrought in and subdued by him to what his work, regarded as a composition for literary purposes, required. Occurring in conversation, breaking out in familiar correspondence, they are magnificent, inimitable; nothing more is required of them; thus thrown out anyhow, they serve their turn and fulfil their function. And therefore I should not wonder if really Carlyle lived, in the

long run, by such an invaluable record as that correspondence
between him and Emerson, of which we owe the publication
to Mr. Charles Norton,—by this and not by his works, as
Johnson lives in Boswell, not by his works. For Carlyle's
5 sallies, as the staple of a literary work, become wearisome; and
as time more and more applies to Carlyle's works its stringent
test, this will be felt more and more. Shakespeare, Molière,
Swift,—they too had, like Carlyle, the devouring eye and
the portraying hand. But they are great literary masters, they
10 are supreme writers, because they knew how to work into a
literary composition their materials, and to subdue them to the
purposes of literary effect. Carlyle is too wilful for this, too
turbid, too vehement.

You will think I deal in nothing but negatives. I have been
15 saying that Emerson is not one of the great poets, the great
writers. He has not their quality of style. He is, however, the
propounder of a philosophy. The Platonic dialogues afford us
the example of exquisite literary form and treatment given to
philosophical ideas. Plato is at once a great literary man and a
20 great philosopher. If we speak carefully, we cannot call
Aristotle or Spinoza or Kant great literary men, or their productions great literary works. But their work is arranged with
such constructive power that they build a philosophy and are
justly called great philosophical writers. Emerson cannot, I
25 think, be called with justice a great philosophical writer. He
cannot build; his arrangement of philosophical ideas has no
progress in it, no evolution; he does not construct a philosophy. Emerson himself knew the defects of his method, or
rather want of method, very well; indeed, he and Carlyle
30 criticise themselves and one another in a way which leaves
little for any one else to do in the way of formulating their
defects. Carlyle formulates perfectly the defects of his friend's
poetic and literary production when he says of the "Dial":
"For me it is too ethereal, speculative, theoretic; I will have
35 all things condense themselves, take shape and body, if they
are to have my sympathy." And, speaking of Emerson's orations he says: "I long to see some concrete Thing, some
Event, Man's Life, American Forest, or piece of Creation,

which this Emerson loves and wonders at, well *Emersonised,*
—depictured by Emerson, filled with the life of Emerson, and
cast forth from him, then to live by itself. If these orations balk
me of this, how profitable soever they may be for others, I
will not love them." Emerson himself formulates perfectly   5
the defect of his own philosophical productions when he
speaks of his "formidable tendency to the lapidary style. I
build my house of boulders." "Here I sit and read and write,"
he says again, "with very little system, and as far as regards
composition, with the most fragmentary result; paragraphs   10
incompressible, each sentence an infinitely repellent particle." Nothing can be truer; and the work of a Spinoza or
Kant, of the men who stand as great philosophical writers,
does not proceed in this wise.

Some people will tell you that Emerson's poetry indeed is   15
too abstract, and his philosophy too vague, but that his best
work is his *English Traits.* The *English Traits* are, beyond
question, very pleasant reading. It is easy to praise them, easy
to commend the author of them. But I insist on always trying
Emerson's work by the highest standards. I esteem him too   20
much to try his work by any other. Tried by the highest
standards, and compared with the work of the excellent markers and recorders of the traits of human life,—of writers like
Montaigne, La Bruyère, Addison,—the *English Traits* will not
stand the comparison. Emerson's observation has not the dis- 25
interested quality of the observation of these masters. It is the
observation of a man systematically benevolent, as Hawthorne's observation in *Our Old Home* is the work of a man
chagrined. Hawthorne's literary talent is of the first order. His
subjects are generally not to me subjects of the highest inter- 30
est; but his literary talent is of the first order, the finest, I
think, which America has yet produced,—finer, by much, than
Emerson's. Yet *Our Old Home* is not a masterpiece any more
than *English Traits.* In neither of them is the observer disinterested enough. The author's attitude in each of these cases 35
can easily be understood and defended. Hawthorne was a
sensitive man, so situated in England that he was perpetually
in contact with the British Philistine; and the British Philistine

is a trying personage. Emerson's systematic benevolence comes from what he himself calls somewhere his "persistent optimism"; and his persistent optimism is the root of his greatness and the source of his charm. But still let us keep our literary
5 conscience true, and judge every kind of literary work by the laws really proper to it. The kind of work attempted in the *English Traits* and in *Our Old Home* is work which cannot be done perfectly with a bias such as that given by Emerson's optimism or by Hawthorne's chagrin. Consequently,
10 neither *English Traits* nor *Our Old Home* is a work of perfection in its kind.

Not with the Miltons and Grays, not with the Platos and Spinozas, not with the Swifts and Voltaires, not with the Montaignes and Addisons, can we rank Emerson. His work of
15 various kinds, when one compares it with the work done in a corresponding kind by these masters, fails to stand the comparison. No man could see this clearer than Emerson himself. It is hard not to feel despondency when we contemplate our failures and shortcomings: and Emerson, the least self-flatter-
20 ing and the most modest of men, saw so plainly what was lacking to him that he had his moments of despondency. "Alas, my friend," he writes in reply to Carlyle, who had exhorted him to creative work,—"Alas, my friend, I can do no such gay thing as you say. I do not belong to the poets, but only to a
25 low department of literature,—the reporters; suburban men." He deprecates his friend's praise; praise "generous to a fault," he calls it; praise "generous to the shaming of me,—cold, fastidious, ebbing person that I am. Already in a former letter you had said too much good of my poor little arid book, which is
30 as sand to my eyes. I can only say that I heartily wish the book were better; and I must try and deserve so much favour from the kind gods by a bolder and truer living in the months to come,—such as may perchance one day relax and invigorate this cramp hand of mine. When I see how much work is to be
35 done; what room for a poet, for any spiritualist, in this great, intelligent, sensual and avaricious America,—I lament my fumbling fingers and stammering tongue." Again, as late as 1870, he writes to Carlyle: "There is no example of constancy

like yours, and it always stings my stupor into temporary recovery and wonderful resolution to accept the noble challenge. But 'the strong hours conquer us;' and I am the victim
of miscellany,—miscellany of designs, vast debility, and pro-
crastination." The forlorn note belonging to the phrase "vast   5
debility," recalls that saddest and most discouraged of writers,
the author of *Obermann*, Senancour, with whom Emerson
has in truth a certain kinship. He has in common with Senancour his pureness, his passion for nature, his single eye; and
here we find him confessing, like Senancour, a sense in him-   10
self of sterility and impotence.

And now I think I have cleared the ground. I have given up
to envious Time as much of Emerson as Time can fairly expect ever to obtain. We have not in Emerson a great poet, a
great writer, a great philosophy-maker. His relation to us is   15
not that of one of those personages; yet it is a relation of, I
think, even superior importance. His relation to us is more like
that of the Roman Emperor Marcus Aurelius. Marcus Aurelius
is not a great writer, a great philosophy-maker; he is the friend
and aider of those who would live in the spirit. Emerson is the   20
same. He is the friend and aider of those who would live in
the spirit. All the points in thinking which are necessary for
this purpose he takes; but he does not combine them into a
system, or present them as a regular philosophy. Combined in
a system by a man with the requisite talent for this kind of   25
thing, they would be less useful than as Emerson gives them to
us; and the man with the talent so to systematise them would
be less impressive than Emerson. They do very well as they
now stand;—like "boulders," as he says;—in "paragraphs incompressible, each sentence an infinitely repellent particle."   30
In such sentences his main points recur again and again, and
become fixed in the memory.
We all know them. First and foremost, character. Character
is everything. "That which all things tend to educe,—which
freedom, cultivation, intercourse, revolutions, go to form and   35
deliver,—is character." Character and self-reliance. "Trust thyself! every heart vibrates to that iron string." And yet we have

our being in a *not ourselves*. "There is a power above and
behind us, and we are the channels of its communications." But
our lives must be pitched higher. "Life must be lived on a
higher plane; we must go up to a higher platform, to which
5 we are always invited to ascend; there the whole scene
changes." The good we need is for ever close to us, though
we attain it not. "On the brink of the waters of life and truth,
we are miserably dying." This good is close to us, moreover,
in our daily life, and in the familiar, homely places. "The
10 unremitting retention of simple and high sentiments in obscure
duties,"—that is the maxim for us. "Let us be poised and wise,
and our own to-day. Let us treat the men and women well,—
treat them as if they were real; perhaps they are. Men live in
their fancy, like drunkards whose hands are too soft and
15 tremulous for successful labour. I settle myself ever firmer in
the creed, that we should not postpone and refer and wish, but
do broad justice where we are, by whomsoever we deal with;
accepting our actual companions and circumstances, however
humble or odious, as the mystic officials to whom the universe
20 has delegated its whole pleasure for us." "Massachusetts, Connecticut River, and Boston Bay, you think paltry places, and
the ear loves names of foreign and classic topography. But
here we are; and if we will tarry a little we may come to
learn that here is best. See to it only that thyself is here."
25 Furthermore, the good is close to us *all*. "I resist the scepticism
of our education and of our educated men. I do not believe
that the differences of opinion and character in men are or-
ganic. I do not recognise, beside the class of the good and the
wise, a permanent class of sceptics, or a class of conservatives,
30 or of malignants, or of materialists. I do not believe in two
classes." "Every man has a call of the power to do something
unique." Exclusiveness is deadly. "The exclusive in social life
does not see that he excludes himself from enjoyment in the
attempt to appropriate it. The exclusionist in religion does not
35 see that he shuts the door of heaven on himself in striving
to shut out others. Treat men as pawns and ninepins, and you
shall suffer as well as they. If you leave out their heart you
shall lose your own." "The selfish man suffers more from his
selfishness than he from whom that selfishness withholds some

important benefit." A sound nature will be inclined to refuse
ease and self-indulgence. "To live with some rigour of temperance, or some extremes of generosity, seems to be an asceticism
which common good-nature would appoint to those who are
at ease and in plenty, in sign that they feel a brotherhood with   5
the great multitude of suffering men." Compensation, finally, is
the great law of life; it is everywhere, it is sure, and there is
no escape from it. This is that "law alive and beautiful, which
works over our heads and under our feet. Pitiless, it avails itself of our success when we obey it, and of our ruin when we   10
contravene it. Men are all secret believers in it. It rewards
actions after their nature. The reward of a thing well done
is to have done it." "The thief steals from himself, the
swindler swindles himself. You must pay at last your own
debt."   15
     This is tonic indeed! And let no one object that it is too
general; that more practical, positive direction is what we
want; that Emerson's optimism, self-reliance, and indifference
to favourable conditions for our life and growth, have in them
something of danger. "Trust thyself;" "what attracts my atten-   20
tion shall have it;" "though thou shouldst walk the world over,
thou shalt not be able to find a condition inopportune or ignoble;" "what we call vulgar society is that society whose poetry
is not yet written, but which you shall presently make as enviable and renowned as any." With maxims like these, we   25
surely, it may be said, run some risk of being made too well
satisfied with our own actual self and state, however crude and
imperfect they may be. "Trust thyself?" It may be said that
the common American or Englishman is more than enough disposed already to trust himself. I often reply, when our sec-   30
tarians are praised for following conscience: Our people are
very good in following their conscience; where they are not
so good is in ascertaining whether their conscience tells them
right. "What attracts my attention shall have it?" Well, that is
our people's plea when they run after the Salvation Army, and   35
desire Messrs. Moody and Sankey. "Thou shalt not be able to
find a condition inopportune or ignoble?" But think of the
turn of the good people of our race for producing a life of
hideousness and immense ennui; think of that specimen of your

own New England life which Mr. Howells gives us in one of
his charming stories which I was reading lately; think of the
life of that ragged New England farm in the *Lady of the
Aroostook;* think of Deacon Blood, and Aunt Maria, and the
5 straight-backed chairs with black horse-hair seats, and Ezra
Perkins with perfect self-reliance depositing his travellers in the
snow! I can truly say that in the little which I have seen of the
life of New England, I am more struck with what has been
achieved than with the crudeness and failure. But no doubt
10 there is still a great deal of crudeness also. Your own novelists
say there is, and I suppose they say true. In the New England, as in the Old, our people have to learn, I suppose, not
that their modes of life are beautiful and excellent already;
they have rather to learn that they must transform them.
15   To adopt this line of objection to Emerson's deliverances
would, however, be unjust. In the first place, Emerson's points
are in themselves true, if understood in a certain high sense;
they are true and fruitful. And the right work to be done, at
the hour when he appeared, was to affirm them generally and
20 absolutely. Only thus could he break through the hard and
fast barrier of narrow, fixed ideas which he found confronting him, and win an entrance for new ideas. Had he attempted developments which may now strike us as expedient,
he would have excited fierce antagonism, and probably ef-
25 fected little or nothing. The time might come for doing other
work later, but the work which Emerson did was the right
work to be done then.
       In the second place, strong as was Emerson's optimism, and
unconquerable as was his belief in a good result to emerge
30 from all which he saw going on around him, no misanthrop-
ical satirist ever saw shortcomings and absurdities more
clearly than he did, or exposed them more courageously.
When he sees "the meanness," as he calls it, "of American politics," he congratulates Washington on being "long already
35 happily dead," on being "wrapt in his shroud and for ever
safe." With how firm a touch he delineates the faults of your
two great political parties of forty years ago! The Democrats,
he says, "have not at heart the ends which give to the name

of democracy what hope and virtue are in it. The spirit of our American radicalism is destructive and aimless; it is not loving; it has no ulterior and divine ends, but is destructive only out of hatred and selfishness. On the other side, the conservative party, composed of the most moderate, able, and cultivated 5 part of the population, is timid, and merely defensive of property. It vindicates no right, it aspires to no real good, it brands no crime, it proposes no generous policy. From neither party, when in power, has the world any benefit to expect in science, art, or humanity, at all commensurate with the re- 10 sources of the nation." Then with what subtle though kindly irony he follows the gradual withdrawal in New England, in the last half century, of tender consciences from the social organisations,—the bent for experiments such as that of Brook Farm and the like,—follows it in all its "dissidence of dissent 15 and Protestantism of the Protestant religion!" He even loves to rally the New Englander on his philanthropical activity, and to find his beneficence and its institutions a bore! "Your miscellaneous popular charities, the education at college of fools, the building of meeting-houses to the vain end to which 20 many of these now stand, alms to sots, and the thousand-fold relief societies,—though I confess with shame that I sometimes succumb and give the dollar, yet it is a wicked dollar which by and by I shall have the manhood to with-hold." "Our Sunday schools and churches and pauper societies 25 are yokes to the neck. We pain ourselves to please nobody. There are natural ways of arriving at the same ends at which these aim but do not arrive." "Nature does not like our be-nevolence or our learning much better than she likes our frauds and wars. When we come out of the caucus, or the 30 bank, or the Abolition Convention, or the Temperance meet-ing, or the Transcendental Club, into the fields and woods, she says to us: 'So hot, my little Sir?' "

Yes, truly, his insight is admirable; his truth is precious. Yet the secret of his effect is not even in these; it is in his temper. 35 It is in the hopeful, serene, beautiful temper wherewith these, in Emerson, are indissolubly joined; in which they work, and have their being. He says himself: "We judge of a man's wis-

dom by his hope, knowing that the perception of the inexhaustibleness of nature is an immortal youth." If this be so,
how wise is Emerson! for never had man such a sense of the
inexhaustibleness of nature, and such hope. It was the ground
5   of his being; it never failed him. Even when he is sadly avow-
ing the imperfection of his literary power and resources, la-
menting his fumbling fingers and stammering tongue, he adds:
"Yet, as I tell you, I am very easy in my mind and never dream
of suicide. My whole philosophy, which is very real, teaches
10   acquiescence and optimism. Sure I am that the right word
will be spoken though I cut out my tongue." In his old age,
with friends dying and life failing, his tone of cheerful, for-
ward-looking hope is still the same: "A multitude of young
men are growing up here of high promise, and I compare
15   gladly the social poverty of my youth with the power on
which these draw." His abiding word for us, the word by
which being dead he yet speaks to us, is this: "That which
befits us, embosomed in beauty and wonder as we are, is
cheerfulness and courage, and the endeavour to realise our as-
20   pirations. Shall not the heart, which has received so much,
trust the Power by which it lives?"

     One can scarcely overrate the importance of thus holding
fast to happiness and hope. It gives to Emerson's work an
invaluable virtue. As Wordsworth's poetry is, in my judgment,
25   the most important work done in verse, in our language, during the present century, so Emerson's *Essays* are, I think, the
most important work done in prose. His work is more important than Carlyle's. Let us be just to Carlyle, provoking
though he often is. Not only has he that genius of his which
30   makes Emerson say truly of his letters, that "they savour always of eternity." More than this may be said of him. The
scope and upshot of his teaching are true; "his guiding genius,"
to quote Emerson again, is really "his moral sense, his perception of the sole importance of truth and justice." But consider
35   Carlyle's temper, as we have been considering Emerson's; take
his own account of it: "Perhaps London is the proper place
for me after all, seeing all places are *im*proper: who knows?
Meanwhile, I lead a most dyspeptic, solitary, self-shrouded life;

consuming, if possible in silence, my considerable daily allot-
ment of pain; glad when any strength is left in me for working,
which is the only use I can see in myself,—too rare a case of
late. The ground of my existence is black as death; too black,
when all *void* too; but at times there paint themselves on it   5
pictures of gold, and rainbow, and lightning; all the brighter
for the black ground, I suppose. Withal, I am very much of a
fool."—No, not a fool, but turbid and morbid, wilful and
perverse. "We judge of a man's wisdom by his hope."

    Carlyle's perverse attitude towards happiness cuts him off   10
from hope. He fiercely attacks the desire for happiness; his
grand point in *Sartor,* his secret in which the soul may find
rest, is that one shall cease to desire happiness, that one should
learn to say to oneself: "What if thou wert born and predes-
tined not to be happy, but to be unhappy!" He is wrong; Saint   15
Augustine is the better philosopher, who says: "Act we *must*
in pursuance of what gives us most delight." Epictetus and
Augustine can be severe moralists enough; but both of them
know and frankly say that the desire for happiness is the root
and ground of man's being. Tell him and show him that he   20
places his happiness wrong, that he seeks for delight where
delight will never be really found; then you illumine and further him. But you only confuse him by telling him to cease to
desire happiness, and you will not tell him this unless you are
already confused yourself.   25

    Carlyle preached the dignity of labour, the necessity of
righteousness, the love of veracity, the hatred of shams. He is
said by many people to be a great teacher, a great helper for
us, because he does so. But what is the due and eternal result
of labour, righteousness, veracity?—Happiness. And how are   30
we drawn to them by one who, instead of making us feel that
with them is happiness, tells us that perhaps we were predes-
tined not to be happy but to be unhappy?

    You will find, in especial, many earnest preachers of our
popular religion to be fervent in their praise and admiration   35
of Carlyle. His insistence on labour, righteousness, and veracity pleases them; his contempt for happiness pleases them too.
I read the other day a tract against smoking, although I do not

happen to be a smoker myself. "Smoking," said the tract, "is liked because it gives agreeable sensations. Now it is a positive objection to a thing that it gives agreeable sensations. An earnest man will expressly avoid what gives agreeable sensations."
5   Shortly afterwards I was inspecting a school, and I found the children reading a piece of poetry on the common theme that we are here to-day and gone to-morrow. I shall soon be gone, the speaker in this poem was made to say,—

         And I shall be glad to go,
10   For the world at best is a weary place,
         And my pulse is getting low.

How usual a language of popular religion that is, on our side of the Atlantic at any rate! But then our popular religion, in disparaging happiness here below, knows very well what it is
15   after. It has its eye on a happiness in a future life above the clouds, in the New Jerusalem, to be won by disliking and rejecting happiness here on earth. And so long as this ideal stands fast, it is very well. But for very many it now stands fast no longer; for Carlyle, at any rate, it had failed and vanished.
20   Happiness in labour, righteousness and veracity,—in the life of the spirit,—here was a gospel still for Carlyle to preach, and to help others by preaching. But he baffled them and himself by preferring the paradox that we are not born for happiness at all.
25   Happiness in labour, righteousness and veracity; in all the life of the spirit; happiness and eternal hope;—that was Emerson's gospel. I hear it said that Emerson was too sanguine; that the actual generation in America is not turning out so well as he expected. Very likely he was too sanguine as to
30   the near future; in this country it is difficult not to be too sanguine. Very possibly the present generation may prove unworthy of his high hopes; even several generations succeeding this may prove unworthy of them. But by his conviction that in the life of the spirit is happiness, and by his hope that this
35   life of the spirit will come more and more to be sanely understood, and to prevail, and to work for happiness,—by this

conviction and hope Emerson was great, and he will surely prove in the end to have been right in them. In this country it is difficult, as I said, not to be sanguine. Very many of your writers are over-sanguine, and on the wrong grounds. But you have two men who in what they have written show their sanguineness in a line where courage and hope are just, where they are also infinitely important, but where they are not easy. The two men are Franklin and Emerson.[1] These two are, I think, the most distinctively and honourably American of your writers; they are the most original and the most valuable. Wise men everywhere know that we must keep up our courage and hope; they know that hope is, as Wordsworth well says,—

> The paramount *duty* which Heaven lays,
> For its own honour, on man's suffering heart.

But the very word *duty* points to an effort and a struggle to maintain our hope unbroken. Franklin and Emerson maintained theirs with a convincing ease, an inspiring joy. Franklin's confidence in the happiness with which industry, honesty, and economy will crown the life of this work-day world, is such that he runs over with felicity. With a like felicity does

[1] I found with pleasure that this conjunction of Emerson's name with Franklin's had already occurred to an accomplished writer and delightful man, a friend of Emerson, left almost the sole survivor, alas! of the famous literary generation of Boston,—Dr. Oliver Wendell Holmes. Dr. Holmes has kindly allowed me to print here the ingenious and interesting lines, hitherto unpublished, in which he speaks of Emerson thus:—

> Where in the realm of thought, whose air is song,
> Does he, the Buddha of the West, belong?
> He seems a wingéd Franklin, sweetly wise,
> Born to unlock the secrets of the skies;
> And which the nobler calling—if 'tis fair
> Terrestrial with celestial to compare—
> To guide the storm-cloud's elemental flame,
> Or walk the chambers whence the lightning came
> Amidst the sources of its subtile fire,
> And steal their effluence for his lips and lyre?

Emerson run over, when he contemplates the happiness eternally attached to the true life in the spirit. You cannot prize
him too much, nor heed him too diligently. He has lessons for
both the branches of our race. I figure him to my mind as
visible upon earth still, as still standing here by Boston Bay,
or at his own Concord, in his habit as he lived, but of height-
ened stature and shining feature, with one hand stretched out
towards the East, to our laden and labouring England; the
other towards the ever-growing West, to his own dearly-loved
America,—"great, intelligent, sensual, avaricious America." To
us he shows for guidance his lucid freedom, his cheerfulness
and hope; to you his dignity, delicacy, serenity, elevation.

George Sand

In a letter dated yesterday, Mr. Matthew Arnold sends us the following reflections on the place in literature of George Sand, suggested by the memorial just erected to her at La Châtre:—

To-day a statue of George Sand is unveiled at La Châtre, a little town of Berry, not far from Nohant, where she lived. She could hardly escape a statue, but the present is not her hour, and the excuses for [not] taking part in to-day's ceremony prove it. Now is the hour of the naturalists and realists, of the great work, as it is called, and solid art of Balzac, which M. Daudet and other disciples are continuing; not of the work of humanitarians and idealists like George Sand and her master, Rousseau. The work, whether of idealists or of realists, must stand for what it is worth, and must pay the penalty of its defects. George Sand has admirably stated the conditions under which Rousseau's work was produced: "Rousseau had within him the love of goodness and the enthusiasm for beauty—and he knew nothing of them to start with. The absence of moral education had prolonged the childhood of his spirit beyond the ordinary term. The reigning philosophy of his time was not moralist; in its hatred of unjust restraints, it left out the chapter of duty altogether. Rousseau, more logical and more serious than the rest, came then to perceive that liberty was not all, and that philosophy must be a virtue, a religion, a social law."

Of George Sand herself, too, we may say that she suffered from the absence of moral education, and had to find out for herself that liberty is not all, and that philosophy must be a virtue, a religion, a social law. Her work, like Rousseau's, has

faults due to the conditions under which it arose—faults of declamation, faults of repetition, faults of extravagance. But do not let us deceive ourselves. Do not let us suppose that the work of Rousseau and George Sand is defective because those
5   writers are inspired by the love of goodness and the desire for beauty, and not, according to the approved recipe at present, by a disinterested curiosity. Do not let us assume that the work of the realists is solid—that the work of Balzac, for instance, will stand, that the work of M. Daudet will stand, because it is
10   inspired by a disinterested curiosity.

The best work, the work which endures, has not been thus inspired. M. Taine is a profound believer in the motive of disinterested curiosity, a fervent admirer of the work of Balzac. He even puts his name in connection with that of Shakspeare,
15   and appears to think that the two men work with the same motive. He is mistaken. The motive of Shakspeare, the master-thought at the bottom of Shakspeare's production, is the same as the master-thought at the bottom of the production of Homer and Sophocles, Dante and Molière, Rousseau and
20   George Sand. With all the differences of manner, power, and performance between these makers, the governing thought and motive is the same. It is the motive enunciated in the burden to the famous chorus in the "Agamemnon"—τὸ δ'εὖ νικάτω, "Let the good prevail." Until this is recognized, Shakspeare's work
25   is not understood. We connect the word morality with preachers and bores, and no one is so little of a preacher and bore as Shakspeare; but yet, to understand Shakspeare aright, the clue to seize is the morality of Shakspeare. The same with the work of the older French writers, Molière, Montaigne, Rabelais. The
30   master-pressure upon their spirit is the pressure exercised by this same thought: "Let the good prevail." And the result is that they deal with the life of all of us—the life of man in its fulness and greatness.

The motive of Balzac is curiosity. The result is that the mat-
35   ter on which he operates bounds him, and he delineates not the life of man but the life of the Frenchman, and of the Frenchman of these our times, the *homme sensuel moyen*. Balzac deals with this life, delineates it with splendid ability, loves it, and is bounded by it. He has for his public the lovers and seekers

of this life everywhere. His imitators follow eagerly in his track, are more and more subdued by the material in which they work, more and more imprisoned within the life of the average sensual man, until at last we can hardly say that the motive of their work is the sheer motive of curiosity, it has 5 become a mingled motive of curiosity, cupidity, lubricity. And these followers of Balzac, in their turn, have some of them high ability, and they are eagerly read by whosoever loves and seeks the life they believe in.

Rousseau, with all his faults, yet with the love of goodness 10 and the enthusiasm for beauty moving him, is even to-day more truly alive than Balzac, his work is more than Balzac's a real part of French literature. A hundred years hence, this will be far more apparent than it is now. And a hundred years hence George Sand, the disciple of Rousseau, with much of Rous- 15 seau's faults, but yet with Rousseau's great motive inspiring her—George Sand, to whom the French literature of to-day is backward to do honour—George Sand will have established her superiority to Balzac as incontestably as Rousseau. In that strenuous and mixed work of hers, continuing from "Indiana," 20 in 1832, to her death in 1876, we may take "Mauprat," "La Petite Fadette," "Jean de la Roche," "Valvêdre," as characteristic and representative points; and re-reading these novels, we shall feel her power. The novel is a more superficial form of literature than poetry, but on that very account more attrac- 25 tive. In the literature of our century, if the work of Goethe is the greatest and wisest influence, if the work of Words-worth is the purest and most poetic, the most varied and at-tractive influence is, perhaps, the work of George Sand. "Bien dire, c'est bien sentir," and her ample and noble style rests upon 30 large and lofty qualities. To-day, with half-hearted regard, her countrymen will unveil her statue in the little town by the meadows of the poplar-bordered Indre, the river which she has immortalized—

Still glides the stream, and shall not cease to glide— 35
while she, like so many of "the great, the mighty, and the wise," seems to have had her hour and to have passed away. But in her case we shall not err if we adopt the poet's faith,
And feel that she is greater than we know.

Hamlet Once More

At the very moment when Mr. Wilson Barrett is bringing out "Hamlet" at the Princess's, there comes into my hands "Shakspeare and Montaigne, an Endeavour to Explain the Tendency of 'Hamlet' from Allusions in Contemporary Works," by Mr.
5   Jacob Feis, an author not before known to me. Mr. Feis seeks to establish that Shakspeare in "Hamlet" identifies Montaigne's philosophy with madness, branding it as a pernicious one, as contrary to the intellectual conquests his own English nation has made when breaking with the Romanist dogma. "Shak-
10 speare," says Mr. Feis, "wished to warn his contemporaries that the attempt of reconciling two opposite circles of ideas —namely, on the one hand the doctrine that we are to be guided by the laws of nature, and on the other the yielding ourselves up to superstitious dogmas which declare human
15 nature to be sinful, must inevitably produce deeds of madness."

Mr. Feis's name has a German look, and the first instinct of the "genuine British narrowness" will be to say that here is another German critic who has discovered a mare's nest.
20 "Hamlet dies wounded and poisoned, as if Shakspeare had intended expressing his abhorrence of so vacillating a character, who places the treacherous excesses of passion above the power of that human reason in whose free service alone Greeks and Romans did their most exalted deeds of virtue." Shak-
25 speare is "the great humanist," in sympathy with the clear unwarped reason of "a living Horace or Horatio," an Horatio intrepid as the author of "Non vultus instantis tyranni." This is fantastic. Far from abhorring Hamlet, Shakspeare was prob-

ably in considerable sympathy with him; nor is he likely to have thought either that salvation for mankind was to be had from the Odes of Horace.

Mr. Feis is too entire, too absolute. Nevertheless his book is of real interest and value. He has proved the preoccupation 5 of Shakspeare's mind when he made "Hamlet" with Montaigne's "Essays." John Sterling had inferred it, but Mr. Feis has established it. He shows how passage after passage in the second quarto of "Hamlet," published in 1604, has been altered and expanded in correspondence with things in the first 10 English translation of Montaigne's "Essays," Florio's, published in 1603. The "Essays" had already passed through many editions in French, and were known to Shakspeare in that language. Their publication in English was an event in the brilliant and intellectual London world, then keenly interested in 15 the playhouses; and Shakspeare, in revising his "Hamlet" in 1604, gives proof of the actual occupation of his patrons with the Englished Montaigne, and confirms, too, the fact of his own occupation with the "Essays" previously.

For me the interest of this discovery does not lie in its show- 20 ing that Shakspeare thought Montaigne a dangerous author, and meant to give in Hamlet a shocking example of what Montaigne's teaching led to. It lies in its explaining how it comes about that "Hamlet," in spite of the prodigious mental and poetic power shown in it, is really so tantalising and 25 ineffective a play. To the common public "Hamlet" is a famous piece by a famous poet, with crime, a ghost, battle, and carnage; and that is sufficient. To the youthful enthusiast "Hamlet" is a piece handling the mystery of the universe, and having throughout cadences, phrases, and words full of the 30 divinest Shakspearian magic; and that, too, is sufficient. To the pedant, finally, "Hamlet" is an occasion for airing his psychology; and what does pedant require more? But to the spectator who loves true and powerful drama, and can judge whether he gets it or not, "Hamlet" is a piece which opens, indeed, 35 simply and admirably, and then: "The rest is puzzle!"

The reason is, apparently, that Shakspeare conceived this play with his mind running on Montaigne, and placed its ac-

tion and its hero in Montaigne's atmosphere and world. What
is that world? It is the world of man viewed as a being *ondoyant
et divers*, balancing and indeterminate, the plaything of cross
motives and shifting impulses, swayed by a thousand subtle
influences, physiological and pathological. Certainly the action
and hero of the original Hamlet story are not such as to compel the poet to place them in this world and no other, but
they admit of being placed there, Shakspeare resolved to
place them there, and they lent themselves to his resolve. The
resolve once taken to place the action in this world of problem,
the problem became brightened by all the force of Shakspeare's faculties, of Shakspeare's subtlety. "Hamlet" thus
comes at last to be not a drama followed with perfect com-
prehension and profoundest emotion, which is the ideal for
tragedy, but a problem soliciting interpretation and solution.

It will never, therefore, be a piece to be seen with pure
satisfaction by those who will not deceive themselves. But
such is its power and such is its fame that it will always continue to be acted, and we shall all of us continue to go and
see it. Mr. Wilson Barrett has put it effectively and finely on
the stage. In general the critics have marked his merits with
perfect justice. He is successful with his King and Queen. The
King in "Hamlet" is too often a blatant horror, and his Queen
is to match. Mr. Willard and Miss Leighton are a King and
Queen whom one sees and hears with pleasure. Ophelia, too—
what suffering have Ophelias caused us! And nothing can
make this part advantageous to an actress or enjoyable for the
spectator. I confess, therefore, that I trembled at each of Miss
Eastlake's entrances; but the impression finally left, by the
madness scene more especially, was one of approval and respect. Mr. Wilson Barrett himself, as Hamlet, is fresh, natural,
young, prepossessing, animated, coherent; the piece moves. All
Hamlets whom I have seen dissatisfy us in something. Macready wanted person, Charles Kean mind, Fechter English;
Mr. Wilson Barrett wants elocution. No ingenuity will ever
enable us to follow the drama in "Hamlet" as we follow the
first part of "Faust," but we may be made to feel the noble

poetry. Perhaps John Kemble, in spite of his limitations, was the best Hamlet after all. But John Kemble is beyond reach of the memory of even

AN OLD PLAYGOER

A Word More about America

When I was at Chicago last year, I was asked whether Lord
Coleridge would not write a book about America. I ventured
to answer confidently for him that he would do nothing of the
kind. Not at Chicago only, but almost wherever I went, I was
asked whether I myself did not intend to write a book about
America. For oneself one can answer yet more confidently
than for one's friends, and I always replied that most assuredly
I had no such intention. To write a book about America, on the
strength of having made merely such a tour there as mine was,
and with no fuller equipment of preparatory studies and of
local observations than I possess, would seem to me an im-
pertinence.

It is now a long while since I read M. de Tocqueville's famous work on Democracy in America. I have the highest respect for M. de Tocqueville; but my remembrance of his book
is that it deals too much in abstractions for my taste, and that it
is written, moreover, in a style which many French writers
adopt, but which I find trying—a style cut into short paragraphs and wearing an air of rigorous scientific deduction
without the reality. Very likely, however, I do M. de Tocqueville injustice. My debility in high speculation is well known,
and I mean to attempt his book on Democracy again when I
have seen America once more, and when years may have
brought to me, perhaps, more of the philosophic mind. Meanwhile, however, it will be evident how serious a matter I
think it to write a worthy book about the United States, when
I am not entirely satisfied with even M. de Tocqueville's.

But before I went to America, and when I had no expectation of ever going there, I published, under the title of "A

Word about America," not indeed a book, but a few modest remarks on what I thought civilisation in the United States might probably be like. I had before me a Boston newspaper-article which said that if I ever visited America I should find there such and such things; and taking this article for my text 5 I observed, that from all I had read and all I could judge, I should for my part expect to find there rather such and such other things, which I mentioned. I said that of aristocracy, as we know it here, I should expect to find, of course, in the United States the total absence; that our lower class I should 10 expect to find absent in a great degree, while my old familiar friend, the middle class, I should expect to find in full possession of the land. And then betaking myself to those playful phrases which a little relieve, perhaps, the tedium of grave disquisitions of this sort, I said that I imagined one would just 15 have in America our Philistines, with our aristocracy quite left out and our populace very nearly.

An acute and singularly candid American, whose name I will on no account betray to his countrymen, read these observations of mine, and he made a remark upon them to me 20 which struck me a good deal. Yes, he said, you are right, and your supposition is just. In general, what you would find over there would be the Philistines, as you call them, without your aristocracy and without your populace. Only this, too, I say at the same time: you would find over there something 25 besides, something more, something which you do not bring out, which you cannot know and bring out, perhaps, without actually visiting the United States, but which you would recognise if you saw it.

My friend was a true prophet. When I saw the United States 30 I recognised that the general account which I had hazarded of them was, indeed, not erroneous, but that it required to have something added to supplement it. I should not like either my friends in America or my countrymen here at home to think that my "Word about America" gave my full and final 35 thoughts respecting the people of the United States. The new and modifying impressions brought by experience I shall communicate, as I did my original expectations, with all good faith,

and as simply and plainly as possible. Perhaps when I have yet again visited America, have seen the great West, and have had a second reading of M. de Tocqueville's classical work on Democracy, my mind may be enlarged and my present im-
5 pressions still further modified by new ideas. If so, I promise to make my confession duly; not indeed to make it, even then, in a book about America, but to make it in a brief "Last Word" on that great subject—a word, like its predecessors, of open-hearted and free conversation with the readers of this
10 Review.

I suppose I am not by nature disposed to think so much as most people do of "institutions." The Americans think and talk very much of their "institutions"; I am by nature inclined to call all this sort of thing *machinery*, and to regard rather
15 men and their characters. But the more I saw of America, the more I found myself led to treat "institutions" with increased respect. Until I went to the United States I had never seen a people with institutions which seemed expressly and thoroughly suited to it. I had not properly appreciated the
20 benefits proceeding from this cause.

Sir Henry Maine, in an admirable essay which, though not signed, betrays him for its author by its rare and characteristic qualities of mind and style—Sir Henry Maine in the *Quarterly Review* adopts and often reiterates a phrase of M. Scherer, to
25 the effect that "Democracy is only a form of government." He holds up to ridicule a sentence of Mr. Bancroft's History, in which the American democracy is told that its ascent to power "proceeded as uniformly and majestically as the laws of being and was as certain as the decrees of eternity." Let us be
30 willing to give Sir Henry Maine his way, and to allow no magnificent claim of this kind on behalf of the American democracy. Let us treat as not more solid the assertion in the Declaration of Independence, that "all men are created equal, are endowed by their Creator with certain inalienable rights,
35 among them life, liberty, and the pursuit of happiness." Let us concede that these natural rights are a figment; that chance and circumstance, as much as deliberate foresight and design,

have brought the United States into their present condition, that moreover the British rule which they threw off was not the rule of oppressors and tyrants which declaimers suppose, and that the merit of the Americans was not that of oppressed men rising against tyrants, but rather of sensible young people 5 getting rid of stupid and overweening guardians who misunderstood and mismanaged them.

All this let us concede, if we will; but in conceding it let us not lose sight of the really important point, which is this: that their institutions do in fact suit the people of the United States 10 so well, and that from this suitableness they do derive so much actual benefit. As one watches the play of their institutions, the image suggests itself to one's mind of a man in a suit of clothes which fits him to perfection, leaving all his movements unimpeded and easy. It is loose where it ought to be loose, and it 15 sits close where its sitting close is an advantage. The central government of the United States keeps in its own hands those functions which, if the nation is to have real unity, ought to be kept there; those functions it takes to itself and no others. The State governments and the municipal governments provide 20 people with the fullest liberty of managing their own affairs, and afford, besides, a constant and invaluable school of practical experience. This wonderful suit of clothes, again (to recur to our image), is found also to adapt itself naturally to the wearer's growth, and to admit of all enlargements as they 25 successively arise. I speak of the state of things since the suppression of slavery, of the state of things which meets a spectator's eye at the present time in America. There are points in which the institutions of the United States may call forth criticism. One observer may think that it would be well if the 30 President's term of office were longer, if his ministers sate in Congress or must possess the confidence of Congress. Another observer may say that the marriage laws for the whole nation ought to be fixed by Congress, and not to vary at the will of the legislatures of the several States. I myself was much struck 35 with the inconvenience of not allowing a man to sit in Congress except for his own district; a man like Wendell Phillips was thus excluded, because Boston would not return him. It is

as if Mr. Bright could have no other constituency open to him
if Rochdale would not send him to Parliament. But all these
are really questions of *machinery* (to use my own term), and
ought not so to engage our attention as to prevent our seeing
that the capital fact as to the institutions of the United States
is this: their suitableness to the American people and their
natural and easy working. If we are not to be allowed to say,
with Mr. Beecher, that this people has "a genius for the organisation of States," then at all events we must admit that in
its own organisation it has enjoyed the most signal good fortune.

Yes; what is called, in the jargon of the publicists, the political problem and the social problem, the people of the United
States does appear to me to have solved, or Fortune has solved
it for them, with undeniable success. Against invasion and
conquest from without they are impregnably strong. As to
domestic concerns, the first thing to remember is, that the
people over there is at bottom the same people as ourselves, a
people with a strong sense for conduct. But there is said to be
great corruption among their politicians and in the public
service, in municipal administration, and in the administration
of justice. Sir Lepel Griffin would lead us to think that the administration of justice, in particular, is so thoroughly corrupt,
that a man with a lawsuit has only to provide his lawyer with
the necessary funds for bribing the officials, and he can make
sure of winning his suit. The Americans themselves use such
strong language in describing the corruption prevalent amongst
them that they cannot be surprised if strangers believe them.
For myself, I had heard and read so much to the discredit of
American political life, how all the best men kept aloof from
it, and those who gave themselves to it were unworthy, that I
ended by supposing that the thing must actually be so, and the
good Americans must be looked for elsewhere than in politics.
Then I had the pleasure of dining with Mr. Bancroft in Washington; and however he may, in Sir Henry Maine's opinion,
overlaud the pre-established harmony of American democracy,
he had at any rate invited to meet me half a dozen politicians
whom in England we should pronounce to be members of
Parliament of the highest class, in bearing, manners, tone of feel-

ing, intelligence, information. I discovered that in truth the practice, so common in America, of calling a politician "a thief,"
does not mean so very much more than is meant in England
when we have heard Lord Beaconsfield called "a liar" and Mr.
Gladstone "a madman." It means, that the speaker disagrees with   5
the politician in question and dislikes him. Not that I assent, on
the other hand, to the thick-and-thin American patriots, who
will tell you that there is no more corruption in the politics
and administration of the United States than in those of
England. I believe there *is* more, and that the tone of both is   10
lower there; and this from a cause on which I shall have to
touch hereafter. But the corruption is exaggerated; it is not the
wide and deep disease it is often represented; it is such that
the good elements in the nation may, and I believe will,
perfectly work it off; and even now the truth of what I   15
have been saying as to the suitableness and successful working of American institutions is not really in the least affected
by it.

Furthermore, American society is not in danger from revolution. Here, again, I do not mean that the United States are   20
exempt from the operation of every one of the causes—such
a cause as the division between rich and poor, for instance—
which may lead to revolution. But I mean that comparatively
with the old countries of Europe they are free from the danger of revolution; and I believe that the good elements in them   25
will make a way for them to escape out of what they really
have of this danger also, to escape in the future as well as now
—the future for which some observers announce this danger
as so certain and so formidable. Lord Macaulay predicted that
the United States must come in time to just the same state of   30
things which we witness in England; that the cities would fill
up and the lands become occupied, and then, he said, the
division between rich and poor would establish itself on the
same scale as with us, and be just as embarrassing. He forgot
that the United States are without what certainly fixes and   35
accentuates the division between rich and poor—the distinction
of classes. Not only have they not the distinction between
noble and bourgeois, between aristocracy and middle class;
they have not even the distinction between bourgeois and

peasant or artisan, between middle and lower class. They have
nothing to create it and compel their recognition of it. Their
domestic service is done for them by Irish, Germans, Swedes,
negroes. Outside domestic service, within the range of conditions which an American may in fact be called upon to
traverse, he passes easily from one sort of occupation to another, from poverty to riches, and from riches to poverty.
No one of his possible occupations appears degrading to him
or makes him lose caste; and poverty itself appears to him as
inconvenient and disagreeable rather than as humiliating. When
the immigrant from Europe strikes root in his new home, he
becomes as the American.

It may be said that the Americans, when they attained their
independence, had not the elements for a division into classes,
and that they deserve no praise for not having invented one.
But I am not now contending that they deserve praise for their
institutions, I am saying how well their institutions work. Considering, indeed, how rife are distinctions of rank and class in
the world, how prone men in general are to adopt them, how
much the Americans themselves, beyond doubt, are capable of
feeling their attraction, it shows, I think, at least strong good
sense in the Americans to have forborne from all attempt to
invent them at the outset, and to have escaped or resisted
any fancy for inventing them since. But evidently the United
States constituted themselves, not amid the circumstances of a
feudal age, but in a modern age; not under the conditions of an
epoch favourable to subordination, but under those of an
epoch of expansion. Their institutions did but comply with
the form and pressure of the circumstances and conditions
then present. A feudal age, an epoch of war, defence, and
concentration, needs centres of power and property, and it re-
inforces property by joining distinctions of rank and class with
it. Property becomes more honourable, more solid. And in
feudal ages this is well, for its changing hands easily would
be a source of weakness. But in ages of expansion, where men
are bent that every one shall have his chance, the more readily
property changes hands the better. The envy with which its
holder is regarded diminishes, society is safer. I think whatever

may be said of the worship of the almighty dollar in America, it is indubitable that rich men are regarded there with less envy and hatred than rich men are in Europe. Why is this? Because their condition is less fixed, because government and legislation do not take them more seriously than other people, make 5 grandees of them, aid them to found families and endure. With us, the chief holders of property are grandees already, and every rich man aspires to become a grandee if possible. And therefore an English country-gentleman regards himself as part of the system of nature; government and legislation have 10 invited him so to do. If the price of wheat falls so low that his means of expenditure are greatly reduced, he tells you that if this lasts he cannot possibly go on as a country-gentleman; and every well-bred person amongst us looks sympathising and shocked. An American would say: "Why should he?" The 15 Conservative newspapers are fond of giving us, as an argument for the game-laws, the plea that without them a country-gentleman could not be induced to live on his estate. An American would say: "What does it matter?" Perhaps to an English ear this will sound brutal; but the point is that the 20 American does not take his rich man so seriously as we do ours, does not make him into a grandee; the thing, if proposed to him, would strike him as an absurdity. I suspect that Mr. Winans himself, the American millionaire who adds deer-forest to deer-forest, and will not suffer a cottier to keep a 25 pet lamb, regards his own performance as a colossal stroke of American humour, illustrating the absurdities of the British system of property and privilege. Ask Mr. Winans if he would promote the introduction of the British game-laws into the United States, and he would tell you with a merry laugh 30 that the idea is ridiculous, and that these British follies are for home consumption.

The example of France must not mislead us. There the institutions, an objector may say, are republican, and yet the division and hatred between rich and poor is intense. True; 35 but in France, though the institutions may be republican, the ideas and morals are not republican. In America not only are the institutions republican, but the ideas and morals are prevail-

ingly republican also. They are those of a plain, decent middle
class. The ideal of those who are the public instructors of the
people is the ideal of such a class. In France the ideal of the
mass of popular journalists and popular writers of fiction, who
5   are now practically the public instructors there, is, if you
could see their hearts, a Pompadour or du Barry/*régime*, with
themselves for the part of Faublas. With this ideal prevailing,
this vision of the objects for which wealth is desirable, the
possessors of wealth become hateful to the multitude which
10 toils and endures, and society is undermined. This is one of the
many inconveniences which the French have to suffer from
that worship of the great goddess Lubricity to which they are
at present vowed. Wealth excites the most savage enmity there,
because it is conceived as a means for gratifying appetites of the
15 most selfish and vile kind. But in America Faublas is no more
the ideal than Coriolanus. Wealth is no more conceived as the
minister to the pleasures of a class of rakes, than as the minister
to the magnificence of a class of nobles. It is conceived as a thing
which almost any American may attain, and which almost
20 every American will use respectably. Its possession, therefore,
does not inspire hatred, and so I return to the thesis with which
I started—America is not in danger of revolution. The division
between rich and poor is alleged to us as a cause of revolution
which presently, if not now, must operate there, as elsewhere;
25 and yet we see that this cause has not there, in truth, the characters to which we are elsewhere accustomed.

A people homogeneous, a people which had to constitute
itself in a modern age, an epoch of expansion, and which has
given to itself institutions entirely fitted for such an age and
30 epoch, and which suit it perfectly—a people not in danger of
war from without, not in danger of revolution from within—
such is the people of the United States. The political and social
problem, then, we must surely allow that they solve successfully. There remains, I know, the human problem also; the
35 solution of that too has to be considered; but I shall come to
that hereafter. My point at present is, that politically and so-
cially the United States are a community living in a natural
condition, and conscious of living in a natural condition. And

being in this healthy case, and having this healthy conscious-
ness, the community there uses its understanding with the
soundness of health; it in general sees its political and social
concerns straight, and sees them clear. So that when Sir Henry
Maine and M. Scherer tell us that democracy is "merely a form   5
of government," we may observe to them that it is in the
United States a form of government in which the community
feels itself in a natural condition and at ease; in which, consequently, it sees things straight and sees them clear.

More than half one's interest in watching the English people   10
of the United States comes, of course, from the bearing of
what one finds there upon things at home, amongst us English
people ourselves in these islands. I have frankly recorded what
struck me and came as most new to me in the condition of the
English race in the United States. I had said beforehand, in-   15
deed, that I supposed the American Philistine was a livelier
sort of Philistine than ours, because he had not that pressure
of the Barbarians to stunt and distort him which befalls his
English brother here. But I did not foresee how far his superior liveliness and naturalness of condition, in the absence of   20
that pressure, would carry the American Philistine. I still use
my old name *Philistine*, because it does in fact seem to me as
yet to suit the bulk of the community over there, as it suits
the strong central body of the community here. But in my
mouth the name is hardly a reproach, so clearly do I see the   25
Philistine's necessity, so willingly I own his merits, so much I
find of him in myself. The American Philistine, however, is
certainly far more different from his English brother than I
had beforehand supposed. And on that difference we English
of the old country may with great profit turn our regards for   30
awhile, and I am now going to speak of it.

Surely if there is one thing more than another which all the
world is saying of our community at present, and of which the
truth cannot well be disputed, it is this: that we act like people
who do not think straight and see clear. I know that the   35
Liberal newspapers used to be fond of saying that what charac-
terised our middle class was its "clear, manly intelligence,
penetrating through sophisms, ignoring commonplaces, and

giving to conventional illusions their true value." Many years
ago I took alarm at seeing the *Daily News* and the *Morning
Star*, like Zedekiah the son of Chenaanah, thus making horns of
iron for the middle class and bidding it "Go up and prosper!"
and my first efforts as a writer on public matters were
prompted by a desire to utter, like Micaiah the son of Imlah,
my protest against these misleading assurances of the false
prophets. And though often and often smitten on the cheek,
just as Micaiah was, still I persevered; and at the Royal Institution I said how we seemed to flounder and to beat the air, and
at Liverpool I singled out as our chief want the want of lucidity. But now everybody is really saying of us the same
thing: that we fumble because we cannot make up our mind,
and that we cannot make up our mind because we do not
know what to be after. If our foreign policy is not that of "the
British Philistine, with his likes and dislikes, his effusion and
confusion, his hot and cold fits, his want of dignity and of the
steadfastness which comes from dignity, his want of ideas and
of the steadfastness which comes from ideas," then all the
world at the present time is, it must be owned, very much
mistaken.

Let us not, therefore, speak of foreign affairs; it is needless,
because the thing I wish to show is so manifest there to everybody. But we will consider matters at home. Let us take the
present state of the House of Commons. Can anything be more
confused, more unnatural? That assembly has got into a condition utterly embarrassed, and seems impotent to bring itself
right. The members of the House themselves may find entertainment in the personal incidents which such a state of confusion is sure to bring forth abundantly, and excitement in the
opportunities thus often afforded for the display of Mr. Gladstone's wonderful powers. But to any judicious Englishman
outside the House the spectacle is simply an afflicting and
humiliating one; the sense aroused by it is not a sense of delight
at Mr. Gladstone's tireless powers, it is rather a sense of disgust
at their having to be so exercised. Every day the House of
Commons does not sit judicious people feel relief, every day
that it sits they are oppressed with apprehension. Instead of

being an edifying influence, as such an assembly ought to be, the House of Commons is at present an influence which does harm; it sets an example which rebukes and corrects none of the nation's faults, but rather encourages them. The best thing to be done at present, perhaps, is to avert one's eyes from the House of Commons as much as possible; if one keeps on constantly watching it welter in its baneful confusion, one is likely to fall into the fulminating style of the wrathful Hebrew prophets, and to all it "an astonishment, a hissing, and a curse."

Well, then, our greatest institution, the House of Commons, we cannot say is at present working, like the American institutions, easily and successfully. Suppose we now pass to Ireland. I will not ask if our institutions work easily and successfully in Ireland; to ask such a question would be too bitter, too cruel a mockery. Those hateful cases which have been tried in the Dublin Courts this last year suggest the dark and ill-omened word which applies to the whole state of Ireland—*anti-natural*. *Anti-natural, anti-nature*—that is the word which rises irresistibly in my mind as I survey Ireland. Everything is unnatural there—the proceedings of the English who rule, the proceedings of the Irish who resist. But it is with the working of our English institutions there that I am now concerned. It is unnatural that Ireland should be governed by Lord Spencer and Mr. Campbell Bannerman—as unnatural as for Scotland to be governed by Lord Cranbrook and Mr. Healy. It is unnatural that Ireland should be governed under a Crimes Act. But there is necessity, replies the Government. Well, then, if there is such evil necessity, it is unnatural that the Irish newspapers should be free to write as they write and the Irish members to speak as they speak—free to inflame and further exasperate a seditious people's minds, and to promote the continuance of the evil necessity. A necessity for the Crimes Act is a necessity for absolute government. By our patchwork proceedings we set up, indeed, a make-believe of Ireland's being constitutionally governed. But it is not constitutionally governed; nobody supposes it to be constitutionally governed, except, perhaps, that born swallower of all clap-trap, the British Philistine. The Irish themselves, the all-important personages in this case, are not taken in; our make-believe does not produce in them the very least gratitude, the very least softening. At the same time it adds an hundred fold to the difficulties of an absolute government.

5   The working of our institutions being thus awry, is the working of our thoughts upon them more smooth and natural? I imagine to myself an American, his own institutions and his habits of thought being such as we have seen, listening to us as we talk politics and discuss the strained state of things over

10 here. "Certainly these men have considerable difficulties," he would say; "but they never look at them straight, they do not think straight." Who does not admire the fine qualities of Lord Spencer?—and I, for my part, am quite ready to admit that he may require for a given period not only the present Crimes

15 Act, but even yet more stringent powers of repression. *For a given period*, yes!—but afterwards? Has Lord Spencer any clear vision of the great, the profound changes still to be wrought before a stable and prosperous society can arise in Ireland? Has he even any ideal for the future there, beyond

20 that of a time when he can go to visit Lord Kenmare, or any other great landlord who is his friend, and find all the tenants punctually paying their rents, prosperous and deferential, and society in Ireland settling quietly down again upon the old basis? And he might as well hope to see Strongbow come to

25 life again! Which of us does not esteem and like Mr. Trevelyan, and rejoice in the high promise of his career? And how all his friends applauded when he turned upon the exasperating and insulting Irish members, and told them that he was "an English gentleman"! Yet, if one thinks of it, Mr. Trevelyan

30 was thus telling the Irish members simply that he was just that which Ireland does not want, and which can do her no good. England, to be sure, has given Ireland plenty of her worst, but she has also given her not scantily of her best. Ireland has had no insufficient supply of the English gentle-

35 man, with his honesty, personal courage, high bearing, good intentions, and limited vision; what she wants is statesmen with just the qualities which the typical English gentleman has

not—flexibility, openness of mind, a free and large view of things.

Everywhere we shall find in our thinking a sort of warp inclining it aside of the real mark, and thus depriving it of value. The common run of peers who write to the *Times* about reform of the House of Lords one would not much expect, perhaps, to "understand the signs of this time." But even the Duke of Argyll, delivering his mind about the land-question in Scotland, is like one seeing, thinking, and speaking in some other planet than ours. A man of even Mr. John Morley's gifts is provoked with the House of Lords, and straightway he declares himself against the existence of a Second Chamber at all; although—if there be such a thing as demonstration in politics—the working of the American Senate demonstrates a well-composed Second Chamber to be the very need and safe-guard of a modern democracy. What a singular twist, again, in a man of Mr. Frederic Harrison's intellectual power, not, perhaps, to have in the exuberance of youthful energy weighted himself for the race of life by taking up a grotesque old French pedant upon his shoulders, but to have insisted, in middle age, in taking up the Protestant Dissenters too; and now, when he is becoming elderly, it seems as if nothing would serve him but he must add the Peace Society to his load! How perverse, yet again, in Mr. Herbert Spencer, at the very mo-ment when past neglects and present needs are driving men to co-operation, to making the community act for the public good in its collective and corporate character of *the State*, how perverse to seize this occasion for promulgating the ex-tremest doctrine of individualism; and not only to drag this dead horse along the public road himself, but to induce Mr. Auberon Herbert to devote his days to flogging it!

We think thus unaccountably because we are living in an unnatural and strained state. We are like people whose vision is deranged by their looking through a turbid and distorting atmosphere, or whose movements are warped by the cramping of some unnatural constraint. Let us just ask ourselves, looking at the thing as people simply desirous of finding the truth, how

men who saw and thought straight would proceed, how an
American, for instance—whose seeing and thinking has, I have
said, if not in all matters, yet commonly in political and social
concerns, this quality of straightness—how an American
5   would proceed in the three confusions which I have given as
instances of the many confusions now embarrassing us: the
confusion of our foreign affairs, the confusion of the House
of Commons, the confusion of Ireland. And then, when we
have discovered the kind of proceeding natural in these cases,
10   let us ask ourselves, with the same sincerity, what is the cause
of that warp of mind hindering most of us from seeing straight
in them, and also where is our remedy.

The Angra Pequeña business has lately called forth from all
sides many and harsh animadversions upon Lord Granville,
15   who is charged with the direction of our foreign affairs. I
shall not swell the chorus of complainers. Nothing has happened but what was to be expected. Long ago I remarked that
it is not Lord Granville himself who determines our foreign
policy and shapes the declarations of Government concerning
20   it, but a power behind Lord Granville. He and his colleagues
would call it the power of public opinion. It is really the
opinion of that great ruling class amongst us on which Liberal
Governments have hitherto had to depend for support—the
Philistines or middle class. It is not, I repeat, with Lord
25   Granville in his natural state and force that a foreign Government has to deal; it is with Lord Granville waiting in devout
expectation to see how the cat will jump—and that cat the
British Philistine! When Prince Bismarck deals with Lord
Granville, he finds that he is not dealing mind to mind with
30   an intelligent equal, but that he is dealing with a tumult of
likes and dislikes, hopes and fears, stock-jobbing intrigues,
missionary interests, quidnuncs, newspapers—dealing, in short,
with *ignorance* behind his intelligent equal. Yet ignorant as
our Philistine middle class may be, its volitions on foreign
35   affairs would have more intelligibility and consistency if
uttered through a spokesman of their own class. Coming
through a nobleman like Lord Granville, who has neither the
thoughts, habits, nor ideals of the middle class, and yet wishes

to act as proctor for it, they have every disadvantage. He
cannot even do justice to the Philistine mind, such as it is, for
which he is spokesman; he apprehends it uncertainly and expounds it ineffectively. And so with the house and lineage of
Murdstone thundering at him (and these, again, through Lord   5
Derby as their interpreter) from the Cape, and the inexorable
Prince Bismarck thundering at him from Berlin, the thing
naturally ends by Lord Granville at last wringing his adroit
hands and ejaculating disconsolately: "It is a misunderstanding
altogether!" Even yet more to be pitied, perhaps, was the hard   10
case of Lord Kimberley after the Majuba Hill disaster. Who
can ever forget him, poor man, studying the faces of the
representatives of the dissenting interest and exclaiming: "A
sudden thought strikes me! May we not be incurring the sin of
blood-guiltiness?" To this has come the tradition of Lord   15
Somers, the Whig oligarchy of 1688, and all Lord Macaulay's
Pantheon.

I said that a source of strength to America, in political and
social concerns, was the homogeneous character of American
society. An American statesman speaks with more effect the   20
mind of his fellow-citizens from his being in sympathy with it,
understanding and sharing it. Certainly one must admit that if,
in our country of classes, the Philistine middle class is really
the inspirer of our foreign policy, that policy would at least
be expounded more forcibly if it had a Philistine for its spokes- 25
man. Yet I think the true moral to be drawn is rather, perhaps,
this: that our foreign policy would be improved if our whole
society were homogeneous.

As to the confusion in the House of Commons, what, apart
from defective rules of procedure, are its causes? First and   30
foremost, no doubt, the temper and action of the Irish members. But putting this cause of confusion out of view for a
moment, every one can see that the House of Commons is far
too large, and that it undertakes a quantity of business which
belongs more properly to local assemblies. The confusion from   35
these causes is one which is constantly increasing, because, as
the country becomes fuller and more awakened, business
multiplies, and more and more members of the House are in-

clined to take part in it. Is not the cure for this found in a
course like that followed in America, in having a much less
numerous House of Commons, and in making over a large
part of its business to local assemblies, elected, as the House
5   of Commons itself will henceforth be elected, by household
suffrage? I have often said that we seem to me to need at
present, in England, three things in especial: more equality,
education for the middle classes, and a thorough municipal
system. A system of local assemblies is but the natural com-
10   plement of a thorough municipal system. Wholes neither too
large nor too small, not necessarily of equal population by any
means, but with characters rendering them in themselves fairly
homogeneous and coherent, are the fit units for choosing these
local assemblies. Such units occur immediately to one's mind in
15   the provinces of Ireland, the Highlands and Lowlands of
Scotland, Wales north and south, groups of English counties
such as present themselves in the circuits of the judges or
under the names of East Anglia or the Midlands. No one will
suppose me guilty of the pedantry of here laying out definitive
20   districts; I do but indicate such units as may enable the reader
to conceive the kind of basis required for the local assemblies
of which I am speaking. The business of these districts would
be more advantageously done in assemblies of the kind; they
would form a useful school for the increasing number of aspi-
25   rants to public life, and the House of Commons would be
relieved.

The strain in Ireland would be relieved too, and by natural
and safe means. Irishmen are to be found, who, in desperation
at the present state of their country, cry out for making Ire-
30   land independent and separate, with a national Parliament in
Dublin, with her own foreign office and diplomacy, her own
army and navy, her own tariff, coinage and currency. This is
manifestly impracticable. But here again let us look at what is
done by people who in politics think straight and see clear;
35   let us observe what is done in the United States. The Government at Washington reserves matters of imperial concern, matters such as those just enumerated, which cannot be relinquished without relinquishing the unity of the empire. Neither

does it allow one great South to be constituted, or one great West, with a Southern Parliament, or a Western. Provinces that are too large are broken up, as Virginia has been broken up. But the several States are nevertheless real and important wholes, each with its own legislature; and to each the control, 5 within its own borders, of all except imperial concerns is freely committed. The United States Government intervenes only to keep order in the last resort. Let us suppose a similar plan applied in Ireland. There are four provinces there, forming four natural wholes—or perhaps (if it should seem expedient 10 to put Munster and Connaught together) three. The Parliament of the empire would still be in London, and Ireland would send members to it. But at the same time each Irish province would have its own legislature, and the control of its own real affairs. The British landlord would no longer 15 determine the dealings with land in an Irish province, nor the British Protestant the dealings with church and education. Apart from imperial concerns, or from disorder such as to render military intervention necessary, the government in London would leave Ireland to manage itself. Lord Spencer and 20 Mr. Campbell Bannerman would come back to England. Dublin Castle would be the State-House of Leinster. Land-questions, game-laws, police, church, education, would be regulated by the people and legislature of Leinster for Leinster, of Ulster for Ulster, of Munster and Connaught for Munster and Con- 25 naught. The same with the like matters in England and Scotland. The local legislatures would regulate them.

But there is more. Everybody who watches the working of our institutions perceives what strain and friction is caused in it at present, by our having a Second Chamber composed al- 30 most entirely of great landowners, and representing the feelings and interests of the class of landowners almost exclusively. No one, certainly, under the conditions of a modern age and our actual life, would ever think of devising such a Chamber. But we will allow ourselves to do more than merely state this 35 truism, we will allow ourselves to ask what sort of Second Chamber people who thought straight and saw clear would, under the conditions of a modern age and of our actual life,

naturally make. And we find, from the experience of the
United States, that such provincial legislatures as we have just
now seen to be the natural remedy for the confusion in the
House of Commons, the natural remedy for the confusion in
5   Ireland, have the further great merit besides of giving us the
best basis possible for a modern Second Chamber. The United
States Senate is perhaps, of all the institutions of that country,
the most happily devised, the most successful in its working.
The legislature of each State of the Union elects two senators
10 to the Second Chamber of the national Congress at Washington. The senators are the Lords—if we like to keep, as it is
surely best to keep, for designating the members of the
Second Chamber, the title to which we have been for so many
ages habituated. Each of the provincial legislatures of Great
15 Britain and Ireland would elect members to the House of
Lords. The colonial legislatures also would elect members to
it; and thus we should be complying in the most simple and yet
the most signal way possible with the present desire of both
this country and the colonies for a closer union together, for
20 some representation of the colonies in the Imperial Parliament.
Probably it would be found expedient to transfer to the Second
Chamber the representatives of the Universities. But no scheme
for a Second Chamber will at the present day be found solid
unless it stands on a genuine basis of election and representa-
25 tion. All schemes for forming a Second Chamber through
nomination, whether by the Crown or by any other voice, of
picked noblemen, great officials, leading merchants and bankers,
eminent men of letters and science, are fantastic. Probably they
would not give us by any means a good Second Chamber. But
30 certainly they would not satisfy the country or possess its
confidence, and therefore they would be found futile and
unworkable.
    So we discover what would naturally appear the desirable
way out of some of our worst confusions to anybody who
35 saw clear and thought straight. But there is little likelihood,
probably, of any such way being soon perceived and followed
by our community here. And why is this? Because, as a community, we have so little lucidity, we so little see clear and

think straight. And why, again, is this? Because our community is so little homogeneous. The lower class has yet to show what it will do in politics. Rising politicians are already beginning to flatter it with servile assiduity, but their praise is as yet premature, the lower class is too little known. The upper class and the middle class we know. They have each their own supposed interests, and these are very different from the true interests of the community. Our very classes make us dim-seeing. In a modern time, we are living with a system of classes so intense, a society of such unnatural complication, that the whole action of our minds is hampered and falsened by it. I return to my old thesis: inequality is our bane. The great impediments in our way of progress are aristocracy and Protestant dissent. People think this is an epigram; alas, it is much rather a truism!

An aristocratical society like ours is often said to be the society from which artists and men of letters have most to gain. But an institution is to be judged, not by what one can oneself gain from it, but by the ideal which it sets up. And aristocracy —if I may once more repeat words which, however often repeated, have still a value from their truth—aristocracy now sets up in our country a false ideal, which materialises our upper class, vulgarises our middle class, brutalises our lower class. It misleads the young, makes the worldly more worldly, the limited more limited, the stationary more stationary. Even to the imaginative, whom Lord John Manners thinks its sure friend, it is more a hindrance than a help. Johnson says well: "Whatever makes the past, the distant, or the future, predominate over the present, advances us in the dignity of thinking beings." But what is a Duke of Norfolk or an Earl [of] Warwick, dressed in broadcloth and tweed, and going about his business or pleasure in hansom cabs and railways like the rest of us? Imagination herself would entreat him to take himself out of the way, and to leave us to the Norfolks and Warwicks of history.

I say this without a particle of hatred, and with esteem, admiration, and affection for many individuals in the aristocratical class. But the action of time and circumstance is fatal.

If one asks oneself what is really to be desired, [not] what is expedient, one would go far beyond the substitution of an elected Second Chamber for the present House of Lords. All confiscation is to be reprobated, all deprivation (except in bad cases

5   of abuse) of what is actually possessed. But one would wish, if one set about wishing, for the extinction of title after the death of the holder, and for the dispersion of property by a stringent law of bequest. Our society should be homogeneous, and only in this way can it become so.

10   But aristocracy is in little danger. "I suppose, sir," a dissenting minister said to me the other day, "you found, when you were in America, that they envied us there our great aristocracy." It was his sincere belief that they did, and such probably is the sincere belief of our middle class in general; or at any

15 rate, that if the Americans do not envy us this possession, they ought to. And my friend, one of the great Liberal party which has now, I suppose, pretty nearly run down its deceased wife's sister, poor thing, has his hand and heart full, so far as politics are concerned, of the question of church disestablishment. He

20 is eager to set to work at a change which, even if it were desirable (and I think it is not), is yet off the line of those reforms which are really pressing.

     Mr. Lyulph Stanley, Professor Stuart, and Lord Richard Grosvenor are waiting ready to help him, and perhaps Mr.

25 Chamberlain himself will lead the attack. I admire Mr. Chamberlain as a politician because he has the courage—and it is a wise courage—to state large the reforms we need, instead of minimising them. But like Saul before his conversion, he breathes out threatenings and slaughter against the Church,

30 and is likely, perhaps, to lead an assault upon her. He is a formidable assailant, yet I suspect he might break his fingernails on her walls. If the Church has the majority for her, she will of course stand. But in any case this institution, with all its faults, has that merit which makes the great strength of

35 institutions—it offers an ideal which is noble and attaching. Equality is its profession, if not always its practice. It inspires wide and deep affection, and possesses, therefore, immense strength. Probably the Establishment will not stand in Wales,

probably it will not stand in Scotland. In Wales it ought not, I think, to stand. In Scotland I should regret its fall; but Presbyterian churches are born to separatism, as the sparks fly upward. At any rate, it is through the vote of local legislatures that disestablishment is likely to come, as a measure required in certain provinces, and not as a general measure for the whole country. In other words, the endeavour for disestablishment ought to be postponed to the endeavour for far more important reforms, not to precede it. Yet I doubt whether Mr. Chamberlain and Mr. Lyulph Stanley will listen to me when I plead thus with them; there is so little lucidity in England, and they will say I am priest-ridden.

One man there is, whom above all others I would fain have seen in Parliament during the last ten years, and beheld established in influence there at this juncture—Mr. Goldwin Smith. I do not say that he was not too embittered against the Church; in my opinion he was. But with singular lucidity and penetration he saw what great reforms were needed in other directions, and the order of relative importance in which reforms stood. Such were his character, style, and faculties, that alone perhaps among men of his insight he was capable of getting his ideas weighed and entertained by men in power; while amid all favour and under all temptations he was certain to have still remained true to his insight, "unshaken, unseduced, unterrified." I think of him as a real power for good in Parliament at this time, had he by now become, as he might have become, one of the leaders there. His absence from the scene, his retirement in Canada, is a loss to his friends, but a still greater loss to his country.

Hardly inferior in influence to Parliament itself is journalism. I do not conceive of Mr. John Morley as made for filling that position in Parliament which Mr. Goldwin Smith would, I think, have filled. If he controls, as Protesilaos in the poem advises, hysterical passion (the besetting danger of men of letters on the platform and in Parliament) and remembers to approve "the depth and not the tumult of the soul," he will be powerful in Parliament; he will rise, he will come into office; but he will not do for us in Parliament, I think, what Mr.

Goldwin Smith would have done. He is too much of a partisan. In journalism, on the other hand, he was as unique a
figure as Mr. Goldwin Smith would, I imagine, have been in
Parliament. As a journalist, Mr. John Morley showed a mind
5   which seized and understood the signs of the times; he had
all the ideas of a man of the best insight, and alone, perhaps,
among men of his insight, he had the skill for making these
ideas pass into journalism. But Mr. John Morley has now left
journalism. There is plenty of talent in Parliament, plenty of
10 talent in journalism, but no one in either to expound "the
signs of this time" as these two men might have expounded
them. The signs of the time, political and social, are left, I
regret to say, to bring themselves as they best can to the notice
of the public. Yet how ineffective an organ is literature for
15 conveying them compared with Parliament and journalism!
    Conveyed somehow, however, they certainly should be, and
in this disquisition I have tried to deal with them. But the
political and social problem, as the thinkers call it, must not so
occupy us as to make us forget the human problem. The
20 problems are connected together, but they are not identical.
Our political and social confusions I admit; what Parliament is
at this moment, I see and deplore. Yet nowhere but in England
even now, not in France, not in Germany, not in America,
could there be found public men of that quality—so capable
25 of fair dealing, of trusting one another, keeping their word to
one another—as to make possible such a settlement of the
Franchise and Seats Bills as that which we have lately seen.
Plato says with most profound truth: "The man who would
think to good purpose must be able to take many things into
30 his view together." How homogeneous American society is,
I have done my best to declare; how smoothly and naturally
the institutions of the United States work, how clearly, in
some most important respects, the Americans see, how straight
they think. Yet Sir Lepel Griffin says that there is no country
35 calling itself civilised where one would not rather live than in
America, except Russia. In politics I do not much trust Sir
Lepel Griffin. I hope that he administers in India some district
where a profound insight into the being and working of insti-

tutions is not requisite. But, I suppose, of the tastes of himself and of that large class of Englishmen whom Mr. Charles Sumner has taught us to call the class of gentlemen, he is no untrustworthy reporter. And an Englishman of this class would rather live in France, Spain, Holland, Belgium, Germany, Italy, Switzerland, than in the United States, in spite of our community of race and speech with them! This means that, in the opinion of men of that class, the human problem at least is not well solved in the United States, whatever the political and social problem may be. And to the human problem in the United States we ought certainly to turn our attention, especially when we find taken such an objection as this; and some day, though not now, we will do so, and try to see what the objection comes to. I have given hostages to the United States, I am bound to them by the memory of great, untiring, and most attaching kindness. I should not like to have to own them to be of all countries calling themselves civilised, except Russia, the country where one would least like to live.

A Comment on Christmas

Bishop Wilson is full of excellent things, and one of his apophthegms came into my mind the other day as I read an angry and unreasonable expostulation addressed to myself. Bishop Wilson's apophthegm is this: *Truth provokes those*
5 *whom it does not convert.* "Miracles," I was angrily reproached for saying, "do not happen, and more and more of us are becoming convinced that they do not happen; nevertheless, what is really best and most valuable in the Bible is independent of miracles, and for the sake of this, I constantly read the
10 Bible myself, and I advise others to read it also." One would have thought that at a time when the French newspapers are attributing all our failures and misfortunes to our habit of reading the Bible, and when our own Lieutenant-Governor of Bengal is protesting that the golden rule is a delusion and a
15 snare for practical men, the friends of the old religion of Christendom would have had a kindly feeling towards anyone,—whether he admitted miracles or not,—who maintained that the root of the matter for all of us was in the Bible, and that to the use of the Bible we should still cling. But no;
20 *Truth provokes those whom it does not convert.* So angry are some good people at being told that miracles do not happen, that if we say this, they cannot bear to have us using the Bible at all, or recommending the Bible. Either take it and recommend it with its miracles, they say, or else leave it alone,
25 and let its enemies find confronting them none but orthodox defenders of it like ourselves.

The success of these orthodox champions is not at all commensurate with their zeal; and so, in spite of rebuke, I find myself, as a lover of the Bible, perpetually tempted to substi-

tute for their line of defence a different method, however it
may provoke them. Christmas comes round again, and brings
the most beautiful and beloved festival of the Christian year.
What is Christmas, and what does it say to us? Our French
friends will reply that Christmas is an exploded legend, and 5
says to us nothing at all. The *Guardian*, on the other hand, lays
it down that Christmas commemorates the miracle of the Incarnation and that the truth of this miracle is the fundamental
truth for Christians. Which is right, the *Guardian* or our
French friends? Or are neither the one nor the other of them 10
right, and is the truth about Christmas something quite different from what either of them imagine? The enquiry is
profitable; and I kept Christmas, this last winter, by following
it.

Who can ever lose out of his memory the roll and march of 15
those magnificent words of prophecy, which, ever since we
can remember, we have heard read in church on Christmas-
day, and have been taught to regard as the grand and wonderful prediction of "the miracle of the Incarnation?" "The Lord
himself shall give you a sign: Behold, a virgin shall conceive, 20
and bear a son, and shall call his name Immanuel. Butter and
honey shall he eat, until he shall know to refuse the evil and
choose the good. For before the child shall know to refuse the
evil and choose the good, the land that thou abhorrest shall be
forsaken of both her kings." We all know the orthodox inter- 25
pretation. Immanuel is Jesus Christ, to be born of the Virgin
Mary; the meaning of the name Immanuel, *God with us*, signi-
fies the union of the divine nature and ours in Christ, God and
man in one Person. "Butter and honey shall he eat,"—the
Christ shall be very man, he shall have a true human body, he 30
shall be sustained, while he is growing up, with that ordinary
nourishment wherewith human children are wont to be fed.
And the sign that the promised birth of Immanuel, God and
man in one Person, from the womb of a virgin, shall really
happen, is this: the two kings of Syria and Israel who are now, 35
in the eighth century before Christ, threatening the kingdom
of Judah, shall be overthrown, and their country devastated.

"*For* before the child shall know,"—before this promised coming of Jesus Christ, and as a sign to guarantee it, the kings of Syria and Israel shall be conquered and overthrown. And conquered and overthrown they presently were.

5 But then comes the turn of criticism. The study of history, and of all documents on which history is based, is diligently prosecuted; a number of learned, patient, impartial investigators read and examine the prophets. It becomes apparent what the prophets really mean to say. It becomes certain that in the

10 famous words read on Christmas-day the prophet Isaiah was not meaning to speak of Jesus Christ to be born more than seven centuries later. It becomes certain that his Immanuel is a prince of Judah to be born in a year or two's time. It becomes certain that there is no question at all of a child miraculously con-

15 ceived and born of a virgin. What the prophet declares is that a young woman, a damsel, at that moment unmarried, shall have time, before certain things happen, to be married and to bear a son, who shall be called Immanuel. There is no question in the name *Immanuel* of a union of the human and divine na-

20 tures, of God and man in one Person. "God present with his people and protecting them" is what the prophet means the name to signify. In "Butter and honey shall he eat," there is no question of the Christ's being very man, with a true human body. What the prophet intends to say is, that when the prince

25 Immanuel, presently to be born, reaches adult age, agriculture shall have ceased in the desolated realm of Judah itself; the land, overrun by enemies, shall have returned to a wild state, the inhabitants shall live on the produce of their herds and on wild honey. But before this comes to pass, before the visitation

30 of God's wrath upon the kingdom of Judah, and while the prince Immanuel is still but a little child, not as yet able to discern betwixt good and evil, "to refuse the evil and choose the good," the present enemies of Judah, the kings of Syria and Israel, shall be overthrown and their land made desolate.

35 Finally, this overthrow and desolation are not, with the prophet, the sign and guarantee of Immanuel's coming. Immanuel is himself intended as a sign; all the rest is accompaniment of this sign, not proof of it.

This, the true and sure sense of those noble words of prophecy which we hear read on Christmas-day, is obscured by slight errors in the received translation, and comes out clearer when the errors are corrected:—

"The Lord himself shall give you a sign: Behold, the damsel 5 shall conceive, and bear a son, and shall call his name Immanuel.

"Milk-curd and honey shall he eat, when he shall know to refuse the evil and choose the good.

"For before the child shall know to refuse the evil and choose the good, the land shall be forsaken, whose two kings 10 make thee afraid."

Syria and Israel shall be made desolate in Immanuel's infancy, says the prophet; but the chastisement and desolation of Judah also, he declares, shall follow later, by the time Immanuel is a youth. Farther yet, however, Isaiah carries his 15 prophecy of Immanuel and of the events of his life. In his manhood, the prophet continues, Immanuel, the promised child of the royal house of David, shall reign in righteousness over a restored, far-spreading, prosperous, and peaceful kingdom of the chosen people. "Of the increase of his government and 20 peace there shall be no end, upon the throne of David, and upon his kingdom." This completion of the prophecy, too, we hear read in church on Christmas-day. Naturally, the received and erroneous interpretation, which finds, as we have seen, in the first part of the prophecy "the miracle of the Incarnation," 25 governs our understanding of the latter part also. But in the latter part, as well as in the former, the prophet undoubtedly has in view, not a scion of the house of David to be born and to reign seven centuries later, but a scion of the house of David to be born immediately; a scion who in his youth should see 30 Judah afflicted, in his manhood should reign over Judah restored and triumphant.

Well, then, the "miracle of the Incarnation," the preternatural conception and birth of Jesus Christ, which the Church celebrates at Christmas, and which is, says the *Guardian*, the 35 fundamental truth for Christians, gets no support at all from the famous prophecy which is commonly supposed to announce it. Need I add that it gets no support at all from any

single word of Jesus Christ himself, from any single word in
the letters of Paul, Peter, James, or John? The miraculous conception and birth of Jesus is a *legend*, a lovely and attractive
legend, which soon formed itself, naturally and irresistibly,
5   around the origin of the Saviour; a legend which by the end
of the first century had established itself, and which passed
into two out of the four Gospel narratives that in the century
following acquired canonicity. In the same way, a precisely
similar legend formed itself around the origin of Plato, al-
10   though to the popular imagination Plato was an object incomparably less fitted to offer stimulus. The father of Plato, said
the Athenian story, was upon his marriage warned by Apollo
in a dream that his wife, Perictiona, was about to bring forth
a babe divinely conceived, and that he was to live apart from
15   her until the child had been born. Among the students of
philosophy, who were Plato's disciples, this story, although
authorised by his family, languished and died. Had Plato
founded a popular religion the case would have been very
different. Then the legend would have survived and thriven;
20   and for Plato, too, there would have certainly been a world-
famous "miracle of the Incarnation" investing his origin. But
Plato, as Bossuet says, formed fewer disciples than Paul formed
churches. It was these churches, this multitude, it was the
popular masses with their receptivity, their love of wonders,
25   with all their favouring native tendencies of mind, heart, and
soul, which made the future of the Christian legend of the
miracle of the Incarnation.

But because the story of the miracle of the Incarnation is a
legend, and because two of the canonical Gospels propound
30   the legend seriously, basing it upon an evidently fantastic use
of the words of prophecy, and because the festival of Christmas adopts and consecrates this legend, are we to cast the
Gospels aside, and cast the celebration of Christmas aside; or
else are we to give up our reason and common sense, and to
35   say that things are not what they are, and that Isaiah really
predicted the preternatural conception and birth of Jesus
Christ, and that the miracle of the Incarnation really happened
as the *Guardian* supposes, and that Christians, in commemorat-

ing it, commemorate a solid fact of history, and a fact which is the fundamental truth for Christians? By no means. The solid fact of history marked by Christmas is the birth of Jesus, the miraculous circumstances with which that birth is invested and presented are legendary. The solid fact in itself, the birth of Jesus with its inexhaustible train of consequences, its "unspeakable riches," is foundation enough, and more than enough, for the Christmas festival; yet even the legend and miracle investing the fact, and now almost inseparable from it, have, moreover, their virtue of symbol.

Symbol is a dangerous word, and we ought to be very cautious in employing it. People have a difficulty in owning that a thing is unhistorical, and often they try to get out of the difficulty by saying that the thing is symbolical. Thus they think to save the credit of whoever delivered the thing in question, as if he had himself intended to deliver it as symbolical and figurative, not as historical. They save it, however, at the expense of truth. In very many cases undoubtedly, when this shift of symbol is resorted to for saving the credit of a narrator of legend, the narrator had not himself the least notion that what he propounded was figure, but fully imagined himself to be propounding historical fact. The Gospel narrators of the miracle of the Incarnation were in this position of mind; they did not in the least imagine themselves to be speaking symbolically. Nevertheless, a thing may have important value as symbol, although its utterer never told or meant it symbolically. Let us see how this is so with the Christian legend of the Incarnation.

In times and among minds where science is not a power, and where the preternatural is daily and familiarly admitted, the pureness and elevation of a great teacher strike powerfully the popular imagination, and the natural, simple, reverential explanation of his superiority is at once that he was born of a virgin. Such a legend is the people's genuine construing of the fact of his unique pureness. In his birth, as well as in his life and teaching, this chosen one has been pure,—has been unlike other men, and above them. Signal and splendid is the pureness of Plato; noble his serene faith, that "the conclusion has long

been reached that dissoluteness is to be condemned, in that it
brings about the aggrandisement of the lower side in our nature, and the defeat of the higher." And this lofty pureness of
Plato impressed the imagination of his contemporaries, and
5   evoked the legend of his having been born of a virgin. But
Plato was, as I have already said, a philosopher, not the founder
of a religion; his personality survived, but for the intellect
mainly, not for the affections and imagination. It influenced
and affected the few, not the many,—not the masses which
10 love and foster legend. On the figure of Jesus also the stamp of
a pureness unique and divine was seen to dwell. The remark
has often been made that the pre-eminent, the winning, the
irresistible Christian virtues, were charity and chastity. Perhaps the chastity was an even more winning virtue than the
15 charity; it offered to the Pagan world, at any rate, relief from a
more oppressive, a more consuming, a more intolerable bondage. Chief among the beatitudes shone, no doubt, this pair:
*Blessed are the poor in spirit, for theirs is the kingdom of
heaven,* and, *Blessed are the pure in heart, for they shall see
20 God;* and of these two, the second blessing may have brought
even the greater boon. Jesus, then, the bestower of this precious blessing, Jesus, the high exemplar and ideal of pureness,
was born of a virgin. And what Jesus brought was not a philosophy, but a religion; he gave not to the few, but to the
25 masses, to the very recipients whom the tender legend of his
being born of the gracious Virgin, and laid in the humble
manger, would suit best; who might most surely be trusted
to seize upon it, not to let it go, to delight in it and magnify
it for ever.
30   So the legend of the miraculous conception and birth of
Jesus, like the legend of the miraculous conception and birth
of Plato, is the popular homage to a high ideal of pureness, it
is the multitude's way of expressing for this its reverence. Of
such reverence the legend is a genuine symbol. But the impor-
35 tance of the symbol is proportional to the scale on which it
acts. And even when it acts on a very large scale, still its virtue will depend on these two things further: the worth of the
idea to which it does homage, and the extent to which its

recipients have succeeded in penetrating through the form of the legend to this idea.

And first, then, as to the innate truth and worth of that idea of pureness to which the legend of the miracle of the Incarnation does homage. *Blessed are the pure in heart, for they shall see God,* says Jesus. *God hath not called us unto impureness, but unto holiness,* adds his apostle. Perhaps there is no doctrine of Christianity which is exposed to more trial amongst us now, certainly there is none which will be exposed, so far as from present appearances one can judge, to more trial in the immediate future, than this. *Let us return to nature,* is a rising and spreading cry again now, as it was at the Renascence. And the Christian pureness has so much which seems to contradict nature, and which is menaced by the growing desire and determination to return to nature! The virtue has suffered more than most virtues in the hands of hypocrites; and with hypocrites and hypocrisy, as a power in human life, there is an increasing impatience. But the virtue has been mishandled, also, by the sincere; by the sincere, but who are at the same time over-rigid, formal, sour, narrow-minded; and these, too, are by no means in the ascendant among us just now. Evidently, again, the virtue has been mishandled by many of the so-called saints, and by the asceticism of the Catholic Church; for these have so managed things, very often, as to turn and rivet the thoughts upon the very matter from which pureness would avert them and get them clear, and have to that extent served to endanger and impair the virtue rather than forward it. Then, too, with the growing sense that gaiety and pleasure are legitimate demands of our nature, that they add to life and to our sum of force, instead of, as strict people have been wont to say, taking from it,—with this growing sense comes also the multiplication everywhere of the means of gaiety and pleasure, the spectacle ever more prominent of them and catching the eye more constantly, an ever larger number of applicants pressing forward to share in them. All this solicits the senses, makes them bold, eager, and stirring. At the same time the force of old sanctions of self-restraint diminishes and gives way. The belief in a magnified and non-natural man, out of

our sight, but proved by miracles to exist and to be all-powerful, who by his commands has imposed on us the obligation of
self-restraint, and who will punish us after death in endless
fire if we disobey, will reward us in Paradise if we submit,—
5   this belief is rapidly and irrecoverably losing its hold on men's
minds. If pureness or any other virtue is still to subsist, it
must subsist nowadays not by authority of this kind enforcing
it in defiance of nature, but because nature herself turns out to
be really for it.
10   Mr. Traill has reminded us, in the interesting volume on
Coleridge which he has recently published, how Coleridge's
disciple, Mr. Green, devoted the last years of his life to elabo-
rating, in a work entitled *Spiritual Philosophy: founded on the
Teaching of the late Samuel Taylor Coleridge*, the great
15   Coleridgian position "that Christianity, rightly understood, is
identical with the highest philosophy, and that, apart from all
question of historical evidence, the essential doctrines of Christianity are necessary and eternal truths of reason,—truths
which man, by the vouchsafed light of nature and without aid
20   from documents or tradition, may always and everywhere discover for himself." We shall not find this position established or
much elucidated in *Spiritual Philosophy*. We shall not find it
established or much elucidated in the works of Coleridge's immediate disciples. It was a position of extreme novelty to take
25   at that time. Firmly to occupy it, resolutely to maintain it,
required great boldness and great lucidity. Coleridge's position
made demands upon his disciples which at that time it was almost impossible they should fulfil; it embarrassed them, forced
them into vagueness and obscurity. The most eminent and
30   popular among them, Mr. Maurice, seems never quite to have
himself known what he himself meant, and perhaps never really
quite wished to know. But neither did the master, as I have
already said, establish his own position; there were obstacles in
his own character, as well as obstacles in his circumstances, in
35   the time. Nevertheless it is rightly called "the great Coleridgian
position." It is at the bottom of all Coleridge's thinking and
teaching; it is true; it is deeply important; and by virtue of it
Coleridge takes rank, so far as English thought is concerned, as

an initiator and founder. The "great Coleridgian position," that apart from all question of the evidence for miracles and of the historical quality of the Gospel narratives, the essential matters of Christianity are necessary and eternal facts of nature or truths of reason, is henceforth the key to the whole de- 5 fence of Christianity. When a Christian virtue is presented to us as obligatory, the first thing, therefore, to be asked, is whether our need of it is a fact of nature.

Here the appeal is to experience and testimony. His own experience may in the end be the surest teacher for every man; 10 but meanwhile, to confirm or deny his instinctive anticipations and to start him on his way, testimony as to the experience of others, general experience, is of the most serious weight and value. We have had the testimony of Plato to the necessity of pureness, that virtue on which Christianity lays so much 15 stress. Here is yet another testimony out of the same Greek world,—a world so alien to the world in which Christianity arose; here is the testimony of Sophocles. "Oh that my lot might lead me in the path of holy *pureness* of thought and deed, the path which august laws ordain, laws which in the 20 highest heaven had their birth; . . . the power of God is mighty in them, and groweth not old." That is the testimony of the poet Sophocles. Coming down to our own times, we have again a like testimony from the greatest poet of our times, Goethe; a testimony the more important, because Goethe, like 25 Sophocles, was in his own life what the world calls by no means a purist. "May the idea of *pureness*," says Goethe, "extending itself even to the very morsel which I take into my mouth, become ever clearer and more luminous within me!"

But let us consult the testimony not only of people far over 30 our heads, such as great poets and sages; let us have the testimony of people living, as the common phrase is, in the world, and living there on an every-day footing. And let us choose a world the least favourable to purists possible, the most given to laxity,—and where indeed by this time the reign of the great 35 goddess Lubricity seems, as I have often said, to be almost established,—the world of Paris. Two famous women of that world of Paris in the seventeenth century, two women not

altogether unlike in spirit, Ninon de l'Enclos and Mme. de Sévigné, offer, in respect to the virtue with which we are now occupied, the most striking contrast possible. Both had, in the highest degree, freedom of spirit and of speech, boldness,
5   gaiety, lucidity. Mme. de Sévigné, married to a worthless husband, then a widow, beautiful, witty, charming, of extraordinary freedom, easy and broad in her judgments, fond of enjoyment, not seriously religious,—Mme. de Sévigné, living in a society where almost everybody had a lover, never took one.
10 The French commentators upon their incomparable countrywoman are puzzled by this. But really the truth is, that not from what is called high moral principle, not from religion, but from sheer elementary soundness of nature and by virtue of her perfect lucidity, she revolted from the sort of life so
15 common all around her, was drawn towards regularity, felt antipathy to blemish and disorder. Ninon, on the other hand, with a like freedom of mind, a like boldness and breadth in her judgments, a like gaiety and love of enjoyment, took a different turn, and her irregular life was the talk of her cen-
20 tury. But that lucidity, which even all through her irregular life was her charm, made her say at the end of it: "All the world tells me that I have less cause to speak ill of time than other people. However that may be, could anybody have proposed to me beforehand the life I have had, I would have
25 hanged myself." That, I say, is the testimony of the most lucid children of this world, as the testimony of Plato, Sophocles, and Goethe is the testimony of the loftiest spirits, to the natural obligation and necessity of the essentially Christian virtue of pureness. So when legend represents the founder of Chris-
30 tianity and great exemplar of this virtue as *born of a virgin*, thus doing homage to pureness, it does homage to what has natural worth and necessity.

But we have further to ask to what extent the recipients of the legend showed themselves afterwards capable, while firmly
35 believing the legend and delighting in it, of penetrating to that virtue which it honoured, and of showing their sense that accompanying the legend went the glorification of that virtue. Here the Collects of the Church which have come down to us

from Catholic antiquity,—from the times when all legend was most unhesitatingly received, most fondly loved, most delighted in for its own sake,—are the best testimony. Now the Collect for Christmas-day,—that very day on which the miracle of the Incarnation is commemorated, and on which we might expect the legend's miraculous side to be altogether dominant,—firmly seizes the homage to pureness and renovation which is at the heart of the legend, and holds it steadily before us all [at] Christmas-time. "Almighty God," so the Collect runs, "who hast given us thine only-begotten Son to take our nature upon him, and as at this time to be born of a pure virgin, grant that we being regenerate, and made thy children through adoption and grace, may daily be renewed by thy Holy Spirit." [1] The miracle is amply and impressively stated, but the stress is laid upon the work of regeneration and inward renewal, whereby we are to be made sons of God, like to that supreme Son whose pureness was expressed through his being born of a pure virgin. It is as, in celebrating at Easter the miracle of the Resurrection, the Church, following here St. Paul, seizes and elevates in the Collect for Easter Eve [2] that great "secret of Jesus" which underlies the whole miraculous legend of the Resurrection, but which could arrive at the general heart of mankind only through materialising itself in that legend.

So manifest is it that there is that true and grand and profound doctrine of the *necrosis,* of "dying to re-live," underlying all which is legendary in the presentation of the death and resurrection of Jesus by our Gospels,—so manifest is it that St. Paul seized upon the doctrine and elevated it, and that the Church has retained it,—that one can find no difficulty, when the festival of Easter is celebrated, in fixing one's thoughts upon the doctrine as a centre, and in receiving all

[1] The point in the Collect is taken from the Mozarabic Breviary at Lauds: "Nos a mundanis contagiis munda, et in hoc mundo mundos nos esse constitue."

[2] The point here is taken from a Benediction of St. Gregory for the First Sunday in Easter: "Resuscitet vos de vitiorum sepulchris qui eum resuscitavit a mortuis." See Blunt's *Annotated Book of Common Prayer.*

the miraculous story as poetry naturally investing this and doing homage to it. But there is hardly a fast or a festival of the Christian year in which the underlying truth, the beneficent and forwarding idea, clothed with legend and miracle

5 because mankind could only appropriate it by materialising it in legend and miracle, is not apparent. Trinity Sunday is an exception, but then Trinity Sunday does not really deal with Gospel story and miracle, it deals with speculation by theologians on the divine nature. Perhaps, considering the results of

10 their speculation, we ought now rather to keep Trinity Sunday as a day of penitence for the aberrations of theological dogmatists. It is, however, in itself admissible and right enough that in the Christian year one day should be given to considering the aspects by which the human mind can in any degree

15 apprehend God. But Trinity Sunday is, as I have said, an exception. For the most part, in the days and seasons which the Church observes, there is commemoration of some matter declared in Scripture, and combined and clothed more or less with miracle. Yet how near to us, under the accompanying in-

20 vestment of legend, does the animating and fructifying idea lie! —in Lent, with the miracle of the temptation, the idea of self-conquest and self-control; in Whitsuntide, with the miracle of the tongues of fire, the idea of the spirit and of inspiration.

What Christmas primarily commemorates is the birthday of

25 Jesus,—Jesus, the bringer to the world of the new dispensation contained in his method and secret, and in his temper of sweet reasonableness for applying these. But the religion of Christendom has in fact made the prominent thing in Christmas a miracle, a legend; the miracle of the Incarnation, as it is called, the

30 legend of Jesus having been born of a virgin. And to those who cannot bring themselves to receive miracle and legend as fact, what Christmas, under this popularly established aspect of it, can have to say to us, what significance it can contain, may at first sight seem doubtful. Christmas might at first appear to be

35 the one great festival which is concerned wholly with mere miracle, which fixes our attention upon a miracle and nothing else. But when we come to look closer, we find that even in the case of Christmas the thing is not so. That on which Christmas,

even in its popular acceptation, fixes our attention, is that to which the popular instinct, in attributing to Jesus his miraculous Incarnation, in believing him born of a pure Virgin, did homage:—pureness. And this to which the popular instinct thus did homage, was an essential characteristic of Jesus and 5 an essential virtue of Christianity, the obligation of which, though apt to be questioned and discredited in the world, is at the same time nevertheless a necessary fact of nature and eternal truth of reason. And fondly as the Church has cherished and displayed the Christmas miracle, this, the true sig- 10 nificance of the miraculous legend for religion, has never, the Christmas Collect shows us, been unknown to her, never wholly lost out of sight. As time goes on, as legend and miracle are less taken seriously as matters of fact, this worth of the Christmas legend as symbol will more and more come into 15 view. The legend will still be loved, but as poetry,—as poetry endeared by the associations of some two thousand years; religious thought will rest upon that which the legend symbolises.

It is a mistake to suppose that rules for conduct and recom- 20 mendations of virtue, presented in a correct scientific statement, or in a new rhetorical statement from which old errors are excluded, can have anything like the effect on mankind of old rules and recommendations to which we have been long accustomed, and with which our feelings and affections have 25 become intertwined. Pedants always suppose that they can, but that this mistake should be so commonly made, proves only how many of us have a mixture of the pedant in our composition. A correct scientific statement of rules of virtue has upon the great majority of mankind simply no effect at all. 30 A new rhetorical statement of them, appealing, like the old familiar deliverances of Christianity, to the heart and imagination, can have the effect which those deliverances had, only when they proceed from a religious genius equal to that from which those proceeded. To state the requirement is to declare 35 the impossibility of its being satisfied. The superlative pedantry of Comte is shown in his vainly imagining that he could satisfy it; the comparative pedantry of his disciples is shown by the degree in which they adopt their master's vain imagination.

The really essential ideas of Christianity have a truth, depth, necessity, and scope, far beyond anything that either the adherents of popular Christianity, or its impugners, at present suppose. Jesus himself, as I have remarked elsewhere, is even the better fitted to stand as the central figure of a religion, because his reporters so evidently fail to comprehend him fully and to report him adequately. Being so evidently great and yet so uncomprehended, and being now inevitably so to remain for ever, he thus comes to stand before us as what the philosophers call an *absolute*. We cannot apply to him the tests which we can apply to other phenomena, we cannot get behind him and above him, cannot command him. But even were Jesus less of an *absolute*, less fitted to stand as the central figure of a religion than he is, even were the constitutive and essential ideas of Christianity less pregnant, profound, and far-reaching than they are, still the personage of Jesus, and the Christian rules of conduct and recommendations of virtue, being of that indisputable significance and worth which in any fair view to be taken of them they are, and also so widely known and loved from of old, would have a value and a substantiality for religious purposes which no new apparitions and constructions can possibly have. No new constructions in religion can now hope to found a common way, hold aloft a common truth, unite men in a common life. And yet how true it is, in regard to mankind's conduct and course, that, as the *Imitation* says so admirably, "Without a way there is no going, without a truth, no knowing, without a life, no living." *Sine viâ non itur, sine veritate non cognoscitur, sine vitâ non vivitur.* The way, truth, and life have been found in Christianity, and will not now be found outside of it. Instead of making vain and pedantic endeavours to invent them outside of it, what we have to do is to help, so far as we can, towards their continuing to be found inside of it by honest and sane people, who would be glad to find them there if they can accomplish it without playing tricks with their understanding; to help them to accomplish this, to remove obstacles out of the way of their doing so.

Far from having anything to gain by being timid and reticent, or else vague and rhetorical, in treating of the miraculous element in the Bible, he who would help men will probably now do most good by treating this element with entire unreserve. Let him frankly say, that miracle narrated in the Bible is as legendary as miracle narrated anywhere else, and not more to be taken as having actually happened. If he calls it symbolical, let him be careful to admit that the narrators did not mean it for symbol, but delivered it as having actually happened, and in so delivering it were mistaken. Let him say that we can still use it as poetry, and that in so using it we use it better than those who used it as matter of fact; but let him not leave in any uncertainty the point that it is as poetry that we do use it. Let no difficulties be slurred over or eluded. Undoubtedly a period of transition in religious belief, such as the period in which we are now living, presents many grave difficulties. Undoubtedly the reliance on miracles is not lost without some danger; but the thing to consider is that it *must* be lost, and that the danger must be met, and, as it can be, counteracted.

If men say, as some men are likely enough to say, that they altogether give up Christian miracles and cannot do otherwise, but that then they give up Christian morals too, the answer is, that they do this at their own risk and peril; that they need not do it, that they are wrong in doing it, and will have to rue their error. But for my part, I prefer at present to affirm this reality of Christian morals simply and barely, not to give any rhetorical development to it. Springs of interest for the emotions and feelings this reality possesses in abundance, and hereafter these springs may and will most beneficially be used by the clergy and teachers of religion, who are the best persons to turn them to account. As they have habitually and powerfully used the springs of emotion contained in the Christian legend, so they will with time come to use the springs of emotion contained in the Christian reality. But there has been so much vagueness, and so much rhetoric, and so much licence of affirmation, and so much treatment of what cannot be known as if it were well known, and of what is poetry and legend as if it were essential solid fact, and of what is investment and

dress of the matter as if it were the heart of the matter, that
for the present, and when we are just at the commencement of
a new departure, I prefer, I say, to put forward a plain, strict
statement of the essential facts and truths consecrated by the
5   Christian legend, and to confine myself to doing this. No
doubt, not even those facts and truths can produce their full
effect upon men when exhibited in a mere naked statement.
Nevertheless, the most important service we can render to
Christianity, at the present moment, is perhaps not so much to
10 work upon men's feelings with rhetoric about it, as to show
to their understandings what its essential facts and truths really
are.

Therefore, when we are asked: What really is Christmas,
and what does it celebrate? we answer: The birthday of Jesus.
15 But what, then, is the miracle of the Incarnation? A homage
to the virtue of pureness, and to the manifestation of this virtue
in Jesus. What is Lent, and the miracle of the temptation? A
homage to the virtue of self-control and to the manifestation
of this virtue in Jesus. What does Easter celebrate? Jesus vic-
20 torious over death by dying. By dying how? Dying to re-live.
To re-live in Paradise, in another world? No, in this. But if in
this, what is the kingdom of God? The ideal society of the
future. Then what is immortality? To live in the eternal order,
which never dies. What is salvation by Jesus Christ? The at-
25 tainment of this immortality. Through what means? Through
faith in Jesus, and appropriation of his method, secret, and
temper.

Men's experience of the saving results of the method and
secret and temper of Jesus, imperfectly even as his method and
30 secret and temper have been extricated and employed hitherto,
makes truly the strength of that wonderful Book, in which,
with an immense vehicle of legend and miracle, the new
dispensation of Jesus and the old dispensation which led up to
it are exhibited and brought to mankind's knowledge; makes
35 the strength of the Bible, and of the religion and churches
which the Bible has called into being. We may remark that
what makes the attraction of a church is always what is consonant in it to the method and secret and temper of Jesus, and

productive, therefore, of the saving results which flow from these. The attraction of the Catholic Church is unity; of the Protestant sects, conscience; of the Church of England, abuses reformed but unity saved. I speak of that which, in each of these cases, is the attraction, the promise apparently held out; I do not say that the promise is made good. The attraction, in each case, is something given by the line of Jesus. That which makes the weakness and danger of a church, again, is just that in it which is not consonant to the line of Jesus. Thus the danger of the Catholic Church is its obscurantism; of the Protestant sects, their contentiousness; of the Church of England, its deference to station and property. I said in a discourse at the East-end of London that ever since the appearance of Christianity *the prince of this world is judged*. The *Guardian* was much alarmed at my saying that, and reproved me for saying it. I will urge nothing in answer, except that this deference to the *prince of this world*, to the susceptibilities of station and property, which has been too characteristic of the Church of England in the past,—a deference so signally at variance with the line of Jesus,—is at the same time just what now makes the Church of England's weakness and main danger.

As time goes on, it will be more and more manifest that salvation does really depend on conformity to the line of Jesus; and that this experience, and nothing miraculous or preternatural, is what establishes the truth and necessity of Christianity. The experience proceeds on a large scale, and therefore slowly. But even now, and imperfectly moreover as the line of Jesus has been followed hitherto, it can be seen that those nations are the soundest which have the most seriously concerned themselves with it and have most endeavoured to follow it. Societies are saved by following it, broken up by not following it; and as the experience of this continually proceeds, the proofs of Christianity are continually accumulating and growing stronger. The thing goes on quite independently of our wishes, and whether we will or no. Our French neighbours seem perfectly and scornfully incredulous as to the cogency of the beatitude which pronounces blessing on the pure in heart; they would not for a moment admit that nations perish through the service of the great goddess Lubricity. On the contrary, more and more of them, great and small, philosophers as well as the vulgar, maintain this service to be the most natural and reasonable thing in the world. Yet really this service broke up the great Roman Empire in the past, and is capable, it will be found, of breaking up any number of societies.

Or let us consider that other great beatitude and its fortunes, the beatitude recommending the Christian virtue of charity: "Blessed are the poor in spirit, for theirs is the kingdom of heaven." Many people do not even understand what it is which this beatitude means to bless; they think it recommends humbleness of spirit. Ferdinand Baur, whose exegesis of texts from the Gospels is more valuable than his criticism of the mode in which the Gospels were composed, has very well pointed out that the persons here blest are not those who are humble-spirited, but those who are in the intention and bent of their spirit,—in mind, as we say, and not in profession merely,—indifferent to riches. Such persons, whether they possess riches or not, really regard riches as something foreign to them, something not their own, and are thus, in the phrase of another text where our received translation is misleading, *faithful* as regards riches. "If ye have not been faithful in that which is foreign to you, who will give you that which is your own?" The faithfulness consists in having conquered the temptation to treat that for which men desire riches, private possession and personal enjoyment, as things vital to us and to be desired. Wherever there is cupidity, in short, there the blessing of the Gospel cannot rest. The actual poor, therefore, may altogether fail to be objects of that blessing, the actual rich may be objects of it in the highest degree. Nay, the surest of means to restore and perpetuate the reign of the selfish rich, if at any time it have been menaced or interrupted, is cupidity, envy, and hatred in the poor. And this, again, is a witness to the infallibility of the line of Jesus. We must come, both rich and poor, to prefer the common good, the interest of "the body of Christ,"—to use the Gospel phrase,—the body of Christ of which we are members, to private possession and personal enjoyment.

This is Christian charity, and how rare, how very rare it is, we all know. In this practical country of ours, where possessing property and estate is so loved, and losing them so dreaded, the opposition to Christian charity is almost as strong as that to Christian purity in France. The *Saturday Review* is in general respectful to religion, sane in behaviour, in matters of criticism reasonable. But let it imagine property and privilege threatened, and instantly what a change! There seems to rise before one's mind's eye a sort of vision of an elderly demoniac, surrounded by a troop of younger demoniacs of whom he is the owner and guide, all of them suddenly foaming at the mouth and crying out horribly. The attachment to property and privilege is so strong, the fear of losing them so agitating. But the line of Jesus perpetually tends to establish itself, as I have said, independently of our wishes, and whether we will or no. And undoubtedly the line of Jesus is: "How hardly shall they that have riches enter into the kingdom of God!" In other words: "How hardly shall those who cling to private possessions and personal enjoyment, who have not brought themselves to regard property and riches as foreign and indifferent to them, who have not annulled self and placed their happiness in the common good, make part of the ideal society of the future!"

The legend of Christmas is a homage to the Christian virtue of pureness; and Christmas, with its "miracle of the Incarnation," should turn our thoughts to the certainty of this virtue's final victory, against all difficulties. And with the victory of this virtue let us associate the victory of its great fellow-virtue of Christian charity, a victory equally difficult but equally certain. The difficulties are undeniable, but here, however, the signs of the times point far more to the emergence and progress of the virtue than to its depression. Who cannot see that the idea of the common good is acquiring amongst us, at the present day, a force altogether new? that for instance, in cases where, in the framing of laws and in the interpretation of them by tribunals, regard to property and privilege used to be, one may say, paramount, and the idea of the common good hardly considered at all, things are now tending quite the other way; the pretensions of property and privilege are se-

verely scrutinised, the claims of the common good entertained
with favour.

An acceleration of progress in the spread of ideas of this
kind, a decline of vitality in institutions where the opposite
ideas were paramount, marks the close of a period. Jesus announced for his own period such a close; a close necessitated
by the emergence of the new, the decay of the old. He announced it with the turbid figures familiar through prophecy
to his hearers' imagination, figures of stupendous physical
miracle, a break-up of nature, God coming to judgment. But
he did not announce under these figures, as our Bibles make
him announce, the end of *the world;* he announced "the end
of *the age,*" "the close of *the period.*" That close came, as he
had foretold; and a like "end of the age" is imminent, wherever
a certain stage is reached in the conflict between the line of
Jesus and the facts of that period through which it takes its
passage. Sometimes we may almost be inclined to augur that
from some such "end of the age" we ourselves are not far
distant now; that through dissolution,—dissolution peaceful if
we have virtue enough, violent if we are vicious, but still dissolution,—we and our own age have to pass, according to the
eternal law which makes dissolution the condition of renovation. The price demanded, according to the inexorable conditions on which the kingdom of God is offered, for the mistakes of our past, for the attainment of our future, this price
may perhaps be required sooner than we suppose, required
even of us ourselves who are living now: "Verily I say unto
you, it shall be required *of this generation.*"

Preface
[to *Discourses in America*]

Of the three discourses in this volume, the second was originally given as the Rede Lecture at Cambridge, was recast for
delivery in America, and is reprinted here as so recast. The
first discourse, that on "Numbers," was originally given in
New York. It was afterwards published in the *Nineteenth Cen-*   5
tury, and I have to thank Mr. Knowles for kindly permitting
me to reprint it now. The third discourse, that on "Emerson,"
was originally given in Emerson's "own delightful town,"
Boston.

    I am glad of every opportunity of thanking my American   10
audiences for the unfailing attention and kindness with which
they listened to a speaker who did not flatter them, who would
have flattered them ill, but who yet felt, and in fact expressed,
more esteem and admiration than his words were sometimes,
at a hasty first hearing, supposed to convey. I cannot think   15
that what I have said of Emerson will finally be accounted
scant praise, although praise universal and unmixed it certainly is
not. What high esteem I feel for the suitableness and easy play
of American institutions I have had occasion, since my return
home, to say publicly and emphatically. But nothing in the   20
discourse on "Numbers" was at variance with this high esteem,
although a caution, certainly, was suggested. But then some
caution or other, to be drawn from the inexhaustibly fruitful
truth that moral causes govern the standing and the falling of
States, who is there that can be said not to need?   25

    All need it, we in this country need it, as indeed in the dis-
course on "Numbers" I have by an express instance shown.
Yet as regards us in this country at the present moment, I am

tempted, I confess, to resort to the great truth in question, not
for caution so much as for consolation. Our politics are "battles of the kites and the crows," of the Barbarians and the
Philistines; each combatant striving to affirm himself still, while
5   all the vital needs and instincts of our national growth demand,
not that either of the combatants should be enabled to affirm
himself, but that each should be transformed. Our aristocratical
class, the Barbarians, have no perception of the real wants of
the community at home. Our middle classes, the great Philis-
10 tine power, have no perception of our real relations to the
world abroad, no clue, apparently, for guidance, wherever
that attractive and ever-victorious rhetorician, who is the Minister of their choice, may take them, except the formula of that
submissive animal which carried the prophet Balaam. Our af-
15 fairs are in the condition which, from such parties to our politics, might be expected. Yet amid all the difficulties and morti-
fications which beset us, with the Barbarians impossible, with
the Philistines determining our present course, with our rising
politicians seeking only that the mind of the Populace, when
20 the Populace arrives at power, may be found in harmony
with the mind of Mr. Carvell Williams, which they flatter
themselves they have fathomed; with the House of Lords a
danger, and the House of Commons a scandal, and the general
direction of affairs infelicitous as we see it,—one consolation
25 remains to us, and that no slight or unworthy one. Infelicitous
the general direction of our affairs may be; but the individual
Englishman, whenever and wherever called upon to do his
duty, does it almost invariably with the old energy, courage,
virtue. And this is what we gain by having had, as a people, in
30 the ground of our being, a firm faith in conduct; by having believed, more steadfastly and fervently than most, this great law
that moral causes govern the standing and the falling of men
and nations. The law gradually widens, indeed, so as to include
light as well as honesty and energy; to make light, also, a moral
35 cause. Unless we are transformed we cannot finally stand, and
without more light we cannot be transformed. But in the
trying hours through which before our transformation we

have to pass, it may well console us to rest our thoughts upon
our life's law even as we have hitherto known it, and upon all
which even in our present imperfect acception of it it has done
for us.

Appendix One:
Reports of Public Lectures and Brief Notes
to the Press

[OCCASIONAL NOTES]

Mr. Matthew Arnold writes to us as follows:—"I have just been reading the vigorous article in yesterday's *Daily Telegraph* about "the French gag" with which the Government are going to stop free debate in England. I notice that the 5 racy and idiomatic writer does not say *bâillon*. May I ask why we all persist in saying *clôture?* Is it for the pleasure of describing the circumflex when we write the word, and of pronouncing the French *u* when we speak it? Or is it from the mere English love of whatever is complicated and not simple? 10 We all say *enclosure, disclosure,* every day of our lives. But *closure* itself, also, in its uncompounded state, is a perfectly good English word; a word used by Chaucer, Shakspeare, Boyle, Atterbury, and Pope."

—*Pall Mall Gazette*, February 14, 1882, p. 3.

[MR. ARNOLD AND THE LITERARY CLASS]

15 MR. MATTHEW ARNOLD was tendered an informal reception by the Authors Club at the Hotel Dam, [New York City, on February 28, 1882. . . . He] was welcomed by Professor Charlton T. Lewis, to whose greeting he made the following response:

20 "GENTLEMEN: I have been received in this country with unbounded kindness. Much of that kindness, though it has gratified me, has also surprised me, I was so little prepared for it. But for your kindness, gentlemen, and for the kindness of the Club of Authors, I feel better prepared, on account of the

kindness I have experienced from the literary class at home.
Gentlemen, I owe everything to the literary class—to the
class of writers. Here in this Club of Authors and in the pri-
vacy of this family circle I will make a confession to you, and
reveal to you the insecurity of my position. [Laughter.] Gen- 5
tlemen, that great public to which we all speak has never quite
comprehended what I am after, and so far as it has comprehended it, it does not much like it. [Laughter.] If it were not
for the literary class having given me its support the great public would never have attended to me at all, and at this moment 10
if the literary class withdrew its support from me, the public
would entirely cease to attend to me. [Several voices "No!
No!"] Yes, gentlemen, it would cease to attend to me, and
it would give itself up to charmers such as the Rev. Joseph
Cook. [Laughter.] Now to what do I owe this support—this 15
generous support of the literary class? I owe it, I believe, to
their finding in me that which pleased Gil Blas in the road to
Merida when he cried, '*Le coeur au métier.*' Put your heart
into your business. I believe that I have '*le coeur au métier,*'
and that it is on that account the class has been favorable to 20
me. We all know what has been said with more or less truth,
of the irritability, the envy and the jealousy of the literary
class; but I believe that they recognize when a man pursues
the profession of literature with his heart in his work and
takes it seriously and with conscience, and that they feel a 25
favor toward him in consequence. If they do not recognize
it and do not feel a favor toward him in consequence, who
will? I make no distinction between the literary class in England and that here. Here, as in England, I believe that there
is very much against any one who pursues literature seriously 30
and with conscience. Society will always try to impose its decisions and its preferences upon a man of letters; the crowd
will always try to impose its decisions and preferences upon
him; journalism, which is not quite the same as literature, will
always try to impose its decisions and impressions upon him. 35
Unless, gentlemen, we ourselves take our work seriously the
case is lost. [Applause.] Gentlemen, in thanking you cordially
as I do, and in taking a grateful leave of you, and of this coun-

try, from which I am about to sail almost immediately, suffer
me to leave with you these words, *Le coeur au métier.*"
[On Saturday, March 1, Arnold lectured on "Literature and
Science" at Chickering Hall.] He was introduced . . . by Mr.
5　Joseph H. Choate, to whose address he replied:
"I speak to-night for the last time in America, and I speak
in the same hall in which I spoke first, and when, I am sorry
to say, owing to being unaccustomed to speaking before large
assemblies, I was not well heard. If practice could cure that
10　defect I ought now to be cured, for I have gone on speaking
ever since until I am almost tired of the sound of my own
voice. Yet, now that the end has come, I cannot help regretting
it; I have been met with such kindness everywhere. I wish to
express my gratitude for the kindness with which you have
15　received me, and the indulgence with which you have heard
me; my interest in this great country and its inexhaustible resources; and my hearty desire to visit it again before I die."
Mr. Arnold then spoke of literary and scientific education,
and was repeatedly interrupted by applause, which broke out
20　again in a hearty manner at the close of the address.
　　　　　　　　　—*The Critic and Good Literature* (New York),
　　　　　　　　　　　　　　　　　March 8, 1884, p. 113.

[MENDACIOUS PERSONAL GOSSIP]

To the Editor of The Nation:
　　Sir: Considering the deference in thought and conduct
25　shown toward women in this country, perhaps the most mali-
cious story set afloat in connection with the recent visit of
Mr. Matthew Arnold is that for which a respectable Boston
weekly journal made itself responsible, namely: that Mr. Arnold, from the vantage ground of a seat in a street-car in that
30　city, entered into conversation with a lady swinging by a strap
in front of him, and, having inquired of her the location of the
Hotel Vendome, promised her his seat when he should leave
the car.
　　Mr. Arnold's attention having been called to this particu-
35　larly spiteful publication, he replies, under date of April 18,
as follows:

"The incident is a fabrication; but why give things of this kind importance by noticing them?"

The query accompanying the denial would indicate that Mr. Arnold does not quite understand us yet. Would it be subjecting him to further castigation to make a further quota- 5 tion from his letter?

"Mendacious personal gossip is the bane of American journalism."

                                 * * *

WASHINGTON, April 30, 1884.   10
     —*The Nation* (New York), May 8, 1884, pp. 404–5.

[JEWS' FREE SCHOOL DINNER]

A banquet, in aid of the funds of the Jews' Free School, was held on Wednesday night [May 21, 1884], in the great hall of the "Criterion," Piccadilly. The Right Hon. A. J. Mundella, Vice-President of the Committee of Council on Education, 15 presided. [After toasts to the Queen, the Prince of Wales, the clergy, the army, navy, and reserve forces, the Chairman said:]

I have now the honour of calling upon one of the most distinguished of living Englishmen, whom we are proud to number among the great supporters of the Education Department. 20 [Applause.] My friend Mr. Matthew Arnold, senior Inspector of Schools, and I am proud to say one of our greatest living critics and one of our greatest living poets, will now address you. [Applause.]

MR. MATTHEW ARNOLD, M.A., in proposing "The Houses 25 of Parliament," said—I have been entrusted with a toast, although all America will tell you that I am no orator. But it is less difficult to speak among old friends—and, gentlemen, the Free School and I—as by your kind cheers you have shown me that you are aware—are old friends. I may almost adopt 30 Grattan's famous words, and say that I sat by the Free School's cradle; and the Free School is now so full of life and prosperity that it will certainly follow my hearse. It is now a great many years ago since I had the honour to be the agent for introducing the Free School among State-aided schools. I still remem- 35 ber, as if it were yesterday, that morning, just at this season of

the year, when I first visited the great school in Bell Lane,
and found my friend Mr. Angel waiting for me at the door;
found the Baroness Lionel and Lady de Rothschild, the wife
of your then president, Sir Anthony, waiting for me inside—
5   the Baroness Lionel, who has passed away, with her energy,
her imagination, her generosity—[Hear, hear]—Lady de Rothschild, in whom we can still love and admire that beauty of
character and that charm of goodness of which nobody but
herself seems to remain unconscious. But, gentlemen, I must
10 not forget that I have a toast to propose to you—"The Houses
of Parliament." Surely it was a strange notion in the managers
of your dinner to entrust that toast to me, an aged and pensive
outsider. [Laughter.] I suppose those who are in the Parliamentary game may get pleasure from its excitement, but I can
15 hardly imagine a cold looker-on finding in the spectacle of it
at present much to inspire him with happy thoughts or to suggest to him smooth things to say; but, still, however distressing
a spectacle Parliament may at times offer, Parliament is nevertheless the necessary organ through which our national life
20 has to be carried on. We are bound therefore to be as hopeful
about it as we can. And in Parliament, as elsewhere, the young
will often afford to us grounds for hope—[Hear, hear];—the
young with their vitality, their audacity. [Hear, hear and
laughter.] Their revolt against used-up routine. [Hear, hear.]
25 We have present here this evening a young but already distinguished politician—[Applause]—Lord Randolph Churchill,
who supplies us with plenty of hope of this kind. [Hear, hear.]
He has vitality, he has audacity—[Laughter]—he has sufficient
spirit of revolt. [Hear, hear.] I couple the name of Lord Ran-
30 dolph Churchill with the toast of The Two Houses of Parliament. I wish him a brilliant, a fortunate and a useful career.
[Applause.]

     [Lord Randolph Churchill's response was the principal
speech of the evening, along with the remarks of Mundella
that followed it.]
                    —*The Jewish Chronicle*, Supplement, May 23, 1884, p. 2.

[SOHO CLUB AND HOME FOR WORKING GIRLS]

A festival dinner in connexion with this institution was held at
the Langham Hotel on Wednesday evening [July 9, 1884],
his Royal Highness the Duke of Cambridge presiding. . . .
Mr. Matthew Arnold, in speaking to the toast ["Prosperity to
the Soho Club and Home for Working Girls"], said that he   5
had been for more than 30 years inspecting schools in Westminster, and had been all that time familiar with the district
of Soho. There was one thing in the district of Soho that always struck him as characteristic of it, and that was its turn
for gaiety, which was due partly to foreign admixture and   10
partly to its having been once inhabited by the rich and gay.
Miss Stanley, in her home and club in Soho, and by those
agencies of social intercourse and recreation which she so
well knew how to employ, did her best to give to the toiling
and indigent classes in the neighbourhood some share in the   15
gaiety, the variety, the beauty, and the cheerfulness of life.
                    —*The Times*, July 11, 1884, p. 4, col. 3.

[MR. MATTHEW ARNOLD ON AMERICA]

Dr. Robert Laird Collier, writing in the *Boston Herald*, gives
an account of an interview with Mr. Matthew Arnold, in
which Mr. Arnold spoke as follows:—   20
    I have been asked by representatives of the *Pall Mall Ga-
zette* and other London papers to be "interviewed," and have
always declined the honour, and furthermore have promised
Mr. Knowles, of the *Nineteenth Century*, that if I have any
thing to say about America I will send it to him. But I have   25
no present intention either to write or say anything. It was
very shocking to see that miserable hoax printed in the Chicago
Tribune, purporting to give some criticisms I had made
through the *Pall Mall Gazette*. Since its publication I have received many letters from friends in Chicago, who feel justly   30
aggrieved that such reflections should come from my pen. It
is simply preposterous to suppose that I could repay their hos-

pitality and the great kindness they showed me by such criticism. Such an act on my part would have been monstrous and unpardonable. I met many most charming people in Chicago, and have there friends to whom I am deeply attached. It is
5 true I did not care for Chicago; it is too "new," and as we would say in England, "too beastly prosperous." I would not go to see the pig-sticking at the stock-yards. Certainly not! Why should I wish to see pig-sticking? Still, as I have said, nowhere did I meet more charming people than in Chicago. I
10 liked Milwaukee and St. Louis better as cities, but I prefer Philadelphia to any American city. Chestnut-street is like Bond-street. Philadelphia is so respectable. There are traces, certainly, of Quaker rigidity, but at the same time great refinement.
15   I everywhere met with kindness and affectionateness, and came home feeling that the Americans are indeed a very warmhearted people. My wife and daughter were loath to quit the country, so appreciative were they of the universal civility and goodness shown them and myself. We enjoyed all we saw,
20 and the affectionate people most of all. Yes, I must say they are an affectionate people. I met more social refinement than I had expected. Still, all I had written of society in America holds true. The Americans are a commercial people, with the intellectual limitations of such. The conditions make them a
25 commercial people; they could not be otherwise, situated as they are. They have a vast continent, and all its resources are to be developed. Business absorbs the time and powers of the men as it does not in Europe; consequently there is in America no class of gentlemen as in England, although everywhere
30 there are individuals equal to any gentleman in the world.
    And the ladies are more charming. I have never met such takingness. The young ladies are most engaging. While many of the gentlemen have the tone of feeling and the speech of English gentlemen, the ladies are much more engaging than
35 English ladies—are better informed and more capable in conversation. It is this takingness or engagingness in all American ladies that really quite fascinated me—the young ladies are so well posted and converse so pleasingly.
                    —*Pall Mall Gazette*, July 17, 1884, p. 10.

[OLIVER WENDELL HOLMES]

[Arnold responded to the request of *The Critic* for a tribute
to the seventy-fifth birthday anniversary of Oliver Wendell
Holmes with this note:]
To the Editors of The Critic:
Pray let my voice be admitted to swell the chorus of good   5
wishes to the excellent veteran of letters and delightful man
whose birthday is August the 29th. What an auspicious birthday—within one day of Goethe's!
                                        Matthew Arnold.
Athenaeum Club, Pall Mall, S.W., August 6th, 1884.   10
        —*The Critic and Good Literature* (New York),
                              August 30, 1884, p. 97.

[A LAY SERMON:
ON THE UNVEILING OF A MOSAIC IN
WHITECHAPEL]

I come here to-day in deference to a summons I could not
resist, a summons from Mr. Watts himself, the author of the
beautiful work of art which has just been unveiled on St.   15
Jude's church. In former times, as Mr. Courtney has mentioned, I was tolerably acquainted with the East-end of London from inspecting the schools here. But for a long time my
work has lain elsewhere, and in my leisure I have not come
here. I will tell you the reason. If we go from here westward   20
we come through the City to the West-end and there we see
a possessing class spending and enjoying, and in the City we
see a trading class desiring nothing better than to possess and
enjoy too; and these are the before-the-scenes, as one may say,
of our national world. They produce what is called the na-   25
tional fabric of British civilization, the marvellous work and
wonders of British enterprise. Then at the East-end we have
what may be called the "behind-the-scenes" of English civilization. You know that behind the scenes at a theatre you see
a number of men in their shirt-sleeves, dusty boards and   30
benches, and odds and ends of things, and that always has

seemed to me to be a representation of what the east of London is by comparison with the brilliant spectacle which is seen further west. And not only is there this "behind-the-scenes" to be seen in the east of London, but there may also
5 be conceived here as presented to our view a great receptacle and limbo in which the people who have failed and fallen or been hurt and wounded, and whom the excess of production and competition which the trading classes carry on has turned out—a great receptacle and limbo in which these poor people
10 exist as well as they can. When English people speak of English life and of our national civilization they naturally think chiefly of the spectacle which is to be seen westward, in the City and at the West-end, and this spectacle everybody is struck with and very many—the majority, perhaps—praise and
15 admire. And when the possessing and trading classes get a peep behind the scenes, there is soon some one to pull the curtain. As to the life of the spending and enjoying class we are told that luxury is good for trade. As for the trade and the trading classes, though occasionally there are murmurs
20 and complaints of over-production, over-competition, and depression, there comes an authority, a great authority, such as Mr. Giffen—who, no doubt, is a friend of the chairman's [laughter and "Hear, hear"]—a political economist who tells us in imposing letters to *The Times*, which *The Times* prints in
25 imposing type, that all is for the best and that the more competition the more prosperity. And so with the spectacle of our civilization most people are well satisfied.

But there are two sorts of people who have always been, or generally been, dissatisfied and malcontents—the poets and
30 the saints. [Laughter.] It happens that I was brought up under the influence of a poet who was very much dissatisfied with the proceedings of the middle and upper classes among us, and who, indeed, called them idolatry. "Avarice and expense are idols, and these they adore." This poet convinced me, and
35 therefore I have spent most of my leisure time, not among the lower classes, but in preaching to the upper classes in my own feeble way, and in telling them that their idolatrous world could not stand, and that already one began to hear formidable

cracks in it, and to see it beginning to sway ominously to and fro. Some there are, however, who came to the East-end, though I did not; and these are the saints—some from those classes who possess and enjoy and from the class that is aspiring to possess and enjoy. They, dissatisfied with merely living the   5
life of those classes, came to the East-end, and such men are the true saviours of society. [Cheers.] Their names pass, everything passes, but that matters little—their names are written in the Book of Life. There is written a name which, perhaps, by this time is beginning to wax faint in the memories of men,   10
because he has now been dead some years—the name of Denison. There is written another name which the chairman has already mentioned—the name of the admirable young man whose memory will be preserved by this hall in which I speak —the name of Toynbee. I cannot forbear to say that I myself   15
knew, when I inspected schools here, one of those men—(Mr. Arnold met him once in Spitalfields and asked, "Ill and overworked, how fare you in this scene?")—a man fruitful in good works, cheerful, devoted, indefatigable. That man I have never seen since, and I do not know whether he is alive or not; some   20
here will perhaps know him by name—William Tyler. Then there is the man whom we are met to-day to honour, who has been here 12 years—Mr. Barnett. [Cheers.]

The first means which people think of in coming to help a neighbourhood of this kind is naturally religion. We have   25
just had here a great attempt to move this neighbourhood by means of an agency of this kind—the machinery of the East London Mission. Religion, when used in this way, is naturally presented under the preternatural and miraculous aspect which popular Christianity assumes. People are told to give a hearty   30
assent to Christianity in this preternatural and miraculous aspect. They are told also—and this we must never forget—to be sober, patient, charitable, kind; and then they are told that after this life they will wake up in a world as little like Whitechapel as possible. [Hear.] An aspect of the Christian Gospel,   35
which in the past has been a stay to millions, and which is still a stay to many, shall never be spoken of by me with hostility; but I have long been convinced that to very many, and above

all to very many of those whom you have to reach here, Christianity as thus presented appears something neither entirely solid nor verifiable. There is, no doubt, a profounder, and at present little recognized, aspect of the Christian religion in which it is solid and verifiable. But to seize this aspect the standard of life must be raised, and it cannot be seized until the domestic affections and the social impulses have been cultivated, until the sense of beauty has been quickened, until the pleasures of art have been laid open. Some have come here with a wish to cultivate and appeal to the social sympathies. Mr. Barnett's originality has been that, besides his labours as a parish clergyman, he has appealed to this sense of beauty, that he has desired, in the words of the tablet placed beside the mosaic, he has striven, to "make the lives of his neighbours brighter by bringing within their reach the influence of beauty." It is with this object that he has set on foot these art exhibitions which have attracted so much attention outside the limits of the East-end, which have already exercised a great and powerful influence here, which have already given an access to art to hundreds who had none before, and which will, no doubt, produce still greater influence in the future.

Nevertheless, that saying remains true—"Whosoever drinketh of this water shall thirst again." No doubt the social sympathies, the feeling for beauty, the pleasure of art, if left merely by themselves, if untouched by what is the deepest thing in human life—religion—are apt to become ineffectual and superficial. The art which Mr. Barnett has done his best to make known to the people here, the art of men like Mr. Watts, the art manifested in works such as that which has just now been unveiled upon the walls of St. Jude's Church, this art has a deep and powerful connexion with religion. You have seen the mosaic, and you have read, perhaps, the scroll which explains it. There is a figure of Time—a strong young man full of hope, energy, daring, venture, moving on to take possession of life; and beside him there is that beautiful figure of Death, representing the breakings off, the cuttings short, the baffling disappointments, the heart-piercing separations from which the fullest life and the most fiery energy cannot exempt us. Step out as you will, strong and bold young man, that mournful figure must go hand in hand with you for ever. These two figures belong, if you will, to art. But who is the third figure, with the weighing scales and the sword of fire? We are told by the text which is engraved on the scroll: "The Eternal (the scroll, however, has 'the Lord') is a God of judgment: blessed are all they that wait for Him." The figure is that of Judgment, and that figure, I say, belongs to religion. The text which explains the figure is taken from one of the Hebrew prophets. But an even more striking text is furnished us from the sayings of the founder of Christianity, when he was about to leave the world and to leave behind him his disciples, who, so long as He lived, had Him to come to and had Him to do, as one may say, all their thinking for them. He told them that when He was gone they should find a new source of thought and feeling open itself within them; that this new source of thought and feeling should be a comforter to them, and that it should convince the world of many things. Among other things, he said it should convince the world of judgment, because "the Prince of this world is judged." That is a text which we shall do well to lay to heart and consider along with the text from the Prophets which is printed beside it.

More and more it has become manifest that the Prince of this world is really judged—that the Prince of this world, which is the perpetual idol of selfishly possessing and enjoying, and the worlds fashioned under the inspiration of this idol, are judged. One world and another have gone to pieces because they were fashioned under the inspiration of this idol, and that is a consoling and edifying thought. Above all, it is a consoling and edifying thought for those classes, which—in comparison with the great possessing and trading classes, which may be described as the fortunate classes—may be called the sacrificed classes. True, if the sacrificed classes merely in their turn, under the influence of hatred or cupidity, desire to change and destroy in order to possess and enjoy, their world too will be idolatrous; the old world will continue to stand for the present, or, at any rate, their new world will not take its place. True, into the old world, fashioned as we have said,

much of human virtue has entered, and that may often make
it pardonable and even lovable; but still, considering how much
good it has left undone and how much positive ill it has done,
we may be allowed to be satisfied when the time comes for
5 its departing. There will always be an infinite charm in the
ideal presented by the Christian religion of the new world to
rise after the Prince of this world and this idolatrous world
are judged. There will always be an infinite charm in such expressions as "The consolation of Israel," "The restoration of
10 all things," "A new Heaven and a new earth," "The Kingdom
of God." But I say, however great might be that charm for
the man of soul, that charm is perhaps greatest for the sacrificed classes, and it is good for them to have this ideal before
them, to have before their eyes in a crowded street like this
15 a monument which recalls it to them.

People are always tempted to ask when they entertain ideals
of this kind, "Will the change come soon; will the renovation
be in our own time?" There are seasons, and this in which we
live is perhaps one of them, when the crackings which we
20 hear, and the swayings and the rockings which we see, and
the signs and warnings on every side seem to say that the
change cannot be very far off. But we must remember at the
same time how short our time here is. We must remember
what the philosopher so well says—that men always are im-
25 patient, and for precipitating things. We must remember what
contradiction the course of events perpetually offers to such
an ideal as that of the Kingdom of God. We must remember
the delays and the deferments which it is certain to meet with.
We must remember the obstacles perpetually opposed, not only
30 by the selfish among mankind, but also "by the fears of the
brave and the follies of the wise." Let us therefore beware of
expecting that any renovation upon which we have set our
hearts will come immediately, but let us also be thankful to be
reminded that whether it comes late or soon the Prince of this
35 world is judged, and that the renovation will surely come
sooner or later. This it is which makes faith and hope to be
among the primal virtues, because they keep alive in us confidence in our ideal when events might otherwise shake it.

Faith and hope would not be virtues if the exercise of them was easy. It is because the exercise of them is hard that they become virtues, and that they are a beauty and a merit. [Cheers.]

> And oh, when nature sinks, as oft she may,
> Through long-lived pressure of obscure distress,   5
> Still to be strenuous for the bright reward,
> And in the soul admit of no decay,
> Brook no continuance of weak-mindedness,
> Great is the glory, for the strife is hard.

[Cheers.]   10

—The Times, December 1, 1884, p. 10, cols. 4-5.

[DULWICH COLLEGE]

Yesterday afternoon the prizes were distributed to the successful boys of Dulwich College by Mr. Matthew Arnold.

After distributing the prizes, Mr. Matthew Arnold, who on rising was greeted with loud cheers, said,—It is true, as Mr.   15
Welldon has told you, that, though I have not infrequently been asked to give away prizes on occasions of this kind, I have till now always declined to do so. On the present occasion, however, the case is different. Your distinguished Head Master, Mr. Welldon, has been appointed to Harrow, and is   20
bringing to a close his administration of Dulwich. The conjunction of these two names, Harrow and Dulwich, had an effect upon me which I could not resist. The great school to which Mr. Welldon is going, Harrow, is a school with which, though I was at another school myself, I am yet connected   25
on account of my children by memories which I can never lose, of kindness which I can never repay. The great school which Mr. Welldon is leaving, Dulwich, happens to be a signal and splendid type of just that description of school which I have long desired, and vainly desired, to see put at the dis-   30
posal of the professional and trading classes throughout this country. [Cheers.] When I look at your buildings, at your grounds, at your equipment of every kind—when I see the

sort of head master with whom you are parting, the sort of
head master chosen as his successor, the sort of staff by which
they are surrounded—when I see all these, and then think how
very, very seldom the English middle class elsewhere finds it-
5 self with advantages of this kind, and how very, very little
they in general seem to care whether they possess them or not,
I am filled with admiration of Dulwich, and with astonishment,
I must say, at the indifference which people outside Dulwich
seem to feel to their own clear interest. But expressions of as-
10 tonishment and impatience are not of much use; the thing is
to consider what hope we may entertain for the future. And
I am bound to say that I do not see much hope in the future
of the public institution throughout this country of schools
like Dulwich. I regret that it should be so, but such is the case.
15 In America, in the colonies, and, finally, in our own country
also the tendency will rather be, it seems to me, to strengthen
and enlarge more or less the instruction given in the schools
which we call elementary—schools for the mass of the community—to say that that instruction, indeed, is indispensable
20 for every citizen, that it is all the instruction which is strictly
necessary, and that whoever wants more instruction than that
must get it at his own expense as he can. Under these circumstances, the future of high culture and high studies must depend most upon the love of individuals for them and the
25 faith of individuals in them. Perhaps this has always been their
best support, and it is a support which, happily for mankind,
will, I believe, never fail. [Cheers.] In communities where there
are no endowments these will be the only support of high
studies and fine culture. But human nature is weak, and I pre-
30 fer, I confess, that these supports, however strong and stanch
they may be, of high studies and fine culture should not have
the whole weight thrown upon them, should not be the only
supports. Here is the great advantage of endowments. [Hear,
hear.] Endowments and public foundations fix and fortify
35 our profession of faith and love towards high studies and serious
culture. [Cheers.] But endowments are sporadic; they alight
here, and they do not alight there. Dulwich is no part, alas!
of a complete public school system. Dulwich itself, like Eton

and Winchester and Harrow, is but a lucky accident; but in
the absence of any complete system of higher schools, and in
the growing improbability of this want being made good, the
value, the importance, the responsibility of lucky accidents
like Dulwich increases, let me tell you, a thousand fold. More   5
particularly is this the case with regard to the great school
where I have just had the honour to-day of distributing the
prizes. Dulwich is the very type of the schools which the
English middle classes, had they and their politicians been wise,
would, I think, in their day of power, which is now, perhaps,   10
passing from them, have endeavoured to institute for themselves everywhere. Something at least you do here to remedy
their grave omission. May you prosper in the future as in
the past you have prospered. May you shine forth as a bright
example of what a school for the English middle classes should   15
be, and may you do what a single school can to repair, so far
as in you lies, the intellectual poverty and effacement to which
in general those classes have, through their own neglect, condemned themselves. [Cheers.]
                    —*The Times*, July 30, 1885, p. 8, col. 2.   20

[NATIONAL EISTEDDFOD OF WALES]

[Arnold attended the sessions of the National Eisteddfod of
Wales in 1885 at Aberdare as guest of Lord Aberdare, who as
H. A. Bruce had formerly been Vice-President of the Committee of Council for Education. On the second day, August
26, Arnold was on the platform when J. C. Parkinson spoke   25
on "The Celtic Race and Literature," an address that drew
heavily on Arnold's *On the Study of Celtic Literature* and
paid tribute to Arnold's presence: "No living Englishman has
more justly appreciated and honoured the Celtic genius than
Mr. Matthew Arnold, whose presence is the crowning compli-   30
ment to this Eisteddfod." Lord Aberdare proposed the vote of
thanks to Parkinson, and called on Arnold to second the pro-
posal.]
    Mr. Matthew Arnold, who seconded the vote, received quite
an ovation. He said he was honoured by the commission to   35

second the vote of thanks. That commission would give him nothing but pleasure if it were not accompanied by the intimation that he was to say something more tomorrow. [Applause.] If he might be allowed to say of an address which
5 contained so many kind things of himself, it was one full of interest. He had very great pleasure in seconding the vote. [Applause.]

[On the following day, August 27, during an interval between the appearance of the choirs in choral competition,
10 Arnold was again called upon to speak, this time by Archdeacon Griffiths:]

Mr. Matthew Arnold said that in this great building, which was a monument to the turn of the Celtic race for the gigantic, and, he must say also, so far as speaking was concerned, of the
15 impossible—[laughter and appause]—he was rather surprised that they should even wish to hear any speaker unless he was such an elocutionist as the Archdeacon of Llandaff. But he knew that even in the ages of faith confessors and martyrs were personages of interest, and he supposed that they re-
20 membered that he (the speaker) had suffered something for the sake of Eisteddfodau, and that, therefore, they kindly wished to hear him. It was true that, twenty years ago, he wrote a letter to his friend, Sir Hugh Owen—an excellent Welshman—[applause]—in which he expressed his interest
25 in Eisteddfodau and what they indicated. [Applause.] He wished to say that he retained that interest still, and that the sight of this immense audience exceeded anything he supposed possible. [Hear, hear.] But this audience also exceeded what it was possible for his voice to reach, and therefore, having ex-
30 pressed his interest in Eisteddfodau, he meant to take his leave of them and sit down. [Laughter and applause.]

—*Western Mail*, August 27, 1885, p. 3, col. 8;
August 28, p. 3, col. 4.

Appendix Two:
Arnold's Version of Isaiah

[ISAIAH OF JERUSALEM]

PRELUDE

(I)

1

1 THE vision of Isaiah the son of Amoz, which he saw concerning Judah and Jerusalem in the days of Uzziah, Jotham, Ahaz, and Hezekiah, kings of Judah.

2 HEAR, O heavens, and give ear, O earth! for the LORD hath spoken:—"I have nourished and brought up children, and they have rebelled against me.

3 "The ox knoweth his owner, and the ass his master's crib: but Israel doth not know, my people doth not consider."

4 Ah sinful nation, a people laden with iniquity, a seed of evildoers, children that are corrupters: they have forsaken the LORD, they have provoked the Holy One of Israel unto anger, they are gone away backward.

5 Why should ye be stricken any more? ye will revolt more and more: the whole head is sick, and the whole heart faint.

6 From the sole of the foot even unto the head there is no soundness in it; but wounds, and bruises, and putrefying sores: they have not been pressed, neither bound up, neither mollified with ointment.

7 Your country is desolate, your cities are burned with fire: your land, strangers devour it in your presence, and it is desolate, as overthrown by strangers.

8 And the daughter of Zion is left as a cottage in a vineyard, as a lodge in a garden of cucumbers, as a besieged city.

9 Except the L ORD of hosts had left unto us a very small remnant, we should have been as Sodom, and we should have been like unto Gomorrah.

10 H EAR the word of the L ORD, ye rulers of Sodom! give ear unto the law of our God, ye people of Gomorrah!

11 To what purpose is the multitude of your sacrifices unto me? saith the L ORD: I am full of the burnt offerings of rams, and the fat of fed beasts; and I delight not in the blood of bullocks, or of lambs, or of he goats.

12 When ye come to appear before me, who hath required this at your hand, to tread my courts?

13 Bring no more vain oblations; incense is an abomination unto me; the new moons and sabbaths, the calling of assemblies, I cannot away with; it is iniquity, even the solemn meeting.

14 Your new moons and your appointed feasts my soul hateth: they are a trouble unto me; I am weary to bear them.

15 And when ye spread forth your hands, I will hide mine eyes from you: yea, when ye make many prayers, I will not hear: your hands are full of blood.

16 Wash you, make you clean; put away the evil of your doings from before mine eyes; cease to do evil;

17 Learn to do well; seek judgment, correct the oppressor, judge the fatherless, plead for the widow.

18 Come now, and let us reason together, saith the L ORD: though your sins be as scarlet, they shall be as white as snow; though they be red like crimson, they shall be as wool.

19 If ye be willing and obedient, ye shall eat the good of the land:

20 But if ye refuse and rebel, ye shall be devoured with the sword: for the mouth of the L ORD hath spoken it.

21 How is the faithful city become an harlot! it was full of judgment; righteousness lodged in it; but now murderers.

22 Thy silver is become dross, thy wine mixed with water:

23 Thy princes are rebellious, and companions of thieves:

every one loveth gifts, and followeth after rewards: they judge not the fatherless, neither doth the cause of the widow come unto them.

24 Therefore saith the Lord, the Lᴏʀᴅ of hosts, the mighty One of Israel:—"Ah, I will ease me of mine adversaries, and avenge me of mine enemies:

25 "And I will turn my hand upon thee, and purely purge away thy dross, and take away all thine alloy:

26 "And I will restore thy judges as at the first, and thy counsellers as at the beginning: afterward thou shalt be called, The city of righteousness, the faithful city."

27 Zion shall be redeemed through judgment, and her converts through righteousness.

28 And the destruction of the transgressors and of the sinners shall be together, and they that forsake the Lᴏʀᴅ shall be consumed.

29 For they shall be ashamed of the oaks which ye have desired, and ye shall be confounded for the gardens that ye have chosen.

30 For ye shall be as an oak whose leaf fadeth, and as a garden that hath no water.

31 And the strong shall be as tow, and his work as a spark, and they shall both burn together, and none shall quench them.

CALAMITIES FOR JUDAH

(II–V)

2

1 Tʜᴇ word that Isaiah the son of Amoz saw concerning Judah and Jerusalem.

2 "Aɴᴅ it shall come to pass in the last days, that the mountain of the Lᴏʀᴅ's house shall be established in the top of the mountains, and shall be exalted above the hills; and all nations shall flow unto it.

3 "And many people shall go and say, 'Come ye, and let us

go up to the mountain of the Lord, to the house of the God of Jacob; and he will teach us of his ways, and we will walk in his paths:' for out of Zion shall go forth the law, and the word of the Lord from Jerusalem.

4 "And he shall judge among the nations, and shall rebuke many people: and they shall beat their swords into plowshares, and their spears into pruninghooks: nation shall not lift up sword against nation, neither shall they learn war any more."

5 O house of Jacob, come ye, and let us walk in the light of the Lord!

6 Therefore thou hast forsaken thy people the house of Jacob, because they be replenished from the east, and are soothsayers like the Philistines, and they please themselves in the children of strangers.

7 Their land also is full of silver and gold, neither is there any end of their treasures; their land is also full of horses, neither is there any end of their chariots:

8 Their land also is full of idols; they worship the work of their own hands, that which their own fingers have made:

9 And the mean man boweth down, and the great man humbleth himself: therefore forgive them not!

10 Enter into the rock, and hide thee in the dust, for fear of the Lord, and for the glory of his majesty!

11 The lofty looks of man shall be humbled, and the haughtiness of men shall be bowed down, and the Lord alone shall be exalted in that day.

12 For the day of the Lord of hosts shall be upon every thing that is proud and lofty, and upon every thing that is lifted up; and it shall be brought low:

13 And upon all the cedars of Lebanon, that are high and lifted up, and upon all the oaks of Bashan,

14 And upon all the high mountains, and upon all the hills that are lifted up,

15 And upon every high tower, and upon every fenced wall,

16 And upon all the ships of Tarshish, and upon all pleasant pictures.

17 And the loftiness of man shall be bowed down, and the haughtiness of men shall be made low: and the LORD alone shall be exalted in that day.

18 And the idols he shall utterly abolish.

19 And they shall go into the holes of the rocks, and into the caves of the earth, for fear of the LORD, and for the glory of his majesty, when he ariseth to shake terribly the earth.

20 In that day a man shall cast his idols of silver, and his idols of gold, which they made each one for himself to worship, to the moles and to the bats;

21 To go into the clefts of the rocks, and into the crevices of the crags, for fear of the LORD, and for the glory of his majesty, when he ariseth to shake terribly the earth.

22 Cease ye from man, whose breath is in his nostrils: for wherein is he to be accounted of?

3

1 For, behold, the Lord, the LORD of hosts, doth take away from Jerusalem and from Judah the stay and the staff, the whole stay of bread, and the whole stay of water,

2 The mighty man, and the man of war, the judge, and the prophet, and the prudent, and the ancient,

3 The captain of fifty, and the honourable man, and the counseller, and the cunning artificer, and the master of the spell.

4 And I will give children to be their princes, and babes shall rule over them.

5 And the people shall be oppressed, every one by another, and every one by his neighbour: the child shall behave himself proudly against the ancient, and the base against the honourable.

6 When a man shall take hold of his brother of the house of his father, saying, Thou hast clothing, be thou our ruler, and let this ruin be under thy hand:

7 In that day shall he swear, saying, I will not be an healer; for in my house is neither bread nor clothing: make me not a ruler of the people.

8 For Jerusalem is ruined, and Judah is fallen: because their

tongue and their doings are against the LORD, to provoke the eyes of his glory.

9 The shew of their countenance doth witness against them; and they declare their sin as Sodom, they hide it not. Woe unto their soul! for they have rewarded evil unto themselves.

10 Say ye to the righteous, that it shall be well with him: for they shall eat the fruit of their doings.

11 Woe unto the wicked! it shall be ill with him: for the reward of his hands shall be given him.

12 As for my people, children are their oppressors, and women rule over them. O my people, they which lead thee cause thee to err, and destroy the way of thy paths.

13 The LORD standeth up to plead, and standeth to judge the people.

14 The LORD will enter into judgment with the ancients of his people, and the princes thereof: for ye have eaten up the vineyard; the spoil of the poor is in your houses.

15 What mean ye that ye beat my people to pieces, and grind the faces of the poor? saith the Lord GOD of hosts.

16 MOREOVER the LORD saith:—
Because the daughters of Zion are haughty, and walk with stretched forth necks and wanton eyes, walking and mincing as they go, and making a tinkling with their feet:

17 Therefore the Lord will smite with a scab the crown of the head of the daughters of Zion, and the LORD will discover their secret parts.

18 In that day the Lord will take away the bravery of their tinkling ornaments about their feet, and their headbands, and their round tires like the moon,

19 The earrings, and the bracelets, and the mufflers,

20 The bonnets, and the ornaments of the legs, and the girdles, and the scent-bottles, and the amulets,

21 The rings, and nose-jewels,

22 The changeable suits of apparel, and the mantles, and the wimples, and the pockets,

23 The looking-glasses, and the fine linen, and the hoods, and the vails.

24 And it shall come to pass, that instead of sweet smell there shall be stink; and instead of a girdle a rent; and instead of well set hair baldness; and instead of a stomacher a girding of sackcloth; and branding instead of beauty.

25 Thy men shall fall by the sword, and thy mighty in the war.

26 And her gates shall lament and mourn; and she being desolate shall sit upon the ground.

4

1 And in that day seven women shall take hold of one man, saying, We will eat our own bread, and wear our own apparel: only let us be called by thy name, to take away our reproach!

2 IN that day shall the Branch of the LORD be beautiful and glorious, and the fruit of the land shall be excellent and comely for them that are escaped of Israel.

3 And it shall come to pass, that he that is left in Zion, and he that remaineth in Jerusalem, shall be called holy, even every one that is written among the living in Jerusalem;

4 When the Lord shall have washed away the filth of the daughters of Zion, and shall have purged the blood of Jerusalem from the midst thereof, by the spirit of judgment, and by the spirit of burning.

5 And the LORD will create upon every dwelling place of mount Zion, and upon her assemblies, a cloud and smoke by day, and the shining of a flaming fire by night: for upon all the glory shall be a defence.

6 And there shall be a tabernacle for a shadow in the daytime from the heat, and for a place of refuge, and for a covert from storm and from rain.

5

1 Now will I sing to my wellbeloved a song of my beloved touching his vineyard. My wellbeloved hath a vineyard in a very fruitful hill:

2   And he fenced it, and gathered out the stones thereof,
     and planted it with the choicest vine, and built a tower in
     the midst of it, and also made a winepress therein: and he
     looked that it should bring forth grapes, and it brought
     forth wild grapes.

3   And now, O inhabitants of Jerusalem, and men of Judah,
     judge, I pray you, betwixt me and my vineyard.

4   What could have been done more to my vineyard, that I
     have not done in it? wherefore, when I looked that
     it should bring forth grapes, brought it forth wild
     grapes?

5   And now go to; I will tell you what I will do to my
     vineyard: I will take away the hedge thereof, and it shall
     be eaten up; and break down the wall thereof, and it shall
     be trodden down:

6   And I will lay it waste: it shall not be pruned, nor digged;
     but there shall come up briers and thorns: I will also com-
     mand the clouds that they rain no rain upon it.

7   For the vineyard of the LORD of hosts is the house of Is-
     rael, and the men of Judah his pleasant plant: and he
     looked for judgment, but behold oppression; for righ-
     teousness, but behold a cry.

8   WOE unto them that join house to house, that lay field
     to field, till there be no place, that they may be placed
     alone in the midst of the earth!

9   In mine ears saith the LORD of hosts, Of a truth many
     houses shall be desolate, even great and fair, without in-
     habitant.

10   Yea, ten acres of vineyard shall yield one bath, and the
     seed of an homer shall yield an ephah.

11   Woe unto them that rise up early in the morning, that
     they may follow strong drink; that continue until night,
     till wine inflame them!

12   And the harp, and the viol, the tabret, and pipe, and wine,
     are in their feasts: but they regard not the work of the
     LORD, neither consider the operation of his hands.

13   Therefore my people are gone into captivity, because they

have no knowledge: and their honourable men are famished, and their multitude dried up with thirst.

14 Therefore hell hath enlarged herself, and opened her mouth without measure: and their glory, and their multitude, and their pomp, and he that rejoiceth, shall descend into it.

15 And the mean man shall be brought down, and the mighty man shall be humbled, and the eyes of the lofty shall be humbled:

16 But the LORD of hosts shall be exalted in judgment, and God that is holy shall be sanctified in righteousness.

17 Then shall the lambs feed after their manner, and the waste places of the fat ones shall strangers eat.

18 Woe unto them that draw iniquity with cords of vanity, and sin as it were with a cart rope:

19 That say, Let him make speed, and hasten his work, that we may see it: and let the counsel of the Holy One of Israel draw nigh and come, that we may know it!

20 Woe unto them that call evil good, and good evil; that put darkness for light, and light for darkness; that put bitter for sweet, and sweet for bitter!

21 Woe unto them that are wise in their own eyes, and prudent in their own sight!

22 Woe unto them that are mighty to drink wine, and men of strength to mingle strong drink:

23 Which justify the wicked for reward, and take away the righteousness of the righteous from him!

24 Therefore as the fire devoureth the stubble, and the flame consumeth the chaff, so their root shall be as rottenness, and their blossom shall go up as dust: because they have cast away the law of the LORD of hosts, and despised the word of the Holy One of Israel.

25 Therefore is the anger of the LORD kindled against his people, and he hath stretched forth his hand against them, and hath smitten them: and the hills do tremble, and their carcases are as dung in the midst of the streets. For all this his anger is not turned away, but his hand is stretched out still.

26 And he will lift up an ensign to the nations from far, and will hiss unto them from the end of the earth: and, behold, they shall come with speed swiftly.

27 None shall be weary nor stumble among them; none shall slumber nor sleep; neither shall the girdle of their loins be loosed, nor the latchet of their shoes be broken:

28 Whose arrows are sharp, and all their bows bent, their horses' hoofs shall be counted like flint, and their wheels like a whirlwind:

29 Their roaring shall be like a lion, they shall roar like young lions: yea, they shall roar, and lay hold of the prey, and shall carry it away safe, and none shall deliver it.

30 And in that day there shall be roaring over it like the roaring of the sea: and if one look unto the land, behold darkness and sorrow, and the light is darkened in the heavens thereof.

VISION

(VI)

6

1 IN the year that king Uzziah died I saw also the Lord sitting upon a throne, high and lifted up, and his train filled

2 the temple. Above it stood the seraphims: each one had six wings; with twain he covered his face, and with twain

3 he covered his feet, and with twain he did fly. And one cried unto another, and said:—
Holy, holy, holy, is the LORD of hosts: the whole earth is full of his glory.

4 AND the posts of the door moved at the voice of him that cried, and the house was filled with smoke. Then said I:—

5 Woe is me! for I am undone; because I am a man of unclean lips, and I dwell in the midst of a people of unclean lips: for mine eyes have seen the King, the LORD of hosts.

6 THEN flew one of the seraphims unto me, having a live coal in his hand, which he had taken with the tongs from
7 off the altar: and he laid it upon my mouth, and said:— Lo, this hath touched thy lips; and thine iniquity is taken away, and thy sin purged.

8 ALSO I heard the voice of the Lord, saying, Whom shall I send, and who will go for us?
9 Then said I, Here am I; send me. And he said:— Go, and tell this people, Hear ye indeed, but understand not; and see ye indeed, but perceive not.
10 Make the heart of this people gross, and make their ears heavy, and shut their eyes; lest they see with their eyes, and hear with their ears, and understand with their heart, and convert, and be healed.

11 THEN said I, Lord, how long? And he answered:— Until the cities be wasted without inhabitant, and the houses without man, and the land be utterly desolate,
12 And the LORD have removed men far away, and there be a great forsaking in the midst of the land.
13 Even if yet in it shall be a tenth, it shall return, and shall be consumed: but as a terebinth tree, and as an oak, whose substance is in them, when they are cut down, so the substance thereof shall be a holy seed.

IMMANUEL

(VII–XII)

7

1 AND it came to pass in the days of Ahaz the son of Jotham, the son of Uzziah, king of Judah, that Rezin the king of Syria, and Pekah the son of Remaliah, king of Israel, went up toward Jerusalem to war against it, but
2 could not prevail against it. And it was told the house of

David, saying, Syria is confederate with Ephraim. And
his heart was moved, and the heart of his people, as the
3   trees of the wood are moved with the wind. Then said the
Lord unto Isaiah, Go forth now to meet Ahaz, thou, and
Shear-Jashub [1] thy son, at the end of the conduit of the
4   upper pool in the highway of the fuller's field; and say
unto him:—
Take heed, and be quiet; fear not, neither be fainthearted
for the two tails of these smoking firebrands, for the fierce
anger of Rezin with Syria, and of the son of Remaliah.
5   Because Syria, Ephraim, and the son of Remaliah, have
taken evil counsel against thee, saying,
6   Let us go up against Judah, and vex it, and let us make a
breach therein for us, and set a king in the midst of it,
even the son of Tabeal—
7   Thus said the Lord God: It shall not stand, neither shall
it come to pass.
8   For the head of Syria is Damascus, and the head of Damascus is Rezin; and within three-score and five years
shall Ephraim be broken, that it be not a people,
9   And the head of Ephraim is Samaria, and the head of
Samaria is Remaliah's son. If ye will not believe, surely ye
shall not be established.

10-11   MOREOVER the Lord spake again unto Ahaz, saying: Ask
thee a sign of the Lord thy God; ask it either in the depth
12   or in the height above. But Ahaz said: I will not ask,
13   neither will I tempt the Lord. And he said:—
Hear ye now, O house of David; Is it a small thing for
you to weary men, but will ye weary my God also?
14   Therefore the Lord himself shall give you a sign; Behold,
the virgin shall conceive, and bear a son, and shall call his
name Immanuel.
15   Milk-curd and honey shall he eat, when he shall know to
refuse the evil, and choose the good.
16   For before the child shall know to refuse the evil, and

---

[1] "The remnant shall return."

choose the good, the land shall be forsaken, whose two kings make thee afraid.

17 The LORD shall bring upon thee, and upon thy people, and upon thy father's house, days that have not come, from the day that Ephraim departed from Judah; even the king of Assyria.

18 And it shall come to pass in that day, that the LORD shall hiss for the fly that is in the uttermost part of the rivers of Egypt, and for the bee that is in the land of Assyria.

19 And they shall come, and shall rest all of them in the desolate valleys, and in the holes of the rocks, and upon all thorns, and upon all bushes.

20 In the same day shall the Lord shave with a rasor that is hired, namely, by them beyond the river, by the king of Assyria, the head, and the hair of the legs: and it shall also consume the beard.

21 And it shall come to pass in that day, that a man shall nourish a young cow, and two sheep;

22 And it shall come to pass, for the abundance of milk that they shall give he shall eat curds: for milk-curd and honey shall every one eat that is left in the land.

23 And it shall come to pass in that day, that every place shall be, where there were a thousand vines at a thousand silverlings, it shall even be for briers and thorns.

24 With arrows and with bows shall men come thither; because all the land shall become briers and thorns.

25 And on all hills that are digged with the mattock, thou shalt not come thither for fear of briers and thorns: but it shall be for the sending forth of oxen, and for the treading of lesser cattle.

8

1 MOREOVER the Lord said unto me, Take thee a great tablet, and write in it with pen of the people concerning Spoil-
2 speedeth-prey-hasteth.[1] And I took unto me faithful wit-

---

[1] Maher-shalal-hash-baz.

nesses to record, Uriah the priest, and Zechariah the son
3 of Jeberechiah. And I went unto the prophetess; and she
conceived, and bare a son. Then said the Lord to me:—
Call his name "Spoil-speedeth-prey-hasteth."

4 For before the child shall have knowledge to cry, My
father, and my mother! the riches of Damascus and the
spoil of Samaria shall be taken away before the king of
Assyria.

5 The Lord spake also unto me again, saying:—
6 Forasmuch as this people refuseth the waters of Shiloah
that go softly, and rejoice in Rezin and Remaliah's son;
7 Now therefore, behold, the Lord bringeth up upon them
the waters of the river, strong and many, even the king
of Assyria, and all his glory: and he shall come up over
all his channels, and go over all his banks.
8 And he shall pass through Judah; he shall overflow and go
over, he shall reach even to the neck; and the stretching
out of his wings shall fill the breadth of thy land, O Immanuel!

9 Associate yourselves, O ye peoples, and ye shall be
broken in pieces; and give ear, all of ye of far countries:
gird yourselves, and ye shall be broken in pieces; gird
yourselves, and ye shall be broken in pieces!
10 Take counsel together, and it shall come to nought; speak
the word, and it shall not stand: for "God-is-with-us!" [1]
11 For the Lord spake thus to me with a strong hand, and
instructed me that I should not walk in the way of this
people, saying:—
12 "Say ye not, A confederacy! wheresoever this people shall
say, A confederacy! neither fear ye their fear, nor be
afraid.
13 "Sanctify the Lord of hosts himself; and let him be your
fear, and let him be your dread.
14 "And he shall be for a sanctuary; but for a stone of stum-
bling and for a rock of offence to both the houses of Israel,

---

[1] Immanuel.

for a gin and for a snare to the inhabitants of Jerusalem.
15 "And many among them shall stumble, and fall, and be broken, and be snared, and be taken.
16 "Bind up the testimony, seal the law among my disciples!"—

17 AND I will wait upon the LORD, that hideth his face from the house of Jacob, and I will look for him.
18 Behold, I, and the children whom the LORD hath given me, are for signs and for tokens in Israel from the LORD of hosts, which dwelleth in mount Zion!
19 And when they shall say unto you, Seek unto them that have familiar spirits, and unto wizards that chirp, and that mutter—should not a people seek unto their God? for the living should they seek unto the dead?
20 "To the law and to the testimony!"—if they speak not according to this word, it is because for them there is no light of dawn.
21 And they shall pass along, hardly bestead and hungry: and it shall come to pass, that when they shall be hungry, they shall fret themselves, and curse their king and their God; and shall look upward,
22 And shall look unto the earth; and behold trouble and darkness, dimness of anguish! and they shall be driven to darkness.

9

1 NEVERTHELESS the dimness shall not remain unto that which was vexed: as aforetime did come shame unto the land of Zebulun and the land of Naphtali, so afterward cometh honour; to the way of the sea, beyond Jordan, the border of the Gentiles.
2 The people that walked in darkness have seen a great light: they that dwell in the land of the shadow of death, upon them hath the light shined.
3 Thou hast multiplied the nation, thou hast increased the joy: they joy before thee according to the joy in harvest, and as men rejoice when they divide the spoil.

4 For thou hast broken the yoke of his burden, and the staff of his shoulder, the staff of his oppressor, as in the day of Midian.

5 For all the trampling of the warrior with confused noise, and the war-cloak rolled in blood—they shall be for burning and fuel of fire.

6 For unto us a child is born, unto us a son is given: and the government shall be upon his shoulder: and his name shall be called Wonderful Counseller, Mighty God, Everlasting Father, Prince of Peace.

7 Of the increase of his government and peace there shall be no end, upon the throne of David, and upon his kingdom, to order it, and to establish it with judgment and with righteousness from henceforth even for ever. The zeal of the LORD of hosts will perform this.

8 THE Lord sent a word into Jacob, and it hath lighted upon Israel.

9 And all the people shall know, even Ephraim and the inhabitant of Samaria, that say in their pride and stoutness of heart:

10 "The bricks are fallen down, but we will build with hewn stones: the sycomores are cut down, but we will change them into cedars"—

11 Therefore the LORD shall set up the overthrowers of Rezin against them, and join their enemies together;

12 The Syrians before, and the Philistines behind; and they shall devour Israel with open mouth. For all this his anger is not turned away, but his hand is stretched out still.

13 For the people turneth not unto him that smiteth them, neither do they seek the LORD of hosts.

14 Therefore the LORD will cut off from Israel head and tail, palm-branch and rush, in one day.

15 The ancient and honourable, he is the head; and the prophet that teacheth lies, he is the tail.

16 For the leaders of this people cause them to err; and they that are led of them are destroyed.

17 Therefore the Lord shall have no joy in their young men,

neither shall have mercy on their fatherless and widows: for every one is an hypocrite and an evildoer, and every mouth speaketh folly. For all this his anger is not turned away, but his hand is stretched out still.

18 For wickedness burneth as the fire: it shall devour the briers and thorns, and shall kindle in the thickets of the forest, and they shall mount up like the lifting up of smoke.

19 Through the wrath of the LORD of hosts is the land darkened, and the people shall be as the fuel of the fire: no man shall spare his brother.

20 And he shall snatch on the right hand, and be hungry; and he shall eat on the left hand, and they shall not be satisfied: they shall eat every man the flesh of his own arm:

21 Manasseh, Ephraim; and Ephraim, Manasseh: and they together shall be against Judah. For all this his anger is not turned away, but his hand is stretched out still.

10

1 Woe unto them that decree unrighteous decrees, and that write grievousness which they have prescribed;

2 To turn aside the needy from judgment, and to take away the right from the poor of my people, that widows may be their prey, and that they may rob the fatherless!

3 And what will ye do in the day of visitation, and in the desolation which shall come from far? to whom will ye flee for help? and where will ye leave your glory?

4 Without me they shall bow down among the prisoners, and they shall fall under the slain. For all this his anger is not turned away, but his hand is stretched out still.

5 O ASSYRIAN, the rod of mine anger, and the staff in mine hand for mine indignation!

6 I send him against an hypocritical nation, and against the people of my wrath do I give him a charge, to take the

spoil, and to take the prey, and to tread them down like the mire of the streets.

7 Howbeit he meaneth not so, neither doth his heart think so; but it is in his heart to destroy and cut off nations not a few.

8 For he saith: "Are not my princes altogether kings?

9 "Is not Calno as Carchemish? is not Hamath as Arpad? is not Samaria as Damascus?

10 "As my hand hath found the kingdoms of the idols—and whose graven images did excel them of Jerusalem and of Samaria—

11 "Shall I not, as I have done unto Samaria and her idols, so do to Jerusalem and her idols?"

12 Wherefore it shall come to pass, that when the Lord hath performed his whole work upon mount Zion and on Jerusalem, I will punish the fruit of the stout heart of the king of Assyria, and the glory of his high looks.

13 For he saith: "By the strength of my hand I have done it, and by my wisdom; for I am prudent: and I have removed the bounds of the people, and have robbed their treasures, and I have put down the inhabitants like a valiant man:

14 "And my hand hath found as a nest the riches of the people: and as one gathereth eggs that are left, have I gathered all the earth; and there was none that moved the wing, or opened the mouth, or chirped."

15 Shall the axe boast itself against him that heweth therewith? or shall the saw magnify itself against him that shaketh it? as if the rod did shake itself against them that lift it, or as if the staff did lift that which is no wood!

16 Therefore shall the Lord, the Lord of hosts, send among his fat ones leanness; and under his glory he shall kindle a burning like the burning of a fire.

17 And the light of Israel shall be for a fire, and his Holy One for a flame: and it shall burn and devour his thorns and his briers in one day;

18 And shall consume the glory of his forest, and of his fruitful field, both soul and body: and they shall be as when a sick man fainteth.

19 And the remainder of the trees of his forest shall be few, that a child may write them.

20 And it shall come to pass in that day, that the remnant of Israel, and such as are escaped of the house of Jacob, shall no more again stay upon him that smote them; but shall stay upon the LORD, the Holy One of Israel, in truth.

21 "The-remnant-shall-return," [1] even the remnant of Jacob, unto the mighty God.

22 For though thy people Israel be as the sand of the sea, only a remnant of them shall return: a consumption is decreed, flooding in with righteousness.

23 For the Lord GOD of hosts shall make a consumption, even determined, in the midst of all the earth.

24 THEREFORE thus saith the Lord GOD of hosts: O my people that dwellest in Zion, be not afraid of the Assyrian, when he shall smite thee with a rod, and shall lift up his staff against thee, after the manner of Egypt.

25 For yet a very little while, and the indignation shall cease, and mine anger shall be for their destruction.

26 And the LORD of hosts shall stir up a scourge for him according to the slaughter of Midian at the rock of Oreb: and as his rod was upon the sea, so shall he lift it up after the manner of Egypt.

27 And it shall come to pass in that day, that his burden shall be taken away from off thy shoulder, and his yoke from off thy neck, and the yoke shall break because of the fatness.

28 HE is come to Aiath, he is passed to Migron! at Michmash he hath laid up his carriages:

29 They are gone over the passage: they have taken up their lodging at Geba; Ramah is afraid; Gibeah of Saul is fled.

30 Lift up thy voice, O daughter of Gallim: cause it to be heard unto Laish, O poor Anathoth!

31 Madmenah is removed; the inhabitants of Gebim gather their stuff to flee.

[1] Shear-jashub.

32   As yet shall he remain at Nob that day: he shall shake his hand against the mount of the daughter of Zion, the hill of Jerusalem.

33   Behold! the Lord, the LORD of hosts, shall lop the bough with terror: and the high ones of stature shall be hewn down, and the haughty shall be humbled.

34   And he shall cut down the thickets of the forest with iron, and Lebanon shall fall by a mighty one.

11

1   AND there shall come forth a rod out of the stem of Jesse, and a Branch shall grow out of his roots:

2   And the spirit of the LORD shall rest upon him, the spirit of wisdom and understanding, the spirit of counsel and might, the spirit of knowledge and of the fear of the LORD;

3   And shall make him of quick understanding in the fear of the LORD: and he shall not judge after the sight of his eyes, neither reprove after the hearing of his ears:

4   But with righteousness shall he judge the poor, and reprove with equity for the meek of the earth: and he shall smite the earth with the rod of his mouth, and with the breath of his lips shall he slay the wicked.

5   And righteousness shall be the girdle of his loins, and faithfulness the girdle of his reins.

6   The wolf also shall dwell with the lamb, and the leopard shall lie down with the kid; and the calf and the young lion and the fatling together; and a little child shall lead them.

7   And the cow and the bear shall feed; their young ones shall lie down together: and the lion shall eat straw like the ox.

8   And the sucking child shall play on the hole of the asp, and the weaned child shall put his hand on the cockatrice' den.

9   They shall not hurt nor destroy in all my holy mountain:

for the earth shall be full of the knowledge of the Lord, as the waters cover the sea.

10 And in that day there shall be a root of Jesse, which shall stand for an ensign of the people; to it shall the Gentiles seek: and his rest shall be glorious.

11 And it shall come to pass in that day, that the Lord shall set his hand again the second time to recover the remnant of his people, which shall be left, from Assyria, and from Egypt, and from Pathros, and from Cush, and from Elam, and from Shinar, and from Hamath, and from the islands of the sea.

12 And he shall set up an ensign for the nations, and shall assemble the outcasts of Israel, and gather together the dispersed of Judah from the four corners of the earth.

13 The envy also of Ephraim shall depart, and the adverse ones of Judah shall be cut off: Ephraim shall not envy Judah, and Judah shall not vex Ephraim.

14 But they shall fly upon the shoulders of the Philistines toward the west; they shall spoil them of the east together: they shall lay their hand upon Edom and Moab; and the children of Ammon shall obey them.

15 And the Lord shall utterly destroy the tongue of the Egyptian sea; and with his mighty wind shall he shake his hand over the river, and shall smite it into seven streams, and make men go over dryshod.

16 And there shall be an highway for the remnant of his people, which shall be left, from Assyria; like as it was to Israel in the day that he came up out of the land of Egypt.

12

1 And in that day thou shalt say: O Lord, I will praise thee! though thou wast angry with me, thine anger is turned away, and thou comfortest me.

2 Behold, God is my salvation; I will trust, and not be afraid: for the Lord JEHOVAH is my strength and my song; he also is become my salvation.

3 Therefore with joy shall ye draw water out of the wells of salvation.

4 And in that day shall ye say: Praise the Lord, call upon his name, declare his doings among the peoples, make mention that his name is exalted.

5 Sing unto the Lord; for he hath done excellent things: this is known in all the earth.

6 Cry out and shout, thou inhabitant of Zion! for great is the Holy One of Israel in the midst of thee.

[Arnold omits 13:1. For 13:2–14:23, see pp. 362–65.]

THE BURDENS

(XIV, 24–XXIII)

14

24 The Lord of hosts hath sworn, saying: Surely as I have thought, so it shall come to pass; and as I have purposed, so shall it stand:

25 That I will break the Assyrian in my land, and upon my mountains tread him under foot: then shall his yoke depart from off them, and his burden depart from off their shoulders.

26 This is the purpose that is purposed upon the whole earth: and this is the hand that is stretched out upon all the nations.

27 For the Lord of hosts hath purposed, and who shall disannul it? and his hand is stretched out, and who shall turn it back?

28 In the year that King Ahaz died was this burden:—

29 Give not thyself wholly to joy, Philistia, because the rod of him that smote thee is broken! for out of the serpent's root shall come forth a cockatrice, and his fruit shall be a fiery flying serpent.

30 And the firstborn of the poor shall feed, and the needy shall lie down in safety: and I will kill thy root with famine, and he shall slay thy remnant.

31 Howl, O gate; cry, O city; Philistia, thou art wholly dissolved! for there cometh from the north a smoke, and none is away from his fellow in his ranks.

32 What shall one then answer the messengers of the nations? —That the LORD hath founded Zion, and it is a refuge unto the poor of his people.

15

1 THE burden of Moab:—
Because in a night Ar of Moab is laid waste, and brought to silence! because in a night Kir of Moab is laid waste and brought to silence!

2 He is gone up to Bajith, and to Dibon, the high places, to weep! Moab shall howl upon Nebo, and upon Medeba: on all their heads shall be baldness, and every beard cut off.

3 In their streets they shall gird themselves with sackcloth: on the tops of their houses, and in their streets, every one shall howl, weeping abundantly.

4 And Heshbon shall cry, and Elealeh: their voice shall be heard even unto Jahaz: therefore the armed soldiers of Moab shall cry out; his life shall be grievous unto him.

5 My heart doth cry out for Moab! his fugitives shall flee unto Zoar, the heifer of three years old: for by the mounting up of Luhith, with weeping shall they go it up; for in the way of Horonaim they shall raise up a cry of destruction.

6 For the waters of Nimrim shall be desolate: for the grass is withered away, the herb faileth, there is no green thing.

7 Therefore the abundance they have gotten, and that which they have laid up, shall they carry away over the brook of the willows.

8 For the cry is gone round about the borders of Moab;

the howling thereof unto Eglaim, and the howling thereof unto Beer-elim.

9 For the waters of Dimon shall be full of blood: for I will bring more upon Dimon, lions upon him that escapeth of Moab, and upon the remnant of the land.

16

1 SEND ye the lamb to the ruler of the land from Sela to the wilderness, unto the mount of the daughter of Zion!

2 For it shall be, that, as a wandering bird cast out of the nest, so the daughters of Moab shall be at the fords of Arnon.

3 "Take counsel, execute judgment; make thy shadow as the night in the midst of the noonday; hide the outcasts; bewray not him that wandereth.

4 "Let Moab's outcasts dwell with thee! be thou a covert to them from the face of the spoiler: for the extortioner is at an end, the spoiler ceaseth, the oppressors are consumed out of the land.

5 "And in mercy shall the throne be established: and there shall sit upon it in truth, in the tabernacle of David, one judging, and seeking judgment, and hasting righteousness."

6 —We have heard of the pride of Moab; he is very proud: even of his haughtiness, and his pride, and his wrath: but his lies shall not be so.

7 Therefore shall Moab howl for Moab, every one shall howl: for the foundations of Kir-hareseth shall ye mourn; surely they are stricken.

8 For the fields of Heshbon languish, and the vine of Sibmah: the lords of the heathen have broken down the principal plants thereof, that came even unto Jazer, that wandered through the wilderness: her branches were stretched out, they were gone over the sea.

9 Therefore I will bewail with the weeping of Jazer the vine of Sibmah: I will water thee with my tears, O Heshbon, and Elealeh! for the shouting for thy summer fruits and for thy harvest is fallen.

10 And gladness is taken away, and joy out of the plentiful field; and in the vineyards there shall be no singing, neither shall there be shouting: the treaders shall tread out no wine in their presses; I have made their vintage shouting to cease.

11 Wherefore my bowels do sound like an harp for Moab, and mine inward parts for Kir-haresh.

12 And it shall come to pass, when it is seen that Moab wearieth himself on the high place, and cometh to his sanctuary to pray, he shall not prevail.

13 THIS is the word that the LORD hath spoken concerning
14 Moab in the former time. But now the LORD hath spoken, saying:—

Within three years, as the years of an hireling, and the glory of Moab shall be contemned, with all that great multitude; and the remnant shall be very small and feeble.

17

1 THE burden of Damascus:—
Behold, Damascus is taken away from being a city, and it shall be a ruinous heap.

2 The cities of Aroer are forsaken: they shall be for flocks, which shall lie down, and none shall make them afraid.

3 The fortress also shall cease from Ephraim, and the kingdom from Damascus; and the remnant of Syria shall be as the glory of the children of Israel, saith the LORD of hosts.

4 And in that day it shall come to pass, that the glory of Jacob shall be made thin, and the fatness of his flesh shall wax lean.

5 And it shall be as when the harvestman gathereth the corn, and reapeth the ears with his arm; and it shall be as he that gathereth ears in the valley of Rephaim.

6 Yet gleanings shall be left in it, as at the shaking of an olive tree, two or three berries in the top of the uppermost bough, four or five in the outmost fruitful branches thereof, saith the LORD God of Israel.

7   At that day shall a man look to his Maker, and his eyes
    shall have respect to the Holy One of Israel.

8   And he shall not look to the altars, the work of his hands;
    neither shall respect that which his fingers have made,
    either the groves, or the images.

9   In that day shall his strong cities be as the ruins in the
    thickets and in the heights, which they left because of the
    children of Israel: and there shall be desolation.

10 Because thou hast forgotten the God of thy salvation, and
    hast not been mindful of the rock of thy strength, there-
    fore thou hast planted a pleasant planting, and hast set it
    with strange slips;

11 In the day thou madest thy plant to grow, and in the
    morning thou madest thy seed to flourish: but the harvest
    shall be a heap for the day of wounding and of desperate
    sorrow.

12 WOE to the multitude of many people, which make a
    noise like the noise of the seas; and to the rushing of na-
    tions, that make a rushing like the rushing of mighty
    waters!

13 The nations shall rush like the rushing of many waters:
    but God shall rebuke them, and they shall flee far off,
    and shall be chased as the chaff of the mountains before
    the wind, and like a rolling thing before the whirlwind.

14 And behold at eveningtide trouble; and before the morn-
    ing he is not! This is the portion of them that spoil us,
    and the lot of them that rob us.

18

1   WOE for the land buzzing with wings, which is beyond
    the rivers of Ethiopia;

2   That sendeth ambassadors by the sea, even in vessels of
    bulrushes upon the waters! Go, ye swift messengers, to
    the nation long-shanked and smooth, to the people terrible
    from their beginning hitherto; the nation of great might
    and victorious, whose land the rivers divide.

3 All ye inhabitants of the world, and dwellers on the earth, see ye, when he lifteth up an ensign on the mountains! and when he bloweth a trumpet, hear ye!

4 For so the LORD said unto me: I will take my rest, and I will consider in my dwelling place like a clear heat upon herbs, and like a cloud of dew in the heat of harvest.

5 For afore the harvest, when the bud is perfect, and the sour grape is ripening in the flower, he shall both cut off the sprigs with pruning hooks, and take away and cut down the branches.

6 They shall be left together unto the fowls of the mountains, and to the beasts of the earth: and the fowl shall summer upon them, and all the beasts of the earth shall winter upon them.

7 In that time shall the present be brought unto the LORD of hosts of a people long-shanked and smooth, and from a people terrible from their beginning hitherto; a nation of great might and victorious, whose land the rivers divide, to the place of the name of the LORD of hosts, the mount Zion.

19

1 THE burden of Egypt:—
Behold, the LORD rideth upon a swift cloud, and shall come into Egypt: and the idols of Egypt shall be moved at his presence, and the heart of Egypt shall melt in the midst of it.

2 And I will set the Egyptians against the Egyptians; and they shall fight every one against his brother, and every one against his neighbour: city against city, and kingdom against kingdom.

3 And the spirit of Egypt shall fail in the midst thereof; and I will destroy the counsel thereof: and they shall seek to the idols, and to the charmers, and to them that have familiar spirits, and to the wizards.

4 And the Egyptians will I give over into the hand of a

cruel lord; and a fierce king shall rule over them, saith
the Lord, the Lᴏʀᴅ of hosts.

5 And the waters shall fail from the sea, and the river shall
be wasted and dried up.

6 The river-streams shall become stinking, the channels of
Egypt shall be emptied and dried up: the reeds and flags
shall wither.

7 The meadow-flats by the stream, by the mouths of the
stream, and every seed-field by the stream, shall wither,
be driven away, and be no more.

8 The fishers also shall mourn, and all they that cast angle
into the stream shall lament, and they that spread nets
upon the waters shall languish.

9 Moreover they that work in fine flax, and they that weave
cotton, shall be confounded.

10 And the foundations of the land shall be broken; all that
labour for hire shall be troubled at heart.

11 Surely the princes of Zoan are fools, the counsel of the
wise counsellers of Pharaoh is become brutish! how say ye
unto Pharaoh, "I am the son of the wise, the son of ancient kings"?

12 Where are they? where are thy wise men? and let them
tell thee now, and let them know what the Lᴏʀᴅ of hosts
hath purposed upon Egypt.

13 The princes of Zoan are become fools, the princes of
Noph are deceived; they have also seduced Egypt, even
they that are the stay of the tribes thereof.

14 The Lᴏʀᴅ hath mingled a perverse spirit in the midst
thereof: and they have caused Egypt to err in every work
thereof, as a drunken man staggereth in his vomit.

15 Neither shall there be any work for Egypt, which the
head with the tail, the palm-branch with the rush, may do.

16 In that day shall Egypt be like unto women: and it shall
be afraid and fear because of the shaking of the hand of
the Lᴏʀᴅ of hosts, which he shaketh over it.

17 And the land of Judah shall be a terror unto Egypt, every
one that maketh mention thereof shall be afraid in himself, because of the counsel of the Lᴏʀᴅ of hosts, which he
hath determined against Egypt.

18 In that day shall five cities in the land of Egypt speak the language of Canaan, and swear to the LORD of hosts; one shall be called "The city of destruction of idols."

19 In that day shall there be an altar to the LORD in the midst of the land of Egypt, and a pillar at the border thereof to the LORD.

20 And it shall be for a sign and for a witness unto the LORD of hosts in the land of Egypt: for they shall cry unto the LORD because of the oppressors, and he shall send them a saviour, and a great one, and he shall deliver them.

21 And the LORD shall be known to Egypt, and the Egyptians shall know the LORD in that day, and shall do sacrifice and oblation; yea, they shall vow a vow unto the LORD, and perform it.

22 And the LORD shall smite Egypt: he shall smite and heal it: and they shall return even to the LORD, and he shall be intreated of them, and shall heal them.

23 In that day shall there be a highway out of Egypt to Assyria, and the Assyrian shall come into Egypt, and the Egyptian into Assyria, and the Egyptians shall worship with the Assyrians.

24 In that day shall Israel be the third with Egypt and with Assyria, even a blessing in the midst of the earth,

25 Wherewith the LORD of hosts shall bless, saying: Blessed be Egypt my people, and Assyria the work of my hands, and Israel mine inheritance.

20

1 IN the year that Tartan came unto Ashdod (when Sargon the king of Assyria sent him—the same fought against
2 Ashdod, and took it), at the same time spake the LORD by Isaiah the son of Amoz, saying:—
Go and loose the sackcloth from off thy loins, and put off thy shoe from thy foot.

AND he did so, walking naked and barefoot.

3 And the LORD said:—
Like as my servant Isaiah hath walked naked and barefoot

three years for a sign and wonder upon Egypt and upon Ethiopia;

4 So shall the king of Assyria lead away the Egyptians prisoners, and the Ethiopians captives, young and old, naked and barefoot, even with their buttocks uncovered, to the shame of Egypt.

5 And they shall be afraid and ashamed of Ethiopia their expectation, and of Egypt their glory.

6 And the inhabitant of this coast shall say in that day: Behold, so fareth it with our hope, whither we fled for help to be delivered from the king of Assyria; and how shall we escape?

21

[For 21:1–10, see pp. 361–62.]

11 THE burden of Dumah:—
One calleth to me out of Seir: Watchman, what of the night? Watchman, what of the night?

12 The watchman said: The morning cometh, and also the night; if ye will inquire, inquire ye: return, come!

13 THE burden upon Arabia:—
In the desert in Arabia shall ye lodge, O ye travelling companies of Dedanim!

14 The inhabitants of the land of Tema brought water to him that was thirsty, they prevented with their bread him that fled.

15 For they fled from the swords, from the drawn sword, and from the bent bow, and from the grievousness of war.

16 For thus hath the Lord said unto me: Within a year, according to the years of an hireling, and all the glory of Kedar shall fail;

17 And the residue of the number of archers, the mighty men of the children of Kedar, shall be diminished: for the LORD God of Israel hath spoken it.

22

1 THE burden of the valley of vision:—
   What aileth thee now, that thou art wholly gone up to
   the housetops?

2 Thou that art full of stirs, a tumultuous city, a joyous
   city! thy slain men are not slain with the sword, nor dead
   in battle.

3 All thy rulers are fled together, they are bound—and no
   bow-shot! all that are found in thee are bound together,
   while that they hasted to flee afar.

4 Therefore said I: Look away from me; I will weep bitterly, labour not to comfort me, because of the spoiling
   of the daughter of my people.

5 For it is a day of trouble, and of treading down, and of
   perplexity, by the Lord GOD of hosts in the valley of vision,
   of breaking down the walls, and of crying to the mountains.

6 And Elam bare the quiver with chariots of men and horsemen, and Kir uncovered the shield.

7 And it shall come to pass, that thy choicest valleys shall
   be full of chariots, and the horsemen shall set themselves
   in array at the gate.

8 And he withdraweth the covering of Judah, and thou
   hast looked in that day to the armour of the House of the
   Forest;

9 Ye have seen also the breaches of the city of David, that
   they are many: and ye gathered together the waters of
   the lower pool;

10 And ye have numbered the houses of Jerusalem, and the
   houses have ye broken down to fortify the wall;

11 Ye make also a ditch between the two walls for the water
   of the old pool;—but ye have not looked unto the maker
   thereof, neither had respect unto him that fashioned it
   long ago.

12 And in that day did the Lord GOD of hosts call to weeping, and to mourning, and to baldness, and to girding with
   sackcloth:

13 And behold joy and gladness, slaying oxen, and killing
    sheep, eating flesh, and drinking wine; let us eat and drink,
    for to morrow we shall die!

14 And it was revealed in mine ears by the Lord of hosts:
    Surely this iniquity shall not be purged from you till ye
    die, saith the Lord God of hosts.

15 Thus saith the Lord God of hosts:—
    Go, get thee unto this treasurer, even unto Shebna, which
    is over the house, and say:

16 What hast thou here? and whom hast thou here? that thou
    hast hewed thee out a sepulchre here, as he that heweth
    him out a sepulchre on high, and that graveth an habita-
    tion for himself in a rock?

17 Behold, the Lord will carry thee away with a mighty cap-
    tivity, and will surely grasp thee.

18 He will surely violently turn thee and toss thee like a ball
    into a large country: there shalt thou die, and there the
    chariots of thy glory shall be, thou shame of thy lord's
    house!

19 And I will drive thee from thy station, and from thy state
    shall he pull thee down.

20 And it shall come to pass in that day, that I will call my
    servant Eliakim the son of Hilkiah:

21 And I will clothe him with thy robe, and strengthen him
    with thy girdle, and I will commit thy government into
    his hand: and he shall be a father to the inhabitants of
    Jerusalem, and to the house of Judah.

22 And the key of the house of David will I lay upon his
    shoulder; so he shall open, and none shall shut; and he
    shall shut, and none shall open.

23 And I will fasten him as a nail in a sure place; and he
    shall be for a glorious throne to his father's house.

24 And they shall hang upon him all the glory of his father's
    house, the offspring and the issue, all vessels of small quan-
    tity, from the vessels of cups, even to all the vessels of
    flagons.

25 In that day, saith the Lord of hosts, shall the nail that is

fastened in the sure place be removed, and be cut down,
and fall; and the burden that was upon it shall be cut off:
for the LORD hath spoken it.

23

1 THE burden of Tyre:—
Howl, ye ships of Tarshish! for it is laid waste, so that
there is no house, no entering in: from the land of Chittim it is revealed to them.

2 Be still, ye inhabitants of the isle! thou whom the merchants of Zidon, that pass over the sea, have replenished.

3 And by great waters the seed of Nile, the harvest of the
river, was her revenue; and she was a mart of nations.

4 Be thou ashamed, O Zidon! for the sea hath spoken, even
the strength of the sea, saying: I travail not, nor bring
forth children, neither do I nourish up young men, nor
bring up virgins.

5 When that the report cometh unto Egypt, then shall they
be sorely pained at the report of Tyre.

6 Pass ye over to Tarshish; howl, ye inhabitants of the isle!

7 Is this your joyous city, whose antiquity is of ancient
days? whose feet did carry her afar off to sojourn?

8 Who hath taken this counsel against Tyre, the crowning
city, whose merchants are princes, whose traffickers are
the honourable of the earth?

9 The LORD of hosts hath purposed it, to stain the pride of
all glory, and to bring into contempt all the honourable
of the earth.

10 Pass through thy land as a river, O daughter of Tarshish:
there is no more band!

11 He stretched out his hand over the sea, he shook the kingdoms: the LORD hath given a commandment against Canaan, to destroy the strongholds thereof.

12 And he said, Thou shalt no more rejoice, O thou humbled
virgin, daughter of Zidon! arise, pass over to Chittim;
there also shalt thou have no rest.

13 Behold the land of the Chaldeans! this people is not, the

Assyrian hath made it to be for beasts that dwell in the wilderness: they did set up the towers thereof, they raised up the palaces thereof; and he brought it to ruin.

14 Howl, ye ships of Tarshish! for your strength is laid waste.

15 AND it shall come to pass in that day, that Tyre shall be forgotten seventy years, according to the days of one king; after the end of seventy years shall Tyre sing as an harlot:—

16 "Take an harp, go about the city, thou harlot that hast been forgotten; make sweet melody, sing many songs, that thou mayest be remembered!"

17 And it shall come to pass after the end of seventy years, that the LORD will visit Tyre, and she shall turn to her hire, and shall commit fornication with all the kingdoms of the world upon the face of the earth.

18 And her merchandise and her hire shall be holiness to the LORD: it shall not be treasured nor laid up; for her merchandise shall be for them that dwell before the LORD, to eat sufficiently, and for seemly clothing.

[For chapters 24–27, see pp. 369–75.]

THE WOES

(XXVIII–XXXIII)

28

1 WOE to the crown of pride of the drunkards of Ephraim, whose glorious beauty is a fading flower, which is on the head of the fat valleys of them that are overcome with wine!

2 Behold, the Lord hath a mighty and strong one, which, as a tempest of hail and a destroying storm, as a flood of mighty waters overflowing, shall cast down to the earth with the strong hand.

3 The crown of pride of the drunkards of Ephraim shall be trodden under feet.

4 And the glorious beauty, which is on the head of the fat valley, shall be a fading flower, and as the hasty fruit before the summer; which when he that looketh upon it seeth, while it is yet in his hand he eateth it up.

5 In that day shall the LORD of hosts be for a crown of glory, and for a diadem of beauty, unto the residue of his people,

6 And for a spirit of judgment to him that sitteth in judgment, and for strength to them that turn back the battle at the gate.

7 BUT these, also, have erred through wine, and through strong drink are out of the way; the priest and the prophet have erred through strong drink, they are swallowed up of wine, they are out of the way through strong drink; they err in vision, they stumble in judgment.

8 For all tables are full of vomit and filthiness, so that there is no place clean.

9 "Whom will he teach knowledge? and whom will he make to understand doctrine? them that are weaned from the milk, and drawn from the breasts?

10 "For precept must be upon precept, precept upon precept; line upon line, line upon line; here a little, and there a little."

11 YEA, with stammering lips and another tongue will he speak to this people!

12 To whom he said: This is the rest wherewith ye may cause the weary to rest, and this is the refreshing; yet they would not hear.

13 But the word of the LORD was unto them precept upon precept, precept upon precept; line upon line, line upon line; here a little, and there a little; that they might go, and fall backward, and be broken, and snared, and taken.

14 Wherefore hear the word of the LORD, ye scornful men, that rule this people which is in Jerusalem!

15 Because ye have said, We have made a covenant with death, and with hell are we at agreement; when the overflowing scourge shall pass through, it shall not come unto

us: for we have made lies our refuge, and under falsehood
have we hid ourselves:

16 Therefore thus saith the Lord God: Behold, I lay in Zion
for a foundation a stone, a tried stone, a precious corner
stone, a sure foundation: he that believeth shall not take
flight.

17 Judgment also will I lay for a line, and righteousness for
a plummet: and the hail shall sweep away the refuge of
lies, and the waters shall overflow the hiding place.

18 And your covenant with death shall be disannulled, and
your agreement with hell shall not stand; when the overflowing scourge shall pass through, then ye shall be trodden down by it.

19 From the time that it goeth forth it shall take you: for
morning by morning shall it pass over, by day and by
night: and it shall be a vexation only to understand the
report.

20 For the bed is shorter than that a man can stretch himself
on it: and the covering narrower than that he can wrap
himself in it.

21 For the Lord shall rise up as in mount Perazim, he shall be
wroth as in the valley of Gibeon; that he may do his work,
his strange work; and bring to pass his act, his strange act.

22 Now therefore be ye not mockers, lest your bands be
made strong: for I have heard from the Lord God of hosts
a consumption, even determined upon the whole earth.

23 Give ye ear, and hear my voice; hearken, and hear my
speech!

24 Is the plowman plowing alway to sow? is he opening and
breaking the clods of his ground?

25 When he hath made plain the face thereof, doth he not
cast abroad the fitches, and scatter the cummin, and cast in
wheat in rows, and the barley in its appointed place and
the rie on the border thereof?

26 For his God doth instruct him to discretion, and doth
teach him.

27 For the fitches are not threshed with a threshing instru-

ment, neither is a cart wheel turned about upon the cummin; but the fitches are beaten out with a staff, and the cummin with a rod.

28 Bread corn is threshed; howbeit he will not ever be threshing it, nor break it with the wheel of his cart, nor bruise it with his horses.

29 This also cometh forth from the LORD of hosts, which is wonderful in counsel, and excellent in working.

29

1 WOE to Ariel, to Ariel, the city where David dwelt! Add ye year to year; let them kill the sacrifices;

2 Then I will distress Ariel, and there shall be heaviness and sorrow—and then it shall be unto me as Ariel.

3 For I will camp against thee round about, and will lay siege against thee with a mount, and I will raise forts against thee.

4 And thou shalt be brought down, and shalt speak out of the ground, and thy speech shall be low out of the dust, and thy voice shall be, as of a ghost, out of the ground, and thy speech shall whisper out of the dust.

5 And then the multitude of thine enemies shall be made like small dust, and the multitude of the terrible ones shall be as chaff that passeth away: yea, it shall be at an instant suddenly.

6 Thou shalt be visited of the LORD of hosts with thunder, and with earthquake, and great noise, with storm and tempest, and the flame of devouring fire.

7 And the multitude of all the nations that fight against Ariel, even all that fight against her and her munition, and that distress her, shall be as a dream of a night vision.

8 It shall even be as when an hungry man dreameth, and, behold, he eateth; but he awaketh, and his soul is empty! or as when a thirsty man dreameth, and, behold, he drinketh; but he awaketh, and, behold, he is faint, and his soul hath appetite! so shall the multitude of all the nations be, that fight against mount Zion.

9 STAND ye still, and wonder! blind ye your eyes, and grow blind! They are drunken, but not with wine; they stagger, but not with strong drink.

10 For the LORD hath poured out upon you the spirit of deep sleep, and hath closed your eyes, the prophets; and your rulers, the seers, hath he covered.

11 And the vision of all this is become unto you as the words of a book that is sealed, which men deliver to one that is learned, saying, Read this, I pray thee: and he saith, I cannot; for it is sealed:

12 And the book is delivered to him that is not learned, saying, Read this, I pray thee: and he saith, I am not learned.

13 For thus hath the Lord said: Forasmuch as this people draw near me with their mouth, and with their lips do honour me, but have removed their heart far from me, and their fear toward me is taught by the precept of men;

14 Therefore, behold, I will proceed to do a marvellous work among this people, even a marvellous work and a wonder; for the wisdom of their wise men shall perish, and the understanding of their prudent men shall disappear.

15 WOE unto them that seek deep to hide their counsel from the LORD, and their works are in the dark, and they say, Who seeth us? and who knoweth us?

16 Surely ye are perverse! is the potter like as the clay, for the work to say of him that made it, He made me not? or for the thing framed to say of him that framed it, He had no understanding?

17 Is it not yet a very little while, and Lebanon shall be turned into a fruitful field, and the fruitful field shall be esteemed as a forest?

18 And in that day shall the deaf hear the words of the book, and the eyes of the blind shall see out of obscurity, and out of darkness.

19 The meek also shall increase their joy in the LORD, and the poor among men shall rejoice in the Holy One of Israel.

20 For the terrible one is brought to nought, and the scorner

is consumed, and all that watch for iniquity are cut off:

21 That make a man an offender for a word, and lay a snare for him that reproveth in the gate, and turn aside the just for a thing of nought.

22 Therefore thus saith the LORD, who redeemed Abraham, concerning the house of Jacob: Jacob shall not now be ashamed, neither shall his face now wax pale.

23 But when he and his children see the work of mine hands in the midst of him, they shall sanctify my name, and sanctify the Holy One of Jacob, and shall fear the God of Israel.

24 They also that erred in spirit shall come to understanding, and they that murmured shall learn doctrine.

30

1 WOE to the rebellious children, saith the LORD, that take counsel, but not of me; and that weave a confederacy, but not by my spirit, that they may add sin to sin:

2 That walk to go down into Egypt, and have not asked at my mouth; to strengthen themselves in the strength of Pharaoh, and to trust in the shadow of Egypt!

3 Therefore shall the strength of Pharaoh be your shame, and the trust in the shadow of Egypt your confusion.

4 For his princes were at Zoan, and his ambassadors came to Hanes.

5 They were all ashamed of a people that could not profit them, nor be an help nor profit, but a shame, and also a reproach.

6 THE burden of the beasts of the south:—
"Through the land of trouble and anguish, from whence come the young and old lion, the viper and fiery flying serpent, they will carry their riches upon the shoulders of young asses, and their treasures upon the bunches of camels, to a people that shall not profit them.

7 "For the Egyptians shall help in vain, and to no purpose;

therefore have I cried concerning this: Proud Rahab is
Shabeth sit-still!"

8   Now go, write it before them in a tablet, and note it in
a book, that it may be for the time to come for ever and
ever.

9   For this is a rebellious people, lying children, children that
will not hear the law of the Lord:

10   Which say to the seers, See not! and to the prophets,
Prophesy not unto us right things, speak unto us smooth
things, prophesy deceits,

11   Get you out of the way, turn aside out of the path, cause
the Holy One of Israel to cease from before us!

12   Wherefore thus saith the Holy One of Israel: Because ye
despise this word, and trust in oppression and perverseness,
and stay thereon;

13   Therefore this iniquity shall be to you as a breach ready
to fall, swelling out in a high wall, whose breaking cometh
suddenly at an instant.

14   And he shall break it as the breaking of the potters' vessel
that is broken in pieces; he shall not spare: so that there
shall not be found in the bursting of it a sherd to take fire
from the hearth, or to take water withal out of the pit.

15   For thus saith the Lord God, the Holy One of Israel: In
returning and rest shall ye be saved; in quietness and in
confidence shall be your strength: and ye would not.

16   But ye said, No; for we will fly upon horses; therefore
shall ye flee: and, We will ride upon the swift; therefore
shall they that pursue you be swift.

17   One thousand shall flee at the rebuke of one; at the rebuke of five shall ye flee: till ye be left as a beacon upon
the top of a mountain, and as an ensign on an hill.

18   And therefore will the Lord wait before he be gracious
unto you, and therefore will he delay before he have
mercy upon you: for the Lord is a God of judgment:
blessed are all they that wait for him!

19   For the people shall dwell in Zion at Jerusalem: thou shalt
weep no more! he will be very gracious unto thee at the

voice of thy cry; when he shall hear it, he will answer thee.

20 And though the Lord give you the bread of adversity, and the water of affliction, yet shall not thy teachers be removed into a corner any more, but thine eyes shall see thy teachers:

21 And thine ears shall hear a word behind thee, saying, "This is the way, walk ye in it," when ye turn to the right hand, and when ye turn to the left.

22 Ye shall defile also the covering of thy graven images of silver, and the ornament of thy molten images of gold: thou shalt cast them away as a defiled cloth; thou shalt say unto it, Get thee hence.

23 Then shall he give rain for thy seed, that thou sowest the ground withal; and bread of the increase of the earth, and it shall be fat and plenteous: in that day shall thy cattle feed in large pastures.

24 The oxen likewise and the young asses that ear the ground shall eat clean provender, which hath been winnowed with the shovel and with the fan.

25 And there shall be upon every high mountain, and upon every high hill, rivers and streams of waters in the day of the great slaughter, when the towers fall.

26 Moreover, the light of the moon shall be as the light of the sun, and the light of the sun shall be sevenfold, as the light of seven days, in the day that the LORD bindeth up the breach of his people, and healeth the stroke of their wound.

27 BEHOLD, the name of the LORD cometh from far, burning with his anger, and the burden thereof is heavy: his lips are full of indignation, and his tongue as a devouring fire,

28 And his breath as an overflowing stream reaching to the midst of the neck, to winnow the nations with the fan of destruction: and there shall be a bridle in the jaws of the peoples causing them to err.

29 Ye shall have a song, as in the night when the holy solemnity is kept; and gladness of heart, as when one goeth with

a pipe to come into the mountain of the LORD, to the mighty One of Israel.

30 And the LORD shall cause his glorious voice to be heard, and shall shew the lighting down of his arm, with the indignation of his anger, and with the flame of a devouring fire, with scattering, and tempest, and hailstones.

31 For through the voice of the LORD shall the Assyrian be beaten down, when the LORD shall smite with a rod.

32 And every stroke of the staff of judgment, which the LORD shall lay upon him, it shall be with tabrets and harps: and in battles of his brandished arm will he fight against him.

33 For Tophet is ordained of old; yea, for the king it is prepared; he hath made it deep and large: the pile thereof is fire and much wood; the breath of the LORD, like a stream of brimstone, doth kindle it.

31

1 WOE to them that go down to Egypt for help; and stay on horses, and trust in chariots, because they are many; and in horsemen, because they are very strong; but they look not unto the Holy One of Israel, neither seek the LORD!

2 Yet he also is wise, and will bring evil, and will not call back his words: but will arise against the house of the evil-doers, and against the help of them that work iniquity.

3 Now the Egyptians are men, and not God; and their horses flesh, and not spirit. When the LORD shall stretch out his hand, both he that helpeth shall fall, and he that is holpen shall fall down, and they all shall fail together.

4 For thus hath the LORD spoken unto me: Like as the lion and the young lion growling over his prey, when a multitude of shepherds is called forth against him, he will not be afraid of their voice, nor abase himself for the noise of them: so shall the LORD of hosts come down to fight for mount Zion, and for the hill thereof.

5 As birds flying round, so will the LORD of hosts defend

Jerusalem; defending also he will deliver it; and passing over he will preserve it.

6 Turn ye unto him from whom the children of Israel have deeply revolted!

7 For in that day every man shall cast away his idols of silver, and his idols of gold, which your own hands have made unto you for a sin.

8 Then shall the Assyrian fall with the sword, not of a mighty man; and the sword, not of a mean man, shall devour him: but he shall flee from the sword, and his young men shall be for bondsmen.

9 And his rock, it shall pass away for fear, and his princes shall flee from their ensign, saith the Lord, whose fire is in Zion, and his furnace in Jerusalem.

32

1 BEHOLD, the king shall reign in righteousness, and princes shall rule in judgment;

2 And a man shall be as an hiding place from the wind, and a covert from the tempest; as rivers of water in a dry place, as the shadow of a great rock in a weary land.

3 And the eyes of them that see shall not be dim, and the ears of them that hear shall hearken.

4 The heart also of the rash shall understand knowledge, and the tongue of the stammerers shall be ready to speak plainly.

5 The vile person shall be no more called noble, nor the worker of mischief said to be worthy.

6 For the vile person doth speak villainy, and his heart doth work iniquity, to practise hypocrisy, and to utter error against the Lord, to make empty the soul of the hungry, and he doth cause the drink of the thirsty to fail.

7 The instruments also of the worker of mischief are evil: he deviseth wicked devices to destroy the poor with lying words, even when the needy speaketh right.

8 But the noble deviseth noble things; and staunch to noble things shall he stand.

9 RISE up, ye women that are at ease; hear my voice, ye careless daughters; give ear unto my speech!

10 A year and a day, and ye shall be troubled, ye careless women! for the vintage shall fail, the gathering shall not come.

11 Tremble, ye women that are at ease; be troubled, ye careless ones: strip you, and make you bare, and gird sackcloth upon your loins!

12 They shall beat the breast for the pleasant fields, for the fruitful vine.

13 Upon the land of my people shall come up thorns and briers; yea, upon all the houses of joy in the joyous city:

14 Because the palaces shall be forsaken; the uproar of the city shall be desolate; the hill and tower shall be for dens for ever, a joy of wild asses, a pasture of flocks;

15 Until the spirit be poured upon us from on high, and the wilderness be a fruitful field, and the fruitful field be counted for a forest.

16 Then judgment shall dwell in the wilderness, and righteousness remain in the fruitful field.

17 And the work of righteousness shall be peace; and the effect of righteousness quietness and assurance for ever.

18 And my people shall dwell in a peaceable habitation, and in sure dwellings, and in quiet resting places.

19 And it shall hail, and the forest shall be brought down; and the city shall be low, in a low place.

20 Blessed are ye that sow beside all waters, that send abroad the feet of the ox and the ass!

33

1 WOE to thee that spoilest, and thou wast not spoiled; and dealest injuriously, and they dealt not injuriously with thee! when thou shalt cease to spoil, thou shalt be spoiled; and when thou shalt make an end to deal injuriously, they shall deal injuriously with thee.

2 O LORD, be gracious unto us; we have waited for thee! be

thou their arm every morning, our salvation also in the time of trouble!

3 At the noise of the tumult the peoples fled; at the lifting up of thyself the nations were scattered.

4 And your spoil shall be gathered like the gathering of the caterpillar: as the running to and fro of locusts shall men run upon them.

5 The LORD is exalted; for he dwelleth on high: he hath filled Zion with judgment and righteousness.

6 And the stability of thy times shall be wisdom, and knowledge, and strength of salvation: the fear of the LORD is their treasure.

7 BEHOLD, their valiant ones cry without: the ambassadors of peace weep bitterly.

8 The highways lie waste, the wayfaring man ceaseth: he hath broken the covenant, he hath despised the cities, he regardeth no man.

9 The land mourneth and languisheth: Lebanon is ashamed and hewn down: Sharon is like a wilderness; and Bashan and Carmel shake off their leaves.

10 Now will I rise, saith the LORD; now will I be exalted; now will I lift up myself.

11 Ye shall conceive chaff, ye shall bring forth stubble: your breath, as fire, shall devour you.

12 And the peoples shall be as the burnings of lime: as thorns cut up shall they be burned in the fire.

13 Hear, ye that are far off, what I have done! and, ye that are near, acknowledge my might!

14 The sinners in Zion are afraid; fearfulness hath surprised the hypocrites. "Who among us shall dwell with the devouring fire? who among us shall dwell with everlasting burnings?"

15 He that walketh righteously, and speaketh uprightly; he that despiseth the gain of oppressions, that averteth his hands from holding of bribes, that stoppeth his ears from hearing of blood, and shutteth his eyes from seeing evil—

16 He shall dwell on high: his place of defence shall be the munitions of rocks: bread shall be given him; his waters shall be sure.

17 Thine eyes shall see the king in his beauty: they shall behold the land spreading very far forth.

18 Thine heart shall meditate the terror. Where is the assessor? where is the weigher? where is he that counted the towers?

19 Thou seest no more the fierce people, the people of a dark speech that thou canst not perceive, of a stammering tongue that thou canst not understand.

20 Look upon Zion, the city of our solemnities! thine eyes shall see Jerusalem a quiet habitation, a tabernacle that shall not be taken down; not one of the stakes thereof shall ever be removed, neither shall any of the cords thereof be broken.

21 But there the glorious LORD will dwell with us: a place of broad rivers and streams, wherein shall go no galley with oars, neither shall gallant ship pass thereby.

22 For the LORD is our judge, the LORD is our lawgiver, the LORD is our king; he will save us.

23 Thy tacklings are loosed; they hold not firm their mast, they keep not spread the sail!—but then is the prey of a great spoil divided; the lame take the prey.

24 And the inhabitant shall not say, "I am sick!" the people that dwell therein shall be forgiven their iniquity.

[For chapters 34–35, see pp. 366–68.]

SENNACHERIB

(XXXVI–XXXIX)

36

1 Now it came to pass in the fourteenth year of king Hezekiah, that Sennacherib king of Assyria came up against all

2 the defenced cities of Judah, and took them. And the king

of Assyria sent Rabshakeh from Lachish to Jerusalem
unto king Hezekiah with a great army. And he stood by
the conduit of the upper pool in the highway of the ful-
3 ler's field. Then came forth unto him Eliakim, Hilkiah's
son, which was over the house, and Shebna the scribe,
4 and Joah, Asaph's son, the recorder. And Rabshakeh said
unto them: Say ye now to Hezekiah, Thus saith the great
king, the king of Assyria, What confidence is this wherein
5 thou trustest? I say, sayest thou (but they are but vain
words), I have counsel and strength for war: now on
6 whom dost thou trust, that thou rebellest against me? Lo,
thou trustest in the staff of this broken reed, on Egypt;
whereon if a man lean, it will go into his hand, and pierce
it: so is Pharaoh king of Egypt to all that trust in him.
7 But if thou say to me, We trust in the LORD our God: is it
not he, whose high places and whose altars Hezekiah hath
taken away, and said to Judah and to Jerusalem, Ye shall
8 worship before this altar? Now therefore strike a bargain,
I pray thee, with my master the king of Assyria, and I will
give thee two thousand horses, if thou be able on thy part
9 to set riders upon them. How then wilt thou turn away
the face of one captain of the least of my master's servants,
and put thy trust on Egypt for chariots and for horse-
10 men? And am I now come up without the LORD against
this land to destroy it? the LORD said unto me, Go up
against this land, and destroy it.
11 Then said Eliakim and Shebna and Joah unto Rabshakeh:
Speak, I pray thee, unto thy servants in the Syrian language, for we understand it; and speak not to us in the
Jews' language, in the ears of the people that are on the
12 wall. But Rabshakeh said, Hath my master sent me to thy
master and to thee to speak these words? hath he not sent
me to the men that sit upon the wall, that they may eat
their own dung, and drink their own piss with you?
13 Then Rabshakeh stood, and cried with a loud voice in the
Jews' language, and said: Hear ye the words of the great
14 king, the king of Assyria. Thus saith the king, Let not
Hezekiah deceive you: for he shall not be able to deliver

15 you. Neither let Hezekiah make you trust in the LORD, saying, the LORD will surely deliver us; this city shall not
16 be delivered into the hand of the king of Assyria. Hearken not to Hezekiah; for thus saith the king of Assyria: Make an agreement with me by a present, and come out to me; and eat ye every one of his vine, and every one of his fig tree, and drink ye every one the waters of his own cistern;
17 until I come and take you away to a land like your own land, a land of corn and wine, a land of bread and vine-
18 yards. Beware lest Hezekiah persuade you, saying, The LORD will deliver us. Hath any of the gods of the nations delivered his land out of the hand of the king of Assyria?
19 Where are the gods of Hamath and Arphad? where are the gods of Sepharvaim? and have they delivered Samaria
20 out of my hand? Who are they among all the gods of these lands, that have delivered their land out of my hand, that the LORD should deliver Jerusalem out of my hand?
21 But they held their peace, and answered him not a word: for the king's commandment was, saying, Answer him not.
22 Then came Eliakim, the son of Hilkiah, that was over the household, and Shebna the scribe, and Joah, the son of Asaph, the recorder, to Hezekiah with their clothes rent,

37

1 and told him the words of Rabshakeh. And it came to pass, when king Hezekiah heard it, that he rent his clothes, and covered himself with sackcloth, and went into the
2 house of the LORD. And he sent Eliakim, who was over the household, and Shebna the scribe, and the elders of the priests covered with sackcloth, unto Isaiah the prophet
3 the son of Amoz. And they said unto him: Thus saith Hezekiah, This day is a day of trouble, and of rebuke, and of blasphemy; for the children are come to the birth,
4 and there is not strength to bring forth. It may be the LORD thy God will hear the words of Rabshakeh, whom

the king of Assyria his master hath sent to reproach the
living God, and will reprove the words which the Lord
thy God hath heard; wherefore lift up thy prayer for the
5 remnant that is left. So the servants of king Hezekiah came
6 to Isaiah. And Isaiah said unto them: Thus shall ye say
unto your master, Thus saith the Lord, Be not afraid of
the words that thou hast heard, wherewith the servants
7 of the king of Assyria have blasphemed me. Behold, I will
send a breath upon him, and he shall hear a rumour, and
return to his own land; and I will cause him to fall by
the sword in his own land.
8 So Rabshakeh returned, and found the king of Assyria
warring against Libnah: for he had heard that he was de-
9 parted from Lachish. And he heard say concerning Tirhakah king of Ethiopia, He is come forth to make war
with thee. And when he heard it, he sent messengers to
10 Hezekiah, saying: Thus shall ye speak to Hezekiah king
of Judah, saying, Let not thy God, in whom thou trustest, deceive thee, saying, Jerusalem shall not be given into
11 the hand of the king of Assyria. Behold, thou hast heard
what the kings of Assyria have done to all lands by de-
12 stroying them utterly; and shalt thou be delivered? Have
the gods of the nations delivered them which my fathers
have destroyed, as Gozan, and Haran, and Rezeph, and
13 the children of Eden which are in Telassar? Where is the
king of Hamath, and the king of Arphad, and the king of
the city of Sepharvaim, Hena, and Ivah?
14 And Hezekiah received the letter from the hand of the
messengers, and read it: and Hezekiah went up unto the
15 house of the Lord, and spread it before the Lord. And
16 Hezekiah prayed unto the Lord, saying: O Lord of hosts,
God of Israel, that dwellest between the cherubims, thou
art the God, even thou alone, of all the kingdoms of the
17 earth: thou hast made heaven and earth. Incline thine ear,
O Lord, and hear; open thine eyes, O Lord, and see: and
hear all the words of Sennacherib, which hath sent to re-
18 proach the living God. Of a truth, Lord, the kings of Assyria have laid waste all the nations, and their countries,

19 and have cast their gods into the fire: for they were no
gods, but the work of men's hands, wood and stone:
20 therefore, they have destroyed them. Now therefore, O
Lᴏʀᴅ our God, save us from his hand, that all the kingdoms of the earth may know that thou art the Lᴏʀᴅ,
even thou only.
21 Then Isaiah the son of Amoz sent unto Hezekiah, saying:
Thus saith the Lᴏʀᴅ God of Israel, Whereas thou hast
22 prayed to me against Sennacherib king of Assyria, this is
the word which the Lᴏʀᴅ hath spoken concerning him:—

Tʜᴇ virgin, the daughter of Zion, hath despised thee, and
laughed thee to scorn; the daughter of Jerusalem hath
shaken her head at thee.
23 Whom hast thou reproached and blasphemed? and against
whom hast thou exalted thy voice, and lifted up thine eyes
on high? even against the Holy One of Israel.
24 By thy servants hast thou reproached the Lord, and hast
said: "By the multitude of my chariots am I come up to
the height of the mountains, to the sides of Lebanon; and
I will cut down the tall cedars thereof, and the choice fir
trees thereof: and I will enter into the height of his
border, and into his garden-grove of pleasure.
25 "I have digged, and drunk water; and with the sole of
my feet have I dried up all the arms of rivers of Egypt."

26 Hᴀsᴛ thou not heard long ago, how I have done it? and of
ancient times, that I have formed it? now have I brought
it to pass, that thou shouldest be to lay waste defenced
cities into ruinous heaps.
27 Therefore their inhabitants were of small power, they
were dismayed and confounded: they were as the grass
of the field, and as the green herb, as the grass on the
housetops, and as corn blasted before it be grown up.
28 But I know thy abode, and thy going out, and thy coming
in, and thy rage against me.
29 Because thy rage against me, and thy tumult, is come up
into mine ears, therefore will I put my hook in thy nose,
and my bridle in thy lips, and I will turn thee back by
the way by which thou camest.

30 AND this shall be a sign unto thee: Ye shall eat this year such as groweth of itself; and the second year that which springeth the same: and in the third year sow ye, and reap, and plant vineyards, and eat the fruit thereof!

31 And the remnant that is escaped of the house of Judah shall again take root downward, and bear fruit upward:

32 For out of Jerusalem shall go forth a remnant, and they that escape out of mount Zion: the zeal of the LORD of hosts shall do this.

33 Therefore thus saith the LORD concerning the king of Assyria: He shall not come into this city, nor shoot an arrow there, nor come before it with shields, nor cast a bank against it.

34 By the way that he came, by the same shall he return, and shall not come into this city, saith the LORD.

35 For I will defend this city to save it for mine own sake, and for my servant David's sake.

36 THEN the angel of the LORD went forth, and smote in the camp of the Assyrians a hundred and fourscore and five thousand: and when they arose early in the morning, be-

37 hold, they were all dead corpses. So Sennacherib king of Assyria departed, and went and returned, and dwelt at

38 Nineveh. And it came to pass, as he was worshipping in the house of Nisroch his god, that Adrammelech and Sharezer his sons smote him with the sword; and they escaped into the land of Armenia: and Esar-haddon his son reigned in his stead.

38

1 In those days was Hezekiah sick unto death. And Isaiah the prophet the son of Amoz came unto him, and said unto him: Thus saith the LORD, Set thine house in order!

2 for thou shalt die, and not live. Then Hezekiah turned his

3 face toward the wall, and prayed unto the LORD, and said: Remember now, O LORD, I beseech thee, how I have walked before thee in truth and with a perfect heart, and

have done that which is good in thy sight. And Hezekiah
4 wept sore. Then came the word of the LORD to Isaiah, say-
5 ing: Go, and say to Hezekiah, Thus saith the LORD, the
God of David thy father: I have heard thy prayer, I have
seen thy tears; behold, I will add unto thy days fifteen
6 years. And I will deliver thee and this city out of the
hand of the king of Assyria: and I will defend this city.
7 And this shall be a sign unto thee from the LORD, that the
8 LORD will do this thing that he hath spoken; behold, I
will bring again the shadow of the degrees, which is gone
down in the sun dial of Ahaz, ten degrees backward. So
the sun returned ten degrees, by which degrees it was
gone down.

9 THE writing of Hezekiah king of Judah, when he had
been sick, and was recovered of his sickness.

10 I SAID: In the smoothness of my days I shall go to the
gates of the grave; I am deprived of the residue of my
years.
11 I said: I shall not see the LORD, even the LORD, in the land
of the living; I shall behold man no more with the inhabitants of the world.
12 Mine age is departed, and is removed from me as a shepherd's tent; I have cut off, as a weaver, my life, as a
weaver cutteth off the thread; from day even to night
wilt thou make an end of me.
13 I reckoned till morning, that, as a lion, so will he break
all my bones: from day even to night wilt thou make
an end of me.
14 Like a crane or a swallow, so did I chatter: I did mourn
as a dove: mine eyes fail with looking upward: O LORD, I
am oppressed; undertake for me!
15 What shall I say? he hath both promised unto me, and
himself hath done it: I shall go softly all my years in the
contrition of my soul.
16 O Lord, by these things men live, and in all these things
is the life of my spirit! so wilt thou recover me, and make
me to live.

17 Behold, for my peace I had this great bitterness! thou hast in love to my soul delivered it from the pit of corruption: thou hast cast all my sins behind thy back.

18 For the grave cannot praise thee, death cannot celebrate thee: they that go down into the pit cannot hope for thy truth.

19 The living, the living, he shall praise thee, as I do this day: the father to the children shall make known thy truth!

20 The LORD was ready to save me: therefore we will sing my songs to the stringed instruments all the days of our life in the house of the LORD.

21 (For Isaiah had said: Let them take a lump of figs, and lay it for a plaister upon the boil, and he shall recover.

22 Hezekiah also had said, What is the sign that I shall go up to the house of the LORD?)

39

1 AT that time Merodach-baladan, the son of Baladan, king of Babylon, sent letters and a present to Hezekiah: for he

2 had heard that he had been sick, and was recovered. And Hezekiah was glad of them, and shewed them the house of his precious things, the silver, and the gold, and the spices, and the precious ointment, and all the house of his armour, and all that was found in his treasures: there was nothing in his house, nor in all his dominion, that Hezekiah shewed them not.

3 Then came Isaiah the prophet unto king Hezekiah, and said unto him, What said these men? and from whence came they unto thee? And Hezekiah said, They are come

4 from a far country unto me, even from Babylon. Then said he, What have they seen in thine house? And Hezekiah answered, All that is in mine house have they seen: there is nothing among my treasures that I have not

5 shewed them. Then said Isaiah to Hezekiah, Hear the

6 word of the LORD of hosts: Behold, the days come, that all that is in thine house, and that which thy fathers have laid up in store until this day, shall be carried to Babylon:

7 nothing shall be left, saith the LORD. And of thy sons that
shall issue from thee, which thou shalt beget, shall they
take away; and they shall be eunuchs in the palace of the
8 king of Babylon. Then said Hezekiah to Isaiah: Good is
the word of the LORD which thou hast spoken. He said
moreover: Yea, there shall be peace and truth in my days!

[THE GREAT PROPHECY OF
ISRAEL'S RESTORATION]

[In the year 722 B.C. the kingdom of Israel fell; its capital,
Samaria, was taken by Shalmaneser, king of Assyria, and its
ten tribes were carried away into Assyria. Of the chosen people
in the Holy Land, therefore, 'there was none left but the
tribe of Judah only.' The great eastern empire of Assyria was
then at its height of power; Media, Persia, and Babylon were
subject to it, and it was hoping to conquer Egypt, with which
Hoshea, the last king of Israel, had made an alliance. The
kingdom of Judah, also, leaned towards Egypt; for Judah,
though it survived, was tributary to Assyria, and hoped by
help of Egypt to break the Assyrian power. Eight years after
the destruction of the kingdom of Israel, Hezekiah, the king of
Judah, refused to pay his tribute any longer: the king of Assyria, Sennacherib, invaded Egypt and Palestine, but without
success, and his army which appeared before Jerusalem was,
according to the Jewish accounts, destroyed. At this time
Babylon threw off the yoke of Assyria and sent an embassy
to gain the friendship of Hezekiah; Media also made itself independent. Sennacherib regained his hold upon Babylon, but
the end of Assyria's greatness was drawing nigh. She again
lost Babylon; and in the year 625 B.C. the king of Babylon,
in conjunction with the king of Media, took Nineveh and destroyed for ever the Assyrian empire. The kingdom of Media
with Persia, on the one hand, and the kingdom of Babylon,
on the other, were Assyria's heirs and successors. Judah, after
the death of Hezekiah, had no returning gleam of political
prosperity. In 588 B.C., thirty-seven years after the fall of the
kingdom of Assyria, and a hundred and thirty-four years after

the fall of the kingdom of Israel, Nebuchadnezzar king of Babylon made a final invasion of Judah, took Jerusalem, and carried away the king and the chief part of the people to Babylon. But Nebuchadnezzar's brilliant reign founded no enduring power for Babylon. His successors became engaged in war with the Medo-Persian kingdom; and it was this kingdom which was to grow and succeed. Under Cyrus the Persian its fortunes prevailed. In 548 B.C., forty years after the fall of Jerusalem, Cyrus conquered the wealthy Lydian monarchy of Croesus, and the Greek cities on the western coast of Asia Minor; then, in the year 541 B.C., he turned upon Babylon, defended by its walls and waters. Against their enslaver and oppressor the Jewish exiles in Babylon saw uplifted the irresistible sword of God's instrument, this Persian prince, to whose religion the Babylonian idolatry was hateful; a victorious warrior, a wise and just statesman, favourable to Babylon's prisoners and victims, and disposed to restore the exiles of Judah to their own land. Assyria had fallen, Babylon was now falling; and in this supreme hour is heard the voice of God's prophets, commanded to comfort God's people, as follows:—]

(*Isaiah* 40–66)

40

1 COMFORT ye, comfort ye my people, saith your God.

2 Speak ye comfortably to Jerusalem, and cry unto her that her warfare is accomplished, that her iniquity is pardoned; that she receiveth of the LORD's hand double for all her rue.

3 A VOICE of one that crieth! In the wilderness prepare ye the way of the LORD, make straight in the desert a highway for our God.

4 Every valley shall be exalted, and every mountain and hill shall be made low; and the crooked shall be made straight, and the rough places plain;

5 And the glory of the LORD shall be revealed, and all flesh

shall see it together: for the mouth of the LORD hath spoken it.

6   A voice said, Cry! And he said, What shall I cry?—All flesh is grass, and all the goodliness thereof is as the flower of the field:

7   The grass withereth, the flower fadeth, because the spirit of the LORD bloweth upon it: surely the people is grass.

8   The grass withereth, the flower fadeth; but the word of our God shall stand for ever.

9   O THOU that bringest good tidings to Zion, get thee up into the high mountain; O thou that bringest good tidings to Jerusalem, lift up thy voice with strength; lift it up, be not afraid; say unto the cities of Judah, Behold your God!

10   Behold, the Lord GOD will come with strong hand, and his arm shall rule for him: behold, his reward is with him, and his recompence before him.

11   He shall feed his flock like a shepherd: he shall gather the lambs with his arm, and carry them in his bosom, and shall gently lead those that are with young.

12   Who hath measured the waters in the hollow of his hand, and meted out heaven with the span, and comprehended the dust of the earth in a measure, and weighed the mountains in scales, and the hills in a balance?

13   Who hath directed the Spirit of the LORD, or being his counsellor hath taught him?

14   With whom took he counsel, and who instructed him, and taught him in the path of judgment, and taught him knowledge, and shewed to him the way of understanding?

15   Behold, the nations are as a drop of a bucket, and are counted as the small dust of the balance: behold, he taketh up the isles as a very little thing!

16   And Lebanon is not sufficient to burn, nor the beasts thereof sufficient for a burnt offering.

17   All nations before him are as nothing; and they are counted to him less than nothing, and vanity.

18   To whom then will ye liken God? or what likeness will ye compare unto him?

19 The workman melteth an image, and the goldsmith spreadeth it over with gold, and casteth silver chains.

20 He that is too poor for oblation chooseth a tree that will not rot; he seeketh unto him a cunning workman to prepare an image, that shall not be moved.

21 Have ye not known? have ye not heard? hath it not been told you from the beginning? have ye not understood from the foundations of the earth?

22 He that sitteth above the circle of the earth, and the inhabitants thereof are as grasshoppers? that stretcheth out the heavens as a curtain, and spreadeth them out as a tent to dwell in?

23 That bringeth the princes to nothing? he maketh the judges of the earth as vanity.

24 Yea, scarce shall they be planted, yea, scarce shall they be sown, yea, scarce shall their stock take root in the earth; and he shall blow upon them, and they shall wither, and the whirlwind shall take them away as stubble.

25 To whom then will ye liken me, or shall I be equal? saith the Holy One.

26 Lift up your eyes unto the heavens, and behold! who hath created these things? he bringeth out their host by number, he calleth them all by names; by the greatness of his might, for that he is strong in power, not one faileth.

27 Why sayest thou, O Jacob, and speakest, O Israel, My way is hid from the Lord, and my judgment is passed over from my God?

28 Hast thou not known? hast thou not heard, that the everlasting God, the Lord, the Creator of the ends of the earth, fainteth not, neither is weary? there is no searching of his understanding.

29 He giveth power to the faint, and to them that have no might he increaseth strength.

30 Even the youths shall faint and be weary, and the young men shall utterly stumble;

31 But they that wait upon the Lord shall renew their strength; they shall mount up with wings as eagles; they shall run, and not be weary; and they shall walk, and not faint.

41

1 KEEP silence before me, O islands, and let the nations renew their strength! let them come near, then let them speak; let us come near together to judgment.

2 Who raised up from the east the man with whom goeth victory, gave the nations before him, and made him rule over kings? he gave them as the dust to his sword, and as driven stubble to his bow.

3 He pursued them, and passed safely, even by the way that he had not gone with his feet.

4 Who hath wrought and done it? even he that called forth the generations from the beginning: I the LORD, the first, and to the last I am he.

5 Far lands saw it, and feared; the ends of the earth were afraid, draw near, and come.

6 They help every one his neighbour, and every one saith to his brother, Be of good courage.

7 So the carpenter encourageth the goldsmith, and he that smootheth with the hammer him that smiteth the anvil, saying of the solder, It is good: and he fasteneth it with nails, that it should not be moved.

8 But thou, Israel my servant, Jacob whom I have chosen, the seed of Abraham my friend;

9 Thou whom I have taken from the ends of the earth, and called thee from the extreme borders thereof, and said unto thee: Thou art my servant, I have chosen thee, and not cast thee away;

10 Fear thou not, for I am with thee! be not dismayed, for I am thy God! I will strengthen thee, yea, I will help thee, yea, I will uphold thee with the right hand of my righteousness.

11 Behold, all they that were incensed against thee shall be ashamed and confounded! they shall be as nothing; and they that strive with thee shall perish.

12 Thou shalt seek them, and shalt not find them, even them that contended with thee; they that war against thee shall be as nothing, and as a thing of nought.

13 For I the LORD thy God will hold thy right hand, saying unto thee, Fear not; I help thee!

14 Fear not, thou worm Jacob, and thou handful Israel! I help thee, saith the LORD, and thy redeemer is the Holy One of Israel.

15 Behold, I will make thee a new sharp threshing instrument having teeth: thou shalt thresh the mountains, and beat them small, and shalt make the hills as chaff.

16 Thou shalt fan them, and the wind shall carry them away, and the whirlwind shall scatter them; but thou shalt rejoice in the LORD, and shalt glory in the Holy One of Israel.

17 When the poor and needy seek water, and there is none, and their tongue faileth for thirst, I the LORD will hear them, I the God of Israel will not forsake them.

18 I will open rivers on high places, and fountains in the midst of the valleys: I will make the wilderness a pool of water, and the dry land springs of water.

19 I will plant in the wilderness the cedar, the acacia tree, and the myrtle, and the olive tree; I will set in the desert the cypress tree, and the pine, and the box tree together:

20 That they may see, and know, and consider, and understand together, that the hand of the LORD hath done this, and the Holy One of Israel hath created it.

21 PRODUCE your cause, saith the LORD; bring forth your strong reasons, saith the King of Jacob.

22 Let them bring them forth, and shew us what shall happen: let them shew the former things, what they be, that we may consider them, and know the latter end of them; or declare us things for to come.

23 Shew the things that are to come hereafter, that we may know that ye are gods! yea, do good, or do evil, that we may be dismayed, and behold it together!

24 Behold, ye are of nothing, and your work of nought: an abomination is he that chooseth you.

25 I have raised up one from the north, and he shall come: from the rising of the sun, that he should call upon my

name: and he shall come upon princes as upon morter, and as the potter treadeth clay.

26 Who hath declared from the beginning, that we may know? and beforetime, that we may say, It is right! yea, there is none that sheweth, yea, there is none that declareth, yea, there is none that hath heard your words.

27 I the first said to Zion, Behold, behold it! and I gave to Jerusalem one that bringeth good tidings.

28 I look, and there is no one; even among them, and there is no counsellor, that, when I should ask of them, could answer a word.

29 Behold, they are all vanity! their works are nothing: their molten images are wind and confusion.

42

1 BEHOLD my servant, whom I uphold; mine elect, in whom my soul delighteth! I have put my spirit upon him: he shall declare judgment to the Gentiles.

2 He shall not strive, nor cry, nor cause his voice to be heard in the street.

3 A bruised reed shall he not break, and smoking flax shall he not quench: he shall declare judgment with truth.

4 He shall not fail nor be discouraged, until he set judgment in the earth: far lands wait for his law.

5 Thus saith God the LORD, he that created the heavens, and stretched them out; he that spread forth the earth, and that which cometh out of it; he that giveth breath unto the people upon it, and spirit to them that walk therein:

6 I the LORD have called thee in righteousness, and will hold thine hand, and will keep thee, and give thee for a mediator of the people, for a light of the Gentiles;

7 To open the blind eyes, to bring out the prisoners from the prison, and them that sit in darkness out of the prison house;

8 I the LORD: that is my name! and my glory will I not give to another, neither my praise to graven images.

9 Behold, the former things are come to pass, and new things do I declare: before they spring forth I tell you of them.

10 SING unto the LORD a new song, and his praise from the end of the earth, ye that go down to the sea and all that is therein; the isles, and the inhabitants thereof!

11 Let the wilderness and the cities thereof lift up their voice, the villages that Kedar doth inhabit: let the inhabitants of the rock sing, let them shout from the top of the mountains.

12 Let them give glory unto the LORD, and declare his praise in the islands.

13 The LORD shall go forth as a mighty man, he shall stir up his zeal like a man of war: he shall cry, yea, roar: he shall behave himself mightily against his enemies.

14 I have long time holden my peace; I have been still, and refrained myself: now will I cry like a travailing woman; I will destroy and devour at once.

15 I will make waste mountains and hills, and parch up all their herbs; and I will make the rivers dry land, and I will dry up the pools.

16 And I will bring the blind by a way that they knew not, I will lead them in paths that they have not known: I will make darkness light before them, and crooked things straight. These things will I do unto them, and not forsake them.

17 They shall be turned back, they shall be greatly ashamed, that trust in graven images, that say to the molten images, Ye are our gods.

18 Hear, ye deaf! and look, ye blind, that ye may see!

19 Who is blind, but my servant? or deaf, as my messenger that I would send? who is blind as God's liegeman, and blind as the LORD's servant?

20 Seeing many things, but thou observest not; having the ears open, but he heareth not.

21 The LORD was pleased to do it for his righteousness' sake; to magnify the law, and to make it honourable.

22 But this is a people robbed and spoiled; they are all of
them snared in dungeons, and they are hid in prison
houses: they are for a prey, and none delivereth; for a
spoil, and none saith, Restore.

23 Who among you will give ear to this? who will hearken
and hear concerning the fore time?

24 Who gave Jacob for a spoil, and Israel to the robbers?
did not the LORD, he against whom we have sinned? for
they would not walk in his ways, neither were they
obedient unto his law.

25 Therefore he hath poured upon him the fury of his anger,
and the strength of battle; and it hath set him on fire
round about, yet he knew not, and it burned him, yet he
laid it not to heart.

43

1 But now thus saith the LORD that created thee, O Jacob,
and he that formed thee, O Israel! Fear not, for I have
redeemed thee; I have called thee by thy name, thou art
mine!

2 When thou passest through the waters, I will be with
thee, and through the rivers, they shall not overflow
thee: when thou walkest through the fire, thou shalt not
be burned, neither shall the flame kindle upon thee.

3 For I am the LORD thy God, the Holy One of Israel, thy
Saviour: I give Egypt for thy ransom, Ethiopia and Saba
for thee.

4 Because thou art precious in my sight, honourable, and
I have loved thee, therefore will I give men for thee, and
people for thy life.

5 Fear not, for I am with thee! I will bring thy seed from
the east, and gather thee from the west;

6 I will say to the north, Give up! and to the south, Keep
not back! bring my sons from far, and my daughters
from the ends of the earth;

7 Even every one that is called by my name: for I have

created him for my glory, I have formed him, yea, I have made him.

8 Bring forth the blind people that have eyes, and the deaf that have ears!

9 Let all the nations be gathered together, and let the Gentiles be assembled: who among them can declare this? Or let them shew us former things! let them bring forth their witnesses, that they may be justified! let one hear, and say, It is truth!

10 Ye are my witnesses, saith the LORD, and my servant whom I have chosen, that ye may know and believe me, and understand that I am he: before me there was no God formed, neither shall there be after me.

11 I, even I, am the LORD, and beside me there is no saviour.

12 I have declared, and have saved, and I have shewed, and it was no strange god that was among you: therefore ye are my witnesses, saith the LORD, that I am God.

13 Yea, before the day was, I am he, and there is none that can take away out of my hand: I will work, and who shall let it?

14 Thus saith the LORD, your redeemer, the Holy One of Israel: For your sake I have sent to Babylon, and do make them all to flee away, and the Chaldeans upon the ships of their pleasure;

15 I the LORD, your Holy One, the creator of Israel, your King.

16 Thus saith the LORD, which maketh a way in the sea, and a path in the mighty waters;

17 Which bringeth forth the chariot and horse, the army and the power: (they shall lie down together, they shall not rise; they are extinct, they are quenched as tow.)

18 Remember not the former things, neither consider the things of old!

19 Behold, I do a new thing! now it shall spring forth! shall ye not know it? I will even make a way in the wilderness, and rivers in the desert.

20 The beast of the field shall honour me, the jackals and

the ostriches: because I give waters in the wilderness, and rivers in the desert, to give drink to my people, my chosen,

21 This people that I formed for myself; they shall shew forth my praise.

22 BUT THOU hast not called upon me, O Jacob! but thou hast been careless of me, O Israel!

23 Thou hast not brought me the lambs of thy burnt offering, neither hast thou honoured me with thy sacrifices: I have not burdened thee with an offering, nor wearied thee with incense.

24 Thou hast bought me no sweet cane with money, neither hast thou filled me with the fat of thy sacrifices: but thou hast burdened me with thy sins, thou hast wearied me with thine iniquities.

25 I, even I, am he that blotteth out thy transgressions for mine own sake, and will not remember thy sins.

26 Put me in remembrance, let us plead together! declare thou, that thou mayest be justified!

27 Thy first father hath sinned, and thy teachers have transgressed against me.

28 Therefore I have profaned the princes of the sanctuary, and have given Jacob to the curse, and Israel to reproaches.

44

1 Yet now hear, O Jacob, my servant, and Israel, whom I have chosen!

2 Thus saith the LORD that made thee, and formed thee from the womb, which will help thee: Fear not, O Jacob, my servant; and thou, Jeshurun, whom I have chosen!

3 For I will pour water upon him that is thirsty, and floods upon the dry ground: I will pour my spirit upon thy seed, and my blessing upon thine offspring:

4 And they shall spring up as the grass amidst water, as willows by the water courses.

5 One shall say, I am the LORD's, and another shall call himself by the name of Jacob, and another shall subscribe
with his hand unto the LORD, and surname himself by the
name of Israel.

6 THUS saith the LORD the king of Israel, and his redeemer
the LORD of hosts: I am the first, and I am the last; and
beside me there is no God.

7 And who, as I, hath foretold, (let him declare it, and set
it in order for me!) since I appointed the ancient people?
and the things that are coming, and shall come, let them
shew!

8 Fear ye not, neither be afraid! have not I told thee from
aforetime, and have declared it? ye are even my witnesses. Is there a God beside me? yea, there is no God; I
know not any.

9 They that make a graven image are all of them vanity,
and their delectable things shall not profit; and they are
their own witnesses; they see not, nor know, that they
may be ashamed.

10 Who hath formed a god, or molten an image that is
profitable for nothing?

11 Behold, all his fellows shall be ashamed, and the work-
men, that are but men. Let them all be gathered together,
let them stand up; they shall fear, they shall be ashamed
together.

12 The smith with the tongs both worketh in the coals, and
fashioneth it with hammers, and worketh it with the
strength of his arms: yea, he is hungry, and his strength
faileth: he drinketh no water, and is faint.

13 The carpenter stretcheth out his rule; he marketh it out
with a line; he fitteth it with planes, and he marketh it
out with the compass, and maketh it after the figure of a
man, according to the beauty of a man; that it may remain in the house.

14 He heweth him down cedars, and taketh the cypress and
the oak: he chooseth for himself among the trees of the
forest: he planteth an ash, and the rain doth nourish it.

324 Philistinism in England and America

15 Then shall it be for a man to burn, for he will take thereof, and warm himself; yea, he kindleth it, and baketh bread; yea, he maketh a god, and worshippeth it; he maketh it a graven image, and falleth down thereto.

16 He burneth part thereof in the fire; with part thereof he eateth flesh; he roasteth roast, and is satisfied: yea, he warmeth himself, and saith, Aha, I am warm, I have seen the fire!

17 And the residue thereof he maketh a god, even his graven image: he falleth down unto it, and worshippeth it, and prayeth unto it, and saith: Deliver me, for thou art my god!

18 They have not known nor understood; for he hath shut their eyes, that they cannot see, and their hearts, that they cannot understand.

19 And none considereth in his heart, neither is there knowledge nor understanding to say: I have burned part of it in the fire, yea, also I have baked bread upon the coals thereof, I have roasted flesh, and eaten it; and shall I make the residue thereof an abomination? shall I fall down to the stock of a tree?

20 He feedeth on ashes: a deceived heart hath turned him aside, that he cannot deliver his soul, nor say: Is there not a lie in my right hand?

21 Remember this, O Jacob and Israel, for thou art my servant! I have formed thee, thou art my servant: O Israel, thou shalt not be forgotten of me!

22 I have blotted out, as a thick cloud, thy transgressions, and, as a cloud, thy sins: return unto me, for I have redeemed thee.

23 SING, O ye heavens, for the LORD hath done it: shout, ye foundations of the earth: break forth into singing, ye mountains, O forest, and every tree therein! for the LORD hath redeemed Jacob, and glorified himself in Israel.

24 Thus saith the LORD, thy redeemer, and he that formed thee from the womb, I the LORD that maketh all things,

that stretcheth forth the heavens alone, that spreadeth
abroad the earth by myself;

25 That frustrateth the tokens of the liars, and maketh di-
viners mad; that turneth wise men backward, and maketh
their knowledge foolish;

26 That confirmeth his word to his servant, and performeth
his counsel toward his messengers; that saith to Jerusalem, Thou shalt be inhabited! and to the cities of Judah,
Ye shall be built, and I will raise up the decayed places
thereof!

27 That saith to the deep, Be dry, and I will dry up thy
rivers!

28 That saith of Cyrus, He is my shepherd, and shall perform all my pleasure, even saying to Jerusalem, Thou
shalt be built, and to the temple, Thy foundation shall be
laid!

45

1 Thus saith the LORD to his anointed, to Cyrus, whose
right hand I have holden, to subdue nations before him;
and I will ungird the loins of kings, to open before him
the two leaved gates, and the gates shall not be shut;

2 I will go before thee, and make the crooked places
straight: I will break in pieces the gates of brass, and cut
in sunder the bars of iron:

3 And I will give thee the treasures hid in darkness, and
concealed riches of secret places, that thou mayest know
that I am the LORD which call thee by thy name, the
God of Israel.

4 For Jacob my servant's sake, and Israel mine elect, I have
even called thee by thy name: I have surnamed thee,
though thou hast not known me.

5 I am the LORD, and there is none else, there is no God
beside me: I girded thee, though thou hast not known me:

6 That they may know from the rising of the sun, and

from the west, that there is none beside me: I am the
Lord, and there is none else.

7 I form the light, and create darkness: I make peace, and
create evil: I the Lord do all these things.

8 Drop down, ye heavens, from above, and let the skies
pour down righteousness! let the earth open, and bring
forth salvation, and let righteousness spring up together!
I the Lord have created it.

9 Woe unto him that striveth with his Maker! Let the pot-
sherd strive with the potsherds of the earth. Shall the clay
say to him that fashioneth it, What makest thou? or thy
work, He hath no hands?

10 Woe unto him that saith unto his father, What begettest
thou? or to his mother, What hast thou brought forth?

11 Thus saith the Lord, the Holy One of Israel and his
Maker: Ask ye me of things to come concerning my sons?
and concerning the work of my hands command ye me?

12 I have made the earth, and created man upon it: I, even
my hands, have stretched out the heavens, and all their
host have I commanded.

13 I have raised him up in righteousness, and I will direct all
his ways: he shall build my city, and he shall let go my
captives, not for price nor reward, saith the Lord of hosts.

14 Thus saith the Lord: The labour of Egypt, and merchandise of Ethiopia and of the Sabeans, men of stature, shall
come over unto thee, and they shall be thine: they shall
come after thee; in chains they shall come over, and they
shall fall down unto thee, they shall make supplication
unto thee, saying: Surely God is in thee, and there is
none else, there is no God!

15 Verily thou art a God whose way is hidden, O God of
Israel, the Saviour!

16 They shall be ashamed, and also confounded, all of them;
they shall go to confusion together, that are makers of
idols.

17 But Israel shall be saved in the Lord with an everlasting
salvation; ye shall not be ashamed nor confounded, world
without end.

18 For thus saith the LORD that created the heavens, God himself that formed the earth and made it; he hath established it, he created it not in vain, he formed it to be inhabited; I the LORD, and there is none else:

19 I have not spoken in secret, in a dark place of the earth: I said not unto the seed of Jacob, Seek ye me in vain! I the LORD speak uprightly, I declare things that are right.

20 Assemble yourselves and come, draw near together, ye that are escaped of the nations! they have no knowledge that set up the wood of their graven image, and pray unto a god that cannot save.

21 Tell ye, and bring them near, yea, let them take counsel together! who hath declared this from ancient time? who hath told it from that time? have not I the LORD? and there is no God else beside me; a just God and a Saviour; there is none beside me.

22 Look unto me, and be ye saved, all the ends of the earth! for I am God, and there is none else.

23 I have sworn by myself, the word is gone out of my mouth in righteousness, and shall not return, that unto me every knee shall bow, every tongue shall swear.

24 Surely, shall one say, in the LORD have I righteousness and strength! Even to him shall men come, and all that are incensed against him shall be ashamed.

25 In the LORD shall all the seed of Israel be justified, and shall glory.

46

1 BEL boweth down, Nebo stoopeth, their idols are upon the beasts, and upon the cattle: they are borne that ye carried; they are a burden to the weary beast.

2 They stoop, they bow down together; they cannot deliver the burden, but themselves are gone into captivity.

3 Hearken unto me, O house of Jacob, and all the remnant of the house of Israel, which are borne by me from the birth, which are carried from the womb!

4 And even to your old age I am he, and even to hoar hairs

will I carry you: I have made, and I will bear; even I will carry, and will deliver you.

5 To whom will ye liken me, and make me equal, and compare me, that we may be like?

6 They lavish gold out of the bag, and weigh silver in the balance, and hire a goldsmith, and he maketh it a god: they fall down, yea, they worship.

7 They bear him upon the shoulder, they carry him, and set him in his place, and he standeth; from his place shall he not remove: yea, one shall cry unto him, yet can he not answer, nor save him out of his trouble.

8 Remember this, and shew yourselves men! bring it again to mind, O ye transgressors!

9 Remember the former things of old: for I am God, and there is none else; I am God, and there is none like me;

10 Declaring the end from the beginning, and from ancient times the things that are not yet done, saying: My counsel shall stand, and I will do all my pleasure:

11 Calling the eagle from the east, the man that executeth my counsel from a far country: yea, I have spoken it, I will also bring it to pass; I have purposed it, I will also do it.

12 Hearken unto me, ye obdurate, that are far from righteousness!

13 I bring near my righteousness: it shall not be far off, and my salvation shall not tarry: and I will give salvation to Zion; to Israel, my glory.

47

1 COME down, and sit in the dust, O virgin daughter of Babylon, sit on the ground! there is no throne, O daughter of the Chaldeans! for thou shalt no more be called tender and delicate.

2 Take the millstones, and grind meal! uncover thy locks, make bare the leg, uncover the thigh, pass over the rivers!

3 Thy nakedness shall be uncovered, yea, thy shame shall be seen: I will take vengeance, and I will be entreated of for thee by no man.

4 As for our redeemer, the LORD of hosts is his name, the
   Holy One of Israel.

5 Sit thou silent, and get thee into darkness, O daughter of
   the Chaldeans! for thou shalt no more be called, The lady
   of kingdoms.

6 I was wroth with my people, I polluted mine inheritance,
   and gave them into thine hand: thou didst shew them no
   mercy; upon the ancient hast thou very heavily laid thy
   yoke.

7 And thou saidst, I shall be a lady for ever! so that thou
   didst not lay these things to thy heart, neither didst remember the latter end of it.

8 Therefore hear now this, thou that art given to pleasures,
   that dwellest carelessly, that sayest in thine heart: I am,
   and none else beside me; I shall not sit as a widow,
   neither shall I know the loss of children.

9 But these two things shall come to thee in a moment in
   one day, the loss of children, and widowhood: they shall
   come upon thee in their perfection for the multitude of
   thy sorceries, and for the great abundance of thine enchantments.

10 For thou hast trusted in thy wickedness, thou hast said,
   None seeth me! Thy wisdom and thy knowledge, it hath
   perverted thee; and thou hast said in thine heart, I am,
   and none else beside me.

11 Therefore shall evil come upon thee, thou shalt not know
   from whence it riseth; and mischief shall fall upon thee,
   thou shalt not be able to put it off; and desolation shall
   come upon thee suddenly, which thou shalt not know.

12 Stand now with thine enchantments, and with the multitude of thy sorceries, wherein thou hast laboured from
   thy youth! if so be thou shalt be able to profit, if so be
   thou mayest prevail.

13 Thou art wearied in the multitude of thy counsels! Let
   now the astrologers, the stargazers, the prognosticators by
   the new moon, stand up, and save thee from these things
   that shall come upon thee.

14 Behold, they shall be as stubble! the fire shall burn them,
   they shall not deliver themselves from the power of the

flame! it shall not be a coal to warm at, nor a fire for a man to sit before it.

15 Thus shall they be unto thee with whom thou hast laboured, even they with whom thou hast dealt from thy youth: they shall wander every one to his quarter; none shall save thee.

48

1 HEAR ye this, O house of Jacob, which are called by the name of Israel, and are come forth out of the fountain of Judah! which swear by the name of the LORD, and make mention of the God of Israel, but not in truth, nor in righteousness!

2 For they call themselves of the holy city, and stay themselves upon the God of Israel; the LORD of hosts is his name.

3 I have declared the former things from the beginning, and they went forth out of my mouth, and I shewed them; I did them suddenly, and they came to pass.

4 Because I knew that thou art obstinate, and thy neck is an iron sinew, and thy brow brass,

5 I have even from the beginning declared it to thee: before it came to pass I shewed it thee: lest thou shouldest say, Mine idol hath done them, and my graven image, and my molten image, hath commanded them.

6 Thou hast heard—see all this! and will not ye declare it? I shew thee new things from this time, even hidden things, and thou didst not know them.

7 They are created now, and not in the former time; even before this day thou heardest them not; lest thou shouldest say, Behold, I knew them.

8 Yea, thou heardest not, yea, thou knewest not, yea, beforehand thine ear was not opened; for I knew that thou wouldest deal very treacherously, and wast called a transgressor from the womb.

9 For my name's sake will I defer mine anger, and for my praise will I refrain for thee, that I cut thee not off.

10 Behold, I have refined thee, but not gotten therefrom silver; I have tried thee in the furnace of affliction.

11 For mine own sake, even for mine own sake, will I do it: for how should my name be polluted? and I will not give my glory unto another.

12 Hearken unto me, O Jacob and Israel, my called! I am he; I am the first, I also am the last.

13 Mine hand also hath laid the foundation of the earth, and my right hand hath spread out the heavens: when I call unto them, they stand forth together.

14 All ye, assemble yourselves, and hear: which among them hath declared these things? The man whom the LORD loveth will do his pleasure on Babylon, and his chastisement on the Chaldeans.

15 I, even I, have spoken; yea, I have called him: I have brought him, and he shall make his way prosperous.

16 Come ye near unto me, hear ye this: I have not spoken in secret from the beginning; from the time that it was, there am I. (And now the Lord GOD, and his Spirit, hath sent me.)

17 Thus saith the LORD, thy Redeemer, the Holy One of Israel: I am the LORD thy God which teacheth thee to profit, which leadeth thee by the way that thou shouldest go.

18 O that thou hadst hearkened to my commandments! then had thy peace been as a river, and thy righteousness as the waves of the sea:

19 Thy seed also had been as the sand, and the offspring of thy bowels like the grains thereof; his name should not have been cut off nor destroyed from before me.

20 Go ye forth of Babylon, flee ye from the Chaldeans, with a voice of singing declare ye, tell this, utter it even to the end of the earth! say ye: The LORD hath redeemed his servant Jacob,

21 And they thirsted not when he led them through the deserts; he caused the waters to flow out of the rock for them; he clave the rock also, and the waters gushed out.

22 No peace, saith the LORD, unto the wicked!

49

1 LISTEN, O isles, unto me; and hearken, ye people, from far! The LORD hath called me from the womb: from the bowels of my mother hath he made mention of my name.

2 And he hath made my mouth like a sharp sword; in the shadow of his hand hath he hid me, and made me a polished shaft; in his quiver hath he hid me;

3 And said unto me, Thou art my servant, O Israel, in whom I will be glorified.

4 Then I said: I have laboured in vain, I have spent my strength for nought, and in vain; yet surely my righteousness is with the LORD, and my recompence with my God.

5 And now, saith the LORD that formed me from the womb to be his servant, to bring Jacob again to him, and that Israel may be gathered; (for I have honour in the eyes of the LORD, and my God is my strength;)

6 And he said: It is a small thing that thou shouldest be my servant to raise up the tribes of Jacob, and to restore the preserved of Israel; I will also give thee for a light to the Gentiles, that my salvation may be unto the ends of the earth!

7 Thus saith the LORD, the Redeemer of Israel, his Holy One, to him whom man despiseth, to him whom the people abhorreth, to a servant of tyrants: Kings shall see and arise, princes also shall worship, because of the LORD that is faithful, the Holy One of Israel, and he chose thee.

8 Thus saith the LORD: In an acceptable time have I heard thee, and in a day of salvation have I helped thee; and I will preserve thee, and give thee for a mediator of the people, to establish the land, to cause to inherit the desolate heritages;

9 That thou mayest say to the prisoners, Go forth! to them that are in darkness, Shew yourselves! They shall feed in the ways, and their pastures shall be in all high places;

10 They shall not hunger nor thirst, neither shall the heat nor sun smite them; for he that hath mercy on them shall

lead them, even by the springs of water shall he guide them.

11 And I will make all my mountains a way, and my highways shall be cast up.

12 Behold. these shall come from far; and, lo, these from the north and from the west; and these from the land of Sinim.

13 Sing, O heavens, and be joyful, O earth, and break forth into singing, O mountains! for the LORD hath comforted his people, and doth have mercy upon his afflicted.

14 But Zion said: The LORD hath forsaken me, and my Lord hath forgotten me!—

15 Can a woman forget her sucking child, that she should not have compassion on the son of her womb? yea, they may forget, yet will I not forget thee!

16 Behold, I have graven thee upon the palms of my hands! thy walls are continually before me!

17 Thy children shall make haste; thy destroyers and they that made thee waste shall go forth of thee.

18 Lift up thine eyes round about, and behold! all these gather themselves together, and come to thee. As I live, saith the Lord, thou shalt surely clothe thee with them all, as with an ornament, and bind them on thee, as a bride doeth.

19 For thy waste and thy desolate places, and the land of thy destruction, shall even now be too narrow by reason of the inhabitants, and they that swallowed thee up shall be far away.

20 The children which thou shalt have, after thou hast lost the other, shall say again in thine ears: The place is too strait for me; give place to me that I may dwell.

21 Then shalt thou say in thine heart: Who hath begotten me these, seeing I have lost my children, and am desolate, a captive, and removing to and fro? and who hath brought up these? Behold, I was left alone; these, where had they been?

22 Thus saith the Lord GOD: Behold, I will lift up mine hand to the Gentiles, and set up my standard to the nations; and

they shall bring thy sons in their arms, and thy daughters shall be carried upon their shoulders.

23 And kings shall be thy nursing fathers, and their queens thy nursing mothers: they shall bow down to thee with their face toward the earth, and lick up the dust of thy feet; and thou shalt know that I am the Lord; for they shall not be ashamed that wait for me.—

24 Shall the prey be taken from the mighty, or the captivity of the righteous be loosed?—

25 But thus saith the Lord: Even the captives of the mighty shall be taken away, and the prey of the terrible shall be loosed: for I will contend with him that contendeth with thee, and I will save thy children.

26 And I will feed them that oppress thee with their own flesh, and they shall be drunken with their own blood, as with new wine; and all flesh shall know that I the Lord am thy Saviour, and thy Redeemer the mighty One of Jacob.

50

1 Thus saith the Lord, Where is the bill of your mother's divorcement, whom I have put away? or which of my creditors is it to whom I have sold you? Behold, for your iniquities have ye sold yourselves, and for your transgressions is your mother put away.

2 Wherefore, when I came, was there no man? when I called, was there none to answer? Is my hand shortened at all, that it cannot redeem? or have I no power to deliver? Behold, at my rebuke I dry up the sea, I make the rivers a wilderness; their fish stinketh, because there is no water, and dieth for thirst.

3 I clothe the heavens with blackness, and I make sackcloth their covering.

4 The Lord God hath given me the tongue of the learned, that I should know how to speak a word in season to him that is weary: he wakeneth morning by morning, he wakeneth mine ear to hear as the learned.

5 The Lord G<small>OD</small> hath opened mine ear, and I was not rebellious, neither turned away back.

6 I gave my back to the smiters, and my cheeks to them that plucked off the hair: I hid not my face from shame and spitting.

7 For the Lord G<small>OD</small> will help me, therefore shall I not be confounded; therefore have I set my face like a flint, and I know that I shall not be ashamed.

8 He is near that justifieth me. Who will contend with me? let us stand together! who is mine adversary? let him come near to me!

9 Behold, the Lord G<small>OD</small> will help me; who is he that shall condemn me? lo, they all shall wax old as a garment, the moth shall eat them up.

10 Who is among you that feareth the L<small>ORD</small>? let him obey the voice of his servant! that walketh in darkness, and hath no light? let him trust in the name of the L<small>ORD</small>, and stay upon his God!

11 Behold, all ye that kindle a fire, that compass yourselves about with burning darts: get ye into the flame of your fire, and among the darts that ye have kindled! This shall ye have of mine hand: ye shall lie down in sorrow!

51

1 Hearken to me, ye that follow after righteousness, ye that seek the L<small>ORD</small>! look unto the rock whence ye are hewn, and to the hole of the pit whence ye are digged.

2 Look unto Abraham your father, and unto Sarah that bare you; for I called him when he was alone, and blessed him, and increased him.

3 For the L<small>ORD</small> shall comfort Zion, he will comfort all her waste places, and he will make her wilderness like Eden, and her desert like the garden of the L<small>ORD</small>; joy and gladness shall be found therein, thanksgiving and the voice of melody.

4 Hearken unto me, my people, and give ear unto me, O

my nation! for a law shall proceed from me, and I will
make my judgment to rest for a light of the Gentiles.

5   My righteousness is near, my salvation is gone forth, and
mine arms shall judge the people; far lands shall wait upon
me, and on mine arm shall they trust.

6   Lift up your eyes to the heavens, and look upon the earth
beneath! for the heavens shall vanish away like smoke,
and the earth shall wax old like a garment, and they that
dwell therein shall die in like manner; but my salvation
shall be for ever, and my righteousness shall not be abolished.

7   Hearken unto me, ye that know righteousness, the people
in whose heart is my law! fear ye not the reproach of
men, neither be ye afraid of their revilings.

8   For the moth shall eat them up like a garment, and the
worm shall eat them like wool; but my righteousness shall
be for ever, and my salvation from generation to generation.

9   Awake, awake, put on strength, O arm of the LORD!
awake, as in the ancient days, in the generations of old.
Art thou not it that hath cut Rahab, and wounded the
dragon?

10 Art thou not it which hath dried the sea, the waters of
the great deep? that hath made the depths of the sea a
way for the ransomed to pass over?

11 Even so the redeemed of the LORD shall return, and come
with singing unto Zion, and everlasting joy shall be upon
their head: they shall obtain gladness and joy, and sorrow
and mourning shall flee away.

12 I, even I, am he that comforteth you! who art thou, that
thou shouldest be afraid of a man that shall die, and of the
son of man which shall be made as grass?

13 And forgettest the LORD thy maker, that hath stretched
forth the heavens, and laid the foundations of the earth?
and hast feared continually every day because of the
fury of the oppressor, as if he were ready to destroy? and
where is the fury of the oppressor?

14 The captive exile shall very soon be loosed; he shall not die in the pit, neither shall his bread fail.

15 For I am the Lᴏʀᴅ thy God, that divided the sea, whose waves roared: The Lᴏʀᴅ of hosts is his name.

16 And I have put my words in thy mouth, and I have covered thee in the shadow of mine hand, that I may plant the heavens, and lay the foundations of the earth, and say unto Zion: Thou art my people!

17 Awake, awake, stand up, O Jerusalem, which hast drunk at the hand of the Lᴏʀᴅ the cup of his fury! thou hast drunken the dregs of the cup of trembling, and wrung them out.

18 None to guide her among all the sons whom she hath brought forth! neither any to take her by the hand of all the sons that she hath brought up!

19 These two things are come unto thee: who shall be sorry for thee? desolation with destruction, and famine with the sword: by whom shall I comfort thee?

20 Thy sons have fainted, they lie at all corners of the streets, as a wild bull in a net: they are full of the fury of the Lᴏʀᴅ, the rebuke of thy God.

21 Therefore hear now this, thou afflicted, and drunken, but not with wine!

22 Thus saith thy Lord the Lᴏʀᴅ, and thy God that pleadeth the cause of his people: Behold, I have taken out of thine hand the cup of trembling, even the dregs of the cup of my fury; thou shalt no more drink it again:

23 But I will put it into the hand of them that afflict thee, which have said to thy soul, Bow down, that we may go over! and thou hast laid thy body as the ground, and as the street to them that went over.

52

1 Awake, awake, put on thy strength, O Zion! put on thy beautiful garments, O Jerusalem, the holy city! for hence-

forth there shall no more come into thee the uncircumcised and the unclean.

2 Shake thyself from the dust, arise, and sit up, O Jerusalem! loose thyself from the bands of thy neck, O captive daughter of Zion!

3 For thus saith the Lord: Ye have sold yourselves for nought, and ye shall be redeemed without money.

4 For thus saith the Lord God: My people went down aforetime into Egypt to sojourn there, and the Assyrian oppressed them for nought.

5 Now therefore what have I here, saith the Lord, that my people is taken away for nought? they that rule over them make them to howl, saith the Lord, and my name continually every day is blasphemed.

6 Therefore my people shall know my name: therefore they shall know in that day that I am he that doth speak: behold, it is I!

7 How beautiful upon the mountains are the feet of him that bringeth good tidings, that publisheth peace! that bringeth good tidings of good, that publisheth salvation! that saith unto Zion, Thy God reigneth!

8 Thy watchmen lift up the voice, with the voice together do they sing; for eye to eye they do behold, how that the Lord doth bring again Zion.

9 Break forth into joy, sing together, ye waste places of Jerusalem! for the Lord hath comforted his people, he hath redeemed Jerusalem.

10 The Lord hath made bare his holy arm in the eyes of all the nations, and all the ends of the earth shall see the salvation of our God.

11 Depart ye, depart ye, go ye out from thence, touch no unclean thing! go ye out of the midst of her! be ye clean, that bear the vessels of the Lord!

12 For ye shall not go out with haste, nor go by flight; for the Lord will go before you, and the God of Israel will be your rereward.

13 Behold, my servant shall prosper, he shall be exalted and extolled, and be very high.

14 As many were astonied at thee—his visage was so marred more than any man, and his form more than the sons of men—

15 So shall many nations exult in him: kings shall shut their mouths before him: for that which had not been told them shall they see, and that which they had not heard shall they consider.

53

1 Who believed our report, and to whom was the arm of the LORD revealed?

2 For he grew up before him as a slender plant, and as a root out of a dry ground: he had no form nor comeliness, and when we saw him, there was no beauty that we should desire him.

3 He was despised and rejected of men, a man of sorrows, and acquainted with grief; and we hid as it were our faces from him; he was despised, and we esteemed him not.

4 Surely he hath borne our griefs, and carried our sorrows! yet we did esteem him stricken, smitten of God, and afflicted.

5 But he was wounded for our transgressions, he was bruised for our iniquities: the chastisement of our peace was upon him, and with his stripes we are healed.

6 All we like sheep were gone astray, we were turned every one to his own way; and the LORD hath laid on him the iniquity of us all.

7 He was oppressed, and he was afflicted, yet he opened not his mouth: as a lamb is brought to the slaughter, and as a sheep before her shearers is dumb, so he opened not his mouth.

8 He was taken from prison and from judgment; and who of his generation regarded it, why he was cut off out of the land of the living? for the transgression of my people was he stricken!

9 And he made his grave with the wicked, and with sinners

in his death; although he had done no violence, neither was any deceit in his mouth.

10 Yet it pleased the LORD to bruise him; he hath put him to grief! When he hath made his soul an offering for sin, he shall see his seed, he shall prolong his days, and the pleasure of the LORD shall prosper in his hand:

11 He shall see of the travail of his soul, and shall be satisfied; by his knowledge shall my righteous servant justify many; for he shall bear their iniquities.

12 Therefore will I divide him his portion with the great, and he shall divide the spoil with the strong! because he hath poured out his soul unto death: and he was numbered with the transgressors; and he bare the sin of many, and made intercession for the transgressors.

54

1 SING, O barren, thou that didst not bear! break forth into singing, and cry aloud, thou that didst not travail with child! for more are the children of the desolate than the children of the married wife, saith the LORD.

2 Enlarge the place of thy tent, and let them stretch forth the curtains of thine habitations! spare not, lengthen thy cords, and strengthen thy stakes!

3 For thou shalt break forth on the right hand and on the left; and thy seed shall inherit the Gentiles, and make the desolate cities to be inhabited.

4 Fear not, for thou shalt not be ashamed! neither be thou confounded, for thou shalt not be put to shame! for thou shalt forget the shame of thy youth, and shalt not remember the reproach of thy widowhood any more.

5 For thy Maker is thine husband, the LORD of hosts is his name: and thy Redeemer the Holy One of Israel, the God of the whole earth shall he be called.

6 For the LORD hath called thee as a woman forsaken and grieved in spirit, and a wife of youth, when thou wast refused, saith thy God.

7 For a small moment have I forsaken thee, but with great mercies will I gather thee.

8 In a little wrath I hid my face from thee for a moment; but with everlasting kindness will I have mercy on thee, saith the LORD thy Redeemer.

9 For this is as the waters of Noah unto me; for as I have sworn that the waters of Noah should no more go over the earth, so have I sworn that I would not be wroth with thee, nor rebuke thee.

10 For the mountains shall depart, and the hills be removed; but my kindness shall not depart from thee, neither shall the covenant of my peace be removed, saith the LORD that hath mercy on thee.

11 O thou afflicted, tossed with tempest, and not comforted! behold, I will lay thy stones with fair colours, and lay thy foundations with sapphires;

12 And I will make thy windows of agates, and thy gates of carbuncles, and all thy borders of pleasant stones.

13 And all thy children shall be taught of the LORD; and great shall be the peace of thy children.

14 In righteousness shalt thou be established: be thou far from anguish, for thou shalt not fear! and from terror, for it shall not come near thee!

15 Behold, if any gather together against thee, it is not by me: whosoever shall gather together against thee shall come over unto thy part.

16 Behold, I have created the smith that bloweth the coals in the fire, and that bringeth forth a weapon by his work; and I have created the waster to destroy.

17 No weapon that is formed against thee shall prosper; and every tongue that shall rise against thee in judgment thou shalt condemn. This is the heritage of the servants of the LORD, and their righteousness of me, saith the LORD.

55

1 Ho, every one that thirsteth, come ye to the waters, and he that hath no money! come ye, buy, and eat! yea, come, buy wine and milk without money and without price!

2 Wherefore do ye spend money for that which is not

bread, and your labour for that which satisfieth not? hearken diligently unto me, and eat ye that which is good, and let your soul delight itself in fatness.

3 Incline your ear, and come unto me! hear, and your soul shall live! and I will make an everlasting covenant with you, even the sure mercies of David.

4 Behold, I appointed him for a lawgiver to the nations, a prince and commander to the nations.

5 Behold, thou shalt call nations that thou knowest not, and nations that knew not thee shall run unto thee, because of the Lord thy God, and for the Holy One of Israel; for he hath glorified thee.

6 Seek ye the Lord while he may be found! call ye upon him while he is near!

7 Let the wicked forsake his way, and the unrighteous man his thoughts; and let him return unto the Lord, and he will have mercy upon him, and to our God, for he will abundantly pardon!

8 For my thoughts are not your thoughts, neither are your ways my ways, saith the Lord.

9 For as the heavens are higher than the earth, so are my ways higher than your ways, and my thoughts than your thoughts.

10 For as the rain cometh down, and the snow from heaven, and returneth not thither, but watereth the earth, and maketh it bring forth and bud, that it may give seed to the sower, and bread to the eater:

11 So shall my word be that goeth forth out of my mouth; it shall not return unto me void, but it shall accomplish that which I please, and it shall prosper in the thing whereto I sent it.

12 For ye shall go out with joy, and be led forth with peace: the mountains and the hills shall break forth before you into singing, and all the trees of the field shall clap their hands.

13 Instead of the thorn shall come up the fir tree, and instead of the brier shall come up the myrtle tree; and it shall be to the Lord for a name, for an everlasting sign that shall not be cut off.

56

1   Thus saith the Lord: Keep ye judgment, and do justice! for my salvation is near to come, and my righteousness to be revealed.

2   Blessed is the man that doeth this, and the son of man that layeth hold on it! that keepeth the sabbath from polluting it, and keepeth his hand from doing any evil.

3   Neither let the son of the stranger, that hath joined himself to the Lord, speak, saying, The Lord hath utterly separated me from his people! neither let the eunuch say, Behold, I am a dry tree!

4   For thus saith the Lord unto the eunuchs that keep my sabbaths, and choose the things that please me, and take hold of my covenant:

5   Even unto them will I give in mine house and within my walls a place and a name better than of sons and of daughters; I will give them an everlasting name, that shall not be cut off.

6   Also the sons of the stranger, that join themselves to the Lord, to serve him, and to love the name of the Lord, to be his servants, every one that keepeth the sabbath from polluting it, and taketh hold of my covenant;

7   Even them will I bring to my holy mountain, and make them joyful in my house of prayer: their burnt offerings and their sacrifices shall be accepted upon mine altar; for mine house shall be called an house of prayer for all people.

8   The Lord God, which gathereth the outcasts of Israel, saith: Yet will I gather others to him, beside those that are gathered unto him.

9   All ye beasts of the field, come to devour, yea, all ye beasts of the forest!

10 His watchmen are blind, they are all ignorant; they are all dumb dogs, they cannot bark; sleeping, lying down, loving to slumber.

11 Yea, they are greedy dogs which can never have enough,

and they are shepherds that cannot understand: they all look to their own way, every one for his gain, one and all of them.

12 Come, say they, I will fetch wine, and we will fill ourselves with strong drink; and to morrow shall be as this day, and much more abundant.

57

1 The righteous perisheth, and no man layeth it to heart; and merciful men are taken away, none considering that the righteous is taken away because of the evil.

2 He shall enter into peace! they shall rest in their beds, whoso walked in his uprightness.

3 But draw near hither, ye sons of the sorceress, the seed of the adulterer and the whore!

4 Against whom do ye sport yourselves? against whom make ye a wide mouth, and draw out the tongue? are ye not children of transgression, a seed of falsehood;

5 Enflaming yourselves with idols under every green tree, slaying the children in the valleys under the clifts of the rocks?

6 Among the smooth stones of the valley is thy portion; they, they are thy lot! even to them hast thou poured a drink offering, thou hast offered a meat offering. Should I receive comfort in these?

7 Upon a lofty and high mountain hast thou set thy bed: even thither wentest thou up to offer sacrifice.

8 Behind the doors also and the posts hast thou set up thy remembrance: thou hast discovered thyself to another than me, and art gone up; thou hast enlarged thy bed, and made thee a covenant with them; thou lovedst their bed where thou sawest it.

9 And thou wentest unto Moloch with ointment, and didst increase thy perfumes, and didst send thy messengers far off, and didst go down even deep into hell.

10 Thou art wearied in the greatness of thy way, yet saidst thou not, There is no hope! thou hast yet found strength in thine hand, therefore thou wast not discouraged.

11 And of whom hast thou been afraid or feared, that thou hast lied, and hast not remembered me, nor laid it to thy heart? have not I held my peace even of old? and thou fearest me not.

12 I declare thy salvation! and thy handiwork, it shall not profit thee.

13 When thou criest, let thy companies of idols deliver thee! but the wind shall carry them all away, vanity shall take them. But he that putteth his trust in me shall possess the land, and shall inherit my holy mountain.

14 Thus shall it be said: Cast ye up, cast ye up, prepare the way, take the stumblingblock out of the way of my people!

15 For thus saith the high and lofty One that inhabiteth eternity, whose name is Holy: I dwell in the high and holy place, with him also that is of a contrite and humble spirit, to revive the spirit of the humble, and to revive the heart of the contrite ones.

16 For I will not contend for ever, neither will I be always wroth; for the spirit should fail before me, and the souls which I have made.

17 For the iniquity of his covetousness was I wroth, and smote him: I hid me, and was wroth, and he went on frowardly in the way of his heart.

18 I have seen his ways, and will heal him! I will lead him also, and restore comforts unto him and to his mourners.

19 I create the fruit of the lips! Peace, peace to him that is far off, and to him that is near, saith the LORD, and I will heal him!

20 But the wicked are like the troubled sea, when it cannot rest, whose waters cast up mire and dirt.

21 No peace, saith my God, to the wicked!

58

1 CRY aloud, spare not, lift up thy voice like a trumpet, and shew my people their transgression, and the house of Jacob their sins!

2 Yet they seek me daily, and desire to know my ways, as a

nation that did righteousness, and forsook not the ordinance of their God: they ask of me the ordinances of judgment, they desire that God should draw nigh to them.

3 Wherefore have we fasted, say they, and thou seest not? wherefore have we afflicted our soul, and thou takest no knowledge?—Behold, in the day of your fast ye find pleasure, and exact all your labours!

4 Behold, ye fast for strife and debate, and to smite with the fist of wickedness! your fast this day is not a fast, to make your voice to be heard on high.

5 Is it such a fast that I have chosen? such a day that a man doth afflict his soul? is it to bow down his head as a bulrush, and to spread sackcloth and ashes under him? wilt thou call this a fast, and an acceptable day to the LORD?

6 Is not this the fast that I have chosen? to loose the bands of wickedness, to undo the heavy burdens, and to let the oppressed go free, and that ye break every yoke?

7 Is it not to deal thy bread to the hungry, and that thou bring the poor that are cast out to thy house? when thou seest the naked, that thou cover him; and that thou hide not thyself from thine own flesh?

8 Then shall thy light break forth as the morning, and thine health shall spring forth speedily, and thy righteousness shall go before thee, the glory of the LORD shall be thy rereward.

9 Then shalt thou call, and the LORD shall answer; thou shalt cry, and he shall say, Here I am! If thou take away from the midst of thee the yoke, the putting forth of the finger, and speaking vanity;

10 And if thou draw out thy soul to the hungry, and satisfy the afflicted soul; then shall thy light rise in obscurity, and thy darkness be as the noon day.

11 And the LORD shall guide thee continually, and satisfy thy soul in drought, and make fat thy bones; and thou shalt be like a watered garden, and like a spring of water, whose waters fail not.

12 And they that shall be of thee shall build the old waste places: thou shalt raise up the ruins of many generations;

and thou shalt be called, The repairer of the breach, The restorer of paths to dwell in.

13 If thou turn away thy foot from the sabbath, from doing thy pleasure on my holy day, and call the sabbath a delight, the holy of the Lord, honourable; and shalt honour him, not doing thine own ways, nor finding thine own pleasure, nor speaking thine own words;

14 Then shalt thou delight thyself in the Lord, and I will cause thee to ride upon the high places of the earth, and feed thee with the heritage of Jacob thy father; for the mouth of the Lord hath spoken it.

59

1 Behold, the Lord's hand is not shortened, that it cannot save, neither his ear heavy, that it cannot hear;

2 But your iniquities have separated between you and your God, and your sins have hid his face from you, that he will not hear.

3 For your hands are defiled with blood, and your fingers with iniquity; your lips have spoken lies, your tongue hath muttered perverseness.

4 None calleth for justice, nor any pleadeth for truth: they trust in vanity, and speak lies; they conceive mischief, and bring forth iniquity.

5 They hatch cockatrice' eggs, and weave the spider's web: he that eateth of their eggs dieth, and that which is crushed breaketh out into a viper.

6 Their webs shall not become garments, neither shall they cover themselves with their works: their works are works of iniquity, and the act of violence is in their hands.

7 Their feet run to evil, and they make haste to shed innocent blood: their thoughts are thoughts of iniquity; wasting and destruction are in their paths.

8 The way of peace they know not, and there is no right in their goings: they have made them crooked paths; whosoever goeth therein shall not know peace.

9 Therefore is judgment far from us, neither doth justice

overtake us: we wait for light, but behold obscurity; for brightness, but we walk in darkness.

10 We grope for the wall like the blind, and we grope as if we had no eyes: we stumble at noon day as in the night; we are in desolate places as dead men.

11 We roar all like bears, and moan sore like doves: we look for judgment, but there is none; for salvation, but it is far off from us.

12 For our transgressions are multiplied before thee, and our sins testify against us; for our transgressions are with us, and as for our iniquities, we know them;

13 In transgressing and lying against the LORD, and departing away from our God, speaking oppression and revolt, conceiving and uttering from the heart words of falsehood.

14 And justice is turned away backward, and righteousness standeth afar off; for truth is fallen in the street, and equity cannot enter.

15 Yea, truth faileth! and he that departeth from evil maketh himself a prey.

And the LORD saw it, and it displeased him that there was no judgment.

16 And he saw that there was no man, and wondered that there was no intercessor: therefore his arm brought salvation unto him, and his righteousness, it sustained him.

17 For he put on righteousness as a breastplate, and an helmet of salvation upon his head; and he put on the garments of vengeance for clothing, and was clad with zeal as a cloke.

18 According to their deeds, accordingly he will repay; fury to his adversaries, recompence to his enemies; to the far lands he will repay recompence.

19 So shall they fear the name of the LORD from the west, and his glory from the rising of the sun, when the enemy shall come in like a flood, whom the Spirit of the LORD shall drive.

20 And a redeemer shall come to Zion, and unto them that turn from transgression in Jacob, saith the LORD.

21 As for me, this is my covenant with them, saith the LORD:

My spirit that is upon thee, and my words which I have put in thy mouth, shall not depart out of thy mouth, nor out of the mouth of thy seed, nor out of the mouth of thy seed's seed, saith the LORD, from henceforth and for ever.

60

1 ARISE, shine, for thy light is come, and the glory of the LORD is risen upon thee!

2 For, behold, darkness doth cover the earth, and gross darkness the nations! but the LORD shall arise upon thee, and his glory shall be seen upon thee.

3 And the Gentiles shall come to thy light, and kings to the brightness of thy rising.

4 Lift up thine eyes round about, and see! all they gather themselves together, they come to thee! thy sons shall come from far, and thy daughters shall be carried upon the arm.

5 Then thou shalt see and rejoice, and thine heart shall flutter and be enlarged; because the abundance of the sea shall be converted unto thee, the treasures of the Gentiles shall come unto thee.

6 The multitude of camels shall cover thee, the dromedaries of Midian and Ephah; all they from Sheba shall come, they shall bring gold and incense, and they shall shew forth the praises of the LORD.

7 All the flocks of Kedar shall be gathered together unto thee, the rams of Nebaioth shall minister unto thee: they shall come up with acceptance on mine altar, and I will glorify the house of my glory.

8 —Who are these that fly as a cloud, and as the doves to their windows?

9 Surely the isles do wait upon me, and the ships of Tarshish in front, to bring thy sons from far, their silver and their gold with them, for the name of the LORD thy God, and for the Holy One of Israel, because he hath glorified thee!

10 And the sons of strangers shall build up thy walls, and

their kings shall minister unto thee; for in my wrath I smote thee, but in my favour have I had mercy on thee.

11 Therefore thy gates shall be open continually, they shall not be shut day nor night; that men may bring unto thee the treasures of the Gentiles, and that their kings may be brought.

12 For the nation and kingdom that will not serve thee shall perish; yea, those nations shall be utterly wasted.

13 The glory of Lebanon shall come unto thee, the cypress tree, the pine tree, and the box together, to beautify the place of my sanctuary; and I will make the place of my feet glorious.

14 The sons also of them that afflicted thee shall come bending unto thee; and all they that despised thee shall bow themselves down at the soles of thy feet, and they shall call thee, The city of the LORD, the Zion of the Holy One of Israel.

15 Whereas thou hast been forsaken and hated, so that no man went through thee, I will make thee an eternal excellency, a joy of many generations.

16 Thou shalt also suck the milk of the Gentiles, and shalt suck the breast of kings; and thou shalt know that I the LORD am thy Saviour, and thy Redeemer the mighty One of Jacob.

17 For brass I will bring gold, and for iron I will bring silver, and for wood brass, and for stones iron: I will also make thy officers peace, and thine exactors righteousness.

18 Violence shall no more be heard in thy land, wasting nor destruction within thy borders; but thou shalt call thy walls Salvation, and thy gates Praise.

19 The sun shall be no more thy light by day, neither for brightness shall the moon give light unto thee; but the LORD shall be unto thee an everlasting light, and thy God thy glory.

20 Thy sun shall no more go down, neither shall thy moon withdraw itself; for the LORD shall be thine everlasting light, and the days of thy mourning shall be ended.

21 Thy people also shall be all righteous; they shall inherit the land for ever: the branch of my planting, the work of my hands, that I may be glorified.

22 A little one shall become a thousand, and a small one a strong nation: I the LORD will hasten it in his time.

61

1 THE Spirit of the Lord GOD is upon me; because the LORD hath anointed me to preach good tidings unto the afflicted; he hath sent me to bind up the brokenhearted, to proclaim liberty to the captives, and the opening of the prison to them that are bound;

2 To proclaim the acceptable year of the LORD, and the day of vengeance of our God; to comfort all that mourn;

3 To appoint unto them that mourn in Zion, to give unto them beauty for ashes, the oil of joy for mourning, the garment of praise for the spirit of heaviness; that they might be called trees of righteousness, the planting of the LORD, that he might be glorified.

4 And they shall build the old wastes, they shall raise up the former desolations, and they shall repair the waste cities, the desolations of many generations.

5 And strangers shall stand and feed your flocks, and the sons of the alien shall be your plowmen and your vine-dressers.

6 But ye shall be named the Priests of the LORD: men shall call you the Ministers of our God: ye shall eat the riches of the Gentiles, and in their glory shall ye boast your-selves.

7 For your shame ye shall have double; and for confusion shall my people rejoice in their portion: therefore in their land they shall possess the double; everlasting joy shall be unto them.

8 For I the LORD love judgment, I hate robbery and wrong; and I will give them their reward in truth, and I will make an everlasting covenant with them.

9 And their seed shall be known among the Gentiles, and

their offspring among the people: all that see them shall acknowledge them, that they are the seed which the LORD hath blessed.

10 I WILL greatly rejoice in the LORD, my soul shall be joyful in my God; for he hath clothed me with the garments of salvation, he hath covered me with the robe of righteousness, as a bridegroom decketh himself with ornaments, and as a bride adorneth herself with her jewels.

11 For as the earth bringeth forth her bud, and as the garden causeth the things that are sown in it to spring forth; so the Lord GOD will cause righteousness and praise to spring forth before all the nations.

62

1 For Zion's sake will I not hold my peace, and for Jerusalem's sake I will not rest, until the righteousness thereof go forth as brightness, and the salvation thereof as a lamp that burneth.

2 And the Gentiles shall see thy righteousness, and all kings thy glory; and thou shalt be called by a new name, which the mouth of the LORD shall name.

3 Thou shalt also be a crown of glory in the hand of the LORD, and a royal diadem in the hand of thy God.

4 Thou shalt no more be termed Forsaken, neither shall thy land any more be termed Desolate; but thou shalt be called My delight is in her, and thy land Married; for the LORD delighteth in thee, and thy land shall be married.

5 For as a young man marrieth a virgin, so shall thy sons marry thee; and as the bridegroom rejoiceth over the bride, so shall thy God rejoice over thee.

6 —'I have set watchmen upon thy walls, O Jerusalem, which shall never hold their peace day nor night.'—Ye that are the LORD's remembrancers, keep not silence,

7 And give him no rest, till he establish, and till he make Jerusalem a praise in the earth!

8 The LORD hath sworn by his right hand, and by the arm

of his strength: Surely I will no more give thy corn to
be meat for thine enemies, and the sons of the stranger
shall not drink thy wine for the which thou hast laboured!

9 But they that have harvested it shall eat it, and praise the
LORD; and they that have gathered thy wine shall drink it,
in the courts of my holiness.

10 Go through, go through the gates; prepare ye the way of
the people! cast up, cast up the highway! gather out the
stones! lift up a standard for the nations!

11 Behold, the LORD hath proclaimed unto the end of the
world: Say ye to the daughter of Zion, Behold, thy salvation cometh! behold, his reward is with him, and his
recompence before him!

12 And they shall call them, The holy people, The redeemed
of the LORD; and thou shalt be called, Sought out, A city
not forsaken.

63

1 WHO is this that cometh from Edom, with dyed garments
from Bozrah? this that is glorious in his apparel, travelling
in the greatness of his strength?—'I that speak in righteousness, mighty to save.'—

2 Wherefore art thou red in thine apparel, and thy garments like him that treadeth in the winefat?

3 —'I have trodden the winepress alone, and of the nations
there was none with me; then trod I them in mine anger,
and trampled them in my fury, and their blood was
sprinkled upon my garments, and I have stained all my
raiment.

4 'For the day of vengeance is in mine heart, and the year
of my redeemed is come.

5 'And I looked, and there was none to help, and I wondered that there was none to uphold; therefore mine own
arm brought salvation unto me, and my fury, it upheld me.

6 'And I tread down the people in mine anger, and make
them drunk in my fury, and I bring down their strength
to the earth.'—

7   I WILL mention the lovingkindnesses of the LORD, and the praises of the LORD, according to all that the LORD hath bestowed on us; and the great goodness toward the house of Israel, which he hath bestowed on them according to his mercies, and according to the multitude of his lovingkindnesses.

8   For he said, Surely they are my people, children that will not lie! so he was their Saviour.

9   In all their affliction he was afflicted, and the angel of his presence saved them: in his love and in his pity he redeemed them; and he bare them and carried them all the days of old.

10   But they rebelled, and vexed his holy Spirit; therefore he was turned to be their enemy, and he fought against them.

11   Then remembered his people the days of old and Moses, saying: Where is he that brought them up out of the sea with the shepherd of his flock? where is he that put his holy Spirit within them?

12   That led them by the right hand of Moses with his glorious arm, dividing the water before them, to make himself an everlasting name?

13   That led them through the deep, as an horse in the desert, and they did not stumble?

14   As a beast goeth down into the valley, the Spirit of the LORD caused them to rest: so didst thou lead thy people, to make thyself a glorious name.

15   Look down from heaven, and behold from the habitation of thy holiness and of thy glory! where is thy zeal and thy strength, the sounding of thy bowels and of thy mercies toward me? are they restrained?

16   Doubtless thou art our father, though Abraham be ignorant of us, and Israel acknowledge us not! thou, O LORD, art our Father! our Redeemer is thy name from everlasting!

17   O LORD, why hast thou made us to err from thy ways, and hardened our heart from thy fear? Return for thy servants' sake, the tribes of thine inheritance!

18   The people of thy holiness have had possession but a little

while: our adversaries have trodden down thy sanctuary.
19 We are thine! thou never barest rule over them; they were not called by thy name.

64

1 Oh that thou wouldest rend the heavens, that thou wouldest come down! that the mountains might flow down at thy presence,
2 As the fire burneth the stubble, the fire causeth the water to boil! to make thy name known to thine adversaries, that the nations may tremble at thy presence!
3 When thou didst terrible things which we looked not for, thou camest down, the mountains flowed down at thy presence.
4 For since the beginning of the world men have not heard, nor perceived by the ear, neither hath the eye seen, O God, beside thee, who hath prepared such things for him that waiteth for him.
5 Thou meetest him that rejoiceth and worketh righteousness, those that remember thee in thy ways.
   Behold, thou art wroth (for we have sinned) with thy people continually!—and shall we be saved?
6 We are all even as the unclean, and all our righteousnesses are as filthy rags; and we all are faded as a leaf, and our iniquities, like the wind, do take us away.
7 And there is none that calleth upon thy name, that stirreth up himself to take hold of thee; for thou hast hid thy face from us, and hast consumed us, because of our iniquities.
8 But now, O Lord, thou art our father! we are the clay, and thou our potter, and we all are the work of thy hand.
9 Be not wroth very sore, O Lord, neither remember iniquity for ever! behold, see, we beseech thee, we are all thy people!
10 Thy holy cities are a wilderness, Zion is a wilderness, Jerusalem a desolation.
11 Our holy and our beautiful house, where our fathers

praised thee, is burned up with fire; and all our pleasant things are laid waste.

12 Wilt thou refrain thyself for these things, O LORD? wilt thou hold thy peace, and afflict us very sore?

65

1 I GAVE ear to them that asked not for me, I am found of them that sought me not. I said, Behold me, behold me, unto a nation that called not upon my name.

2 I have spread out my hands all the day unto a rebellious people, which walketh in a way not good, after their own thoughts;

3 A people that provoketh me to anger continually to my face; that sacrificeth in the gardens, and burneth incense upon the tiles;

4 Which remain among the graves, and lodge in the monuments; which eat swine's flesh, and broth of abominable things is in their vessels;

5 Which say: Stand by thyself, come not near to me, for I am holier than thou! These are a smoke in my nose, a fire that burneth all the day.

6 Behold, it is written before me; I will not keep silence, but will recompense, even recompense into their bosom,

7 Your iniquities, and the iniquities of your fathers together, saith the LORD, which have burned incense upon the mountains, and blasphemed me upon the hills; therefore will I measure the reward of their former work into their bosom.

8 Thus saith the LORD: As the new wine is found in the grape-cluster, and one saith, Destroy it not, for a blessing is in it! so will I do for my servants' sakes, that I may not destroy them all.

9 And I will bring forth a seed out of Jacob, and out of Judah an inheritor of my mountains; and mine elect shall inherit it, and my servants shall dwell there.

10 And Sharon shall be a fold of flocks, and the valley of Achor a place for the herds to lie down in, for my people that have sought me.

11 But ye are they that forsake the LORD, that forget my holy mountain, that prepare a table for Fortune, and that furnish the drink-offering unto that which destineth.

12 Therefore will I destine you to the sword, and ye shall all bow down to the slaughter; because when I called, ye did not answer, when I spake, ye did not hear, but did evil before mine eyes, and did choose that wherein I delighted not.

13 Therefore thus saith the Lord GOD: Behold, my servants shall eat, but ye shall be hungry; behold, my servants shall drink, but ye shall be thirsty; behold, my servants shall rejoice, but ye shall be ashamed;

14 Behold, my servants shall sing for joy of heart, but ye shall cry for sorrow of heart, and shall howl for vexation of spirit.

15 And ye shall leave your name for a curse unto my chosen; for the Lord GOD shall slay you, and call his servants by another name;

16 That he who blesseth himself in the earth shall bless himself in the God of truth, and he that sweareth in the earth shall swear by the God of truth; because the former troubles are forgotten, and because they are hid from mine eyes.

17 For, behold, I create new heavens and a new earth; and the former shall not be remembered, nor come into mind.

18 But be ye glad and rejoice for ever in that which I create; for, behold, I create Jerusalem a rejoicing, and her people a joy!

19 And I will rejoice in Jerusalem, and joy in my people; and the voice of weeping shall be no more heard in her, nor the voice of crying.

20 There shall be no more thence an infant of days, nor an old man that hath not filled his days; for the child shall die an hundred years old, and the sinner being an hundred years old shall be accursed.

21 And they shall build houses, and inhabit them; and they shall plant vineyards, and eat the fruit of them.

22 They shall not build, and another inhabit; they shall not plant, and another eat; for as the days of a tree are the

days of my people, and mine elect shall long enjoy the work of their hands.

23 They shall not labour in vain, nor bring forth for trouble; for they are the seed of the blessed of the LORD, and their offspring with them.

24 And it shall come to pass, that before they call, I will answer; and while they are yet speaking, I will hear.

25 The wolf and the lamb shall feed together, and the lion shall eat straw like the bullock, and dust shall be the serpent's meat. They shall not hurt nor destroy in all my holy mountain, saith the LORD.

66

1 THUS saith the LORD: The heaven is my throne, and the earth is my footstool; where is the house that ye build unto me, and where is the place of my rest?

2 For all those things hath mine hand made, and all those things were, saith the LORD; but to this man will I look, even to him that is meek and of a contrite spirit, and trembleth at my word.

3 He that killeth an ox is the same that slayeth a man; he that sacrificeth a lamb, the same that cutteth a dog's throat; he that offereth an oblation, offereth swine's blood; he that burneth incense, is he that blesseth an idol. Yea, they have chosen their own ways, and their soul delighteth in their abominations!

4 I also will choose to mock them, and will bring their fears upon them; because when I called, none did answer, when I spake, they did not hear; but they did evil before mine eyes, and chose that in which I delighted not.

5 Hear the word of the LORD, ye that tremble at his word: Your brethren that hated you, that cast you out for my name's sake, said, Let the LORD be glorified, and let your joy appear! but they shall be ashamed.

6 —A voice of noise from the city, a voice from the temple, a voice of the LORD that rendereth recompence to his enemies!

7 Before she travailed, she brought forth: before her pain came, she was delivered of a man child.

8 Who hath heard such a thing? who hath seen such things? Shall a land be brought forth in one day, or shall a nation be born at once? for as soon as Zion travailed, she brought forth her children.

9 Shall I bring to the birth, and not cause to bring forth? saith the LORD; shall I cause to bring forth, and shut the womb? saith thy God.

10 Rejoice ye with Jerusalem, and be glad with her, all ye that love her! rejoice for joy with her, all ye that mourn for her!

11 That ye may suck, and be satisfied with the breasts of her consolations; that ye may milk out, and be delighted with the abundance of her glory.

12 For thus saith the LORD: Behold, I will extend peace to her like a river, and the glory of the Gentiles like a flowing stream: then shall ye suck, ye shall be borne upon her sides, and be dandled upon her knees.

13 As one whom his mother comforteth, so will I comfort you, and ye shall be comforted in Jerusalem.

14 And when ye see this, your heart shall rejoice, and your bones shall flourish like an herb; and the hand of the LORD shall be known toward his servants, and his indignation toward his enemies.

15 For, behold, the LORD will come with fire, and with his chariots like a whirlwind, to render his anger with fury, and his rebuke with flames of fire.

16 For by fire and by his sword will the LORD plead with all flesh, and the slain of the LORD shall be many.

17 They that sanctify themselves, and purify themselves in the gardens behind one chief in the midst, eating swine's flesh, and the abomination, and the mouse, shall be consumed together, saith the LORD.

18 For I know their works and their thoughts.

IT shall come, that I will gather all nations and tongues; and they shall come, and see my glory.

19 And I will set a sign among them, and I will send those
    that escape of them unto the nations, to Tarshish, Phul
    and Lud that draw the bow, to Tubal and Javan, to the
    isles afar off, that have not heard my fame, neither have
    seen my glory; and they shall declare my glory among
    the Gentiles.

20 And they shall bring all your brethren for an offering
    unto the Lord out of all nations upon horses, and in
    chariots, and in litters, and upon mules, and upon drome-
    daries, to my holy mountain Jerusalem, saith the Lord, as
    the children of Israel bring an offering in a clean vessel
    into the house of the Lord.

21 And of them also will I take for priests and for Levites,
    saith the Lord.

22 For as the new heavens and the new earth, which I will
    make, shall remain before me, saith the Lord, so shall your
    seed and your name remain.

23 And it shall come to pass, that from one new moon to
    another, and from one sabbath to another, shall all flesh
    come to worship before me, saith the Lord.

24 And they shall go forth, and look upon the carcases of
    the men that have transgressed against me; for their worm
    shall not die, neither shall their fire be quenched, and
    they shall be an abhorring unto all flesh.

APPENDIX

THE following shorter prophecies, relating in general to the
same times and circumstances as the preceding [chapts. 40–66],
but which became incorporated with earlier prophecies, are
here disengaged, and are given in the connexion and order to
which they seem naturally to belong.

THE FIRST VISION

(The prophet is in Babylon, living amongst its people, and
partaking of its secure and magnificent life. Suddenly a vision

reveals to him the conquest of Babylon by the Median army under Cyrus. This vision is to be conceived as a little anterior to the Great Prophecy.)

Isaiah 21, 1–10

21

1 THE burden of the desert of the sea.

As whirlwinds in the south pass through; so it cometh from the desert, from a terrible land.

2 A grievous vision is declared unto me! the robber robbeth, and the spoiler spoileth. Go up, O Elam! besiege, O Media: all the sighing thereof have I made to cease.

3 Therefore are my loins filled with pain; pangs have taken hold upon me, as the pangs of a woman that travaileth: I was bowed down at the hearing of it; I was dismayed at the seeing of it.

4 My heart panted, fearfulness affrighted me: the night of my pleasure hath he turned into fear unto me.

5 Prepare the table, watch the watch, eat, drink.—*Rise, ye princes, anoint the shield!*

6 FOR thus hath the LORD said unto me: Go, set a watchman, let him declare what he seeth;

7 And if he see a train of couples of horsemen, a train of asses, a train of camels, let him hearken diligently with much heed.

8 And he cried as a lion: My lord, I stand continually upon the watch-tower in the daytime, and I am set in my ward whole nights.

9 AND, behold, there cometh a train of men, with couples of horsemen!
And he answered and said: Babylon is fallen, is fallen! and all the graven images of her gods he hath broken unto the ground.

10 O my threshing-ground and thou son of my floor! that
    which I have heard of the Lord of hosts, the God of
    Israel, have I declared unto you.

THE KING OF BABYLON

(This prophecy may not improperly follow the preceding.
It belongs to much the same date and circumstances; but the
Median invasion has come yet nearer, and the overthrow of
Babylon, the death and dishonour of its king, stand before the
prophet's mind certain and clear, and fill him with exultation.)

Isaiah 13, 2-22; 14, 1-23

13

2 Lift ye up a banner upon the high mountain, exalt the
   voice unto them, shake the hand, that they may go in to
   the gates of the nobles!
3 I have commanded my consecrated ones, I have also called
   my mighty ones for mine anger, even my proudly rejoicing ones.
4 The noise of a multitude in the mountains, like as of a
   great people! a tumultuous noise of the kingdoms of
   nations gathered together! the Lord of hosts mustereth
   the host of the battle.
5 They come from a far country, from the end of heaven,
   even the Lord and the weapons of his indignation, to
   destroy the whole land!
6 Howl ye! for the day of the Lord is at hand: it shall
   come as a destruction from the Almighty.
7 Therefore shall all hands be faint, and every man's heart
   shall melt,
8 And they shall be afraid: pangs and sorrows shall take
   hold of them; they shall be in pain as a woman that travaileth: they shall be amazed one at another; their faces
   shall be as flame-faces.
9 Behold, the day of the Lord cometh, cruel both with

wrath and fierce anger, to lay the land desolate! and he shall destroy the sinners thereof out of it.

10 For the stars of heaven and the constellations thereof shall not give their light: the sun shall be darkened in his going forth, and the moon shall not cause her light to shine.

11 And I will punish the world for their evil, and the wicked for their iniquity; and I will cause the arrogancy of the proud to cease, and will lay low the haughtiness of the terrible.

12 I will make a man more precious than fine gold; even a man than the golden wedge of Ophir.

13 Therefore I will shake the heavens, and the earth shall remove out of her place, in the wrath of the LORD of hosts, and in the day of his fierce anger.

14 And it shall be as the chased roe, and as sheep that no man gathereth: they shall every man turn to his own people, and flee every one into his own land.

15 Every one that is found shall be thrust through; and every one that is overtaken shall fall by the sword.

16 Their children also shall be dashed to pieces before their eyes; their houses shall be spoiled, and their wives ravished.

17 Behold, I will stir up the Medes against them, which shall not regard silver; and as for gold, they shall not delight in it.

18 Their bows also shall dash the young men to pieces; and they shall have no pity on the fruit of the womb; their eye shall not spare children.

19 And Babylon, the glory of kingdoms, the beauty of the Chaldees' excellency, shall be as when God overthrew Sodom and Gomorrah.

20 It shall never be inhabited, neither shall it be dwelt in from generation to generation: neither shall the Arabian pitch tent there; neither shall the shepherds make their fold there.

21 But wild beasts of the desert shall lie there; and their houses shall be full of doleful creatures; and ostriches shall dwell there, and satyrs shall dance there.

22 And the wild beasts of the waste shall cry in their lofty

houses, and jackals in their pleasant palaces: and her time is near to come, and her days shall not be prolonged.

14

1 For the LORD will have mercy on Jacob, and will yet choose Israel, and set them in their own land: and the strangers shall be joined with them, and they shall cleave to the house of Jacob.

2 And the heathen shall take them, and bring them to their place; and the house of Israel shall possess them in the land of the LORD for servants and handmaids: and they shall take them captives, whose captives they were; and they shall rule over their oppressors.

3 AND it shall come to pass in the day that the LORD shall give thee rest from thy sorrow, and from thy fear, and from the hard bondage wherein thou wast made to serve,

4 That thou shalt take up this proverb against the king of Babylon, and say:—
How hath the oppressor ceased! the stress of the exactor ceased!

5 The LORD hath broken the staff of the wicked, and the sceptre of the rulers.

6 He who smote the people in wrath with a continual stroke, he that ruled the nations in anger, is persecuted, and none hindereth.

7 The whole earth is at rest, and is quiet: they break forth into singing.

8 Yea, the fir trees rejoice at thee, and the cedars of Lebanon, saying: Since thou art laid down, no feller is come up against us!

9 Hell from beneath is moved for thee to meet thee at thy coming: it stirreth up the dead for thee, even all the chief ones of the earth; it hath raised up from their thrones all the kings of the nations.

10 All these shall speak and say unto thee: 'Art thou also become weak as we? art thou become like unto us?'

11 Thy pomp is brought down to the grave, and the noise of thy viols: the worm is spread under thee, and the worms cover thee.

12 How art thou fallen from heaven, O Lucifer, son of the morning! how art thou cut down to the ground, which didst weaken the nations!

13 For thou saidst in thine heart: I will ascend into heaven, I will exalt my throne above the stars of God; I will sit also upon the mount of assembly, in the ends of the north:

14 I will ascend above the heights of the clouds; I will be like the most High.

15 Yet thou shalt be brought down to hell, to the sides of the pit!

16 They that see thee shall narrowly look upon thee, and consider thee, saying: Is this the man that made the earth to tremble, that did shake kingdoms?

17 That made the world as a wilderness, and destroyed the cities thereof? that loosed not his prisoners to their homes?

18 All the kings of the nations, even all of them, lie in glory, every one in his own house.

19 But thou art cast out of thy grave like a rejected branch! thou art clothed around with them that are slain, that are thrust through with a sword, that go down to the stones of the pit! as a carcase trodden under feet!

20 Thou shalt not be joined with them in burial, because thou hast destroyed thy land, and slain thy people: the seed of evildoers shall no more be named.

21 Prepare slaughter for his children for the iniquity of their fathers! that they do not rise, nor possess the land, nor fill the face of the world with foes.

22 For I will rise up against them, saith the LORD of hosts, and cut off from Babylon the name, and remnant, and son, and grandson, saith the LORD.

23 I will also make it a possession for the hedgehog, and pools of water; and I will sweep it with the besom of destruction, saith the LORD of hosts.

EDOM AND ISRAEL

(See the introductory note to chapter 63 of the Great Prophecy
[pp. 431–32]. In the crash and revolution of the epoch of Babylon's fall, Edom, that old and bitter enemy of Israel, shall be
visited with God's vengeance and utterly wasted. Edom's
savage exultation at Nebuchadnezzar's conquest of Jerusalem
is familiar to us all from the 137th Psalm: "Remember the
children of Edom, O Lord, in the day of Jerusalem, how they
said: Down with it, down with it, even to the ground!" Compare Jeremiah xlix. 7–22; and Ezekiel xxv. 12–14, and xxxv; and
Obadiah. Israel, on the other hand, shall return in safety and
joy to Zion. This prophecy supposes the same situation of
things as the Great Prophecy.)

Isaiah 34, 35

34

1 COME near, ye nations, to hear! and hearken, ye people!
   let the earth hear, and all that is therein; the world, and
   all things that come forth of it.

2 For the indignation of the LORD is upon all nations, and
   his fury upon all their armies: he hath utterly destroyed
   them, he hath delivered them to the slaughter.

3 Their slain also shall be cast out, and their stink shall
   come up out of their carcases, and the mountains shall be
   melted with their blood.

4 And all the host of heaven shall be dissolved, and the
   heavens shall be rolled together as a scroll; and all their host
   shall fall down, as the leaf falleth off from the vine, and as
   a falling fig from the fig tree.

5 For my sword hath been bathed in heaven! behold, it
   shall come down upon Edom, and upon the people of
   my curse, to judgment!

6 The sword of the LORD is filled with blood, it is made fat
   with fatness, and with the blood of lambs and goats, with
   the fat of the kidneys of rams: for the LORD hath a sacri-

fice in Bozrah, and a great slaughter in the land of Edom.

7 And the buffaloes shall fall down with them, and the bullocks with the bulls; and their land shall be soaked with blood, and their dust made fat with fatness.

8 For it is the day of the LORD's vengeance, and the year of recompences for the controversy of Zion.

9 And the streams thereof shall be turned into pitch, and the dust thereof into brimstone, and the land thereof shall become burning pitch.

10 It shall not be quenched night nor day; the smoke thereof shall go up for ever: from generation to generation it shall lie waste; none shall pass through it for ever and ever.

11 But the pelican and the hedgehog shall possess it; the ostrich also and the raven shall dwell in it: and he shall stretch out upon it the line of confusion, and the weights of emptiness.

12 The nobles thereof shall no more call a king to the kingdom, and all her princes shall be nothing.

13 And thorns shall come up in her palaces, nettles and brambles in the fortresses thereof: and it shall be an habitation of jackals, and a court for the ostrich.

14 The wild cat and the wolf shall meet there, and the satyr shall cry to his fellow: the night-demon also shall rest there, and find for herself a place of rest.

15 There shall the arrow-snake make her nest, and lay, and hatch, and gather under her shadow: there shall the vultures also be gathered, every one with her mate.

16 Seek ye out of the book of the LORD, and read! no one of these shall fail, none shall want her mate: for his mouth it hath commanded, and his spirit it hath gathered them.

17 And he hath cast the lot for them there, and his hand hath divided it unto them by line: they shall possess it for ever, from generation to generation shall they dwell therein.

35

1 THE wilderness and the solitary place shall be glad; and the desert shall rejoice, and blossom as the rose.

2 It shall blossom abundantly, and rejoice even with joy and singing: the glory of Lebanon shall be given unto it, the excellency of Carmel and Sharon; they shall see the glory of the LORD, and the excellency of our God.

3 Strengthen ye the weak hands, and confirm the feeble knees!

4 Say to them that are of a fearful heart: Be strong, fear not! behold, your God cometh with vengeance, even God with a recompence; he will come and save you.

5 Then the eyes of the blind shall be opened, and the ears of the deaf shall be unstopped.

6 Then shall the lame man leap as an hart, and the tongue of the dumb sing: for in the wilderness shall waters break out, and streams in the desert.

7 And the parched ground shall become a pool, and the thirsty land springs of water: in the habitation of jackals, where each lay, shall be grass with reeds and rushes.

8 And an highway shall be there, and a way; and it shall be called, The way of holiness; the unclean shall not pass over it, but it shall be for those: the wayfarer, though a fool, shall not err therein.

9 No lion shall be there, nor any ravenous beast shall go up thereon, it shall not be found there; but the redeemed shall walk there:

10 And the ransomed of the LORD shall return, and come to Zion with songs and everlasting joy upon their heads: they shall obtain joy and gladness, and sorrow and sighing shall flee away.

EARLY DAYS OF RETURN

(Babylon had now fallen and Israel was restored. But the wars, revolutions, and world-ruin, amidst which the downfall of Babylon took place, still continued. Cyrus perished miserably in an obscure war with a barbarous foe (B.C. 529); then came the storm of Egypt's invasion by his son, the furious Cambyses (B.C. 525). The air was full of rumours, and the earth of agitations; on the other hand, Jerusalem found itself, by God's wonderful leading and favour, restored. But the infant community there, though replaced in its home, was short of numbers, feeble, and fearful. The prophet animates and uplifts it by the assurance of its divine destinies.)

Isaiah 24–27

24

1 BEHOLD, the LORD maketh the earth empty, and maketh it waste, and turneth it upside down, and scattereth abroad the inhabitants thereof.

2 And it shall be, as with the people, so with the priest; as with the servant, so with his master; as with the maid, so with her mistress; as with the buyer, so with the seller; as with the lender, so with the borrower; as with the taker of usury, so with the giver of usury to him.

3 The land shall be utterly emptied, and utterly spoiled: for the LORD hath spoken this word.

4 The earth mourneth and fadeth away, the world languisheth and fadeth away, the haughty people of the earth do languish.

5 The earth also is defiled under the inhabitants thereof; because they have transgressed the laws, changed the ordinance, broken the everlasting covenant.

6 Therefore hath the curse devoured the earth, and they that dwell therein are desolate: therefore the inhabitants of the earth are burned, and few men left.

7 The new wine mourneth, the vine languisheth, all the merryhearted do sigh.

8 The mirth of tabrets ceaseth, the noise of them that rejoice endeth, the joy of the harp ceaseth.

9 They shall not drink wine with a song; strong drink shall be bitter to them that drink it.

10 The city is solitary and broken down: every house is shut up, that no man may come in.

11 There is a crying for wine in the streets; all joy is darkened, the mirth of the land is gone.

12 In the city is left desolation, and the gate is smitten with destruction.

13 Thus shall it be in the midst of the earth among the nations, as the shaking of an olive tree, and as the gleaning of grapes when the vintage is done.

14 They shall lift up their voice, they shall sing for the majesty of the Lord, they shall cry aloud from the sea.

15 Wherefore glorify ye the Lord in the east, even the name of the Lord God of Israel in the coasts of the sea!

16 From the uttermost part of the earth have we heard songs: Glory to the righteous! But I said, My leanness, my leanness, woe unto me! the robber robbeth; yea, the robber robbeth very sore.

17 Fear, and the pit, and the snare, are upon thee, O inhabitant of the earth!

18 And it shall come to pass, that he who fleeth from the noise of the fear shall fall into the pit; and he that cometh up out of the midst of the pit shall be taken in the snare: for the windows from on high are open, and the foundations of the earth do shake.

19 The earth is utterly broken down, the earth is clean dissolved, the earth is moved exceedingly.

20 The earth doth reel to and fro like a drunkard, and doth sway like a hammock; the transgression thereof is heavy upon it; and it shall fall, and not rise again.

21 And it shall come to pass in that day, that the Lord shall punish the host of heaven in the height, and the kings of the earth upon the earth.

22 And they shall be gathered together, as prisoners are gathered in the pit, and shall be shut up in the prison, and after many days shall they be visited.

23 Then the moon shall be confounded, and the sun ashamed, when the Lord of hosts shall reign in mount Zion, and in Jerusalem, and before his ancients gloriously.

25

1   O LORD, thou art my God! I will exalt thee, I will praise thy name; for thou hast done wonderful things; thy counsels of old are faithfulness and truth.

2   For thou hast made of a city an heap; of a defenced city a ruin: a palace of strangers to be no city; it shall never be built.

3   Therefore shall the strong people glorify thee, the city of the terrible nations shall fear thee.

4   For thou hast been a strength to the poor, a strength to the needy in his distress, a refuge from the storm, a shadow from the heat, when the blast of the terrible ones was as a storm against the wall.

5   Thou dost bring down the noise of strangers, as the heat in a dry place; as the heat by the shadow of a cloud, so the song of the terrible ones is brought low.

6   And in this mountain shall the LORD of hosts make unto all people a feast of fat things, a feast of wines on the lees, of fat things full of marrow, of wines on the lees well refined.

7   And he will destroy in this mountain the face of the covering cast over all people, and the vail that is spread over all nations.

8   He will swallow up death in victory; and the Lord GOD will wipe away tears from off all faces; and the rebuke of his people shall he take away from off all the earth: for the LORD hath spoken it.

9   And it shall be said in that day, Lo, this is our God! we have waited for him, and he will save us: this is the LORD! we have waited for him, we will be glad and rejoice in his salvation.

10   For in this mountain shall the hand of the LORD rest, and Moab shall be trodden down in his place, even as straw is trodden down in the dung-pool.

11   And they shall spread forth their hands in the midst thereof, as one that swimmeth spreadeth forth his hands

to swim: and he shall bring down their pride together with the wiles of their hands.

12   The fortress of the high fort of thy walls shall he bring down, lay low, and bring to the ground, even to the dust.

26

1   IN that day shall this song be sung in the land of Judah:— We have a strong city; salvation will God appoint for walls and bulwarks.

2   Open ye the gates, that the righteous nation which keepeth the truth may enter in!

3   Thou wilt keep him in perfect peace, whose mind is stayed on thee; because he trusteth in thee.

4   Trust ye in the LORD for ever! for in the LORD JEHOVAH is everlasting strength:

5   For he bringeth down them that dwell on high; the lofty city, he layeth it low; he layeth it low, even to the ground; he bringeth it even to the dust.

6   The foot shall tread it down, even the feet of the poor, and the steps of the needy.

7   The way of the just is made smooth: thou, most upright, dost make smooth the path of the just!

8   Yea, in the way of thy judgments, O LORD, have we waited for thee! the desire of our soul was to thy name, and to the remembrance of thee.

9   With my soul have I desired thee in the night; yea, with my spirit within me do I seek thee early! for when thy judgments are in the earth, the inhabitants of the world will learn righteousness.

10   Let favour be shewed to the wicked, so will he not learn righteousness: in the land of uprightness will he deal unjustly, and will not behold the majesty of the LORD.

11   LORD, thy hand is very high, but they see it not; they will not see! they shall see, and be ashamed at thy jealousy for the people; yea, the fire of thine enemies shall devour them!

12 Lord, thou wilt ordain peace for us: for thou also hast wrought all our works for us.

13 O Lord our God, other lords beside thee have had dominion over us; but of thee only will we make mention, of thy name!

14 They are dead, they shall not live! they are deceased, they shall not rise! because thou hast visited and destroyed them, and made all their memory to perish.

15 Thou dost increase the nation, O Lord, thou dost increase the nation! thou art glorified: thou enlargest all the borders of the land.

16 Lord, in trouble they sought thee; they poured out a prayer when thy chastening was upon them.

17 Like as a woman with child, that draweth near the time of her delivery, is in pain, and crieth out in her pangs; so have we been in thy sight, O Lord!

18 We have been with child, we have been in pain, we have as it were brought forth wind; we have not wrought any deliverance in the earth, neither are inhabitants of the land born unto it.

19 —Thy dead men shall live! my dead body, it shall arise! Awake and sing, ye that dwell in dust; for a dew of life is thy dew, and the earth shall bring forth the dead!

20 Come, my people, enter thou into thy chambers, and shut thy doors about thee: hide thyself as it were for a little moment, until the indignation be overpast.

21 For, behold, the Lord cometh out of his place to punish the inhabitants of the earth for their iniquity: the earth also shall disclose her blood, and shall no more cover her slain.

27

1 In that day the Lord with his sore and great and strong sword shall punish leviathan the shooting serpent, even

leviathan that coiling serpent; and he shall slay the dragon that is in the sea.

2 In that day sing ye thus of the fair vineyard:—

3 'I the LORD do keep it; I water it every moment: lest any hurt it, I keep it night and day.

4 'Fury is not in me: let them set the briers and thorns against me! I will go through them in battle, I will burn them together.

5 'Or else let them take hold of my strength! let them make peace with me; let them make peace with me!'

6 He shall cause them that come of Jacob to take root: Israel shall blossom and bud, and fill the face of the world with fruit.

7 Hath he smitten him, as he smote those that smote him? or is he slain according to the slaughter of them that slew him?

8 In measure, chasing her forth, thou punishedst her; driving her out with a rough wind in the day of the east wind.

9 By this therefore shall the iniquity of Jacob be purged, and this is all the fruit of putting off his sin: when he maketh all the stones of the altar as chalkstones that are beaten in sunder, that the groves and images shall stand up no more.

10 For the defenced city shall be desolate, and the habitation forsaken, and left like a wilderness: there shall the calf feed, and there shall he lie down, and consume the green boughs thereof.

11 When the branches thereof are withered, they shall be broken off: the women shall come, and set them on fire: for it is a people of no understanding: therefore he that made them will not have mercy on them, and he that formed them will shew them no favour.

12 And it shall come to pass in that day, that the LORD shall sift corn from the channel of the river unto the stream of Egypt, and ye shall be gathered one by one, O ye children of Israel!

13 And it shall come to pass in that day, that the great trumpet shall be blown, and they shall come which were for-

lorn in the land of Assyria, and the outcasts in the land
of Egypt, and shall worship the LORD in the holy mount at
Jerusalem.

NOTES

PRELUDE

(CHAPTER 1)

WE are to conceive of this prophecy as an introductory piece,
or overture, opening the way and striking the tone for all that   5
follows, and establishing the point of view from which Isaiah,
about the year 700 B.C., wished the series of his prophecies to
be read and the history of the preceding half-century to be
regarded. The chosen people had known during this time both
prosperity and adversity, but by neither had it been instructed.   10
The historical sketch given in the Introduction (pp. 108–14)
should be read with attention.

2. *The Lord.*—In the text, as in our Bibles generally, this
word LORD, when it stands, as here, for Jehovah, or the Eternal,
is printed in capitals; when it stands (as in verse 24 of this   15
chapter, for instance) simply for the Hebrew word meaning
lord, then it has only its first letter a capital one. In the notes
it will not be necessary to observe this distinction.

3. *Doth not know.*—To whom he belongs.

7. *Your country is desolate.*—Both in the war with Syria   20
and Israel this had been seen, and it was now seen again in the
invasion of Sennacherib.

8. *Lodge in a garden of cucumbers.*—Dr. Kitto says:—"Cucumbers, melons, and similar products are seldom (in the Holy
Land) protected by enclosures, but cultivated in large open   25
fields, quite exposed to the depredations of men or beasts. To
prevent this, a slight artificial mount is raised, if required, and
on this is constructed a frail hut or booth, such as is used in the
vineyard also, just sufficient for one person, who, in this con-
fined solitude, remains constantly watching the ripening crop.   30
Very often has our travelling party paused on arriving at such

melon-grounds to bargain with the watchman for a supply of his refreshing fruit; and on such occasions—often seeing no object around to a great distance in the plain but this one man and his solitary shed—we have been most forcibly reminded of the peculiar appropriateness of the image of desolation suggested by the prophet."

9. *A very small remnant.*—"We came within a very little of perishing entirely," is all that the prophet here means. *Remnant* is not used in the sense in which it is used in "the remnant shall return" (x, 21).

12. *To tread my courts.*—To crowd trampling into God's courts, to attend his services, is not what he requires.

27. *Zion shall be redeemed.*—A sifting judgment, and the establishment of righteousness, shall redeem Zion.

29. *The oaks.*—The evergreen oaks of the idolatrous groves and gardens.

CALAMITIES FOR JUDAH

(Chapters 2–5)

This prophecy, following the Prelude, and forming the real beginning to the Book of Isaiah, belongs to the time of Jotham and of Isaiah's early career, when Judah was, to outward view, still prosperous. We may place its date about the year 740 B.C.

2. *And it shall come to pass, etc.*—The prophecy opens with three verses (2–4) which we find nearly in the same words in Micah also (iv, 1–3). In each case the words are probably a quotation from an older prophet. They fix the ideal for Zion and its people: after exhibiting the ideal, Isaiah proceeds to show how far his countrymen depart from it.

5. *O House of Jacob.*—A call from the prophet to his own people.

6. *Thou hast.*—The Eternal is addressed.

ib. The east.—Uzziah had recovered for Judah the port at the head of the Gulf of Akaba on the Red Sea, Elath (II Kings, xiv, 22). In his reign and that of his son Jotham trade from this port on the south-east brought into Judah wealth, but also for-

eign manners and idolatries. In the reign of Ahaz and afterwards there was a like importation from the north-east, from
Syria and Assyria.

ib. Soothsayers.—The practice of magic was adopted from
the Philistines, whom Uzziah conquered; Judah grew familiar-   5
ised with foreigners, and fond of them and their usages, and
came to rely on the same sources of strength as they.

9. *And the mean man, etc.*—Men of all conditions, small and
great, betook themselves to idolatry, so as to provoke the coming of a day of the Eternal, a day of judgment.   10

13. *Upon all the cedars.*—The day of judgment is presented
as bringing to nothing all the greatness of nature, and all the
greatness and art of man.

16. *Ships of Tarshish.*—From the port of Elath Jewish fleets,
in Uzziah's time, traded with Tartessus at the mouth of the   15
Guadalquivir.

ib. Pleasant pictures.—All sorts of objects of art pleasant to
the eye are included.

3

3. *The master of the spell.*—More literally *the master of
muttering*, one skilled in magical arts and incantations.   20

4. *Children to be their princes.*—Jotham's son Ahaz and the
insolent young nobles surrounding him are here indicated.

6. *When a man shall take, etc.*—In the miserable anarchy
prevailing, no man is willing to assume headship and responsibility.   25

8. *Jerusalem is ruined.*—Compare Micah, iii, 12—"Zion shall
be plowed as a field, and Jerusalem shall become heaps." Jeremiah tells us (xxvi, 18,19) that after this prophecy of Micah the
king and people of Judah "did fear the Lord, and besought the
Lord, and the Lord repented him of the evil which he had pro-   30
nounced against them." But in the later years of Hezekiah,
when his ministers and people were seeking the Egyptian alliance, and the amendment of Judah had proved transitory, the
threatening pronouncement reappears. See Isaiah, xxxii, 14.

378 Philistinism in England and America

12. *Women rule over them.*—The youthful, sensual, and foolish Ahaz was under the influence of the harem.

24. *Branding.*—Inflicted on the captive by the conqueror.

4

1. *And in that day seven women, etc.*—Zion shall be so desolate of men that its proud daughters, instead of being wooed, shall compete in wooing, for the sake of the mere protection of his name, any surviving man that they can find.

2. *The Branch.*—See xi, 1, and xxxii, 1. After the purging judgment the saved remnant of Israel shall live under a righteous king, "the fruit of the land," its choice and blessed product.

5. *A cloud and smoke, etc.*—A reminiscence of the protection formerly given to Israel by the pillar of cloud and pillar of fire in the wilderness, after the escape from Egypt.

5

1. *Now will I sing to my wellbeloved.*—"I" is the prophet, "my wellbeloved" is the Eternal, to whom the prophet sings a parabolic song, supposed to proceed from the Eternal himself, touching his vineyard,—his chosen land and people.

10. *Bath, homer, ephah.*—Hebrew measures. A bath is from seven to eight gallons. Ten acres, therefore, of vineyard were to yield but seven and a half gallons of wine. An ephah is the tenth part of a homer; the produce, therefore, was to be but a tenth of the grain sown.

17. *The lambs feed after their manner.*—Where once was Jerusalem, the flocks of strangers shall graze at will, of strangers who succeed to the possessions of the once-powerful native lords.

18. *Draw iniquity, etc.*—Sinners contemptuous and incredulous of divine judgment are represented as in their folly dragging eagerly along their iniquity and their sin, to their ruin.

26. *The nations from far.*—Assyria and others, executors of God's judgments.

30. *Over it.*—Over the invaders' prey, Judah.

VISION

(CHAPTER 6)

1. *In the year that king Uzziah died.*—This year of Isaiah's vision and consecration was probably the year 740 B.C. Jotham, on account of the leprosy of his father Uzziah, acted as regent for some years before Uzziah's death.

ib. His train filled the temple.—The *train* means the flowing skirts of God's robes; the *temple* means the heavenly temple, not the temple at Jerusalem.

2. *Above it stood the seraphims.*—The seraphims are conceived floating above the train of God. How they are to be imagined is to be gathered from this verse. The word *seraph* seems to have generally had the meaning of a fiery flying dragon.

13. *So the substance thereof shall be a holy seed.*—As life remains in the stump of trees which have been cut down, and as new shoots spring from it, so from the stock of the burned and purged tenth of the chosen people shall come a living growth.

IMMANUEL

(CHAPTERS 7–12)

For history see the Introduction [pp. 108–14]. The date of the invasion of Judah by the kings of Syria and Israel, and of Isaiah's meeting with Ahaz, who had succeeded his father Jotham on the throne of Judah, was probably about 732 B.C.

2. *Ephraim.*—Of the ten tribes which formed the northern kingdom, the kingdom of Israel, Ephraim was the chief, and it was also the seat of the capital, Samaria. Its name is therefore often used to designate the whole northern kingdom.

3. *Shear-jashub.*—The first appearance of this mystic name, *The remnant shall return.* For its importance see the Preface [pp. 110–12].

6. *The son of Tabeal.*—Tabeal was probably a Syrian prince, and his son was a favourite of the two kings, Rezin and Pekah.

5　　8. *And within threescore and five years, etc.*—Many critics are for omitting this second part of the verse as a later interpolation. Whether we omit it or retain it the passage is not so clearly self-explaining as might be wished. As it stands it seems to mean:—Judah's enemies are but a poor pair; one of them, Ephraim, will go to pieces within about half a century; the other is of like kind.

11. *Either in the depth.*—Either from the underworld or from the world of air.

14. *Behold the virgin, etc.*—Immanuel is addressed in the next chapter (verse 8) as a prince of Judah. "The virgin," therefore, is to be married to one of the house of David, and is within a year's time to bear a prince of Judah. The prince meant cannot be Hezekiah, for Hezekiah was at the time of this prophecy nearly grown up.

20　　15. *Milk-curd and honey.*—See below, 21–25. By the time the virgin's child, the young prince of Judah, comes to years of discretion, warfare shall have made his country desolate, agriculture shall be abandoned in Judah, men shall subsist on the produce of their wandering herds and on wild honey.

25　　16. *Before the child.*—Much before the child comes to years of discretion, at a time quite near, a time only a year or two hence (see viii, 4), Syria and Israel shall be conquered by the king of Assyria.

17. *The Lord shall bring upon thee.*—The prophet returns to Judah. Syria and Israel shall be conquered; but the chastisement of Judah also shall follow later.

ib. Ephraim departed from Judah.—The separation of the two kingdoms of Judah and Israel in Rehoboam's time is meant.

18. *The fly, etc.*—The lowlands of Egypt, up to the head of the streams of the Delta, were the haunt of flies, as the mountain-lands of Assyria were the haunt of wild bees.

20. *Shall the Lord shave with a rasor that is hired.*—The

Eternal shall bring his instrument, the king of Assyria, from beyond the river Euphrates, to inflict upon Judah conquest, servitude, and dishonour. The shaving of the head, body, and beard marks the loss of manhood.

21. *A man shall nourish, etc.*—See note on verse 15. After the conquest, the desolated land shall be used by its inhabitants merely for pasture and for hunting, not for agriculture as at present.

23. *Silverlings.*—The silverling, or silver shekel, was worth about 2s. 3d.

8

1. *With pen of the people.*—In large plain handwriting, which he who runs may read.

4. *Before the child shall have knowledge to cry.*—Within a year or two, before the child presently to be born can speak plain. See the Introduction [p. 112]. In fact, by 730 B.C., two years from the time when Isaiah spoke, Tiglath-pileser had crushed the kingdom of Syria and chastised the kingdom of Israel.

6. *The waters of Shiloah.*—The spring and pool of Shiloah or Siloah, in the valley on the south-east side of Jerusalem, is taken to represent the source of refreshment and life in the Lord's Zion. The prophecy is against both Judah and Israel ("both the houses of Israel," verse 14), but verses 6 and 7 apply particularly to Israel, ruled by Remaliah's son, Pekah, and in alliance with Rezin, king of Syria. In verse 8 the prophet passes to Judah.

9. *Associate yourselves, O ye peoples.*—The power of Assyria, figured by the river Euphrates, shall overflow Israel and Judah; but the triumph of the heathen over the kingdom of the Eternal and his Immanuel shall not endure.

12. *Say ye not, A confederacy.*—Do not share in the panics of your nation about alliances formed against it.

14. *A sanctuary.*—A sanctuary to the prophet himself, to the "*remnant*" of the Jewish nation, to the disciples (see verse 16) of the Eternal. The Eternal speaks.

18. *Behold, I and the children.*—The prophet speaks. The children are Shear-jashub, "The remnant shall return," and Maher-shalal-hash-baz, "Spoil speedeth, prey hasteth." See the Preface [pp. 110–13].

19. *That chirp and that mutter.*—The low indistinct voice of the dead whom the wizards profess to raise, and for whom they speak, is meant.

ib. Unto the dead.—The spirits of the dead which the necromancers profess to evoke.

9

1. *That which was vexed.*—The northern border of the Holy Land on both sides of the Jordan was most exposed to the invasions of Syria and Assyria, the great Gentile kingdoms to the north and north-east, and was naturally the first part of Palestine to suffer. See II Kings, xv, 29. Tiglath-pileser invaded Naphtali and Zebulun (answering to what was afterwards Upper and Lower Galilee), and, to the east of the Jordan, he invaded the half tribe of Manasseh, with Gad and Reuben, and deported the inhabitants of all of them to Assyria. The affliction which began here, and afterwards spread farther, shall not, the prophet says, be permanent.

ib. The way of the sea.—*The sea* is commonly taken to mean the Sea of Galilee; but more probably it is the Mediterranean, with which Zebulun was in contact at Carmel. Zebulun is spoken of in Genesis (xlix, 13) as a maritime tribe:—"Zebulun shall dwell at the haven of the sea, and he shall be for an haven of ships; and his border shall be unto Zidon."

4. *The staff of his shoulder.*—The disciplining staff or rod laid by his oppressor upon Israel's neck, shoulders, and back.

ib. As in the day of Midian.—In Immanuel's reign God's people shall be delivered from their conquerors and oppressors, as Gideon delivered them from the Arabian tribes of the Midianites. See Judges, vii, viii.

6. *His name.*—The "name" given to Immanuel consists of eight appellations, in four pairs.

8. *A word into Jacob.*—The word is to the whole people of

both Judah and Israel; but what follows next applies specially
to Israel or Ephraim. Judah comes in at verse 21.

10. *The bricks are fallen down.*—Instead of repenting,
Ephraim proposes to restore and augment his worldly strength
by the use of stronger materials.   5

11. *The overthrowers of Rezin.*—The Assyrians who had
crushed Rezin of Syria.

14. *Palm-branch and rush.*—The handsome palm-branch is
opposed to the valueless rush as the head to the tail, the honourable to the ignoble.   10

18. *It shall devour the briers and thorns.*—Judgment shall
fall first upon individuals (the briers and thorns), then upon
the mass of the nation (the thickets of the forest).

10

5. *O Assyrian.*—So far as to the judgment upon God's
people. But the instrument of this judgment, Assyria, far from   15
regarding itself as God's instrument against Israel and Judah, is
proud and self-sufficient, and shall in its turn be brought low.

9. *Is not Calno as Carchemish, etc.*—These are vassal territories of the king of Assyria. Calno, afterwards Ctesiphon, is
on the Tigris, Carchemish (Circesium) on the Euphrates, Ar-   20
pad in the neighbourhood of Aleppo, Hamath (Epiphania) on
the Orontes. The king of Assyria ranks the God of Israel with
the gods of these vassal territories, who have failed to save
them.

15. *As if the rod, etc.*—As it is the living arm wielding the   25
staff, axe, or saw, and not the instrument itself, which really
does the work, so it is the Eternal wielding his instrument
Assyria, and not Assyria itself, that is to be magnified.

21. *The-remnant-shall-return.*—This is the translation of
Shear-jashub, the symbolical name of Isaiah's son. However   30
numerous be the people of Israel and Judah, only a remnant of
them shall be saved, and shall found the felicity of the future.

26. *Midian at the rock of Oreb.*—See Judges, vii, 25. Assyria
shall fall before God's people, as Midian and Egypt formerly
did.   35

27. *The yoke shall break.*—The *remnant*, God's true people, shall be so strong and stout that Assyria's yoke on their neck shall be burst asunder by their stoutness.

28. *He is come to Aiath, etc.*—The conquering march of
5 the Assyrians through Judah, from the north southwards to Jerusalem, is described. Nob, the last-named place on the conquerors' march, is within sight of Jerusalem itself.

34. *He shall cut down.*—"He" is the Eternal. The thickets are the rank and file of the king of Assyria's army; Lebanon,
10 with its grand cedars, represents his mighty men.

11

1. *A rod out of the stem of Jesse.*—The Immanuel of chapters vii and ix.

3. *Shall not judge, etc.*—Shall not decide and censure hastily and passionately.

15 10. *His rest.*—The seat and firmly-established throne of Immanuel.

11. *To recover the remnant of his people.*—The deportation by Tiglath-pileser of the tribes on the northern frontier of Palestine has been mentioned in the note to ix, 1. Between that
20 time and the year 700 B.C. the whole population of the northern kingdom had been deported, after the fall of Samaria.

ib. From Pathros, etc.—Pathros is Upper Egypt; Cush is Ethiopia; Elam is Susistan, east of the Tigris; Shinar is on the Euphrates, and formed part of Babylonia; Hamath (already
25 mentioned in x, 9) is Epiphania on the Orontes.

ib. The islands of the sea.—The coasts and islands of the Mediterranean.

15. *The tongue of the Egyptian sea.*—The tongue or inlet of sea running up between Egypt and Arabia, the Gulf of
30 Suez.

ib. The river.—Euphrates. By cutting channels to carry off its waters men shall be able to cross it dryshod.

12

4. *Among the peoples.*—The blessed reign of Immanuel has carried the knowledge of the Eternal among all nations.

THE BURDENS

(CHAPTERS 14,24 – 23,18)

In the last half of the eighth century before Christ Palestine and the neighbouring countries repeatedly felt the arm of Assyria, and such visitations caused Isaiah to utter his *burdens,* or oracular sentences of doom, upon the countries visited. These, as they now stand, we may suppose him to have collected and republished at the end of the century, with new touches thrown in, and with a sentence upon the conquering Assyria itself for preface. 5

14

29. *The rod of him that smote thee.*—Uzziah had been victorious over the Philistines (II Chron., xxvi, 6), but in the reign of his grandson Ahaz they in their turn invaded Judah and occupied some of its towns (II Chron., xxviii, 18). The power of Judah, "of him that smote them," had been brought low by the alliance against Ahaz of the kings of Syria and Israel. The prophet warns the Philistines not to be over-elated at Judah's weakness, for they shall feel the hand of a more formidable conqueror, Assyria. In fact, Tiglath-pileser at the end of the reign of Ahaz chastised, we are told, the Philistines and received their submission. Subsequently revolting, they were again invaded and chastised by Tiglath-pileser's successors, Sargon and Sennacherib. 10 15 20

31. *O gate.*—The gates of the Philistian fortresses were famous for their strength.

ib. There cometh from the north.—The well-disciplined army of Assyria is meant. 25

32. *What shall one then answer.*—This is one of the touches probably added during Sennacherib's invasion, when the other Palestinian nations were in communication with Judah as to means of resisting the common foe.

15

1. *The burden of Moab.*—Tiglath-pileser chastised the Moabites and received their submission; and again, after they had revolted on Sennacherib's accession, the king of Moab submitted himself to Sennacherib. The places named in the burden
5   are places belonging to the Moabites; Ar of Moab (Areopolis) and Kir of Moab (Kir-hareseth) are their two chief towns.

5. *The heifer.*—The strong fortress of Zoar, on a hill near the Dead Sea, is compared to a heifer of three years old, full of strength and not yet tamed to the plough.
10   7. *The brook of the willows.*—A brook on the southern border of Moab, forming the boundary between Moab and Edom.

9. *Dimon.*—Dimon is the Dibon of verse 2, a place about an hour's journey off the river Arnon. The *b* is changed into *m*
15   to get the signification of "blood."

16

1. *Send ye the lamb, etc.*—The fugitives of Moab have fled as far as Sela (Petra) in Edom. They are bidden by the prophet to send their tribute of lambs from thence through the wilderness to Jerusalem, to the king there, their proper ruler. The
20   Moabites had formerly been subject to David.

2. *The daughters of Moab.*—The frightened and uncertain fugitives shall be at the fords of Arnon, the river of Moab, like birds cast out of the nest.

3. *Take counsel, etc.*—This verse and the two verses follow-
25   ing are the appeal which the tribute-bringing envoys of Moab make to the strong and just ruler of Jerusalem.

6. *We have heard, etc.*—This is the prophet's answer in the name of Judah.

ib. His lies shall not be so.—Things shall not go as he falsely
30   vaunts they will.

8. *The vine of Sibmah, etc.*—The vineyards and wine of Sibmah in Moab were famous. The cultivation of the excellent vine of Moab extended northward and westward to Heshbon

and the Dead Sea. The conqueror brings it all to an end, whereat the prophet is moved with pity.

12. *The high place.*—The high place and sanctuary of Chemosh the god of Moab.

13. *This is the word, etc.*—The foregoing prophecy may be supposed to have been uttered when Moab was overrun by the armies of Tiglath-pileser, Shalmaneser, or Sargon. At the end of the century, after the rising of Moab against Sennacherib, the prophet republishes his former utterance with a prediction of new and speedy ruin added.

14. *The years of an hireling.*—Strictly counted, as a hireling counts the time which he has to serve.

17

1. *The burden of Damascus.*—This prophecy belongs to the time of Tiglath-pileser and his chastisement of Syria and Israel.

2. *The cities of Aroer.*—There were two Aroers in the territory of the tribes of Israel on the east of Jordan. As Aroer means *laid bare*, the name is a symbol of the desolation of the whole country.

5. *Rephaim.*—A plain abounding in corn to the south-west of Jerusalem. Of Israel, as of Judah, there shall be a remnant saved, a remnant like the few ears of corn which escape the reaper, like the few olives which escape the gatherer.

9. *As the ruins in the thickets and in the heights.*—The cities of Israel shall be as the ruins of the Canaanitish cities left in the thickets and in the heights after the conquest of Canaan by the Israelites.

10. *Strange slips.*—The idolatry of Israel is expressed under the figure of a planting or garden set with "strange slips" of divinities adopted from their heathen neighbours.

12. *Woe to the multitude, etc.*—The kingdoms of this world, which now serve as God's instrument for the punishment of his people, shall finally perish themselves.

18

1. *Woe for the land buzzing with wings, etc.*—Compare "the
fly that is in the uttermost part of the rivers of Egypt," vii, 18.
The numberless flies of the rivers of the interior of Africa are
meant. The "rivers of Ethiopia" are the Blue and White Nile;
5   the "land" is the country between them and to the south of
them, the Meroe of the Greeks, Nubia and Abyssinia. The king
of Ethiopia, Shabak, had dispossessed the Egyptian king and
had retained a preponderance, which in the last quarter of the
eighth century B.C. enabled him and his successor to govern
10 the policy of Egypt and of the princes of the Delta. In the year
720 Shabak, having joined in the movement against Assyria,
was defeated by Sargon at Raphia in Southern Palestine. His
successor was defeated in the same region by Sennacherib nine-
teen years later. The prophecy is probably to be assigned to
15 this later period. Assyria is too strong for the Ethiopians, for
whom the prophet has clearly a kindness; but the Eternal in
his own time will bring Assyria to ruin, and will receive the
worship of Ethiopia.

2. *Vessels of bulrushes.*—Boats made of papyrus, used by
20 the dwellers on the Nile.

ib. Go, ye swift messengers.—The prophet sends a message
to all the widespread, great, and warlike Ethiopian people, to
the effect that the Eternal is preparing a cure for the present
distress.

25 *ib. A nation long-shanked and smooth.*—Herodotus calls the
Ethiopians "the tallest and finest of men," and mentions also
their smooth and shining skin, due, it was said, to the water of
a certain spring (Herod., iii., 20, 23).

ib. The rivers.—The Blue and White Nile.

30 4. *Like a clear heat.*—The Eternal lets Assyria ripen until
the hour of its ruin comes.

7. *In that time.*—See the end of note to verse 1.

19

1. *The burden of Egypt.*—Egypt at this time, as has been
mentioned, felt the pressure of Ethiopia, the suzerain of the

weak princes of the Delta. These princes shared in the defeats of Raphia in 720, and of Altaku, or Eltekeh, in 701. It was a time of confusion and helplessness for Egypt, in spite of its antiquity, civilisation, and pretensions; and the Jewish reliance upon Egyptian power, in the struggle with Assyria, was per- 5 fectly vain.

4. *A cruel lord.*—The king of Ethiopia. The establishment of the first king of the Ethiopian dynasty had been attended with cruel treatment of the dispossessed king of Egypt.

5. *The waters shall fail.*—The political confusion in Egypt 10 brought about anarchy, stoppage, and social distress.

11. *Zoan.*—Zoan is Tanis, a chief city of Lower Egypt, near the Pelusian mouth of the Nile; Noph (verse 13) is Memphis.

15. *The head with the tail, etc.*—Images for the upper and lower classes. 15

18. *In that day.*—For Egypt the final solution shall be, as for Ethiopia, conversion to Israel's God, the Eternal, and peace in that conversion.

23. *Shall worship.*—The Egyptians together with the Assyrians shall worship the Eternal. 20

20

1. *Tartan came unto Ashdod.*—Tartan is a military title, like *generalissimo.* Ashdod, the strong city of the Philistines, was taken by Sargon's general about 711 B.C. The reduction and occupation by the Assyrians of the Palestinian fortresses was preliminary to the conquest of Egypt. Isaiah foretells that con- 25 quest, which was accomplished, however, not by Sargon, but by Esar-haddon, the son of Sennacherib.

6. *Of this coast.*—Of Palestine. The court of Jerusalem and the people of Judah rely upon Egypt and Ethiopia for aid against Assyria, and Egypt and Ethiopia are themselves As- 30 syria's prey.

21

11. *The burden of Dumah.*—Edom or Idumæa is probably called Dumah, *silence*, by a play of words to express the deso-

lation coming upon the land. Seir is the well-known mountain
of Edom. We hear of the Edomites being subdued both by
Tiglath-pileser and by Sennacherib.

12. *The watchman.*—The watchman is the prophet in Jeru-
5   salem, answering the appeal of Edom. He sees but a troubled
future for Edom, day breaking for it to be followed again by
darkness and night; only one counsel he can give: *Return,
come!* be converted to the God of Israel!

13. *The burden upon Arabia.*—Tiglath-pileser subdued the
10 Arab tribes; Sargon also subdued the nomads of "remote Arabia
which had never before given tribute to Assyria." Herodotus
speaks of Sennacherib as "king of the Arabians and Assyrians."
This prophecy shows us the Arab caravans unable to travel
securely for fear of the soldiery of the invaders. The Dedanim,
15 Tema, and Kedar are tribes and places of Arabia.

16. *The years of an hireling.*—See note on xvi, 14.

22

1. *The valley of vision.*—The valley of vision is Jerusalem,
where the prophet's house stood in the lower town between
Mount Moriah and Mount Zion. The Assyrian is in Palestine,
20 Jerusalem is in danger. The defences and cisterns of the city
are being hurriedly repaired; but there is no amendment of
life, no seriousness, and no force. Jerusalem is in gaiety and
revel; the citizens go up upon their flat roofs for pleasure
parties, or in curiosity about the approaching soldiery of the
25 invader.

3. *All thy rulers.*—As if it had already happened, the prophet
sees the disaster sure to befall such a nation and government as
those of Judah in conflict with such an enemy as Assyria. The
prophecy belongs probably to the time of the projected al-
30 liance with Egypt, either in Sargon's reign or at the accession
of Sennacherib.

5. *Crying to the mountains.*—Cries of despair ascending to
the hills which stood about Jerusalem, and echoed back from
them.

35 6. *Elam . . . Kir.*—Contingents of the Assyrian army,

troops from Elam or Susistan, a part of Persia, and from the banks of the river Cyrus in Armenia.

8. *He withdraweth.*—"He" is the Eternal, who withdraws the covering or curtain from Jerusalem and lets it be seen in its weakness.

ib. The House of the Forest.—The arsenal. See I Kings, vii, 2. It was built by Solomon, and having "four rows of cedar pillars, with cedar beams upon the pillars," was thence called "the house of the forest of Lebanon."

15. *This treasurer.*—The treasurer of the Jewish king was his chief minister, a high steward, or mayor of the palace.

16. *What hast thou here?*—The unpopular Shebna was an alien, with no right in Jerusalem, and no family stock there.

19. *Shall he pull thee down.*—"He" is the Eternal.

20. *I will call my servant Eliakim.*—A little later (xxxvi, 3) we find Eliakim in the post of mayor of the palace, and Shebna in that of scribe or secretary.

24. *They shall hang upon him.*—All his connexions, small and great, shall prosper through his rise.

23

1. *The burden of Tyre.*—Shalmaneser besieged Tyre, with what final result is not known. In the rising of the Phœnician cities after Sennacherib's accession Isaiah saw fresh calamity for Tyre.

ib. Ye ships of Tarshish.—Tarshish, or Tartessus, is the mining country outside the Straits of Gibraltar, at the mouth of the Guadalquivir, with which Phœnicia traded.

ib. From the land of Chittim.—The Tarshish fleet is supposed to have reached Chittim, or Cyprus, on its voyage home, and there to learn the fall of Tyre.

3. *The harvest of the river.*—The Tyrian traders went to Egypt for grain.

4. *Zidon.*—Zidon, the other great Phœnician city, shares with Tyre the shame of loss of trade and decline.

5. *Egypt.*—Egypt, of which Tyre was so good a customer, shall grieve at Tyre's fall.

6. *The isle.*—Tyre was built on an island. The Phœnicians are bidden to betake themselves to Tarshish, now that they have lost Tyre.

10. *Pass through thy land as a river.*—With Tyre's fall the band of subjection is loosed for the colonies and countries dependent on Tyre; they are free.

11. *He stretched out, etc.*—"He" is the Eternal; Canaan, in the latter part of the verse, is Phœnicia.

13. *Behold the land of the Chaldeans.*—The Phœnicians are told to mark the fate of Babylonia, which in 704 B.C. had risen against Sennacherib, and had just been subdued by him and heavily punished. The prophecy probably dates from Sennacherib's invasion of Palestine in 701 B.C., after his victory over Merodach-baladan, king of Babylon.

15. *Seventy years, according to the days of one king.*—A long uneventful period of subjugation is foretold for Tyre; then she shall recover her trade and wealth, but shall bestow them on the Eternal's service. By *the days of one king* is meant the uniform course of life under one ruler and policy; by *seventy years*, as by *threescore and five years* (vii, 8) is meant a certain considerable term of years.

17. *Her hire.*—The trade of Tyre is signified by this figure of hire and fornication.

THE WOES

(CHAPTERS 28–33)

The Burdens are concerned with foreign nations mainly; in the Woes, the prophet comes nearer home, dealing with the history of the chosen people from the fall of Samaria in 721 B.C. down to Sennacherib's invasion in 701 B.C. The prophecy which comes first belongs clearly to the beginning of this period. The prophecies which follow cannot be assigned with certainty to any particular year. It is sometimes urged that they must belong to the early years of the period; because they prophesy disaster to Jerusalem, while, at the end of the period, it is Sennacherib's disaster, not Jerusalem's, which Isaiah is prophesying. But, on the one hand, the ruin of the sinful Jerusalem was always an article of faith with Isaiah, although the insolent and unrighteous heathen invader may provoke chastisement. On the other hand, the tone of emotion in these chapters is such that they may better be referred to the ago- 5 nising crisis which followed Sennacherib's accession in 705 than to any earlier time.

28

1. *The crown of pride.*—The vine-clad hill of Samaria, the capital of Ephraim. The rich and beautiful vegetation crown- ing this hill is figured as being at the same time a crown to the 10 heads of the revelling and riotous nobles of Ephraim.

7. *But these, also.*—Not the nobles, priests, and prophets of Ephraim only, of the northern kingdom, but those of Judah likewise.

9. *Whom will he teach.*—The words of the drunken nobles 15 of Judah to Isaiah. The repetitions in the next verse are prob- ably meant to reproduce the speech of drunken men.

11. *With stammering lips.*—With speech hard to catch and indistinctly understood like that of these drunkards, even with the speech of the Assyrian invader. The Assyrians spoke a 20 Semitic dialect imperfectly comprehended by the Hebrews.

15. *We have made a covenant with death.*—The alliance with Egypt, which the nobles and court of Jerusalem were secretly preparing as the means of deliverance from Assyria, is probably here meant. The "overflowing scourge" is Assyria. 25

21. *As in mount Perazim, etc.*—Two defeats which David inflicted on the Philistines. See I Chron., xiv, 10–16.

ib. His strange work.—The strangeness is in God's now working the defeat of his own chosen people.

23. *Give ye ear, etc.*—The prophet concludes with a par- 30 able, illustrating God's ways with his people from the simple operations of the tiller of the ground. As the tiller of the ground is not always ploughing and breaking it open, so God is not always afflicting and punishing, but only long enough to prepare his people's hearts to receive the seed of righteousness. 35

25. *The fitches.*—"Fitches" is only an old form of the word "vetches."

27. *The fiitches are not threshed.*—As the husbandman has divers modes of treatment, some harder, others gentler, for the different objects of his care, so has God for his people.

29

1. *Ariel.*—Ariel, meaning "the Lion of God," is Jerusalem, the unconquered fortress-city of David.

ib. Add ye year to year.—Let the year go round with its feasts and sacrifices; then shall come a visitation from the Eternal upon Jerusalem; but afterwards it shall be his own Jerusalem again. The date of this prophecy is between 705 and 701 B.C., during the revolts and agitations which followed the accession of Sennacherib, and while the court party at Jerusalem were secretly planning their alliance with Egypt.

9. *Stand ye still and wonder.*—Spoken to the politicians and people of Judah, misled by their prophets and failing to comprehend their situation. The failure is in the learned and unlearned alike.

15. *Woe unto them.*—The secret planners of the Egyptian alliance.

16. *Is the potter like as the clay.*—Do these profound politicians suppose that they and their policy shape the course of things, not the Eternal?

17. *Lebanon shall be turned.*—A little while, and the Eternal shall change all that state of things which now is, and which seems permanent; the forest (Lebanon) shall become field, and the field forest; in the deaf and blind (the ignorant common people) shall be awakened knowledge of the Eternal and joy in him.

20. *The terrible one.*—The oppressive magnates, the court and politicians, of Jerusalem, shall pass away.

23. *In the midst of him.*—By "him" is meant Jacob.

30

2. *Pharaoh.*—A general name for each successive ruler of Egypt, like Cæsar for the ruler of Rome. The princes of the Delta were Pharaohs. But the over-lord or suzerain of Egypt was now the Ethiopian Shabatok, the son of the Shabak who was defeated by Sargon at Raphia in 720 B.C.

4. *Zoan . . . Hanes.*—Cities of Lower and Middle Egypt, and residences of princes. Zoan is Tanis, Hanes is Anusis afterwards Heracleopolis. (See xix. 11.)

5. *They were all ashamed.*—The princes and ambassadors of Judah can get nothing by their journey to Egypt but shame and disappointment; Egypt is of no use.

6. *The burden of the beasts of the south.*—Now follows, in this and the next verse, an oracular sentence on the vanity of the embassy to Egypt. The beasts of the south are the animals of interior Africa.

7. *Proud Rahab.*—Rahab, meaning *pride*, is a Biblical name for Egypt; but Rahab, or Egypt the proud, is really, says the prophet, *Shabeth*, the sitting-still, the do-nothing.

8. *Now go, etc.*—The prophet is commanded to write, and keep for a testimony against his countrymen, this oracle concerning the folly of their recourse to Egypt.

16. *We will fly upon horses.*—We will have horses and chariots and the famous Egyptian cavalry.

18. *Therefore will the Lord wait.*—The day of mercy cannot arrive until the actual things have passed away, and the people is purged to a "remnant."

25. *The day of the great slaughter.*—Compare ii, 12–15. The day of the Lord will destroy all in which the rulers of Judah, as it now is, place their trust. "The towers fall," but streams of water spring forth in the hills for the righteous to whom belongs the new world.

29. *The holy solemnity.*—The Passover.

33. *Tophet.*—The place of abomination in the valley of Hinnom, where men burned their children in sacrifice to Moloch. The Moloch-pile, says the prophet, is ready for the *melech* (king) of Assyria.

31

4. *Like as the lion.*—Not Egypt shall save Judah, but the Eternal.

8. *Not of a mighty man, etc.*—A sword, not of man at all, but of God.

9. *His rock.*—The "rock" of the Assyrian is his king, Sennacherib, who shall take to flight.

32

1. *The king.*—God's judgment accomplished, the "remnant" established, the Assyrian put to flight, Immanuel, the saviour king of chapters ix and xi, shall begin his reign with princes and ministers of his own stamp.

2. *A man.*—King and princes shall be the people's protectors instead of being its oppressors.

3. *The eyes of them that see, etc.*—The mental and spiritual deficiencies of the people shall be cured.

9. *Rise up, ye women.*—Compare the prophet's like strain some forty years earlier, iii, 16.

14. *The hill and tower.*—Ophel, the fortified south-eastern slope of Mount Moriah, with the watch-tower thereon.

15. *The fruitful field be counted for a forest.*—In the new time the splendour of righteousness shall be such that what now passes for fruitful field (morally) shall then seem but forest and wilderness.

19. *And it shall hail, and the forest shall be brought low.*— In the time of judgment, which must precede the reign of Immanuel, the now powerful kingdom of this world, Assyria (described under figure of the "forest," x, 34), shall be brought down by the hail-storm of God's wrath.

ib. And the city shall be low.—The same storm shall lay low the "city" also, the actual sinful Jerusalem that rejects God's word.

20. *Blessed are ye, etc.*—Blessed is "the remnant," which after that time of destruction shall have the land at its free disposal for either tilling or pasture.

33

In this prophecy we are clearly in 701 B.C., at the moment when the Assyrian invader is encamped in Judah, ravaging its lands, taking its towns one after the other, threatening Jerusalem. We have seen the dealings of Hezekiah and his court with Egypt. They had also taken part in the rising of Palestine 5 against Sennacherib, so far as to receive from the revolted Ekronites their king, Padi, who had remained faithful to Assyria, and to imprison him at Jerusalem. When Sennacherib formed the siege of Lachish in Judah, Hezekiah, alarmed, sent ambassadors to make his submission (II Kings, xviii, 14–16). 10 Sennacherib received his submission and presents; but immediately afterwards, unwilling apparently to leave so strong a place as Jerusalem in the hands of a faithless tributary, he sent a division of his army thither to demand its surrender. Indignation at the invader's violence and perfidy, confidence in the 15 future of Zion notwithstanding the doomed sinners whom the actual Zion contains, are now the foremost thoughts with Isaiah. See Introduction, pp. 113–14.

1. *Woe to thee, etc.*—The prophet addresses the Assyrian invader. 20

2. *Their arm.*—Judah's.

4. *Your spoil.*—The Assyrians are addressed. In the preceding verse "thyself" is of course the Eternal.

6. *Thy times.*—Judah is addressed.

7. *Their valiant ones.*—These are the magnates of Judah 25 sent as ambassadors to Sennacherib at Lachish, and who have discovered that the surrender of Jerusalem will be required as well as their presents and tribute.

8. *The highways lie waste.*—Owing to the presence of the Assyrian host in the country. 30

ib. He hath broken the covenant.—Sennacherib, after accepting Hezekiah's submission, had then demanded, further, the surrender of Jerusalem.

11. *Ye shall, etc.*—The Assyrians are addressed.

13. *Ye that are near.*—The prophet now addresses his own 35 countrymen.

17. *Shall behold the land spreading.*—Shall see the borders of the kingdom extended as in the time of David and Solomon.

18. *The terror.*—Of the Assyrian conquests.

ib. Where is the assessor, etc.—Where is now the foreigner who assessed the tribute, and weighed it when paid, and who counted the towers of our fortresses in order to besiege them?

19. *Of a dark speech.*—See note on xxviii, 11.

21. *A place of broad rivers.*—No earthly waters, but the river of the peace of God. Compare Isaiah lxvi, 12.

23. *Thy tacklings are loosed.*—Judah is addressed. After a moment of alarm and danger, Judah shall see the Assyrians in retreat and shall despoil them.

SENNACHERIB

(CHAPTERS 36–39)

See the introductory note to the last chapter.

36

1. *Now it came to pass, etc.*—See Introduction, p. 118 and p. 128, for the reasons for thinking that the words, "Now it came to pass in the fourteenth year of king Hezekiah," ought to stand not here but at the beginning of chap. xxxviii. The present chapter should begin: "Now Sennacherib, etc." We are in this chapter not at the fourteenth year of Hezekiah's reign, but at the twenty-fourth.

2. *Rabshakeh.*—This, like Tartan in xx, 1, is not the man's own name but a title. Rabshakeh means "chief officer."

3. *Eliakim . . . Shebna.*—See xxii, 15–25, and notes.

7. *Whose high places.*—Hezekiah had put down the idolatrous worship throughout his kingdom (II Kings xviii, 4); and the Assyrian treats this as an outrage upon the God of the land.

ib. Before this altar.—Before the altar in Jerusalem only.

8. *I will give thee.*—A sarcasm on the weakness of Judah.

Even if you give them horses, they have not soldiers to put upon them.

11. *The Syrian language.*—Hezekiah's ministers beg Rabshakeh to speak Aramaic, not Hebrew, that the common people may not understand them.

12. *That they may eat, etc.*—Who have to undergo siege and its extremities of famine for your pleasure.

17. *Until I come, etc.*—According to the Assyrian system, the inhabitants of Judah were to be finally deported as those of Israel had been.

19. *Hamath and Arphad.*—See note on x, 9.

ib. Sepharvaim.—Sippara, or the sun-city, in Mesopotamia, on the Euphrates.

37

8. *Libnah.*—Like Lachish, one of the cities of Judah. Sennacherib probably moved from Lachish hither in order to meet the army of Tirhakah.

9. *Tirhakah.*—Sennacherib defeated the army of Egypt and Ethiopia at Altaku, in the south of Palestine. But it is doubtful how far his victory was complete; at all events it did not enable him to effect the conquest of Egypt. Tirhakah, or Taharka, did not come to the throne until 692 B.C., so that he is probably here called "king of Ethiopia," as commanding for Shabatok, his predecessor, the son of Shabak.

12. *Gozan and Haran, etc.*—Territories and places of Mesopotamia conquered by Shalmaneser. The "children of Eden" are the Bit-Adini, or tribe of Adini; Telassar, or Asshur's Hill, is probably a new name given to their place of dwelling by the conqueror.

13. *Hena and Ivah.*—These places cannot be identified, but were probably in Mesopotamia.

24. *To the sides of Lebanon.*—Lebanon stands for Israel, the northern kingdom. After felling and destroying there, the Assyrian invader will now pass on to the hill of Zion at the

farther end of Palestine, and to the royal palace of the kings of Judah.

25. *I have digged, etc.*—The Assyrian king's march against Egypt is in the prophet's mind. He makes the king boast of providing water for his army in crossing the desert, and of turning the streams which defended the Egyptian towns.

30. *A sign unto thee.*—Judah and its king are addressed. For two years the invader's presence in the country shall prevent regular cultivation; then the land shall be rid of him, and the tiller of the ground shall resume his occupation.

36. *Then the angel, etc.*—See Introduction, p. 113. See also Herodotus, ii, 141, for a different account of this disaster to Sennacherib's army. According to Herodotus, the disaster took place at Pelusium, on the border of Egypt, and was due to a plague of field mice devouring the bow-strings, leathern shield-straps, etc., of the Assyrians.

38. *His sons smote him.*—As Sennacherib's death and Esarhaddon's accession did not occur till 680 B.C. this verse is probably a later addition. But see Introduction, p. 128.

38

This chapter relates events which happened in 711 B.C., and should probably, as has been already said, commence thus: "Now it came to pass in the fourteenth year of king Hezekiah, that in those days was Hezekiah sick unto death."

10. *In the smoothness.*—In the midst of the even-flowing, natural course of my days.

16. *By these things men live.*—By these divine promises and their fulfilment.

22. *What is the sign.*—See verse 7.

39

1. *Merodach-baladan.*—In 711 B.C. this vassal king was preparing to revolt against Sargon, and would therefore gladly seize the opportunity of communicating with Hezekiah in view of his alliance. In 709 the revolt was crushed, and the

stronghold of the Bit-Yakin, the children or tribe of Yakin, in Southern Babylonia, into which Merodach-baladan had thrown himself, was taken and destroyed. But Merodach-baladan escaped, and in 704 we find him in revolt against Sennacherib, and again defeated. "I victoriously entered his palace at Babylon," says Sennacherib in an inscription, "and opened his treasures." Merodach-baladan survived, however, to revolt yet once more against Sennacherib on the Assyrian king's return from Palestine, and to be once more defeated.

6. *Shall be carried to Babylon.*—Nebuchadnezzar's conquest and Judah's captivity did not come until 588 B.C., one hundred and twenty years later. The capital of the great king in 711 was Nineveh. But Babylon was in Sargon's time a royal residence of the king of Assyria, and the most famous city in his dominions; when therefore the vassal king of Babylon visited Hezekiah, Isaiah might naturally use Babylon, Merodach-baladan's capital, for the representative city of the great power threatening Judah's existence.

(CHAPTER 40)

For the circumstances under which this Chapter opens see the Note on pp. 312–13.

The *Greek* Version mentioned in these notes is that of the Septuagint, or Seventy, begun at Alexandria in the third century before Christ, but not completed till the following century. It is the version which we find generally used and quoted in the New Testament. The *Vulgate* is the Latin Version of St. Jerome, made from the Hebrew at the beginning of the fifth century after Christ. It is the authorised version of the Church of Rome, and up to the Reformation was the Bible of Christendom; only for the Psalms a yet earlier Latin version, made from the Greek, not the Hebrew, and merely corrected by Jerome, maintained its ground; of this version the Latin headings to the Psalms in the Prayer-Book are relics. The *Chaldaic* Version and paraphrase was formerly thought to be nearly contemporary with the Christian era, or a little anterior to it; a considerable weight of opinion now, however, seems to be in favour of assigning this version to the third and fourth centuries after Christ. In any case it possesses great interest, having been made by learned Jews, in an idiom akin to the Hebrew, and which was the idiom in common use in Palestine at the Christian era. In this idiom were interpreted the Scriptures at those 'readings in the Synagogue every Sabbath-day' which we find mentioned in the New Testament; and much of these old interpretations and explanations is probably incorporated in the Chaldaic paraphrase. Other versions will be mentioned in the following notes, but they do not require special remark here.

1. *Comfort ye, comfort ye my people.*—Sometimes *my people* is erroneously taken for the nominative of address, as if the meaning were: Be comforted, my people. It is not so: the prophets are commanded to comfort the people. 'Prophets, prophesy consolations,' is the opening in the Chaldaic version. And in the Greek the word *priests* is supplied at the beginning of the second verse. But the right word to supply is *prophets*.

6. *And he said, What shall I cry?*—*He* is the prophet to whom the command to cry came. The Greek and the Vulgate have *I said;* the Arabic version supplies, as a subject to *said,* the words *He who was commanded.* But this is not necessary. The air is full of inspiration, of divine calls and prophetic voices, and the forms of expression are naturally rapid and elliptical. After a pause, it is given to the prophet what he shall cry.

9. *O thou.*—Here the opening ends, and the main subject,—Israel's restoration by the Almighty God of Israel,—is directly entered on.

15. *The isles.*—See note on verse 1 of the following chapter.

16. *And Lebanon is not sufficient to burn.*—The trees of Lebanon are not enough for wood on the fire of sacrifice.

18. *To whom then will ye liken God?*—How should the image-deities of idolatrous Babylon be compared to this almighty and unsearchable God of Israel?

20. *He that is too poor for oblation.*—Probably a contrast is intended between the costly idol of metal and the cheaper idol of wood, just as we find the two kinds of idols put side by side again at c. 44, vv. 12–17. So blinded are these heathens,

the Prophet means, that every man must have his idol; he who is too poor for oblation, who is still more, therefore, too poor to have his molten image with work of silver and gold, will yet have his image of wood.

23. *That bringeth the princes to nothing.*—After these words, in order to complete the sense, *Have ye not known him?* should be repeated from v. 21.

26. *Their host.*—The host of the stars.

27. *Why sayest thou, O Jacob.*—How then can Jacob and Israel be faint-hearted, or despair of their restoration, when this unmatchable, all-powerful, unwearying God is their God? Compare c. 49, v. 14.

ib. My judgment is passed over.—Is neglected. My God neglects (Israel is supposed to say) to judge my cause and to give sentence for me.

(CHAPTER 41)

To make still clearer the contrast between the power and wisdom of the God of Israel and of the gods of the heathen, these latter are challenged to show and compare their performances beside His.

1. *O islands.*—Literally, *coast-lands,* with especial reference to the coasts and islands of the Mediterranean, and, as these were westerly to the Jews, to the west; but used also generally in the sense of *far lands, distant regions.*

ib. Renew their strength.—Collect all their force to answer me.

2. *The man.*—The man called is Cyrus, from Persia, which is easterly both to Babylonia and to Palestine. Cyrus had the character of a mild and just prince; and Xenophon, the Greek historian, chose him for his ideal of a virtuous ruler. The Persians themselves said, according to Herodotus, that Darius was a hucksterer, Cambyses a master, but Cyrus a father. But it specially weighed, besides, with the Jews, that his religion, the religion of Persia, rejected and forbade idols like the religion of Israel. With this character to mark his religion, and pursuing, too, a policy favourable to the Jews, Cyrus came to be spoken of by them almost as a servant of the true God like

themselves. See Ezra i. 2: 'Thus saith Cyrus King of Persia, *The Lord God of heaven* hath given me all the kingdoms of the earth.'

2. *Gave the nations before him.*—First the kingdom of the Medes, then Lydia the kingdom of the rich Crœsus, and the Greek cities of Asia Minor; all conquered by Cyrus before his enterprise against Babylon.

3. *Even by the way that he had not gone.*—Even in his marches through new and unknown countries Cyrus was guided prosperously to his goal, as God's instrument.

8. *But thou, Israel.*—Amid the conquest, panic, and hurried recourse of the heathens to their idols, Israel has a secure upholder and restorer in the Lord his God.

17. *When the poor and needy seek water.*—On the march of the suffering exiles through the desert between Babylon and the Holy Land, in the promised and approaching return of the Jews to their country. In these regions water is almost the first object of a man's thoughts. The Ghassanides, one of the most powerful divisions of the Arabian race, took their name from a spring of water they fell in with on their march across the desert from Arabia into Syria. God promises his people to provide water in the wilderness and on the bare highlands for them, and verdure in the desert, that their return may be made easier.

21. *Produce your cause.*—Israel having been exhorted and encouraged, the discourse turns again to the heathen and their false gods, who had been challenged to a competition with the Lord.

22. *Let them shew the former things.*—Let the gods of the heathen show what counsel and warning they have given to their dependents in former times, and let us see whether it has been verified; or let them give some counsel and warning to them now, and let us see whether it will be verified.

25. *One from the north, and . . . from the rising of the sun.*—Cyrus from Persia, which is to the north and east of Babylon.

26. *Who hath declared.*—Who of the false gods can point to warnings and prophecies fulfilled, as the God of Israel can?

What have they to produce like the Lord's sentence passed two hundred years ago on Assyria in its pride of power: 'When the Lord hath performed his whole work upon Mount Zion and on Jerusalem, *I will punish the fruit of the stout heart of the king of Assyria, and the glory of his high looks*' (Isaiah x. 12),—and since fulfilled in Assyria's fall? What can they produce like the Lord's sentence passed sixty years ago on Babylon in its pride of power: 'I will punish the king of Babylon and that nation for their iniquity, and the land of the Chaldeans, and will make it a perpetual desolation' (Jeremiah xxv. 12),—and now being fulfilled in Babylon's danger and fast-approaching fall? Nothing of this kind can they produce, and they are all vanity.

27. *I gave to Jerusalem.*—Israel had prophets and true counsellors from his God, while the heathen from their false gods had none.

(CHAPTER 42)

Israel, the object of this divine favour and these divine purposes, is now more closely considered, his true mode of working is declared, his blindness and shortcomings are reproved.

1. *Behold my servant, whom I uphold; mine elect.*—The Greek supplies, '*Jacob* my servant, *Israel* mine elect.' The whole passage, vv. 1–4, is applied to Christ in the New Testament, St. Matth. xii. 17–21; but neither the Greek version nor the Hebrew original are there closely followed. The occasion of quoting the passage is Jesus Christ's charge to those whom he healed that they should not make him known, the point primarily to be illustrated being Christ's mild, silent, and uncontentious manner of working.

2. *He shall not strive.*—More literally, shall not *clamour*: shall not speak with the high, vehement voice of men who contend. God's servant shall bring to men's hearts the word of God's righteousness and salvation by a gentle, inward, and spiritual method.

3. *A bruised reed.*—Suffering and failing hearts he shall treat tenderly, and restore them by mildness, not severity.

6. *For a mediator of the people, for the light of the Gen-*

tiles.—We are familiar with the application of this to Christ; but it is said in the first instance of the ideal Israel, immediately represented to the speaker by God's faithful prophets bent on declaring his commandments and promises, and by the pious
5 part of the nation, persisting, in spite of their exile among an idolatrous people, in their reliance on God and in their pure worship of him. The ideal Israel, thus conceived, was to be God's mediator with the more backward mass of the Jewish nation, and the bringer of the saving light and health of the
10 God of Israel to the rest of mankind.

9. *The former things are come to pass.*—Such as the prophesied fall of Assyria.

ib. And new things do I declare.—The approaching fall of Babylon and the restoration of Israel.

15 10. *Sing unto the Lord.*—In the convulsions of war and change coming upon the earth God's arm was about to be shown in the overthrow of idolatrous Babylon, and in the restoration of his chosen people; hence this song of triumph.

ib. Ye that go down to the sea, and all that is therein.—
20 Compare Psalm xcvi. 11: 'Let the sea make a noise, and all that therein is.'

11. *The wilderness and the cities thereof.*—The great expanse of desert country between Babylonia, Palestine, and Arabia, with nomad tribes masters of it, and settlements scat-
25 tered through it where there is water. Kedar is the name of an Arabian people, descended from Ishmael, lying in the north of Arabia, next to their brother race, Nebaioth, the Nabathæans. See Gen. xxv. 13.

ib. The inhabitants of the rock.—The country above spoken
30 of is by no means one great plain of sand, but has stony regions (Arabia Petræa), hills, and rock-forts. These are often contrasted with the undefended habitations of the nomad Arabs. 'We Bedouins,' says one of these Arabs, in the sixth century after Christ, to the poet Imroulcays, who sought his protec-
35 tion, 'live in the plains, and have no castles where we can make our guests safe: go to the Jew Samuel in his castle of El-Ablak.' The fidelity of this Jewish lord of an Arabian rock-fort became a proverb.

12. *In the islands.*—See note to c. 41, v. 1.

15. *I will make the rivers dry land,* &c.—The great rivers of Mesopotamia, from the nature of the country through which they flow, have from the earliest times offered scope for large engineering operations, both civil and military. Mr. Layard speaks thus of the ruins of a great stone-dam he found in the Tigris: 'It was one of those monuments of a great people, to be found in all the rivers of Mesopotamia, which were undertaken to ensure a constant supply of water to the innumerable canals spreading like network over the surrounding country, and which, even in the days of Alexander, were looked upon as the works of an ancient nation.' Engineering works for a military object, besides the operations on the Gyndes and Euphrates attributed to Cyrus, are continually mentioned. For example, Arabian writers relate how Zebba (probably the Zenobia of our histories) built two fortresses, one on the right, the other on the left bank of the Euphrates, and connected them by a tunnel, which she made by damming and turning the Euphrates when its waters were low, executing a deep cutting in its bed, bricking the cutting over, and then turning the waters back again. She hoped thus to have always a sure place of refuge, but an enemy who was at war with her got the secret of the tunnel, met her at its mouth in the second fortress when she fled from the first, and slew her.

16. *And I will bring the blind,* &c.—I will bring my faint-hearted, incredulous, and undiscerning people safe through the desert to their own land.

19. *Who is blind, but my servant.*—Israel, as a whole, is faint-hearted, is slow to understand God's great purposes for it, and incredulous of them, in spite of all the experience it has had of God's guidance.

21. *The Lord was pleased,* &c.—The Lord took Israel for his chosen people, in order to exalt his law, the law of righteousness, committed to Israel; Israel is conquered, despoiled, and captive; how can such things befall God's chosen people? Clearly, because of Israel's sins; because, though the chosen people, Israel would not walk in God's ways. Let Israel now return to them and be saved.

(CHAPTER 43)

And saved Israel shall be, the next chapter continues; his
sons shall be gathered from all the regions where they are
dispersed, and shall be brought with safety and victory, as of
old from the bondage of Egypt, to their own land.

5   3. *I give Egypt for thy ransom, Ethiopia and Saba for thee.*
—In the crash now begun, the new conquering power, Persia,
was about to attack and overturn other powers besides Babylon. Cambyses, the son of Cyrus, conquered Egypt and invaded Ethiopia. Saba is Meroe on the Upper Nile. The Persian
10   king was to set free the chosen people; these other peoples,
given into his hand, were to be as a ransom and a substitute
for the delivered Israel.

        8. *Bring forth the blind people that have eyes.*—Set free my
people Israel, who have been blind to my ways but shall see
15   them, and deaf to my word but shall hearken to it.

        9. *Let all the nations.*—The heathen and their gods are
again challenged as in c. 41. See note to v. 26 of that chapter.

        10. *Ye are my witnesses,* &c.—Israel is here addressed, both
the blind and faint-hearted mass of the nation, and the faithful
20   and believing few.

        14. *And the Chaldeans upon the ships of their pleasure.*—
'I make the Chaldeans to flee upon the barks that had before
served for their pleasure.' The great feature of Babylon was
its river, the Euphrates, with its quays, bridges, cuts, and
25   artificial lakes; it served alike for use and pleasure.

        16. *Which maketh a way in the sea.*—A remembrance of
the march out of Egypt and of Pharaoh's overthrow.

        20. *The beasts of the field shall honour me.*—I will provide
water in the desert for my returning people on their march
30   through it; and by this the wild creatures of the desert, which
usually suffer by the drought prevailing there, shall profit.

        23. *Thou hast not brought me the lambs.*—Compare Ps. l. 8:
'I will not reprove thee because of thy sacrifices or for thy
burnt-offerings, because they were not always before me.' The
35   sacrificial service of the temple necessarily ceased during the
exile at Babylon; God has no concern for this, neither does

he plague his people about it; his concern is because his people plague *him* with their sins.

24. *No sweet cane.*—A spice reed, *calamus aromaticus,* used for the holy anointing oil. See Exod. xxx. 23, where it is called 'sweet calamus,' and mentioned along with cinnamon.

26. *Let us plead together.*—As the heathen and their deities were challenged recently, so Israel is now challenged to try its cause with God.

27. *Thy first father.*—Jacob, by whose representative name the Jewish people is throughout addressed. See Hos. xii. 2, 3: 'The Lord will punish Jacob according to his ways, according to his doings will he recompense him; he took his brother by the heel in the womb,' &c. But probably a general sense is meant to be given to the expression: 'thy forefathers,' 'thy race from its first beginning.'

28. *The princes of the sanctuary.*—The chief priests. See Jer. lii. 24.

(CHAPTER 44)

Nevertheless, Israel shall be restored, and so evidently blest that other nations shall attach themselves to him, call themselves by his name, and become servants of his God. For his God is the only God, the idols are vanity. Amidst the joy of the whole earth, God will perform his promise and restore Israel by the hand of Cyrus.

2. *Jeshurun.*—Probably a diminutive of endearment, coming originally from Jashar, *upright,* and with a force something like that of *Goodchild.* The Greek has, *my beloved Israel,* the Vulgate, *rectissime,* Luther, *Frommer,* 'pious one.'

7. *The ancient people.*—More literally, the *everlasting* people; Israel, the chosen, eternal people of God.

ib. Let them shew.—A challenge as at c. 41, vv. 21–26; see the notes there.

8. *They are their own witnesses.*—They themselves have the plain evidence of the nullity of their gods; but they are blind to it, that they may come to shame and ruin.

11. *That are but men.*—That are mere mortal men, and yet make gods!

12. *The smith.*—There is here mention, first, of the molten image made by the smith, and then of the cheaper wooden image made by the carpenter. See c. 40, v. 20, and the note there.

ib. Yea, he is hungry.—This god-maker is hungry and faint, even at the very time he is at his god-making!

27. *That saith to the deep,* &c.—There is reference here to the Israelites' passage of the Red Sea, and probably also to the operations of Cyrus in drying and turning the rivers of Babylon.

(CHAPTER 45)

Cyrus is God's instrument, and those Jews that have difficulty in recognising him as such, are warned not to be more wise than God. God has raised up Cyrus and is directing his wars, that Israel may be saved, and that the world may be saved with Israel in Israel's God, the sole source of salvation.

1. *To his anointed, to Cyrus.*—The Vulgate keeps the Greek word for *anointed*, and has *Christo meo Cyro*.

ib. I will ungird the loins.—To gird the loins is to make fit for action and to fill with strength; so to *un*gird them is to make powerless for action and to leave defenceless.

ib. To open before him the two-leaved gates, &c.—The gates of Babylon and the other cities besieged by Cyrus.

4. *I have surnamed thee.*—'My shepherd.' See the last verse of the preceding chapter.

8. *Drop down, ye heavens,* &c.—Compare Deut. xxxii. 2: 'My doctrine shall drop as the rain, my speech shall distil as the dew,' &c.

ib. Have created him.—Cyrus.

9. *Woe unto him.*—God here turns to Israel, who was looking for 'a rod out of the stem of Jesse' to restore the Jews in triumph to Jerusalem, and was little prepared to accept an alien deliverer like Cyrus. 'Will Israel be more wise than God who made him and the world and rules them in his own manner?' is the substance of this and the following verses.

ib. Thy work.—In common speech we should say, *one's* work. Shall one's work say of him that fashioneth it, &c.

11. *Ask ye me of things to come*, &c.—See note to v. 9. Will ye take the disposition of things out of my hands, and direct me how I am to deal with my own chosen people?

13. *I have raised him*, &c.—*Him* is Cyrus, *my city* is Jerusalem, *my captives* are the Jews.

14. *The labour of Egypt*, &c.—See c. 43, v. 3, and the note there. Saba, or Meroe, on the Upper Nile, was the centre of a great caravan trade between Ethiopia, Egypt and North Africa, Arabia and India. Herodotus speaks (iii. 20) of the Ethiopians as 'the tallest of men.'

ib. Shall come over unto thee.—*Thee* is Israel. The conquest of strange nations by Cyrus shall acquaint these nations with Israel and Israel's God, and make them see that only in this God is salvation.

ib. In chains.—After their conquest by Cyrus.

15. *Thou art a God that hidest thyself.*—A God that is unsearchable, whose ways, though excellent, are not as man's ways, and whose footsteps are not known.

19. *I have not spoken in secret.*—My oracles have not been hidden and ambiguous, my promises and threatenings have been distinct and clear. See note to c. 41, v. 26.

20. *Ye that are escaped of the nations.*—The great convulsion of Cyrus's conquests is supposed to be over, and the remnants of the conquered nations are called upon to leave their idols, and to know and acknowledge the God of Israel.

(CHAPTER 46)

The idols of Babylon fall, and their captive worshippers, instead of being sustained by them, have to put them on beasts of burden to be carried; the God of Israel is no idol to be carried on beasts of burden or on men's shoulders, he carries his people. He has called Cyrus and will save Israel in his own manner.

1. *Bel boweth down, Nebo stoopeth.*—Babylonian idols. In the star-worship of Babylon, Bel was the planet Jupiter; it has been conjectured that Nebo was the planet Mercury. The temple of Bel was one of the wonders of Babylon. The gods of the conquered people were carried off into captivity

along with the people. So Jeremiah says (xlviii. 7) of Chemosh
the god of Moab: 'Chemosh shall go into captivity with his
priests and his princes.'

1. *They are borne that ye carried.*—The Babylonians are
addressed. The idols that they used to carry with honour in
their religious processions, are now packed on horses and
bullocks and borne by the weary beasts away.

2. *They could not deliver the burden.*—The false gods
could not deliver their own images, borne into captivity.

8. *Shew yourselves men.*—Not such children as to con-
found me with these dumb idols, who cannot counsel or save.

11. *Calling an eagle from the east.*—Cyrus from Persia.

12. *Ye obdurate.*—Spoken to those Jews who were slow
to believe in their deliverance through Cyrus.

(CHAPTER 47)

An outburst of triumph on the approaching fall of luxurious,
tyrannous, superstitious Babylon.

1. *Daughter of the Chaldeans.*—Chaldæa was the country,
Babylon the capital.

2. *Take the millstones*, &c.—Perform the offices of a slave,
thou who hast been so luxurious!

ib. Uncover thy locks, &c.—Struggle along on thy way
into captivity, squalid and half-clad, thou who hast been so
delicate!

6. *Upon the ancient.*—Israel. Israel *the ancient*, Israel *in his
old age*, is used to heighten the picture of cruelty. *Ancient*
here must not be paralleled with *ancient* in c. 44, v. 7, 'the
ancient people;' the word in the original is not the same there
as here, and means there *eternal*, God's chosen and eternal
people.

9. *The loss of children and widowhood.*—Babylon is said
to lose her children inasmuch as she loses her citizens, and to
be a widow inasmuch as she loses her king.

ib. The multitude of thy sorceries.—The 'magicians, astrologers, and sorcerers' of Babylon are familiar to us from the
book of Daniel. See Dan. ii. 2.

14. *It shall not be a coal to warm at*, &c.—Not a pleasant,
warmth-giving fire, but a devouring, destructive one.

15. *They with whom thou hast dealt.*—The magicians and astrologers of Babylon, with whose arts she has so busied herself, and on whom she has so relied, shall fail her in her day of trouble; they shall either be destroyed or flee.

(CHAPTER 48)

Israel is warned against his old hardness of heart, and bidden to receive the declaration of that which is God's present will, —the deliverance of Israel through Cyrus. But for the wicked, let Israel know, there is no deliverance.

3. *I have declared the former things.*—Such as the fall of Assyria and of Babylon. See c. 41, v. 26, and the note there.

6. *Thou hast heard; see all this!*—The Vulgate well translates, *Quæ audisti, vide omnia!* All that was before prophesied to thee, the fall of these mighty kingdoms, behold it fulfilled!

ib. I shew thee new things.—What these 'new things' are, namely, the deliverance through Cyrus, will be distinctly declared at v. 14.

11. *Will I do it.*—Deliver thee.

14. *Which among them.*—Among the false gods and the false prophets of the heathen.

ib. The Lord hath loved him.—*Him* is Cyrus. The Lord hath loved Cyrus; Cyrus will do the Lord's pleasure on Babylon, and the Lord's arm shall be, by Cyrus, on the Chaldeans.

16. *Come ye near unto me,* &c.—In this verse the Prophet, charged with these messages from God, speaks in his own name, and testifies to his countrymen that he has from the beginning pointed out to them God's hand and beck in these great events now happening.

21. *And they thirsted not,* &c.—This is what the delivered are to sing. On their return from Babylon, as in old time on their return from Egypt, they have been led safely through the desert and supplied with water.

22. *No peace.*—This is the note of warning, coming in at the close of the strain of promise.

At the end of this chapter there is a kind of pause in the discourse, which enters upon a second stage in the next chapter.

(CHAPTER 49)

The Prophet, who had appeared in v. 16 of the preceding chapter, comes forth in this chapter more distinctly. Speaking in the name of Israel, the true Israel, the pious and persisting part of his nation, he announces God's calling and purposes
5   for this Israel of whom he is the representative. God will not only restore the Jewish nation through this true Israel, full of faith and of courage for the promised restoration; he will also bring the Gentiles to himself through its light and leading. It is true, many of the Jews are incredulous and desponding;
10   but vain are their fears; God will not forsake his people.

2. *He hath made my mouth like a sharp sword.*—Compare Heb. iv. 12: 'The word of God is quick, and powerful, and sharper than any two-edged sword,' &c.

6. *It is a small thing*, &c.—See the introduction to this
15   chapter.

8. *A mediator of the people.*—The same expression as at c. 42, v. 6; see the note there. 'The people' is the Jewish people as opposed to the Gentiles.

ib. To establish the land.—The Holy Land, which was to be
20   restored and re-settled.

9. *The prisoners.*—The exiled and captive Israelites.

ib. Their pastures shall be in all high places.—See c. 41, v. 17, and the note there.

11. *My highways shall be exalted.*—Built up so as to form
25   a high and clear causeway to travel on.

12. *The land of Sinim.*—Probably China, which may have been known to the dwellers in Babylon as the name of a distant land, beyond India. It seems used here to imply the farthest parts of the world.

30   14. *But Zion said.*—The great body of the Jews were made despondent by their long adversity, and thought God had left them and would never restore them. Compare c. 40, v. 27: 'Why sayest thou, O Jacob, and speakest, O Israel, My way is hid from the Lord, and my judgment is passed over from my
35   God?'

16. *Graven thee upon the palms of my hands.*—As some-

thing to be ever remembered by me. See Deut. vi. 8: 'And thou shalt bind them (God's words) for a sign upon thine hand, and they shall be as frontlets between thine eyes.' Here the object for remembrance is conceived as written on something like paper, and then attached to the hands or face; in the text it is conceived as graven directly upon the hands. In Persia at this day people wear talismans, called *forms*, representing a star with five rays, each ray having written on it an important text of the Koran, and in the middle of the star is written the name of God. These are now talismans, but they were originally *reminders*, to keep God and certain thoughts concerning him ever at hand. Their use throws light on the expressions, 'to trust in God's *name*,' 'to fear the *name*,' 'to rejoice in the *name*,' 'to believe in the *name*,' which so often occur in the Bible.

18. *All these.*—The scattered and exiled children of Zion.

19. *They that swallowed thee up.*—Zion's foreign conquerors and occupiers shall evacuate her, and leave her to her own children.

20. *The place is too strait for me.*—A picture of the fulness and prosperity, after her restoration, of the desolate and empty Jerusalem of the time of the exile.

21. *Then shalt thou say*, &c.—The expressions in this verse are to be closely noted, for the discourse returns to them at the beginning of the next chapter. Zion complains that she is (1) a mother who has lost her children, and (2) a wife whom her husband (God) has abandoned.

24. *Shall the prey.*—Shall Israel be really rescued from such a power as Babylon? Yes.

(CHAPTER 50)

In the first three verses the thread of the discourse is directly continued from the last chapter. At v. 4 the Prophet, as the true Israel (see the introduction to the last chapter), speaks again of himself and his mission.

1. *Thus saith the Lord*, &c.—See v. 21 of the preceding chapter. Zion complains that her children are lost, and she is divorced. God answers: Can a writing of divorcement (St.

Matth. v. 31) be shown against me, as in a man's case, to prove
a formal divorce? or, have I creditors to whom, as a human
debtor, I sell my children? Zion is abandoned, and her children lost to her, but for a time, because of her sins and while
5   her sins last.

2. *Wherefore, when I came*, &c.—The faint-heartedness of
the bulk of the Jewish people, despondent and inert about the
promised restoration, is rebuked, and God's almighty power
to effect his designs is set forth.

10   10. *Who is among you.*—God speaks.

11. *Behold, all ye that kindle a fire.*—This is said to the Jews,
who receive with incredulity, anger, and persecution, God's
message and messenger. In this, as in the preceding verse, it is
God who speaks; and he warns these Jews that their anger and
15   violence shall be turned against themselves, and they shall 'lie
down in sorrow.' See c. 66, v. 24.

(Chapter 51)

This chapter continues the encouragement given at v. 10 of
the preceding chapter. The faithful of Israel shall be brought
to the land of promise like their father Abraham, and shall be
20   blest and multiplied there; they shall be the means of extending
God's salvation to the rest of the world. Let not man make
them afraid; the Lord is with them, who brought them out of
Egypt; who afflicted them, but will now save them and afflict
their oppressors.

25   1. *The rock*, &c.—Abraham and Sarah, the progenitors of
Israel.

2. *I called him alone.*—When he was but one, God called
him, to make him a great nation. Compare Ezek. xxxiii. 24:
'Abraham was one, and he inherited the land.'

30   5. *Mine arms shall judge.*—The common figure of the
actual arm or hand of God swaying human affairs.

9. *Cut Rahab and wounded the dragon.*—Rahab, 'the
Proud,' is Egypt; the dragon is probably the crocodile of the
Nile, the emblematic beast of Egypt. As God smote Egypt of
35   old, and delivered his people, so he will deliver them now.

12. *Afraid of a man.*—Such as thy oppressor, the king of Babylon, whom thou fearedst so, and who is now falling.

16. *That I may plant the heavens,* &c.—The new heavens and the new earth. Compare c. 65, v. 17.

18. *None to guide her.*—What follows is a picture of the misery wrought by Nebuchadnezzar's siege and destruction of Jerusalem.

19. *These two things.*—Desolation and destruction of the land is one of the two things; famine and slaughter of the people the other.

21. *Not with wine.*—Dizzy and staggering, not with wine, but with affliction from God.

23. *Laid thy body as the ground and as the street.*—A trait of the humiliation of the conquered and the insolence of the conqueror in Eastern kingdoms. So it is related that when Sapor king of Persia got on horseback, his prisoner, the Roman emperor Valerian, had to kneel down and make his back a step for him.

(CHAPTER 52)

The strain of the previous chapter is continued. Israel shall be restored, and the mountains of Judah and the waste places of Jerusalem shall rejoice at the triumphal return to Zion of the Lord with his people. This strain ends with v. 12.

3. *Ye have sold yourselves for nought.*—This is the same sort of argumentation as at c. 50, v. 1; see the note there. Egypt and Assyria acquired no perpetual rights over Israel, they never became his purchasers and legal owners; so it is now with Babylon; Babylon has no permanent property in Israel whom it so heavily oppresses; therefore the Lord, who punished Israel by giving him over for a time to his enemies, will now restore him.

7. *Thy watchmen.*—The prophets, who with joy announce God's return with his redeemed people to Zion.

11. *From thence.*—From Babylon, on their march home to the Holy Land.

ib. The vessels of the Lord.—The holy vessels of the Temple,

which had been carried off to Babylon, and which Cyrus
restored to the returning Jews. See Ezra i. 7, 8: 'Also Cyrus
the king brought forth the vessels of the house of the Lord,
which Nebuchadnezzar had brought forth out of Jerusalem,
5 and had put them in the house of his gods; even those did
Cyrus king of Persia bring forth by the hand of Mithredath the
treasurer, and numbered them unto Sheshbazzar the prince of
Judah.'

   12. *With haste.*—With haste and by flight, as ye did from
10 Egypt. The exodus from Babylon shall be not like this, but
public and triumphant.

   13. *Behold my servant,* &c.—This and the two following
verses belong to the next chapter. They declare the future
glory of God's persecuted servant.

15   14. *His visage was so marred.*—See c. 50, v. 6.

   15. *So shall many nations exult in him.*—The Vulgate has
asperget gentes multas, 'he shall sprinkle many nations;' and
so, too, has our Bible. The Greek has: 'Many nations shall be
in admiration at him.' The Chaldaic has, 'he shall *rout,*' or
20 '*scatter.*'

   ib. Kings shall shut their mouths before him.—In sign of
reverence.

(CHAPTER 53)

The application of this well-known chapter to Jesus Christ
will be in every one's mind. But it must be our concern here
25 to find out its primary historical import, and its connexion
with the discourse where it stands. On this the 50th chapter
throws much light; see particularly vv. 5–9. There we find
ill-usage and persecution of God's servant: 'I gave my back
to the smiters and my cheeks to them that plucked off the
30 hair; I hid not my face from shame and spitting.' In Jeremiah
(c. 11, v. 19) we find this persecution of God's servant, at the
hands of those who would not receive his word, threatening
to proceed even to killing: 'I was like a lamb or an ox that is
brought to the slaughter; and I knew not that they had de-
35 vised devices against me, saying, Let us destroy the tree with
the fruit thereof, and let us cut him off from the land of the

living, that his name may be no more remembered.' From the same prophet we find that in the case of Urijah, brought from Egypt and put to death under Jehoiakim, the persecution *did* proceed even to killing (Jer. xxvi. 23). From the New Testament we learn the same thing: 'Ye are witnesses unto yourselves, that ye are the children of them which killed the prophets;'—'Jerusalem, that killest the prophets' (St. Matth. xxiii. 31, 37). Leaving the Bible, from Josephus we learn the same; from the Jewish traditions, too, the same. According to these traditions, Isaiah himself was put to death by Manasseh. Adding all this to the data furnished by this 53rd chapter itself, we have for the original subject of this chapter a martyred servant of God, recognisable by the Jews of the exile under the allusions here made to him, who eminently fulfilled the ideal of the servant of God, the true Israel, the mediator of the people and the light of the Gentiles, presented in this series of chapters; and whose death, crowning his life and reaching men's hearts, made an epoch of victory for this ideal.

More, as to the first and historical meaning, cannot be said with certainty. Many attempts have been made at an identification of this 'man of sorrows' with his primary historical original, in addition to the identification of him with Christ; he has been said to be Hezekiah, Josiah, Isaiah himself, Jeremiah; but there are no sufficient grounds to establish his identity with any one of them.

The purport of the chapter is as follows. The Prophet, speaking as one of the Jewish people (as in c. 42, v. 24: 'The Lord, he against whom *we* have sinned') declares how God's faithful servant, the bearer of his commands and promises, despised, persecuted, and at last taken away from prison and judgment to die, was stricken for the iniquities of the people, bare their sins, healed them by his sufferings, and would finally, in spite, nay, by means of his death, prevail and triumph.

1. *Who believed our report.*—Literally, 'our *hearing*,' which the Greek and the Vulgate have. The report we gave of God's commands and promises and of the glorification of his servant. See the last three verses of the preceding chapter; see also

c. 49, vv. 1–8, and c. 50, vv. 7–11. The Prophet speaks in the
first verse as one of God's messengers; immediately afterwards he begins to speak as one of the sinful and undiscerning
people.

5   2. *Before him.*—Before the Lord.
       ib. A slender plant.—The word in the original means merely
a young shoot, a sapling. Not a *tender* plant, which implies
beauty, delicacy, and fostering care, but a *slender* plant, 'as a
root out of a dry ground,' thin and insignificant.

10   3. *We hid as it were our faces.*—In contempt and disgust.
       5. *The chastisement of our peace.*—The chastisement by
which our peace is won.

       7. *He was oppressed and he was afflicted.*—The Vulgate,
which throughout this chapter translates so as to heighten the

15   identification with Christ, has here: *Oblatus est quia ipse voluit,*
He was offered because he himself chose to be. It is remarkable
that in several places in this chapter the old Latin version
which the Vulgate superseded is more faithful to the original
than the Vulgate itself.

20   8. *He was taken,* &c.—Taken away from prison and from
judgment to a violent death. This and the preceding verse
are quoted in Acts viii. 32, 33, as the passage of Scripture
which the Ethiopian eunuch was reading when Philip joined
him. This verse is there quoted according to the Greek version,

25   which mistakes the original: 'In his humiliation his judgment
was taken away, and who shall declare his generation? for his
life is taken from the earth.'
       ib. Who of his generation.—Who of his contemporaries
recognised the true meaning of his death? that he died, not, as

30   we thought, by his own fault, but for us and because of our
sins.
       ib. My people.—The Prophet speaks as in God's name. The
Vulgate here makes God himself speak, and say: *Propter scelus
populi mei percussi eum,* Because of the wickedness of my

35   people I smote him.
       9. *He made his grave with the wicked.*—Compare Jer. xxvi.
23, as to the burial of the prophet Urijah: 'And they fetched
forth Urijah out of Egypt and brought him unto Jehoiakim

the king; who slew him with the sword, and cast his dead body into the graves of the common people.'

11. *He shall see of the travail of his soul.*—He shall see the fruits of his sufferings in the many whom his life and death have turned to God and saved.

ib. By his knowledge.—Compare c. 50, v. 4: 'The Lord GOD hath given me the tongue of the learned, that I should know how to speak a word in season to him that is weary,' &c. In this and the following verse God himself speaks.

(CHAPTER 54)

God's people thus purged and healed shall be eternally established; Israel shall extend his borders and multiply his sons; his enemies shall come over to him; this is the heritage of the servants of the Lord and their promised justification through God's righteous servant.

1. *Sing, O barren.*—Zion is addressed as at c. 49, vv. 18–21, and with the same promises. See the notes there. The captivity in Babylon is Zion's widowhood without her husband, the Lord; the slaughter and diminution of her people are her childlessness; this is to be more than made good after her restoration.

2. *Lengthen thy cords,* &c.—Images taken from the pitching of tents.

6. *A wife of youth.*—And therefore beloved.

9. *This is as the waters of Noah unto me.*—I deal with my people respecting this their captivity in Babylon, as I dealt with them respecting Noah's flood. The words which follow explain the particular dealing meant.

15. *Whosoever shall gather together against thee,* &c.—It had been already promised that the Gentiles should resort to Israel for salvation; here it is added that even those who try to be his enemies shall come over to him.

16. *Behold I have created,* &c.—Destroyers and destruction are God's work; they reach those only whom he means them to reach, and he does not mean them to reach Israel.

17. *Their righteousness of me.*—This is what was promised at v. 11 of the preceding chapter: 'By his knowledge shall my

righteous servant justify many.' In the original, the same word
stands both for *justification* and for *righteousness*, and what is
said here is: 'This is the heritage of the servants of the Lord
and their promised justification by me through means of my
5 righteous servant.'

(CHAPTER 55)

The Jewish people are urged to take the freely offered salvation now close at hand; but are warned that they can have it
only on condition of amending their lives.

1. *Ho, every one that thirsteth.*—Compare St. John vii. 37:
10 'Jesus stood and cried, saying, If any man thirst let him come
unto me and drink.'

3. *The sure mercies of David.*—The same sure, unfailing
mercies which I showed to David.

4. *Behold, I appointed him.*—I gave formerly the nations
15 into David's hand; so will I now into yours.

5. *Thou shalt call a nation,* &c.—See the preceding chapter,
v. 3. See also c. 52, v. 15; and c. 45, v. 14, and the notes there.

12. *For ye shall go out with joy.*—On the return to the
Holy Land. See c. 52, v. 12, and the note there.

(CHAPTER 56)

20 The warning is continued. Righteousness is needed, in order
to lay hold on God's coming salvation; but, with righteousness,
the stranger may lay hold on it as well as Israel. At v. 8 the
discourse turns abruptly, with severe threatenings, to the sloth-
ful and sinful part of the nation and their faithless guides.

25 1. *Do justice! for my salvation is near.*—This is nearly the
same as John the Baptist's preaching, St. Matth. iii. 2: 'Repent
ye, for the kingdom of heaven is at hand.'

2. *That keepeth the sabbath.*—This seems at variance with
Isaiah, c. 1, v. 13: 'The new moons and sabbaths I cannot
30 away with.' But that related to a time when the kingdom of
Judah yet stood, when the service of the Temple was in full
course, the whole exterior part of the Jews' religion splendid
and prominent. At such a time, a prophet might naturally undervalue the whole of this exterior part in comparison with the

inward part. But during the exile in Babylon all the services and sacrifices of the Temple had ceased, and the one testimony of faithfulness to their religion which the Jews among an idolatrous people could give was the observance of their Sabbath; their Sabbath was the one outward thing which brought their religion to their mind. Hence its observance acquired quite a special value.

3. *Neither let the son of the stranger,* &c.—By the law of Moses, eunuchs and strangers were not to enter into the congregation of the Lord. See Deut. xxiii. 1–8. This exclusion was now to cease. A stricter and narrower policy, however, prevailed under Ezra and Nehemiah after the return (Neh. xiii. 1–3), and in general the views of the priesthood were, on a point like this, less liberal than those of the prophets. But our prophet's whole conception of the Gentiles in relation to the religion of Israel is unexampled in the Old Testament for its admirable width, depth, and grandeur.

ib. Eunuch.—It must be remembered that, attached to a great Eastern court like that of Babylon, were a multitude of eunuchs, some of whom had perhaps adopted the religion of Israel. It is probable, also, that some of the Jewish youths were taken for the court-service as eunuchs, and their countrymen would afterwards have been likely to abhor them on that account. These considerations will enable us the better to feel the exquisite tenderness and mercifulness of this passage.

5. *Better than of sons.*—A better and more enduring name than he could have had through children born to him to keep up his name and the name of his family.

7. *Mine house shall be called an house of prayer.*—The words quoted by Jesus Christ when he cleared the temple. See St. Matth. xxi. 13.

9. *All ye beasts of the field.*—There is here an abrupt turn to the faithless part of the Jewish nation, under their negligent rulers and guides. The barbarous idolatrous nations are called, as beasts of the field and forest, to devour this easy prey.

10. *His watchmen.*—His chief men, princes, priests, and prophets.

(CHAPTER 57)

The insensibility and idolatry of the unfaithful part of the Jewish nation are reproved. The restoration of Israel is, indeed, willed by God, but it is for the righteous only.

1. *The righteous perisheth,* &c.—We are taken back to the subject of c. 53: 'Who of his generation regarded it, why he was cut off out of the land of the living?' The wicked cannot understand the meaning of the life and death of the righteous; how his perishing is not his fault, but the fault of the evil around him.

3. *But draw near,* &c.—The righteous dies and is at rest; but ye, what will ye make at last of your derision of the righteous, and of the follies and idolatries wherein ye trust? Nothing.

ib. Sons of the sorceress, &c.—Ye who have mixed yourselves up with the sorceries and idolatries of Babylon. The figure of adultery, &c., has reference to this idolatrous unfaithfulness. We find again in chapters 65 and 66 that many of the Jews in Babylon gave themselves to this, and thought it really religion and a way of safety out of their troubles.

4. *Against whom.*—The idolatrous Jews mocked and despised the pious and persisting servant of God.

5. *Under every green tree.*—The idolatrous worship in the consecrated groves of the false gods, so often mentioned in Scripture.

ib. Slaying the children in the valleys.— The most famous sacrifices of this kind were those in the valley of Hinnom. See Jeremiah vii. 31. They were made to Moloch, the king of heaven, the god of the Ammonites. But through all the kindreds of the Semitic race (to which the Babylonians, too, belonged) sacrifices of this sort seem to have been in use.

6. *They, they are thy lot.*—To them thou attachest thy luck, thy fortune. The worship of stones is a very early form of idolatry, and originated, probably, in the veneration paid to meteoric stones,—stones which, as the people said, 'fell down from heaven.' But the worship extended to other stones also. Traces of this worship occur in Genesis, in Jacob's consecration of the stones in his passage by Bethel. 'And Jacob rose up early in the morning, and took the stone that he had

put for his pillows, *and set it up for a pillar, and poured oil upon the top of it.*' Gen. xxviii. 18. The Greeks, too, had this stone worship; 'In the earlier times,' says the Greek traveller Pausanias, 'all the Greeks worshipped, in place of images of the gods, undressed stones.' We find the name *Bætylia* given to these stones, and it has even been conjectured that this name comes from Bethel.

7. *Upon a lofty and high mountain.*—The worship 'in high places' is well known.

ib. Thy bed.—The idolatry of the Jews is throughout spoken of under the figure of adultery, as unfaithfulness to God.

8. *Thy remembrance.*—Probably, small images like those of the Roman Penates or household gods, which were in every private family, and were the objects of prayers and offerings.

ib. Thou hast enlarged thy bed.—Still the figure of adultery against God committed with the false gods of Babylon.

9. *And thou wentest,* &c.—See v. 5 and the second note there. The idolatrous Jews offered precious ointment and frankincense to Moloch. Moloch was the king of heaven, but these Jews sought out all idolatrous worships and false gods, down to the gods of the underworld.

10. *Thou art wearied.*—Nothing could convince these idolatrous Jews of the folly of their misplaced trust and vain worship.

11. *And of whom hast thou been afraid.*—How could thy calamities, and the fear of thy Babylonian tyrant, make thee so superstitious and forgetful?

14. *Cast ye up.*—As before; make a clear and smooth highway for my returning people.

15. *Of a contrite and humble spirit.*—This should be noted as, what may be called, *the new test* of religion, brought in,— or at any rate first set in clear light,—by this Prophet. See also c. 66, v. 2, where this *test* is again given. Compare, too, c. 42, v. 2.

19. *I create the fruit of the lips.*—I create comfort and joy of heart, and so give cause for the outpourings of praise and thankfulness from those whom I save.

ib. Peace to him that is far off.—Again this Prophet's large conception of the extent, reaching to the Gentiles as well as Jews, of God's salvation. St. Paul quotes these words in Eph. ii. 17: 'Christ came and preached peace to you (the Gentiles) which were afar off, and to them that were nigh.'

5   21. *No peace.*—Again this warning as to the sole condition upon which God's salvation can be had. See the last verse of c. 48.

(CHAPTER 58)

Reproof continues. External worship is insufficient; a change of heart, mildness and mercy, are requisite in order that God's salvation offered to Israel may take effect.

10   1. *Cry aloud.*—God speaks to the prophet.

3. *Wherefore have we fasted?*—Besides the regular fasts of the Jewish religion, there were, during the captivity in Babylon, special fasts appointed as days of repentance and prayer for Israel.

15   *ib. Exact all your labours.*—Make your dependents do all the work you want done. Oppression, fault-finding, and harshness go on during the fast just the same.

4. *To be heard on high.*—If ye wish your voice and your prayer to be heard by God in heaven, this is not the sort of

20   fast to induce him to listen.

9. *The putting forth of the finger.*—Mockery and insolence towards the pious and persisting part of the nation.

13. *The sabbath.*—For the special importance of the Sabbath during the captivity in Babylon see c. 56, v. 2, and the

25   note there.

14. *The high places of the earth.*—In early times and in the warfare of early times the high and rocky situations were also the strong and defensible situations, and therefore he who oc-

30   cupied them was formidable and powerful.

(CHAPTER 59)

Israel's sins are what make Israel's misery and defer his salvation. But God, because Israel is his chosen instrument, will himself interpose to break up the unrighteous kingdoms of the world and to restore Israel.

3. *Your hands are defiled.*—This and what follows is a picture of the sins of the unfaithful part of the Jewish nation during the captivity in Babylon, and in spite of the lessons taught by that captivity.

5. *They hatch cockatrice' eggs.*—They hatch mischief. Cockatrice is compounded of the words *cock* and *adder*, and is a fabled venomous serpent bred from an egg. Serpents do not lay eggs, but bring forth their young alive.

ib. Weave the spider's web.—They spin vain, foolish schemes, which can only come to nought.

7. *Their feet run to evil.*—Quoted in the Epistle to the Romans (iii. 15), to prove the guiltiness before God of the Jews under their law.

9. *Therefore is judgment gone from us.*—Here the person changes, and the Prophet speaks as himself one of the sinful people, and offers up in his own name and theirs a sort of confession of sins.

ib. We wait for light, &c.—See the preceding chapter, v. 3: 'Wherefore have we fasted, and thou seest not?' Now the people know and confess the reason;—because of their sins.

10. *We grope for the wall.*—A picture of the helplessness and hopelessness of the Jewish exiles.

11. *We roar all like bears, and moan sore like doves.*—We complain loudly and obstreperously, and we complain with whining and moaning; in vain, because our heart is not right with God.

15. *He that departeth from evil maketh himself a prey.*— Again a reference, probably, to the subject of the 53rd chapter, —the death of the patient and innocent servant of God.

ib. And the Lord saw it, &c.—Israel, God's chosen instrument, failed to put down iniquity,—nay, himself fell into it. Therefore God, by the wars and convulsions which shatter the world, will himself destroy the wicked, both Jew and Gentile, and will bring about, through these wars and convulsions, the restoration of Zion and of the remnant of the true Israelites, and the salvation of the world through the light that shall spring from them.

18. *According to their deeds, &c.*—The enemies of the

Lord, whoever and wherever they are, Jew or Gentile, near
or far, shall be visited and smitten.

19. *When the enemy.*—Cyrus. See c. 45, v. 1. Cyrus and his
conquests are to be God's instruments of punishment to an
5   unrighteous world, of restoration to the true Israelites.

20. *And a redeemer shall come to Zion,* &c.—The primary
historical application of this is still to Cyrus, or, more strictly,
to the salvation which was to arise for Zion, and through Zion
for the world, out of that great storm of war and change
10   in which Cyrus was the chief human agent. St. Paul, in Rom.
xi. 26, quotes the Greek version, which differs from the original: 'There shall come out of Sion the deliverer, and shall
turn away ungodliness from Jacob.' The best Greek text has
not 'out of Sion,' as St. Paul quotes, but 'for Sion's sake.'

15   21. *My spirit that is upon thee.*—The Prophet here declares
God's promise to Israel that the line of prophets of God should
not fail.

(CHAPTER 60)

The Prophet, who has just announced '*A redeemer shall
come to Zion,*' now describes Zion as it shall be after its res-
20   toration.

1. *Arise, shine.*—Zion is addressed; the Greek, the Vulgate,
and the Chaldaic insert the explanatory word 'Jerusalem.'

2. *Darkness doth cover the earth.*—The kingdoms of the
earth are breaking up amid gloom and misery; with Israel
25   alone is light and joy in the Lord.

3. *And the Gentiles shall come to thy light.*—It shall be seen
that Israel alone has in the Lord the secret of light and joy,
and the heathen nations shall come to share it with Israel. See
c. 45, v. 14, and the notes there.

30   4. *Thy sons shall come from far.*—See c. 49, v. 22: 'The
Gentiles . . . shall bring thy sons in their arms, and thy
daughters shall be carried upon their shoulders.' The nations
amongst which the Jews are scattered shall bring them back to
the Holy Land, with offerings and treasures to restore the
35   Temple service and rebuild Jerusalem.

5. *The abundance of the sea.*—The riches of the coast-lands of the West, the Mediterranean countries, 'the isles.' More fully at v. 9.

6. *The multitude of camels.*—In this and the following verse are enumerated nations and contributions of the inland country to the south and south-east of Palestine, Arabian tribes and their respective products; in verses 8 and 9, those of the Mediterranean sea-board and the west. Midian and Ephah, with their caravan trade, Kedar (see c. 42, v. 11) and Nebaioth, with their flocks, are tribes of Northern Arabia; Sheba, with its gold and frankincense, is in Arabia Felix, to the south of them.

8. *Who are these that fly as a cloud?*—The Prophet has pictured the approach of the caravans of inland Arabia; now he pictures the approach of the fleets from the coast-lands of the Mediterranean. The fleets with their sails, as seen afar off, are compared to a cloud, or to a flock of white doves flying towards their dovecote.

9. *Tarshish.*—The Greek Tartessus, a Phœnician settlement at the mouth of the Guadalquivir, outside the Straits of Gibraltar, and representing to the Hebrews the farthest west. It was the port whence the rich mineral produce of Spain was shipped by the Phœnicians.

11. *Therefore thy gates shall be open continually.*—This trait, with many others in the present chapter, is repeated in the picture of the new Jerusalem in the Book of Revelation (xxi. 25). Here the open gates have their special reason assigned: to admit the ever in-streaming world, with its offerings and homage.

12. *For the nation and kingdom.*—Every nation shall fall unless it serves the Lord, the righteous God, the God of Israel, through whom alone is salvation. The figure of serving Israel means serving the God of Israel.

13. *The glory of Lebanon.*—A reminiscence of the building of Solomon's temple, and of the contributions to it of cedar-wood out of Lebanon (1 Kings v. 1–11), which are to be repeated now for the rebuilding of the Temple.

16. *Thou shalt also suck.*—See v. 11.

17. *For brass,* &c.—The more valuable, for the less valuable thou hast lost.

ib. Thy officers peace.—The restored Zion shall have peace-loving and righteous rulers.

21. *Thy people also shall be all righteous.*—The stress is on *all.* See c. 54, v. 13; c. 57, v. 13; and the twice-repeated warning: 'No peace, saith my God, to the wicked!'

ib. The branch.—This is in apposition with *they.* They, the branch of my planting, the work of my hands, shall inherit the land for ever. In this and the concluding verse God himself speaks.

At the end of this chapter is a pause.

(CHAPTER 61)

The Prophet speaks in his own name, as at c. 50, v. 4, which should be compared with the opening of this chapter. See also the opening of c. 49. He declares for whom his ministry and God's promises are intended, sums up the blessings of the new era at hand, and professes his joy and thankfulness for it.

1. *Unto the afflicted.*—The Vulgate, which the English Authorised Version follows, has *mansuetis,* 'the meek;' the Greek has 'the poor.' It will be remembered how (St. Luke iv. 18) Jesus Christ reads out this passage in the synagogue at Nazareth, and applies it to himself and his ministry. St. Luke uses the Greek, and makes Christ say 'the poor.'

ib. Liberty to the captives.—The expressions, 'liberty to the captives,' 'opening of the prison to the bound,' 'acceptable year of the Lord,' are all expressions with a special meaning for the Jews from the year of jubilee, when by the law of Moses the slave recovered his liberty. *Acceptable year* is more properly *gracious year,* or, *year of grace of the Lord.*

3. *Beauty for ashes.*—Beauty means *ornament* here; the signs of joy instead of the signs of mourning.

5. *And strangers.*—The Jews, a nation of God's servants appointed to initiate the rest of the world into his service, are to give themselves to this sacred and priestly labour, while the rest of the world do their secular labour for them.

7. *For your shame ye shall have double.*—See c. 40, v. 2: 'Jerusalem receiveth of the Lord's hand double for all her rue.'

ib. My people.—One of the sudden changes of person so common with this Prophet. *Ye* and *they* both relate to God's people, Israel.

10. *I will greatly rejoice.*—The Prophet speaks as already possessing by anticipation the blessings promised, and as filled with gratitude for them.

(CHAPTER 62)

For these blessings the Prophet will not cease to pray and wrestle, until they arrive, and the glorious salvation of the renewed Zion shines forth.

1. *Righteousness.*—More properly here *saving health*. The Vulgate, to make the application to Christ evident, translates: 'Until her *Just One* go forth as brightness, and her *Saviour* be lighted as a lamp.'

2. *New name.*—We have again, in the Book of Revelation, this bestowal of a *new name* upon those whom God has redeemed and renewed.

4. *My delight is in her, and thy land Married.*—In the Hebrew, Hephzibah and Beulah.

6. *I have set watchmen.*—God declares that he has set his watchmen, his angels, upon the walls of Jerusalem, to remind him of her continually. Compare c. 49, v. 16. The Prophet entreats these watchmen to ply their office without ceasing, until Jerusalem is restored.

10. *Go through, go through.*—Compare c. 40, v. 3. The immediate return of the Lord with his chosen people to Jerusalem is announced, and preparations for the triumphal march and entry are to be made.

ib. Lift up a standard for the nations.—In order that 'the Gentiles shall come to thy light, and kings to the brightness of thy rising.' See c. 60, v. 3.

(CHAPTER 63)

So sure are God's purposes that even if mortal instruments (such as Cyrus) fail, God himself will do the work upon the

enemies of Israel. The Prophet selects Edom as a kindred and neighbour people of Israel, and yet their ancient and specially bitter enemy (compare c. 34; compare also Obadiah, and Ezek. xxxv. 5, and Ps. cxxxvii. 7), who had assisted Nebuchadnezzar
5   in the destruction of Jerusalem. In a kind of short drama, of sublime grandeur, the Prophet exhibits God himself as returning from executing vengeance upon Edom.

After the 6th verse the subject changes, and the Prophet, reverting to God's old mercies towards Israel, supplicates for
10   their renewal.

1. *Who is this?*—A conqueror with blood-stained garments is supposed to appear. The spectators ask, Who is he?—He is the Lord.

ib. Bozrah.—A place in Hauran, to the north of Edom as
15   marked in the maps, but the territory of the Edomites reached there after the downfall of the Jewish kingdom. Bozrah, or Bostra, afterwards became a place of importance; the fairs of Bozrah and Damascus are mentioned as the two great Syrian fairs which Mahomet in his youth visited.

20   *ib. I that speak.*—God answers. In the next verse the spectators again question; in the three following verses God speaks.

4. *I looked, and there was none to help.*—The year of God's redeemed has come (see c. 61, v. 1, and the note there), the time for the restoration of Israel that the world might be
25   saved through Israel; the kings of the earth and the revolutions of states might fail or delay in bringing about God's designs for Israel; then God himself must interpose.

7. *I will mention.*—Here the short drama, or vision, of the Divine Conqueror of Edom ends; the Prophet reverts to God's
30   old loving-kindnesses and the deliverance from Egypt, and implores a return of the like dealings.

13. *As an horse in the desert.*—As the free, light-stepping horse of the Arab in the desert.

14. *As the beast.*—As the cattle go instinctively down to
35   sheltered places for their rest, so Israel was led to places of rest and security.

15. *The sounding of thy bowels.*—The metaphor is from

strings tightly stretched, and giving, therefore, a louder and deeper sound.

16. *Though Abraham be ignorant of us.*—Though we are in exile, strangers to the Holy Land and the polity founded by our fathers.

18. *Our adversaries.*—Babylon and the heathen nations.

(CHAPTER 64)

The supplication goes on without interruption, but it passes into a confession of sins in the name of the whole people,— sins that had grown up amidst the despair and misery of the exile,—and ends with an appeal to God's grace and mercy.

1. *That thou wouldest rend the heavens.*—That thou would-est appear once more in fire, as formerly on Sinai.

4. *Who hath prepared.*—Before *who* supply, to complete the sense, *a God.*

5. *That rejoiceth.*—In the Lord. Compare Psalm xcvii. 12: '*Rejoice in the Lord*, ye righteous.'

ib. Wroth with them continually.—With thy people Israel. One of the changes of person already noticed as frequent with this Prophet.

(CHAPTER 65)

God makes answer to the foregoing supplication. He has called his people, but in vain; they have been obstinately deaf to him, unfaithful and superstitious. The unfaithful shall be punished; but a faithful remnant shall be saved and restored to Zion, and for them the promises shall take effect.

1. *I gave ear to them*, &c.—Quoted from the Greek version, but with a transposition of the two clauses, by St. Paul in the Epistle to the Romans, x. 20: 'I was found of them that sought me not, I was made manifest unto them that asked not after me.' St. Paul applies this verse to the Gentiles, and the verse following to Israel. Here both verses apply to Israel.

3. *Gardens.*—The gardens and sacred groves of the false gods. See c. 1, v. 29: 'Ye shall be confounded for the gardens that ye have chosen.'

3. *The tiles.*—The roof-tiles of the flat-roofed Eastern houses, where the Chaldeans practised their star-worship. See Zephaniah i. 4, 5: 'I will cut off them that worship the host of heaven upon the housetops.'

4. *Remain among the graves,* &c.—The Greek adds, in explanation, 'for the sake of visions.' What is meant is the heathen practice called *incubatio,*—passing the night on tombs or in sacred places for the sake of apparitions and revelations expected there.

ib. Which eat swine's flesh, &c.—Which use for their sacrifices, and for their feasts after their sacrifices, things unclean and forbidden to Israel.

5. *Which say, Stand by thyself.*—Yet doing all this out of superstition, and out of the vain notion that it will be of religious avail to them, they insolently repel their unsuperstitious and faithful brethren as less holy than themselves.

ib. These are a smoke in my nose, &c.—Make my nostrils to smoke with wrath, and my wrath to burn like fire.

7. *Burned incense upon the mountains,* &c.—The so often mentioned idolatrous worship upon the high places. See c. lvii. v. 7.

8. *As the new wine,* &c.—The juice that shall one day be wine is in the grape-cluster, and the grape-cluster is preserved for its sake; so Israel shall be preserved, for the sake of the life and blessing to come from it.

9. *My mountains.*—The mountains of Judah in general, and the hills of Zion and Moriah in particular.

10. *Sharon.*—The strip of western coast from Joppa northwards to Cæsarea. The valley of Achor is opposed to it, as being in the east of the Holy Land, by Jericho.

11. *Fortune.*—In the original, *Fortune* and *that which destineth* are Gad and Meni. Gad means *luck,* Meni means *fate* or *destiny.* They are Babylonian names of two stars, or, stardeities; probably of the two planets held to be fortunate, Jupiter and Venus. Or, Meni may be the planet Saturn, the unlucky star, opposed to Jupiter, the star of good luck.

15. *By another name.*—A name like, *The blessed of the Lord.* See v. 23.

17. *I create new heavens.*—With the break-up of the heathen kingdoms and the restoration of Israel begins a new epoch.

20. *There shall be no more*, &c.—Child and man shall alike attain to a patriarchal age. The child shall grow up and come to old age; the sinner shall be an old man when his curse overtakes him.

22. *As the days of a tree.*—Man's life shall have, instead of its present brief term, the far longer term allotted to the life of trees.

25. *Dust shall be the serpent's meat.*—The serpent shall be harmful no more, but shall be content to feed on dust, an innocent food.

(Chapter 66)

The discourse is continued from the preceding chapter.

God declares his chief pleasure to be in piety; the sacrifices of the superstitious and unfaithful Jews shall avail them nothing, while, on the other hand, the triumph of their faithful brethren is immediately approaching. Swiftly shall Zion rise again from her ruins; then shall be held a day of the Lord to sift the unfaithful from among the righteous, and to punish them and all their like; the whole world shall afterwards flow to Zion and worship before God.

1. *The heaven is my throne*, &c.—Stephen quotes this in his speech before the council. After saying, 'Howbeit the most High dwelleth not in temples made with hands,' he goes on, 'As saith the prophet,' and quotes this passage. See Acts vii. 48–50.

2. *But to this man*, &c.—See c. 57, v. 15. The line of thought seems to be as follows: The temple is going to be rebuilt, and men's thoughts will be concentrated upon this work made with hands; in Babylon the unfaithful Jews have just shown, by even adopting the rites and sacrifices of the heathen, how prone men are to rely upon the outward parts of religion; at this moment, therefore, God will declare that what he regards is not these things, but inward religion; lowliness, contrition, and awe of his word.

3. *He that killeth an ox.*—These superstitious Jews in Babylon, who thought to be more religious than their brethren by
multiplying ceremonies and sacrifices, even those of the heathen, included in the jumble of observances to which they were
thus led, human sacrifices and rites the most repulsive and
abominable, far more than enough to countervail the other
sacrifices by which they thought, perhaps, to replace the suspended worship of the Temple. To this their superstitious unfaithfulness and self-will brought them, and to a neglect or
violation of all that God really regards.

5. *Ye that tremble at his word.*—This is addressed to the
faithful part of the nation. Their superstitious brethren had
scornfully repelled them, thinking that they glorified God by
doing so, and by multiplying the observances which constituted, they hoped, their own superior holiness: God was
indeed about to be glorified, but by the restoration of Zion
and the triumph of the faithful few, to the discomfiture of the
faint-hearted clingers to Babylon.

6. *A voice of noise*, &c.—The restoration is supposed to be
taking place. The three following verses describe its incomparable suddenness and rapidity.

12. *The glory of the Gentiles.*—See c. 60, v. 5.

14. *The hand of the Lord*, &c.—When Zion is rebuilt the
Lord will hold a great day of judgment there, to sift out and
punish his enemies.

16. *All flesh.*—Not the Jews only, but *all flesh;* and the
wicked of *all flesh* shall perish.

17. *The gardens.*—As before, the consecrated groves and
gardens of the heathen deities.

ib. *One chief in the midst.*—The *choragus* or ringleader in
the idolatrous processions and ceremonies.

ib. *Swine's flesh.*—Such uncleanness and abomination for
Israel as has already been mentioned at v. 3, and in c. 65,
v. 4, and in c. 57, vv. 5–9.

18. *It shall come.*—After this vengeance on the wicked God
will gather the world to Zion to see his glory and to worship
him.

19. *Those that escape of them.*—See c. 45, v. 20: 'Assemble

yourselves . . . ye that are escaped of the nations.' See also v. 14 of the same chapter. Those who remain of the warring nations, after the wars and destructions coming upon the earth, having been converted themselves to the God of Israel, shall go to all parts of the world spreading God's name, and setting at liberty the widely dispersed Israelites, whom they shall bring back to Jerusalem as an offering to the Lord.

ib. Tarshish, Phul, and Lud, &c.—The prophet goes from west to east in his enumeration. For Tarshish see c. 60, v. 9, and the note there. Phul is the country mentioned with Lud in Ezekiel, xxvii. 10, and by him there called Phut, where the Greek and the Vulgate translate *Libyans.* In the text now before us the Greek has Phud or Phut after the Hebrew, but the Vulgate translates *Africa.* An African people is meant, and an African people famous in the use of the bow, which the Ethiopians, for example, were. Lud is Lydia, the well-known western kingdom of Asia Minor, conquered by Cyrus before his march against Babylon. Tubal is a people in the north-east of Asia Minor. Javan is Greece, Ionia; Homer has the word Iaones, which is very near Javan; and a Greek note-writer to another poet says: 'The barbarians call all the Greeks *Iaones.*' The *sign* mentioned at the beginning of this verse consists in the converted Gentiles going to convert the more distant heathen world, and to bring the scattered Israelites home.

20. *And they shall bring,* &c.—Compare c. 43, v. 5; and c. 49, v. 12 and v. 22.

ib. An offering.—The restored Israelites shall be offered by their Gentile liberators to the Lord in Zion, as gifts are offered to the Temple.

21. *For priests and for Levites.*—Of the Gentiles also shall priests and Levites for God's service be taken. Originally priests and Levites had been taken from the tribe of Levi only, but at c. 61, v. 6 it was said of the Israelites generally: 'Ye shall be named the priests of the Lord; men shall call you the ministers of our God.' And now, finally, our Prophet's horizons widen yet more, and he admits to the priesthood and ministry of God the Gentiles also.

23. *From one new moon,* &c.—Every new moon and every

sabbath shall all flesh, Gentile as well as Jew, worship before the Lord.

24. *The men that have transgressed.*—The unfaithful and unrighteous who in the day of God's judgment have been separated and slain. See v. 16.

ib. Their worm shall not die, &c.—This expression is adopted in the New Testament: 'Where their worm dieth not, and the fire is not quenched' (St. Mark ix. 44).

THE FIRST VISION

(Chapter 21)

1. *The desert of the sea.*—The sea is the Persian Gulf to the south-east of Babylon. This heading was not improbably prefixed to the prophecy by an ancient annotator.

ib. As whirlwinds in the south, &c.—As the whirlwind passes through the desert by the sea to the south of Babylon, through that terrible land of storms and desolation, so passes the invading host through that desert, coming upon Babylon.

2. *The robber.*—The Babylonian conqueror continues to plunder and afflict the captive Jews.

ib. Elam.—The Elymais of the Greeks, the country below Susa, at the head of the Persian Gulf, and south-east of Babylon. It joins Persia proper and belonged to the Persian Empire after Cyrus had founded this.

ib. Thereof.—Of the captive Israel, whom the Median conquest of Babylon is to deliver.

3. *Filled with pain.*—The prophet has lived in Babylon and with its people until his lot seems bound up with theirs, and the first hearing of their suddenly approaching ruin fills him with dismay.

4. *The night of my pleasure.*—The nightly feastings and rejoicings of luxurious Babylon.

5. *Prepare the table,* &c.—Babylon is feasting securely.

ib. Rise, ye princes.—On a sudden is heard the watchman's cry of alarm to the princes of Babylon to oil their shields, to get ready against approaching danger.

6. *Set a watchman.*—The watchman is here the spirit of vision of the prophet himself. The Median and Persian host is described, with its various composition. Strabo mentions the use of asses by the mounted troops of certain Asiatic nations.

8. *As a lion.*—The watchman, impatient, cries in a loud and angry voice, like that of a lion, to complain of his long and vain watching. But, even while he cries, the invading column appears; and his next cry is to announce: Babylon is fallen.

9. *He hath broken.*—Cyrus, an enemy to the Babylonian idolatry.

10. *O my threshing-ground,* &c.—Under the figure of a threshing-ground and the *son of a threshing-floor* (i.e. the corn threshed upon it) the prophet describes his own beaten, crushed and pounded people.

THE KING OF BABYLON

(CHAPTER 13)

The invading host of Cyrus is at hand; the Jewish exiles in Babylon are directed to signal to the invaders to draw nigh, and to enter the proud city, which shall be dismayed and destroyed.

2. *Shake the hand.*—Beckon with the hand to the invaders.

ib. The nobles.—Of Babylon.

3. *My consecrated ones.*—God calls Cyrus and his host 'my consecrated ones' because they are his appointed instruments to work his vengeance on Babylon.

4. *In the mountains.*—The mountains between Media and the plain of the Euphrates, where the invading host, drawn from many and far nations, is mustered.

6. *Howl ye.*—Babylon and its people are addressed.

8. *As flame-faces.*—Lurid with terror.

10. *The stars of heaven,* &c.—Hebrew prophecy habitually applied to 'a day of the Lord,' such as the downfall of a mighty city or empire, figures drawn from great convulsions of nature. See c. 34, and the notes there.

14. *It shall be as the chased roe.*—The mixed multitude from all lands, who were brought together in great and rich

Babylon, shall be dismayed and dispersed at its fall, and shall
wander back as they can to the countries from whence they
came.

17. *The Medes.*—Cyrus was a Persian, and Persia afterwards
gave its name to the empire; but at this time the Persians were
only known as a contingent of the Median host, and the invading power is spoken of as *the Medes, Media.* The same in
Jeremiah li. 11.

ib. Which shall not regard silver.—The Medes are presented
as a rude, raw, and fierce people, caring more for bloodshed
than for wealth and luxury.

19. *The Chaldees.*—The people of Babylonia.

20. *The Arabian.*—The wandering Arab from the wastes of
neighbouring Arabia.

21. *Satyrs.*—Wild men with the hair and characters of the
goat. In the neighbourhood of the ruins of Babylon the belief
in such creatures as haunting the ruins still subsists.

(CHAPTER 14)

The Jews shall return home, and instead of being bondsmen
to the stranger, they shall rule the stranger; and then they shall
sing a song of triumph over their fallen tyrant, the king of
Babylon.

1. *The strangers.*—Those of the mixed multitude, gathered
in Babylon from all lands, who shall escort the Jews on their
return to Palestine, and serve them there.

4. *Proverb.*— *Proverb* is used for a taunting speech or song.
What follows may with advantage be compared, for weight
and splendour of diction, with the great *commos* at the beginning of the Chœphorœ of Æschylus.

8. *The fir-trees rejoice.*—The king of Babylon can invade
Syria and his other neighbouring countries, and waste them,
and cut down their forests, no more.

10. *All these shall speak*, &c.—The kings who are already in
Scheol, or Hades, shall rise up from their thrones in curiosity
when the great king of Babylon comes down among them,
fallen like themselves and extinguished. Their address to him

ends with the words *like unto us;* in the next verse the prophet speaks again.

12. *Lucifer.*—The bright and glorious morning-star, used as an image of the king of Babylon in his day of splendour. From the occurrence of the name Lucifer in this verse to de- 5 note a great enemy of God, it came to be transferred by the Fathers, and in the popular use of the Middle Age, to Satan himself.

13. *The mount of assembly, in the ends of the north.*—The mount of assembly of the Gods of the heathen, placed by the 10 Asiatic nations in the sacred north. Compare the Mount Meru of Indian religion, the sacred mountain of the Gods, in the Himalayas, on the extreme north of India.

18. *In his own house.*—His grave, the house of the grave. Other kings have honourable burial; the king of Babylon, slain 15 in the massacre when Babylon was taken, lies cast out like a false and dishonoured scion of royalty, a trampled carcase, covered only by the bodies of the slain.

22. *For I will rise.*—With the preceding verse the 'proverb' against the king of Babylon ends; in what follows the prophet 20 speaks in the Lord's name.

23. *I will sweep it with the besom of destruction.*—After the massacre on the night of the taking of Babylon, when Belshazzar was slain, Cyrus spared the city, and proposed to make it the third city of his empire (coming after Susa and Ecbatana), 25 and his winter-residence. He laid upon it, however, a heavy tribute. Under Darius Hystaspes it rose in revolt, and when it was at last taken after a long siege, it suffered very severely, and never recovered itself. Alexander meant to restore it, but was prevented by death. Under his successors its true desola- 30 tion began, after the foundation of Seleucia in its neighbourhood; Babylon was *exhausta vicinitate Seleuciæ*, says the elder Pliny. Its condition since that time, and at present, well answers in general to the description by prophecy of its utter desolation and ruin. 35

EDOM AND ISRAEL

(Chapter 34)

This chapter announces the ruin of Edom and its people.

4. *The host of heaven shall be dissolved*, &c.—The usual figures of prophecy for describing a 'day of the Lord.' The figures of this verse are adopted almost word for word in Revelation, vi. 13, 14.

5. *My sword hath been bathed.*—God speaks. The Vulgate has *inebriatus est gladius*. Bathed as in the wine of God's fury and made drunken.

6. *Blood of lambs and goats.*—Under the figure of a great sacrifice of lambs, goats, rams, bullocks, &c., is described the slaughter of the people and princes of Edom.

ib. Bozrah.—See note on lxiii. 1, of the Great Prophecy.

9. *Burning pitch.*—Figures drawn from the destruction of Sodom and Gomorrah. Compare xiii. 19.

11. *The line of confusion*, &c.—The measuring-line and measuring-weights of ruin and desolation.

14. *The satyr.*—See note to xiii. 21.

ib. The night-demon.—Lilith, corresponding to the *Lamia* of Greek and Roman demonology, a she-demon haunting waste places and supposed to be especially fatal to children.

15. *And lay, and hatch.* See note to lix. 5.

16. *Seek ye out of the book of the Lord, and read.*—The prophet means the book of his own prophecy. Read and mark it well, he says; everything which it announces shall come to pass. Compare Isaiah xxx. 8: 'Now go, write it before them in a table, and note it in a book, that it may be for the time to come for ever and ever.'

ib. Of these.—Of these creatures of the wilderness and desolation.

(Chapter 35)

In contrast to the ruin of Edom the Prophet now describes Israel's triumphant march home through the blossoming wilderness. For similar pictures compare in the Great Prophecy xli. 18, 19; xliii. 20; xlviii. 21; li. 3, 11 (where the last verse of the present chapter occurs over again); and lv. 12, 13.

2. *The excellency of Carmel and Sharon.*—See note to lxv. 10, in the Great Prophecy.

8. *An highway shall be there.*—Compare lxii. 10.

ib. For those.—For the chosen people, who shall find the way so plain and easy that the weakest can march in it without difficulty.

EARLY DAYS OF RETURN

(CHAPTER 24)

This chapter declares what trouble and dissolution prevail on earth in this day of God's judgments.

5. *Broken the everlasting covenant.*—Not the special covenant with Israel, but God's everlasting covenant with the whole human race. Compare Genesis ix. 16: 'And the bow shall be in the cloud; and I will look upon it, that I may remember the everlasting covenant between God and every living creature of all flesh that is upon the earth.'

10. *The city is solitary.*—Dominating the picture of the general distress, is always the image of Babylon in ruin, great and luxurious Babylon, then recently fallen.

13. *As the shaking of an olive-tree.*—Compare Isaiah xvii. 6. Among the nations of the earth men shall be scarce as the single olives left to be shaken down, or the few grapes left to be gleaned, after the harvest is gathered. Those who remain shall glorify God and his dealings.

14. *The sea.*—The Mediterranean, around which sea all this history is transacted.

15. *The coasts of the sea.*—The western sea, the Mediterranean, and thus as the *west* contrasting with the *east* in the parallel clause preceding.

16. *But I said.*—The prophet, speaking as one of the scanty and trembling remnant of Israel, newly re-established in Jeru-

salem, refuses to be glad and hopeful amid the violence and confusion prevailing around him.

16. *The robber robbeth.*—The same expression is used in the First Vision. Here it is general, denoting the world-wide confusion prevalent. See xxi. 2.

18. *The windows from on high are open.*—A figure taken from the deluge to signify the flood of ruin submerging everything.

21. *The host of heaven.*—The offending powers of heaven and the offending kings of earth shall be punished together.

22. *Visited.*—For their final sentence and punishment.

23. *His ancients.*—The elders in Jerusalem, destined to rule with God in the reign of saints.

(CHAPTER 25)

In the twenty-first verse of the preceding chapter the prophet had turned to the great future of God's triumph and glory which was to follow the present tribulation; he now goes on in the same strain.

2. *Thou hast made of a city an heap.*—The Prophet dwells on the impressive lesson of God's judgments conveyed by the recent fall of Babylon.

ib. A palace of strangers.—Of strangers and enemies to Israel.

3. *The strong people.*—This is probably said generally, and not with any special reference to the Medes who had conquered Babylon.

4. *A storm against the wall.*—The Chaldee paraphrase has, *a storm which overthrows a wall*. And this is probably the right sense; a storm so violent that it sweeps down walls before it.

5. *As the heat in a dry place.*—The clause following gives the mode in which the heat is brought down,—namely, by the shadow of clouds. As clouds quell heat, so God quells the tumult of 'the strange children' (Ps. xviii. 46, Prayer-Book Version).

6. *Unto all people a feast.*—The familiar figure of the kingdom of God as a feast at which all nations come and sit down.

'Many shall come from the east and west, and shall sit down with Abraham, and Isaac, and Jacob, in the kingdom of heaven:' Matth. viii. 11.

7. *And he will destroy in this mountain.*—The mountain is of course Zion. There is no sublimer text on the sublime theme here treated than this and the following verse.

8. *He will swallow up death in victory.*—St. Paul quotes this text, 1 Cor. xv. 54. The Greek Bible of the Seventy does not take the words thus, but the Greek versions of Aquila, Symmachus, and Theodotion do, and Theodotion has the same words as St. Paul.

ib. The rebuke of his people.—The reproach of failure cast on the people of righteousness.

10. *Moab.*—Moab is, with Edom, the standing type of the bitter and eternal enemy of God's people, and the triumph of God's people involves always vengeance upon Moab and Edom. Compare xxxiv, xxxv. Ezekiel puts Moab and Edom together, as offenders against Israel. See Ezek. xxv. 8–14.

11. *They shall spread forth.*—The wily Moab tries to save himself by swimming in the filthy pool where he is trodden down; but in vain.

12. *Thy walls.*—Moab is addressed. *He* refers to God.

(CHAPTER 26)

The strain of elation and of trust in God continues. But the prophet, after celebrating the fall of those who have lorded it over God's people, turns his eyes upon the restored remnant and cannot but perceive how small and ineffectual it is, how far its actual power falls short of its high hopes and destinies. But the people of righteousness shall re-live; the earth shall give up God's saints, who are dead, to live with their re-animated nation, and to do God's work and share his reign when the present tyranny and tribulation are overpast.

1. *Salvation will God appoint.*—God's salvation shall be in place of walls and bulwarks to his Zion. Compare the Great Prophecy, lx. 18.

5. *The lofty city.*—Again the prophet recurs to Babylon and its recent fall.

10. *So will he not learn.*—The prosperity of the wicked misleads men; unless unrighteousness is punished, mankind will not quit it.

13. *Other lords.*—The former captors and oppressors of Israel, with especial reference to Babylon. They are now visited and destroyed.

15. *Thou dost increase.*—God is now restoring and exalting Israel again, and giving to him wide dominion.

16. *Lord, in trouble we sought thee,* &c.—But Israel, speaking by the prophet's voice, sees with disquietude and discouragement how ineffectual are his actual means, how little he has yet performed, how small are his present numbers.

19. *Thy dead men shall live.*—Sublimely recovering himself, the prophet cries that God's saints (*Thy dead men*), though they are dead, shall live, and, with the lifeless but re-animated body of the restored exiles (*my dead body*), shall found the kingdom of righteousness, after the present distress.

ib. A dew of life.—Literally 'a dew of lights.' *Light* and *life* are in the Bible, as is well known, interchangeable ideas.

ib. Thy dew.—God's dew.

ib. The earth shall bring forth the dead.—It may easily be conceived how this magnificent verse, taken literally, became a signal text for the doctrine of the resurrection of the dead which from this time onward began to prevail among the Jews. Compare Ezek. xxxvii. 1–14, and Dan. xii. 2.

20. *Come, my people.*—God's voice exhorts Israel to patience and quiet until the storms of the troubled present shall have blown over.

21. *The earth also shall disclose.*—Iniquity shall no more remain hidden and unpunished.

(CHAPTER 27)

The prophet continues to depict God's care for the city and people of righteousness, and their assured permanency.

1. *Leviathan,* &c.—Probably the great Asiatic empires in general are here meant, and not any two of them in particular. 'The dragon' is the Biblical name for Egypt.

2. *The fair vineyard.*—A common Biblical figure for Israel. Compare Psalm lxxx. 8.

4. *Fury is not in me,* &c.—God is a gracious God, full of love and care for his vineyard; but if he is provoked by enemies of his vineyard (the briers and thorns) he will scatter 5 and consume them, if indeed they do not (as they had better) prevent his wrath by humbling themselves and making peace with him.

7. *Hath he smitten him,* &c.—Israel has been punished, but not as his enemies and destroyers have been punished. Exile 10 was in God's eyes a sufficient punishment for Israel, and his putting away idolatry is a sufficient title for re-admission to God's favour. Not such is Babylon's punishment and end, for Babylon is 'a people of no understanding.'

10. *There shall the calf feed,* &c.—Babylon shall be aban- 15 doned to desolation; the leafage of its gardens shall be browsed by animals or broken off for the oven.

12. *The Lord shall sift corn.*—Under the figure of sifting corn is announced the final collection and restoration of all the true Israel, however outcast and scattered. The *river* is 20 Euphrates; the *stream of Egypt* is the torrent-bed of El Arisch, marking the boundary between Palestine and Egypt.

13. *Assyria . . . Egypt.*—The prophet reverts to old scenes of Israel's captivity to figure the house of bondage from which God's people shall be eternally delivered. 25

Critical and Explanatory Notes

References to Arnold's diary-notebooks are drawn from H. F. Lowry, K. Young, and W. H. Dunn, eds., *The Note-Books of Matthew Arnold* (London: Oxford University Press, 1952), supplemented by W. B. Guthrie, ed., *Matthew Arnold's Diaries: the Unpublished Items* (Ann Arbor: University Microfilms, 1959). Arnold's correspondence with his publishers is quoted from W. E. Buckler, ed., *Matthew Arnold's Books* (Geneva: Droz, 1958). Most quotations from his other letters are taken from the collection by G. W. E. Russell, where they can be found under their dates; the collection has been published in so many editions that page references are not helpful. A very few quotations are from unpublished letters; most of these can be traced through Arthur Kyle Davis's *Matthew Arnold's Letters: a Descriptive Checklist* (Charlottesville: The University Press of Virginia, 1968). Notes to cancelled passages of an essay are placed after the other notes to that essay.

[A WORD ABOUT AMERICA]

Arnold's first essay on America had a long gestation. When he saw Thomas Wentworth Higginson's review of *Mixed Essays* in the *North American Review* for July, 1879, he wrote to Henry James: "I want a few words of confirmation or of dissuasion from you before I write a page or two which I have it in my head to write about America. I don't know whether you saw what Mr. (Colonel?) Higginson said in the last North American Review— of my never, in my social disquisitions, using the materials offered me by America. You will find it at any Club. The truth is, I have my ideas about America, but never having been there, I am extremely shy of bringing them out." (He was at that very time reading *Roderick Hudson*, to which he would allude in the essay.) Presumably in the autumn of the same year he saw by some

449

means the comment on himself in the *Boston Daily Advertiser* for
November 18. James Russell Lowell's arrival as United States minister in London in 1880 led to a meeting with him and a friendly
correspondence that set Arnold to reading Lowell's essays in the
early spring of 1882. By that time Arnold was at last working on
his essay and was beginning to make plans for a lecture tour in
America for the following winter (a tour subsequently deferred
until the winter of 1883–84). Thus the essay was almost deliberately a forerunner of the *Discourses in America,* and indeed contains the seeds of the lecture on "Numbers." Arnold was pleased
with its reception: "I think you would have liked it," he wrote to
M. E. Grant Duff on July 29. "One had to trust a great deal to
one's 'flair,' but I think my 'flair' served me here pretty well. At
any rate, Henry James, the novelist, being asked by [James T.]
Knowles [editor of the *Nineteenth Century*] to write a reply to
it, said after reading it that he could not write a reply to it, it was
so true, and carried him so along with it."—*Letters,* ed. Russell.
On May 18 he acknowledged a note from Lowell with the remark: "We may have types of Philistine that you have not, but
whoever neither *is* καλὸς κᾱγαθός, nor has the ideal of becoming so,
is surely a Philistine, and I imagine there are but too many of such
people, on both sides the Atlantic. John Morley, who has seen
you [i.e., America] with his own eyes, wrote to me that he was
particularly pleased with my insisting on its being just the same
people there and here. He added, that you had one or two advantages which we have not, and three or four disadvantages; perhaps
it may be more true to say, reversing the proportion, that you have
three or four advantages as compared with us, and one or two
disadvantages." He wrote the essay between April 8 and 16, 1882, it
was published in the *Nineteenth Century* for May, and he received
£50 in payment. It has been edited, with notes, by Kenneth Allott,
Five Uncollected Essays of Matthew Arnold (Liverpool: University Press, 1953).

   1:1–12. Lowell's essay first appeared in the *Atlantic Monthly*
XXIII, 82–94 (January, 1869); it was republished in his *My Study
Windows* (Boston and London, 1871). Arnold quotes from the
final paragraph. His diary shows that he was reading "in Lowell"
on March 29 and April 6, 1882. "A consummation devoutly to be
wished" is *Hamlet* III, i, 63–64.

   1:16–19. Higginson, "Recent Essays," *North American Review*
CXXIX, 98–99 (July, 1879)—a review of *Mixed Essays* and other
books.

1:19–2:21. "Novelists and Critics of American Manners," *Boston Daily Advertiser*, Tuesday, November 18, 1879, p. 2, col. 2, referring to the review by Harriet Waters Preston of Arnold's *Mixed Essays* in the *Atlantic Monthly* XLIV, 675–78 (November, 1879). Arnold draws entirely from the newspaper, not from the *Atlantic*, and the newspaper's quotations from p. 677 of the review are not quite *verbatim;* moreover the word "vulgarity" is not Arnold's but the reviewer's. Henry James was by this time living in England; the novelist Howells was editor of the *Atlantic Monthly* from 1871 to 1881. As Arnold was about to board the train at St. Pancras station for Liverpool and America in the autumn of 1883, he praised Henry James to an interviewing reporter: "There is nothing objectionable in his books. They can be put into anybody's hands." He said he had been reading Howells with great pleasure: "His 'Lady of the Aroostook' is delightful, and strikes me as his best work."—*Pall Mall Gazette*, November 2, 1883, p. 11.

2:22–23. But he had quoted with approval the passage from Renan he repeats in the present essay, p. 14. And Professor Kenneth Allott indicates other passages in Arnold's public writings and private letters that say much the same thing.—*Five Uncollected Essays*, p. viii.

2:26–27. For example, "Look at America; it is the same race; whether we are first or they, Anglo-Saxonism triumphs," and "America is just ourselves, with the Barbarians quite left out, and the Populace nearly."—"My Countrymen" (1866) and Preface to *Culture and Anarchy* (1869), *Prose Works*, ed. Super, V, 30, 243.

3:3–8. *Works and Correspondence* (London: Rivingtons, 1852), II, 435, in an Appendix of detached notes; jotted in one of Arnold's "General Note-Books."—*Note-Books*, ed. Lowry, p. 538.

3:12–13. In fact, Arnold was thinking of making a lecture tour of America the following autumn; he actually made it in the winter of 1883–84 and he visited the United States again in the summer of 1886, by which time his daughter had married an American.

3:26–29. Jonah 1:1–3.

3:31–34. Heinrich von Ewald, *Commentary on the Prophets of the Old Testament*, tr. J. Frederick Smith (London, 1881), V, 97. Arnold's pocket diary indicates that he was reading "in Jonah" from April 10–15, 1882, and "in Ewald" from April 16–27.—*Note-Books*, ed. Lowry, p. 603.

4:4–5. Arnold had been using this description repeatedly in the past three or four years: in "Equality" (1878), "Irish Catholicism and British Liberalism" (1878), " 'Ecce, Convertimur ad Gentes' "

(1879), "Wordsworth" (1879), "The Future of Liberalism" (1880), and "The Incompatibles" (1881).—*Prose Works*, ed. Super, VIII, 299, 302, 345; IX, 8, 38, 158, 273.

4:7–11. "Condescension in Foreigners," final paragraph.

4:17–29. H. Hussey Vivian, *Notes of a Tour in America, from August 7th to November 17th, 1877* (London, 1878), p. 233. The *Notes* were first published in *The Cambrian*, a Swansea newspaper. Henry Hussey Vivian (1821–94), who developed his family copper smelting business into one of the largest metallurgical plants in the world, sat as a Liberal in Parliament from 1852 to 1893, when he was made Baron Swansea. Arnold's pocket diary shows him reading Vivian's book from April 3–8, 1882.

5:12–19. See p. 1:19n.

5:24–25. This sentence is the germ of the lecture on "Numbers" that Arnold wrote for his American lecture tour.

6:8–13, 17–27. See p. 1:19n.

7:6–7. *Roderick Hudson*, James's first novel, was published in book form in 1876. A revised London edition in three volumes came out in 1879. In the late summer of that year, Arnold wrote to James: "We like Roderick extremely, but are not through him yet. I read a chapter or two aloud the evenings I am at home, and he is religiously kept for this purpose; I am a good deal away just at this time, and so we do not get him so often as we could wish. But your writing is so good and so *fin* that it bears being taken slowly." A year and a half after the publication of this essay, on December 11, 1883, Arnold lectured on "Literature and Science" in Northampton, Massachusetts.

7:18–21. See p. 2:26–27n.

8:11–18. A combination of statements made in leading articles of *The Nonconformist* XXIV, 966 (November 30, 1864) and *The Daily News*, December 7, 1864, p. 4, cols. 3–4, quoted in "My Countrymen" (1866).—*Prose Works*, ed. Super, V, 5.

8:20–21. "Ye are the salt of the earth."—Matthew 5:13.

8:21–24. Speech at Leeds, October 8, 1866, reported next day in *The Morning Star*, p. 2, col. 5, and *The Times*, p. 7, col. 5; jotted in Arnold's pocket diary for October 12 and quoted in "Culture and Its Enemies" (1867).—*Note-Books*, ed. Lowry, pp. 36–37; *Prose Works*, ed. Super, V, 108.

8:26–37. Speech introducing R. W. Dale's lecture on "The Rise of Evangelical Nonconformity," given in Islington on February 10, 1880, reported in *The Times* next day, p. 11, cols. 1–2, and quoted in "The Future of Liberalism" (1880).—*Prose Works*, ed. Super, IX, 154.

9:2–13. Bright spoke in this manner at a banquet at Rochdale, December 18, 1879, to welcome T. B. Potter, M. P., on his return from America; reported in *The Times* next day, p. 4, cols. 1–4. In his pocket diary for the 19th Arnold wrote: "In to-day's *Times: Bright's Speech on United States.—Note-Books*, ed. Lowry, p. 329. See "Numbers" (1883), p. 144.

9:22. "By their fruits ye shall know them."—Matthew 7:20.

9:27–29, 33–35. See p. 1:19n.

10:6–9. See *Culture and Anarchy* (1868), *Prose Works*, ed. Super, V, 186.

10:9–13. Arnold's pat description of the middle class at this time; see "Equality" (1878), "Irish Catholicism and British Liberalism" (1878), " 'Porro Unum Est Necessarium' " (1878), "The Future of Liberalism" (1880), "The Incompatibles" (1881), and "An Unregarded Irish Grievance" (1881).—*Prose Works*, ed. Super, VIII, 302, 322, 362, 369; IX, 148, 276, 296. He jotted the expression in his pocket diary for March 22, 1879, and June 13, 1880, as well as in one of his "General Note-Books."—*Note-Books*, ed. Lowry, pp. 317, 339, 542.

10:15–17. Arnold listed these "instincts" or "powers" in "Equality" (1878), the Preface to *Mixed Essays* (1879), "A Speech at Eton" (1879), "The Future of Liberalism" (1880), and "The Incompatibles" (1881).—*Prose Works*, ed. Super, VIII, 287, 372; IX, 26–27, 142, 271, and Indexes, *s.v.* "civilization, powers of" and "powers of life." These "powers" were central to his argument in "Literature and Science" (1882): see pp. 61–62.

10:26–28. Arnold no doubt read some of the American criticisms of *Literature and Dogma*.

10:32–11:7. R. W. Dale, *Impressions of America* (New York, 1879), pp. 167, 201. "To a Nonconformist traveling in America, one of the freshest sensations arises from the absence of an ecclesiastical establishment."—p. 169. *Whitaker's Almanack*, an annual compendium of information that has been published since 1868 (for 1869), listed 175 sects in England and Wales in 1882. Dale, one of the leading Nonconformist ministers, was an acquaintance of Arnold's. See "The Church of England" (1876), *Prose Works*, ed. Super, VIII, 84–85. He spent seven or eight weeks in the United States in the early autumn of 1877.

11:8–10. Arnold's authority is Dale, p. 201.

454   *Critical and Explanatory Notes*

12:9–12, 24–28. "Condescension in Foreigners," ¶9, 18, 9.

14:1–3. *Ibid.*, ¶21.

14:3–8. *Questions contemporaines* (2nd ed.; Paris, 1868), p. vii (Preface), quoted by Arnold in his Preface to *Culture and Anarchy* (1869), *Prose Works*, ed. Super, V, 241. Arnold jotted the quotation in one of his "General Note-Books."—*Note-Books*, ed. Lowry, p. 498.

14:8–10. Arnold attributed this expression to Michelet in a letter to Clough about February 24, 1848, and jotted it in his pocket diary for April 27, 1877.—*Letters of Matthew Arnold to Arthur Hugh Clough*, ed. H. F. Lowry (London: Oxford University Press, 1932), p. 66; *Note-Books*, ed. Lowry, p. 276.

14:13. Quinion was manager of the wine importing firm of Edward Murdstone, David Copperfield's stepfather (see line 30). Arnold chose Murdstone, Quinion, and the schoolmaster Creakle as types of the English middle class in "The Incompatibles" (1881), *Prose Works*, ed. Super, IX, 274–82.

14:15–23. André Theuriet, quoted by *The Pall Mall Gazette*, September 12, 1881, p. 5; jotted in Arnold's pocket diary for July 30.—*Note-Books*, ed. Lowry, p. 356. Theuriet (1833–1907) was a novelist of provincial life in France. The *Pall Mall* draws upon Theuriet's essay on Twain in *Parlement*—one of a series by him on "Poets and Humourists." He found the vogue for Twain a sign of the vulgarity, the "rustic tastes" of the American public, evidence of the evil effects of democracy upon literature.

16:1–17:16. Isabella L. Bird, *A Lady's Life in the Rocky Mountains* (New York, 1879–80), pp. 44 or 49 ("make myself agreeable"), 50 ("catch and saddle a horse"), 51–57 (with omissions). She was on her way from Cheyenne, Wyoming, through Fort Collins to Estes Park, not "on her journey from Denver to the Rocky Mountains." Miss Bird (1831–1904), author also of books of travel in Hawaii and Japan, made her journey to the Rockies by herself in the autumn of 1873 and wrote her account of it in the form of letters to her sister, "without the remotest idea of publication"; they appeared serially in the *Leisure Hour* in 1878 and then as a book, which occurs on a reading list in Arnold's pocket diary for 1880.—*Note-Books*, ed. Lowry, p. 598. On March 28, 1882, he jotted, "extract in Miss Bird." The Covenanters were rigorously doctrinal Scottish Calvinists. Thomas Boston, a Scottish Presbyterian minister, published his *Human Nature in its Fourfold State* in 1720; it went through several dozen editions in the next century and a half.

17:38–18:1. "Is there no balm in Gilead."—Jeremiah 8:22.

18:17. "Ah, the rowdy Philistine!" said Arminius von Thunder-ten-Tronckh by way of recognizing the Young Lion of *The Daily Telegraph.—Friendship's Garland* (1870), *Prose Works,* ed. Super, V, 346–47.

18:24–25. Arnold cited this remark in "The Incompatibles" (1881) in a similar context and in "An Unregarded Irish Grievance" (1881).—*Prose Works,* ed. Super, IX, 284, 305. Lord Frederick went to Dublin on May 6, 1882—a week after this essay appeared—as successor to Arnold's brother-in-law W. E. Forster as chief secretary for Ireland and was assassinated while walking in Phoenix Park on the day of his arrival.

18:29. "While ye have light, believe in the light, that ye may be the children of light."—John 12:36. The expression, a favorite of Arnold's, occurs also in Luke 16:8, Ephesians 5:8, and I Thessalonians 5:5.

18:38. Charles Guiteau shot President Garfield in Washington on July 2, 1881. He attempted to support his defence of insanity by unruly behavior in the courtroom during his ten-week trial, in the course of which the lawyers were almost as outrageous as the prisoner. He was convicted on January 25, 1882, and executed on June 30.

19:3–6. "Condescension in Foreigners," ¶20.

19:6–17. The Coercion Act, which gave the authorities a right to arrest and detain persons suspected of subversive activities in Ireland, made no distinction between subjects of the Crown and others in Ireland, and the legal net caught some dozen American citizens, most or all of them Irishmen who had been naturalized in the United States, then returned and resumed their domicile in Ireland. The outraged American press demanded strong measures to protect American citizens, and in February, 1882, the House of Representatives called upon the President to provide detailed information as to American citizens arrested in Ireland. Lowell, as United States minister in London, made his report on March 14. A mass meeting at the Cooper Union in New York on April 3 was one of many attacks on his conduct. See H. E. Scudder, *James Russell Lowell, a Biography* (Boston, 1901), II, 280–93. The report in *The Times* (April 5, p. 5, cols. 3–5) of the Cooper Union meeting carries the tone, but not quite the language, Arnold cites. "This very week" would be about April 15.

19:23. Grub Street, the London street which in the eighteenth century became symbolic of the impoverished hack writer, was the address from which Arnold dated his satiric *Friendship's Garland* letters in 1866–70.

19:26–31. Arnold's essay on "Copyright" (1880) was in part a reply to S. S. Conant's article on "International Copyright," *Macmillan's Magazine* XL, 151–61 (June, 1879).—*Prose Works*, ed. Super, IX, 127–35. Conant, managing editor of *Harper's Weekly*, reaffirmed his view in *The Academy* XVI, 125–26 (August 16, 1879).

19:34. Horace *Odes* I. iii. 9.

20:17–19. Edward L. Pierce, *Memoir and Letters of Charles Sumner, 1811–1845* (Boston, 1877), II, 215 (letter of July 8, 1842), quoted by Arnold in "Equality" (1878) and several times thereafter.—*Prose Works*, ed. Super, VIII, 283–84, 338, 359–60.

21:18–19. See p. 14:1–3.

21:22. "But one thing is needful" ("Porro unum est necessarium"), from Luke 10:42, is the title Arnold gave to the chapter of *Culture and Anarchy* in which he discussed the religion of the middle class.

21:35–22:1. "Réflexions et Maximes," *Oeuvres de Vauvenargues*, ed. D.-L. Gilbert (Paris, 1857), I, 386–87 (nos. 133, 135 and footnote). Arnold's pocket diary shows that he was reading in Vauvenargues almost daily while he was writing this essay.

23:14–16. Arnold may have drawn his list from James Fraser, *Report [to the Schools Inquiry Commission] on the Common School System of the United States, &c.* (London, 1866), pp. 19, 141, *et passim.* But "astrology" is surely, in Arnold's essay, a slip for "astronomy." Dale also comments on American education.

23:17–18. Réflexions et Maximes," I, 399 (no. 217, footnote).

23:28–29. P. T. Barnum's greatest achievement as a proprietor of the Barnum and Bailey Circus was the purchase in January, 1882, of Jumbo, an African elephant thought to be the largest in the world, from the London Zoological Society, who had exhibited him in Regent's Park for seventeen years. Though he was sold because his temper was becoming uncertain, there was outraged protest from the newspapers and from the entire British public. The Queen and the Prince of Wales demanded that the contract be broken. Lowell, the American minister, remarked at a banquet in London that "the only burning question between England and America is Jumbo." The sale was not overthrown, however, even by a suit in the Court of Chancery; Jumbo arrived in New York on Easter Sunday, April 9, 1882, and for three and a half years was the most popular attraction of the circus. He was killed by a railway locomotive while the circus was loading on September 15,

1885, his skeleton was presented to the Museum of Natural History in New York, and his mounted hide is still to be seen in the Barnum Museum of Tufts University in Medford, Massachusetts. —Irving Wallace, *The Fabulous Showman* (New York: Alfred Knopf, 1959), pp. 289–95.

[AN ETON BOY]

With King Cetywayo coming to London and the subject of frequent newspaper articles, interest in the recent Zulu War was still strong enough to warrant the publication of this essay in the *Fortnightly Review* for June, 1882. Though Arnold speaks of having come upon the memoir of Lieutenant Mynors by chance, the essay is the sort of thing he did occasionally, especially in his later years, to oblige a friend; there is no reference to it, however, in his published correspondence. He wrote the article between April 29 and May 17, and was paid £25 for it by the publisher of the *Fortnightly*. The abundance of quotation from Mynors gives the essay a political and social tone quite unlike Arnold's usual tone; it reminds us, however, of his recurring sense of the pathos of the early death of a promising and bright young man. Arnold's nephew, Thomas's son Arthur, also died in the Zulu War.

24:2–4. In *A French Eton* (1864), *Schools and Universities on the Continent* (1868), and more recently in " 'Ecce, Convertimur ad Gentes' " (1879) and "An Unregarded Irish Grievance" (1881). —*Prose Works*, ed. Super, II, IV, IX.

24:16. The earliest use of "modus vivendi" cited by the *N.E.D.* is from *Notes and Queries* for August 9, 1879, p. 109, which said: "This formula is in daily use to express a practical compromise."

24:29. "Marriage with a deceased wife's sister" was the aim of a recurrent bill proposed by the "political Dissenters," recurrently ridiculed by Arnold, most notably in *Culture and Anarchy*, chapt. vi (1868) and *Friendship's Garland*, Letter VIII (1869).—*Prose Works*, ed. Super, V, 205–8, 313–18.

25:1–2. "Now his parents went to Jerusalem every year at the feast of the passover, . . . after the custom of the feast."—Luke 2:41–42. Arnold frequently made sport of the Birmingham Nonconformist Liberals led by Joseph Chamberlain and Jesse Collings, though he was not without respect for them as well. See Introduction to *God and the Bible* (1874), *Prose Works*, ed. Super, VII, 145, and Index to later volumes in that edition. The term "caucus," long common in the United States, was used in England by Lord Beaconsfield in 1878 with reference to the Birmingham Liberal

"Six Hundred," a committee aimed at securing concerted political action for the party in that constituency. The Caucus-race in *Alice in Wonderland* was more than a decade earlier, and of course no one knew what it meant.

25:4–15. Mary Raleigh, ed., *Alexander Raleigh: Records of His Life* (Edinburgh, 1881), p. 53. Raleigh wrote "and we shall look back on." Raleigh (1817–80) was an Independent (Congregational) preacher who ended his ministry as successor to Arnold's acquaintance Dr. John Stoughton at Kensington Chapel. A friend of Raleigh's records that Arnold's definition of God as a *"Power not ourselves which makes for righteousness"* was one of Raleigh's favorite aversions. "He was never tired of inveighing against its insufficiency, its cumbrousness, its ugliness, though no man lived more entirely in its meaning."—p. 233. In one of his last addresses Raleigh also used Arnold's expression "stream of tendency," meaning, however, merely "trend" or "practice."—p. 285. Stamford Hill, where Raleigh preached from 1871 to 1875, is the main road north from Stoke Newington, in North London.

26:9–10. The Conservatives, Arnold said, habitually relied on the authority of "our traditional, existing social arrangements." See "The Future of Liberalism" (1880), *Prose Works*, ed. Super, IX, 143.

26:12–13. "Verily I say unto you, That a rich man shall hardly enter into the kingdom of heaven. And again I say unto you, It is easier for a camel to go through the eye of a needle, than for a rich man to enter into the kingdom of God."—Matthew 19:23–24 (Mark 10:24–25, Luke 18:24–25).

26:21–22. "The battle of Waterloo was won on the playing fields of Eton" was a remark attributed (probably apocryphally) to the great Duke of Wellington by Montalembert, *De l'Avenir politique de l'Angleterre* (1855), chapt. xi, ¶4.

27:4–5. An echo of George Sand's words: "Le sentiment de la vie idéale, qui n'est autre que la vie normale telle que nous sommes appelés à la connaître" ("the sentiment of the ideal life, which is none other than man's normal life as we shall some day know it"). —*Journal d'un Voyageur pendant la guerre* (4th ed.; Paris, 1871), p. 2, jotted in Arnold's pocket diary for May 21, 1877, and quoted in his essay on George Sand (1877).—*Note-Books*, ed. Lowry, p. 277; *Prose Works*, ed. Super, VIII, 219.

27:11–15. *Letters and Diary of the late Arthur C. B. Mynors, Lieut. 3rd Batt., 60th Rifles, who died at Fort Pearson, Natal, the 25th day of April, 1879, from 19th February, the date of his sailing for Natal, to the 15th of April; together with some other letters and notices relating to him* (Margate: H. Keble, Steam Printer, "Gazette" Office, Albert Terrace, 1879). "The volume has been printed, not for publication, but for private circulation among his relatives and friends."—Preface, p. 7.

27:19–20. Arnold matriculated at Oxford on November 28, 1840. Mynors' father, Robert, was at Christ Church from 1837 to 1841; an uncle, Edmund, was an undergraduate with Arnold at Balliol College from 1841, and another uncle, Walter, was an undergraduate at Oriel College from 1845, while Arnold was a fellow there. The family seats were at Treago, Herefordshire, and Evancoyd, Radnorshire. Young Arthur matriculated at Christ Church, Oxford, in 1875, and was commissioned 2nd lieutenant on May 11, 1878.

27:25–28:3. From a memorial paragraph to Mynors in the *Eton College Chronicle,* June 20, 1879, quoted on p. 66 of the *Letters and Diary.* "Election" of scholars for the coming year at Eton took place on the last Monday of July; it was a time of great festivity and marked the end of the school year.

28:1. The Zulu War began in January, 1879, with the invasion of Zululand by a British force under Lt.-General Frederic Thesiger, Lord Chelmsford, after an ultimatum to the Zulu king Cetywayo from the British high commissioner Sir Bartle Frere was unanswered. Most of Chelmsford's central column was overwhelmed and slaughtered on January 22 at Isandhlwana; another column under Col. Charles Knight Pearson garrisoned Ekowe, where they were cut off until Chelmsford's relief reached them on April 3. On the day before the relief Chelmsford's camp was attacked by a force of about 10,000 Zulus at Ginginhlovo, but the Zulus were repulsed.

28:7–30. *Letters and Diary,* pp. 9–10. Durrant's Hotel, Manchester Square, was where Mynors' family was staying in London.

28:32–29:36. *Ibid.,* pp. 11–13.

29:37–39. *Ibid.,* p. 14.

30:1–25. *Ibid.,* pp. 15–16. *The Graphic* on March 1 printed sketches of the embarkation of the 60th Rifles at Gravesend and of the steamship *Dublin Castle* lying there at anchor (p. 204). Other sketches from shipboard appeared on March 15 (p. 272) and March 29 (the negro minstrelsy, p. 308). There are sketches of the battle of Ginginhlovo on May 17 (pp. 480–81) and of the 60th Rifles relieving Ekowe on May 24 (pp. 500, 508, 517).

30:26–28. *Letters and Diary,* p. 17.

30:28–31. *Ibid.*, p. 18.

30:33–31:25. *Ibid.*, pp. 20–21.

31:26–31. *Ibid.*, pp. 21–23. Mynors calls the fort "Etshowe," *The Graphic* uses Arnold's spelling.

31:33–33:16. *Ibid.*, pp. 23–26, with variants.

33:17–34:3. *Ibid.*, pp. 26–27. Lt.-Col. Edward Hopton of the 88th Foot is described in the Preface as "a very old and much esteemed friend of the family."

34:6–36:13. *Ibid.*, pp. 28–31, with variants. W. L. Pemberton and F. W. Northey were lieutenant-colonels in the 60th regiment, The King's Royal Rifle Corps; Arthur Tufnell became a major during the campaign, C. P. Cramer was a captain, and R. H. Gunning was a lieutenant. G. C. J. Johnson was a lieutenant in the 99th.

36:23–38:26. *Ibid.*, pp. 32–37, with variants.

38:27–41:20. *Ibid.*, pp. 38–43, with variants. Edward T. H. Hutton, a fellow lieutenant, became a captain shortly thereafter. Capt. the Hon. Keith Turnour was son of the fourth Earl Winterton.

41:28–42:26. *Ibid.*, pp. 44–46.

42:30–43:2. *Ibid.*, pp. 49–50.

43:3–5. *Ibid.*, pp. 47, 66 (memorial paragraph in the *Eton College Chronicle*).

43:5–12. *Ibid.*, p. 48.

43:30–44:19. *Ibid.*, pp. 54–55, 66, 51–52, with variants.

44:19–23. *Ibid.*, p. 85. The memorial volume prints the commemorative sermon preached in the College Chapel on July 6, 1879, by the Rev. Edmond Warre, a master at Eton from 1861 and headmaster after 1884.

44:36. "The old order changeth, yielding place to new."—Tennyson, "The Passing of Arthur," line 408.

45:14. *La Fille Élisa* (1877) is a novel by Edmond de Goncourt about a young lady of ill repute. *Nana* (1880), a novel by Zola, tells the story of a courtesan of the "demi-monde" of the second Empire; it is a sequel of *L'Assommoir*, and Arnold read it in the summer of 1882.

45:23. Thucydides conceived that his account of the Peloponnesian War would be "a possession for ever."—I, xxii, 4. See p. 165:4.

45:27–28. "A Letter to a Noble Lord" (1796), three-fifths through. The quotation, a favorite of Arnold's, occurs repeatedly in his *Note-Books* and his prose works.

[A SEPTUAGENARIAN POET]

Arnold was speaking to Edith Simcox about Rossetti on May 2, 1882, when she brought up the name of one of the late poet's friends, W. B. Scott, who had just then published a new book of poems. Arnold expressed his distress that so little notice had been given to the publication and promised a review in *The Pall Mall Gazette* if Scott would send him a copy. Since the *Pall Mall* had already designated another reviewer, however, Arnold sent his remarks to the *St. James's Gazette*, a rival evening paper founded about two years earlier by Frederick Greenwood. (He had edited the *Pall Mall* for fifteen years from its founding in 1865 until his resignation when that paper passed from George Smith's ownership to Yates Thompson's.) Arnold reported to Miss Simcox: "There was very little of mine, because I wanted to give as much as possible of my author. I rather fancied this volume at the expense of the much more ambitious *Year of the World*, which probably, being an unsound production, is a special favourite with its parent; but I think that I gave the best things of the new volume, and Lord Houghton, who read the notice without knowing who wrote it, was much struck with the extracts and said he should buy the book. I make it such a point of conscience to try to keep my word when I have half promised a notice that I wished you to know that I had kept it." He received three guineas in payment for the article which appeared on June 2. It was identified as Arnold's by Roger L. Brooks, " 'A Septuagenarian Poet': an Addition to the Matthew Arnold Bibliography," *Modern Philology* LVII, 262–63 (May, 1960).

46:1–2. Tennyson was born in 1809, Browning in 1812, W. B. Scott on September 12, 1811.

46:10–11. *The Year of the World; a Philosophical Poem on "Redemption from the Fall"* (Edinburgh: William Tait; London: Simpkin and Marshall, 1846). Arnold quotes from pp. ix–x and 7. The poem is in five parts, principally in blank verse. Scott sent a copy of the volume to Emerson, whose letter of acknowledgment he subsequently printed in his *Autobiographical Notes* (New York, 1892), I, 240.

47:5–9. The present volume, one hundred short poems dedicated to W. M. Rossetti "in memory of the friendship of half a lifetime," carries on p. iii as epigraph the opening lines of the four-teenth-century Scottish poet John Barbour's *Bruce*.

47:10–17. "Rosabell," the story in a variety of lyric measures of a country lass who fell from virtue, was first published in Leigh Hunt's *Monthly Repository* in February-March 1838. Later Scott altered the name to "Mary Anne, as more indicative of the humble rank of my heroine." He printed yet another version in his *Autobiographical Notes*, I, 135–52. The passage Arnold quotes is in sec. 13, p. 149.

47:21. *Year of the World*, p. x (Preface).

47:26. Tennyson's "The Revenge: a Ballad of the Fleet" was first published in the *Nineteenth Century* for March, 1878; his "Despair" appeared in the same journal in November, 1881. "Did you ever?" remarked Arnold to his sister about one of Tennyson's magazine poems about this time (May 15, 1880).

47:29–52:4. "Old, Old Story" is printed on pp. 49–52 of *A Poet's Harvest Home*, and is divided into two parts, the first part ending with the line "Ask *her* now. . . ." "An Autumn Evening" appears on pp. 136–37, "Adieu" on p. 150, "Rose-leaves" on p. 98, "To the Dead" (subtitled "A Paraphrase") on p. 59.

51:15–16. Dante Gabriel Rossetti died on April 9, 1882.

51:28. "Great plainness of speech" is Arnold's own language, p. 47:25–26.

52:6. An Egyptian nationalist movement led by Arabi Pasha was moving toward a crisis when Arnold wrote: riots broke out on June 11 and a month later the British fleet bombarded the fortifications of Alexandria. The Irish problem was of course perennial; the most recent crisis was the assassination of the Irish Secretary, Lord Frederick Cavendish, and his under-secretary in Phoenix Park, Dublin, on May 6.

[LITERATURE AND SCIENCE]

From time to time in his later years Arnold wrote an essay which summed up in itself the essence of all his previous writings on an aspect of human thought—was the epitome, the almost perfect statement of his doctrine. Such an essay, quite intentionally, was his Rede lecture at Cambridge on "Literature and Science," later adapted for his lecture tour in America and by far the most popular of his discourses with his American audiences: it was, as he told his sister Mrs. Forster on October 5, 1883, "in general my

doctrine on Studies as well as I can frame it."—*Letters*, ed. Russell.
As early as the concluding pages of his report on Continental
education to the Schools Inquiry Commission (1868) Arnold
wrote: "The ideal of a general, liberal training is, to carry us to a
knowledge of ourselves and the world. We are called to this
knowledge by special aptitudes which are born with us; the grand
thing in teaching is to have faith that some aptitudes of this kind
everyone has. This one's special aptitudes are for knowing men,—
the study of the humanities; that one's special aptitudes are for
knowing the world,—the study of nature. The circle of knowledge
comprehends both, and we should all have some notion, at any
rate, of the whole circle of knowledge. The rejection of the
humanities by the realists, the rejection of the study of nature by
the humanists, are alike ignorant."—*Prose Works*, ed. Super, IV,
300. In his General Report for 1876 to the Education Department,
Arnold discussed briefly the appropriate balance between hu-
manistic subjects and scientific ones, and even used some of the
same illustrations he was to use again in the Rede lecture. "To
have the power of using, which is the thing wished, these data of
natural science, a man must, in general, have first been in some
measure *moralised;* and for moralising him it will be found not
easy, I think, to dispense with those old agents, letters, poetry,
religion. So let not our teachers be led to imagine, whatever they
may hear and see of the call for natural science, that their literary
cultivation is unimportant. The fruitful use of natural science itself
depends, in a very great degree, on having effected in the whole
man, by means of letters, a rise in what the political economists
call *the standard of life*."—Arnold, *Reports on Elementary Schools,
1852–1882*, ed. F. Sandford (London, 1889), p. 200; ed. F. S.
Marvin (London, 1908), p. 178.

The address T. H. Huxley gave at the opening of Sir Josiah
Mason's new Science College in Birmingham on October 1, 1880,
was almost explicitly a challenge to his good friend Arnold. "In
[the] belief [of the great majority of educated Englishmen],
culture is obtainable only by a liberal education; and a liberal education is synonymous, not merely with education and instruction
in literature, but in one particular form of literature, namely, that
of Greek and Roman antiquity. They hold that the man who has
learned Latin and Greek, however little, is educated; while he who
is versed in other branches of knowledge, however deeply, is a
more or less respectable specialist, not admissible into the cultured
caste. The stamp of the educated man, the University degree, is

not for him. I am too well acquainted with the generous catholicity of spirit, the true sympathy with scientific thought, which pervades the writings of our chief apostle of culture to identify him with these opinions; and yet one may cull from one and another of those epistles to the Philistines, which so much delight all who do not answer to that name, sentences which lend them some support."—"Science and Culture," *Science and Culture and Other Essays* (London, 1881), p. 8. A leading article in *The Times* for October 2 (p. 9, cols. 4–6) makes Arnold's reply almost by anticipation, and calls Arnold "at once the most formidable and the most temperate champion of the Humanities."

But the issue had been joined even earlier. In December, 1874, and January, 1875, C. A. Appleton sent a series of letters to *The Times* deprecating the aims of Owens College, Manchester, and was answered in *The Manchester Weekly Times* by "Verax" (Henry Dunckley), whose essay on "Industry and Culture" belittles the actual achievement of Oxford.—*Letters of "Verax"* (Manchester, 1878), pp. 150–58.

Arnold delivered the Rede lecture to a crowded audience in the Senate House at Cambridge on June 14, 1882, and was paid £9 4s. 6d. Its publication in the *Nineteenth Century* for August brought him £40. (An honorary doctorate of laws he was to have received on the occasion of the lecture was deferred for a year because of the assassination of Lord Frederick Cavendish, son of the chancellor of the university.) The approbation of James Russell Lowell, American minister to London, may have been partly responsible for Arnold's choosing the lecture for his American tour a year later (a tour he already had on his mind and had discussed with Lowell by this time). He wrote to Lowell: "I am glad you like my Cambridge discourse; I suppose the friends of physical science are to the full as exuberant in America, just now, as they are here. Statesmen (Gladstone himself excepted) read less and less, and the less they read, the more is all public regulation of studies likely to go in favour of natural science." He fitted the lecture with a new introduction for the American tour, where he was somewhat overwhelmed by its popularity. "At present I am bored by having to repeat my Literature and Science so often. There is a perfect craze in New England for hearing it, but I hope the big cities will be more rational," he wrote to his sister Frances on November 27, 1883. To his younger daughter he wrote the day before, as he faced the prospect of delivering it twice on successive nights, "They are all eager to hear [it] out here, because the question is so much discussed in relation to the schools here, and everybody cares about schools. I get as sick of the lecture myself as Lord Hartington is said to get of his own speeches before he is through with them." The young ladies of Wellesley College endeared themselves to him by telegraphing to beg for the lecture on Emerson, "which will be an agreeable change to me after for ever giving the lecture on Literature and Science. Here in New England every one is full of the Education question, and of the contest between letters and science more particularly; and all the country places want to hear me on Literature and Science."—*Letters*, ed. Russell. The American version of the lecture was published in *The Manhattan* III, 323–32 (April, 1884), and brought him £50. A year later Arnold asked his son-in-law in New York to obtain a copy of this printing for use in the collected *Discourses in America*, only to learn that the journal was now defunct and the article unobtainable. "I must now set to work to correct the copy I lectured from, but as I had remodelled the thing a good deal for the Manhattan it is a bore having to go over the ground again. I hope the £50 Mr. [William Henry] Forman paid me for that article did not hasten his catastrophe," he wrote to his daughter.

On his American tour Arnold delivered the lecture on "Literature and Science" twenty-nine times: first on November 9 in the College Church at Dartmouth College, Hanover, N. H.; then on November 16 in Trinity Episcopal Church, Haverhill, Massachusetts; on November 17 in a matinee performance in Chickering Hall, Boston; on November 19 in the Academy of Music, Brooklyn; on November 20 in the Second Presbyterian Church, Princeton, New Jersey; on November 21 in the New Haven Opera House, New Haven, Connecticut; on November 23 in the Channing Memorial Church, Newport, Rhode Island; on November 26 at Newton, Massachusetts; on November 27 in Horticultural Hall, Worcester, Massachusetts; on November 30 at Salem, Massachusetts; on December 3 in Sayles Memorial Hall at Brown University, Providence; on December 5 in the Music Hall at Taunton, Massachusetts; on December 7 in the College Hall at Amherst College, Amherst, Massachusetts; on December 11 in the Social Hall at Smith College, Northampton, Massachusetts; on December 17 at the Congregational Church in Washington, D. C.; on December 18 in Mozart Hall, Richmond, Virginia; on January 2 in Lester Hall, Binghamton, New York; on January 5 at Swarthmore College, Swarthmore, Pennsylvania; on January 9 at Colgate University, Hamilton, New York; on January 11 at Wells College,

Aurora, New York; on January 12 at the Music Hall Building in Buffalo; on January 16 at Oberlin College, Oberlin, Ohio; on January 18 in University Hall, Ann Arbor, Michigan; on January 25 at Madison, Wisconsin; on January 28 at Galesburg, Illinois; on February 12 in Shaftesbury Hall, Toronto; on February 18 in Quebec; on February 20 in Montreal, and finally on March 1 in Chickering Hall, New York City, his farewell lecture of the tour. After his return to England he delivered it before the Literary and Scientific Society at Loughborough on October 23 and then to an audience of from 2000 to 2500 in Kinnaird Hall, Dundee, on October 27. His custom when he lectured in Britain was to accept only reimbursement for railway travel, but having failed to make that limitation clear to the authorities of the Armistead Trust in Dundee, who arranged the lecture there, he accepted their check for £7 10s. An excellent study of this lecture and its context in Arnold's thought is Fred A. Dudley, "Matthew Arnold and Science," *PMLA* LVII, 275–94 (March, 1942). J. M. Robertson, in *Modern Humanists* (1891), sets beside this lecture a passage from a letter written by Arnold's father on May 9, 1836: "If one might wish for impossibilities, I might then wish that my children might be well versed in physical science, but in due subordination to the fulness and freshness of their knowledge on moral subjects. This, however, I believe cannot be; and physical science, if studied at all, seems too great to be studied ἐν παρέργῳ: wherefore, rather than have it the principal thing in my son's mind, I would gladly have him think that the sun went round the earth, and that the stars were so many spangles set in the bright blue firmament. Surely the one thing needful for a Christian and an Englishman to study is Christian and moral and political philosophy, and then we should see our way a little more clearly without falling into Judaism, or Toryism, or Jacobinism, or any other *ism* whatever."—A. P. Stanley, *The Life and Correspondence of Thomas Arnold, D. D.,* chapt. VIII.

53:10–22. *Republic* VI, 495 D–E.

53:24–54:4. *Theaetetus* 172–73.

54:9–10. "Nous avons changé tout cela," replied Sganarelle when, having declared that the human heart is on the right side, he was challenged by the old-fashioned view that it is in fact on the left. —Molière, *Le Médecin malgré lui*, II, iv.

54:10–11. "Literary Ethics," three-fourths through; *Nature, Addresses, and Lectures.* Arnold's "modern majority" is a misprint for Emerson's "modern majesty"; see Textual Notes.

54:38–55:3. *Republic* IX, 591 B–C, jotted in Arnold's pocket diary for July 4, 1880, at the end of 1882 and 1883, on October 19, 1884, and in one of his "General Note-Books," sometimes with the heading "Importance of Choice of Studies."—*Note-Books*, ed. Lowry, pp. 339, 386, 402, 408, 540.

55:23–26. Huxley cited Mason's aim of providing young men with "sound, extensive, and practical scientific knowledge," and his prohibition of "mere literary instruction and education."— "Science and Culture," pp. 5–6. Sir Josiah Mason (1795–1881) started life as a vegetable huckster, became a manufacturer of steel pens and plated spoons, forks, etc., and accumulated more than £500,000, most of which he put to charitable uses, including the establishment of an almshouse, an orphanage, and the Science College. This last, formerly in Edmund Street near the Birmingham Town Hall, has now been absorbed into the University of Birmingham, of which indeed it was the first home (1900).

56:13–28. "The Function of Criticism at the Present Time" (1864), *Prose Works*, ed. Super, III, 261, 283–84; quoted by Huxley, "Science and Culture," pp. 8–9.

56:29–57:7. "Science and Culture," pp. 9–10. The expression "criticism of life" Arnold first used in the essay on "Joubert" (1864), *Prose Works*, ed. Super, III, 209.

57:28–33. Quoted in [Mark Pattison], "F. A. Wolf," *North British Review* XLII, 262 (June, 1865), an essay cited by Arnold in *Schools and Universities on the Continent* (1868), *Prose Works*, ed. Super, IV, 186.

58:13–17. "Science and Culture," pp. 8–9, 14–15.

59:7–20. *Ibid.*, pp. 11–12, 15–16.

60:5–6. Huxley speaks of "the classical scholars, in their capacity of Levites in charge of the ark of culture and monopolists of liberal education," and later refers to them as "the Levites of culture."—*Ibid.*, pp. 3, 6. By command of the Lord, the Levites were guardians of the sacred tabernacle of the Israelites and all the vessels thereof, and likewise of the ark of the covenant.—Numbers 1:50, 3:31; Exodus 38:21.

60:8. When Nebuchadnezzar king of Babylon conquered Judah, he carried out of Jerusalem "all the treasures of the house of the Lord, and the treasures of the king's house, and cut in pieces all the vessels of gold which Solomon king of Israel had made in the temple of the Lord."—II Kings 24:13. It is tempting also to see an allusion to Nebuchadnezzar's losing his reason, so that "he was driven from men, and did eat grass as oxen."—Daniel 4:33.

60:14–16. Arnold repeated the first part of this observation in his introduction to *Isaiah of Jerusalem;* see p. 106:17 and note.

60:31–33. Three myths, from Arnold's point of view.

61:1–3. "Science and Culture," p. 7.

61:3–8. Charles Watkins Merrifield, F. R. S., speaking at the Glasgow meeting of the Association in September, 1876; *Report of the Forty-Sixth Meeting of the British Association for the Advancement of Science* (London, 1877), Part II, 213. Arnold quoted this remark in his General Report as inspector of schools for 1876.—*Reports on Elementary Schools,* ed. F. Sandford (London, 1889), p. 199; ed. F. S. Marvin (London, 1908), p. 177. "Esaias is very bold," wrote St. Paul to the Romans, 10:20.

61:35–62:1. Arnold first listed these powers in "Equality" (1878), and referred to them frequently thereafter.—*Prose Works,* ed. Super, VIII, 287.

63:12–14. Plato *Symposium* 206 A, in the language of Shelley's translation; jotted in Arnold's pocket diary for May 31, 1868, and October 7 and 14, 1877.—*Note-Books,* ed. Lowry, pp. 76, 284.

63:25–26. "M. Littré . . . traces up . . . all our impulses into two elementary instincts, the instinct of self-preservation and the reproductive instinct."—*Literature and Dogma* (1871), chapt. i; *Prose Works,* ed. Super, VI, 174.

64:1–2. James Joseph Sylvester (1814–97) was, as Arnold says, recognized as one of the foremost mathematicians of his day. When the Johns Hopkins University was founded in Baltimore in 1877, he became professor of mathematics there and founded the *American Journal of Mathematics.* He was still in Baltimore when Arnold lectured there in December, 1883, but immediately thereafter returned to England to become Savilian professor of geometry at Oxford. He was extraordinarily fertile of mind and stimulating in conversation. Like Arnold he was a member of the Athenaeum Club.

64:3–7. In the first version of "Literature and Science," delivered as the Rede Lecture at Cambridge; see Textual Notes. Cambridge was noted for its predominance in mathematics and science, Oxford in the humanities.

64:21–23. *The Descent of Man,* Part III, chapt. xxi, ¶7; jotted in Arnold's pocket diary for July 19, 1882.—*Note-Books,* ed. Lowry, p. 377.

64:25–28. "Science and Culture," p. 15.

65:6–8. *Ibid.*

65:21. Darwin died on April 19, 1882.

65:35. Michael Faraday (1791–1867), the physicist and chemist, was brought up in and remained for life a member of the sect founded by the Scottish religious leader Robert Sandeman (1718–71), a group which believed in weekly communion, the kiss of peace, ceremonial washing of feet, a community of goods, and the refusal to eat blood meats.

66:7–10. "Science and Culture," p. 11.

67:7. "Scholarly and pious persons, worthy of all respect, favour us with allocutions upon the sadness of the antagonism of science to their mediaeval way of thinking."—*ibid.*, p. 16.

67:17. In *Literature and Dogma* (1873), Arnold makes a comparable appeal to experience in support of his doctrine that "there rules an enduring Power, not ourselves, which makes for righteousness."—*Prose Works*, ed. Super, VI, 370.

67:28. Arnold quoted this line, without translation, as a touchstone passage in his essay on "Byron" (1881).—*Prose Works*, ed. Super, IX, 231.

67:31–32. *Ethics*, IV, xviii, scholium; jotted in Arnold's pocket diary for July 17, 1870, at the beginning of 1876, and in one of his "General Note-Books."—*Note-Books*, ed. Lowry, pp. 131, 242, 530.

67:35–36. Luke 9:25.

68:26–28. See p. 59:9, 16.

69:22–32. *Macbeth*, V, iii, 40; this paraphrase is jotted at the end of Arnold's pocket diary for 1877. He commented upon it in his General Report as inspector of schools for 1876.—*Reports on Elementary Schools*, ed. Sandford, p. 198; ed. Marvin, p. 176. The thesis was a recurring one with him: in 1852 (his first report), "Young men, whose knowledge of grammar, of the minutest details of geographical and historical facts, and above all of mathematics, is surprising, often cannot paraphrase a plain passage of prose or poetry without totally misapprehending it," and in 1874, "The candidate has to paraphrase a passage of English poetry, and no exercise can better show his range of ideas and quickness of apprehension."—ed. Sandford, pp. 19, 175–76; ed. Marvin, pp. 16, 156. "National schools" are those conducted by the National Society for Promoting the Education of the Poor in the Principles of the Established Church throughout England and Wales.

70:4–12. Arnold alludes to H. Hussey Vivian, *Notes of a Tour in America* (London, 1878), especially p. 233. See p. 4:17n.

70:34–35. Huxley, "Science and Culture," p. 19.

70:38. For this instinct see p. 63:25n.

71:12. Lady Jane Grey (1537–54) at the age of thirteen was described by Roger Ascham as incredible in her accomplishment in writing and speaking Greek, to which accomplishment she added Latin, French, Italian, and Hebrew. A cousin of Edward VI and like him a Protestant, she was married to a son of the Duke of Northumberland and was proclaimed queen on the death of Edward. But Edward's Catholic sister Mary was able to enforce her own succession, and Lady Jane and her husband were beheaded when she was only 16.

71:13–14. At Cambridge the women's colleges were Girton (founded 1869) and Newnham (founded 1871); Anne Jemima Clough, sister of Arnold's friend, was first head of the latter. At Oxford, Lady Margaret Hall was founded in 1878, Somerville Hall in 1879; the other colleges for women there are of later date. Bedford College, London, was founded as early as 1849.

71:19–20. An epitaph made for him during his life, quoted in Charles Clément, *Michel-Ange, Léonard de Vinci, Raphaël* (Paris, 1861), p. 191, and jotted in one of Arnold's "General Note-Books" with the heading, "The Ancients Unattainable."—*Note-Books*, ed. Lowry, p. 446.

72:6. Ruskin delivered the Rede Lecture on May 24, 1867, and received an honorary LL.D. at that time. He was soon to resume his professorship at Oxford when Arnold spoke.

72:31. "He shall not strive, nor cry."—Matthew 12:19. Arnold used the phrase frequently, from the time he wrote his "Lines Written in Kensington Gardens" (1852).

[NOTES ON CANCELLED PASSAGE]

546:29. Proverbs 21:30.

546:31–32. See the Introduction to *Literature and Dogma* (1871) and an essay that was in some ways a forerunner of the present lecture, the Preface to *A Bible-Reading for Schools* (1872).— *Prose Works*, ed. Super, VI, 164–67 and VII, 499–501.

547:19–20. See p. 55:23–26n.

547:29–31. Sir Charles Lyell (1797–1875), geologist, laid the foundation for Darwin's theory of evolution by demonstrating that the geological history of the earth was far longer than had formerly been supposed, and that geological change was far more gradual. Sir Charles Bell (1774–1842), anatomist, made significant discoveries about the functions of nerves. H. M. S. *Challenger*, a naval corvette fitted out for scientific research, returned in May, 1876, from a three and a half year cruise that produced significant results in a wide range of scientific areas.

547:38–548:1. Connop Thirlwall, *Letters Literary and Theological*, ed. J. J. S. Perowne and L. Stokes (London, 1881), p. 147 (June 8, 1836). Thirlwall, a graduate of Cambridge, was bishop of St. David's from 1840 until his death in 1875.

548:15. The annual conference of the National Union of Elementary Teachers was held at Sheffield on April 11, 1882.

548:25. The vice-chancellor of the University of Cambridge in 1882 was Dr. James Porter, master of Peterhouse.

548:27–29. Sir Robert Rede died in 1519, leaving an endowment for three lectures to be delivered annually at Cambridge in perpetuity, one in humanity, one in logic, and one in philosophy. A reorganization of the endowment in 1858 provided for one annual lecture to be delivered by a man of eminence in science or literature who should be designated each year by the vice-chancellor.

549:3–5. Oxford was the center of support for Charles I in the Civil Wars; it was the seat of the court and Royalist Parliament from the latter part of 1643 to the spring of 1645. Methodism sprang from the group (including Charles Wesley and George Whitefield) that about 1730 came under the influence at Oxford of John Wesley, fellow of Lincoln College. Tractarianism was the movement that took form about 1833 under the leadership of E. B. Pusey, John Keble, and John Henry Newman, all then or recently fellows of Oriel College. Ritualism was an offspring of Tractarianism within the Anglican Church.

549:6. Charles Simeon (1759–1836), vicar of Holy Trinity, Cambridge, was a leading evangelical, a founder of the Church Missionary Society and a supporter of the British and Foreign Bible Society. He had many disciples among the younger men at the University.

549:8. Arnold's interest in John Smith (1618–52) and other Cambridge Platonists or Latitudinarians such as Benjamin Whichcote and Henry More was most evident in his essay on "A Psychological Parallel" (1876), reprinted in *Last Essays on Church and Religion.—Prose Works*, ed. Super, VIII, 111–47.

[A LIVERPOOL ADDRESS]

In response to an invitation from the principal, G. H. Rendall, Arnold on September 30, 1882, delivered the address at the opening of the winter session of the Liverpool University College before a crowded audience in the small concert room of St. George's Hall—some 1200 people present, Arnold was told. The Earl of Derby, president of the University College and like Arnold an Old Rugbeian, was in the chair. Arnold "has left his mark on the literature," he said in his introductory remarks, and then no doubt with Arnold's recently-published "Literature and Science" in mind he added, "and when I say the literature I mean on the intellectual life, of our country and our time. If such a being exists among men as a really original thinker, Mr. Arnold has a claim to that title; and to the merits of original thought he has added the equally rare qualifications of a style so artistic as to be, or at least to seem to be, absolutely without art."

There was some awkwardness in the circumstance that the principal business of the session was the awarding of prizes to the students of the medical school, and Arnold had really nothing to say to the medical students. But he also put off the writing until the very last minute. He was visiting his son Richard in Manchester, "much bothered by my discourse and very bilious. . . . I finished by noon on Friday [the day before the address was given] but I could not get properly to work at the writing out," for his son wanted to show him some new lodgings he was about to take. "I wrote out two or three pages before dinner, and went off at a quarter past seven, very indisposed and cross," to dine with his nephew. "When we got home I began writing out again, found a good deal to alter, so did not dare leave it to the next morning for fear I should have to read the thing half written, and, in short, sat up till ten minutes past five working at it." He slept until eight, then took the train to Liverpool, left his things at the station and went directly to a ceremonial champagne luncheon for about thirty, "chiefly doctors, but you know I like doctors." Then to the hall for the lecture. "I was very well received. I think the discourse gave satisfaction, though I thought it was horrid while I was writing it out." After a reception, he went to Lord Derby's seat at Knowsley, seven miles away, where he was a guest for two nights. —Letter to his wife, October 1, 1882; *Letters,* ed. Russell. His fatigue may have had something to do with the response of an anonymous writer in the *Liverpool Daily Post* on October 4, quoted by Professor Allott: Arnold was "a gentleman of quiet and not very distinguishable appearance, who reads monotonously from a paper and never attempts an oratorical effect either by voice or action. . . . When his own world will not take a man seriously, there is generally a reason for it. And the reason may be found in Mr. Arnold's manner. . . . When you have once heard him read something he has written, with the elocution of a worn and weary curate—a mechanical clerical delivery only varied when the falling inflection at the end of a sentence is especially deep and sickly like Mr. Bancroft's in Captain Hawtrey—you feel that the power of this distinguished man is not increased by personal acquaintance. His manner shows extreme lassitude, and when in his languid way he vindicates some of his old utterances, you wonder how he could ever have had the courage to utter them."—"Strangers on the Platform," XIV.

The Liverpool papers reported the address in full, but Arnold kept the reports in the London papers to a summary, for he had already promised the address to Knowles, editor of the *Nineteenth Century;* it appeared in the November number and brought Arnold £33 in payment. It has been reprinted at the university where it was delivered by Kenneth Allott, *Five Uncollected Essays of Matthew Arnold* (Liverpool: University Press, 1953).

75:17–21. The principal was G. H. Rendall, son of the Rev. F. Rendall, assistant master in classics and a house master at Harrow School. Arnold moved from London to Harrow in 1868 in order to send his sons to the school, and two of them died while he lived there. He moved to his home in Cobham in 1873. The younger Rendall was a Moniter (one of the top boys) when "Budge" Arnold entered the bottom of the Fourth Form in April, 1868.

75:22–23. "In those days came John the Baptist, preaching in the wilderness of Judaea."—Matthew 3:1.

75:30–32. The Royal Institution school (founded 1819), the Liverpool Institute (1825), and the Liverpool College (1840) were semiprivate schools founded by public subscription. The Institute was a development of the Mechanics' Institute and was under the proprietorship of the subscribers.

77:28. I.e., Lord Derby.

77:32–38. Arnold alludes to his tour of the Continent in 1865 to gather information on behalf of the Schools Inquiry Commission,

and to the conclusion of his report to that Commission. See
Prose Works, ed. Super, IV, 328.

79:27. Owens College, Manchester, was opened in 1851 with
money bequeathed by John Owens, who foresaw its development
into a university. It was incorporated into the Victoria University
in 1880, along with (soon thereafter) University College, Liverpool, and the College of Science, Leeds. The independence granted
to the two latter institutions early in the present century left
Owens College the single college of Victoria University. Regius
professorships are professorships supported by the crown or government; bursaries, like scholarships, are forms of financial assistance for students.

80:1–2. The original attempt to establish a nonsectarian London
University as a teaching and examining body failed of securing a
charter; the teaching functions were assigned to relatively autono-
mous units established in various interests—University College was
nonsectarian, King's College was Anglican—and the University of
London became merely an examining body, both for its constituent units and after 1858 for whoever else might present himself.

80:20. Two years after Arnold spoke, University College, Liverpool, was admitted as a college of the Victoria University (the
"new northern University" of p. 81:19), which granted the
degrees. The University of Liverpool was chartered in 1903.

81:13–14. From 1858 the universities of Oxford and Cambridge
examined schoolboys who presented themselves at two levels,
those under fifteen (or sixteen for Cambridge) and those under
eighteen; examinations were held simultaneously at the universities and at other places, and success in the higher level was
rewarded at Oxford by the title of associate in arts.

82:5–9. Bransby Blake Cooper, *The Life of Sir Astley Cooper*
(London, 1843), II, 53; jotted in Arnold's pocket diary for September 9, 1872, and February 9, 1879.—*Note-Books*, ed. Lowry, pp.
181–82, 316. Sir Astley Cooper (1768–1841) was a well-known
surgeon and author of surgical and anatomical treatises; John Keats
attended his lectures while a student at Guy's Hospital.

82:10–11. "Don't think; try; be patient; be accurate," quoted in
John Baron, *Life of Edward Jenner* (London, 1838), I, 124, and
referred to by Sir James Paget, *The Hunterian Oration . . . at
the Royal College of Surgeons of England on the 13th of February 1877* (London, 1877), p. 15; jotted in Arnold's pocket diary
for February 16, 1879, and in one of his "General Note-Books."—

Note-Books, ed. Lowry, pp. 316, 512. John Hunter (1728–93), surgeon and teacher of both Cooper and Jenner (the discoverer of vaccine), is commemorated by an annual oration. Arnold (perhaps deliberately) failed to convey Hunter's point, and his quotation was greeted with laughter and applause by his Liverpool audience. Lord Derby commented that there was nothing in Arnold's lecture to exercise the patience of anyone, while there was a great deal to make one think. About the time Arnold began his Oxford studies, Dr. Thomas Arnold, canvassing possible careers for his sons, remarked that none of them seemed inclined to follow medicine.—A. P. Stanley, *Life of Arnold,* letter of September 22, 1841.

82:33–83:5. Alexander, Lord Cockburn, *Life of Lord Jeffrey* (Edinburgh, 1852), II, 142. Arnold omits the sentence with which this comment was introduced: "Did you ever hear that most of the Quakers die of stupidity—actually and literally?" Francis Jeffrey was one of the founders and for a long time editor of the *Edinburgh Review* and author of many papers of literary criticism published in that journal. He became Lord Jeffrey more than twenty years after the anecdote to which Arnold alludes.

83:14–17. In "Falkland" (1877), the essay to which Goldwin Smith replied, Arnold used this expression with reference to the seventeenth-century Puritans, who in his opinion left their mark on the life of the English middle class and of all Americans. The application to America is made explicit in "A Word about America" (1882), p. 17. See *Prose Works,* ed. Super, VIII, 201, 295.

83:27–30. See p. 61:35n.

84:34–35. "Energy and honesty" were the characteristics Arnold ascribed to the English as early as "The Literary Influence of Academies" (1864), in contrast to "openness of mind and flexibility of intelligence" which were "remarkable characteristics of the French people in modern times."—*Prose Works,* ed. Super, III, 237; and see "My Countrymen" (1866) and "On the Study of Celtic Literature" (1866), *Ibid.,* V, 13 and III, 341.

85:27. Arnold first called conduct "three-fourths, at the lowest computation, of human life" in the opening chapter of *Literature and Dogma* (1871).—*Prose Works,* ed. Super, VI, 173.

86:5–9. Quoted from Jules Michelet, *Histoire de France* (nouv. éd.; Paris, 1876), XVIII, 149 ("Louis XV," chapter ix), jotted in Arnold's pocket diary for April 10 and 17, 1875, March 11, 1882, and in one of his "General Note-Books." The quotation from Voltaire by itself is jotted in the diary at the end of 1878, at the beginning of 1879, and in a "General Note-Book"; it comes from a letter to P. de Cideville, February 18, 1737.—*Oeuvres complètes* (Paris, 1880), XXXIV, 215; Arnold, *Note-Books,* ed. Lowry, pp. 228–29, 371–72, 506, 310, 313, 512. In "Falkland" (1877) Arnold described Luther as a "Philistine of genius"; in " 'Porro Unum Est Necessarium' " (1878) he developed at some length the notion of Voltaire as the embodiment of the French quality of logic and lucidity—"Voltaire, the French Luther of the eighteenth century." —*Prose Works,* ed. Super, VIII, 206, 363.

87:3. The Salvation Army was founded in 1878, officially named in 1880. In the Popular Edition of *God and the Bible* (1884) Arnold spoke of "a materialistic fairy-tale like that of the Salvation Army."—*Prose Works,* ed. Super, VII, 372.

87:14–16. Edward Bouverie Pusey, regius professor of Hebrew and canon of Christ Church, Oxford, from 1828, died at the age of 82 on September 16, 1882, about a fortnight before Arnold's address. His adherence to the Tractarian movement gave it weight and the name "Puseyism"; he remained a very conservative member of the Church of England, an Anglican Catholic but not a Roman Catholic.

87:16–19. Thomas Mozley (1806–93), older brother of J. B. Mozley, to whose lectures *On Miracles* Arnold referred in *God and the Bible,* was a pupil of Newman's at Oriel College, Oxford, and married Newman's sister. His two-volume *Reminiscences, Chiefly of Oriel College and the Oxford Movement* (London, 1882) was on Arnold's reading list the year it was published.— *Note-Books,* ed. Lowry, p. 604.

87:19–20. The Rev. S. F. Green, rector of St. John the Evangelist, Miles Platting, Manchester, was imprisoned in Lancaster Gaol from March, 1881, to November, 1882, for disobeying his bishop's inhibition against ritualistic practices; he was therefore in prison when Arnold spoke.

[A FRENCH WORTHY]

From the time Arnold was introduced to Jean-Jacques Rapet through Guizot on his official visit of inquiry into French popular education in 1859, the two were in frequent correspondence. Rapet made an official visit to England in May, 1862, and Arnold showed him around. In October, 1864, Rapet gratified Arnold by reporting the praise of his article on Academies that was current in Paris.

Arnold of course renewed the acquaintance on his official visit to France for the Schools Inquiry Commission of 1865. It may have been Rapet who called to Arnold's attention the French educational statistics he himself had helped to compile, which Arnold used in " 'Porro Unum Est Necessarium' " (1878). And so when Rapet died Arnold wrote to John Morley, editor of *The Pall Mall Gazette*, on October 24, 1882: "Shall I write a page or a page and a half about him for you? . . . The French *Journal des Instituteurs* has had a long article on him. He had 'morality,' so you will not be surprised to hear that I knew him."—*Letters*, ed. Russell. The article was not easy, however; two weeks later (November 6) Arnold wrote to his sister Frances: "I did not write yesterday, because I wanted to finish a short notice of poor old Rapet, the French inspector who guided me so well at my first visit to French schools, and whom Guizot esteemed so highly: I think his daughter will like it, and there are one or two things to be said in connexion with him which it may be useful to say. But he has given me a bad week, though it is only a two column affair, for the Pall Mall. It is the shaping a thing that worries me; the mere writing it, when one is fairly launched, is not so bad; but the difference even in this respect between verse and prose is curious. Before I could shape this notice of Rapet I accumulated matter enough in my thoughts for an article of twenty pages; then by a process of selection one had to use of this what would make the best article of two pages. I am not going to write anything more between this and Christmas—on that I am determined." (This last resolution, it will be seen, was short lived.) The article appeared anonymously on the front page of the *Pall Mall* for November 8, and Arnold received £3 in payment. It has been reprinted in F. Neiman, ed., *Essays, Letters, and Reviews by Matthew Arnold* (Cambridge, Mass., 1960).

89:7. Port Royal, a thirteenth-century Cistercian convent in the country some twenty miles southwest of Paris, became in the seventeenth century a center for Jansenists, with their strong moral and spiritual seriousness. A place of retreat for men and a school were established there. The tragic dramatist Racine was educated in the school and Pascal lived at Port Royal for much of his last eight years. Ste.-Beuve's longest single work is his five-volume *Port-Royal* (1840–59).

89:10–11. Henri François d'Aguesseau (1668–1751), chancellor of France and one of the greatest legal minds of his era, was brought up under Jansenist influence and wrote philosophical and historical treatises as well as books on jurisprudence. Vauvenargues (1715–47) was author of a collection of *Maximes* and *Réflexions* Arnold was reading a few months before he wrote this essay. The letters of Marie de Rabutin-Chantal, Marquise de Sévigné (1626–96) were constant favorites of his which he was also reading in 1882, and the *Pensées* of Joseph Joubert (1754–1824) were the subject of one of the earlier *Essays in Criticism* (1864). Émile Littré (1801–81), positivist thinker whose French dictionary and critical writings Arnold admired, died only about a year before this essay was published.

89:17. Roger de Rabutin, comte de Bussy (1618–93), cousin of Mme. de Sévigné and one of her correspondents, was disgraced at court for profligacy and after a year in the Bastille was banished to his Burgundian estates for the final seventeen years of his life.

89:22–90:2. Arnold's most extended handling of the then relatively new (and in the twentieth century much discredited) science of ethnology was in his lectures *On the Study of Celtic Literature* (1866). F. E. Faverty's illuminating study, *Matthew Arnold the Ethnologist* (Evanston: Northwestern University Press, 1951) does not allude to the refinement of Arnold's analysis of the French race to the present essay, which was hardly accessible when Faverty wrote. See also "Numbers" (1883), pp. 155–56.

90:7–8. The Department of Ain is on the eastern border of France, near Geneva; its capital is Bourg. The nearest large city is Lyons.

90:12. Jean-Baptiste Girard (1765–1850), Johann Heinrich Pestalozzi (1746–1827), and Philip Emanuel von Fellenberg (1771–1844) were all Swiss educational reformers.

90:13. Joseph-Marie, baron de Gérando (1772–1842) was a successful public administrator and office-holder under Bonaparte, the restored Bourbons, and Louis-Philippe.

90:15–17. Périgueux is a town of southwestern France, northeast of Bordeaux. François Guizot (1787–1874), minister of Public Instruction under Louis-Philippe and later his chief minister, was author of the education statute of 1833 which Arnold described in 1860 as "truly the root of the present system of primary instruction in France."—*Prose Works*, ed. Super, II, 67.

90:27, 32. The *Cours d'études des écoles primaires: Exercices et devoirs pour chaque jour de l'année* was published in 1860–61, with the teacher's manual a decade and a half later. Rapet's *Manuel de morale et d'économie politique, à l'usage des classes ouvrières* was published in 1858.

90:38–91:3. It was to Arnold himself that Guizot thus pointed out Rapet in 1859.—*The Popular Education of France, Prose Works*, ed. Super, II, 31.

91:14–15. Ambroise Rendu (1778–1860), whose *Essai sur l'instruction publique* Arnold used in preparing his report on elementary education in France (1860), is described by Arnold as "Inspector-General and afterwards Councillor of the University, [who] distinguished himself by his labours in the cause of public education."—*Prose Works*, ed. Super, II, 43.

92:8–9. Pierre-Paul Royer-Collard (1763–1845) was first president of the Commission of Public Instruction under the restored monarchy of 1815. Victor Cousin (1792–1867), the philosopher, was minister of Public Instruction in 1840. His successor in that office was Abel-François Villemain (1790–1870) and his predecessor was Narcisse-Achille, comte de Salvandy (1795–1856), who also served from 1845 to 1848. Arnold conversed with Guizot, Cousin, and Villemain on his official tour of France in 1859.

92:15–17. *Marc-Aurèle et la fin du monde antique* (Paris, 1882), p. 637 (chapt. xxxiv, halfway through), jotted in Arnold's pocket diary for July 30, 1882.—*Note-Books*, ed. Lowry, p. 378.

[AT THE PRINCESS'S]

In October, 1879, the young playwright Henry Arthur Jones (1851–1929), struck by Arnold's essay on "The French Play in London," addressed him a letter of appreciation and sent him copies of two of his plays. His farce, *A Clerical Error*, was just then opening at the Court Theatre, Sloane Square; "I must try and see [it]—which is far better than reading—some night that I am in town," Arnold told him. Three years later Jones asked Arnold to be present at the opening night of *The Silver King* at the Princess's Theatre, and Arnold accepted. On November 19, 1882, he wrote to John Morley, who had recently become editor of *The Pall Mall Gazette:* "Shall I write you a letter with the impressions called forth by the first representation of *The Silver King*? I had not been at the Princess's for years, and several things occurred to me. I waited till your theatrical critic (who is he?) had fired his shot, but there is nothing in his satire [November 18, pp. 4–5] to make my letter unsuitable. At the same time, you may have had enough of the subject. I know nothing of the author personally, but he wrote saying he had nourished himself on my works and wished I would go to his first representation. I resisted, but went at last, expecting to be bored, but am highly pleased. I should sign 'An Old Playgoer.'" He corrected the proof about December 4; when the letter did not appear on the 5th, he was seized with "the horrid suspicion" that he had failed to post it. But he had done so, and his letter appeared on December 6.— *Letters*, ed. Russell. He received £3 in payment. (The *Pall Mall's* regular reviewer, incidentally, had been very warm in his praise of the play—"one of the best melodramas of recent years.")

This and the four other pieces in *The Pall Mall Gazette* signed "An Old Playgoer" were gathered in the DeLuxe edition of Arnold's works (1903–4) and have since been published separately as *Letters of an Old Playgoer* by Brander Matthews (New York: Columbia University, 1919); they were never collected by Arnold himself. William Archer's *About the Theatre: Essays and Studies* (London, 1886) provides a context for Arnold's short critiques, especially in the long survey of the London stage from 1882 to 1886 called "Are We Advancing" and the chapter on "Shakespeare and the Public." Ten letters from Arnold to Jones survive.

94:2–4. The Princess's Theatre, on Oxford Street near Oxford Circus, was erected in 1830 on the site of an earlier theater that burned. It was named "The Princess's" in 1840. In 1880 it was demolished and rebuilt. On February 21, 1848, Macready began an engagement of twelve nights at the theater, during which he presented eight Shakespearean plays with Mrs. Fanny Kemble Butler (1809–93) as his leading lady—an actress with whom he was profoundly dissatisfied.—*The Diaries of William Charles Macready*, ed. William Toynbee (London, 1912), II, 385–87. Arnold wrote to Clough at Oxford from Lansdowne House on March 6, 1848: "You must come this week if you come but on my conscience I do not think it is worth while. The squalor of the place, the faint earthy orange smell, the dimness of the light, the ghastly ineffectualness of the sub-actors, the self-consciousness of Fanny Kemble, the harshness of Macready, the unconquerable difficulty of the play, altogether gave me sensations of wretchedness during the performance of Othello the other night I am sure you would have shared with me had you been there. I go no more, except to accompany you." And two days later: "Come this week if possible. . . . You cannot be sure beforehand of what you will see. Macbeth is the best—or Wolsey [*Henry VIII*]."—*The Letters of Matthew Arnold to Arthur Hugh Clough*, ed. H. F. Lowry (London: Oxford University Press, 1932), pp. 72, 74. Macready's repertoire at the Princess's included also *King Lear, Julius Caesar* (Brutus), *Hamlet, Virginius, Richelieu,* and *Werner.*

94:18. *The Lights o' London,* an early hit by the very prolific playwright George R. Sims (1847–1922) ran for more than 200 performances at the Princess's from September 10, 1881. It was admired for its realistic scenes of London low life.

94:22–24. Arnold quoted these words as by "the most delicate of living critics" (presumably Sainte-Beuve) in *On Translating Homer* (1861), *Prose Works,* ed. Super, I, 102.

94:25–26. Jones's *The Silver King,* written in collaboration with Henry Herman, opened at the Princess's on November 16, 1882, and ran for nearly 300 performances there. It is printed in *Representative Plays by Henry Arthur Jones,* ed. Clayton Hamilton (Boston: Little, Brown, and Company, 1925), I, 1–109. The editor's introduction has much to say of Arnold's encouragement of Jones.

95:13. See *The Tempest,* IV, i, 47.

95:16–19. Wilson Barrett (1847–1904) was leading actor and manager of the Princess's from 1881 to 1886, and a playwright as well, later best known for writing and acting in *The Sign of the Cross.* He had produced and acted in *A Clerical Error,* Jones's first London play. Charles Coote, who took the part of the murdered Geoffrey Ware's clerk, did not subsequently make a name for himself in the theater. Mary Eastlake played Denver's wife.

95:24. Both *The Athenaeum* and *The Saturday Review* on November 25 treat the play simply as the melodrama it is. In general, they agree with Arnold's judgment of the play. The former review (p. 707) is amused at the hero's bravado in the ruffians' lair, the latter (p. 701) suggests that "the recital of a long and absurd dream might with advantage be omitted" and praises Coote's excellent performance. It ridicules the "stilts" on which the morning papers had mounted to praise the play.

95:33. Transpontine ("across the bridge") alludes to the kind of melodrama currently being staged in the Surrey theaters south of the Thames in London.

96:3–4. See *Hamlet,* III, ii, 22–23.

96:12–14. A young man named Wilfred Denver with a lovely wife, two darling children (a boy and a girl), and a faithful servant, is ruined by gambling and drink through the machinations of his wife's rejected suitor Geoffrey Ware. In a drunken fury he goes to murder his tormentor, and finds a band of jewel thieves

at work in the man's home. They drug him, and when they are
surprised again at their job by Ware's return, murder Ware with
Denver's gun, and bolt. Denver, waking, believes he has carried
out his plan and flees in an ill-fitting sailor suit on the 7:35 express
from Euston. He leaps from the train before it reaches Rugby,
and luckily, for it crashes into some goods wagons loaded with
petroleum and all the passengers in Denver's carriage are consumed to cinders in the flames. Denver, presumed dead, makes his
way to Nevada, strikes a rich vein of silver, and after three and a
half years returns to find his wife and children and faithful servant destitute, starving, and about to be evicted from their cottage
by a heartless landlord, coincidentally the murdering cracksman.
Denver rescues them, establishes them in the country mansion
which had been his wife's when he courted her, and might have
lived contentedly,—might even have taken his family to Nevada,
where the law could not reach him,—but for a terrible nightmare
of the Lord's vengeance for the murder he still believes he has
committed. And so, disguising himself as a half-witted deaf beggar,
he makes his way into the dockside warehouse meeting room of
the thieves, overhears their quarrelling and acknowledgment of
the murder, reveals himself and flourishing a crowbar walks
from the room as four desperate men cry helplessly, "Stop him!
Stop him!" "Stop me! The whole world shall not stop me now!"
he proclaims, and bangs the door behind him. And so the murderer
is apprehended, the family is reestablished in prosperity, and
Denver's name is cleared. There is enough deliberate comedy at
critical moments in the play, quite apart from the over-elaborate
working of coincidence and dramatic irony, to suggest that the
author's tongue is not always flat in his mouth, but all the reviews
indicate that the performance was quite straightforward. William
Archer remarks on its curious moral values in *About the Theatre*,
pp. 87–89.

    96:20–28. Acts 19:35. See Arnold's use of this passage again in
his lecture on "Numbers" (1883), p. 154:31–32, and in "A Comment on Christmas" (1885), p. 227:35–36. In "The French Play in
London" (1879), Arnold deals severely with the recent English
imitations of the French contemporary drama.—*Prose Works*, ed.
Super, IX, 78–79.

[AN OLD PLAYGOER AT THE PLAY]

Arnold received £2 in payment for this second letter over the signature "An Old Playgoer," which was published in *The Pall Mall Gazette* for March 30, 1883.

97:1. The Olympic Theatre, on Wych Street, Strand, was rebuilt after a fire in 1849, and finally closed in 1899 when the area was rebuilt to form Aldwych and Kingsway. *Forget-Me-Not,* a comedy by F. C. Grove and Herman Charles Merivale, opened at the Lyceum Theatre on August 21, 1879; it was revived at the Prince of Wales's on February 21, 1880, and at the Olympic on January 6, 1883.

97:7. The Cretan Epimenides, sent into the country to recover a stray sheep, fell asleep at noonday in a cave and remained asleep for fifty-seven years; when he awoke, unaware that he had taken more than a short nap, he was bewildered at finding others in possession of his father's farm and house.—Diogenes Laertius I. x.

97:14. Geneviève Ward (1837–1922), later Dame Geneviève, New York born actress, had an operatic career until illness deprived her of her singing voice in 1863. A decade later she began a distinguished career on the stage. She managed the Lyceum for the season in which she first appeared as Stephanie de Mohrivart in *Forget-Me-Not,* a part she ultimately played over two thousand times in all parts of the world. She continued to act almost to the year of her death.

97:27-28. Article 148 of the French Civil Code provided that a son under 25, a daughter under 21, could not contract a marriage without the consent of their father and mother. "In case of disagreement, the consent of the father is sufficient."

98:11. For M. Blowitz see p. 161:12n.

98:17-18. *A Great Catch,* a comedy, opened at the Olympic on March 17, 1883. Geneviève Ward played the part of the heroine, Mrs. de Motteville.

99:12-16. Herbert (later Sir Herbert) Beerbohm Tree (1853–1917) was relatively new to the stage when he played the foolish Lord Boodle in *A Great Catch,* a performance described by *The Athenaeum* as "a singularly diverting piece of character acting."—March 24, p. 387. Lucy Buckstone died in 1893 at the age of 34; W. H. Vernon died in 1905, at 71.

99:28–30. As has been noted, Miss Ward was, like Howells, an American.

[ISAIAH OF JERUSALEM]

In May, 1872, Arnold published a version of the last twenty-seven chapters (the Babylonian chapters) of the book of Isaiah as a reading book for schools. At Christmas, 1875, he published a finer edition of the same chapters, with an appendix made up of his version of four parts of the earlier chapters that were associated by the biblical critics with the Babylonian chapters, or at least were dissociated from the rest of the first thirty-nine. (His Introduction to this work appears in *Prose Works*, ed. Super, VII, 51–72.) On February 20, 1878, he reminded Macmillan to send him an interleaved copy of the whole book of Isaiah, so that he might work at leisure on the chapters he had not yet done (the suggestion is that he merely entered necessary corrections to the Authorized Version, and used the blank leaves to do so). Not until 1882 was he beginning to reckon the prospect of completing the version in calculating his income from Macmillan. On March 27, 1883, he wrote: " 'Isaiah of Jerusalem' is ready for the printer, except the short notes which I shall add when I have the printed and re-arranged text before me. I have an article on Isaiah in the forthcoming XIXth Century, and another in the May number, and a good deal of them I shall use for the Introduction. I will keep my corrected Isaiah by me for the next fortnight, till I have finished the second article; then the printer shall have it. What I want to know is, how long will it take to print the text (about 40 chapters) so that I may have it before me for writing the notes, which are to come all together at the end? I suppose July would not be a bad time to bring out such a book, or even the beginning of August; it is indispensable it should appear before the Old Testament of the Revisers, but this cannot, I hear, come till next year, so we are quite safe." The Preface went to the printer, R. & R. Clark of Edinburgh, by the middle of July, the text and notes by the end of the month. "The book should be a handsome one," Arnold told the publisher; "I have never done a piece of work that pleases me more."—Buckler, *Matthew Arnold's Books*, pp. 116, 123–24. It came out about November 20, while Arnold was in America. A copy went to Charles Eliot Norton, to whom Arnold remarked a year later: "With a book of this kind it is particularly hard to make an impression in England at this moment; the new world thinks it knows all about the matter, and that nothing is to be made of it, and is sick of it; the old world profoundly distrusts the dealings with it of an innovator such as I am, wants no change in its ideas on the subject, and draws its bed-clothes over its ears. But the book will be useful some day, perhaps."—*Letters*, ed. Russell. Arnold was paid £50 each for the two articles which became the Preface, when they appeared in the *Nineteenth Century* for April and May, 1883. The articles contained several paragraphs of remarks on the Revised Version of the New Testament and some parallels between the politics of Isaiah's Palestine and modern Europe that were dropped from the Introduction (see Textual Notes), and some samples of Arnold's forthcoming version.

100:1–2. The Revised Version of the Old Testament in English, begun by a company of twenty-seven revisers on June 30, 1870, in consequence of a resolution of the Convocation of the Province of Canterbury, was completed on June 20, 1884, and published early in the following year.

100:8–13. Joseph Butler, "Six Sermons . . . upon Public Occasions," IV, ¶6–7 ("Children in Charity Schools"); *Works*, ed. W. E. Gladstone (Oxford, 1896), II, 343–44.

101:1–2. The First Lesson at Morning Prayer on Christmas Day is Isaiah 9:1–8. Arnold quotes the Authorized Version of verse 5, which in the Revised Version would become: "For all the armour of the armed man in the tumult, and the garments rolled in blood, shall even be for burning, for fuel of fire," with "For every boot of the booted warrior" as alternative to the opening words. The First Lesson at Evening Prayer is Isaiah 7:10–17.

101:13–16. *The Prophets of Israel and Their Place in History* (New York, 1882), p. 276 (Lecture VI, second-last paragraph).

101:17–19. See notes to pp. 103:16–18, 107:3. Cheyne's 5th ed., revised, of the 1880 version reads: "Yea, every boot of him that stamped with noise, and the cloak rolled in blood—they are to be burned up as fuel of fire." In the Preface to this edition, Cheyne remarks: "Mr. Matthew Arnold (in his *Isaiah of Jerusalem*) censures the translation in the present work precisely as if its object was the same as that of my earlier attempt [1870]. I have not recalled the latter, [which aimed at reconciling in some degree English style and Hebrew scholarship]; indeed, it partly supplements the present work, especially in the introduction, which contains a moderate statement of the anti-traditional point of view scarcely as yet superseded."—(New York, 1892), I, ix.

102:5–6. The Revised Version of the New Testament in English was published in 1881.

103:16–18. "A clear sense is the indispensable thing. Even where the authorised version seems wrong, I have not always, if its words give a clear sense, thought it necessary to change them."—Introduction to Arnold's version of Isaiah XL–LXVI (1872), *Prose Works*, ed. Super, VII, 56:12–15 (and see variant to that passage). In a brief, on the whole complimentary, review of that book, T. K. Cheyne remarked: "He fails to observe that such 'noble and consecrated expressions' are sometimes . . . entirely wrong, and commonly among the chief obstacles to understanding the Scriptures."—*Academy* IX, 163 (February 19, 1876).

104:20–22. Isaiah 7:12. Arnold's bad example was Cheyne's version.

104:32–34. Arnold made the same remark in his Introduction to Isaiah XL–LXVI (1872), *Prose Works,* ed. Super, VII, 59.

106:17–18. "All knowledge may be in itself good," remarked Arnold in his Preface to Johnson's *Six Chief Lives of the Poets* (1878), perhaps alluding to the opening words of Aristotle *de Anima* or to "Scire aliquid laus est," Dionysius Cato *Disticha de Moribus* IV, 29.—*Prose Works,* ed. Super, VIII, 312:10 and note. "All knowledge is interesting to a wise man," he remarked in "Literature and Science" (1882), p. 60:14–15.

107:3. Thomas Kelly Cheyne (1841–1915), a student of Ewald's and a late addition to the company engaged in preparing the Revised Version of the Old Testament, himself published two versions of Isaiah, one in 1870 and the other in 1880–81. As director of the theological department of *The Academy* he reviewed in that journal, over his signature, both of Arnold's versions of Isaiah (February 19, 1876, and December 22, 1883). Arnold subsequently had some friendly correspondence with him on scriptural translation, but nothing with reference to Isaiah has survived.

107:6–7. Campegius Vitringa (c. 1659–1722), Dutch exegete, published his two folio volumes of commentary on Isaiah in 1714 and 1720. H. F. W. Gesenius (1786–1842), professor of theology at Halle, published a commentary on Isaiah in 1820–21. Heinrich von Ewald (1803–75), professor at Göttingen, published *Die Propheten des Alten Bundes* in 1840 (second ed., 1867–68). Franz Julius Delitzsch (1813–90), professor at Rostock, Erlangen, and Leipzig, published his *Biblischer Commentar über den Prophet Jesaia* in 1866.

107:12–20. Delitzsch, *Biblical Commentary on the Prophecies of Isaiah*, tr. James Martin (Edinburgh, 1877), I, 83–85, 98–99.

107:26. See p. 110:23–24 and n.

108:11–12. The Scottish theologian and Semitic scholar William Robertson Smith (1846–94), one of the Company of Revisers of the Old Testament, like Cheyne had studied at Göttingen. Arnold has already cited his lectures.

109:26. Arnold repeatedly told his countrymen that they had "an upper class materialised, a middle class vulgarised, and a lower class brutalised." See "Equality" (1878), "Irish Catholicism and British Liberalism" (1878), and "Wordsworth" (1879), *Prose Works*, ed. Super, VIII, 299, 345; IX, 38.

109:35–110:6. "Six Sermons . . . upon Public Occasions," II, ¶8 ("Before the Corporation of London"); *Works*, ed. Gladstone, II, 302 (with omissions).

110:19–30. See Isaiah 7:14, 8:8, 7:3 (10:21); 8:1, 3.

111:7. The expression is from Revelation 11:15.

111:18. Isaiah 22:1, 5.

113:35–37. At the village of La Albuera, thirteen miles southeast of Badajoz, in Spain, some 30,000 British, Portuguese and Spanish troops under Marshal Beresford on May 16, 1811, defeated a somewhat smaller French army under Marshal Soult in a very bloody battle that cost the British more than half their force. The French retired without relieving the siege of Badajoz, but the British and their allies gave up the siege a few weeks later in the face of renewed pressure. Sir William Napier, without distorting the barrenness of the victory, is eloquent in his description of his countrymen's performance (a passage which much enhanced the reputation of his *History*): "Suddenly and sternly recovering, they closed on their terrible enemies, and then was seen with what a strength and majesty the British soldier fights. . . . Nothing could stop that astonishing infantry . . . ; their flashing eyes were bent on the dark columns in their front; their measured tread shook the ground; their dreadful volleys swept away the head of every formation; their deafening shouts overpowered the dissonant cries that broke from all parts of the tumultuous crowd, as foot by foot, and with a horrid carnage, it was driven by the incessant vigour of the attack to the farthest edge of the hill. . . . The rain flowed after in streams discoloured with blood, and 1500 unwounded men, the remnant of 6000 unconquerable British soldiers, stood triumphant on the fatal hill."—*History of the War in the Peninsula*

(London, 1828–40), Book XII, end of chapt. vi. The *Victoires, conquêtes, désastres, revers et guerres civiles des Français de 1792 à 1815*, a huge compilation edited by General C. T. Beauvais and other Napoleonic soldiers soon after Waterloo, aimed at refurbishing the glory of the French soldier and flattering the chauvinism of the military by portraying twenty-three years of victory against the single day of defeat. The work, largely drawn from the files of the government newspaper, the *Moniteur*, was immensely popular but historically worthless.

113:37–38. In Isaiah 37:36–38 it is said that the angel of the Lord smote in the camp of the Assyrians 185,000 men, "and when they arose early in the morning, behold, they were all dead corpses." Thereupon Sennacherib returned to his capital of Nineveh and was assassinated. But sober historical evaluation makes it clear that the Assyrians suffered no such loss, for their power was not threatened by rebellion, and furthermore Sennacherib lived another twenty years. The Assyrian account may be found in D. D. Luckenbill, ed., *The Annals of Sennacherib* (Chicago, 1924).

114:6–7. Isaiah 32:1–2.

114:10–11. John Davison, *Discourses on Prophecy* (London, 1824), p. 420; (4th ed., Oxford, 1839), p. 319 (Discourse VI, part iv); quoted in *Literature and Dogma, Prose Works*, ed. Super, VI, 386:36–37.

114:16–17. *Analogy* II, iv, ¶8; *Works*, ed. Gladstone, I, 251; quoted in *St. Paul and Protestantism* and *Literature and Dogma, Prose Works*, ed. Super, VI, 87, 386. Butler's word was "precipitating," not "anticipating."

117:11–14. Isaiah 9:6–7, 11:1, 4:2, 11:4.

117:15–18. Isaiah 49:7, Matthew 12:19, Isaiah 42:2.

118:18–23. Delitzsch, tr. Martin, I, 56–57; II, 84, 122–27.

119:36–120:3. Isaiah, chapts. 9–11.

120:20. "The meek shall inherit the earth."—Psalm 37:11. See Jesus in the Sermon on the Mount, Matthew 5:5.

122:30–38. Edition of 1892, I, 125–27 (introduction to Isaiah, chapt. xxi).

123:5. Isaiah 14:4.

123:30. Ewald deals with Isaiah in the second and fourth volumes of his *Commentary on the Prophets of the Old Testament*, tr. J. Frederick Smith (London, 1876, 1880). For the Burden of Moab, see II, 135–50.

124:16. Robert Lowth (1710–87) first published his new translation of Isaiah in 1778. It was several times republished in the nineteenth century.

124:29–32. Ewald, II, 173; see Cheyne (1892), I, 142.

125:5–13. Ewald, II, 79–81.

126:1–5. Cheyne (1892) argues for the hypothetical invasion of Judaea by Sargon.—I, 68–69. Both he and Ewald place chapt. i "in the middle of the Book," Ewald after chapt. xvii.—II, 117–32.

127:32–35. See II Kings 18:13–19:37.

128:6. See Ewald, II, 261–65 (where only 37:22–35 are admitted as genuine, out of chapts. xxxvi–xxxix); and see Cheyne (1892), I, 209; II, 188–89.

128:8–9. See II Chronicles 26:22, 32:32.

129:9–11. "Jehovah of hosts" was Robertson Smith's expression (e.g., at p. 242); Cheyne's 1892 version of the passage is: "Therefore—it is an oracle of the Lord, Jehovah Sabáoth, the Hero of Israel."

129:17–20. Cheyne's 1892 edition reads: " . . . good, the land shall become deserted, at whose two kings thou fearest horribly."

[NOTES ON CANCELLED PASSAGES]

555:18–20. "Maximen und Reflexionen," *Werke* (Stuttgart, 1833), XLIX, 64; (Weimar, 1897), XLVIII, 179; jotted in one of Arnold's "General Note-Books."—*Note-Books*, ed. Lowry, p. 522.

556:33–41. John William Burgon (1813–88), whose poem "Petra" won the Newdigate prize in 1845 (two years after Arnold's "Cromwell"), attacked the Revised Version of the New Testament in three articles in the *Quarterly Review* (October, 1881–April, 1882), and reprinted them as *The Revision Revised* (London, 1883). He became dean of Chichester in 1875.

557:19–20. "The instinct of self-preservation in humanity" was one of the two great motives of human existence (along with the instinct for reproduction) according to a statement Arnold attributed to Émile Littré in *Literature and Dogma* (1871).—*Prose Works*, ed. Super, VI, 174. To this instinct Arnold ascribed even such apparent work of chance as the survival of the manuscripts of Aristophanes, whereas those of Menander were (he supposed) all lost.—"On the Modern Element in Literature" (1857/1869), *Prose Works*, ed. Super, I, 29.

557:29–31. "Thou wilt not leave my soul in hell" is the Authorized Version of the quotation in Acts 2:27 of Psalm 16:10. The Revised Version substituted "Hades" for "hell" in Acts and "Sheol" for "hell" in Psalms (the latter still unpublished, of course, when Arnold wrote). "Virum volitare per ora"—"take wing through the mouths of men"—is from Vergil *Georgics* III, 9.

557:36–37. "Deliver me from offendiculum of scrupulousness" was a prayer of Joseph Butler late in life, surviving in manuscript.— *Works*, ed. W. E. Gladstone (Oxford, 1896), II, 424, quoted by Arnold in "A Psychological Parallel" (1876), *Prose Works*, ed. Super, VIII, 132.

558:4–5. Hesiod *Works and Days* 40, quoted by Plato *Republic* V, 466C and *Laws* 690E.

559:26. Spencer Perceval (1762–1812), a protégé of the younger Pitt's, became prime minister in 1809, at a time when English affairs in the Peninsular War were exceedingly difficult, and within a year he had also to face a Regency at home because of the insanity of George III. He was assassinated in the lobby of the House of Commons on May 11, 1812.

559:29–30. In "My Countrymen" (1866), *Prose Works*, ed. Super, V, 29. The proprietor of *The Times* was John Walter (1818–94), third successive bearer of that name to own the newspaper from its founding.

560:5. Samuel Smith (1836–1906), a cotton-broker of Liverpool, was elected to Parliament at a Liverpool bye-election in December, 1882. "A zealous presbyterian of Liberal views, he . . . constantly spoke in the House of Commons on moral, social, religious, currency, and Indian questions. Critics likened him to Jeremiah, but he was sincere and well-informed," said G. L. Norgate in the *D. N. B.* In 1875 he was one of those who invited Moody and Sankey to Liverpool. Christian Socialism, a term first used by F. D. Maurice, Charles Kingsley, and others in mid century, was embraced by the interdenominational Christian Socialist League of the early 1880's.

561:26–27. This is Cheyne's reading of Isaiah 9:5, and Cheyne was one of the Revisers. See p. 101:17–19 and note to 101:1–2.

561:31–33. "Isaïe qui a vu la gloire de Nabuchodonosor et son orgueil insensé longtemps avant sa naissance, a prédit sa chute soudaine et celle de son empire. . . . En exécution du décret de Dieu, Cyrus se fait tout à coup une ouverture dans Babylone. . . . Ainsi fut livrée en proie *aux Mèdes et aux Perses, et à Cyrus*, comme avoient dit les prophètes, *cette superbe Babylone* [see Isaiah 13:7, 21:2, etc.]—Bossuet, *Discours sur l'histoire universelle*, pt. II,. chapt. vi; *Oeuvres complètes*, ed. F. Lachat (Paris, 1864), XXIV, 419, 421.

561:42–562:4. The (Episcopal) Church of Ireland was disestablished by Gladstone in July, 1869, in response, as Arnold believed, to the English Nonconformist dislike of establishments, not out of a sense of justice to the Irish Catholics. Hence his use here of the names of two leaders of the disestablishment movement. Henry Richard (1812–88), Welsh Congregationalist minister, was a member of Parliament from 1868, leader (to use Arnold's term) of the party of Savages against the party of Simpletons who supported church privilege unswervingly.—"Falkland" (1877), *Prose Works*, ed. Super, VIII, 205. Edward Miall (1809–81), member of Parliament from 1852 to 1874, was founder in 1844 of the British Anti-State Church Association, which soon became the Society for the Liberation of Religion from State Patronage and Control. He was founder and editor of *The Nonconformist*, weekly newspaper of the Congregationalists. The proposed disestablishment of the Irish church was the subject of a substantial section of *Culture and Anarchy* (1868) and, after disestablishment was accomplished, of a little-known but delightfully ironic letter to *The Pall Mall Gazette* on August 2, 1869, "A Recantation and Apology."— *Prose Works*, ed. Super, V, 193–99, 319–24.

562:26. The fall of Sebastopol to the French, Turkish and British forces on September 9, 1855, after a siege of nearly a year, marked the effective end of the Crimean war.

562:28. John Carvell Williams (1821–1909) was for more than fifty years a leader of the Liberation Society.

562:32–33. Sermon IV of the *Six Sermons*, preached May 9, 1745, for the Yearly Meeting of the Children in Charity Schools.—*Works*, ed. Gladstone, II, 339–60.

566:20–21. See p. 114:17.

566:24. "Maximen und Reflexionen," *Werke* (Stuttgart, 1833), XLIX, 100, jotted at the beginning of Arnold's pocket diary for 1878 and quoted in his sketch of Edoardo Fusco (1876).—*Note-Books*, ed. Lowry, p. 291; *Prose Works*, ed. Super, VIII, 8.

566:40–42. Isaiah 6:5.

[ADDRESS TO THE WORDSWORTH SOCIETY]

When Professor W. A. Knight invited Arnold to join the Wordsworth Society (moved, no doubt, by the publication of Arnold's volume of Selections from Wordsworth), Arnold replied: "Do not think me rude if I say that I cannot belong to your Wordsworth Club: I have in like manner refused to belong to the Shakspeare Society. Life is too short for these things—at least *my* life, as school-inspecting has made it, is." But the invitation to preside at the meeting for 1883 was not so easily declined. The session was held in the hall of Westminster School on May 2; Arnold wrote to his wife immediately thereafter: "The speech is over, and I got through pretty well. The grave would have been cheerful compared to the view presented by the Westminster Chamber and the assembled Wordsworth Society when I came upon the platform. The hall was not full, the worthy Knight having rather muddled things, and the Society is not composed of people of a festive type. But my darling Lucy looked charming. . . . Coleridge, who proposed a vote of thanks to me, was very sweet.—The papers were awfully boring, except Stopford Brooke's, which was saved by his Irish oratorical manner. I have quite been bilious for the last day or two, and truly when I saw the society dons met before me my tongue clave to the roof of my mouth, and I nearly began to retch. However, it is over, and now I have no more speechifying in prospect."—*Letters*, ed. Russell. "The meeting place was certainly rather depressing, and the audience not bursting with liveliness," he told Knight a fortnight later. He arranged to have his remarks published in *Macmillan's Magazine* for June and was paid £5 for the publication. The report published in the *Transactions* was printed from the *Macmillan's* article, but with a few corrections Arnold forwarded to Knight; the remark about the Wordsworth photographs was added at Knight's request, presumably not having been made at the meeting. The *Transactions* version has been published in F. Neiman, ed., *Essays, Letters, and Reviews by Matthew Arnold* (Cambridge, Mass., 1960).

When Arnold died in April, 1888, Wordsworth's grandson Gordon Wordsworth journeyed all the way from the Lake District to Laleham for the funeral. "It was a real tribute of affection," wrote Arnold's widow to Gordon's mother; "I liked to know that the grandson of him, whom my beloved Matt so venerated & admired, was with us on that last sad day."

131:24–25. Sonnet, "To the Memory of Raisley Calvert," line 6; Sonnet, "Written in London, September, 1802," line 11.

131:26-132:1. *The Excursion*, I, 397–400.

132:3–4. "Ode to Duty," final line.

132:14. John Duke, Lord Coleridge, was Arnold's friend from

boyhood; he was president of the Wordsworth Society in 1882. The promised paper was in fact never read. But at the conclusion of the present meeting Lord Coleridge moved a vote of thanks to Arnold as president:

"I have been asked to do something which some one must do, which all of you desire should be done, and which, in one respect perhaps, there is hardly any one present who can do with greater propriety than myself, namely, to move a vote of thanks to Mr. Matthew Arnold for his address, and for being our President for the year. He has told us how very old he is, and how very grave and solemn he has become, to which every one who looks at him, and listens to him, and reads him, must at once entirely assent. He tells us that he has withdrawn from the world, that he longs to enter a cell, to go into a monastery; and he has described the charms of reflection and meditation with much personal appreciation and characteristic accuracy. But though he has done that, and come here to preside over us, I am sure none of us would have thought that these were his peculiar and characteristic qualities upon any authority less cogent than his own. For my own part, having been brought up with him from a child, I may say that the statement comes upon me as a complete, an interesting, and a pleasurable surprise. With regard to Wordsworth, however, of all living men he has probably done most to bring back and place upon its true grounds the devotion to that great Poet. I should say, moreover, that he is fitly our President, because not only is he perhaps the greatest of English critics, but because he is, if not the greatest, at any rate the most exquisite, of English poets. Those of us who have had the pleasure to live for many years in the light of his friendship know him also to be the most generous, the most steadfast, the most loyal of friends. As his oldest living friend, and as one who yields to no man in admiration for him, as well as one who has owed him much for many, many years, I gladly take the opportunity of moving this vote of thanks."

132:17. Stopford Brooke's paper "On Wordsworth's *Guide to the Lakes*" was published in the *Transactions*, no. 5, pp. 25–35.

132:20–21. Aubrey de Vere's "Remarks on the Personal Character of Wordsworth's Poetry" were printed in the *Transactions*, no. 5, pp. 13–21, and reprinted in de Vere's *Essays, Chiefly Literary and Ethical* (London, 1889), pp. 319–29. His "Recollections of Wordsworth" may be found in his *Essays, Chiefly on Poetry* (London, 1887), II, 275–95. Isabella Fenwick, thirteen years younger than Wordsworth, became his and his family's close friend for the last dozen years of his life; in 1841 she took a house at Ambleside to be near them. To her Wordsworth dictated an extensive series of valuable notes on his poems.

132:25–26. William Angus Knight (1836–1916), professor of moral philosophy in the University of St. Andrews and editor of Wordsworth's works and correspondence, was permanent honorary secretary of the Wordsworth Society from its founding in September, 1880, to its dissolution on February 17, 1887.

132:28–29. In the *Transactions*, no. 3 (1882), pp. 56–76, Knight published a descriptive catalogue of thirty-eight portraits of Wordsworth, of which he reproduced five photographically, on elegant mountings (pp. 79–91): a miniature on ivory by Margaret Gillies (1841), Haydon's portrait (1842), the American artist Henry Inman's portrait (1844), the bust by Angus Fletcher, brother of Lady Richardson (1844), and the posthumous Westminster Abbey statue by Frederick Thrupp (1852). Arnold used the Haydon portrait as frontispiece for his own selection from Wordsworth's poetry.

133:8–10. Presumably the final sonnet of the River Duddon series, "After-Thought." The phrase "We see into the life of things" is from line 49 of "Tintern Abbey."

133:16–20. Ed. E. Castle (Berlin, 1916), I, 354 (February 11 and 9, 1831).

133:29. "Tintern Abbey," line 48.

134:11–12. *The Excursion*, IV, 238.

134:14–15. Lines 5–6 of the sonnet beginning "Here pause: the poet claims at least this praise."

[AN OLD PLAYGOER ON "IMPULSE"]

Arnold's letter to *The Pall Mall Gazette* on B. C. Stephenson's *Impulse*, the third letter signed merely "An Old Playgoer," was published on May 25, 1883, and brought in response a letter in defence of Stephenson the next night. Arnold's line of reasoning respecting *Impulse* is much like what he said four years earlier about another English adaptation of a French play, *Pink Dominos*, in "The French Play in London" (1879), *Prose Works*, ed. Super, IX, 79, 85. Arnold received £4 15s in payment for this letter and the next one.

135:1. B. C. Stephenson's drama *Impulse* opened at the St. James's Theatre on December 9, 1882. It was altered from *La Maison du Mari*, by Xavier du Montépin and Victor Kervani, produced in

Paris in 1873. The theater, in King Street, St. James's, one of the most delightful in London, opened in 1835 and has only recently (1957) been demolished.

135:6–7. *De Imitatione Christi*, III, xliv, 5–7, jotted in Arnold's pocket diary for January 18, 1880, January 10, 1882, and at the beginning of 1883 and 1885.—*Note-Books*, ed. Lowry, pp. 334, 369, 388, 411. ("It is better to pass by many things with a deaf ear, and meditate rather matters which concern your peace.")

135:21. Flaubert's *Madame Bovary* was published in 1857.

136:2–3. See *Hamlet*, III, ii, 24–25.

136:10. The Abbé Prévost's *Manon Lescaut* was published in 1731.

136:15–16. Three of the most popular plays in the repertoire of the *Comédie française* in London in the summer of 1879 were by the younger Alexandre Dumas (1824–95). Victorien Sardou (1831–1908), like Dumas a member of the Academy, was one of the most popular and prolific dramatists of his day, a writer of comedies and history plays. See p. 140:22n.

136:32. See p. 137:36–38n.

137:16. William Hunter Kendal (1843–1917) and his wife Madge Robertson (1849–1935) played the same engagements from 1875 until their retirement in 1908. She became a Dame of the British Empire in 1926. They were partners in the management of the St. James's Theatre for nine years, beginning in 1879. In *Impulse* both played secondary roles.

137:26–31. Mrs. Macdonald was played by Linda Dietz, Victor de Riel by Arthur Dacre.

137:31–32. "Simia quam similis turpissuma bestia nobis" is attributed to Ennius in Cicero *De natura deorum* I. xxxv. 97; see *Ennianae Poesis Reliquiae*, ed. J. Vahlen (new ed.; Leipzig, 1903), p. 211 (Satires, line 69). ("How like is the ape, that vilest of beasts, to ourselves.")

137:36–38. The "journals of society" were a group of weekly papers following in the footsteps of *Vanity Fair* (started November 7, 1868). Two of the most successful were *The World*, a Wednesday paper started July 8, 1874, by Edmund Yates, who had been on the staff of Dickens's *All the Year Round*, and *Truth*, a Thursday paper started January 4, 1877, by Henry Labouchere, who had been on the staff of *The World* from its beginning. See "Joseph de Maistre on Russia," *Prose Works*, ed. Super, IX, 91. "*Impulse* is the silly and unmeaning title of an excellent play, produced, with well-merited success, at the St. James's Theatre on Saturday evening."—*The World*, December 13, 1882, p. 10. "It is on the whole an excellent comedy. The story is interesting, and in the main well developed, and there are a good many telling situations. As a concession to English morals, it is assumed that the lady who runs away from her husband with a Frenchman is—up to the very moment when she leaves her home—a faithful wife, which is slightly improbable."—*Truth*, January 18, 1883, p. 81. The two editors carried on something of a running dialogue with each other as "Edmund" and "Henry" in the pages of their journals.

137:37. Psalm 42:7.

137:38–138:4. Labouchere from 1880 was a radical member of Parliament from Northampton, with Charles Bradlaugh as his colleague. Bradlaugh, a professed atheist, was repeatedly barred from his seat in the House for his refusal to take the oath, and was only finally seated in 1886. For earlier references to his Reform activity, see *Culture and Anarchy* and *Friendship's Garland, Prose Works*, ed. Super, V, *passim*.

138:4–5. Byron, *Childe Harold*, IV, 1269.

[AN OLD PLAYGOER AT THE LYCEUM]

Arnold wrote his short article on Irving's performance of *Much Ado about Nothing* on May 24–26, 1883. "I send you one more theatre letter," he wrote to John Morley, editor of *The Pall Mall Gazette*, on the 27th. "The Lyceum really deserved one. But it is my last, and I must now prepare for the invasion of America. . . . It is kind of you to like my letters to the *P. M. G.*—the last flicker of that nearly exhausted rushlight, but your affectionate friend." —*Letters*, ed. Russell. The letter was published on May 30. When Arnold got to New York in October, he found Irving's company performing there, and again in Boston when he arrived a week or so later.

139:1–7. Ouloug-beb, who preferred reading *Zadig* to the *Thousand and One Nights* and the *Thousand and One Days*, is reported to have had this conversation with his sultanas by Voltaire in the second paragraph of the "Epistle Dedicatory" of *Zadig* (1747).

139:8. Henry Irving, long actor-manager at the Lyceum Theatre, produced *Much Ado about Nothing*, with Ellen Terry as his leading lady, beginning October 11, 1882. Theirs was a partnership at that theater that began in 1878 with *Hamlet* and lasted until 1902. Irving was knighted in 1895 and died in 1905 at the age of 67,

Ellen Terry became a Dame of the British Empire in 1925 and died in 1928 at the age of 81. The theater, one of London's largest, was opened in 1834 on the site of an earlier theater on Wellington Street, Strand. A successor that preserves some features of Irving's theater was scheduled for demolition in 1939 in a scheme to rebuild the area; it was spared by the intervention of the war and still stands in all its elegance as "the world's most famous dance hall."

139:9–10. See p. 137.

139:11–15. *Much Ado about Nothing*, I, i, 251–52; II, i, 29–31.

139:17–18. Fred Archer (1857–86) was England's leading jockey; by the end of his career he had ridden over 8,000 races and won more than a third of them. William Marwood (1820–83), public hangman, invented the "long drop" which instantly killed by dislocating the vertebrae instead of bringing death by slow strangulation. His *Life* was published in 1883.

139:19–20. For Henry Labouchere, see p. 137:38n. In a review of the production of *The Comedy of Errors* at the Strand earlier in the year, *Truth's* critic praised the company for taking freedoms with Shakespeare's text instead of adopting it literally: "We should have been bored to death with an impossible play, whereas, as it is, we are fairly amused with a very decent farce."—January 25, 1883, p. 117.

139:25–27; 140:1–6, 12–14. *Much Ado*, I, i, 39–42; II, i, 38–42; II, i, 50–52.

140:15. See p. 137:38n.

140:22. *Heartsease*, an adaptation by James Mortimer of the younger Dumas' *La Dame aux camélias*, opened at the Princess's on June 5, 1875, and was revived at the Court on May 1, 1880. *La Dame aux camélias* (1852) was in turn Dumas' adaptation of one of his own novels; it is best remembered as the basis of Verdi's opera *La Traviata*. For *Impulse* see pp. 135–38.

141:12. Johnston Forbes-Robertson (1853–1937) began his theatrical career in 1874. Arnold may have seen him in *Heartsease* at the Court Theatre in 1880. He joined the company at the Lyceum for the revival of *Much Ado*. His was a long career as actor and manager with a wide range of classic and modern roles. He was knighted in 1913.

141:13. William Terriss died in 1897 at the age of 50, stabbed to death outside the Adelphi Theatre.

141:18. William Farren was the second in a line of four generations of actors of the same name, reaching from the eighteenth

century to 1937. He retired in 1855 and died in 1861 at the age
of 75. Robert Keeley (1793–1869) was praised by Dickens as a
superb Dogberry and even better Verges.

141:20. Charles Kemble (1775–1854) was performing in *Much
Ado* before Arnold was born, but Arnold may have seen him as
Benedick at Covent Garden in the spring of 1840. He was the
father of the Fanny Kemble Arnold saw at the Princess's with
Macready in 1848, and younger brother of John Philip Kemble.

142:9. *Fédora*, an adaptation by Herman Charles Merivale from
the French of Sardou, opened on May 5, 1883, at the Haymarket.

[NUMBERS]

When Arnold sailed for America on October 13, 1883, he had with
him specially printed copies of a revised "Literature and Science"
and the lecture on "Numbers" written for the American tour. "I
have nearly broken my heart over [the latter], with which I mean
to open in New York, but I begin to think it will do after all.
But we shall see," he wrote to G. W. Smalley only ten days
earlier. The substance of the lecture was foreshadowed in his little-
known review of Curtius's *History of Greece* in 1876: "The sixteen years of the administration of Eubulus (B.C. 354–338) mark
. . . a critical time in Athenian history. . . . 'He based his policy
upon the low and vulgar inclinations of humanity, and by satisfying these estranged his fellow-citizens from all more serious endeavours.' . . . One can well understand that the deterioration
worked by such a leading was fatal. What one asks oneself is,
why the faultier side in the Athenian character, the side which
made the reign of Eubulus possible, should have finally prevailed
rather than the nobler side, the side which made possible the reign
of Pericles? One asks oneself whether it is inevitable, then, that
the faultier side of a national character should be always the one
to prevail finally; and whether, therefore, since every national
character has its faultier side, the greatness of no great nation can
be permanent. And the answer probably is that the greatness cannot be permanent of any nation which is not great by its mere
material numbers as well as by its qualities. Great qualities are bal-
anced by faults, and in any community there will be more individuals with the faults of their nation than with its great qualities.
Now, in a small community like Athens, a community counting its
members by thousands instead of by millions, there is not a suffi-

cient recruiting-ground from which to draw ever-fresh supplies of men of the better type, capable of maintaining their country's greatness at a high level permanently, or of bringing it back there after it has for a time retrograded owing to faults or misfortunes." —*Prose Works,* ed. Super, V, 291–92. Clearly, then, whatever the tone of the lecture itself, it grew out of a context of Arnold's fear of the apparently unrestrained American democracy. His very recent work with the book of Isaiah of course provided him with something of a text for his discourse. "It was expedient in [America], where plain truth is not palatable, to lead up to the dangers of America through those of England and France," Arnold wrote to Fontanès after his return. "Tell me what you think of it, and what Scherer thinks of it," he added.

At the outset Arnold was fearful that he could not make himself heard in a large room: "The lecture itself is all right, but I am not at all sure about my delivery of it," he wrote to his sister as he faced the opening lecture at Chickering Hall on October 30, eight days after he landed. His fears were justified by the event: the audience of about 1300 was largely unable to hear the distinguished guest, "but they remained to the end, were perfectly civil and attentive, and applauded me when I had done," he wrote to her after the lecture. Discouraged as he was almost to the point of abandoning the tour, he set himself to taking elocution lessons, and the London papers, which followed his tour with lively interest, reported that he was "plainly heard" when he repeated the lecture in Boston a week later (though in a hall that held only 900). As the tour progressed and he became more familiar with his own words, further difficulties were removed: "The lecture on Numbers . . . is a sort of lay sermon, and the people are beginning to like it much," he wrote to another sister from Cincinnati. "I now *speak* it almost entirely, as it is getting lodged in my memory. In these large halls it is almost necessary to speak, as any stoppage to the voice, such as a book or paper coming between the speaker's mouth and the audience, is fatal. Of course, if you are near-sighted and have to hold your manuscript close to your face, the stoppage is worse still."—*Letters,* ed. Russell. The London papers reported with some delight that American newspapers were experiencing great difficulty with "the goddess of lubricity."

Not wishing his lectures to lose their freshness, he asked the help of George Washburn Smalley, London correspondent of the *New York Tribune,* to persuade the newspapers to limit the extent of their reporting his text. Smalley complied by writing to the New

York editors, then was much embarrassed when the London papers reported that his own newspaper ignored the request with a full two-column summary. Arnold himself was less displeased by the breach of agreement than he might have been, since, as he reported to his sisters back home, General Grant called "at the *Tribune* Office to thank them for their good report of the main points of my lecture, as he had thought the line taken so very important, but had heard imperfectly! Now I should not have suspected Grant of either knowing or caring anything whatever about me and my productions."—*Letters*, ed. Russell.

He delivered the lecture on "Numbers" eighteen times: on October 30 in Chickering Hall, New York; on November 7 in Horticultural Hall, Boston; on November 13 in Bridgeport, Connecticut; on November 15 in Hartford, Connecticut; on December 12 at Concord, Massachusetts; on December 20 in the Academy of Music at Baltimore; on December 26 in Association Hall at Philadelphia; on January 15 in a theater at Cleveland, Ohio; on January 17 in Merrill Hall, Detroit; on January 21 in the Unitarian Church, Milwaukee; on January 22 in the Central Music Hall, Chicago; on January 30 at St. Louis; on February 4 in the Plymouth Church, Indianapolis; on February 6 in Smith and Nixon's Hall, Cincinnati; on February 13 in Shaftesbury Hall, Toronto; on February 16 in the Grand Opera House, Ottawa; on February 19 at Montreal; and on February 21 in the First Parish Church, Portland, Maine. It was published in the *Nineteenth Century* for April, 1884, after his return, and brought him £50.

143:1–2. Boswell, *Life of Johnson*, April 7, 1775.

143:11–13. Joseph Butler, Sermon VII, "Upon the Character of Balaam," ¶16.—*Works*, ed. W. E. Gladstone (Oxford, 1896), II, 134. This proposition, first quoted by Arnold in his essay on "Bishop Butler and the Zeit-Geist" (1876; *Prose Works*, ed. Super, VIII, 12), was one he quoted or alluded to frequently in his later writings.

144:15–20. See p. 9:2–13 and n.

144:29. Matthew 22:14. Plato speaks similarly: " 'Many,' as they say in the mysteries, 'are the thyrsus-bearers, but few are the mystics,'—meaning, as I interpret the words, 'the true philosophers.' "—Phaedo 69 C-D (tr. Jowett).

144:31–32. "Many Called, Few Chosen," final paragraph; *Parochial Sermons* (London and Oxford, 1840), V, 304. Arnold quoted this remark in "The Bishop and the Philosopher" (1863), *Prose Works*, ed. Super, III, 44.

145:22–146:2. Plato *Republic* VI, 496.

146:13. Eubulus (c. 405–330 B. C.), an honest and efficient Athenian politician, was able through rational financial administration to double or treble the public revenues in a time of great difficulty. But the defeat of the Athenians and Thebans by Philip of Macedon at Chaeronea in 338 foreshadowed the speedy end of Athenian independence. Plato died in 347.

146:14–26, 32–34, 37–38. Ernst Curtius, *History of Greece,* tr. A. W. Ward (London, 1873), V, 138–39, 134 (Book VII, chapt. ii, halfway through). Arnold modified Ward's translation, which read: "the germs of the pernicious," "interests of the citizens were . . . serious affairs," "Famous *hetaerae* formed the chief topic of the town-talk," and "uttered at jovial banquets were with great ardour repeated about town." Arnold quoted part of this passage in his review of Curtius, March 25, 1876.—*Prose Works,* ed. Super, V, 291.

146:36–37. An allusion to "Plain Language from Truthful James," a humorous ballad by the American western writer Bret Harte: "the heathen Chinee" had a smile that "was childlike and bland." Harte's collection of short stories, *The Luck of Roaring Camp,* was on Arnold's reading list for 1881.—*Note-Books,* ed. Lowry, p. 601.

147:25–26, 29–32. Isaiah 10:22, 6:13. The latter passage is in neither the language of the Authorized Version nor quite that of Arnold's recently-published *Isaiah of Jerusalem* (see pp. 269, 111: 27–30). Newman, in the sermon Arnold cited on p. 144, also made much of the concept of the "remnant" and cited, among other scriptural passages, Isaiah 10:22.

147:37. Isaiah 28:1, 7. ("Woe . . . to the drunkards of Ephraim" and "they err in vision.")

148:4–5. Samaria was the chief city of Ephraim, in the Northern Kingdom, Jerusalem the chief city of Judah, in the Southern Kingdom. See p. 379.

148:21–29. See Isaiah 7:14; 9:6–21, and pp. 119:36–120:3.

149:5–6. "Seventy weeks are determined upon thy people . . . to bring in everlasting righteousness."—Daniel 9:24.

149:27–29. "A state without the means of some change is without the means of its conservation."—Burke, *Reflections on the Revolution in France,* beginning of ¶33.

151:11–16. Psalm 50:23, Isaiah 1:16, Psalm 1:2, 119:97 (and see Joshua 1:8, Psalm 1:2).

151:26. Charles Bradlaugh (1833–91), advocate of free thought

and one of the leaders of the mass meeting called by the Reform
League at Hyde Park in 1866, was before the public eye at this
time because, though repeatedly elected to Parliament from
Northampton after 1880, he was denied his seat in the House of
Commons until January 13, 1886. "Why is Mr. Bradlaugh not yet
a Dean?" asked a satirical Matthew Arnold, writing from Grub
Street in 1870.—*Friendship's Garland, Prose Works*, ed. Super, V,
343.

151:34–152:2. Arnold cited this passage with some emphasis in
"Bishop Butler and the Zeit-Geist" (1876), *Prose Works*, ed.
Super, VIII, 26:12–14; and see *God and the Bible* (1875), VII, 385.

152:14–17. Plato Gorgias 521D, jotted in Arnold's pocket diary
for September 26, 1872 and February 23, 1873, and quoted in his
Preface to *Higher Schools and Universities in Germany* (1874)
and "The Incompatibles" (1881).—*Note-Books*, ed. Lowry, pp.
183, 196; *Prose Works*, ed. Super, VII, 130; IX, 268.

152:34–35. For Arnold's view of the English conquests and confiscations and the penal laws in Ireland, see the long pair of essays
on "The Incompatibles" (1881), *Prose Works*, ed. Super, IX, 238–
85. The mid-nineteenth century had seen massive emigration of
the Irish to America, hence Arnold's suggestion that it would be
indiscreet of him to criticize Ireland before an American audience.

153:28. See the opening of "Falkland" (1877), *Prose Works*, ed.
Super, VIII, 188.

154:17–23. January 25, 1863; printed by A. F. Powell, "Sainte-
Beuve and Matthew Arnold—an Unpublished Letter," *French
Quarterly* III, 154 (September, 1921). Ste.-Beuve wrote "traversé
notre littérature et notre poésie par . . . ."

154:30–32. Acts 19:35.

155:4. Translated as "wantonness" in the Authorized Version of
Romans 13:13, and II Peter 2:18, "lasciviousness" in I Peter 4:3.
Plato uses the word in a passage Jowett translates: "Little by
little this spirit of licence, finding a home, imperceptibly penetrates
into manners and customs; whence, issuing with greater force, it
invades contracts between man and man, and from contracts goes
on to laws and constitutions, in utter *recklessness*, ending at last,
Socrates, by an overthrow of all rights, private as well as public."
—*Republic* IV, 424 D-E. Gaylord C. LeRoy discusses the political
and social background of Arnold's remarks on lubricity in "Arnold
and Aselgeia," *Bulletin of the New York Public Library* LXVII
301–6 (May, 1963). From the time of the defeat of the French by
the Germans in 1870, Arnold believed that their national character

had been undermined by sensuality, but LeRoy conceives that Arnold's moralistic attitude springs less from a personal psychic cleavage than from an obsessive political fear: often "expansionist" and the champion of the anti-aristocratic movement in the modern world, Arnold swings on the other hand to a "frantic condemnation of Jacobinism," "a fear of insurrection—insurrection of the working class, insurrection of man's repressed instinctual self."

155:11–14. "La nature ne tient pas du tout à ce que l'homme soit chaste."—*Souvenirs d'enfance et de jeunesse* (Paris, 1883), p. 359. 'C'est peut-être après tout le libertin qui a raison et qui pratique la vraie philosophie de la vie."—pp. 149–50.

155:31–156:6. Arnold here summarizes the description of the ethnology of the French he gave in *On the Study of Celtic Literature* (1866), *Prose Works*, ed. Super, III, 349–50.

156:19–21. Arnold quoted this expression in "A French Elijah" (1871), in his review of Renan's *La Réforme intellectuelle et morale* (1872) and in "Equality" (1878).—*Prose Works*, ed. Super, VII, 11, 44; VIII, 292.

157:34. Arnold applies this expression to France in *Literature and Dogma* (1873) and frequently thereafter.—*Prose Works*, ed. Super, VI, 390, and note to VIII, 223:38.

158:25–27. See p. 143:1–2.

159:17–23. An allusion to Renan's second Letter to Strauss in *La Réforme intellectuelle et morale* (Paris, 1871), p. 204; cited in Arnold's review of that book, *Prose Works*, ed. Super, VII, 45.

160:7–8. "Know ye not that the unrighteous shall not inherit the kingdom of God? Be not deceived: neither fornicators, . . . nor adulterers . . . shall inherit the kingdom of God."—I Corinthians 6:9–10.

160:16–18. *Republic* IX, 588–89.

160:20–25. William Paley, Sermon XIV, "How Virtue Produces Belief, and Vice Unbelief," ¶4; *Sermons* (London, 1828), p. 69; jotted in Arnold's pocket diary for September 12, 1883.—*Note-Books*, ed. Lowry, p. 398.

161:9. "He that is perverse in his ways shall fall at once."—Proverbs 28:18. The word is a favorite of the author of Proverbs, but occurs elsewhere in the Bible: e.g., "a perverse and crooked generation" (Deuteronomy 32:5) and "O faithless and perverse generation" (Matthew 17:17, Luke 9:41).

161:12. Henri Georges Opper de Blowitz (1825–1903) became Paris correspondent of *The Times* in 1871.

161:18–19. Isaiah 31:2.

161:35–37. One is tempted to believe this sentence needs to be clarified by emendation, e.g.: "of inexorable fatality of operation, of the moral failure of the unsound majority to impair . . ." See p. 163:3–4.

163:13–14. Isaiah 10:21, 6:10.

163:33–36. Letter from Cologne, June 9, 1828.—A. P. Stanley, *The Life and Correspondence of Thomas Arnold, D. D.* (13th ed.; London, 1882), II, 324 (Appendix D, IV).

[EMERSON]

Emerson's death on April 27, 1882, led Arnold to propose to Macmillan (who in the summer of 1867 carried a letter of introduction to Emerson from Arnold) the publication of an English edition of Emerson; "for £50 I would write you an introduction," he wrote on May 21. Macmillan before Emerson's death had arranged to bring out such an edition, with a Preface by John Morley, and was in fact at that moment assembling the materials, but invited Arnold to write his essay for *Macmillan's Magazine.* In November he promised the article for Whitsuntide, 1883; by Easter it was to be ready after the summer holidays: "I want to read all Emerson's things again before writing it." Then in mid-July, with the American lecture tour taking shape, the essay was further deferred, and later was planned for delivery there.—Buckler, *Matthew Arnold's Books,* pp. 160–62. On the eve of his departure he wrote to his sister Mrs. Forster: "I have not yet written a line, and, of course, this is a cause of anxiety; but to attempt to write it in this last distracted week would probably be vain, and all I do is to re-read Emerson, and to consider what other people I may take in connexion with him. I have a strong sense of his value, which I am glad to say has deepened instead of diminishing on re-reading him. I always found him of more use than Carlyle, and I now think so more than ever. I should like to slip away from New York and see Concord, and the grave where Emerson is buried, and Boston Bay, all by myself, and then to write my lecture with this local impression fresh upon me." "I shall be glad to have it to think of on the voyage," he wrote to his sister Frances. From New York he reported to her: "I did a good deal of reading [on the voyage]— half a volume of Emerson's *Essays,* and the two thick volumes of his correspondence with Carlyle—the best memorial of Carlyle, I am inclined to think, which exists. My lecture on Emerson is pretty well formed in my head, and the passages marked which I mean to use for it—but oh, my dear Fan, how and when am I to write it? The blaring publicity of this place is beyond all that I had any idea of." "At present I must give every spare moment to that horrid lecture," he wrote to his younger daughter a few days later. "I am getting on a little with the Emerson lecture, but there will be a good deal of pressure to finish it amid all the interruptions besetting me," he wrote on October 28.—*Letters*, ed. Russell. Arnold arrived in Boston on November 5, delivered his first lecture there ("Numbers") two days later, and had a busy social life between half a dozen other New England lecture engagements until he left for Brooklyn on November 19. Some time before that date he sent his very rough draft of the "Emerson" to a Boston printer to have a lecture copy made up (as he had done with the other two lectures before he left England); the Boston printer demanded a fair copy, Charles Eliot Norton assured him that the Harvard University Press could read *any* manuscript and supervised its printing there. Arnold corrected proofs on the train between Princeton and New York (for New Haven) on November 21; both rough draft and lecture copy are now in the Houghton Library of Harvard University. (The Harvard printer's misreadings occasionally found a permanent place in the published essay.) On December 1 he gave the lecture for the first time, in Chickering Hall, Boston. "I cannot be quite sure how they will like it here, but I am satisfied with it, and so would Emerson himself have been, I think, and it will be liked in England, and will help his fame there," he wrote to his sister Frances a few days earlier. "So many of the less wealthy class wish to hear it that it is to be repeated in Tremont Temple, . . . with a charge of half a dollar, instead of a dollar," he wrote to his daughter about the same time.

He delivered the lecture eighteen times in all on his American tour: in Chickering Hall, Boston, on December 1; in Union Hall, Cambridge, on December 4; in the Wellesley College Chapel, Wellesley, on December 6 ("the young ladies . . have telegraphed to beg for the lecture on Emerson, which will be an agreeable change to me after for ever giving the lecture on Literature and Science"); in the hall of Phillips Academy, Andover, on December 13; in the Tremont Temple, Boston, on December 14; in the Academy of Music, Baltimore, on December 22; in Association Hall, Philadelphia, on December 28; in the Lafayette Reformed Church, Jersey City, on December 29; in the Long Island Historical Society building, Brooklyn, on January 3; in Association Hall, New York City, on January 4; in the Vassar College

Chapel, Poughkeepsie, New York, on January 7; in the Opera House, Utica, New York, on January 10; in the Central Music Hall, Chicago, on January 24; at St. Louis on February 1; in Smith and Nixon's Hall, Cincinnati, on February 8; at Cleveland, Ohio, on February 9; at Buffalo on February 11; and at Albany, New York, on February 23. England had followed his lecture tour with interest, and his offer of January 1 to give the lecture at the Royal Institution (where he had lectured on "Equality" six years earlier) was gladly accepted by Professor John Tyndall. On Friday evening, March 21, only four days after his landing at Liverpool, he delivered it there "to a large and distinguished audience"; Walter Besant, whose discourse on "The Art of Fiction" was originally planned for that evening, was put off until after Easter. The essay was published in *Macmillan's Magazine* for May, and presumably brought him the £50 contracted for, though there had been a plaintive letter from America to Macmillan: "Of course they are wild to print the 'Emerson' here, and I wish I had him to sell them, but I keep him for you as promised, and at the rate agreed." One of those who wished to publish was Thomas Bailey Aldrich, editor of the *Atlantic Monthly*.

Much has been written about the reception of the lecture in America; the fullest account is in Chilson H. Leonard, *Arnold in America* (Yale University Dissertation, 1932; Ann Arbor: University Microfilms, 1964). "Many here object to my not having praised Emerson all round, but that was impossible. I have given him praise which in England will be thought excessive, probably; but then I have a very, very deep feeling for him. One hears so much of him here, and what one hears is so excellent, that Flu and Lucy, who really know nothing about him, have become quite attached to him," Arnold wrote to his sister Frances on December 8. Emerson's daughter Ellen had written to say that, on the basis of the newspaper account, "she found not a word in the lecture on her father to give her pain," and "his family and literary executor are perfectly satisfied." On December 12 he lectured at Concord. "I did not give the Emerson lecture, as it was a free criticism of him on the literary side, and I did not wish to stand up in his town as a critic of him. . . . We went to Concord at five [in the] afternoon; it is about twenty miles off. The Emersons sent to meet us. They live in the house which Emerson himself built, about a mile from the station; a good house with nine acres of ground. The house is much more English in its distribution and furniture than most of the houses here. I had told Fanny Lucy to expect something like Rydal Mount, but it was nothing like that—all the modern improvements were present. Mrs. Emerson is eighty-one, of great height, and an invalid. She is still one of the handsomest women you ever saw, with manners of high distinction. She was brought up a strict Calvinist, and never approved her husband's views. He called her 'Queeny,' and she does indeed look like a queen and rules the house. We dined at six, and all except Mrs. Emerson went to the lecture along the frozen road by which the British troops retreated—the high road from Concord to Boston. I gave the lecture on Numbers. This morning I left with them, by request, the lecture on Emerson to read, and we departed, after driving round to Concord Bridge and the monument with Dr. Emerson and his sister. It is a very pleasing country—gentle hills, and New England homesteads, and elm-bordered roads (such elms!), and the quiet river flowing through it. Emerson's lines on the monument you know. They are very fine."—*Letters,* ed. Russell. The best word on the lecture is Charles Eliot Norton's account in a letter written to Lowell in England: "[It] is a piece of large, liberal, genuine criticism; but, being criticism, has aroused the provincial ire of the pure disciples. On the whole Howells was right when he said that as he was listening to it he was constantly thinking, 'Ah! that is just what I should have liked to say!' I have read the piece very carefully (for Arnold left it with me to have it printed for him) and I quarrel with no part of it. He has never written anything more picturesque than the opening pages, —never a sincerer criticism or one from so high a point of view." —*Letters of Charles Eliot Norton,* ed. Sara Norton and M. A. De-Wolfe Howe (Boston, 1913), II, 167 (misdated). The lecture is in fact one of Arnold's best and most engaging essays in criticism.

As for Arnold's long-standing admiration for Emerson, it is perfectly genuine. His earliest volume of poems contained a sonnet "Written in Emerson's *Essays.*" He met Emerson in London in April, 1848, through Clough. Clough sent Emerson a copy of *The Strayed Reveller* (1849), and then, when he went out to Boston in 1852, one persistent question in Arnold's letters was, "What does Emerson say to my poems?" "Make him look at [them]." (The *Empedocles on Etna* volume, which Clough reviewed for the *North American Review.*) Arnold sent Emerson *Last Words on Translating Homer* (1862) for its concluding remarks on Clough, and *A French Eton* (1864) with a letter that said: "I look back with great satisfaction to having made your personal acquaintance when you were here some years ago, and I can never forget the refreshing and quickening effect your writings had upon me at a critical time of my life." When Emerson sent a book to Arnold by the hand of Moncure D. Conway, Arnold wrote to Conway on November 8, 1865: "Emerson has always particularly interested me by retaining his reason while Carlyle, his fellow-prophet, lost his; Emerson for some time suffered in popularity from his sobriety, but as the rôle of reason in human affairs begins to get more visibly important, what he lost is being made up to him."—Conway, *Autobiography* (Boston, 1904), facing II, 320. Arnold sent *New Poems* (1867) by the hand of its publisher, Alexander Macmillan: "Some things in [it] you will, I think, read with interest. Your writings have given me and continue to give me so much pleasure and stimulus, that I consider myself almost bound to make an offering to you of any production at all considerable which comes from me; since you are sure to have had some part in it." In the same year Emerson sent Arnold a copy of *May-Day and Other Poems*. While Arnold was on his lecture tour, Mrs. James T. Fields published her recollections of Emerson: "Matthew Arnold was one of the minds and men to whom he constantly reverted with pleasure. Every traveller was asked for the last news of him. . . . '[Arnold] is one of the men one wishes not to lose sight of.' " —"Glimpses of Emerson," *Harper's New Monthly Magazine* LXVIII, 460 (February, 1884). For a fuller discussion of the relationship, see my article, "Emerson and Arnold's Poetry," *Philological Quarterly* XXXIII, 396–403 (October, 1954). Carlyle's impact on Arnold is the subject of Kathleen Tillotson's "Matthew Arnold and Carlyle," *Proceedings of the British Academy* XLII, 133–53 (1956) and D. J. DeLaura, "Arnold and Carlyle," *PMLA* LXXIX, 104–29 (March, 1964). For Newman, see DeLaura's "Matthew Arnold and John Henry Newman: The 'Oxford Sentiment' and the Religion of the Future," *Texas Studies in Literature and Language* VI, 571–702 (Supplement, 1965) and *Hebrew and Hellene in Victorian England* (Austin: University of Texas Press, 1971). And for all three, see my lectures on *The Time-Spirit of Matthew Arnold* (Ann Arbor: The University of Michigan Press, 1970).

165:1. Arnold was an undergraduate at Balliol College, Oxford, from the autumn of 1841 to the autumn of 1844.

165:4. Thucydides asserted that his history was composed as "a possession for ever."—I, xxii, 4. See p. 45:23.

165:23–28. "Peace in Believing" (1839), *Parochial Sermons* (London and Oxford, 1842), VI, 400–401.

165:29. The chapel at Littlemore, a village three miles southeast of Oxford, was in Newman's care as Vicar of St. Mary's, Oxford. He retired to his house at Littlemore as he drew closer to a determination to give up his Anglican titles at St. Mary's and Oriel College.

166:2–3. See Acts 18:3. But the place was Corinth, not Ephesus.

166:7–18. "Worship, a Preparation for Christ's Coming," *Parochial Sermons* (London and Oxford, 1840), V, 2–3, with omission. Though one of the sermons Arnold quotes was published while he was at Oxford, both were preached before he was an undergraduate there. See DeLaura, *Hebrew and Hellene*, pp. 149–50.

166:19–20. "Steeped in sentiment as she lies, spreading her gardens to the moonlight, and whispering from her bowers the last enchantments of the Middle Age, who will deny that Oxford, by her ineffable charm, keeps ever calling us nearer to the true goal of all of us, to the ideal, to perfection, . . . than all the science of Tübingen?"—Preface to *Essays in Criticism* (1865), *Prose Works*, ed. Super, III, 290.

166:27–29. "Death of Edward Irving" (1835), *Critical and Miscellaneous Essays*, *Works* (Centenary edition; London, 1899), XXVIII, 319–20. Carlyle wrote "wore him and wasted him." Irving, three years older than Carlyle and a native of the same part of Scotland, was an immensely popular Presbyterian minister in London from 1822; in 1832 he founded the Holy Catholic Apostolic Church, commonly called the Irvingite church, now housed in Gordon Square. He introduced Carlyle to Jane Welsh, who became Mrs. Carlyle.

167:3–7. *Wilhelm Meister's Apprenticeship*, Book VIII, chapt. viii; *Works* (Centenary ed.), XXIV, 157. Carlyle wrote "the treasure" and "your hearts too."

167:15–18. "Emerson the Lecturer," halfway through; *My Study Windows* (Boston, 1871), pp. 379–81. When Arnold wrote, Lowell was United States minister in London.

167:28–30. "Literary Ethics," second-last paragraph; *Nature, Addresses, and Lectures, Complete Works* (Centenary ed.; Boston, 1903), I, 185–86. Emerson wrote "art, and poetry, and science."

167:31–33. "History," first paragraph; *Essays, First Series*, Centenary ed., II, 3.

167:33–168:6. "Self-Reliance," third paragraph; *Essays, First Series*, Centenary ed., II, 47. Arnold used Emerson's earlier, not final, version: *Essays*, with Preface by Thomas Carlyle (London: James Fraser, 1841), pp. 47–48. Emerson wrote "in the highest mind."

168:21–24. This is Arnold's judgment of Herman Grimm, *Goethe: Vorlesungen gehalten an der Kgl. Universität zu Berlin*, 1877. See "A French Critic on Goethe" (1878), *Prose Works*, ed. Super, VIII, 254–55.

168:32–169:1. "In that gift for 'saying things,' so notable in Pope and Tennyson, he is the chief of American poets. From what other bard have so many original lines and phrases passed into literature, —coins that do not wear out, of standard value, bright and current gold? It is worth while, for the mere effect, to group some of them together, and especially those which, appearing in his first book forty years ago, long since became a constituent part of our literary thought and expression."—E. C. Stedman, "Emerson," *Century Magazine* XXV, 880 (April, 1883); reprinted in his *Poets of America* (Boston, 1885), p. 161. Stedman then quotes thirty-one short passages from Emerson's poems.

169:1–2. The "personal estimate" is the fallacious kind of judgment about poetry which occurs when we allow such matters as personal affection or patriotism to govern our valuation of a work. Arnold distinguishes it from the "real estimate" (p. 168:27) in "The Study of Poetry" (1880), *Prose Works*, ed. Super, IX, 163–64.

169:6–8. *Twelfth Night* II, iv, 117; *Paradise Lost* I, 63; "Ode: On a Distant Prospect of Eton College," line 99.

169:35–36. *Of Education*, two-thirds through; *Works*, ed. Allan Abbott et al. (New York: Columbia University Press, 1931), IV, 286. Milton wrote "simple, sensuous and passionate." Arnold quoted the passage in "Dante and Beatrice" (1863) and at the beginning of "John Keats" (1880); *Prose Works*, ed. Super, III, 8; IX, 205.

170:5–7. I. e., "Concord Hymn" and "Ode Sung in the Town Hall, Concord, July 4, 1857."

170:14–17, 19–22, 26–31. "Voluntaries" III, 13–16; "Sacrifice," and "May-Day," lines 98–103.

171:35. The Transcendentalists were the New England group who espoused the Platonic idealism heralded in Emerson's treatise on *Nature;* they formed a club generally known as the Transcendental Club that held its first meeting at the home of George Ripley in 1836. (Five years later Ripley founded Brook Farm; see p. 181:14.) The best-known statement of the doctrine of the group is Emerson's lecture on "The Transcendentalist" (1841). *The Dial* (1840–44) was the quarterly journal of the group; Emerson was a contributor and ultimately the reluctant editor.

171:37–172:8. *Essays* (London, 1841), p. 169. Arnold quotes the opening two sentences of the essay; the revised version begins with what had been the fifth sentence.—*Essays, First Series;* Centenary ed. II, 169.

172:9–10. Stanley was quarantined for five days at Malta in January–February, 1841. In October, 1878, on a brief visit to America, he stayed with Emerson in Concord.—R. E. Prothero, *The Life and Correspondence of Arthur Penrhyn Stanley* (New York, 1894), I, 278; II, 531. Observe (in the Textual Notes) how Arnold revised to incorporate the Harvard printer's misreading of his "quarantine" as "conversation."

172:32–35. Emerson to Carlyle, October 30, 1840, and August 8, 1839.—*The Correspondence of Thomas Carlyle and Ralph Waldo Emerson, 1834–72,* ed. Charles Eliot Norton (London, 1883), I, 308, 255.

172:35–173:5. Carlyle to Emerson, May 13, 1835.—*Correspondence,* I, 65. Regent Street was a fashionable street in the West End, Crockford's a fashionable gambling establishment, and the allusion to Irish Jesuits depends on the fact that Francis S. Mahony ("Father Prout") was a contributor to *Fraser's Magazine,* in which *Sartor Resartus* was first published.

173:5–10. Carlyle to Emerson, December 8, 1837.—*Correspondence,* I, 140. "There is a man here called John Sterling (*Reverend* John of the Church of England too), whom I love better than anybody I have met with, since a certain sky-messenger [Emerson] alighted to me at Craigenputtock, and vanished in the Blue again." The shovel hat is symbol of holy orders. Carlyle published a biography of Sterling in 1851.

173:11–21. Carlyle to Emerson, November 15, 1838.—*Correspondence,* I, 199. Carlyle wrote "near neighbour, full of quips and cranks, with good humour. . ." and "as snow, will work on you with those large . . ."

173:23–26. September 29, 1844.—*Correspondence,* II, 74.

173:29–30. "I think you have written a wonderful book [*The French Revolution*], which will last a very long time."—Emerson to Carlyle, September 13, 1837; *Correspondence,* I, 129.

174:1–3. The correspondence was published in Boston and London about the middle of February, 1883, some eight months before Arnold left England for America.

174:32–175:5. Carlyle to Emerson, September 26, 1840 (with omission); February 8, 1839.—*Correspondence,* I, 304, 217. Carlyle wrote "they be for others." The latter passage alludes to "The American Scholar," The Divinity School Address and the Dartmouth College oration ("Literary Ethics") of 1837–38.

175:5–12. Emerson to Carlyle, October 30, 1841; May 10, 1838.
—*Correspondence*, I, 345, 161.

175:17, 28. Emerson's *English Traits* was published in 1856, Hawthorne's *Our Old Home* (also an account of England) in 1863.
Hawthorne was American consul in the commercial city of Liverpool from 1853 to 1857.

176:2–3. Perhaps the passage Arnold quotes on p. 182:9–10.

176:21–25. April 25, 1839.—*Correspondence*, I, 238.

176:26–37. Emerson to Carlyle, July 31, 1841, with omissions.
—*Correspondence*, I, 340–42.

176:37–177:5. Emerson to Carlyle, October 15, 1870.—*Correspondence*, II, 334. "Thy strong Hours . . . wasted me" is from
Tennyson's "Tithonus," lines 18–19.

177:13. "Love, friendship, charity, are subjects all | To envious
and calumniating time."—Shakespeare, *Troilus and Cressida*, III,
iii, 173–74.

177:18–20. "Marcus Aurelius . . . remains the especial friend and
comforter of all clear-headed and scrupulous, yet pure-hearted and
upward-striving men, in those ages most especially that walk by
sight, not by faith, but yet have no open vision."—Arnold, "Marcus
Aurelius" (1863), *Prose Works*, ed. Super, III, 156.

177:34–36. "Politics," fourth paragraph from end; *Essays, Second
Series*, Centenary ed., III, 216.

177:36–37. See p. 167:33–34.

178:1–2. See "The Over-Soul," halfway through, and "Nominalist and Realist," three-fourths through; *Essays, First and Second Series*, Centenary ed., II, 280–81; III, 242: "The Maker of all
things and all persons stands behind us and casts his dread omniscience through us over things. . . . The soul's communication of
truth is the highest event in nature. . . . This communication is
an influx of the Divine mind into our mind." "Rightly every man
is a channel through which heaven floweth." In *Literature and
Dogma* Arnold described God as "a power, not ourselves, which
makes for righteousness."—*Prose Works*, ed. Super, VI, 189, 196;
and see Index, *s.v.* "not ourselves."

178:3–6. "New England Reformers," halfway through; *Essays,
Second Series*, Centenary ed., III, 270. Emerson wrote "there the
whole aspect of things changes."

178:7–8. "The Poet," three-fourths through; *Essays, Second Series*, Centenary ed., III, 33.

178:9–11. "Heroism," second-last paragraph; *Essays, First Series*,
Centenary ed., II, 262.

178:11–20. "Experience," two-fifths through (with omission); *Essays, Second Series,* Centenary ed., III, 60–61.

178:20–24. "Heroism," two-thirds through; *Essays, First Series,* Centenary ed., II, 257.

178:25–31. "New England Reformers," immediately following the passage at 178:2–5; *Essays, Second Series,* Centenary ed., III, 270.

178:31–32. "Spiritual Laws," nearly one-third through; *Essays, First Series,* Centenary ed., II, 141. Emerson wrote "somewhat unique."

178:32–38. "Compensation," halfway through; *Essays, First Series,* Centenary ed., II, 110–11. Emerson wrote "the exclusive in fashionable life."

178:38–179:1. "New England Reformers," three-fourths through; *Essays, Second Series,* Centenary ed., III, 277.

179:2–6. "Heroism," fourth paragraph from end; *Essays, First Series,* Centenary ed., II, 261.

179:8–13. "New England Reformers," third paragraph from end (with omissions); *Essays, Second Series,* Centenary ed., III, 283.

179:13–15. "Compensation," three-fifths through; *Essays, First Series,* Centenary ed., II, 114, 113.

179:20–21. "Spiritual Laws," two-fifths through; *Essays, First Series,* Centenary ed., II, 144.

179:21–23. "The Poet," last sentence; *Essays, Second Series,* Centenary ed., III, 42.

179:23–25. "Spiritual Laws," two-fifths through; *Essays, First Series,* Centenary ed., II, 143, slightly abbreviated.

179:35–36. Dwight Lyman Moody (1837–99), a lay evangelist from Chicago, and Ira David Sankey (1840–1908), his organist and hymn-leader, conducted a very successful two-year series of evangelistic revivals in Britain from 1873 to 1875; Arnold himself heard Moody preach. In *God and the Bible* he couples their names with that of the Salvation Army (founded in London in 1878, officially named in June, 1880).—*Prose Works,* ed. Super, VII, 372 and Index.

180:1–7. William Dean Howells's novel, *The Lady of the Aroostook,* was published serially in the *Atlantic Monthly* from November, 1878, to March, 1879, and in volume form very quickly thereafter. Arnold alludes to scenes at the very beginning and the very end, at "a farm-house on the skirts of a village in the hills of Northern Massachusetts"; the heroine is Lydia Blood, but her grandfather is Deacon Latham. Arnold praised this novel on the eve of his departure for America; see p. 451.

180:33–36. "Heroism," final paragraph; *Essays, First Series,* Centenary ed., II, 263, slightly modified.

180:37–181:11. "Politics," halfway through (with omission); *Essays, Second Series,* Centenary ed., III, 210.

181:11–16. For example, in "New England Reformers," ¶4 and one-third through; *Essays, Second Series,* Centenary ed., III, 255–56, 263–67. Brook Farm was a cooperative community established by George Ripley in 1841 at West Roxbury, nine miles from Boston. It was encouraged by the Transcendentalists and Nathaniel Hawthorne was at one time a member. It dissolved in 1847. "The Dissidence of Dissent and the Protestantism of the Protestant Religion" was the motto of *The Nonconformist,* weekly newspaper of the English Congregationalists; it was frequently held up by Arnold as the opposite of "sweetness and light." See *Culture and Anarchy, Prose Works,* ed. Super, V, 101.

181:18–25. "Self-Reliance," ¶7; *Essays, First Series,* Centenary ed., II, 52 (slightly modified).

181:25–33. "Spiritual Laws," ¶8, 7; *Essays, First Series,* Centenary ed., II, 136, 135.

181:37–38. "For in him we live, and move, and have our being."—Acts 17:28.

181:38–182:2. "Spiritual Laws," ¶11; Centenary ed., II, 137–38.

182:8–11. Emerson to Carlyle, July 31, 1841 (with omission).—*Correspondence,* I, 341–42.

182:13–16. Emerson to Carlyle, October 15, 1870.—*Correspondence,* II, 337–38.

182:17. "By [faith] he being dead yet speaketh."—Hebrews 11:4.

182:17–21. "New England Reformers," final paragraph (with omission); *Essays, Second Series,* Centenary ed., III, 285.

182:32–34. From Emerson's diary, October, 1847.—*Correspondence with Carlyle,* II, 148.

182:36–183:8. Carlyle to Emerson, February 8, 1839.—*Correspondence,* I, 214–15.

183:9. See pp. 181:38–182:1.

183:14–15. Book II, chap. ix, "The Everlasting Yea," ¶14.

183:15–17. Arnold quoted this in *Literature and Dogma* (1871) and *God and the Bible* (1875), *Prose Works,* ed. Super, VI, 192; VII, 234.

183:38–184:4. In 1882 Arnold had correspondence with Alfred Arthur Reade, and on November 4 wrote for him a letter on the use of wine which Reade published in his *Study and Stimulants* (Manchester, 1883), pp. 13–14. The volume, a very extensive assembly of such letters solicited by Reade from both sides of the

Atlantic, does not contain the passage Arnold quotes, but Arnold's letter enforces the view he expressed in his lecture: "In general, wine used in moderation seems to add to the *agreeableness* of life, for adults at any rate; and whatever adds to the agreeableness of life adds to its resources and powers."

184:9–11. N. P. Willis, "Saturday Afternoon," lines 26–28, jotted in Arnold's pocket diary for July 29, 1882, where it is attributed merely to "School Reader."—*Note-Books*, ed. Lowry, p. 378.

185:14–15. Sonnet, 1811 ("Here pause: the poet claims at least this praise"), lines 5–6. Wordsworth wrote "that Heaven lays."

185:28–37. "At the Saturday Club," lines 141–50. The poem was published in the *Atlantic Monthly* in January, 1884 (while Arnold was still in America), and in *Before the Curfew and Other Poems*, 1888. "My poem in the Atlantic in which the conjunction [of Emerson and Franklin] occurs was all printed and corrected before Matthew Arnold delivered his lecture in which he married the two names," wrote Holmes to E. P. Whipple, December 31, 1883.—T. F. Currier and E. M. Tilton, *A Bibliography of Oliver Wendell Holmes* (New York: New York University Press, 1953), p. 384.

186:6. *Hamlet* III, iv, 135.

186:10. Emerson to Carlyle, July 31, 1841.—*Correspondence*, I, 342.

[NOTES ON CANCELLED PASSAGES]

571:8. "In Memoriam," line 72.

573:32–33. "New England Reformers," ¶5 from end; *Essays, Second Series*, Centenary ed., III, 281.

573:35–37, 42–574:2. "Spiritual Laws," ¶13 from end and "Compensation," three-fifths through; *Essays, First Series*, Centenary ed., II, 158, 113.

[GEORGE SAND]

On August 2, 1884, *The Times*, in a brief note on new street-names in Paris (p. 5, col. 2), added parenthetically that a statue of George Sand would be dedicated at La Châtre a week from the next Sunday. This note may have been what occasioned Arnold to suggest to Yates Thompson, proprietor of *The Pall Mall Gazette*, that he write a memorial piece on her; Thompson agreed and suggested that the article (contrary to the usual policy) be signed. On August 10, Arnold wrote to W. T. Stead, Thompson's editor: "I have had a week of interruptions, and hardly expected to get anything written about G. Sand; however, I have at last made a start, and tomorrow I hope to send you something."—J. O. Baylen, "Matthew Arnold and the *Pall Mall Gazette*," *South Atlantic Quarterly* LXVIII, 552–53, (Autumn, 1969). He was paid two guineas for the article, which appeared on August 12. A correspondent from Sydenham who signed himself "A Foreign Academician" immediately responded that it was unnecessary for Arnold to reduce Balzac in order to praise George Sand. Alphonse Daudet, whom Arnold called Balzac's "continuator," was infinitely inferior. As for Rousseau, said the correspondent, his great work was his political writing, not *Émile*, *La nouvelle Héloïse*, or the *Confessions*, works far less read than Balzac's novels.—*Pall Mall Gazette*, August 14, p. 3.

187:5–6. "Paris, Sunday, Aug. 10. A statue of George Sand, by Aimé Millet [1819–91; a popular sculptor], was unveiled to-day at La Châtre, the town nearest to Nohant, the village where she spent most of her life. The Academy was asked to send a spokesman; but pleaded that it only honoured its own members, and that deviation from this rule would expose it to constant applications. This was a very naïve admission for a body that has not opened its portals to numerous celebrities far superior to many whom it has admitted."—*The Times*, August 11, 1884, p. 5, cols. 4–5. Though Arnold clearly read this article, he mistook the day of the dedication.

188:12–16. H. Taine, *Histoire de la littérature anglaise* (3rd ed.; Paris, 1873–74), V, 44 (Book V, chapt. i, sec. 2: "Comparaison des passions dans Balzac et dans Dickens"), jotted in Arnold's pocket diary for December 18, 1881. In his diary for October 16, he copied a sentence from IV, 435 (Book IV, Conclusion, sec. i, part 3), in which Taine characterized English literature of the eighteenth century with "faiblesse ou impuissance de la pensée spéculative, de la vraie poésie, du théâtre original, et de tous les genres qui réclament la grande curiosité libre, ou la grande imagination désintéressée."—*Note-Books*, ed. Lowry, pp. 362, 359.

188:23. Line 121.

188:37. Arnold first used this French expression in *Literature and Dogma* (1873), then in his essay on "George Sand" (1877).—*Prose Works*, ed. Super, VI, 390; VIII, 223, and see note at VIII, 437.

189:29–30. Sand, *Journal d'un voyageur* (Paris, 1871), p. 68 (September 29, 1870), jotted in Arnold's pocket diary for May 1, 1881, and at the beginning of 1882 and 1883.—*Note-Books*, ed. Lowry, pp. 353, 366, 389.

189:35–39. Wordsworth, *The River Duddon*, Sonnet XXXIV ("After-thought"), lines 5, 7, 14. Wordsworth wrote "the brave," not "the great," and the final line of the sonnet reads: "We feel that we are greater than we know." See p. 133:9–10.

[HAMLET ONCE MORE]

Arnold's final letter over the signature "An Old Playgoer" appeared in *The Pall Mall Gazette* on October 23, 1884, and brought him £2. By this time Morley had surrendered the editorship of the *Pall Mall* to W. T. Stead, who much altered its editorial policy, and in a manner with which Arnold was not in sympathy. And so when Wilson Barrett's company brought out Bulwer's *Junius* and Arnold was urged to attend the opening night and write an "Old Playgoer" letter about it, he declined. "The play cannot be very good, or Bulwer would have brought it out in his lifetime," Arnold wrote to his daughter Lucy Whitridge on February 24, 1885. "If it is poor I should not like to do execution upon it, as Bulwer was always so studiously kind to me."

190:1–2. Wilson Barrett's *Hamlet* opened at the Princess's on October 16, 1884. The scenes were painted from sketches actually made at Elsinore and there was some attempt to represent medieval life authentically.

190:2–5. London: Kegan Paul, Trench & Co., 1884.

190:9–16. P. 114. And see p. 128.

190:18. An expression from Heine's *Reisebilder* IV: "Englische Fragmente," chapter x, "Wellington," third paragraph from end; quoted by Arnold in "Heinrich Heine" (1863), *Prose Works*, ed. Super, III, 112.

190:20–24. P. 113. The text reads "vacillating and weak-willed."

190:25–27. Horace *Odes* III. iii. 3. See Feis, p. 91. He calls Shakespeare "one of the foremost Humanists in the fullest and noblest meaning of the word" (p. 130), "a veritable Humanist, the truest and greatest" (pp. 209–10).

191:7. John Sterling dealt with the relationship at the beginning of an essay on Montaigne in the *Westminster Review*, American ed., XXXI, 174–90 (July, 1838); reprinted in *Essays and Tales by John Sterling*, ed. J. C. Hare (London, 1848), I, 129–87. Feis cites Sterling's article on p. 130.

191:36. "The rest is silence."—*Hamlet*, V, ii, 369. J. B. Orrick traces Arnold's view of Hamlet to Goethe's *Wilhelm Meisters Lehrjahre*, Book IV, chapter xv, and Book V, chapter iv.— *Matthew Arnold and Goethe, Publications of the English Goethe Society*, n.s., IV (London, 1928), pp. 15–16.

192:2–3. "Certes c'est un subiect merveilleusement vain, divers, et ondoyant, que l'homme: il est malaysé d'y fonder iugement constant et uniforme."—*Essais*, I, i, ¶7.

192:24. Edward Smith Willard (1853–1915) had played the murderous Captain Skinner (the "Spider") in *The Silver King*. Margaret Leighton died in 1908 at the age of 56, Mary Eastlake in 1911 at the age of 55.

192:33–193:3. Macready last played Hamlet at the Haymarket Theatre on January 29, 1851, a few weeks before his retirement. Charles Kean (1811–68) acted the part as late as January, 1858, at the Princess's. Charles Fechter (1824–79), born and trained in France, left his native country because he was discontent with the government's favored treatment of the *Comédie française* and spent his latter years chiefly in London and New York. He performed Hamlet at the Princess's in 1861. John Philip Kemble (1757–1823), traditionally one of the two or three greatest actors of the British stage, made his debut as Hamlet at Drury Lane in 1783, and was painted in that role by the artist Lawrence. He died when Arnold was two months old.

[A WORD MORE ABOUT AMERICA]

Arnold left the United States on the Cunarder *Servia* on March 8, 1884, telling reporters as he left: "I would rather not attempt to give my impressions of America. . . . I shall certainly not write a book on the subject under any circumstances. I am in doubt whether I shall write any kind of article even about it."—*Pall Mall Gazette*, March 10, p. 10. Ten days earlier he wrote a farewell letter to Charles Eliot Norton in Cambridge: "Heine said that at the end of his stay in London he felt himself not to have attained 'one single clear intuition': I will not say that I feel myself precisely in this condition at the end of my stay in America, but I feel myself utterly devoid of all disposition to write and publish my intuitions, clear or turbid."—*Letters*, ed. Russell. And to Henry

James in England he wrote, the day before he sailed: "I hope to shake you by the hand very soon, and to communicate to you— what I have no intention at all of communicating to the public— my 'impressions of America,' or at least some of them." It was hardly to be expected that he should stand by his resolution to say nothing at all; by August 20 he had not only promised Knowles an article for the *Nineteenth Century* of November or December, but was planning to include it and "A Word about America" in a volume with the three lectures of his American tour.—Buckler, *Matthew Arnold's Books*, p. 162. "I find that having been in America wonderfully increases my interest in their men and politics," he wrote to his sister Mrs. Forster on October 18, at the same time expressing the hope that Grover Cleveland would be elected to the presidency. "In some points they are certainly our superiors; but it is not easy to see them and ourselves quite clearly and all round." The excitement attendant on seeing his older daughter Lucy married and departing for New York delayed the fulfillment of his promise to Knowles until January; the essay appeared in the *Nineteenth Century* for February, 1885, and brought Arnold £50. It has been republished in K. Allott, ed., *Five Uncollected Essays of Arnold* (Liverpool, 1953). The reflections on American social conditions promised here were more amply developed in the last essay Arnold wrote, "Civilisation in the United States" (1888).

194:1-2. John Duke Coleridge, Lord Chief Justice of England, who became Lord Coleridge in 1874, was a friend of Arnold's from their university days, as his father had been a friend of Arnold's father. Coleridge visited the United States from August 24 to October 27, and spoke so highly of him in a public address three days after Arnold's arrival that Arnold was somewhat embarrassed, at the same time he was pleased: "I am only afraid of his setting people a little against me by such praise," he wrote to his younger daughter.—*Letters*, ed. Russell. The spate of books about America by English travellers was huge; Arnold alluded to two of them in "A Word about America." But Coleridge fulfilled Arnold's prediction and did not write one.

194:13-14. Alexis de Tocqueville's *Démocratie en Amérique* was first published in 1835. Arnold quoted from it in his Introduction ("Democracy") to *The Popular Education of France* (1861) and again in the Preface to *Mixed Essays* (1879) and "'Ecce Convertimur ad Gentes'" (1879).—*Prose Works*, ed. Super, II, 9; VIII, 371; IX, 10.

194:21. An echo of Frederic Harrison's characterization of

Arnold as lacking in "a system of philosophy with principles coherent, interdependent, subordinate, and derivative."—See *Friendship's Garland* (1871), *Prose Works*, ed. Super, V, 76, 424.

195:18–29. Perhaps James Russell Lowell, if one may make inference from Arnold's letters to him on May 18, 1882, and August 8, 1883.

196:21–29. [H. S. Maine,] "The Nature of Democracy," *Quarterly Review* CLVIII, 299, 304 (October, 1884), reprinted in his *Popular Government* (London, 1885). The article is in part a review of Edmond Scherer, *La Démocratie et la France* (Paris, 1883), from p. 3 of which he quotes the statement Arnold repeats. The Introduction (1844) to Bancroft's *History of the Colonization of the United States* announces his aim of tracing "the steps by which a favoring Providence, calling our institutions into being, has conducted the country to its present happiness and glory." Arnold jotted the quotation from Bancroft in his pocket diary for December 17, 1884.—*Note-Books*, ed. Lowry, p. 409.

197:36–38. In England a member of Parliament need not be, and very frequently is not, a resident of the constituency he represents; in the United States all members of the federal and state legislatures must reside in the district for which they are elected. Wendell Phillips (1811–84), abolitionist and reformer, never held elective office.

198:8. Arnold heard Beecher preach on his first Sunday in America, October 28. See the earlier references to him in *A French Eton* (1864) and the original Preface to *Essays in Criticism* (1865).—*Prose Works*, ed. Super, II, 319; III, 538.

198:22–26. Griffin, *The Great Republic* (London, 1884), pp. 143–45 (the chapter on "Justice"). Sir Lepel Griffin (1838–1908) was a career administrator in the Indian civil service. His article, "A Visit to Philistia," *Fortnightly Review* XLI, 50–64 (January, 1884), describes as an eyewitness the New York appearances of Lord Coleridge, Arnold, and the Lyceum Theatre company of Henry Irving and Ellen Terry. Coleridge, he says, caused consternation by referring to Arnold publicly as "the most distinguished of living Englishmen." His account of Arnold's delivery of his first lecture on "Numbers" in Chickering Hall on October 30 is very unflattering. "The night after his lecture, the well-known journalist, Mr. [Charles Anderson] Dana, in the same hall, repudiated his doctrine, and declared that the facts of America and Europe contradicted his theory; that in England and France there was little or no political progress, that in democratic institutions and the principle of equality were the salvation of the human race; while material triumphs by man over nature contained the condition of progress, a work independent of poets and essayists like Mr. Arnold. There can be no doubt that Mr. Dana truly interprets the feeling of his countrymen, who are satisfied with themselves and do not care to be improved or instructed by any teacher, however illustrious. Mr. Matthew Arnold, piloted by Mr. D'Oyley Carte, and inaudibly lecturing to New York Society, too painfully recalls Samson grinding corn for the Philistines in Gaza."—pp. 62–63. (Chapt. VI of *The Great Republic,* "Sweetness and Light," repeats this account.) The article is on the reading list at the end of Arnold's pocket diary for 1884, and he was reading Griffin in August and September of that year.—*Note-Books,* ed. Lowry, p. 616.

198:34. "I had a men's dinner with dear old Bancroft" (on December 23 or 24, 1883), wrote Arnold to his sister Frances, "which was most interesting, as I met the really best men in Congress; three senators—[Thomas Francis] Bayard [of Delaware], [John] Sherman [of Ohio], and [Randall Lee] Gibson—struck me particularly, as they would be distinguished men in politics anywhere: Gibson for choice; he is senator for Louisiana, and served in the Southern army during the war. The President [Chester A. Arthur] was away when we arrived, and only returned on Christmas day, but he said he should like to receive us, as we were leaving the next morning, so General [Joseph Roswell] Hawley, the senator for Connecticut, took us to the White House at half-past three on Christmas Day afternoon. The house is far handsomer than I expected. The President is a good-looking man, with pleasant, easy manners. He told Lucy that if we would stay on in Washington he would 'make himself personally responsible' for her enjoying her winter there more than even in New York."—*Letters,* ed. Russell; see also his letter to Gladstone, March 26, 1884, in W. H. G. Armytage, "Matthew Arnold and W. E. Gladstone: Some New Letters," *University of Toronto Quarterly* XVIII, 226 (April, 1949). George Bancroft, whose lifetime work was his monumental history of the United States from Columbus to the winning of independence, was then 83. He had been secretary of the navy and then minister to Great Britain (1846–49) under Polk and minister to Berlin (1867–74) under Johnson and Grant.

199:29–34. Macaulay's review of James Mill on Government, four-fifths through: "The increase of population is accelerated by good and cheap government. Therefore, the better the government, the greater is the inequality of conditions. . . . As for America, we appeal to the twentieth century."

201:24–26. Winans (presumably Walter Winans, 1852–1920, grandson of the engineer and railway magnate Ross Winans) purchased large tracts of land in the north of Scotland and took a twenty-year lease on the estate of Kintail, between Inverness-shire and Ross-shire, with the intention of converting it into a deer forest. A cotter on the lands, the cobbler Murdoch Macrae, after repeated warnings ceased to graze his sheep there, but when in July, 1884, he turned a pet lamb that had been hand-fed in the house to graze by the roadside, legal proceedings were entered upon; Winans won the case on appeal, but all the sympathy in the "pet lamb" case was with Macrae. See *The Times*, February 10, 1885, p. 9, col. 5, January 23, 1886, p. 10, col. 3, and January 28, 1886, p. 3, col. 5. A remark in *Truth* on June 14, 1883, indicates that Winans' notoriety was of long standing.

202:6–7. The Duchesse de Pompadour was official mistress of Louis XV of France from 1745 until her death in 1764 at the age of 42. The Comtesse du Barry was his official mistress from 1769 until his death in 1774. *Les Amours du chevalier de Faublas* (1787–90), by Louvet de Couvray, is described by one critic as summing up "la frivolité, le scandale, la débauche, la nudité, l'oubli de tous les devoirs et la sensualité brutale" of eighteenth-century France.

202:16. Coriolanus was spokesman for the aristocracy of Rome, bitterly anti-democratic in his sentiments; therein lies his tragedy in Shakespeare's play.

203:35–204:1. *Morning Star*, December 2, 1864, p. 4, col. 3 (leading article); quoted in "My Countrymen" (1866), *Prose Works*, ed. Super, V, 5–6.

204:1–9. Arnold in "My Countrymen" (p. 5) also quoted praise of the middle class from a leading article in *The Daily News*, December 7, 1864, p. 4, cols. 3–4. When Ahab, king of Israel, wished to persuade Jehoshaphat, king of Judah, to attack the Syrians with him and recapture Ramoth-Gilead, he summoned his prophets, some four hundred men, to deliver the word of the Lord. "And Zedekiah the son of Chenaanah made him horns of iron: and he said, Thus saith the Lord, With these shalt thou push the Syrians, until thou have consumed them. And all the prophets prophesied so, saying, Go up to Ramoth-Gilead, and prosper; for the Lord shall deliver it into the king's hand." But when Ahab pressed yet further, another prophet, Micaiah the son of Imlah, not of this group, asserted that the Lord had put a lying spirit into the mouths of his prophets to compass the king's ruin. Then "Zedekiah the son of Chenaanah went near, and smote Micaiah on the cheek." Ahab angrily cast Micaiah into prison, marched into battle, and was killed.—I Kings 22:11-12, 24; see II Chronicles 18:10-11, 23.

204:9-12. Arnold delivered his lecture on "Equality" at the Royal Institution on February 8, 1878, and his "Liverpool Address" on September 30, 1882.—*Prose Works*, ed. Super, VIII, 277-305; X, 74-88.

204:15-19. "The Future of Liberalism" (1880), *Prose Works*, ed. Super, IX, 148.

204:24-25. Gladstone's government was floundering in its last days; a defeat in the House of Commons on June 8, 1885, some four months after the publication of this essay, forced its resignation. Professor Allott quotes Justin McCarthy's account: "The work of the House of Commons was reduced to a mere scramble. . . . We cannot recollect any time in which the effort at legislation was more barren of results and more bitter in the struggle. . . . The weary session went on, full of quarrel, thorny, and utterly barren."—*A History of Our Own Times* (London, 1900), pp. 107-8.

205:9. Jeremiah 25:18 (see 29:18; 42:18; 44:12, 22; 51:37).

205:15-16. Presumably the "Dublin scandals," in which English officials were prosecuted (and generally acquitted) after allegations against them by the nationalist Irish Press. See p. 206:25-29n.

205:23-24. John Poyntz Spencer, fifth Earl Spencer (1835-1910), an Englishman, was lord-lieutenant of Ireland under Gladstone, 1868-74, 1882-85. Henry Campbell-Bannerman (1836-1908), a Scotsman, was chief secretary for Ireland, 1884-85. As prime minister early in the present century, Campbell-Bannerman carried through Parliament the Deceased Wife's Sister's Marriage Act (1907).

205:25. Gathorne Gathorne-Hardy (1814-1906), an Englishman, became Viscount Cranbrook in 1878. Timothy Michael Healy (1855-1931) was an Irish Member of Parliament, a supporter of Parnell who like Parnell was imprisoned for his part in agrarian agitations. In the present century he became first governor-general of the Irish Free State (1922-28).

205:26. Though when Gladstone took office in 1880 he hoped to pacify Ireland without the aid of the coercion statute the Conservatives had passed, he was unable to carry through Parliament that year the necessary relief for Irish tenants. Land agitation reduced Ireland to chaos, and on January 24, 1881, Arnold's brother-in-law W. E. Forster, the chief secretary for Ireland, introduced his Coercion Bill. Passed with the aid of an innovative resolution to close debate, it suspended the *Habeas Corpus* Act to give the Irish executive an absolute power of arbitrary and preventive arrest. The assassination of Forster's successor Lord Frederick Cavendish on May 6, 1882, brought further disorders, to which the government replied with a new and stiffer Crimes Act, which gave the magistrates the power to hold secret inquiries and examine witnesses upon oath before anyone was definitely charged.—R. C. K. Ensor, *England, 1870–1914* (Oxford: at the Clarendon Press, 1936), pp. 72–77.

206:20. The fourth Earl of Kenmare, who succeeded to the title in 1871, held well over 100,000 acres in Kerry, Cork, and Limerick, in southwestern Ireland. He required a good deal of extraordinary police protection during the agrarian difficulties.

206:24. Richard Strongbow, or Richard de Clare, second Earl of Pembroke, conquered Leinster (the province that included Dublin) in 1168–76 under Henry II.

206:25–29. George Otto Trevelyan (1838–1928), son of Macaulay's sister and biographer of Macaulay, was chief secretary for Ireland, 1882–84, in succession to the assassinated Lord Frederick Cavendish. After what William O'Brien, M.P. for Mallow and editor of the Nationalist newspaper *United Ireland*, considered an evasive answer to a question about the prosecution of an English official of the Dublin post office accused of felony, O'Brien said: "Does the Chief Secretary think I shall give him any information within my power without a guarantee for the safety of the witnesses, because I shall not trust him?" Trevelyan replied, "I may be Chief Secretary for Ireland, but I am an English gentleman (loud cheers [accompanied by the interposition of an Irish member that so was the post office official]), and if a man in putting a question to me tells me that under no circumstances whatever will he trust my statement, I shall not answer him. (Loud cheers.)"—July 10, 1884, reported in *The Times* next day, p. 6, cols. 3–4 and in Hansard's *Parliamentary Debates*. Trevelyan was succeeded by Campbell-Bannerman as chief secretary on October 21.

207:5–6. A bill to extend the county franchise, which since 1867 had been based on different qualifications from the urban franchise, passed the House of Commons in 1884, but was defeated by the House of Lords at its second reading on July 9, 1884. Immediately there was great pressure for reform of the upper house, and even for its abolition. On July 30 John Morley, presiding over a crowded conference of delegates of Liberal associations in St. James's Hall, London, remarked, to a response of loud cheers, with the whole assembly rising and waving their hats: "Be sure that no power on earth can separate henceforth the question of mending the House of Commons from the other question of mending or ending the House of Lords."—*Times*, July 31, 1884, p. 11, col. 4 and p. 9, col. 2. The constitutional crisis was settled by agreement, the franchise bill was passed, and not until 1911 did Morley himself, then a lord, pilot through the upper house the bill by which the Lords' veto was severely limited.

207:7. "Can ye not discern the signs of the times?"—Matthew 16:3. Carlyle used "Signs of the Times" as title of an early essay in the *Edinburgh Review* (June, 1829).

207:8-9. The Duke of Argyll's most recent such delivery was "On the Economic Condition of the Highlands of Scotland," *Nineteenth Century* XIII, 173–98, (February, 1883), in which he compares the prosperity of those regions where ruthless doctrines of "political economy" prevail with the distress of the areas where benevolence and reclamation have too much encouraged the growth of population.

207:16-23. Harrison (1831–1923), a controversialist with whom Arnold delighted to engage, was a follower of Auguste Comte, and as such was satirized in "Anarchy and Authority" (1868) and *Friendship's Garland* (1871).—*Prose Works*, ed. Super, V, 504-6, 353. In 1881–82, distressed by British imperialism as it had taken its direction under Disraeli and was continuing under Gladstone, he, Morley, Spencer, and others founded an Anti-Aggression League, which hoped to be more effective than the much older Peace Society by avoiding the latter's commitment to the principle of nonresistance. But the League was a failure, since the politicians who were at first engaged in it discovered that their interest lay in following the imperialist banner.

207:27. This Burkean conception of the State is frequently repeated by Arnold; see, for example, *The Popular Education of France* (1861), *Prose Works*, ed. Super, II, 26.

207:28-31. In 1884 Herbert Spencer (1820–1903) collected four *Contemporary Review* articles into the book, *The Man versus the State*. Auberon Herbert (1838–1906), a disciple of Spencer's, in the same year published *A Politician in Trouble about His Soul*, reprinted from the *Fortnightly*, at the close of which "Spencerian principles are expounded and the doctrine of *Laissez-faire* is pushed to the extreme point of advocating voluntary taxation."—*D.N.B.*

208:13–28. Angra Pequeña, on the coast of Southwest Africa, was almost unsettled by Europeans, except for missionaries; its proximity to the spreading Cape Colony, however, led to its falling in general within the British sphere of influence in 1876. In 1883 a Bremen merchant named Lüderitz established a trading station there and concluded treaties with the native chiefs by which large tracts of adjacent land were ceded to his company. On April 24, 1884, he transferred his interest to the German government, which on August 7 proclaimed a protectorate over the region. The Berlin Conference of 1884–85 marked out European spheres of influence in Africa (February 26, 1885); the territory then became German Southwest Africa, and remained German until, in consequence of the first world war, it came under the administration of the Union of South Africa. Granville, perennially foreign secretary in the Liberal cabinets after 1870, was generally regarded as lacking in force. Arnold expressed the view of him as spokesman for the Philistines as early as *Friendship's Garland,* Letter IX (1870).— *Prose Works,* ed. Super, V, 330–32; and for Granville's dealings with Bismarck in 1870, see "The Future of Liberalism" (1880), IX, 149.

209:4–6. In "The Incompatibles" (1881) Arnold took John Gordon Sprigg, prime minister of the Cape Colony in 1878–81, 1886–90, etc., as an example of the type of Philistine represented by Murdstone in *David Copperfield.—Prose Works,* ed. Super, IX, 282. The Earl of Derby succeeded the Earl of Kimberley (see p. 209:11) as colonial secretary in December, 1882.

209:8–10. *The Times'* Berlin correspondent, summarizing a German "white book" on Angra Pequeña, quotes Granville as saying to the German *chargé d'affaires* in London late in August, 1884, shortly after he received a memoir of the German position, "Oh, there is a misunderstanding altogether."—Saturday, December 13, 1884, p. 5, col. 4. *The Times* picked up this phrase in a leading article of December 15, p. 9, col. 4.

209:11. The Boer (Dutch) state of Transvaal was annexed by the Conservative government in April, 1877, in the face of a good deal of opposition in England. But the discontent of the Boers led to a revolt in December, 1880. The British forces under Sir George Colley, moving to put down the uprising, were decisively defeated at Majuba Hill on February 27, 1881, Colley was killed in the battle, and by the Pretoria Convention of 1881 Transvaal regained its independence, except for foreign relations. The Earl of Kimberley, colonial secretary in Gladstone's cabinet of 1880, was nominally the responsible minister. Some four years after the publication of this essay, Arnold's younger daughter married Kimberley's son.

209:15–17. John, Lord Somers (1651–1716), a distinguished statesman and constitutional lawyer, presided over the drafting of the Declaration of Rights after the abdication of James II in 1688. The Whig oligarchy, who were responsible for the Glorious Revolution that placed William III on the throne of England in place of James, were the heroes of Macaulay's *History of England;* from them the Liberals of 1880–85 might claim descent.

211:3–4. When Virginia seceded from the Union in 1861, its forty western counties voted against secession and separated themselves from the rest of the state. They became the state of West Virginia in 1863.

211:21–22. Dublin Castle was the administrative seat of the British government in Ireland.

212:9–11. Only in 1913 did the Seventeenth Amendment to the Constitution provide that the United States Senators should be elected by direct vote of the people of the respective states, instead of, as formerly, by the legislatures of the states.

212:21–22. Until the redistribution effected by the Labour government in 1948, the masters of arts of Oxford, Cambridge, and certain other universities sent representatives to the House of Commons. The university electors thus had two votes, one as graduates of the university and one as residents of a geographical constituency.

213:22–24. See p. 4:4–5n.

213:26–27. Lord John Manners (1818–1906), son of the 5th Duke of Rutland (to whose title he succeeded in 1888), was a member of Parliament from 1841 to 1888 (except for 1847–50), and a member of every Conservative cabinet from 1852 to 1892. He wrote several articles for *Blackwood's* in 1884 defending the House of Lords.

213:27. "Something between a hindrance and a help;"—Wordsworth, "Michael," line 189.

214:17–18. The repeated attempts of some Nonconformist members of the Liberal Party to carry through Parliament a bill permitting a man to marry his deceased wife's sister (as in England in the nineteenth century he might not legally do) seemed to Arnold an exercise in futility, and one he repeatedly ridiculed, first and most notably in *Culture and Anarchy* (1868) and *Friendship's Garland*, Letter VIII (1869).—*Prose Works*, ed. Super, V, 205–8, 313–18. See p. 24:29.

214:23–25. Edward Lyulph Stanley (1839–1925) was a member

of the London School Board from 1876 until its abolition in 1904 and a member of Parliament from 1880 to 1885. He was to be a member of the Cross Commission which in 1886 sent Arnold once more to the Continent to enquire into education there. James Stuart (1843–1913) was professor of mechanism at Cambridge; he was elected to Parliament from Hackney Borough in place of the deceased Professor Fawcett late in 1884. Lord Richard Grosvenor (1837–1912) was a member of Parliament from 1861 until he was elevated to the peerage in 1886; he was chief government whip during the Gladstone administration of 1880–85. Joseph Chamberlain (1836–1914), a member of Gladstone's cabinet, clearly grew in Arnold's estimation after the time of the satiric allusion to him in *God and the Bible* (October, 1874).—*Prose Works*, ed. Super, VII, 145.

214:28–29. "And Saul, yet breathing out threatenings and slaughter against the disciples of the Lord, went unto the high priest," and obtained a commission to arrest any of Christ's followers he might find in the synagogues of Damascus. On his journey thither, however, he was blinded by the vision of a great light from heaven and was converted; thereafter known as Paul, he became the greatest theologian and most energetic organizer of the early Church.—Acts 9:1.

215:1–3. Arnold published his essay on "Disestablishment in Wales" in March, 1888; *Prose Works*, ed. Super, vol. XI. The established church in Scotland is Presbyterian; in Wales it was Episcopalian, as it is in England.

215:15. Goldwin Smith (1823–1910), an undergraduate at Magdalen College, Oxford, while Arnold was an undergraduate at Balliol, was vigorously liberal from his youth. He reviewed Arnold's early poems in *The Times*, was a member of the Newcastle Commission that sent Arnold to France in 1859, was regius professor of modern history at Oxford (a chair Dr. Arnold once held) from 1858 to 1866, carried to America in 1864 a letter of introduction to Emerson in which Arnold called him "one of our most powerful and distinguished men of the younger generation," was named professor of history at the newly-formed Cornell University in Ithaca, New York, in 1868, and in 1871 settled permanently in Toronto, though with frequent visits to England. He was pressed to remain in England and stand for Parliament both before his emigration and on his visits, but declined. He several times engaged in controversy with Arnold, not always genially on his part (as in his criticism of Arnold's essay on "Falkland" in

1877), but Arnold's visit to him in Toronto in February, 1884, was most pleasant. He was also a lifelong friend of Lord Coleridge.

215:24–25. Milton's characterization of the loyal seraph Abdiel, *Paradise Lost*, V, 899.

215:31. John Morley (1838–1923) edited the *Fortnightly Review* from 1867 to 1882 and *The Pall Mall Gazette* from 1880 to 1883; Arnold was a contributor to both. A Liberal of the school of Mill, a friend and co-worker of Frederic Harrison's, he was a political writer of great insight and power. He sat in the House of Commons from 1883 to 1908, when he was created Viscount Morley. He was chief secretary for Ireland in 1886 and 1892–95.

215:33–36. Wordsworth, "Laodameia," lines 74–75.

216:10–11. See p. 207:7n.

216:26–27. After the Lords' defeat of his franchise reform bill, Gladstone worked out a compromise with the Conservative leader, Lord Salisbury, which permitted the passage of a bill extending the franchise, providing it should be preceded by agreement on a bill redistributing the seats in Parliament. The reform bill was passed at the end of 1884, the seats bill in 1885.

216:34–36. "A Visit to Philistia," p. 50.

217:2–3. See p. 20:17–19n.

217:14. "He that hath a wife and children hath given hostages to fortune."—Francis Bacon, "Of Marriage and Single Life." Arnold's older daughter Lucy on December 9, 1884, married Frederick W. Whitridge of New York. Arnold and his wife visited the young couple the year after this essay was published.

[A COMMENT ON CHRISTMAS]

"A Comment on Christmas" seems to spring so immediately from newspaper responses to Arnold's "Lay Sermon" in Whitechapel on November 29, 1884 (pp. 249–55), that it is somewhat surprising to see that he had been planning it for nearly two months when he made that address. Percy William Bunting, editor of the *Contemporary Review* from 1882 to 1911, inquired of Arnold what quarrel had led to his discontinuing his contributions to that journal and begged to be allowed to publish something, perhaps on Carlyle. Arnold's reply, dated October 9, 1884, was that he had merely followed James Knowles, who first gave him space in the *Contemporary*, when Knowles founded the *Nineteenth Century*. "I am not disposed to write more at present about Carlyle than I have said in my discourse on Emerson." He did, however, plan an article which Bunting might have. "It will be ready for February, will have for title 'A Christmas Meditation,' and will follow in general the same line of thought and feeling with which *Literature and Dogma* and *God and the Bible* have made the public more or less familiar."—R. L. Lowe, "Matthew Arnold and Percy William Bunting: Some New Letters 1884–1887," *Studies in Bibliography* VII, 199–200 (1955). There were delays and postponements; at length he promised to send it to the printers on March 18, 1885, for the April number. "I am pressed by an article which I am now preparing for the Contemporary—you know how these things worry me and upset me, and I am more pressed than usual," he wrote to his newly-married daughter in America on the 17th; "but somehow I am not quite so much worried, as I know pretty well what I want to say and feel as if it would come easily within the limits proposed. The article will not particularly interest people, but I had promised it." Bunting's terms, whatever they were, seemed to Arnold too liberal; he stipulated only for his customary fee of £50. "I doubted about the article suiting you," he wrote the editor in acknowledging the payment, "but its tone and temper make it possible for a public such as we have at present; vicious attacks on the orthodox position do nothing but harm in every direction. I cannot but hope that the line taken by me will prove, in the times upon which we are entering, to be of use; I feel myself really in sympathy with the religious world far more than with its assailants—even with the religious world as it is at present." On October 11, 1886, he asked Bunting's permission to reprint the article in a volume of Collected Essays he was about to publish; in fact, it appeared at the end of Smith, Elder's "popular edition" of *St. Paul and Protestantism* on January 14, 1887. As Arnold said, the essay aims at summarizing the doctrine of his religious books of the preceding decade, but its concern with the goddess Lubricity links it with the essay on "Numbers" and its concluding turn to an equalitarian economic theory, curious in an essay on religion, may well spring from his recent attempt to present his doctrine to the slum-dwellers of East London and from *The Guardian*'s criticism of what he said on that occasion.

218:4–5. Thomas Wilson, *Maxims of Piety and of Christianity*, ed. Frederic Relton (London, 1898), p. 158; jotted in Arnold's pocket diary for March 30, 1884, at the beginning of 1885, and for January 7, 1885.—*Note-Books*, ed. Lowry, pp. 406, 412, 413.

218:13–14. Sir Augustus Rivers Thompson was lieutenant-governor of Bengal from April 1882 to April 1887.

219:5. "For the world cries your faith is now|But a dead time's exploded dream."—"Stanzas from the Grande Chartreuse" (1855), lines 97–98.

219:6–9. Leading article on Stopford Brooke's secession, November 3, 1880, p. 1497, jotted in Arnold's pocket diary for August 17, 1880, and quoted in the Preface to the Popular Edition (1883) of *Literature and Dogma*, and the article on Christmas signed "E.H.P.," December 20, 1882, p. 1809.—*Note-Books*, ed. Lowry, p. 342; *Prose Works*, ed. Super, VI, 146.

219:19–25. Isaiah 7:14–16; the Authorized Version reads "that he may know," not "until he shall know." For Arnold's own version (p. 221) and his notes, see pp. 270–71, 380. Isaiah VII is the First Lesson at Evening Prayer on Christmas Day.

220:5. E.g., W. Robertson Smith, *The Prophets of Israel and Their Place in History* (New York, 1882), pp. 272–73 (Lecture VI, ¶4 from end).

221:20–22. Isaiah 9:7. This chapter is the First Lesson at Morning Prayer on Christmas Day.

222:6–8. Matthew 1:18–25; Luke 1:26–38.

222:11–17. Diogenes Laertius *Lives of the Philosophers* III, ii.

222:22–23. Panegyric of St. Paul (c. 1659), nearly halfway through.—Bossuet, *Oeuvres choisies*, ed. Jean Calvet (14th ed.; Paris: A. Hatier, 1947), p. 53. Arnold quoted the comparison between St. Paul and Plato as an example of "prose without the note of provinciality—classical prose, prose of the centre," in "The Literary Influence of Academies" (1864) and chose it as one of his two favorite non-Biblical passages of prose in "Fine Passages in Verse and Prose" (1887).—*Prose Works*, ed. Super, III, 246, and XI, Appendix.

222:35. See p. 143:11–13.

223:6–7. "Unto me . . . is this grace given, that I should preach among the Gentiles the unsearchable riches of Christ."—Paul to the Ephesians 3:8.

223:38–224:3. For example, *Republic* IX, 573.

224:18–20. Matthew 5:3, 8.

225:6–7. I Thessalonians 4:7; the Authorized Version reads "uncleanness," not "impureness."

225:38. Arnold first described an anthropomorphic conception of God as a belief in "a magnified and non-natural man" in *St. Paul and Protestantism* (1869), *Prose Works*, ed. Super, VI, 15; and see *Literature and Dogma, ibid.*, 188, 360.

226:10–21. H. D. Traill, *Coleridge* (New York, 1884), p. 175 ("English Men of Letters"). Traill quotes the biographical memoir by John Simon prefixed to Joseph Henry Green's *Spiritual Philosophy* (London, 1865), I, xliii.

226:29–32. In *Literature and Dogma* (1873) Arnold referred to Frederick Denison Maurice (1805–72) as "that pure and devout spirit,—of whom, however, the truth must at last be told, that in theology he passed his life beating the bush with deep emotion and never starting the hare."—*Prose Works*, ed. Super, VI, 383.

227:18–22. *Oedipus Tyrannos* 863–71, jotted in Arnold's pocket diary for July 10, 1887.—*Note-Books*, ed. Lowry, p. 430. This passage was for Arnold the epitome of religious expression: see "Pagan and Mediaeval Religious Sentiment" (1864) and *Literature and Dogma* (1871).—*Prose Works*, ed. Super, III, 231 and VI, 178.

227:27–29. F. W. Riemer, *Mittheilungen über Goethe* (Berlin, 1841), II, 95, jotted in Arnold's pocket diary for March 26, 1871, at the beginning of 1872 and 1875, and in one of his "General Note-Books," and quoted also in the Preface to *Last Essays on Church and Religion* (1877).—*Note-Books*, ed. Lowry, pp. 152, 169, 224, 522; *Prose Works*, ed. Super, VIII, 157–58.

227:35–37. See pp. 154–55.

228:1–2. Marie de Rabutin-Chantal, Marquise de Sévigné (1626–96), a friend of La Rochefoucauld and Madame de La Fayette, was a prolific letter-writer whose correspondence was published in numerous editions after her death. See p. 89:10. Ninon de Lenclos (1620–1705) was famous for her beauty, her wit, and her lovers.

228:21–25. Ninon to St.-Évremond, 1699, quoted by Sainte-Beuve, "Saint-Évremond et Ninon" (May 26, 1851), *Causeries du lundi* (3rd ed.; Paris, 1869), IV, 186; by Arnold in the Preface to *Last Essays on Church and Religion* (1877), *Prose Works*, ed. Super, VIII, 157.

229:20. "Grant, O Lord, that as we are baptized into the death of thy blessed Son our Saviour Jesus Christ, so by continual mortifying our corrupt affections we may be buried with him; and that through the grave, and gate of death, we may pass to our joyful resurrection; for his merits, who died, and was buried, and rose again for us, thy Son Jesus Christ our Lord."

229:21, 26. In *Literature and Dogma* Arnold defined the "secret of Jesus" as *self-renouncement*. "For this world of busy inward movement created by the *method* of Jesus, a rule of action was wanted; and this rule was found in his *secret*. It was this of which the Apostle Paul afterwards possessed himself with such energy, and called it 'the word of the cross,' or *necrosis*, 'dying.'"—*Prose Works*, ed. Super, VI, 291; and for a discussion of *necrosis*, see *St. Paul and Protestantism, ibid.*, 47–49.

229:33–35. The English is not a translation of the Latin, however. See John Henry Blunt, ed., *The Annotated Book of Common Prayer* (London, 1866), p. 76. "Lauds" is the traditional morning prayer of the Western Church, parts of which are combined with Matins into the Morning Prayer service of the Book of Common Prayer. The Mozarabic Rite was used in the Spanish peninsula from the earliest times to the eleventh century.

230:6. Trinity Sunday, one week after Whitsun or Pentecost, is a festival in honor of the Blessed Trinity; its Collect reads: "Almighty and everlasting God, who has given unto us thy servants grace by the confession of a true faith to acknowledge the glory of the eternal Trinity, and in the power of the Divine Majesty to worship the Unity; We beseech thee that thou wouldest keep us stedfast in this faith, and evermore defend us from all adversities."

231:36–232:2. Arnold ridiculed Auguste Comte's "Religion of Humanity" and its English followers (most notably Frederic Harrison and Richard Congreve) at the beginning of "Anarchy and Authority" (1868), but removed the passage from the essay when he reprinted it in *Culture and Anarchy.* He alluded to Harrison's Comtism in "A Word More about America," p. 207:16–20. See *Prose Works,* ed. Super, V, 504–6.

232:6–9. *Literature and Dogma, Prose Works,* ed. Super, VI, 258–65.

232:28–31. *Imitatio* III, lvi, 12–14. "Jesus saith unto him, I am the way, the truth, and the life: no man cometh unto the Father, but by me."—John 14:6.

234:26–27. The method is inwardness or conscience, the secret is self-renouncement, and the temper is sweet reasonableness; see *Literature and Dogma, Prose Works,* ed. Super, VI, 284–301.

235:12–14. John 16:11, which Arnold quoted in his talk given at the unveiling of a mural at St. Jude's Church, Whitechapel, on November 29, 1884. See pp. 253–54.

235:15–16. *The Guardian* complained that according to Arnold's doctrine in the discourse in Whitechapel, "the 'sacrificed classes' are to be consoled and edified by the thought that the rich and powerful will eventually be judged and condemned. . . . This [is] nothing but a Gospel of envy and malice . . . He did not allude to the danger of thinking that poverty and trouble are in themselves meritorious, and will be rewarded; while wealth and power will be punished. . . . The 'sacrificed classes' need to be taught that religion is something more than revenge, and that holiness is not compatible with bitterness."—"Mr. Matthew Arnold's Gospel for the Poor," *The Guardian,* Wednesday, December 10, 1884,

p. 1867. *The Guardian* was a weekly Church of England news-paper published in London. Arnold was very pleased by a letter published in his defence the next week (December 17, p. 1919), signed C. A. Goodhart, vicar of St. Barnabas, Sheffield.

236:13–19. Arnold praises this exegesis from Ferdinand Baur's *Geschichte der christlichen Kirche* (3rd ed.; Tübingen, 1863), I, 26–28—a subtle discussion of the "poor, who have nothing and yet have everything"—in the Preface to *God and the Bible* (1875), *Prose Works*, ed. Super, VII, 374.

236:23–24. Luke 16:12.

236:36–38. Not Gospel, but Romans 12:4–5?

237:2–14. This is not unlike Karl Marx's comment in the 1867 Preface to *Das Kapital:* "The English Established Church . . . will more readily pardon an attack on 38 of its 39 articles than on ⅟₃₉ of its income. Now-a-days atheism itself is *culpa levis,* as compared with criticism of existing property relations."

237:17–18. Mark 10:23, Luke 18:24 (Matthew 19:23).

238:12–13. For example, Matthew 13:39-40, 24:3. The Vulgate expression is *"consummatio saeculi."*

238:27–28. Luke 11:51.

[NOTE ON CANCELLED PASSAGE]

578:15–18. Collect for the sixth Sunday after Epiphany.

[PREFACE TO *Discourses in America*]

The editor of Arnold's letters, his young friend G. W. E. Russell, has noted that the year before Arnold's death Arnold said that *Discourses in America* was the book by which, of all his prose-writings, he should most wish to be remembered. Its three essays are, in fact, epitomes of his writings upon society, education, and literature, and two of them at least, "Literature and Science" and "Emerson," are, for complete competence of style and maturity of thought, among the best things he ever wrote.

The lecture tour was arduous—sixty-five lectures in about four months, on a tour that included Quebec and Portland, Maine; Richmond, Milwaukee, and St. Louis, with many other cities and towns between. His motive was—as a good many of his friends knew—to repay to his publisher George Smith a debt of nearly a thousand pounds he incurred in 1878 to pay his son's gambling obligations at Oxford and to send him off to Australia to find himself again. "This I have enabled myself to clear off, and I have also paid all expenses of the journey," he told Lord Coleridge on his return to London. (In fact, his pocket diaries show that he carried with him from America a draft on Morgan's Bank for £1193 8*s.* 2*d.*, and paid off immediately upon his return a debt to Smith of £959 10*s.* and to his own banker £212.) He placed his tour under the management of D'Oyly Carte, a move he regretted as reducing his income almost by half: "Without running any risk except of the money paid for my passage I might have made 90 per cent. of the profits of my lectures, instead of only 50 per cent. as at present, [besides the expenses of a very costly management]. However, I shall still make a sum which I could have got in no other way, shall have had a most instructive experience of this country and people, and shall have learnt how to proceed if ever I come and lecture here again." Indeed, he had visions of making three or four thousand pounds the next time. As late as September, 1885, he was planning a new lecture tour of America for the autumn of 1886.

His reception was various, but the valedictory of the Boston *Sunday Herald*—"a coarse paper, but perhaps the strongest in America"—pleased him highly and was quoted in England: "The emphatic note of his American visit, was that he kept himself true to conscience, to right principles, to his great office as a constructive critic of literature." Russell's edition of his letters gives a great deal of space to those from America; the fullest account of the tour is C. H. Leonard's *Arnold in America* (Yale University dissertation, 1932; Ann Arbor: University Microfilms, 1964), and an important supplement is D. J. DeLaura, "Matthew Arnold and the American 'Literary Class,'" *Bulletin of the New York Public Library* LXX, 229–50 (April 1966). A significant study of Arnold's impact on America, without especial reference to the lecture tour, is John Henry Raleigh, *Matthew Arnold and American Culture* (Berkeley: University of California Press, 1957).

On August 20, 1884, Arnold proposed to Macmillan that the three lectures, together with "A Word about America" and a projected "Word More about America" be published the following February as "American Addresses, &c." By April 9, 1885, the book had its present title and was presumably limited to the three lectures. Arnold hoped it would appear by Whitsuntide. Simultaneous editions of 1250 copies were published in London and New York, and for them Arnold was paid £75—Buckler, *Matthew Arnold's Books*, pp. 162–63. The book was advertised in London as ready on June 13, at the price of 4*s*. 6*d*., though in fact the publication date was three days later.

239:8–9. "Both for the beauty of the place, and for the friends we made there, Boston lives constantly in our memories; and I can understand perfectly the affection of Bostonians for 'this darling town of ours.' I hope to see it once more, if I live," wrote Arnold to Oliver Wendell Holmes on December 26, 1884.

239:18–20. In "A Word More about America," February, 1885; see pp. 196–98.

240:2–3. "Such bickerings to recount, met oft'n in these our Writers, what more worth is it then to Chronicle the Wars of Kites, or Crows, flocking and fighting in the Air?"—Milton, *History of Britain*, Book IV, near the end; *Works*, ed. G. P. Krapp et al. (New York: Columbia University Press, 1932), X, 191.

240:12–14. Presumably Gladstone, prime minister for the second time, 1880–85. Balaam's ass three times turned aside from the path her master attempted to guide her on, to avoid catastrophe for Balaam, and each time, not perceiving the danger, he beat her. "And the Lord opened the mouth of the ass, and she said unto Balaam, What have I done unto thee, that thou hast smitten me these three times? . . . Am I not thine ass, upon which thou hast ridden ever since I was thine unto this day?"—Numbers 22:28, 30.

240:21. The Congregationalist John Carvell Williams (1821–1907) became secretary of Edward Miall's British Anti-State Church Association three years after its founding in 1844, was responsible for its change of name to the Society for the Liberation of Religion from State Patronage and Control, and remained high in its councils for the rest of his life.

240:22–24. See pp. 204–5, 207–8.

[ON *Cloture*]

242:10–13. Arnold's authority on the use of the word "closure" is presumably Johnson's *Dictionary*. According to the *N.E.D.*, it was *The Pall Mall Gazette* (and therefore Arnold) that established the use of the English form.

[MR. ARNOLD AND THE LITERARY CLASS]

"The business is nearly at an end. It will not have brought the profit which some people expected, but it will bring a good sum, and has shown me how a really large profit may be made if I come again. But when I once get safe over to the other side, shall I ever bring myself to start on such an errand again? To-day I have to visit the Seminary for training Presbyterian ministers—a speech. Later I have to attend a reception given me by the Authors Club— a speech again." So wrote Arnold to his brother as his American lecture tour drew to a close.—*Letters*, ed. Russell. The Authors Club, founded on October 21, 1882, by R. W. Gilder, Brander Matthews, E. C. Stedman, and others, elected Arnold as its first honorary member on October 24, 1883, two days after he landed in New York.—Duffield Osborne, *The Authors Club, An Historical Sketch* (New York, 1913), pp. 3, 7. The report of the address he gave at the reception of February 28 has been reprinted in Fraser Neiman, ed., *Essays, Letters, and Reviews by Matthew Arnold* (Cambridge: Harvard University Press, 1960).

243:14–15. The Rev. Flavius Josephus Cook (1838–1901) for nearly twenty years gave a popular, oracular series of Monday Lectures at Tremont Temple, Boston, on a wide range of subjects of current interest, religious, scientific, social, and philosophical.

243:17–18. Le Sage, *Gil Blas de Santillane*, Book V, chapt. i. Arnold took *Gil Blas* to America with him.—*Note-Books*, ed. Lowry, p. 608.

[MENDACIOUS PERSONAL GOSSIP]

Electric trams were still about six years in the future, but Boston had one of the largest fleets of horse-drawn trams in the United States. They were no favorites of Arnold's: "What it is in the towns, to have practically no cabs and to be obliged to use trams, you cannot imagine, . . . two or three changes, and a walk at each end, and the chance of bad weather," he wrote to his sister Jane from Hartford.—*Letters*, ed. Russell. To Norton he wrote on the eve of his next American journey that even the horse cars would not keep him from Cambridge. The Hotel Vendome, luxurious in its day, stood on Commonwealth Avenue at the corner of Dartmouth Street; it has only recently (1972) been destroyed by fire.

[SPEECH AT THE
JEWS' FREE SCHOOL DINNER]

When Arnold sent Lady de Rothschild a copy of *A Bible Reading for Schools*, his version of the latter part of the Book of Isaiah, he told her (May 17, 1872): "I have sent a copy to Mr. Angel [the Headmaster] as a sort of expression of gratitude for the *ideas* your great Bell Lane Schools have awakened in me." The Jews' Free School in Bell Lane, a short distance east of the Liverpool Street Station and only a few steps from Toynbee Hall, where Arnold spoke on November 29, 1884, was at one time among those Arnold inspected. By 1884 it educated annually over 3,000 Jewish children, considerably more than were educated in the Board schools of London.

245:31–33. In *Friendship's Garland*, Letter VIII (1869), Arnold attributed this saying to John Philpot Curran, not to Grattan.— *Prose Works*, ed. Super, V, 313.

[SOHO CLUB AND HOME FOR WORKING GIRLS]

In early November, 1883, a club-house in Greek Street was opened to accommodate Maude Stanley's Soho Club and Home for Working Girls. *The Pall Mall Gazette* (now edited by W. T. Stead) said two days after Arnold's remarks of July 9, 1884: "Mr. Matthew Arnold is becoming more paradoxical than ever. His recent criticisms on poetry have been somewhat overwhelming, but his latest 'criticism of life'—of life in Soho—is surely the 'crowning wave.' Every one must at some time or another have passed through the district that lies between Soho and Leicester squares, and noted the squalor of its alleys and the almost more depressing shabby-gentility of its larger streets. Here and there in Soho there are restaurants which are still frequented by the judicious, but for the most part it is given up either to factories and workshops or to the small retail dealers who supply the French colony in London. The district wears, however, a very different aspect to Mr. Matthew Arnold, and what has always struck him as the great characteristic of Soho . . . is its 'turn for gaiety.' This state of things he attributes partly to its having been 'once inhabited by the rich and gay,' and partly to 'foreign admixture,' a striking testimony surely to 'the power of manners' and the saving virtue of French civilization."—p. 3, col. 1.

[MR. MATTHEW ARNOLD ON AMERICA]

The Chicago newspaper hoax was a trap laid by *The Chicago News* for *The Chicago Tribune* to catch the latter paper red-handed at stealing news stories from the New York papers and, incidentally, from the foreign news service of the *News* as well. An article purporting to be the first of a series on America contributed by "Mr. Arnold" to the nonexistent "Pall Mall Journal" was planted in a copy of *The New York Tribune* for April 6, 1884, about a fortnight after Arnold's return to London. *The Chicago Tribune* leaped to the bait by reprinting the article—which was very critical of the culture of its city—and drew irate comments from many of Arnold's Chicago acquaintances, including some of his hosts. By April 12, the hoax was confessed. But it brought Arnold no little embarrassment. "I am over-done with letters," he wrote to his sister Frances on April 29. "America adds a strong contingent, especially just now after the hoax played upon the Chicago people—But what newspapers—what a tone and style." Arnold was apparently paid £2 by *The Pall Mall Gazette* for the account of the interview with *The Boston Herald*.

247:18. Robert Laird Collier (1837–90) was a Maryland born Unitarian clergyman who preached in the English industrial cities of Leicester, Birmingham and Bradford from 1881 to 1885.

247:27–29. The fullest account of the hoax, with the entire article attributed to Arnold, is in Chilson H. Leonard, *Arnold in America* (Yale University Dissertation, 1932; Ann Arbor: University Microfilms, 1964), pp. 251–53, 336–40. The perpetrator of the hoax, Melville E. Stone, gives his account in *Fifty Years a Journalist* (New York, 1921), pp. 122–24.

[OLIVER WENDELL HOLMES]

Holmes (substituting for an indisposed Phillips Brooks) wittily introduced Arnold to his audience at the first of his Boston lectures, "Numbers," at Horticultural Hall on November 7, 1883. They met frequently while Arnold was in Boston, and Arnold much liked Holmes. The manuscript of this brief note, actually addressed to J. B. Gilder personally (not "To the Editors of The Critic"), survives in The Pierpont Morgan Library, New York.

[A LAY SERMON]

When the Rev. Charles Anderson moved from the curacy of St. Anne's, Soho, to the vicarage of St. John's, Limehouse, Arnold wrote to him on March 9, 1874: "No words can be too strong to describe the gratitude which society owes to men, who, renouncing the old taste of employing with the multitude a false but powerful fairy-tale in the way of religion, do yet not renounce the taste of conveying religion to the multitude. They are the true civilisers, the true workers for the future; & they will have their reward." This was the sense of what he himself was to say in the same part of London on November 29, 1884. The speech was printed at length in *The Times* the following Monday morning, and in abbreviated form by *The Pall Mall Gazette* in the evening; certain blunders of *The Times* reporter were corrected in the *Pall Mall*, either by Arnold himself or by the assistant editor of the newspaper, E. T. Cook, who was on the platform when Arnold made his speech. There is no record that Arnold was paid by the newspaper. The address was severely criticized in *The Guardian*. The present text is that of *The Times* modified (as indicated in the Textual Notes) from *The Pall Mall Gazette;* the speech was reprinted in its uncorrected form by Fraser Neiman, ed., *Essays, Letters, and Reviews by Matthew Arnold* (Cambridge: Harvard University Press, 1960).

249:14–16. George Frederick Watts's painting, "Time, Death, and Judgment" (one version of which is now in the Tate Gallery, another on a pier beneath the dome of St. Paul's Cathedral) was copied in mosaic by Antonio Salviati (1816–90) for the façade of St. Jude's Church on Commercial Street, Whitechapel, in East London. When the church was demolished in 1925, the mosaic was moved to Endell Street, near old High Holborn (about half a mile directly south of the British Museum), but it is no longer there, the victim of bombing or further demolition. Watts in 1880 painted a portrait of Arnold, now in the National Portrait Gallery.

249:16. Leonard Henry Courtney (1832–1918), later Baron Courtney, who presided over the meeting and introduced Arnold, was Liberal M.P. for Liskeard and was secretary of the Treasury in Gladstone's administration until his resignation two days after this meeting. From 1872 to 1875 he was professor of political economy at University College, London, and from 1865 to 1881 was leader-writer to *The Times.*

249:21. The City, the part of London within the line of the old city walls, is the center of London's commercial and financial activity. It extends along the Thames from the Tower to Temple Bar. Whitechapel is just to the east of the City, the West End is the fashionable residential area of Mayfair, Bayswater, Belgravia, and South Kensington.

250:22. Robert (later Sir Robert) Giffen (1837–1910), assistant secretary to the Board of Trade, was president of the Royal Statistical Society, had been assistant editor of *The Economist,* was one of the founders of *The Statist,* and was a voluminous writer on economic subjects from the free-trade and *laissez-faire* point of view. Like Courtney he was a contributor to the *Fortnightly Review* and friend of its editor John Morley, and like Courtney he was closely associated with Joseph Chamberlain. His most recent letter to *The Times,* printed in the larger type and with the wider spacing reserved for the most important matters, appeared on November 27, 1884, p. 8, cols. 1–2; as Arnold suggests, he asserted that if foreign manufacturers competed with English manufacturers for the English market, "English consumers would be benefited by a cheaper commodity, just as they would by competition springing up at home." It was the doctrine of Pangloss, ridiculed in Voltaire's *Candide,* that "all is for the best in this best of all possible worlds."

250:33–34. Wordsworth. See his sonnet, "Written in London, September, 1802," lines 9–11:
> Rapine, avarice, expense,
> This is idolatry; and these we adore.
> Plain living and high thinking are no more."

Also the first two lines of another sonnet:
> The world is too much with us; late and soon,
> Getting and spending, we lay waste our powers.

251:9. In Philippians 4:1–3, St. Paul pays tribute to his fellow labourers in the gospel, "whose names are in the book of life." The "book of life" appears frequently in Revelation as a record of those who would enter the heavenly city; "and whosoever was not found written in the book of life was cast into the lake of fire."— 21:27, 20:15.

251:11–12. Edward Denison (1840–70), son of the bishop of Salisbury, a wealthy young man, became deeply interested in the condition of the poor in London's East End, took up his residence among them, and studied to find better methods than the dole for dealing with poverty. He was elected to Parliament in November, 1868, but died of consumption only fourteen months later.

251:15. Arnold Toynbee (1852–83), a tutor at Balliol College, Oxford, under Jowett, plunged into the study of economics with a view to improving the condition of the industrial masses. He was associated with Canon Barnett in his work among the East London poor. His friends established Toynbee Hall as a memorial to him, the first "university settlement" or adult education center, designed to encourage closer relations between the working class and those educated at the universities. It was erected in the last six months of 1884 in Commercial Street, next to St. Jude's, and hence was not quite completed when the meeting Arnold addressed was held in it. The historian Arnold J. Toynbee is the nephew of this Arnold Toynbee.

251:21. William Tyler (1812–90), pastor of the Congregational Church, Hanbury St., Spitalfields, to whom Arnold's sonnet "East London" (1867) was addressed, and who was perhaps the somewhat naïve object of Arnold's irony in the final chapter of *Culture and Anarchy* (1868).—*Prose Works*, ed. Super, V, 217.

251:23. Samuel Augustus Barnett (1844–1913), vicar of St. Jude's, was also the first warden of Toynbee Hall.

251:27–28. The Archdeaconry of London's East London Mission was a massive effort to bring Christianity to the slums through services in the parish churches or elsewhere conducted by guest clergy, and with rescue work and refuges, from November 16 to 25, 1884. *The Guardian* regarded Arnold's remark as a sneer and noted that Barnett did not join in the Mission.—"Mr. Matthew Arnold's Gospel for the Poor," December 10, 1884, p. 1867; see p. 235:15–16n.

251:30–252:3. Arnold alludes to a central doctrine of his *Literature and Dogma* and other religious writings. His most recent statement of it was the preface to the Popular Edition of that book (1883), *Prose Works*, ed. Super, VI, 141–46; he was soon to repeat the idea in "A Comment on Christmas," April, 1885.

252:16–21. The temporary art exhibitions continued to thrive. In 1901 the Whitechapel Art Gallery was built to house them, and it is still in use.

252:22–23. John 4:13 (Jesus to the woman of Samaria).

253:5–7. Isaiah 30:18. Arnold preferred "The Eternal" to "The Lord" of the Authorized Version; see p. 104:32–37.

253:18–20. John 16:7–11. "Convince" is an alternative to the Authorized Version's "reprove"; the Revised Version reads "will convict the world in respect of sin."

254:8–11. Luke 2:25, Acts 3:21 ("until the times of restitution of all things"), Revelation 21:1 (Isaiah 65:17, II Peter 3:13). "The Kingdom of God" occurs frequently in the New Testament, especially in the synoptic gospels.

254:24–25. Joseph Butler, *The Analogy of Religion*, II, iv, 8; *Works*, ed. W. E. Gladstone (Oxford, 1896), I, 251.

254:30–31. Samuel Johnson, *The Vanity of Human Wishes*, line 316.

255:4–9. Wordsworth, "To B. R. Haydon," lines 9–14.

[SPEECH AT DULWICH COLLEGE]

Dulwich College was founded in 1616 by Edward Alleyn (1566–1626), the actor, a contemporary of Shakespeare's and a partner with Philip Henslowe in the management of the Rose Theatre and the Fortune Theatre. But it remained almost dormant as a school for over two centuries, until it was reorganized in 1857 and again in 1882. It was decidedly, in Arnold's terms, a "middle class" school, a day school that drew heavily on the parishes of London adjacent to it and sent very few of its boys to the university. His advocacy of schools of this sort, preferably with state support, was continuous from the publication of one of his earliest books, *A French Eton, or Middle Class Education and the State*, in 1864.

255:19–21. The Rev. James E. C. Welldon (1854–1937), translator of Aristotle, was appointed master of Dulwich College in May, 1883, and resigned in July, 1885, to become head master of Harrow, a post he held until 1898. His successor at Dulwich was Arthur Herman Gilkes (1849–1922), who remained there until 1914.

255:24–27. Arnold moved his family from Chester Square, London, to Byron House, Harrow, at the beginning of April, 1868, partly in order to educate his sons at the school there. Both Tom, the eldest, and "Budge," the second son, died at Harrow. In May, 1873, he moved to Pains Hill Cottage, Cobham, Surrey, his home for the rest of his life.

[SPEECH AT THE ABERDARE EISTEDDFOD]

Arnold's letter of September, 1866, to Hugh Owen subjected him to severe criticism from *The Times;* both letter and criticism are quoted in the Introduction to *On the Study of Celtic Literature*,

Prose Works, ed. Super, III, 387–95. The archdeacon of Llandaff in 1884 was John Griffiths.

[ARNOLD'S NOTES TO ISAIAH]

Although Arnold's original version of Isaiah XL–LXVI was intended for schoolchildren, the notes were not significantly revised when the work was republished for adult readers, and indeed all the notes seem more appropriate to a mature audience.

375:23. John Kitto (1804–54), a self-educated lay missionary and popularizer, published his *Pictorial Bible,* with notes, in 1835–38.

403:29–31. Herodotus III, 89.

406:34. Amru'-ul-Qais or Imru'-ul-Qais, Arabian poet of the sixth century.

407:5–12. A. H. Layard, *Nineveh and Its Remains* (5th ed.; London, 1850), I, 8 (chapt. i, halfway through).

413:20. Arnold's catchwords follow the Authorized Version, not his own; so do they also at 414:24, 416:27, and 422:16.

417:15–18. See Gibbon, *Decline and Fall of the Roman Empire,* chapt. x, three-fourths through.

419:8–9. See Josephus *Jewish Antiquities* X, 38.

425:3–7. Pausanias *Description of Greece* VII, xxii, 4; see Sir James Frazer's commentary on this passage. For the term "baetyli" see Pliny *Natural History* XXXVII, 135.

427:7–8. Huxley would have said that Arnold's knowledge of natural history was not perfect.

427:14. Both the Authorized Version and Arnold's read "far from" for "gone from."

430:7. See Isaiah 48:22, 57:21.

431:16. Revelation 2:17, 3:12.

432:17–19. Mohammed, the nephew of a merchant of Mecca, made his first journey with a caravan to Bosra, Syria, at the age of twelve; thereafter he travelled much with the Arabian caravans.

432:34. The Authorized Version and Arnold's read "a beast."

437:21. It is so used by Persian speakers in Aeschylus *Persae* 178, 563.

441:32–33. *Natural History* VI, 122.

446:9. The Authorized Version and Arnold's read "they," not "we."

Textual Notes

[A WORD ABOUT AMERICA]

Ninet. "A Word about America," *Nineteenth Century* XI, 680–96 (May, 1882).

Lit. "A Word about America," *Littell's Living Age* CLIII, 546–56 (June 3, 1882). Not collated.

4:23. hereditary rule, *Ninet.; corrected from Vivian.*
12:24. highest act of *Ninet.; corrected from Lowell.*
16:10. strictest sect *Ninet.; corrected from Bird.*

[AN ETON BOY]

Fortn. "An Eton Boy," *Fortnightly Review* XXXVII (n.s. XXXI), 683–97 (June, 1882).

Lit. "An Eton Boy," *Littell's Living Age* CLIII, 813–21 (June 30, 1882). Not collated.

32:3, 22. Umhloti, Umhali *Fortn. and Mynors; corrected by ed.*
32:33. This afternoon *Fortn.; corrected from Mynors.*
33:12, 27. Undini *Fortn. and Mynors; corrected by ed.*
35:38. and seventy-six *Fortn.; corrected from Mynors.*
37:32. in small parties *Fortn.; corrected from Mynors.*
42:1. he would recover. *Fortn.; corrected from Mynors.*

[A SEPTUAGENARIAN POET]

St. Jas. "A Septuagenarian Poet," *St. James's Gazette,* June 2, 1882, pp. 6–7. Anonymous.

[LITERATURE AND SCIENCE]

Ninet.   "Literature and Science," *Nineteenth Century* XII,
216–30 (August, 1882).

Lit.   "Literature and Science," *Littell's Living Age* CLIV,
579–88 (September 9, 1882). Not collated.

Ecl.   "Literature and Science," *Eclectic Magazine*, n.s.
XXXVI, 550–59 (October, 1882). Not collated.

Manh.   "Literature and Science," *Manhattan* III, 323–32 (April,
1884).

85.   Discourses in | America | by | Matthew Arnold |
London | Macmillan and Co. | 1885
      "Literature and Science," pp. 72–137.

53:1–55:28. *not in Ninet.*

53:23. *no* ¶ *Manh.*

54:3. though *Manh.*

54:9–10. But we have changed *Manh.*

54:10. modern majority *Manh., 85; corrected from Emerson.*

54:31. and for the world's great good, to *Manh.*

55:1. which shall result *Manh.*

55:2–3. wisdom, and will disregard the rest.' I *Manh.*

55:8. *no* ¶ *Manh.*

55:15–17. The question . . . better. *not in Manh.*

55:18. weighs on us still in *Manh.*

55:21. from letters *not in Manh.*

55:23. here in this intensely modern world of the United *Manh.*

55:26–27. is, even more here than in Europe, a *Manh.*

55:29. *The opening five paragraphs in Ninet., as delivered at Cambridge, differ from the opening of Manh. and 85, as delivered in the United States:*

LITERATURE AND SCIENCE. [1]

No wisdom, nor counsel, nor understanding, against the Eternal!
30 says the Wise Man. Against the natural and appointed course of
things there is no contending. Ten years ago I remarked on the
gloomy prospect for letters in this country, inasmuch as while the

[1] Address delivered as 'The Rede Lecture' at Cambridge.

aristocratic class, according to a famous dictum of Lord Beaconsfield, was totally indifferent to letters, the friends of physical
science on the other hand, a growing and popular body, were in
active revolt against them. To deprive letters of the too great place
they had hitherto filled in men's estimation, and to substitute other   5
studies for them, was now the object, I observed, of a sort of cru-
sade with the friends of physical science—a busy host important
in itself, important because of the gifted leaders who march at its
head, important from its strong and increasing hold upon public
favour.   10

I could not help, I then went on to say, I could not help being
moved with a desire to plead with the friends of physical science
on behalf of letters, and in deprecation of the slight which they
put upon them. But from giving effect to this desire I was at that
time drawn off by more pressing matters. Ten years have passed,   15
and the prospects of any pleader for letters have certainly not
mended. If the friends of physical science were in the morning
sunshine of popular favour even then, they stand now in its merid-
ian radiance. Sir Josiah Mason founds a college at Birmingham to
exclude 'mere literary instruction and education;' and at its open-   20
ing a brilliant and charming debater, Professor Huxley, is brought
down to pronounce their funeral oration. Mr. Bright, in his zeal
for the United States, exhorts young people to drink deep of 'Hia-
watha;' and the *Times*, which takes the gloomiest view possible of
the future of letters, and thinks that a hundred years hence there   25
will only be a few eccentrics reading letters and almost every one
will be studying the natural sciences—the *Times*, instead of coun-
selling Mr. Bright's young people rather to drink deep of Homer,
is for giving them, above all, 'the works of Darwin and Lyell and
Bell and Huxley,' and for nourishing them upon the voyage of the   30
'Challenger.' Stranger still, a brilliant man of letters in France,
M. Renan, assigns the same date of a hundred years hence, as the
date by which the historical and critical studies, in which his life
has been passed and his reputation made, will have fallen into neglect, and deservedly so fallen. It is the regret of his life, M. Renan 35
tells us, that he did not himself originally pursue the natural sciences,
in which he might have forestalled Darwin in his discoveries.

What does it avail, in presence of all this, that we find one of
your own prophets, Bishop Thirlwall, telling his brother who was
sending a son to be educated abroad that he might be out of the   40
way of Latin and Greek: 'I do not think that the most perfect
knowledge of every language now spoken under the sun could

compensate for the want of them'? What does it avail, even, that
an august lover of science, the great Goethe, should have said: 'I
wish all success to those who are for preserving to the literature
of Greece and Rome its predominant place in education'? Goethe
5 was a wise man, but the irresistible current of things was not then
manifest as it is now. *No wisdom, nor counsel, nor understanding,
against the Eternal!*
    But to resign oneself too passively to supposed designs of the
Eternal is fatalism. Perhaps they are not really designs of the Eter-
10 nal at all, but designs—let us for example say—of Mr. Herbert
Spencer. Still the design of abasing what is called 'mere literary
instruction and education,' and of exalting what is called 'sound,
extensive, and practical scientific knowledge,' is a very positive
design and makes great progress. The Universities are by no means
15 outside its scope. At the recent congress in Sheffield of elementary
teachers—a very able and important body of men whose movements I naturally follow with strong interest—at Sheffield one of
the principal speakers proposed that the elementary teachers and
the Universities should come together on the common ground of
20 natural science. On the ground of the dead languages, he said, they
could not possibly come together; but if the Universities would
take natural science for their chosen and chief ground instead,
they easily might. Mahomet was to go to the mountain, as there
was no chance of the mountain's being able to go to Mahomet.
25   The Vice-Chancellor has done me the honour to invite me to
address you here to-day, although I am not a member of this great
University. Your liberally conceived use of Sir Robert Rede's lecture leaves you free in the choice of a person to deliver the lecture
founded by him, and on the present occasion the Vice-Chancellor
30 has gone for a lecturer to the sister University. I will venture to
say that to an honour of this kind from the University of Cambridge no one on earth can be so sensible as a member of the University of Oxford. The two Universities are unlike anything else
in the world, and they are very like one another. Neither of them
35 is inclined to go hastily into raptures over her own living offspring
or over her sister's; each of them is peculiarly sensitive to the good
opinion of the other. Nevertheless they have their points of dis-
similarity. One such point, in particular, cannot fail to arrest notice. Both Universities have told powerfully upon the mind and
40 life of the nation. But the University of Oxford, of which I am a
member, and to which I am deeply and affectionately attached, has
produced great men, indeed, but has above all been the source or

the centre of great movements. We will not now go back to the middle ages; we will keep within the range of what is called modern history. Within this range, we have the great movements of Royalism, Wesleyanism, Tractarianism, Ritualism, all of them having their source or their centre in Oxford. You have nothing of the kind. The movement taking its name from Charles Simeon is far, far less considerable than the movement taking its name from John Wesley. The movement attempted by the Latitude men in the seventeenth century is next to nothing as a movement; the men are everything. And this is, in truth, your great, your surpassing distinction: not your movements, but your men. From Bacon to Byron, what a splendid roll of great names you can point to! We, at Oxford, can show nothing equal to it. Yours is the University not of great movements, but of great men. Our experience at Oxford disposes us, perhaps, to treat movements, whether our own, or extraneous movements such as the present movement for revolutionising education, with too much respect. That disposition finds a corrective here. Masses make movements, individualities explode them. On mankind in the mass, a movement, once started, is apt to impose itself by routine; it is through the insight, the independence, the self-confidence of powerful single minds that its yoke is shaken off. In this University of great names, whoever wishes not to be demoralised by a movement comes into the right air for being stimulated to pluck up his courage and to examine what stuff movements are really made of.
Inspirited, then, by this tonic air in which I find myself speaking, I am boldly going to ask   *Ninet.*

5

10

15

20

25

55:34. An . . . anticipate. *not in Ninet.*
55:37–38. sciences strongly move my   *Ninet., Manh.*
56:1. is quite incompetent to   *Ninet., Manh.*
56:2–3. education. His incompetence, however, if he   *Ninet., Manh.*
56:11. may have met with a phrase   *Ninet.*
56:16–17. world. Professor Huxley, in his discourse   *Ninet.*
56:18. at Birmingham   *not in Ninet.*
56:20. these:—'Europe is to be   *Ninet.*
56:23–24. their common outfit   *Ninet.*
56:30–31. remarks that I assert literature   *Ninet.*
56:32. for making us   *Ninet.*
56:36–37. criticism of life which constitutes   *Ninet., Manh.*
57:2. their common outfit   *Ninet., Manh.*

57:16. and . . . man   *not in Ninet., Manh.*

57:18. preachers,   *not in Ninet., Manh.*

57:26–27. which is what people have called humanism, we mean a   *Ninet., Manh.*

57:31. example (says he): a   *Manh.*

57:31, 32. sources . . . are correctly   *Ninet., Manh.*, 85; *corrected from North British.*

58:10. same as to   *Ninet., Manh.*

58:11. with the aim   *Ninet., Manh.*

59:3. poems, histories, and speeches—so   *Ninet.*

59:12. says Professor   *Ninet.*

59:21–22. time we will perhaps touch upon the question of   *Ninet.*

59:37–38. knowing the results of the scientific   *Ninet., Manh.*

60:14. results are established   *Ninet., Manh.*

60:26–27. appeal is to observation and   *Ninet.*

60:31–32. Charon is in his boat on the Styx,   *Ninet.;* Charon is punting his boat on the Styx,   *Manh.*

60:32. Hugo is a truly great poet;   *Ninet.*

60:32–33. or Mr. . . . statesmen;   *not in Ninet., Manh.*

60:35. really happen. *Ninet., Manh.*

61:6. man, in his education, 'has   *Ninet.*

61:8. alternative.' Whether   *Ninet.*

61:12. More . . . reformers.   *not in Ninet.;* ¶But it   *Ninet.*

61:18–19. my acquaintance   *Ninet., Manh.*

61:20–21. of doing them injustice.   *Ninet., Manh.*

61:21–22. ability of the . . . makes them   *Ninet., Manh.*

62:2. and plain lines and not   *Ninet., Manh.*

62:3. fairly true account   *Ninet.*

62:5–7. When . . . wisdom.   *not in Ninet., Manh.*

62:9. will admit   *Ninet., Manh.*

62:10. no ¶   *Ninet., Manh.*

62:11. that these powers just   *Ninet., Manh.*

63:5. We feel, as   *Ninet.*

63:6–7. majority of mankind feel the need   *Ninet.*

63:10–13. ¶The prophetess Diotima explained to Socrates that love is, in fact, nothing but   *Ninet.;* ¶The Mantineian prophetess, Diotima, once explained to Socrates, that love, and impulse, and bent of all kinds, is, in fact, nothing but   *Manh.*

63:13. should be for ever   *Ninet., Manh.*

63:14–16. This . . . form. And therefore   *not in Ninet.*

63:14. assured him,   *Manh.*

63:15–17. desire, and love is only one particular form of it. And this primordial desire   *Manh.*

63:17. This primordial desire it is, *Ninet.*

63:18–19. which causes in us the instinct for relating *Ninet.;* which causes in us the impulse for relating *Manh.*

63:22–24. And . . . instincts. *not in Ninet.*

63:21–25. Such is human nature. Such is human nature; and in seeking to gratify the instinct we are *Ninet.*

63:27–29. ¶Knowledges which cannot be directly related *Ninet.;* ¶But some kinds of knowledge do not directly serve . . . be directly related *Manh.*

63:29–30. for conduct, are instrument-knowledges; *Ninet.*

63:30. to other knowledge, *Ninet.*

63:35. useful to every one *Ninet.*

63:37. My eminent friend, *Manh.*

64:1–2. Sylvester, who holds *Ninet.;* Sylvester, holds *Manh.*

64:3–6. mathematics, is far away in America; and therefore, if in the Cambridge Senate House one may say such a thing without profaneness, I will hazard *Ninet.*

64:4–5. I ventured, *Manh.*

64:7. mathematics, also, goes *Ninet.*

64:11. not stand *Ninet., Manh.*

64:20. and others to that, *Ninet.*

64:21. as the proposition *Ninet.;* as the famous proposition *Manh.*

64:24. reach and importance as *Ninet.*

64:25. Huxley brings us, when *Ninet.*

64:30. should all be *Ninet.*

64:38. sense within them *Ninet., Manh.*

65:1. the sense for *Ninet., Manh.*

65:6. those 'general *Ninet., Manh.*

65:6–7. which have been forced upon us,' says *Ninet.;* which have been forced upon us all,' says *Manh.*

65:7–8. by physical *Ninet., Manh.*

65:16. is so strong *Ninet., Manh.*

65:21. whom we have lately lost, *Ninet.;* whom we lost not long ago, *Manh.*

65:28. natural knowledge of and reasoning *mispr. Manh.*

65:34. are very rare. *Ninet., Manh.*

65:38–66:3. And for one man amongst *Ninet.*

66:3. that for one *Manh.*

66:4–5. are fifty, probably, with the *Ninet., Manh.*

66:6–7. Education . . . demand. *not in Ninet.*

66:6. Education itself lays hold upon us by *Manh.*

66:8–9. its poverty of *Ninet.*

66:13–14. our nursing . . . our nursing   *Ninet.*

66:15. Our Universities came   *Ninet.*

66:17–18. hearts, and so . . . related itself   *Ninet.*

66:18. to the desire . . . the desire   *Ninet., Manh.*

66:19. beauty—the general desire in men, as Diotima said, that good should be for ever present to them. All other   *Ninet.*

66:21–22. upon men's affections by   *Ninet., Manh.*

66:23. conduct and their sense   *Ninet., Manh.*

66:27. that they must and will become   *Ninet.;* soon   *not in Manh.*

67:2. themselves, . . . satisfied,   *not in Ninet.*

67:5. in man's   *Ninet.*

67:6. success of science   *Ninet.*

67:8. letters, have   *Ninet.*

67:9–15. emotions, and how do they exercise it? and if they have it and exercise it, how do they exercise it in relating the results of natural science to man's sense for conduct, his sense for beauty? All these   *Ninet.*

67:17. shows us that   *Ninet.*

67:19–21. power. Next, how do they exercise it? And this is perhaps   *Ninet.*

67:20–21. so as to . . . beauty?   *not in Manh.*

67:23. further,   *Ninet., Manh.*

67:31. with Spinoza,   *Ninet., Manh.*

67:35. to say, 'What   *Ninet., Manh.*

67:36. gained   *mispr. Manh.*

67:37.   *footnote 1 not in Ninet., Manh.*

68:4–5. relating the results   *Ninet.*

68:9–10. moralists are to relate for us the results   *Ninet.*

68:11. our need for . . . our need for   *Ninet., Manh.*

68:12. But   *not in Ninet.*

68:17. that their art,   *Manh.*

68:17–18. find that they have in fact   *Ninet.*

68:28. I could desire no   *Ninet.;* I could desire, for my own part, no   *Manh.*

68:35–36. come to be studied as what they   *Ninet.;* in truth   *not in Manh.*

69:4. ¶Let us, all of us, avoid as much   *Ninet.*

69:11. say to him that   *Ninet.*

69:18. specialists have the gift   *Ninet.*

69:19. will be   *Ninet.*

69:21. only   *not in Ninet., Manh.*

69:22–23. in a training college,   *Ninet., Manh.*

69:24. famous passage in *Manh.*

69:28–30. our primary [our national *Manh.*] schools knew that when a taper burns the wax is converted into carbonic acid and water, and thought *Ninet., Manh.*

69:34. about the converted wax, but *Ninet., Manh.*

70:2. had left things the other *Ninet.*

70:3. our primary schools. *Ninet.*

70:4–5. of Parliament who goes to travel in America, who relates *Ninet.*

70:7. of the country *Ninet.;* of this great continent *Manh.*

70:12. happily secured. *Ninet.*

70:14. himself would hardly *Manh.*

70:15. geology and mining *Ninet.*

70:25–72:16. *Most of this passage forms the concluding paragraph of Ninet., where it occurs after 73:4; see note at that place.*

70:25. would touch *Manh.*

70:34. not a man of English speech models *Manh.*

70:37. gainsayer; *Ninet.*

71:2. conduct, or the instinct for society. If *Manh.*

71:3. literature as it *Ninet., Manh.*

71:4. literature, we *Ninet., Manh.*

71:6–7. making this study more *Ninet.*

71:7–8. now. As I said of humane letters in general, Greek will come to be *Ninet.*

71:8. hope, to be *Manh.*

71:12. did. I *Manh.*

71:12–17. did; perhaps in that chain of forts, with which the fair host of the Amazons is engirdling this University, they are studying *Ninet.*

71:13–17. Amazons is engirdling the English universities, I find that in the happy families of your mixed American universities out *Manh.*

71:19. *no* ¶ *Ninet.*

71:19–20. "The . . . me," *not in Ninet.*

71:21–36. I will not . . . effect. *not in Ninet.*

71:23. of the ancients is *Manh.*

71:24. more crying than in *Manh.*

71:25–26. themselves in our literature and in all our art. *Fit Manh.*

71:28–30. beautiful 'antique symmetry' of Greece; . . . we English fail, and where our execution fails. *Manh.*

71:33–34. from a number of fine . . . about at random on *Manh.*

71:35. it came from all things there being perfectly and sym-
metrically combined   *Manh.*

71:36–37. What must an Englishman feel as to his deficiencies
Ninet.

71:37. about his   *Manh.*

71:38. whereof symmetry   *Ninet., Manh.*

72:5–7. here I have entered Mr. Ruskin's province, and I am well
content to leave not only our street architecture, but also letters
and Greek, under the care of so distinguished a guardian.   *Ninet.*

72:5. here I have touched our friend   *Manh.*

72:8. last, it appears, find flowing   *Manh.*

72:10. that current which seemed   *Manh.*

72:12. this good fellow   *not in Ninet.*

72:15–16. ancestor had latent in him, also,   *Manh.*

72:17. ¶And indeed, to say   *Ninet., Manh.*

72:18. are in danger   *Ninet.*

72:21–23. irresistible. They will be studied more rationally,
Ninet.

72:22–23. will be studied (one may hope) more rationally,   *Manh.*

73:4. *Ninet. concludes:*   ¶And so we have turned in favour of the
humanities the *No wisdom, nor understanding, nor counsel,
against the Eternal!* which seemed against . . . [72:10–14] . . .
humane letters. The time warns me to stop; but most probably,
if we went on, we might arrive at the further conclusion that
our ancestor carried in his nature, also, a necessity for Greek.
The attackers . . . [70:30–71:21] . . . an Italian. What must an
Englishman . . . [71:36–72:7] . . . guardian.   *Ninet.*

[A LIVERPOOL ADDRESS]

Ninet.   "A Liverpool Address," *Nineteenth Century* XII, 710–
               20 (November, 1882).

80:11. and of the utility,   *Ninet.; corrected from Liverpool Daily
Post.*

[A FRENCH WORTHY]

PMG   "A French Worthy," *Pall Mall Gazette,* November 8,
               1882, pp. 1–2. Anonymous.

[AT THE PRINCESS'S]

PMG   "At the Princess's," *Pall Mall Gazette,* December 6, 1882, p. 4. Anonymous.

[AN OLD PLAYGOER AT THE PLAY]

PMG   "An Old Playgoer at the Play," *Pall Mall Gazette,* March 30, 1883, pp. 3–4. Signed "An Old Playgoer."

[ISAIAH OF JERUSALEM]

Ninet.   "Isaiah of Jerusalem," *Nineteenth Century* XIII, 587–603, 779–94 (April, May, 1883). In this edition, pp. 100–115:13, 115:14–130.

Lit.   "Isaiah of Jerusalem," *Littell's Living Age* CLVII, 308–18 (May 5, 1883). The first half only. Not collated.

83is   Isaiah of Jerusalem | in the | Authorised English Version | with | *an Introduction, Corrections, and Notes* | by | Matthew Arnold | Formerly Professor of Poetry in the University of Oxford | and Fellow of Oriel College | London | Macmillan and Co. | 1883
           Introduction, pp. 1–44.

Title: Introduction   *not in Ninet.*

100:1. ¶Goethe's account of beauty is surely the best that has ever been given of it: *Das Schöne ist eine Manifestation geheimer Naturgesetze, die uns ohne dessen Erscheinung ewig wären verborgen geblieben.* 'The beautiful is a manifestation of secret laws of nature, which, but for its apparition, would have for ever remained hidden from us.' Nothing can be truer; we may remember it every time that we look on a lovely face, every time (still more) that we regard a fine work of literature. Yes; what is beautiful attracts us and delights us by virtue of natural laws; but these laws are secret, we cannot draw out the recipe for making the beautiful from them; when, however, the beautiful meets us, and we are attracted and delighted by it, then we find that here we have them manifested. Now the attraction and de- 20

25

light from what is beautiful is thus, as we see, a natural force, and it is moreover one of the most powerful natural forces that act upon mankind. When therefore we have succeeded in enlisting it in support of conduct and religion, we have enlisted a most potent auxiliary. But furthermore, when we have once got this auxiliary, it is necessary to remember that there is something secret and incalculable about its nature. We do not know how it is originated; we cannot break it up and be sure of being able to produce it afresh by methods of our own; if we tamper with it, we are likely to lose it. There it is at present, and it is of a most subtle and fugitive nature; let us treat it, therefore, with all respect.

Thoughts of this kind pass through my mind as I turn over the pages of the revised version of the New Testament. Our established version comes to us from an age of singular power, and has great beauty. This beauty is a source of great power. Use and wont have further added to the power of this beauty by attaching to the old version a thousand sentiments and associations. Altogether, a force of the utmost magnitude has come into being. The revisers seem to me to have been insufficiently aware either of the nature of this force, or of its importance and value. They too much proceed either as if they had the recipe, if they broke up the force of beauty and sentiment attaching to the old version, for producing this force afresh themselves, or else as if the force was a matter of no great importance. In either case they are mistaken. The beauty of the old version is 'a manifestation of *secret* laws of nature,' and neither the revisers nor any of us can be sure of finding the recipe, if we destroy this manifestation, for compounding another as good. And if we think that its beauty does not much matter, then we have nature against us; for a manifestation of beauty is a manifestation of laws of *nature*.

The Dean of Chichester has attacked the revisers with exceeding great vehemence, and many of his reasons for hostility to them I do not share. But when he finally fixes on a test-passage and condemns them by it, he shows, I must say, a genuine literary instinct, a true sense for style, and brings to my mind that to him it was given to produce, long ago, in an Oxford prize-poem, that excellent line describing Petra which Arthur Stanley used to praise so warmly—

A rose-red city, half as old as time.

The Dean of Chichester takes for his test the well-known passage in the first chapter of the Second Epistle of Peter: 'And beside this, giving all diligence, add to your faith virtue; and to virtue knowledge; and to knowledge temperance; and to temperance patience; and to patience godliness; and to godliness brotherly kindness; and to brotherly kindness charity.' By this work of the old translators he then places the work of the revisers: 'Yea, and for this very cause adding on your part all diligence, in your faith supply virtue; and in your virtue knowledge; and in your knowledge temperance; and in your temperance patience; and in your patience godliness; and in your godliness love of the brethren; and in your love of the brethren love.' In merely placing these versions side by side, the Dean of Chichester thinks that he has done enough to condemn the revised version. And so, in truth, he has.

That is to say, he has done enough to condemn it as a substitute for the old version. He has made evident, by a startling example, how it has not the power of beauty and sentiment attaching to the old version, and can never have it. The instinct of self-preservation in humanity will make us retain the old version which has this power. If by an act of authority the new version could be made to supersede the old and the old to go out of use, a blow would be struck at religion in this country far more dangerous to it than the hindrances with which it has to contend now—beer-shops, Dissent, Ritualism, the Salvation Army, and the rest of the long and sad list. The new enemy would be indifference; an ever-growing indifference to a New Testament which failed to delight and move men like the old, and to fix its phrases in their memory. 'Thou wilt not leave his soul in Hades,' is never likely, we may depend upon it, *virûm volitare per ora.*

The revisers have been led away by a very natural desire to correct all the mistakes of the old version, and to make a version which should be perfectly accurate. When once one is engaged, indeed, in a task like that of the revisers, the desire to alter is sure to grow upon one as one proceeds, the '*offendiculum* of scrupulousness,' as Butler calls it, is sure to increase; until at last one is capable of forgetting that even the aorist was made for man and not man for the aorist, and of waging against the past tenses of the old version an often pedantic war. To have fallen into this course of proceeding is so natural, that I

will by no means make it a matter of reproach against the revisers; probably, had I been one of them, I should have fallen
into it myself. But it would have remained none the less true
that this is just one of those cases where 'the half,' as the Greek
5   proverb says, 'is more than the whole;' and that, by resisting the
impulse to alter, by never forgetting that the object in view
was not to make a perfectly accurate translation, but to preserve unimpaired the force of beauty and sentiment residing
in the old version at the same time that one made such correc-
10   tions as were indeed necessary—only by submitting to these
conditions was real success possible to the revisers. As it is, they
have produced a work excellently fitted to help and instruct,
in reading the New Testament, all who do not know Greek;
—a work which in this way will be of invaluable usefulness, and
15   from which every reader will probably import for his own use
into his New Testament such corrections as seem to him urgently needed. But they have not done that which they were
meant to do: they have not given us a version which is just the
old version improved, and which can take the place of it. In
20   fact, a second company of revisers is now needed to go through
the recent revision, and to decide what of it ought to be im-
ported into the established version, and with what modifications.
      Meanwhile the time approaches   *Ninet.*

100:2. Testament, also, to make   *Ninet.*

100:25–26. them! We connect them, at any rate, with truths which
Ninet.

100:27. and they lend   *Ninet.*

101:35. translation of our   *Ninet.*

102:14. have I received   *Ninet.*

102:17–18. it widens one's   *Ninet.*

103:7. *no section division, Ninet.*

105:28. by turning   *Ninet.*

105:35. gate of Jerusalem, bringing   *Ninet.*

106:6. *no section division, Ninet.;* requisite, if   *Ninet.*

108:14. try to   *Ninet.*

108:29. only; and Tirhakah, king of   *Ninet.*

108:36. deliverances, I may speak at more length hereafter. Here I
Ninet.

109:18. Jotham. And soon   *Ninet.*

109:38. changed by that   *Ninet.,* 83is; *corrected from Butler.*

110:27. in a chapter following: *Ninet.*

110:34. luxury, *not in Ninet.*
111:2. nought, the kings *Ninet.*
112:11–12. I for the present, as I have said, do not attempt to discuss. But *Ninet.*
112:19. In 734 B.C. *Ninet.*
113:22–23. In 701 Sennacherib, *Ninet.*
114:13–26. the Remnant. We may touch upon this matter later. At present we do but *Ninet.*
114:28. We will conclude our summary *Ninet.*
114:38. them; by any one *Ninet.*
115:5. conversant. For my part, I often gladly allow myself to employ parallels from such passages, in order to bring out for my own mind the events and personages of Isaiah's time more vividly. What is Assyria but the French empire as it presented itself to the eyes of our fathers—conquering, rapacious, aggressive, insolent, unscrupulous, unrighteous? What is Sennacherib withdrawing baffled from Jerusalem, but Napoleon withdrawing baffled from Moscow? Egypt, of grand appearance but not of real force and vigour answering to it, Egypt august, proud, unwieldy, dilatory, ineffectual, is the Austrian empire. The youthful Ahaz, vain, sensual, and false, is the Prince John of *Ivanhoe.* The pious Hezekiah, with his zeal for strictness in public worship, with his turn for hymnody and for religious literature, with his want of insight and greatness, his errors in policy and his bad ministers, Hezekiah brings always to my mind Mr. Perceval, George the Third's favourite minister; Mr. Perceval, a man exemplary and strictly religious, but narrow and unequal to the situation; capable of pursuing the most deplorable policy and of employing the most unfit men. And as I have formerly likened to Sancho Panza the great *Times* newspaper, following with sighs, shrugs, and remonstrances that arrant adventurer, the modern spirit, so, without offence to the excellent proprietor of the *Times,* let me say that I never can help thinking of him when I read Isaiah's invectives against Hezekiah's Mayor of the Palace, Shebna. Not a word is alleged against Shebna's character; but, like the *Times,* Shebna is the organ of the governing class, the friend and upholder of the established fact—and Isaiah is their mortal enemy. And he sees this Shebna in great prosperity, buying land, building right and left, founding a family. 'What hast thou here and whom hast thou here?' he cries; 'I will drive thee from thy station, and I will call my servant Eliakim,

and I will commit thy government into his hand, and he shall
be a father to the inhabitants of Jerusalem!'[1] It is as if a revolutionary prophet were to see in power the proprietor of the
Times and maintainer of the established fact, and to predict his
having to give place to Mr. Samuel Smith, the newly elected
member for Liverpool, a Christian Socialist. And we find that,
as to the ministers of King Hezekiah and as to the government
of Judah, Isaiah carried his point or nearly carried it; for when
Sennacherib's envoys came to Jerusalem, Shebna was no longer
Mayor of the Palace; Eliakim filled the post instead of him.
Shebna, nevertheless, was Scribe;[2] that is to say, Isaiah had been
allowed to have his way in part, but only in part. A compromise
had been arranged, there had been a shuffling of the cards; Eliakim was now Prime Minister, but Shebna was Secretary of State.
Ah, these politicians! *Ninet.*

115:6. *no section division, Ninet.*

115:9. *that it is not   Ninet.*

115:13. benefit. I have no space left, however, to open this question now; to this question, and to other points still requiring
some notice, I may return hereafter.

But I will not end, even for the present, without seeking to
act up to my own doctrine that the right thing for us to do with
the book of Isaiah is to enjoy it. To enjoy even a chapter of
him is in truth better than to read a thousand pages of comment
on him. After all my comment, let me then refresh my readers
with at least one chapter from Isaiah himself. It shall be a very
noble and characteristic chapter;[3] a chapter which ought probably, if the collection of his prophecies which we possess were
to be properly arranged, to stand the last, and to conclude them.
It admirably illustrates his use of the three *notes* which I have
mentioned as governing his prophecy; and moreover it exhibits the astonishing rapidity of transition, the splendid variety,
the unequalled force, of his mode of employing them.

We are at the moment when the fierce Assyrian giant, the
aggressor, conqueror, and scourge, with *Spoil speedeth prey
hasteth* written on his forehead, is encamped in Judah, ravaging
its lands, taking its towns one after the other, threatening Jerusalem. Him the prophet addresses:—

[1] Isaiah xxii. 15–25.
[2] Isaiah xxxvi. 3.
[3] Chapter xxxiii.

[Arnold gives his own version of the chapter (see pp. 302–4), with footnotes like, but more laconic than, those on pp. 397–98. After quoting verse 1, he remarks:]
Then he strikes the note of *Immanuel:*—
[verses 2–6.] 5
But then recurs the note of *Maher-shalal-hash-baz:*—
[verses 7–9.]
Now sounds again the note of *Immanuel:*—
[verses 10–13 (first half).]
Yes, let Assyria and the nations hear! but then the prophet 10
turns homeward with the note of *Shear-jashub,* of 'Only the remnant.'
[verses 13 (second half) –20.]
Then the note of *Immanuel* joins the note of *The remnant shall return,* and is blended with it:— 15
[verses 21–22.]
Yet once more the note to remind of *Spoil speedeth* and of 'the terror,'—finishing and merged, however, in the notes of victory:—
[verses 23–24.] 20
Of this fine chapter the rendering in our Bibles is often inaccurate, and I have had to alter it. But I have altered it as little as I possibly could, and I should rejoice if the reader happily failed to notice that I had altered it at all. No; decidedly the revisers must not hope to make us enjoy Isaiah by giving us as 25
a rendering of him: *For every boot of him that trampleth noisily. Ninet.*
115:14. *Heading:* ISAIAH OF JERUSALEM. II. *Ninet.*
115:32. prediction. And this supernatural prediction was long thought to add much force and interest to Isaiah's deliverances. 30
How grand, says Bossuet, what a convincing miracle, that the prophet should name Cyrus a century and a half before Cyrus appeared!
Convincing, one may ask, of what? Of its being *a miracle;* of its being, that is, something altogether out of one's experience 35
and contrary to it, something, therefore, baffling and bewildering. How are we furthered, what is really done for us, by Isaiah's naming Cyrus, by his prophesying the capture of Babylon by Cyrus, by his saying, 'Go up, O Elam! besiege, O Media!' some hundred and sixty years, at least, before the Medes and Per- 40
sians under Cyrus took Babylon? Just as much as would be done for us by Milton's having prophesied the disestablishment

of the Irish Church by Mr. Gladstone, by his having cried, 'Go up, O Miall! besiege, O Henry Richard!' some two hundred years before Mr. Gladstone and those his powerful and famous allies executed their achievement. Just as much and just as little.

5   It would be made out that Milton had done something quite out of all common experience, and contrary to it; we should be astonished and puzzled, but not at all furthered. What furthers us is Milton's greatness and sublimity, exhibited under conditions which are accessible to our experience. So with Isaiah,

10 what furthers us is Isaiah's insight and sublimity; and so far as these are shown under natural conditions we shall enjoy them most, for as shown under preternatural conditions they can but astonish us. *Ninet.*

116:8. and sixty years later. *Ninet.;* and fifty years later, *mispr.*

15 83is

116:11–14. prophet. And with these critics I agree; and with that reading of experience which has led them to their conclusion. But what I now wish to insist on is something different. I do not *Ninet.*

20 116:21–22. ¶But Isaiah, some one will say, arrange the Book how you will, *does* predict.—Not supernaturally. He predicts the discomfiture of Sennacherib as a contemporary of the first Napoleon might have predicted his failure in Russia, or as Milton actually predicted disaster to the Church of England. But he

25 does not predict the taking of Babylon any more than contemporaries of the first Napoleon predicted the taking of Sebastopol. He does not mention Cyrus, any more than Milton mentions Mr. Carvell Williams. Isaiah had indeed a sweep of vision, a depth of insight, far beyond Milton's, and which cannot be too

30 much reverenced; but they are not supernatural. If, when the Young Pretender was marching into England and alarm was at its height, some man like Butler (who in that same year 1745 did in fact preach one of his wisest sermons) had said to the English Government, 'The danger from the Jacobites is noth-

35 ing, it will pass away;' but had then pointed to Ireland lying throttled in the gripe of the penal laws, and added, 'There is your danger! there you are accumulating trouble for yourselves in the future,' he would have shown wonderful insight, indeed; insight which neither Butler nor any man then living did ac-

40 tually show. But one cannot say that such a proof of insight, had it been given, would have been preternatural. Well, the prophesying of Isaiah shows an insight of that rare stamp, but

has nothing preternatural. Let us take his famous prophecy of Immanuel as an illustration.

The reader will bear in mind my previous sketch of the situation of events when Isaiah had his meeting with Ahaz, the young king of Judah. The confederate kings of Syria and Ephraim, 5 Rezin of Syria and Pekah son of Remaliah, have invaded Judah, and there is panic at Jerusalem. In the height of the panic, Isaiah goes to meet Ahaz with this message from the Eternal:—[1] [Arnold's version of chapter 7:4-7; see pp. 270-71.] [2]

The threatened danger from Syria and Israel, then, is nothing; 10 and the prophet bids Ahaz ask, if he likes, a sign that so it will prove to be. Ahaz, embarrassed with his formidable comforter, and having his own schemes in his head, replies that he will not presume to ask for a sign. Then Isaiah answers him:— [verses 13-16.] 15

Before a child who is to be born a year hence, a child whose future mother is at this moment unmarried, shall have attained, says the prophet, to the age of reflexion and will, 'shall know to refuse the evil and choose the good,' the dominions of the two dreaded enemies of Ahaz, the kings of Syria and Israel, shall 20 be conquered and desolate. The prophet is speaking in the year 735 B.C. And in fact, whatever Ahaz might do or forbear to do, the conquest by Assyria, within the next twelve or fifteen years, of the kingdoms of Syria and Israel interposed between the northern conqueror and Judah, was a certainty. 25

Well, then, before Immanuel could reach adult age, the lands of Syria and Israel should be forsaken. But twelve or fifteen years hence, when the child presently to be born shall have reached adult age, what then? 'Milk-curd and honey shall he eat, when he shall know to refuse the evil and choose the good.' 30 The real pith of the prophecy is here. It was visible enough that Syria and Israel, which touched frontiers with the aggressive military monarchy of the Assyrians, would be attacked and crushed by it. It was not so visible that Judah which lay beyond, and which imagined itself in danger from Syria and Israel 35 but safe from Assyria, was really in danger from Assyria, not from Syria and Israel. It was not so visible, yet a man of Isaiah's

[1] Isaiah, vii.
[2] [Note to v. 6, "the son of Tabeal":] Probably a Syrian grandee, a favourite of the confederate kings, whom they proposed to place on the 40 throne of Judah.

insight might foresee it and prophesy it; and so Isaiah did, as
follows:—

[verses 17, 21–22, and half of 25.]

That is to say, the land, over-run by enemies, shall return to a
5 wild state, agriculture shall be at an end, the inhabitants shall
have to live on the produce of their herds and on wild honey.
In Immanuel's later life, however, the prophet afterwards adds,
he shall reign in felicity with *the remnant* over a kingdom restored and glorious.

10   Such is really the prophecy to Ahaz. Literally and exactly it
was not fulfilled. Of Immanuel we shall have occasion to speak
later; but it is clear that, within fifteen years from the prophecy
to Ahaz, the time for Judah's ruin had not yet arrived, that it
did not arrive till more than a century afterwards, and that,
15 when it did arrive, the agent of ruin was Babylon, not Assyria.
It is also clear, on the other hand, that with the ruin of Israel,
in 721, that of Judah really began. Judah was directly in the
path of the northern conqueror, whether that conqueror called
itself Babylon or Assyria, and Judah had all the faults which
20 conduct nations to their downfall. Isaiah put the date too near
of what he foresaw, as prophets are apt to do; but he showed a
profound and just insight into the inevitable future course of
events, and his prophecy was substantially true although not true
exactly and preternaturally.

25   Such, then, is the characteristic of the prophet whom we call
Isaiah of Jerusalem. It is his characteristic to deal   *Ninet.*

117:34. was accustomed   *Ninet.*

119:13–15. of contents, at the . . . Isaiah, actually taking place;
   —an   *Ninet.*

119:30. work to the   *Ninet.*

119:34–35. generalities and outpouring.   *Ninet.*

120:16. *no* ¶   *Ninet.*

120:18. triumph; but the unknown   *Ninet.*

120:19–20. announced it.   *Mansueti   Ninet.*

120:25, 28. disciple; there . . . equal; the   *Ninet.*

121:14. *no* ¶   *Ninet.*

121:19. But as they placed   *Ninet.*

121:33. then, is forced   *Ninet.*

122:10. they now stand,   *Ninet.*

122:31. names and circumstances of events produced long after
   their time.   *Ninet.*

123:31. genius, he   *Ninet.*

123:33. He alters *Ninet.*

124:14. especially sensible,—and the English reader, *Ninet.; specially* 83is

124:24. their Bible, such as the English, desire *Ninet.*

125.10. Many editors who *Ninet.*

125:23. it. The *Ninet.*

125:36. the history with *Ninet.*

125:37. history as its *mispr.* 83is

126:15. times; but *Ninet.*

126:20. *no ¶ Ninet.*

127:36. me, in a preceding page, *Early Ninet.*

128:30. there; at *Ninet.*

128:31–32. it, it belongs *Ninet.*

129:4–5. Isaiah?—To sum up the *Ninet.*

129:6, 130:4. *no ¶ Ninet.*

130:4. of the situation, *Ninet.*

130:13–36. *not in Ninet., which proceeds:*

Something I promised to say of the final scope of Isaiah's ideas and Isaiah's prophecy, and as to their real significance and greatness. And here I am come to the end of my space without having been yet able to treat this momentous matter! But whoever will read, as a whole, the Book of Isaiah which I have just been proposing for his adoption, will certainly be in a position to judge for himself the scope of Isaiah's prophecy. Yet something I would willingly say on this subject; it is so great and so fascinating. Perhaps at a future time I may return to it.

Even now, however, let me, before quitting these prophecies, indicate the cause of their extraordinary and tragic impressiveness. It lies in the sense of inexorable fatality which attends and pervades them. Their whole scope, their whole significance, does not lie in this fatality; very far from it. But their extraordinary impressiveness is due to this fatality. Fatality is deeply tragic, and what is deeply tragic is overwhelmingly impressive. On no mimic scene, with no legendary or past personages, was this fatality exhibited by Isaiah; he had to exhibit it pervading the actual history of his country, and the personages involved in it were his contemporaries and himself. Nothing could save Judah but the conversion of the Jewish people; and this conversion was impossible. Nothing could free Isaiah from the mission to preach this conversion, to preach the certainty of ruin without it; and nothing that he could say could make him believed. No eloquence, no energy, no iteration,

could make him believed; and he knew it. This it is which makes
him the most tragic of prophets or poets.

At the outset of his career, in his vision of institution in the
year that king Uzziah died, Isaiah heard the voice of the Lord
5   saying:—
[Arnold's version of chapt. 6:9–10 (p. 269).]
Isaiah asks, 'Lord, how long?' and the answer is:—[verses 11–
12.]
Forty years later, when Isaiah had run a great career, when
10   Sennacherib's invasion was imminent, and even with Sennacherib's discomfiture in prospect, our prophet's language is
just the same. 'Blind ye your eyes,' he cries out to his own
nation, to its leaders and its common people, to its learned and
its unlearned alike—
15   [Arnold's version of 29:9–14 (p. 296).]
True, Isaiah had, to console him, the prospect of the Branch
and the Remnant, of the reign of Immanuel and the saints. He
put his Immanuel too soon, indeed, by seven centuries. He
put his reign of Immanuel and the saints too soon by far more
20   than seven centuries, for it is not come about even yet. Men,
as has been truly said, 'are for anticipating things;' even great
prophets 'are for anticipating things.' To the perversities of the
day we must oppose not a change to appear to-morrow, but, as
Goethe says, *grosse weltgeschichtliche Massen*, the movement
25   and upshot of history on a vast scale. Isaiah foresaw Immanuel
and the reign of saints, he had faith in them, he established the
ideal of them for ever; the movement and upshot of history
has in part brought his immortal prophecy true already, and
will reveal its accomplishment more and more. We do well to
30   to hold fast the animating belief that in nothing will the
prophecy of this sublime seer finally fail, in nothing can it
come short. To Isaiah himself, too, the belief in its certain
accomplishment was animating. Yet how tragic, however glow-
ing may be one's faith in the future, to have to speak to one's
35   own generation and yet to know that one speaks in vain! to
see the politics and society of one's contemporaries, to see them
and to be taking part in them, and all the while to know that
they are inevitably doomed to perish! Of this tragedy the life
of Isaiah was full. It fills his prophecy likewise, and unspeakably
40   impressive and affecting it makes it. 'Woe is me, because I
dwell in the midst of a people of unclean lips; for mine eyes
have seen the King, the Lord of hosts.' *Ninet.*

[ADDRESS TO THE WORDSWORTH SOCIETY]

Macm.   "Address to the Wordsworth Society, May 2nd, 1883,"
          Macmillan's Magazine XLVIII, 154–55 (June, 1883).
Wordsw. "Report of Meeting Held May 2, 1883," *Transactions
          of the Wordsworth Society*, no. 5 (1883).
          Remarks of the President, pp. 4–8.

131:27–29. Excursion, had had held upon him by the Scottish
Church in his   *Macm.*
132:26–30. If . . . work.   *not in Macm.*
132:30–31. matters, too, will come   *Macm.*
133:6. artist; probably,   *Macm.*
133:32. wenn die so   *mispr. Macm., Wordsw.*

[AN OLD PLAYGOER ON "IMPULSE"]

PMG "An Old Playgoer on 'Impulse,' " *Pall Mall Gazette,*
       May 25, 1883, pp. 3–4. Signed "An Old Playgoer."

[AN OLD PLAYGOER AT THE LYCEUM]

PMG "An Old Playgoer at the Lyceum," *Pall Mall Gazette,*
       May 30, 1883, p. 4. Signed "An Old Playgoer."

[NUMBERS]

Ninet. "Numbers; or, the Majority and the Remnant," *Nine-
          teenth Century* XV, 669–85 (April, 1884).
Ecl.   "Numbers; or the Majority and the Remnant," *Eclectic
          Magazine*, n.s. XXXIX, 786–97 (June, 1884). Not col-
          lated.
85   Discourses in | America | by | Matthew Arnold | London |
          Macmillan and Co. | 1885
          "Numbers," pp. 1–71.

143, footnote to title:[1] Address delivered in New York   *Ninet.*
143:3. will call   *Ninet.*

144:30. many are the *Ninet.*

144:35. occasionally. But *Ninet.*

146:9–10. in the last *Ninet.*

147:15. that Athenian *Ninet.*

147:33. Yes, *not in Ninet.*

147:37. them, of Israel *Ninet.*

149:7. the grand glory *Ninet.*

149:11–12. conditions there offered to *Ninet.*

149:17. in nations with *Ninet.*

149:27. suffice. To *Ninet.*

149:38. the State. *Ninet.*

151:3–4. go thoroughly with *Ninet.*

152:15. in his time *not in Ninet.*

153:3. intention to *Ninet.*

154:5. will become *Ninet.*

156:21–25. Let us . . . But, *not in Ninet.;* At any *Ninet.*

157:9–10. direct and just *Ninet.*

159:12. and so accessible; *Ninet.*

159:13. have ever struck *Ninet.*

159:37–38. that it is *Ninet.*

160:11. the goddess is *Ninet.*

160:36. *our* nature, *not in Ninet.*

160:37. deal; that, by her *Ninet.*

161:19. is wise, and will bring evil, and will not call back *Ninet. and Isaiah*

161:37. majority, to destroy States. *Ninet.*

162:23. even in New *Ninet.*

162:25. about you too much. *Ninet.*

163:10–11. must inevitably be impaired *Ninet.*

[EMERSON]

MS   Arnold's manuscript of the essay on "Emerson," written on 41 pp. of various kinds of letter paper, some fair copy, some heavily corrected. Three sheets (pp. 1–10) carry the engraved heading "Halidon Hall," one (pp. 15–18) the heading "Cunard-Royal-Mail-Steamship-'Servia,'" two (pp. 11–12, 19–22) the embossed heading "Education Department, Whitehall." Given by Arnold to Charles Eliot Norton, and now in the Houghton Library of Harvard University.

Harv.   Arnold's lecture copy of "Emerson," 32 pp. printed from *MS* by the printers at the University Press, Harvard, for

Arnold's use, and with his further manuscript revisions.
Given by Arnold to Norton and now in the Houghton
Library of Harvard University.

Variants between *MS* (= *Harv.*) and *Macm.* or 85 are
recorded below and ms revisions on *Harv.* are noted. Except for a very few unrecorded misprints, *Harv.* may be
assumed to agree with *MS*, from which it was printed,
unless there is a separate record of the *Harv.* reading.
Since proofsheets that have not survived presumably in-
tervened between *MS* and *Harv.*, some of the differences
between them may have been Arnold's intention. No attempt is made to follow in detail the process of revision
that took place on *MS* before it was sent to the printer,
though one cancelled passage is recorded.

Macm.   "Emerson," *Macmillan's Magazine* L, 1–13 (May, 1884).
Ecl.   "Emerson," *Eclectic Magazine*, n.s. XL, 109–20 (July,
          1884). Not collated.
85   Discourses in | America | by | Matthew Arnold | London |
          Macmillan and Co. | 1885
          "Emerson," pp. 138–207.

165, footnote to title: ¹Address delivered in Boston, U.S.A.   *Macm.*
165:3. susceptible stage of   *MS*
165:4. for ever.   *MS, Macm.,* 85; forever.   *Harv.*
165:5. in our youth   *not in MS*
165:7. of our youth   *not in MS*
165:12. which today beset men's minds,   *MS*
165:13. very   *not in MS*
165:16. and renew what was to us   *MS, Macm.*
165:16–17. us the most present, the most practical, the most estab-
    lished, the most national institution in the world,—the   *MS*
165:20–21. pulpit, and in the most entrancing voice in the world
    breaking   *MS*
165:22. subtle,   *MS;* subtile,   *Harv., Macm.*
165:22–23. I . . . saying: *not in MS, Harv.; ms revision indicates
    intention to insert something here.*
165:25. struggling and failing,   *not in MS, Macm.,* 85; *added from
    Newman*
166:1. and church   *MS, Harv.;* and the church   *ms revision*
166:3. and sparsely sown   *MS*
166:5. back   *not in MS;* and daily   *MS*
166:7. wellnigh   *MS;* well nigh   *Macm.;* Again . . . him: *not in
    MS*

166:10. by profession *MS, Macm., Newman;* by their profession 85

166:19. those "last *MS;* these "lost *mispr. Harv., Macm.*

166:20. round *MS*

166:26. such . . . as *not in MS*

166:27. on Edward *MS*

166:28. our mad *not in MS; in Harv., &c.*

167:3. in Mignon: *MS;* in "Mignon:" *Harv.;* for Mignon: *Macm.*

167:8. not of the *MS;* not the *Macm.,* 85

167:9. to us *not in MS*

167:11–28. Besides these voices there came from this side of the Atlantic a clear voice which still seemed to him [Arnold] as important as any of them—the voice of Emerson. He was our Newman, and Carlyle, and Göthe. To those of the older generation he was the soul of genius speaking to their bodily ears, visible to their eyes, and that surely was the most potent of influences. But to the younger he was only a voice. *Summary in Chicago Tribune, January 25, 1884, p. 3, col. 5.*

167:17. the distant *MS, Macm.*

167:22. was but a *corrected to* was only a *MS;* was only a *Harv.;* was but a *Macm.,* 85

167:23. But in such wise did he speak, that *MS*

167:26. and Weimar; *MS, Macm.*

168:2. in the same spirit the same *MS*

168:21. lately *not in MS*

168:22. all *not in MS*

168:23. now *not in MS*

168:25. sometimes *not in MS*

168:26. in their judgments some want of *MS*

168:37–38. speech as familiar and . . . quotations. *MS*

169:10–13. It . . . poetry. *not in MS*

169:14. in his poetry *MS*

169:15–16. memory, even of lovers of poetry, at all. Very many passages of *MS;* memory of even most lovers of English poetry. Very many passages of *Macm.*

169:18–19. mentioned, and of a certain circle of adepts. But *MS;* mentioned, and perhaps of a wide *Macm.,* 85; of *om. in later printings of* 85

169:20. of general quotation, *MS*

169:23–24. His . . . poets. *not in MS*

169:31. beautiful and *not in MS*

169:34. that of him *MS*

170:5. work as the famous stanzas on the   *MS;* Bunker's Hill monument   *MS;* Concord Monument   *Harv.*

170:10. give us a sense of   *MS, Macm.*

170:12–13. or two of them.   Take the plain and grand line, which, though not of entire precision in its grammar, is yet in my opinion the finest line he ever wrote: 5
"All, all was given, and only health denied."
Take such a poignant and concise quatrain as this: *MS draft, cancelled*

170:18. again as this:—   *MS, Harv.; as deleted in ms revision*   10

170:25. clearness, but also grace and   *MS*

170:31. And o'er yon hazy crest is   *MS and Emerson;* And in yon hazy west is   *Harv., Macm.*, 85

170:32. the cadence here   *MS, Harv.;* the style and cadence here   *ms revision*

170:34. worthy of Gray.   *MS;* worthy even of Gray.   *Harv., Macm.*, 85

171:7. to Evening loses itself   *MS, Harv.;* to Evening" is like a river which loses itself   *ms revision*

171:9. from . . . quoted,   *not in MS*

171:15. Cowper or Burns make   *MS*

171:16, 18. at knowing . . . to know it;   *MS;* at learning . . . to learn it;   *Harv., Macm.*, 85

171:17. for him, though   *MS*

171:19. be sure that one   *MS, Harv.;* be quite sure that one   *ms revision*

171:26. The School Master of Whittier   *MS;* the "Silent Waters" of Whittier,   *Harv.;* the School Days of Mr. Whittier,   *ms revision*

171:29–30. not even place him among the great men of   *MS;* even *not in Harv.*

171:31–32. Cicero, Plato, Swift, Voltaire—   *MS;* Swift   *omitted Harv., inserted in ms revision*

171:33. style, whose prose   *MS*

171:34. of Emerson himself, like   *MS*

171:36. of Emerson itself is   *MS*

171:38. celestial Venus to   *MS and Emerson;* celestial being to   *Harv., Macm.*, 85

172:7. in question,   *not in MS*

172:9–10. that being in quarantine with some Americans at Malta & *MS;* that being in conversation with some Americans at Milton, and   *Harv.;* that, about the year 1840, being in conversation with some Americans in quarantine at Malta, and   *ms revision*

172:12–13. Essays, then new. The *MS;* Essays. However, the *Harv., Macm.*

172:13. shook their head, *MS*

172:16. have quoted. *MS*

172:17. a style impossible to *MS, Macm.*

172:19. the born man of *MS, Macm.,* 85; the true man of *Harv.*

172:25. he . . . epigrams; *not in MS, Harv.; inserted in ms revision;* epigram; *Macm.,* 85

172:28. in my judgment, *not in MS*

172:31. of great *MS*

172:35. is that of *MS*

172:36. of Sartor," *MS, Harv.;* of "Sartor Resartus," *ms revision*

173:5–6. portrait of his loved John Sterling— *MS*

173:8. only now, now growing *MS only*

173:8–9. and . . . perish, *not in MS; in Harv.*

173:10. in his invitation *Macm.*

173:23. hours *MS, Macm.,* 85; hour *Harv.*

173:27. called a great man of letters, a great writer; *MS*

173:28. men like like Cicero *MS only*

173:30. for his letters and histories. *MS*

173:34. Coming in conversation, *MS, Macm.*

173:36. them; thrown *MS, Harv.;* thus *inserted in ms revision*

174:1. invaluable correspondence as *MS, Harv.;* invaluable record as *ms revision*

174:3. Mr. Norton— . *MS*

174:10. *MS not clear;* know how *Harv.;* knew how *Macm.,* 85

174:15. one of the great men of letters, the great writers. *MS*

174:18. specimens of exquisite *MS*

174:36–37. speaking direct of Emerson's own works he says: *MS*

175:5. Emerson formulates *MS, Harv.;* himself *inserted in ms revision*

175:11. incompressible, *MS, Macm.,* 85; *erroneously altered in later reprints of* 85 *to* incomprehensible

175:22–23. the great markers and recorders *MS; Harv. misprints* masters and readers, *corrected in ms revision*

175:29–35. chagrined. The author's attitude *MS, Harv.; ms revision inserts:* Hawthorne's literary . . . are not generally to me, subjects . . . talent is of the finest kind, finer, a great deal, than Emerson's. Yet "Our . . . disinterested enough.

175:37. situated in England that he was *MS;* situated in life that he is *mispr. Harv.; ms revision corrects:* in England

176:4. But let us *MS*

176:6–7. in "English   *MS;* in the "English   *Harv., etc.*
176:7–8. Home" cannot be done perfectly with   *MS*
176:10. are works of   *MS;* is a work of   *Harv., etc.*
176:15. different kinds,   *MS*
176:22. has exhorted   *MS;* had exhorted   *Harv., etc.*
176:23. can be no   *mispr. Harv.; corrected in ms revision*
176:26. deprecates   *MS;* deprecated   *Harv., Macm.,* 85
176:30. to my eye.   *mispr. Harv.; corrected in ms revision*
176:33. one day relax and   *MS and Emerson;* one day release and
mispr. Harv., Macm., 85
177:13–14. to devouring Time all of Emerson that he can expect
ever to   *MS, Harv.;* as much of Emerson as he   *ms revision*
177:16–17. personages. His relation to us   *MS;* personages; his
Harv.
177:18. of the Emperor   *MS*
177:19. a great writer,   *not in MS, Harv.;* philosophy-maker. He
MS; philosophy-maker; he   *Harv.*
177:22. that are   *MS, Harv.;* which are   *ms revision*
177:25–26. for this, they would   *MS, Harv.;* for this kind of thing,
they would   *ms revision*
177:33. *no ¶   MS, Macm.;* find them.   *mispr. Harv., corrected in
ms revision;* First . . . character.   *not in MS, Harv., inserted in
ms revision;* character—character is   *Macm.*
178:1. power over and   *MS;* power above and   *Harv., etc.*
178:2. But   *not in MS*
178:6. good is ever   *MS;* good we need is ever   *Macm.*
178:8–9. It is close to us in our   *MS, Harv.;* The good is close to
ms revision
178:28. besides   *MS, Harv., Macm.;* beside   85
178:30–31. in two classes."   *MS and Emerson;* in the classes."   30
mispr. Harv., Macm., 85
178:31. classes." "I believe it is the experience of the purest men,
that the net amount of man and man does not much vary."
"Every   *MS*
178:32. unique." Pretension is useless. "Pretension never feigned an   35
act of real greatness. Pretension never wrote an Iliad, nor drove
back Xerxes, nor christianised the world, nor abolished slavery."
Exclusiveness   *MS, Macm.*
179:3. extremes   *MS and Emerson;* extreme   *Harv., Macm.,* 85
179:11. Men are all   *MS and Emerson;* We are all   *Harv., Macm.,*   40
85
179:14. swindles himself." "Always pay, for first or last, you must

pay your entire debt. Persons and events may stand for a time
between you and justice, but it is only a postponement. You must
MS

179:16. ¶Admirable! and let   *MS, Harv.;* ¶Magnificent   *ms revision, cancelled;* ¶This is tonic indeed! And let   *ms revision*

179:20. danger. "The soul always affirms an optimism"; "trust   *MS,
Harv.;* "The . . . optimism"   *cancelled in ms revision*

179:25–28. With . . . they may be.   *not in MS;* "Trust thyself?"
not in Harv., inserted in ms revision; thyself?"—it may   *Macm.*

179:29. the American and Englishman is   *MS, Harv.;* the ordinary
American or Englishman is   *ms revision*

179:30. As I often said when   *MS;* As I often say, when   *Harv.*

179:36. and Messrs. Moody and   *MS;* and hear Moody and   *mispr.
Harv.;* and desire Moody and   *ms revision*

180:3. life of that farm in   *MS;* life of that parson in   *mispr.
Harv., corrected in ms revision*

180:4. Aroostook, of Deacon Blood   *MS;* Aroostook," and of
Dennis Blood   *mispr. Harv.;* Deacon Blood   *ms revision*

180:7–11. I can . . . true.   *not in MS, Harv.;* I can . . . seen of
the country life of England [*sic, erroneously*], I am . . . of
crudeness too.   *added in ms revision*

180:12. learn it may be said not   *MS, Macm.*

180:24. have aroused   *MS;* have caused   *mispr. Harv.;* have excited   *ms revision*

180:28.   as was his   *MS*

180:30. round   *MS, Harv.;* around   *ms revision*

180:32. than he did,   *not in MS, Harv.; added in ms revision*

180:34–36. he boldly congratulates . . . being safely dead and in
his grave.   *MS, Harv.;* he congratulates . . . being long already
happily dead, on being "wrapt . . . safe."   *ms revision*

180:36–37. of the two political parties! The   *MS, Harv.;* of your
two political parties! The   *ms revision*

181:13. last quarter of a century,   *MS*

181:14–15. the bent . . . like,   *not in MS*

181:16. even dares   *MS* (*not clear*); even loves   *Harv., etc.*

181:21. many now stand,   *MS*

181:23. yet   *not in MS*

181:34. ¶His insight   *MS, Harv.;* ¶Yes truly, his insight   *ms revision*

181:35. is not these;   *MS, Harv.;* is not in these;   *ms revision,
Macm.*

181:37. joined, and work, and   *MS, Harv.;* joined; in which they
work, and   *ms revision*

182:3. had a man such sense   MS, *Harv.;* had man such a sense
ms revision

182:17. to us   *not in MS*

182:22. ¶It is impossible to over-rate   MS,*Harv.;* ¶One cannot well
overrate   *ms revision*

182:23–24. It . . . virtue.   *not in MS, Harv.;* added *in ms revision*

182:26. during this century,   MS; I think,   *not in MS*

182:27. is much more   MS

182:30. truly   *not in MS, Harv.;* added *in ms revision*

183:2. for working   MS *and Carlyle;* for writing, *Harv., Macm.,*
85

183:12. great point in   MS

183:19–20. the depth and ground   MS *and ms correction of Harv.'s*
mispr. and good

183:26. no ¶   MS

183:34. in especial   *not in MS, Macm.*

183:38–184:1. although . . . myself.   *not in MS, Harv.;* added *in*
ms revision

184:4. sensations." And the wise man, he [Arnold] supposed, was
to go about seeking how many "agreeable sensations" he could
avoid. *Summary in Chicago Tribune, January 25, 1884, p. 3,*
col. 6.

184:8. in the poem   MS, *Harv.;* in this poem   *ms revision*

184:10–11. a dreary place | And my life is   MS, *Macm.,* 85; *cor-*
rected from Arnold's pocket diary and Willis

184:12–13. side the Atlantic   MS, *Harv.;* of   *inserted in ms revi-*
sion

184:18. now   *not in MS, Macm.;* very   *not in Macm.*

184:20–21. in the life . . . spirit,   *not in MS, Harv.;* inserted *in ms*
revision

184:21. for him to   MS

184:23. by choosing the   MS, *Macm.*

184:25–26. in all the . . . spirit;   *not in MS, Harv.;* added, *but*
without all, *in ms revision*

184:30–31. not to be sanguine.   MS

184:31. But possibly the   MS, *Harv.;* But very possibly the   *ms*
revision

184:32. hopes, several   MS, *Harv.;* hopes; even several   *ms revi-*
sion

184:32–33. succeeding it may   MS

184:34. was happiness   MS, *Harv.;* is happiness   *ms revision*

185:1. he was   MS, *Harv.;* Emerson was   *ms revision*

185:2. in the end   *not in MS, Harv; added in ms revision*
185:3–5. sanguine. You have two   *MS, Harv.;* Many of . . .
grounds. But you   *inserted in ms revision*
185:5–6. show this sanguineness in a case where   *MS*
185:8–9. I think,   *not in MS, Harv.;* and honourably   *not in MS,*
Harv.; the latter inserted in ms revision
185:11. our   *not in MS, Harv.; inserted in ms revision*
185:12. and hope; that hope is,   *MS, Macm.*
185:13. nobly says: *MS*
185:19. which diligence, honesty,   *MS*
185:22–37. *not in MS*
185:31. secret   *Macm., 85; corrected from Holmes*
186:4. I represent him   *MS, Harv.;* I figure him   *ms revision*
186:4–6. mind as still standing there at Concord, in his habit as
MS, Harv.; mind as visible upon earth still, as still standing here
by Boston Bay, or at his own Concord, in his habit as   *ms re-*
vision
186:7. feature, stretching out one hand   *MS, Harv.;* feature, with
one hand stretched out   *ms revision*
186:8. towards our laden and   *MS*
186:9. towards his own dearly loved "great,   *MS*
186:10. sensual and avaricious   *MS, Harv.;* and   *deleted in ms re-*
vision
186:11. guidance his cheerfulness   *MS, Harv.;* lucid freedom, his
inserted in ms revision before cheerfulness
186:12. dignity, serenity, and elevation.   *MS, Harv.;* delicacy,   *in-*
serted, and   *deleted in ms revision*

[GEORGE SAND]

PMG   "George Sand," *Pall Mall Gazette,* August 12, 1884, pp.
1–2.
Ecl.   "George Sand," *Eclectic Magazine,* n.s. XL, 542–43 (October, 1884). Not collated.

187:8. excuses for taking   *PMG; corrected by ed.*

[HAMLET ONCE MORE]

PMG   "Hamlet Once More," *Pall Mall Gazette,* October 23,
1884, p. 4. Signed "An Old Playgoer."

[A WORD MORE ABOUT AMERICA]

Ninet.   "A Word More about America," *Nineteenth Century* XVII, 219–36 (February, 1885).
Lit.   "A Word More about America," *Littell's Living Age* CLXIV, 643–54 (March 14, 1885). Not collated.
Ecl.   "A Word More about America," *Eclectic Magazine*, n.s. XLI, 433–45 (April, 1885). Not collated.

213:30. Earl Warwick   *Ninet.; corrected by ed.*
214:1. [not]   *inserted by ed.*

[A COMMENT ON CHRISTMAS]

Cont.   "A Comment on Christmas," *Contemporary Review* XLVII, 457–72 (April, 1885).
Ecl.   "A Comment on Christmas," *Eclectic Magazine*, n.s. XLI, 836–46 (June, 1885). Not collated.
87   St. Paul | and | Protestantism | *with Other Essays* | by | Matthew Arnold | Formerly Professor of Poetry in the University of Oxford | and Fellow of Oriel College | *Popular Edition* | London | Smith, Elder, & Co., 15 Waterloo Place | 1887 | (*The right of translation is reserved*)
          Reprinted 1888, etc. "A Comment on Christmas," pp. 147–71.

218:1. It is a long time since I quoted Bishop Wilson, but he is full   *Cont.*
218:9. miracles. For   *Cont.*
218:20. convert; so   *Cont.*
218:27. is not commensurate   *Cont.*
218:28. of all rebuke,   *Cont.*
219:8. that the Incarnation is the fundamental   *Cont.*
219:12. inquiry   *Cont.*
220:15. virgin; what . . . says is that   *Cont.*
220:26. realm of Judah; the land,   *Cont.*
221:14. Judah also shall follow   *Cont.*
221:15. Further   *Cont.*
221:31. over it   *Cont.*
222:24–25. receptivity, with their native   *Cont.*
222:34. else to give up our common   *Cont.*

223:34. genuine translation for the fact   *Cont.*
224:8. not the affections and   *Cont.*
224:17. shone this   *Cont.*
224:20. may have been   *Cont.*
224:21. the bringer of this   *Cont.*
225:6. *us to   Cont.*, 87; *corrected from A.V.*
225:17. power in English life, there   *Cont.*
225:22. again, it has been   *Cont.*
225:29. of nature,   *Cont.*
226:25. resolutely to establish it,   *Cont.*
226:34. well as in his   *Cont.*
227:30. *no* ¶   *Cont.*
228:10–11. upon this incomparable woman are   *Cont.*
228:15. all round   *Cont.*

15   229:3–4. testimony. Jesus was manifested, says one of the Epiphany
Collects, "to make us the sons of God and heirs of eternal life,"
and we, having this hope, are to "purify ourselves even as he is
pure." And the Collect for Christmas-day itself—that   *Cont.*
229:9. all Christmas-time.   *Cont.*, 87; *corrected by ed.*
229:10. thy only-begotten   *Cont., Prayer-Book*
229:13. by adoption and   *Cont., Prayer-Book*
229:22–24. Resurrection, and which only through . . . legend
could arrive . . . mankind.   *Cont.*
229:25. ¶It is so manifest that there   *Cont.*
229:28–29. Gospels, it is so manifest that St.   *Cont.*
229:33–38. *not in Cont.*
230:2. And there is   *Cont.*
230:26. temper of *epieikeia,* or sweet   *Cont.*
230:27. applying them.   *Cont.*
230:30. of the Virgin.   *Cont.*
230:33. to say, what   *Cont.*
230:34. first seem doubtful. Christmas   *Cont.*
231:11–12. the . . . us,   *not in Cont.*
231:24–25. to which they have . . . their feelings   *Cont.*
232:20–21. that in any fair view which can be taken   *Cont.*
232:21–22. and also . . . of old,   *not in Cont.*
232:23–24. which no new constructions can   *Cont.*
232:38. this, and to remove   *Cont.*
233:8. careful to mark that   *Cont.*
233:21. *no* ¶   *Cont.*
233:26–27. to say this simply and barely, not   *Cont.*
233:29. this reality   *Cont.;* that reality   87

233:35. in the reality   *Cont.*

234:5–6. this. We make a mistake if we think that even those . . . can now produce   *Cont.*

234:7–12. in such a naked statement, and separately from the poetry and legend with which they are combined, and to which   5
men have been accustomed for centuries. Nevertheless, the important thing at the present moment is not to enlarge upon the effect which the essential facts and truths gain from being still used in that combination, but after indicating this point, and insisting on it, to pass on to show what the essential facts and   10
truths are. *Cont.*

234:14–15. Jesus. What is the   *Cont.*

234:21–22. in this. What, then, is the   *Cont.*

234:25–27. means? Through means of the method and the secret and the temper of Jesus. *Cont.*

234:28. ¶Experience   *Cont.*

234:31. makes the strength   *Cont.*

235:5. cases, is the promise apparently   *Cont.*

235:6–7. The attraction . . . of Jesus.   *not in Cont.*

235:12–13. said the other day, in the East-end of   *Cont.*

235:15–16. was disquieted and alarmed at my saying this. I will urge   *Cont.*

235:17. to . . . *world, not in Cont.*

235:23. on consonance to   *Cont.*

235:35–36. French friends seem   *Cont.*

236:2–3. contrary, many of them maintain   *Cont.*

236:15. has well pointed   *Cont.*

236:25. The fidelity consists   *Cont.*

236:28. cupidity, there the   *Cont.*

236:29. poor may altogether   *Cont.*

236:30. of the blessing;   *Cont.*

236:33. been interrupted, is   *Cont.*

237:3–4. them so hated, the opposition to it is almost   *Cont.*

237:6–7. to religion, intelligent and decorous, in matters of literary and scientific criticism reasonable. *Cont.*

237:19. possessions   *Cont.;* possession   87

237:30. but here the   *Cont.*

238:3. *no* ¶   *Cont.*

238:16. facts of the period   *Cont.*

239:18–19. are not far now;   *Cont.*

238:23. by the inexorable   *Cont.*

[PREFACE TO *Discourses in America*]

85   Discourses in | America | by | Matthew Arnold | London |
     Macmillan and Co. | 1885
     Preface, pp. v–xi.

[A LAY SERMON]

Times   "Mr. Matthew Arnold in Whitechapel," *The Times*, De-
          cember 1, 1884, p. 10, cols. 4–5.
          A full stenographic report in a morning paper.
PMG   "A Lay Sermon by Mr. Matthew Arnold," *Pall Mall Ga-
          zette*, December 1, 1884, p. 6.
          An evening paper's summary of the preceding, with
          paragraphs of quotation. It makes some corrections of *The
          Times* report that may well be Arnold's and are here in-
          corporated.

249:20–23. westward we come to the City and there we see a
     possessing class spending and enjoying, and we see a trading
     Times; westward through the City to the West-end, you meet
     two classes. There is in the West the possessing, the spending,
     and the enjoying class; and in the City there is the trading
     PMG
250:8–9. have turned out—in which it may be conceived as a
     great receptacle and   *Times; corrected by ed.*
250:15–17. And . . . curtain. *PMG; not in Times*
250:28. *no* ¶ *Times, PMG; supplied by ed.*
250:33–34. "Avarice . . . adore." *PMG; not in Times*
250:35–37. leisure time in preaching in my feeble way to these
     classes, and in telling *Times; corrected from PMG*
250:37. idolatrous work *Times, PMG; corrected by ed.*
251:3. and . . . saints *PMG; not in Times*
251:11. name is Denison. *Times;* name of Denison. *PMG*
251:16–18. (Mr. . . . scene?") *PMG; not in Times*
251:22. is a man *Times;* is the name of the man *PMG*
251:24. *no* ¶ *Times;* ¶ *PMG*
251:27–28. a mission to the East-end. *Times;* the machinery . . .
     Mission. *PMG*

251:38–252:3. for very . . . for very . . . Christianity thus . . . appeared . . . neither solid nor   *Times; corrected from PMG*

252:6. of life in religion must   *Times;* of life must   *PMG*

252:8. cultivated and verified,   *Times;* cultivated,   *PMG;* sense of duty   *Times;* sense of beauty   *PMG*

252:11–14. Mr. Barnett's work has been, besides his labours as a parish clergyman, an appeal to the sense of duty, and he has desired in the words of the scroll placed on the wall of the church, "to make   *Times; text follows PMG, which also has parenthetical comment after "beauty":* (not as the *Times* in its otherwise accurate report says "duty"),

252:16. beauty." He has, therefore, set   *Times; corrected from PMG*

252:22. no ¶   *Times, PMG; supplied by ed.*

252:29–30. has just been unveiled, this art has   *Times; corrected from PMG*

252:31–32. You have seen in coming here the mosaic on the walls of St. Jude's Church, and you have   *Times; corrected by ed.*

252:34. adventure,   *Times;* venture,   *PMG*

252:38–253:3. us. Look at that strong and bold young man; that mournful figure must go hand in hand with him for ever; and those two figures, let us admit if you like, belong to art. Who is   *Times; corrected from PMG*

253:4–5. fire? We are told on a scroll. It is thus printed—"The   *Times; corrected from PMG*

253:5–6. (the . . . Lord')   *not in Times*

253:7. are they   *Times;* are all they   *PMG and Isaiah*

253:23. no ¶   *Times;* ¶   *PMG*

253:25, 26, 28. ideal   *Times; corrected from PMG*

253:27–28. has gone . . . it was . . . to the inspiration   *Times; corrected from PMG*

253:30. these classes   *Times;* those classes   *PMG*

253:35, 36, 37. their work . . . old work . . . new work   *Times, PMG; corrected by ed. from lines 27, 38, etc.*

253:37. but at any   *Times; corrected from PMG*

253:38. place. In the old   *Times; corrected from PMG*

254:2–3. considering how much it has   *Times; corrected from PMG*

254:16. no ¶   *Times, PMG; supplied by ed.*

254:23–24. our time is, and what the . . . well said, that   *Times; corrected from PMG*

254:24. are always   *Times;* always are   *PMG*

254:28. delays and adjournments   *Times; corrected from PMG*
254:29–31. obstacles which not only the base and selfish among
mankind but also the fear of the grave and the folly of the world
are perpetually offering.   *Times; corrected from PMG*
255:4, 5, 7. if nature . . . 'Neath long-lived . . . Still in the soul
to admit   *Times, PMG; corrected from Wordsworth*

[ARNOLD'S VERSION OF ISAIAH]

72   *A Bible-Reading for Schools.* | The Great Prophecy | of |
         Israel's Restoration | (Isaiah, Chapters 40–66) | *Arranged
         and Edited for* | *Young Learners* | by | Matthew Arnold,
         D.C.L., | Formerly Professor of Poetry in the University
         of Oxford; | and Fellow of Oriel College. | London: |
         Macmillan and Co. | 1872 | [*All Rights reserved.*]
              Reprinted ("Second Edition," etc.) September and Oc-
         tober, 1872; 1875; 1889.
75is   Isaiah | XL–LXVI | with the | Shorter Prophecies Allied
         to It | *Arranged and Edited* | *With Notes* | by | Matthew
         Arnold | Formerly Professor of Poetry in the University
         of Oxford | and Fellow of Oriel College | London | Mac-
         millan and Co. | 1875 | [*All rights reserved*]
              Also issued with the imprint: New York | Macmillan
         and Co., | 1880
              Adds four passages from earlier chapters, with notes
         upon them (printed in the present edition on pp. 360–
         75, 438–47).
Ninet.   "Isaiah of Jerusalem," *Nineteenth Century* XIII, 587–603,
         779–94 (April, May, 1883).
              Contains Arnold's version of all or parts of chapters 6,
         7, 29, 33
83is   Isaiah of Jerusalem | in the | Authorised English Version |
         with | *an Introduction, Corrections, and Notes* | by | Mat-
         thew Arnold | Formerly Professor of Poetry in the Uni-
         versity of Oxford | and Fellow of Oriel College | London
         | Macmillan and Co. | 1883
              Chapters 1–39, except the portions printed in 75is.

    The Preface (or Introduction) of 72, 75is is printed in volume
VII, 51–72 of the present edition; the Introduction of 83is on
pp. 100–130 of this tenth volume.

Errors in numbering of chapters and verses in Arnold's Notes are silently corrected by the editor.

Epigraph: *"Israel shall be saved in the Lord with an everlasting salvation."* [Isaiah 45:17]   72

269, v. 12. the Eternal have   *Ninet.*

271, v. 17. The Eternal shall   *Ninet.*

296, v. 9. eyes, grow blind!   *Ninet.*

296, v. 10. For the Eternal   *Ninet.*

303, v. 6. is his [Judah's] treasure.   *Ninet.*

303, v. 15. oppressions and averteth   *Ninet.*

304, v. 20. thine eye   *Ninet.*

312:22. according . . . accounts,   *not in* 72

312:27, 38. B.C.   *not in* 72

313:8. prevailed; in   72

313:9. he conquered   72

313:11. B.C.   *not in* 72

316, v. 2. raised up the righteous man from the east, called him to his foot, gave the nations   72 *and A.V.*

318, v. 26. say, He is right!   72; say, He is righteous?   *A.V.*

332, v. 6. is a light thing that   72 *and A.V.*

333, v. 19. shall even now   72 *and A.V.*; shall now   75is

333, v. 22. standard to the people: 72 *and A.V.*

338, v. 8. they behold, how that   72

339, v. 1. believed what we heard,   72

340, v. 10. grief;—when thou hast made his   72

349, v. 2. the darkness shall cover   72 *and A.V.*; *later edd. of* 72 *agree with* 75is

360, 379, 380, 381, 382. *bracketed references inserted by ed.*

401:20. the Introductory Note following the Preface.   72; the Note following the Introduction.   75is

401:26. from the Hebrew   *not in* 72

401:30–31. and . . . Jerome,   *not in* 72

402:2–3. akin to Hebrew,   72

402:21–22. necessary: the air   72

403:26. *The righteous man from the East.*—Cyrus from   72

404:18. thoughts; the Ghassanides,   72

405:7. seventy years ago   72

405:25–26. is Jesus's charge to those he healed   72

409:21. vanity; amidst   72

412:25. picture of oppression. *Ancient*   72

414:9–10. desponding; vain   72

414:14. *is a light thing,*   72

418:23. to Christ 72

419:35–420:4. *believed what we heard.*—See the last verse of the preceding chapter. The Gentiles and their kings had never heard of God's servant; but we Jews, who heard and saw, had we more understanding? 72

420:21. verses *mispr.* 75is

420:22. the place of the Scripture 72 *and Acts*

420:27. taken away from the 72, 75is; *corrected from Acts*

423:5–6. Sabbath, their Sabbath . . . mind; hence 72

423:21. youth were 72

423:30. by Christ 72

424:35–36. occur twice in Genesis, in Jacob's . . . by Bethel, on his way to Mesopotamia and on his return thence. "And Jacob 72

425:2. Gen. xxviii. 18. *not in* 72

426:32. salvation; but 72

427:31–32. it; therefore 72

430:22. Jesus *not in* 72

430:23–24. ministry. He quotes the Greek, and says "the poor." 72

432:3. Obadiah, and *not in* 72

432:31. of like dealings of God with Israel. 72

433:1. lightly stretched, 72; *corrected in later editions*

436:5–6. led rites the most abominable, 72

436:8. Temple; to 72

437:2–3. remain of the nations, 72

438:7–8. and their fire *mispr.* 72

442:12. of Great 75is; *corrected by ed.*

445:1–2. from east . . . Abraham, Isaac 75is; *corrected from A.V.*

Index

A reference to a page of text should be taken to include the notes to that page. Arnold's version of Isaiah and his notes to that version (pp. 259–447) are not indexed here.